# Nazi-Deutsch/Nazi German

# Nazi-Deutsch/Nazi German

*An English Lexicon of the Language
of the Third Reich*

ROBERT MICHAEL
and
KARIN DOERR

*Forewords by*
Paul Rose
Leslie Morris
Wolfgang Mieder

**GREENWOOD PRESS**
Westport, Connecticut • London

Library of Congress Cataloging-in-Publication Data

Michael, Robert, 1936–
    Nazi-Deutsch/Nazi German : an English lexicon of the language of the Third Reich /
Robert Michael and Karin Doerr ; forewords by Paul Rose, Leslie Morris and Wolfgang
Mieder.
       p. cm.
    Includes bibliographical references and index.
    ISBN 0–313–32106–X (alk. paper)
    1. German language—Dictionaries—English.  2. German language—Government
jargon—Dictionaries.  3. National socialism—Terminology—Dictionaries.
4. Nazis—Language—Dictionaries.  5. Germany—History—1933–1945.  6. German
language—Political aspects.  7. Propaganda, German.  I. Title: Nazi-German.
II. Doerr, Karin, 1951–    III. Title.
PF3680.M48   2002
943.086'03—dc21      2001042328

British Library Cataloguing in Publication Data is available.

Library of Congress Catalog Card Number: 2001042328
ISBN: 0-313-32106-X

First published in 2002

Greenwood Press, 88 Post Road West, Westport, CT 06881
An imprint of Greenwood Publishing Group, Inc.
www.greenwood.com

Printed in the United States of America

The paper used in this book complies with the
Permanent Paper Standard issued by the National
Information Standards Organization (Z39.48-1984).

10 9 8 7 6 5 4 3 2 1

# Contents

To the six million dead Jews and to all the victims of Nazism. To those good people in Germany and elsewhere in the world who cared and who helped those on the run from murder. To my friend and colleague, the late Stig Hornshøj-Møller, a brilliant scholar who died in his prime, a human being who devoted his life to gaining and using knowledge to fight against evil.

—Robert Michael

To all those betrayed and injured by German words during the Shoah.

—Karin Doerr

# Foreword

## Paul Rose

The present book by Robert Michael and Karin Doerr, a historian and a Germanist respectively, is an invaluable key that will enable the reader who has no German to gain access to the inner thought patterns and sensibilities of German antisemitic and Nazi mentalities alike. Though there is an enormous public interest in Nazism and the Holocaust, specialists in these fields often are all too aware of the difficulty of conveying the mood, the feel, the logic, which lay beneath the surface of the Third Reich. When a non-German-speaking audience sees Leni Riefenstahl's notorious 1934 Nuremberg Party Rally film *Triumph of the Will*, the English subtitles of Hitler's speeches generally leaves them quite mystified as to why the original German audiences should have found the rhetoric so overwhelming; much of what Hitler says is almost unexceptionable—"patriotism," "rebirth," "mobilization," "order," "dignity," "national community," and so forth. The problem is that these harmless English words do not convey the powerful emotional resonance—almost religious in its intensity—that the original terms carry in German culture. It is this emotionality that completely flooded the German listeners' critical defenses and appealed directly to their whole soul and being—a mood of ecstatic joy reinforced by the sense of excitement and dynamism that was conjured up by the host of new modern jargon words that Nazi-Deutsch invented. When it came to words connected to Jews, of course, the emotional resonance was of very long-standing in German language and culture, and even today German words such as "Jude" (Jew) bear an intensity of revulsion and reaction that is present in no other European language. In the eyes of its inventors, one of the triumphs of this new-speak of Nazi-Deutsch was to transform the traditional language of German antisemitism into something much more modern and suited to the twentieth century.

Through this book a non-German speaker may begin to glimpse and even to experience the emotional rapture that possessed so many Germans exposed to the

Nazi magic, an enchantment that was fortunately elusive to most of those living outside Germany. As will be seen, that same newspeak was an indispensable accessory to the persecution and murder of the European Jews. Scattered through Nazi-Deutsch are to be found the numerous components, some old, some new, that impregnated and animated the new murderous Nazi antisemitism—those medical, religious, biological, economic, racial, cultural, and political components all have left their tedious impact on Nazi-Deutsch. We have known too for a long time just how the SS and the bureaucrats of mass-murder concealed their arrangements in a web of metaphorical, ironic, sometimes half-humorous terms: "Resettlement," "Final Solution," "Evacuation," "Disappearance," "Night and Fog," "Cargo," "Selection," "Annihilation," "Extermination." An English-speaker might find the last two terms, in particular, graphic and realistic enough in their meaning; but here again the peculiarities of German language and its role in both the history of German antisemitism and the Holocaust need to be understood. Above all, there is the constant fluctuation in German antisemitic language between the metaphorical and the physical meaning of words that in English are concrete. Thus, in the Nuremberg trials transcripts we find several pages in both Julius Streicher's and Alfred Rosenberg's trials dealing with what exactly "extermination" and "annihilation" mean, with Rosenberg arguing from the dictionary that they can be used in a harmlessly (?) and purely metaphorical or spiritual sense. The judges at Nuremberg saw through this sophistry and ridiculed it. Unfortunately, there has been a tendency of late to seek to revive this absurd Nuremberg defense not only by such Holocaust deniers as David Irving, but even by serious historians inclined to think that sometimes the historical interpretations that go most against common sense must be the most brilliant.

Many of the terms used in Nazi-Deutsch embody a certain kind of German humor, a certain sarcastic irony that can be a little misleading to someone not acquainted with German culture. One has to beware of taking some of the derogatory terms used for the Nazi elite and Nazi ideas to be somehow proof of a healthy mood of resistance, or of a certain liberal or at least anti-Nazi attitude. More often than not, the prime attitude involved is simply a corrosive cynicism. My own favorite of these terms is the slightly obscene Reichsgletscherspalte (Reich-glacier-crevasse) eponym for the redoubtably glacial Leni Riefenstahl. Caution is, therefore, in order: a derogatory or scornful label does not mean that the user eschewed opportunistic collaboration with Nazi circles. In Germany, all too often, resentment of power went hand in hand with a craven servility.

If Nazi-Deutsch glaringly exposes the uniqueness of Nazism and indeed of German culture, we are still left with some major unresolved, if hotly debated, problems concerning German and Nazi antisemitisms. Was antisemitism all along embedded in German culture? What is the relationship of traditional German antisemitism to other antisemitisms? How did Nazi antisemitism grow out of existing German antisemitic traditions? Did the older German antisemitic traditions lead, through Nazism, to the Holocaust? Robert Michael's thoughtful essay provides an accurate historical context for the reader to ponder these fundamental historical questions. Scholars who are skeptical about tracing unbroken connections between older European antisemitisms, whether Christian or secular, are sometimes too easily satisfied with offering obvious methodological objections to the continuity of European antisemitisms or to the continuity of German anti-semitism. The result is that serious efforts to understand antisemitism and the Holocaust are frequently frustrated. Given the need to be critically minded and to appreciate the complexity of these continuities and connections, and admitting the fact that these may very often be more indirect than they seem at first sight, it is difficult all the same to come away from a reading of the sources assembled in Pro-fessor Michael's essay without feeling that the web of links and influences and con-nections is indeed real and must be taken more seriously than many historians are currently prepared to do.

# Foreword

Leslie Morris

A lexicon of Nazi-Deutsch violates the very principles of secrecy and obfuscation that govern the language of genocide: the lexicon lays bare the range and scope of Nazi language, explicates the terms that were meant to remain obscure, creates lexical order out of the chaos and darkness of this language, and, most significantly, insists on the transparency of this language. Yet the language of genocide is not transparent, but rather opaque: it is language that is denaturalized, stylized, calling attention to itself as language at the same time that it seeks to obscure and sanitize the reality to which it refers. The philosopher Berel Lang, in one of the most interesting critical studies on language and genocide, describes Nazi-Deutsch as a "linguistic lie," in which "moral violation thus takes on the guise of literary form."[1] Lang explains that "as the person who is a liar knowingly affirms what is false, so here a linguistic expression affirms what *it* 'knows' to be false."[2] As such, the lexicon presented here contains a fundamental paradox, as its very existence dismantles the "linguistic lie" that defines the language of genocide. This lexicon of Nazi-Deutsch is thus not only an invaluable resource for understanding the linguistic dimensions to the historical phenomenon of the Holocaust for scholars of German history, culture, and the Holocaust, but it is also a remarkable object in itself, as it is a compilation not only of terms and phrases that shed light on the machinery of destruction of the Third Reich but also of the very obfuscation that lay at the center of this machinery.

It is virtually impossible, in an era in which critical inquiry about the Holocaust and the Third Reich has been marked by meta-reflections about language, violence, memory, testimony, and trauma, to examine language, let alone the language of genocide, as a transparent window into historical or personal experience. Whether or not one subscribes to deconstruction's insistence on language as the site of infinite rupture—where, in Jacques Derrida's formulation, for instance, what remains are words as traces, "cinders," a presence that always marks the absence and the ruptures of history—one cannot deny the extent of the impact of this critical discourse about language and genocide as it has been formulated by, among others, philosophers such as Derrida, Maurice Blanchot, Jean-François Lyotard, and Sarah Kofman.

It is to this discourse that I turn in order to suggest another way of "reading" this lexicon—of moving through the lists of words that are organized alphabetically, and that bring lexical clarity to the language devoted to obscurity. By proclaiming and unmasking the language of death, the language of the perpetrators, the listing of these words in the form of the lexicon is both an act of remembrance and of defiance. In contrast to the function of the list in the culture of memory (for example, Serge Klarsfeld's list of deportees from Drancy to Auschwitz that comprise his 1983 *Memorial to Jews Deported from France 1942–1944*, or the *yizkor-bikher*, the memorial books to the destruction of Eastern European Jewry where the victims of the Holocaust are named and thus remembered), this listing of the words of the Nazi regime does not have an elegiac or memorializing function but rather recalls the historical (and linguistic) moment when the genocide was in the process of being enacted. The scope and range of the lexicon testifies to the magnitude of the Nazi project of the "Endlösung," yet at the same time, what strikes the reader of the lexicon is the sense of fabrication, artifice, and repetition of this "language," a language that Victor Klemperer once described as "*bettelalm*," as language impoverished to the degree that it has to "beg." The language of Nazi-Deutsch is not imaginative, but rather derivative, a langue comprised of startling neologisms and insistent "Germanisms," a language that discloses the "artfulness" of the "design of genocide."[3] Nazi-Deutsch is a language that constantly proclaims its own historicity and that enjoins us, as "readers" of the lexicon, to confront the interstices between language and history.

However, even as we speak of this linguistic entity—or "lie"—that we are calling Nazi-Deutsch, we need to recognize that the term itself would not be found in any dictionary or lexicon on language. Unlike other lost or dead languages (ancient languages, Esperanto, even hieroglyphs), Nazi-Deutsch was never even recognized as language *qua* language but rather as an instrumentalization of the machinery of death. And it is precisely this instrumentalization that strikes the reader of this lexicon of words used not by those for whom the genocide was intended, but rather those who enacted it. Was Heidegger consciously echoing "Nazi-Deutsch" when he spoke, in the Bremen speeches, not of the death camps, but rather of the "fabrication of corpses"? The *Wahrig Deutsches Wörterbuch*, for instance, does not list the term "Nazi-Deutsch" but instead includes, as a secondary meaning of the word "*Nazismus*," "eine vom Nationalsozialismus geprägte sprachliche Wendung" [a linguistic expression that is derived from National Socialism]. Yet if the dictionary contains such examples of *Nazismus*, it does not identify those terms, thus burying a significant historical layer of numerous words within the German language. The lexicon compiled by Robert Michael and Karin Doerr can be seen, then, as doing precisely what the dictionary fails, or refuses, to do.

For this reason, Lang's assertions that Nazi-Deutsch is synonymous with the "literary figure" of the lie is particularly interesting to contemplate in regard to the lexicon presented here in English. This lexicon, with its extensive documentation and memorialization of "the word," accomplishes something that can only take place and be enacted in the realm of language: a translation from a language that is related to, but not quite identical to, what we now think of as the German language. It serves as the echo of voices speaking in a historical period. It not only bears witness to the Shoah, but also, through its documented pages and careful translation, recalls the voices that planned, executed, and enacted the genocide. As such, this lexicon adds a new twist to the conception of language and historical trauma.

Klemperer's insights into the force and power of Nazi-Deutsch—the Lingua Terti Imperii (LTI) that was his ironic name for what we are calling Nazi-Deutsch—are especially relevant and interesting in the wake of recent critical inquiry into the nature of language, narrative, trauma, and history. In his study of LTI, Klemperer, who lived through the Third Reich as a German Jew, takes on the guise not only of philologist but also of anthropologist both inside and outside the culture he is studying. Klemperer maintains that the force of National Socialism was conveyed to the masses not by the speeches of Hitler and Goebbels and their diatribes against the Jews, but rather through linguistic expressions, particular words, and the sentence structures that the Nazi power structure repeated millions of times and that became incorporated into the psyche of the *Volk* mechanically and unconsciously.[4] Klemperer writes of the first word in "Nazi-Deutsch" that he heard—*Strafexpedition*—from a young student he had been acquainted with at the university in Leipzig before the Nazis rose to power. The violence of this one word represents, for Klemperer, the force of language as it is tied to personal experience, for, as he explains, had it not been for the personal connection to the young man, he would have quickly forgotten the word. But the breach of trust that the speaking of this one word *Strafexpedition* brought is associated in his mind with the loss of a friendship. Klemperer paid close attention to the language as it evolved during the Third Reich, noting that words have the potential to be a small can of arsenic—they can be swallowed without being noticed, they seem to not have any effect, and yet after a period of time, the effect of the poison becomes apparent.[5] Writing of the "poison" ("Gift") of LTI, Klemperer asserts in the end that many words and expressions in this "language" should be put "in a mass grave" (27). Does a lexicon of Nazi-Deutsch bury the poison of this language in a mass grave, as Klemperer admonishes, or does it keep it alive? And does it craft the language of the perpetrators into yet another object of "fascinating fascism," or does it dismantle, through its creation of lexical order, the force and power of this language?

This is, I believe, perhaps the most important question that the publication of this lexicon in English raises. It must be stated again that the usefulness of the lexicon for historical research of the Nazi era cannot be disputed. But perhaps a more far-reaching effect of this lexicon is that it will take its place among other texts—documents, testimonies, photographs, narratives, poems, memorials—and enjoin its readers to contemplate the vicissitudes of language, history, and memory to which archival and documentary study of the Holocaust can point.

## Notes

1. Berel Lang, *Act and Idea in the Nazi Genocide* (Chicago: University of Chicago Press, 1990), 91.

2. Ibid.

3. Ibid., 82.

4. See Victor Klemperer, "Sondern der Nazismus glitt in Fleisch und Blut der Menge über durch die Einzelworte, die Redewendungen, die Satzformen, die er ihr in millionen- fachen Wiederholungen aufzwang und die mechanisch und unbewußt übernommen wur- den," in Victor Klemperer, *LTI: Notizbuch eines Philologen* (Leipzig, Germany: Reclam, 1975), 26.

5. Ibid., 27.

# Foreword

## Wolfgang Mieder

The literature on Nazi Germany and the Holocaust is vast and continues to grow as scholars probe ever deeper into this dark period of modern history. Every study represents an addition to the composite picture of this totalitarian state with its policies of mass destruction. By now, much is known about the rise to power of the National Socialists, Adolf Hitler and his criminal inner circle, the path to World War II, the antisemitic propaganda, and the horrific event of the Holocaust. The annihilation of millions of people has also been documented in shocking detail; and much insight has been gained into the role of the perpetrators of these crimes against humanity, the inhumane nonaction against these murderous deeds by the so-called bystanders, and the suffering and merciless killings of innocent victims. In addition to scholarly investigations, there are also invaluable eyewitness accounts in the form of simple personal narratives, of which some have been published as major autobiographies of survivors that have touched the minds and hearts of readers wanting to understand what happened during these modern dark ages.

And yet, one element that surely was of considerable importance in bringing Nazi Germany and the Holocaust about is absent in most of these valuable accounts. This missing link is the use and misuse of the Germany language during this incomprehensible period in Germany history. It must not be forgotten that the chauvinistic escalation toward total war, the absurd racial theories, the antisemitic propaganda, and the meticulously organized and executed destruction of European Jews and other groups of victims could not have succeeded without the communicative power of language. There can and must be no doubt that the devilish and propagandistic misuse and perversion of the German language played a significant role in changing Germany from a democratic and decent nation to one of terror, persecution, and death. In order for the war and mass killings to occur, people needed to be linguistically manipulated to communicate the ill-conceived orders of the Nazi regime, to buy into their underlying supremacist and racial doctrines, and eventually to subscribe to the actual execution of these policies by fighting an absurd European war and carrying out unparalleled genocide. The German language with its long tradition of antisemitic vocabulary and phrases is surely not free of guilt in leading Germany along the path to destruction.

The fact that antisemitism had an especially noticeable history in Germany since the Middle Ages made the German language even more susceptible to its manipulative use by the National Socialists. Stereotypical images and phrases can be traced back to that time, and Martin Luther's violent antisemitism left its mark on later generations of Germans, both in intellectual and theological circles as well as the general population. The propaganda machinery of National Socialism could build on this hateful and discriminatory language. But the Nazis under the linguistic shrewdness of Adolf Hitler and Joseph Goebbels also developed an incredible awareness of how to turn the German language into a most dangerous tool of propaganda. They and their helpers developed a manipulative and aggressive language based on a vocabulary of emotionalism, radicalization, deception, defamation, and brutalization. It must be kept in mind that Germans were not born as National Socialists but rather they were turned into this mind-set and worldview by a steady barrage of Nazi words and slogans in a never-ending flow of proclamations, speeches, radio announcements, films, and so forth. The entire mass media was controlled by the Nazis; and newspapers, magazines, and books all adhered to this language of powerful deception and defamation. By this propagandistic control of language, the Nazis were able to shape not only the communicative process but also the psychological and sociopolitical thinking of most Germans.

There have, of course, by now been numerous studies of this so-called Nazi-Deutsch (Nazi German). One of the earliest investigations was Victor Klemperer's invaluable *LTI* (Lingua Tertii Imperii): *Notizbuch eines Philologen* from 1947, in which this Holocaust survivor and professor of Romance languages describes and analyzes the vocabulary, bureaucratic jargon, metaphors, phrases, and euphemisms of the distorted language of the Third Reich. As well, his voluminous diaries for the years 1933 to 1945 have appeared in both German and English translation. These pages are replete with linguistic comments on how National Socialism changed the cultured German language into an aggressive, hateful, radical, brutal, deceptive, and repetitive tool to be used for mass control and mass killings. There was indeed much linguistic preparation for the war and the final solution with all their inhumane destruction and murder. Klemperer, the literary historian and philologist, was well aware of this when he decided right at the beginning of the Nazi regime to analyze the language of this movement and its leaders. It became obvious to him that language inescapably reveals the thoughts and plans of its users. Quite appropriately, he characterized his linguistic analysis of Nazi-Deutsch by the anti-proverb: "*In lingua veritas.*" The shameful and criminal truth of the Nazis can be seen in their only-too-effective misuse of the German language.

The scholarship on Nazi-Deutsch has hitherto, understandably so, been carried out by German scholars. There have been a few exceptions, with the first English list of Nazi vocabulary assembled by Heinz Paechter and appearing before the end of World War II with the appropriate title of *Nazi-Deutsch: A Glossary of Contemporary German Usage*. But this compilation of 127 pages is long out of print and lacked, of course, the scholarly depth that now, more than half a century later, has been amassed. And yet, these almost exclusively German publications have for the most part not been of much influence on Anglo-American students and scholars of the Holocaust. It is a fact that many of them have no, or only a limited, command of the German language. And even if they actually are fluent in German, they might have difficulty in understanding the at-times-absurd, impenetrable, and euphemistic language of the Nazis. This is, of course, also one of the reasons why German linguists and cultural historians have studied Nazi-Deutsch in such detail. What scholars need, no matter in what language, is a dictionary of the special vocabulary, phrases, slogans, and euphemisms of Nazi German. Such a compilation also needs to include military and governmental terms, hundreds of abbreviations and acronyms, code names, stereotypes, ethnic slurs, and so forth. The list is almost endless, and yet, the present book by Robert Michael and Karin Doerr represents exactly, and to the point, the type of compilation that has long been overdue.

Their new dictionary on Nazi-Deutsch with its two comprehensive and informative introductory essays, "The Tradition of Anti-Jewish Language" and "Nazi-Deutsch: An Ideological Language of Exclusion, Domination, and Annihilation," is indeed a most important research tool for students and scholars of Nazi Germany, World War II, and the Holocaust. It is a treasure trove of disturbing vocabulary, terms, and phrases, and their English translations and explanations are a most welcome addition to the scholarship on Nazi Germany. Each page of this lexicon exposes the German language as a dangerous tool of indoctrination, a violation of civil speech, a sign of propagandistic rhetoric, and an absurd vehicle toward mass hysteria, destruction, and death. Linguistic communication was part and parcel of the Nazi scheme to manipulate the German people into following Nazi ideology and its ruthless proponents into war and the Holocaust. It is difficult to comprehend how this linguistic and semantic manipulation of the German language and its users was possible, but trying to understand this particular manipulation will help in shedding more light on National Socialism and its path of destruction and annihilation.

*Nazi-Deutsch/Nazi German* is a long overdue compilation. It represents a most welcome research tool and it will quickly find appreciative readers. It is one of those rare dictionaries that one wants to read from cover to cover. There are hundreds of revealing pieces of linguistic information on these valuable pages. As a reference work it will serve generations of students and scholars of Nazi Germany well as they continue their search for further keys toward a more complete understanding of what happened during those years of inhumanity. With *Nazi-Deutsch/Nazi German* in hand may readers also keep in mind Victor Klemperer's proverbial claim: "*In lingua veritas*." Language, together with facts, will help people come closer to finding this truth, painful and disturbing as it will doubtlessly continue to reveal itself. The analysis of Nazi-Deutsch in all of its facets must and should remain part of the study of Nazi Germany, World War II, and the Holocaust.

# Preface

This lexicon provides an extensive dictionary of the language of the Third Reich seen through the filter of German National Socialism. It is a research tool in the study of Nazi Germany, World War II, and the Holocaust and an aid to English translation and definition of the German language of that period. In one single volume, it gives access to a specialized vocabulary—namely, the terminology of Nazi ideology; propaganda slogans; military terms; ranks and offices in the Nazi Party, the German (Reich) government, and the armed forces (*Wehrmacht*), along with their numerous abbreviations and acronyms; euphemisms and code names; Germanized words; chauvinistic and antisemitic vocabulary and expressions; military and everyday slang; and racist and sexist slurs. The Appendix contains material we thought too extensive to be placed in the lexicon itself: lists of concentration camps; military, government, and party ranks; the Nazi Party Program; the Hitler oaths; Nazi songs; examples of Nazi material included in children's school textbooks; and the Germanized calendar of months.

Entries have been arranged as follows:

a) the Nazi-German term,

b) its abbreviation if applicable,

c) the literal English translation if necessary,

d) the definition of the term within its Third Reich context in contemporary English,

e) cross-references.

This entry is typical:

a) **Reichsverband deutscher Schriftsteller.**

b) (RDS)

c) Reich league of German writers.

d) From 1933, compulsory membership for German writers, excluding Jews and political opponents of the Nazi Party.

e) *See* Reichsschrifttumskammer.

Robert Michael, Dartmouth, Massachusetts, USA
Karin Doerr, Montréal, Québec, Canada

# Acknowledgments

We would like to thank our colleagues who helped to put us on the right path: Gary Evans, Stefan Gunther, Steven Jacobs, Charlotte Opfermann, and Nancy Rupprecht.

Robert Michael: Without my students and the librarians at the University of Massachusetts–Dartmouth, this book would not and could not have been written. My partner in the project, Karin Doerr, provided not only her indispensable linguistic expertise but also her humane perspective and sympathetic encouragement during this scholarly ordeal. I need most of all to thank my family for their kindness and love in helping me survive the dreadful task of dealing with Nazism for nearly every day of two years: Stephanie, Andrew, Carolyn, and, most of all, Susan.

Karin Doerr:  I am indebted to Concordia University's Inter Library Loans Department for providing me with necessary material at record speed. I am grateful to many colleagues outside my discipline with whom, over the years, I could share ideas, discuss Holocaust-related matters, and work on joint projects. In particular, I thank Kurt Jonassohn, cofounder of the Montreal Institute of Genocide Studies, colleague and friend, for his encouragement and probing questions about Nazi-Deutsch. I also wish to thank Robert Michael for trusting me to be his collaborator. My children, Benjamin and Indira, endured the attention I gave to this work. My immense gratitude goes to Gary Evans, historian, writer, teacher, mentor, for giving me generous professional advice and  support while working on this, at times, trying project.

# The Tradition of
# Anti-Jewish Language

Robert Michael

### Historical and Ideological Background

Nearly two millennia before Adolf Hitler and the Third Reich, the process of de-humanizing the Jews (indeed, inhumanizing them) was well underway. Anti-Jewish myths[1] and images of Jews as evil beings[2] were woven into the languages and minds of Europeans by the leaders of the day. Without this long preparation and the accidents of more recent history, the Holocaust would not have been possible.

The most important church fathers regarded Jews not only as the worst evil-doers of all time—after all, each and every Jew was responsible for murdering Christ—but also as filth, as Satan's associates, and as devils themselves. St. Ambrose sermonized that the synagogue was a "place of unbelief, a home of impiety, a refuge of insanity, damned by God himself"[3] and that Jews "polluted their pre-tended bodily purity with the inner feces of their souls."[4] St. Jerome identified the Jews with Judas and with the immoral use of money, two themes that would be-devil later Christian-Jewish relations. (The young Joseph Goebbels saw the Jews as Judases and Antichrists[5]; Julius Streicher imagined the Jews to be sons of the Devil.[6]) St. Jerome wrote, "If you call [the synagogue] a brothel, a den of vice, the devil's refuge, satan's fortress, a place to deprave the soul, an abyss of every con-ceivable disaster or whatever else you will, you are still saying less than it de-serves."[7] St. Augustine held that the Jews were more like Cains than Judases.[8] The Jews were to suffer death in life.[9] St. John Chrysostom believed that the Jews were not ordinary members of the human race but congenitally evil people who "danced with the Devil."[10] The synagogue was for him "the Devil's house," as were "the souls of the Jews."[11] Just as pigs that refuse to pull the plow are slaughtered, so Jews "grew fit for slaughter."[12]

The church fathers provided a consecrated attack-language that political leaders from Christianized Roman emperors to National Socialists used to attack Jews, Judaism, and Jewishness. They reified anti-Jewish language into public law. In the Christianized Roman Empire, public law called Jews "sacrilegious assemblies," "polluted with the Jewish disease," "contaminated with Jewish sacraments," a "plague that spreads widely," "the abominable and vile," "enemies of the law," "monstrous heretics," "the worst of men," and "blindly senseless." Judaism was "deadly and sacrilegious," "a brothel," "an alien and hostile perversity," "the mark of Jewish filth," "an abominable sect and rite," and "frightful and hideous."[13]

In the Middle Ages, Jews were stateless beings who had no legitimate place in the *societas Christiana*, or the mystical *corpus Christi* of the church. Their status, their very lives, depended on the precarious kindness of the church or Christianized secular authorities. The fundamental Jewish policy of the period was to degrade Jews and alienate them from Christian society.[14] Many Christians, influenced by the church's overt hostility to Jews as "negators and malefactors," vilified Jews and murdered them in large numbers.[15]

Several medieval theologians and popes[16] stated that the Jews were, or should be, permanent slaves to Christians.[17] St. Thomas Aquinas wrote, "Jews, in consequence of their sins, are or were destined to perpetual slavery," and as a result the princes can treat Jewish property as their own.[18] The princes delighted in the church's identification of Jews as slaves, because it justified governmental economic exploitation of the Jewish community.[19] The expropriation of "stateless" Jews was not new to the Third Reich.

Another cause, and consequence, of the miserable and dangerous Jewish condition in medieval Christian Europe was the isolation of the Jewish community.[20] By the end of the twelfth century, the walled ghetto marked most of Christian Europe's towns.[21] Not intended as collecting points on the road to mass murder, which is what the Nazis had in mind, the medieval ghettos nevertheless led to increased Jewish stigmatization; and the ghettos' unhealthful locations, overcrowding, and the legal compulsion forcing the Jews to live there made them dreadful places.

The Nazi stipulation that Jews wear an identifying and stigmatic emblem was also comparable to the medieval church's requirements. Canon 68 of the Fourth Lateran Council in 1215 decreed that the Jews had to be distinguished from Christians "by the quality of their clothes." Thus, secular authorities, pressured by the church, imposed on the Jews the pariah's hat and badge of shame.

There are many parallels between the language of the Holocaust and that of medieval violence against Jews. Crusaders attacked Jews as Europe's "greatest sinners" and despised enemies who must be punished and exterminated[22] "down to the last baby at the breast."[23] Although some medieval Christian murderers allowed Jews to escape death by means of conversion, the Jews' continued existence tested the Christian sense of identity, just as the Jews' presence in Europe between 1933 and 1945 challenged that of the Nazis.[24] Moreover, just as during the Holocaust, medieval synagogues were invaded and burned, often with Jews in them[25]; Torah scrolls were trampled into the mud, torn, and set afire; and Jewish cemeteries were destroyed.[26]

From the twelfth to the twentieth centuries, Christians fantasized that Jews and the devil were involved in a murderous conspiracy, and thousands of Jews were made to pay for this myth with their lives.[27] Jews were perceived as ritual murderers, vampires, desecraters of the Host, and poisoners of the wells. During certain periods, massacres of Jews became chronic. Christian murderers acted "as if they meant to annihilate the whole of Jewry from the face of the earth."[28] None of the events of the 1920s and 1930s was a historical *novum*.

The church and political authorities traditionally sat on their hands during antisemitic outbursts. This was also not new to the Holocaust period. Public policy indicated that Jews were never to have any influence over Christians and were to endure collective punishment for their deicide.[29] The Jews were Christendom's public enemies, capable of any crime, a frightful mixture of Cain and Judas, stateless beings and sinners who must be punished in this world and the next. Papal language refers to "blind Jewish perversion of Faith," "the sons of the crucifiers, against whom to this day the blood cries to the Father's ears," "slaves rejected by God, in whose death they wickedly conspired," "the *perfidia* [treachery] of the Jews," "perpetual slavery," "polluters of the Christian religion," "Jewish blindness," "perversity," "the Jews' damned perfidy," "old and corrupt Jewish blindness," "deadly weeds," "accursed rite," "malicious deceit," "dangerous sickness," and "detestable stubbornness."[30]

## Luther's Antisemitism

During the Reformation, German antisemitism centered around Martin Luther. He was not, nor could he have been, a Nazi. His beliefs were profoundly Christological, whereas the Nazi view seemed more secular. But Martin Luther helped establish the groundwork and vocabulary for Nazi Jew policy. The most popularly read man of his time, by the twentieth century, Luther had become a hero for both Protestant and Catholic antisemites in Germany, including prominent Nazis, among them Streicher and Hitler. Luther's birthday, November 10, is celebrated in Germany as a national holiday; and it served as one of the two days during which the infamous November 1938 Pogrom, *Reichskristallnacht*, took place. The rabbi and scholar Reinhold Lewin, whom the Nazis deported along with his family to their deaths,[31] wrote:

[Luther] profoundly believed that the Jews acted only for the benefit of their own religion and against the interests of Christianity. He expounded this position . . . as a war to the death, and he wrote as a religious fanatic himself. The seeds of Jew hatred that he planted were . . . not forgotten; on the contrary, they continued to spring to life in future centuries. For whoever wrote against the Jews for whatever reason believed that he had the right to justify himself by triumphantly referring to Luther.[32]

The obscene language of street and field pervaded Luther's anti-Jewish rhetoric just as it did the Nazis'. Luther-Deutsch and Nazi-Deutsch had much in common. He called the Jews "learned, shitty, circumcized saints."[33] The synagogue was "an incorrigible whore and an evil slut with whom God ever had to wrangle, scuffle, and fight.... It serves them right that ... instead of the beautiful face of the divine word, they have to look into the devil's black, dark, lying behind, and worship his stench.... You damned Jews ... are not worthy of looking at the outside of the Bible, much less of reading it. You should read only the bible that is found under the sow's tail, and eat and drink the letters that drop from there."[34]

In 1543 Luther was the first to describe in writing the *Judensau*, which pictured the Jew learning the Talmud by kissing, sucking the teats, and eating the feces of a pig. The *Judensau* linked the Jew, the Devil, the ritual-murder defamation, and the blood-libel against the Jews. Luther proclaimed that Jews pretend to know God, in reality they have read this "out of the sow's ass."[35] Jews were full of "the devil's feces ... in which they wallow like swine."[36] No longer God's elect, they were now "polluted so full of the Devil's shit that it oozes out of them from every pore."[37]

Realizing that the Jews would not be converted, Luther implored the German princes to follow a cruel policy, actually carried out four hundred years later by a modern German "prince": Adolf Hitler. It cannot be an accident that both Luther and Hitler advocated the sequential destruction of Jewish religious culture, the abrogation of legal protection, expropriation, forced labor, expulsion, and mass murder.[38]

First, ... set fire to their synagogues or schools....

Second, I advise that their houses also be razed and destroyed.

Third, I advise that all their prayer books and Talmudic writings, in which such idolatry, lies, cursing, and blasphemy are to be taught, be taken from them ... also the entire Bible.... [The Jews] be forbidden on pain of death to praise God, to give thanks, to pray, and to teach publicly among us and in our country.... [T]hey be forbidden to utter the name of God within our hearing.... We must not consider the mouth of the Jews as worthy of uttering the name of God within our hearing. He who hears this name from a Jew must inform the authorities, or else throw sow dung at him when he sees him and chase him away. And may no one be merciful and kind in this regard.

Fourth, I advise that their rabbis be forbidden to teach henceforth on pain of loss of life and limb....

Fifth, I advise that safe-conduct on the highways be abolished completely for the Jews....

Sixth, I advise that usury be prohibited to them and that all cash and treasure ... be taken from them and put aside for safekeeping.... Whenever a Jew is sincerely converted,[39] he should [receive a cash bonus].

Seventh, I recommend putting a flail, an ax, a hoe, a spade, a distaff, or a spindle into the hands of young, strong Jews and Jewesses and letting them earn their bread in the sweat of their brow.... For it is not fitting that they should let us accursed Goyim toil in the sweat of our faces while they, the holy people, idle away their time behind the stove, feasting and farting....[40]

The country and the roads are open for them to proceed to their land whenever they wish. If they did so, we would be glad to present gifts to them on the occasion; it would be good riddance. For they are a heavy burden, a plague, a pestilence, a sheer misfortune for our country."[41]

Luther discussed murder as a final solution if all else failed, and he often believed that all else would fail. Several elements in Luther's program contained murderous implications, and he asked the princes three times to kill Jews who resisted leaving Germany.

I wish and I ask that our rulers who have Jewish subjects exercise a sharp mercy toward these wretched people. . . . They must act like a good physician who, when gangrene has set in, proceeds without mercy to cut, saw, and burn flesh, veins, bone, and marrow. Such a procedure must also be followed in this instance. . . . Deal harshly with them, as Moses did in the wilderness, slaying three thousand lest the whole people perish. [They are a] people possessed.[42]

In at least three other passages, Luther advocated mass murder of Jews. A sermon of 1539 argued, "I cannot convert the Jews. Our Lord Jesus Christ did not succeed in doing it. But I can stop up their mouths so that they will have to lie upon the ground."[43] This Luther-Deutsch is a death threat.[44]

Luther also wrote that Jews, like usurers and thieves, should be executed.

[Today's Jews] are nothing but thieves and robbers who daily eat no morsel and wear no thread of clothing which they have not stolen and pilfered from us by means of their accursed usury. Thus they live from day to day, together with wife and child, by theft and robbery, as arch-thieves and robbers, in the most impenitent security. . . . If I had power over the Jews, as our princes and cities have, I would *deal severely* with their lying mouth. . . . For a usurer is an arch-thief and a robber who should rightly be *hanged* on the gallows seven times higher than other thieves.

The deadly syllogism Luther concocts in this paragraph may be stated as follows:

All thieves and usurers should be executed by hanging.
All Jews are thieves and usurers.
Therefore, all Jews should be hanged.

In *Von den Juden und ihren Lügen* (The Jews and Their Lies) Luther clearly stated that all Jews should be murdered.

We are even at fault in not avenging all this innocent blood of our Lord and of the Christians which they shed for three hundred years after the destruction of Jerusalem, and the blood of the children they have shed since then (which still shines forth from their eyes and their skin). We are at fault in not slaying them.[45]

Foreshadowing the Nazi *Endlösung der Judenfrage* (Final Solution to the Jewish Problem), Luther wrote that "we should step on the heads of these poisonous snakes" and when the Jews disagreed with him, he told them, "shut up, you miserable, screaming Jews."[46] Within Germany, Martin Luther's work has had the authority of Scripture, and his birthday is a national holiday. Because Luther wrote in a stimulating, polemical fashion and he addressed himself to every level of society, he profoundly influenced the attitudes and ideas of the generations that followed, especially the Lutheran clergy,[47] at least through the Nazi period.

During his lifetime, Luther successfully campaigned against the Jews in Saxony, Brandenburg, and Silesia. The Strasbourg city council forbade the sale of Luther's anti-Jewish books when a Lutheran pastor in nearby Hochfelden sermonized that his parishioners should murder the Jews.[48] Lutherans rioted against and expelled Jews from German Lutheran states through the 1580s.[49] At the end of the sixteenth century, both the Catholic Elector of Trier and the Protestant Duke of Brunswick set out to exterminate both witches and Jews. In 1589 the Jews of Halberstadt were charged with being "a peculiar vermin and a people that is insufferable among the Christians."[50] In 1596, Laurentius Fabricius, a professor of Hebrew at Luther's University of Wittenberg, argued that the Jews made themselves "unworthy of eternal life." Judaism "is no more the name of God. [It] has now turned into . . . 'dung,' stinking animal excrement, which Satan has set before the blind Jews to drink and eat."[51]

A Lutheran pamphlet of 1602 may be the modern starting point of the myth of the "Wandering Jew."[52] The publication ran through almost fifty editions within a few years, and the German term *Der Ewige Jude* made its first appearance in 1694.[53] During the nineteenth century, the Wandering Jew became the Eternal Jew (*Der Ewige Jude*), symbol of the Antichrist and death.[54] *Der Ewige Jude* later served as the title of the Nazi propaganda film that may be considered the "blueprint of the Holocaust."[55]

Luther's ideas were further disseminated in 1612 when Vincent Fettmilch reprinted *Von den Juden und ihren Lügen* in order to stir up hatred against the Frankfurt Jews. In 1614 the people of Frankfurt rioted against the Jewish ghetto, where Jewish residences were already marked by insulting signs with pigs and scorpions. Nearly three thousand Jews were killed and the rest expropriated and expelled.[56]

Luther's ideas and feelings about Jews and Judaism served as a basis for the essentially anti-Jewish *Weltanschauung* of many German Christians well into the twentieth century. His influence in Germany had no equivalent elsewhere in Europe. In 1972 Johannes Brosseder of the University of Munich published a huge volume, *Luthers Stellung zu den Juden im Spiegel seiner Interpreten*, including both pre-Nazi and Nazi authors who used Luther to justify their antisemitism.[57] Years before Hitler became chancellor, Julius Streicher's Nazi journal *Der Stürmer* was citing Luther to justify its antisemitism, hailing Luther's determination to rid Germany of the Jewish plague. Many Germans were attracted to Luther because of his antisemitism, especially when combined with his nationalistic views that German values were superior to alien, un-German ideas and that government should hold great authority in the secular sphere.[58] In 1916, when Houston Stewart Chamberlain concluded that Germany needed a savior, "a brave man with the heart of a lion to write the truth," he was quoting from Martin Luther.[59]

Although Adolf Hitler never acknowledged that the *Endlösung der Judenfrage* was based on Luther's ideas, Hitler admired Luther and was quite aware of his antisemitism. Hitler's government closely followed Luther's program for dealing with the Jews, from segregation and loss of rights to expropriation and mass murder. On the stand at the Nuremberg War Crimes Trials, Streicher referred to Luther.

"Dr. Martin Luther," he speculated, "would very probably sit in my place in the defendants' dock today, if this book had been taken into consideration by the Prosecution. In the book, *The Jews and Their Lies*, Dr. Martin Luther writes that the Jews are a serpent's brood, and one should burn down their synagogues and destroy them."[60]

Hitler was also aware of the history of theological antagonism to the Jews, and privately expressed his admiration for the anti-Jewish ideas of "all genuine Christians of outstanding calibre." He mentioned St. John Chrysostom, Pope Gregory VII,[61] St. Thomas Aquinas,[62] Goethe, Father Rohling, Heinrich Treitschke, Richard Wagner,[63] and, especially, Martin Luther. Hitler regarded Luther as "one of the greatest Germans," "the mighty opponent of the Jews," "a great man, a giant," who had found his true identity, as Hitler had, in his antisemitism.

He saw the Jew as we are only now beginning to see him today. But unfortunately too late, and not where he did the most harm—within Christianity itself. Ah, if he had seen the Jew at work there, seen him in his youth! Then he would not have attacked Catholicism, but the Jew behind it. Instead of totally rejecting the Church, he would have thrown his whole passionate weight against the *real* culprits.[64]

In 1932, Hitler, speaking informally in his Munich flat, observed, "Luther, if he could be with us, would give us [National Socialists] his blessing."[65]

Centuries of theological antisemitism (articulated and elaborated by Martin Luther into an especially virulent configuration) argues Christian scholar John Conway "prevented any large-scale mobilization of concern for the Jews" during the Holocaust.[66] On December 17, 1941, seven Lutheran regional-church confederations issued a joint statement that indicated their agreement with the policy of the Third Reich in identifying the Jews with a star, "since after his bitter experience Luther had already suggested preventive measures against the Jews and their expulsion from German territory. From the crucifixion of Christ to today the Jews have fought against Christianity."[67] Even Hitler's Lutheran opponents argued the Jews should be punished.[68]

## Modern German Nationalism and Antisemitism

German nationalism and religious antisemitism combined again at the time of the French Revolution and later during the Holocaust into an explosive brew. The former student of theology Johann Gottlieb Fichte stirred a hate campaign against the Jews based in great part on religious differences between them and Christians. Fichte's *Reden an die deutsche Nation* (Addresses to the German Nation) asserted that only (non-Jewish) Germans could be genuine Christians, since only they were qualified to detect "the seed of truth and life of authentic Christianity." After praising Luther and cursing the pope, Fichte noted, "Authentic religion, in the form of Christianity, was the germ of the modern world. This [Christian] religion must permeate the previous culture of antiquity and thereby spiritualize and sanctify it. . . . The German people have taken this step."[69]

His 1793 essay on the French Revolution argued that Judaism comprised a "state within a state," hostile to, and at war with, all other states of Europe[70]—a concept hinted at in Luther and later made explicit in Paul de Lagarde.[71] Jews were politically alien primarily due to their religious beliefs.

Within all the nations of Europe the Jews comprise a hostile state at perpetual war with their host nations [and] founded on the hatred of the whole human race.... The Jewish nation excludes itself from our [German Christian culture] by the most binding element of mankind—religion.[72]

He criticized the French for their "loving toleration" of "those who do not believe in Jesus Christ," that is, the Jews, for this in effect means an "open denunciation of those who believe in Christ, depriving them of their civic honor and their honestly earned bread." Fichte doubted that Jews could ever "attain a love of justice, mankind, and truth," no matter how much opportunity they were given, for Jews were evil human beings.[73] He argued further—and most notoriously—that Jews should not be awarded civil rights until one night when Christians would "chop off all their heads and replace them with new ones, in which there would not be one single Jewish idea."[74] Fichte may not have been literally advocating physical annihilation of the German Jews, but he clearly wanted to destroy Jewishness. He also suggested expulsion: "I see no other way to protect ourselves from the Jews, except to conquer their Promised Land for them and send all of them there."[75]

Fichte was not alone among contemporary Germans in using the language of violence in regard to the Jews. Other writers applied metaphors of torture and murder to Jews: "beat to death," "exterminate the gnawing worms," "circumcision and castration," and "parasite extermination."[76] The twentieth century would see the actualization of Luther's and Fichte's violent rhetoric. The Nazis first attempted to expel the Jews, but when the rest of the world refused to cooperate with this plan, the Nazis then executed the remaining alternative and "chopped off all their heads." Luther and Fichte's explosive combination of Christian antisemitism and German nationalism, along with racism, would become the fundamental ideological stimulus of the Holocaust.

Despite increasing secularization as in the other European nations, German social, cultural, political, economic, and scientific groups all defined themselves as essentially Christian. This trend would continue well into the twentieth century[77]; even consciously anti-ecclesiastical Christians like Richard Wagner still "retained allegiance to Christian notions and doctrines,"[78] including Christian antisemitism. Antisemitism was widespread in Europe, but the Holocaust had its center in Germany.

After Fichte, Germans of every political stripe and social class argued either that Jews had to convert in order to become full citizens or that they were so soiled by their Jewishness that they were eternal aliens. Many Germans felt that "the Jew was not one of us," that something was wrong with being Jewish, that a Jew could never be fully German.[79] Indeed, Jews were hardly seen as human. They were "the ultimate subhuman—sinister, superstitious, backward, irrational, medieval, stubborn, and filthy."[80]

Most German Christians found ideas of equality and humane treatment for Jews repellent. In February 1832, Ludwig Börne (Judah Baruch) bitterly summed up the predicament of Jews who were making their way into German Christian society: "Some reproach me with being a Jew, some praise me because of it, some pardon me for it, but all think of it."[81] Heinrich Heine observed that Christians considered "Jewishness an incurable malady."[82] The young Chaim Weizmann observed that to the Germans, the Jews were like a splinter in the eye, even if it were gold, it was still an incapacitating irritant.[83]

## Germany at the Center

It is important to note that these anti-Jewish ideas were not held by Germans alone. Many parallels existed in France and other nations. Take, for example, what was demonstrated by the Monument Henry, an extensive record of French opinion at Christmastime in 1898 during the Dreyfus Affair. Coming from a wide range of French society—from workers and farmers, students and soldiers, men and women, and perhaps children—what impresses the reader of these documents expressing hatred, violence, racism, and demands for torture and extermination toward Jews, Judaism, and Jewishness is that they could have been written by Nazis during the 1930s.

Despite these parallel ideas in France, the pragmatic fact is the Holocaust stemmed from Germany; it was initiated and organized by Germans. Long before the birth of the Nazi Party, generation after generation of Germans were indoctrinated into antisemitic ideas by their churches, their parents, and their education. Antisemitism was established long before World War I: "It was never just Hitler and a few Nazis."[84]

Drummers and catalysts, Hitler and the Nazis made sympathetic connections with almost every layer of German society—except for the far Left—and with millions not within Germany.[85] This was made possible, even likely, by a shared Christian antisemitism. The German political, social, and religious elites; the farmers; and the middle classes made the National-Socialist German Workers' Party modern Germany's most popular political party. From the beginning of the post–World War I period—years before Hitler came to power, years before the outbreak of World War II, and years before the death factories of the Third Reich—German awareness of the violence of Nazi language and of the Nazi promises to save Germany by destroying the Jews did nothing to diminish German support for the regime and therefore the "Final Solution to the Jewish Problem." For the Nazis and for most Germans, God's curse on the Jews was clear, and they would not oppose the Nazi government's policy toward the Jews. Yale historian Robert Erickson concluded that German Christian theologians felt themselves "on the same side [as Hitler] of the *Weltanschauungskampf*. [They] saw themselves and were seen by others as genuine Christians acting upon genuine Christian impulses."[86]

Their attitudes toward the Jews were mirrored in those of Dietrich Bonhöffer and Martin Niemöller—the leading anti-Nazis—in the first few years of the Nazi regime.[87] In 1933, Bonhöffer, who later helped German Jews, defended the Reich's anti-Jewish boycott: "The state's measures against the Jewish people are connected . . . in a very special way with the Church. In the Church of Christ, we have never lost sight of the idea that the 'Chosen People,' that nailed the Savior of the world to the cross, must bear the curse of its action through a long history of suffering."[88]

In a sermon of August 1935—three weeks before the first anti-Jewish Nuremberg Decrees were issued—Pastor Niemöller drew half a dozen parallels between the Nazis and their German supporters, and the Jews.[89] He presented the Jews as the paradigmatic evildoers in Christendom. For him, Jewish history was "dark and sinister" and the Jewish people could neither live nor die because it was "under a curse." The Jews are "a highly gifted people which produces idea after idea for the benefit of the world, but whatever it takes becomes poisoned, and all that it ever reaps is contempt and hatred because [always] the world notices the deception and avenges itself in its own way."[90] Niemöller's observations seemed close to those of Hitler's Propaganda Minister Joseph Goebbels, who in a speech of May 1943 asked

What will be the solution of the Jewish question? . . . It is curious to note that the countries where public opinion is rising in favor of the Jews refuse to accept them from us. They call them the pioneers of a new civilizaton, geniuses of philosophy and artistic creation, but when anybody wants them to accept these geniuses, they close their borders; "No, no. We don't want them!" It seems to me to be the only case in the world history where people have refused to accept geniuses.[91]

The leading Roman Catholic prelate of the period, Munich's Cardinal Michael von Faulhaber, regarded the Jews similarly to his Protestant colleagues. In his Advent Sermons for 1933, Faulhaber argued that "Israel had repudiated and rejected the Lord's annointed, had . . . nailed Him to the Cross. Then the veil of the Temple was rent, and with it the covenant between the Lord and His people. The daughters of Sion received the bill of divorce, and from that time forth Assuerus [*Der Erwige Jude*] wanders, forever."[92]

A broad middle-class Christian consensus supported Nazi values.[93] The misery and distress of political-economic crisis, the Third Reich's coercive terror, the brutalization associated with war, and the Nazi promise of great economic gain were crucial factors contributing to the success of the "Final Solution." But those Germans who supported the Nazis did so because they wanted to. They became Nazis because "the Nazis spoke so well to their interests and inclinations."[94] Religious and racist antisemitism prepared, conditioned, and encouraged Germans to collaborate with Hitler's regime and to accept Hitler's "Final Solution to the Jewish Problem. "Without this wide German consensus, the Nazi regime's "antisemitic policies would have remained so many idle fantasies."[95]

Churchgoing Germans were squeamish about anti-Jewish violence on Germany's streets. The Reich government solved this problem by establishing concentration camps and siting the death camps in Poland, for many Germans the *anus mundi*.[96] The reluctance of most of the young anti-Nazi idealists of Helmut von Moltke's Kreisau Circle to concern themselves with the Jews may be traced to their "strong bonds with Christianity, both Lutheran and Catholic, which they regarded 'as the foundation of the moral and religious revival of our people.' "[97] Most conservative German resisters were antisemitic, regarding the Jews as unwanted aliens, never to be permitted German citizenship. These resisters wanted a "volkish Führer state without Hitler."[98]

During the 1930s, most German political parties including the National Socialists had anti-Jewish planks in their platforms. The vast majority of Christian Germans, by their collaboration or silence with the government, seemed to agree with the proposition that the Jews should suffer discrimination, expropriation, or expulsion as part of "God's plan" for them. The Reich's antisemitic legislation was very popular and widely supported.[99] Antisemitism was the norm in Germany during the period when the German government decided to murder all the Jews and the means established to carry out this *Endlösung*.

Although many Germans feared Hitler, many others admired his use of force against Germany's enemies outside and inside the nation.[100] Although he planned ultimately to destroy Christian institutions,[101] Hitler was widely believed when he promised to employ the power of the Third Reich to end disunity and create a Germanic and Christian nation.[102] Germany did not have a commanding Christian voice insisting, "First a human being, then a Christian: this alone is life's order."[103] Instead, the paradigmatic German Christian was Martin Luther.

The language of Nazi-Deutsch confirms that there were few Germans who sensed that Jews were part of the German polity, few who felt that Jews were authentic human beings.

### Christian Racism and Nazi Racism

Long before the Nazis, many Christians found "a horrible and fascinating physical otherness" in Jews.[104] Several church fathers wrote that the Jews were fundamentally and repugnantly alien and that the Jews transmitted indelibly and permanently evil characteristics to their offspring. The second-century Christian apologist Justin Martyr argued that God had given Moses' Law to the Jews in an attempt to keep the inherently sinful Jews' evil in check.[105] St. Augustine observed that no Jew could ever lose the stigma of his forebears' denial and murder of Christ.[106] St. Jerome claimed that all Jews were Judas, innately evil creatures who betrayed the Lord for money.[107] St. Isidore of Seville declared that the Jews' evil character never changes: "Can the Ethiopian change his skin or the leopard his spots?"[108] St. John Chrysostom called Jews deicides with no chance for "atonement, excuse, or defense"[109] and "inveterate murderers, destroyers, men possessed by the devil."[110] In 1134, St. Bernard of Clairvaux wrote that "it is an insult to Christ that the offspring of a Jew has occupied the chair of Peter."[111] St. Thomas Aquinas regarded the Jews as an inherently cruel people.[112] It was because of the Jews' innate cruelty, he charged, that God taught them how to slaughter animals in a kosher, that is, relatively painless, way.[113] At the end of the thirteenth century, "authorities in the hierarchy" refused to admit Jews to conversion.[114] Crusaders[115] often seemed intent on destroying all the Jews, rather than baptizing them because so many were convinced that Jewishness was an inexpungibly evil characteristic.

The most prominent development of the Christian racial idea took place in fifteenth- and sixteenth-century Spain.[116] Spanish theologians believed that "Jews had soiled their furthest descendants . . . corrupted [them] biologically."[117] The major Catholic orders in Spain adopted racist regulations.[118] By the early seventeenth century, even the Jesuits ordered that no man could become a priest unless Christian heritage could be traced back five generations.[119] This "impediment of origin" lasted until after the Holocaust.

In 1604 Father Prudencio de Sandoval wrote, "Who can deny that in the descendants of the Jews there persists and endures the evil inclination of their ancient ingratitude and lack of understanding. [One Jewish ancestor] alone defiles and corrupts him." In 1623 Portuguese scholar Vincente da Costa Mattos held that "a little Jewish blood is enough to destroy the world."[120] Later in the century, Father Francisco de Torrejoncillo warned, "There is no evil the Jews do not desire. . . . To be enemies of Christians, of Christ, and of his Divine Law, it is not necessary to be of a Jewish father and mother. One alone suffices." Christian children must not "be suckled by Jewish vileness because that milk, being of infected persons, can only engender perverse inclinations."[121]

By making the Jews the Devil's people, Martin Luther put them beyond conversion. Trying to convert the Jews, he argued, was like "trying to cast out the devil."[122] "They have failed to learn any lesson from the terrible distress that has been theirs for over fourteen hundred years in exile. . . . Much less do I propose to convert the Jews, for that is impossible."[123] He also wrote:

Speaking to [Jews] about conversion is much the same as preaching the gospel to a sow.

From their youth they have imbibed such venomous hatred against the Goyim from their parents and their rabbis, and they still continuously drink it. . . . It has penetrated flesh and blood, marrow and bone, and has become part and parcel of their nature and their life.

Dear Christian, be advised and so not doubt that next to the devil, you have no more bitter, venomous, and vehement foe than a real Jew who earnestly seeks to be a Jew. . . . Their lineage and circumcision infect them all.

It is impossible to convert the devil and his own, nor are we commanded to attempt this.[124]

Just as an "umbilical relationship" exists between the Old and New Testaments, so is it present in the relationship between Christian and Nazi antisemitism. Hitler's biological racism conflicted with Christian antisemitism but always presupposed it.[125] A purely secular, unchristian racism would have appealed only to the few anti-Christian Nazis who needed a secular justification for their antisemitism.[126] "Dilettante racial theories helped give modern antisemitism the scientific veneer it lacked."[127] Simultaneously rejecting the Church and imitating its Judaeophobia,[128] Hitler agreed with the church's position that Jews were an alien anti-people who must be eliminated. Both Hitler and the church regarded the Jews as their rivals for men's souls, as scapegoats for social movements, revolutions, wars, and economic dislocations that violated their worldviews, and as enemies to be defeated in proof of the victors' metaphysical power over evil and political power over life.

Hitler kept returning to Christian ideas that focused on the Jews' inherent evil and identification with the devil. Hitler argued that the Jew "stops at nothing, and in his vileness he becomes . . . the personification of the devil[;] the symbol of all evil assumes the living shape of the Jew."[129] Like traditional Christian antisemites, Hitler regarded Judaism as the "root of all evil."[130]

Sometimes Hitler spoke in biological-racial terms about the Jews. In 1919 he wrote that "the Jews are unquestionably a race, not a religious community."[131] In *Mein Kampf*, he wrote that the Jew "poisons the blood of others, but preserves his own"; "the lost purity of the blood alone destroys inner happiness forever, plunges man into the abyss for all time, and the consequences can never more be eliminated from body and spirit."[132] In 1942 his table talk included the observation that the way to free Germany of disease was to "dispose of the Jew . . . the racial germ that corrupts the mixture of the blood."[133]

Although some rank-and-file Nazis regarded biological racism[134] with an "official awe" second only to that of *Mein Kampf*, Alfred Rosenberg's secular racism was privately rejected by Hitler's inner circle and by most ordinary Germans. Rosenberg argued that every people possessed a race soul manifesting itself in a political state. He contended that the dialectic that created history was blood against blood. In mythic language, Rosenberg described a world-determining conflict between Aryans and Jews, with the Jews being the only race worth mentioning as a significant rival of the Aryans. The mystical-magical leadership of the Führer would enable the German *Volk* to destroy the Jews and conquer the inferior races by force.[135]

But support for Rosenberg's racist ideas was a minority attitude among the Nazis and certainly among the German people.[136] The Nazi government refused to issue the *Myth of the 20th Century* (it had to be published privately) because Hitler officially stood neutral in matters of religious belief, and he wanted to gather the benefits of friendship of the Christian churches.[137]

In his other books, Rosenberg argued on the basis of religious prejudice, not biological racism. In an essay,[138] he attacked the anti-Christian aspects of the Talmud. Elsewhere,[139] he claimed that the evil "Jewish spirit" created the Talmud, which in turn aggravated bad Jewish character traits. Here Rosenberg also characterized Jews as anti-Christian. In 1932 he contrasted authentic German Christianity with perfidious Jesuitism and Judaism.[140]

In public, Hitler's inner circle may have expressed anti-Jewish biological racism, but in private they ridiculed these racist ideas. Hitler himself dismissed Rosenberg's book.[141] He told Bishop Berning on April 11, 1942, "I must insist that Rosenberg's *Myth of the 20th Century* is not to be regarded as an expression of the official doctrine of the party. . . . Like most of the *Gauleiters*, I have myself merely glanced cursorily at it."[142] Hermann Göring and Josef Goebbels thought Rosenberg's book was ridiculous.[143] Göring called the *Myth* "junk," and Goebbels described it as "*weltanschauliches Gerülpse*," "philosophical belching."[144] G.M. Gilbert, the psychologist who examined the Nazi Nuremberg defendants, reported that none of them had ever even read Rosenberg.[145]

Many antisemites combined their racism with a "spiritual" antisemitism, believing that it was the Jewish spirit that was the real enemy. Paul de Lagarde wrote in 1853 that being German was "not a matter of blood, but of a spiritual state of mind (*Gemüt, nicht Geblüt*)."[146] Although Lagarde was responsible for a virulent biological assault on the Jews—"with trichinae and bacilli one does not negotiate, nor are trichinae and bacilli to be educated; they are exterminated as quickly and thoroughly as possible"[147]—he was in other ways a traditional Christian antisemite. The son of a Lutheran minister, Lagarde had his gravestone carved with the epitaph: "The way of the cross is the road to salvation."[148] Arthur Moeller van den Bruck wrote of "a race of the spirit."[149]

Edouard-Adolphe Drumont, the foremost French antisemite of the nineteenth century, also defined race as Hitler did: "A race, that is to say, a collection of individuals who think the same, a totality representing a certain number of feelings, beliefs, hopes, aptitudes, traditions."[150] Houston Stewart Chamberlain in part rests his anti-Jewish diatribe on the writings of St. Paul: "We must agree with Paul, the apostle, when he says: 'For he is not a Jew who is one outwardly in the flesh, but [a] person is a Jew who is one inwardly, and real circumcision is a matter of the heart—it is spiritual and not literal.'" Chamberlain's very unracist conclusion was that the exceptional Jew could overcome his Jewish spirit to become a real German, "a wholly humanized Jew is no longer a Jew."[151] A few days before Hitler came to power, the bishop of Linz observed that Aryans and Christians together had to fight the "dangers and damages arising out of the Jewish spirit."[152]

Parts of *Mein Kampf* seem much closer to Christian antisemitism than racism. Hitler wrote that the Jew's "spirit is inwardly as alien to true Christianity as his nature two thousand years previous was to the great founder of the new doctrine."[153] Hitler admitted a few months before the end of his life that his biological racism had been a sham. Instead, he believed in "spiritual" racism. He hated metaphysical, not biological, Jewishness; he objected to the "Jewish mind" and to the Jewish religious and cultural values that permeated Jewish thought and behavior.[154] Hitler believed that the only way to eliminate the evil Jewish spirit was to destroy their flesh and blood. Jews were reifications of the Jewish spirit he despised. Hitler suggested that beneath the surface of biological racism, a more essential "spiritual racism" existed: individual Jews embodied an inherently evil Jewish spirit—an idea as old as Christian triumphalism.[155] In 1939 Hitler noted, "I know perfectly well ... that in the scientific sense there is no such thing as [a biological] race."[156] A few months before his death, Hitler again differentiated between a race of the mind and one of the body.[157] He told his last private secretary, close associate, and second-in-command, Martin Bormann, that

we use the term Jewish race as a matter of convenience, for in reality and from the genetic point of view there is no such thing as the Jewish race. There does, however, exist a community. ... It is [a] spiritually homogeneous group [to] which all Jews throughout the world deliberately adhere ... and it is this group of human beings to which we give the title Jewish race.[158]

Denying that the Jews were only "a religious entity," since Jewish atheists existed, Hitler described the Jews as "an abstract race of the mind [that] has its origins, admittedly, in the Hebrew religion. . . . A race of the mind is something more solid, more durable than just a [biological] race, pure and simple."[159]

## Nazi-Deutsch

The history of the Christian world may be viewed as a drama that requires a spirit of evil to establish the identity of the spirit of goodness. As in any drama, once a character is established as evil, when that character suffers and dies, the audience feels justified in its hatred. It was established and then confirmed, and reconfirmed by the churches, that Jews were evil and doing evil to them was authorized, approved, justified, reasonable, indeed a religiously good work. Finally, there came a man who articulated these feelings—already long established in his Christian audience—as well or better than any other and who showed a way to solve the problem that these metaphorically, religiously, historically, and permanently evildoers presented to the world. Thus Hitler, thus the Holocaust, thus Nazi-Deutsch.

Nazi-Deutsch, like all language, sets the parameters for perceptions. Edward Sapir has noted that "we see and hear and otherwise experience very largely as we do because the language habits of our community predispose certain choices of interpretation."[160] Antisemitism ingrained in language demonstrates the "mysterious essential connection" between a thing and its name.[161]

Antisemitic language is not exclusive to Nazism or to Germany. The historical dictionaries of the Western languages reflect and perpetuate negative and hostile stereotypes of Jews. Although there are positive meanings associated with the word Jew, it is the negative ones that are full to the brim with emotional energy, idées-forces. In the seventeenth century, Littré's French dictionary defined "Juif" as someone who lends at usurious rates or anyone who gains money by means of deceit: "He is a young man eager for gain and quite a Jew." In the Oxford English Dictionary, fully half the meanings of "Jew" are offensive, repulsive, if not scurrilous. Jew is applied to a "grasping or extortionate money-lender or usurer, or a trader who drives hard bargains or deals craftily," whereas "to Jew" means to cheat; a "jewbird" has an "ugly, conspicuous beak"; a "jewbush" is one "characterized by powerful emetic and drastic properties," that is, it makes one vomit and die.

The most influential German encyclopedia of the early eighteenth century, Grosses Vollständiges Universal Lexicon, followed Luther's lead in its description of Jews.[162] Its article on Jews contended that once the Jews rejected Jesus as the Christ, they became Satan's people: "And how often have they slaughtered Christian children, crucified them, battered them to pieces! They are the worst thieves, and betrayal is their distinctive insignia. . . . Yes, God has marked them in their very natures. . . . They rouse disgust and horror. . . . [T]hey killed the Son of God, and crucified the Lord of Glory, whose blood still weighs upon them."[163]

In the Deutsches Wörterbuch begun by the Brothers Grimm, "Jude" indicates offensive, slovenly, greedy, deceitful. Their examples are: "Dirty as an old Jew; he stinks like a Jew; to taste like a dead Jew; to borrow like a Jew means worthless; Jew refers to part of a pig's spinal column; to Jew (*jüdeln*) means to talk, bargain, or smell like a Jew. Christians involved in money-lending were called *Kristen-Juden*."[164] Christian usury was termed the "*Judenspiess*," or "Jews' spear."

Of all the languages of Europe, German may have possessed the greatest potential as the language of the "Final Solution." German in particular had already contained a multiplicity of words indicating destruction, four times as many as in French.[165] Nazi-Deutsch added to this array nearly two hundred words and phrases relating to the murder of Jews and other people.

Nazi language followed traditional vocabulary in creating a fictitious Jew. It was this mythical Jew, this false and hateful image of Jews as reflected in language, that led to the mass murder of real Jews. As Aldous Huxley observed, "If you call a man a bug, it means you propose to treat him as a bug." For many Germans and other Europeans, the Jews were not only Christ-killers but *Parasiten* and *Schädlinge*, parasites and vermin. It was no mistake that the poison gas, *Zyklon*, used to murder millions of Jews was an insecticide.

The preexisting language of contempt for Jews was expanded on by the National Socialists.[166] In a literary sense the Nazis may have destroyed "the spirit of the language,"[167] but they also followed centuries-old antisemitic linguistic traditions. A Nazi slogan, "*Die Juden sind unser Unglück*," is often attributed to nineteenth-century historian Heinrich Treitschke, but it originated in Luther's *Von den Juden und ihren Lügen*," where he wrote that the Jews "are a heavy burden, a plague, a pestilence, a sheer misfortune for our country."[168] Hitler and other Nazis employed slogans, quotations, Bible verses, and proverbial expressions[169] to make their points because they sensed that their audience would be receptive to this language.[170]

The National Socialists' vocabulary of vainglorious cant and obfuscating euphemisms endowed their "political revolution" with a unique sense of German rebirth. This "utter debasement of public speech"[171] enabled the leaders of the Third Reich to cut through reason to the emotions, to express what many Germans already felt, to lend government support to popular hates and prejudices and need for power, to smooth the way for Germans—and others—and to see Nazi programs as valid and good, indeed, as worth dying for. Nazi-Deutsch disguised Nazi programs,[172] policies, attitudes, and behaviors from the outside world, from their Jewish and other victims, and perhaps from themselves. During the wartime period of *Sprachregelung* (speech control), the Nazis created terms to disguise the true purpose of their activities, although the insiders knew they referred to the Third Reich's policies and actions against the Jews. Aldo Enzi suggests that the relationship between Nazi-Deutsch and the Third Reich was a two-headed one, like the god Janus. To conceal acts of violence that would offend the ordinary German's sense of human dignity, the Nazis employed

seemingly innocuous words and expressions such as: "preventive detention," "security services," "liquidation," "final solution," "assign to work," "scientific experiments." [Nazi-Deutsch vocabulary contained words that expressed] two aspects, two malleable meanings that could be switched as required—one meaning for the masses . . . and one for the initiated, the rulers, i.e., those in charge.[173]

The Third Reich used euphemistic expressions that referred to appealing ethical values of truth, justice, and loyalty and to mythic heroism and racial purity as tools of persuasion.[174]

Hitler's public speeches[175] and private conversations indicate that Christian antisemitism inspired many of his anti-Jewish ideas, which paralleled those of his listeners.[176] Germans were receptive to this language. The cultural historian George Steiner commented that "Hitler sensed in German another music than that of Goethe, Heine, and Mann; a rasping cadence, half nebulous jargon, half obscenity. And instead of turning away in nauseated disbelief, the German people gave massive echo to the man's bellowing."[177] The centuries of *Judenhaß*, the additional support of antisemitic racial theories, the condoning of antisemitism by many political and religious authorities all conditioned many, if not most, of the German people to follow Hitler into the Holocaust. At a party convention in 1934 Joseph Goebbels called directly for the use of such language: "We must speak the language that the folk understands. Whoever wants to speak to the folk must, as Luther says, pay heed to folk speech."[178] In *Mein Kampf*, Hitler wrote: "I must not measure the speech of a statesman to his people by the impression that it leaves in a university professor, but by the effect it exerts on the people."[179]

## Notes

1. Arthur Cohen, *The Myth of the Judeo-Christian Tradition* (New York: 1963), 52.

2. Jacob Katz, "Was the Holocaust Predictable?" in *The Holocaust as Historical Experience*, ed. Yehuda Bauer and Nathan Rotenstreich (New York: 1981), 34, 36.

3. Robert Wilken, "Insignissima Religio, Certe Licita?" in *The Impact of the Church Upon Its Culture* ed. Jerald Brauer (Chicago: 1968), 63.

4. St. Ambrose, "In Expositionem Evangelii Secundum Lucam," in *Patrologia, Cursus Completus, Series Latina* [hereafter, *PL*], ed. J.-P. Migne (Paris: 1844–1855), 15:1630.

5. Claus-Ekkehard Bärsch. *Erlösung und Vernichtung: Dr. phil. Josef Goebbels: Zur Psyche und Ideologie eines jungen Nationalsozialisten, 1923–1927* (Munich: 1987).

6. Randall L. Bytwerk, *Julius Streicher* (New York: 1983).

7. Quoted from Friedrich Heer, *God's First Love* (New York: 1967), 37.

8. St. Augustine, "Commentaries on Psalms 58 and 59," in *PL*, 36–37:705.

9. Richard L. Rubenstein, *After Auschwitz: Radical Theology and Contemporary Judaism* (Indianapolis, IN: 1966), 74.

10. *Homilies Against Judaizing Christians*, 4.7.4; see also 1.4.1.

11. *Apostolic Constitutions*, 2.61.1; *Homilies Against Judaizing Christians*, 1.3.1, 1.3.5, 1.4.2.

12. *Homilies Against Judaizing Christians*, 1.2.4–1.2.6. See also St. John Chrysostom, *Demonstration to the Jews and Gentiles That Christ Is God*, 4; *Patrologia, Cursus Completus, Series Graeca* (Paris: 1856–1866), 48:819.

13. *Codex Theodosiamus*, 3:1:5, 15:5:5, 16:5:44, 16:7:3, 16:8:7, 16:8:19, 16:8:22, 16:9:4; *Codex Justinianus*, 1:9:3, 1:7:5, and 1:5:7.

14. For a contrary point of view, see Robert Burns, "Antisemitism and Anti-Judaism in Christian History," *The Catholic Historical Review* 20 (1984): 90–93.

15. Robert Chazan sees in the First Crusade's slaughters of Jews in 1096 the emergence of this hostile view of Jews. See Robert Chazan, *European Jewry and the First Crusade* (Berkeley: 1987), 214.

16. Shlomo Simonsohn, *The Apostolic See and the Jews: Documents* (Toronto: 1988), docs. 79 and 82.

17. St. Thomas Aquinas, *De Regimine principum et de regimine Judaeorum* (Turin, Italy: 1924), 117; *Opuscula Omnia* (Paris: 1927), 1:488. See also his *Summa Theologiae* (New York: 1969), 11–11, Q. 10, a. 12, and 111, Q. 68, a. 10 (also called *Summa Theologica*).

18. St. Thomas Aquinas, "Letter to the Duchess of Brabant," in *Church, State, and Jew in the Middle Ages*, ed. Robert Chazan (New York: 1980), 200.

19. Aside from context, there is no way to distinguish between "slave" and "serf" using the medieval Latin word *servus*.

20. Shlomo Simonsohn, *The Apostolic See and the Jews: History* (Toronto: 1991), 139.

21. Lester K. Little, "The Jews in Christian Europe," in *Essential Papers on Judaism and Chistianity in Conflict: From Late Antiquity to the Reformation*, ed. Jeremy Cohen (New York: 1991), 277.

22. Jonathan Riley-Smith, "The First Crusade and the Persecution of the Jews," in *Persecution and Toleration*, ed. W. J. Sheils (n.p., 1984), 51–56; Chazan, *European Jewry*, 80–81.

23. Quote from an anonymous chronicler of Mainz in Adolf Neubauer and Moritz Stern, eds., *Hebräische Berichte über die Judenverfolgungen während der Kreuzzüge* (Berlin: 1892), 176, 169; Robert Chazan, "The Hebrew First-Crusade Chronicles," *Revue des études juives: Historia Judaica* 33 (January–June 1974): 249–250, 253; Bernold, *Chronicle in Monumenta Germaniae Historica, Scriptores* (Hannover, Germany: 1826–1896), 5:465.

24. Gavin I. Langmuir, *History, Religion, and Antisemitism* (Berkeley: 1990), 291; and *Toward a Definition of Antisemitism* (Berkeley: 1990), 97.

25. As at Monieux, Rouen, and Jerusalem. The Crusaders planned to destroy the Jews at prayer on the sabbath in the Speyer synagogue, but the Jews anticipated the Crusaders, and so the slaughter took place outside the synagogue. Norman Golb, "New Light on the Persecution of French Jews at the Time of the First Crusade," in *Medieval Jewish Life*, ed. Robert Chazan (New York: 1976), 24.

26. Jonathan Riley-Smith, *The First Crusade and the Idea of Crusading* (Philadelphia: 1986), 53; Riley-Smith, *The Crusades: A Short History* (New Haven, CT: 1987), 17. This kind of behavior characterized the Nazis as well.

27. For the psychological motivations behind these charges, see Magdalene Schultz, "The Blood Libel: A Motif in the History of Childhood," in *The Blood Libel Legend: A Casebook in Antisemitic Folklore*, ed. Alan Dundes (Madison: 1991), 273–303; Langmuir, *History, Religion, and Antisemitism*, 261.

28. Werner Keller, *Diaspora: The Post-Biblical History of the Jews* (New York: 1966), 237; see also Norman Cohn, *Pursuit of the Millennium* (Oxford: 1980), chap. 7.

29. St. Augustine, "Reply to Faustus, the Manichaean," in *Disputation and Dialogue: Readings from the Jewish-Christian Encounter*, ed. Frank Ephraim Talmage (New York: 1975), 31; and "Commentaries on Psalms 58 and 59," in *PL*, 36–37:705.

30. Solomon Grayzel, *The Church and the Jews in the XIIIth Century* (New York: 1966), Documents 13, 14, 18, 41, 49, 53, 59; Solomon Grayzel, *The Church and the Jews in the XIIIth Century* (Detroit: 1989), Documents 26, 27, 33, 50.

31. Guido Kisch, "Necrologue Reinhold Lewin, 1888-1942," *Historia Judaica* 8 (1946): 217–219.

32. Reinhold Lewin, *Luthers Stellung zu den Juden: Ein Betrag zur Geschichte der Juden während des Reformationszeitalters* (Berlin: 1911), 110.

33. Gerhard Falk, *The Jew in Christian Theology: Martin Luther's Anti-Jewish Vom Schem Hamphoras* (London: 1992), 253.

34. Martin Luther, "Jews," 277, 288, 264–265, 156–157, 164, 256, 212. The Nazis made the same association. See Isaiah Trunk, *Jewish Responses to Nazi Persecution* (New York: 1979), 273.

35. Falk, *Jewish Responses*, 239.

36. *Luther's Werke* (Erlangen, Germany: 1854), 32:298, 282; Hartmann Grisar, *Luther* (St. Louis: 1915), 4:286, 5:406.

37. Falk, *Jewish Responses*, 239–240.

38. Hans Hillerbrand, "Martin Luther and the Jews," in *Jews and Christians: Exploring the Past, Present, and Future*, ed. James H. Charlesworth (New York: 1990), 132.

39. Luther implies that this is impossible.

40. Luther, "Jews," 269–272.

41. Luther, "Jews," 265. This last phrase was employed likewise by the eminent nineteenth-century German historian Heinrich Treitschke, the Pan-German League, and the Nazis.

42. Luther, "Jews," 272, 292.

43. Quoted in Lewin, *Luthers Stellung zu den Juden*, 77. Another advocate of permanently shutting Jewish mouths was St. John Chrysostom (*Homilies Against the Jews*, 5.1.6, 7.2.3).

44. Robert Alter, "From Myth to Murder," *The New Republic* (May 20, 1991): 40.

45. Luther, "Jews," 242, 289, 267.

46. Falk, *Jewish Responses*, 247.

47. Martin Stöhr, "Martin Luther und die Juden," in *Christen and Juden*, ed. Wolf-Dieter Marsch and Karl Thieme (Mainz, Germany: 1961), 127–129; Haim Hillel Ben-Sasson, "Jewish-Christian Disputation in the German Empire," *Harvard Theological Review* 59 (1966): 369–371; Wilhelm Maurer, "Die Zeit der Reformation," in *Kirche and Synagogue*, ed. Karl Rengstorf and Siegfried von Kortzfleisch (Stuttgart, Germany: 1968): 1:378–380; Lewin, *Luthers Stellung zu den Juden*, 110; Heiko Augustinus Oberman, *The Roots of Anti-semitism: In the Age of the Renaissance and Reformation* (Philadelphia: 1981), 9.

48. Salo Baron, *A Social and Religious History of the Jews* (New York: 1952–1969), 13:429, n. 26.

49. Jonathan Israel, *European Jewry in the Age of Mercantilism, 1550–1750* (Oxford: 1989), 12–13.

50. Georg Liebe, *Das Judentum in der deutschen Vergangenheit* (Leipzig, Germany: 1903), 37.

51. Isiah Shachar, *The Judensau* (London: 1974), 87–88, n. 239.

52. R. Edelmann, "Ahasuerus the Wandering Jew: Origin and Background," in *The Wandering Jew: Essays in the Interpretation of a Christian Legend*, ed. Galit Hasan-Rokem and Alan Dundes (Bloomington, IN: 1986), 6.

53. Paul Lawrence Rose, *Revolutionary Antisemitism in Germany from Kant to Wagner* (Princeton, NJ: 1990), 24.

54. Eleonore Sterling, *Judenhass: Die Anfänge des politischen Antisemitismus in Deutschland, 1815–1850* (Frankfurt, Germany: 1969), 56. My late friend, the Danish Holocaust scholar, Stig Møller's term.

55. Stig Møller's phrase.

56. Nicholas De Lange, *Atlas of the Jewish World* (New York: 1984), 44; Heinrich Graetz, *History of the Jews* (Philadelphia: 1940), 4:696-698.

57. Johannes Brosseder, *Luthers Stellung zu den Juden im Spiegel seiner Interpreten* (Munich: 1972).

58. K. von der Bach, *Luther als Judenfeind* (Berlin: 1931); E. Vogelsang, *Luthers Kampf Gegen die Juden* (Tübingen, Germany: 1938); Uriel Tal, *Christians and Jews in Germany: Religion, Politics, and Ideology in the Second Reich, 1870–1914* (Ithaca, NY: 1975).

59. Houston Stewart Chamberlain, *Deutschlands Kampfziel* (Munich: 1916), 61.

60. *Trial of Major War Criminals Before the International Military Tribunal* (Nuremberg, Germany: 1947–1949), 12:318.

61. He forbade "the synagogue of Satan," itself a quotation from Revelations, and "the enemies of Christ" from having any power over Christians. Pope Gregory VII, "Epistola II: Ad Alphonsum Regem Castellae," *Patrologiae Latina* 148, 604–605.

62. Heer, *God's First Love*, 130.

63. George L. Mosse, *Toward the Final Solution: A History of European Racism* (New York: 1978), 205.

64. Heer, *God's First Love*, 284–286.

65. Kurt Ludecke, *I Knew Hitler: A Story of a Nazi Who Escaped the Blood Purge* (London: 1938), 465–466

66. John Conway, "Protestant Missions to the Jews, 1810–1980: Ecclesiastical Imperialism or Theological Aberration?" *Holocaust and Genocide Studies* 1 (1986): 135; Robert P. Ericksen, *Theologians Under Hitler: Gerhard Kittel, Paul Althaus, and Emanuel Hirsch* (New Haven, CT: 1985).

67. Ernst Ehrlich, "Luther und die Juden," in *Die Juden und Martin Luther*, ed. Heinz Kremers et al. (Darmstadt, Germany: 1987), 86.

68. See the section "Germany at the Center" later in this Introduction.

69. Johann Fichte, *Reden an die deutsche Nation*, Sixth Address, Point 81 (1808).

70. The phrase "state within a state" had been used against the French Huguenots, the Jesuits, and Freemasons. See Jacob Katz, "A State Within a State: The History of an Antisemitic Slogan," *Proceedings of the Israel Academy of Sciences and Humanities*, 4(3); and *Jews and Freemasons in Europe, 1723–1939* (Cambridge, MA: 1970), 223–224.

71. Martin Luther, "On the Jews and Their Lies," in *Luther's Works*, ed. and trans. Franklin Sherman (Philadelphia: 1971), 137–138, 265.

72. Johann Fichte, *Beitrag zur Berichtigung der Urteile des Publikums über die französische Revolution*, in *Fichtes Sämtliche Werke* (Berlin: 1845–1846), 6:149–150.

73. Fichte, *Beitrag*, 6:149.

74. Fichte, *Beitrag*, 6:150.

75. Fichte, *Beitrag*, 6:149-50.

76. Sterling, *Judenhass*, 128–129.

77. Tal, *Christians and Jews in Germany*, 291–292; Mosse, *Toward the Final Solution*, esp. 119, 121, 127, and chap. 11.

78. Jacob Katz, *Out of the Ghetto: The Social Background of Jewish Emancipation, 1770–1870* (New York: 1978), 87.

79. Alter, "From Myth to Murder," 34.

80. Sterling, *Judenhass*, 67–68.

81. Hannah Arendt, *The Origins of Totalitarianism* (Cleveland: 1958), 64.

82. Katz, *Out of the Ghetto*, 210.

83. "When someone has something in his eye, he doesn't care whether it is a piece of gold or a piece of mud, he wants it out." Quoted from Fritz Stern, "The Burden of Success: Reflections on German Jewry," in *Dreams and Delusions: The Drama of German History*, ed. Fritz Stern (New York: 1987), n. 111.

84. John Weiss, *Ideology of Death: Why the Holocaust Happened in Germany* (Chicago: 1996), 142.

85. Peter Fritzsche, *Germans into Nazis* (Cambridge, MA: 1998).

86. Ericksen, *Theologians Under Hitler*, 1, 26, 33, 35, 48, 55, 58, 76, 109–119, 199.

87. Both men changed their minds in regard to Jews. Bonhöffer by the late 1930s was helping Jews but, involved in the von Stauffenberg *attentat* against Hitler, was executed.

After the war, Niemöller saw himself and other Lutherans "as guilty as any SS man" in regard to the Holocaust.

88. Dietrich Bonhöffer, *Gesammelte Schriften*, 2:49–50.

89. Martin Niemöller, *Here Stand I!* (New York: 1937), 193–198.

90. Niemöller, *Here Stand I!*, 195.

91. Nuremberg Document, NG 1531.

92. Michael Faulhaber, *Judaism, Christianity, and Germany* (London: 1934), 13–14.

93. Ian Kershaw, *Popular Opinion and Political Dissent in the Third Reich: Bavaria 1933–1945* (London: 1983), 154.

94. Fritzsche, *Germans into Nazis*, 8, 208–209.

95. Robert Gellately, *The Gestapo and German Society: Enforcing Racial Policy, 1933–1945* (New York: 1990), 184.

96. Marcel Ophuls, *The Sorrow and the Pity: A Film* (New York: 1972).

97. Ger van Roon, *Neuordnung im Widerstand* (Munich: 1967), 561.

98. Hermann Graml, Hans Mommsen, et al., *The German Resistance to Hitler* (Berkeley and Los Angeles: 1970), 112f.

99. Detlev Peukert, *Inside Nazi Germany: Conformity, Opposition, and Racism in Everday Life*, trans. Richard Deveson (New Haven, CT: 1987), 60; Gellately, *The Gestapo and German Society*, 206, 207, 214; Ophuls, *The Sorrow and the Pity: A Film*.

100. Kurt Pätzold, "Terror and Demagoguery in the Consolidation of the Fascist Dictatorship in Germany, 1933–34," in *Radical Perspectives on the Rise of Fascism in Germany, 1919–1945*, ed. Michael N. Dobkowski and Isidor Wallimann (New York: 1989).

101. H.R. Trevor-Roper, *Hitler's Secret Conversations, 1941-1944* (New York: 1962), 83–84, 158, 159, 206, 390; John Conway, "Between Cross and Swastika," in *A Mosaic of Victims: Non-Jews Persecuted and Murdered by the Nazis*, ed. Michael Berenbaum (New York: 1990), 181–182; Ian Kershaw, *The "Hitler Myth": Image and Reality in the Third Reich* (Oxford: 1987), 2, 5, 106, 109, 112.

102. Robert Ericksen, "A Radical Minority: Resistance in the German Protestant Church," in *Germans Against Nazism: Nonconformity, Opposition, and Resistance in the Third Reich: Essays in Honor of Peter Hoffman*, ed. Francis R. Nicosia and Lawrence D. Stokes (New York: 1990), 119.

103. This was the motto of Denmark's leading Lutheran humanist Nikolai Grundtvig. See Jaroslav Pelikan, "Grundtvig's Influence," in *The Rescue of the Danish Jews: Moral Courage Under Stress*, ed. Leo Goldberger (New York: 1987), 174, 176–177, 179–180.

104. Alter, "From Myth to Murder," 34, 37–38.

105. *Dialogue with Trypho*, 2:23.

106. Gerhart Ladner, "Aspects of Patristic Anti-Judaism," *Viator* 2 (1971): 362; St. Augustine, *Adversus Judaeos*, 7, 10.

107. St. Jerome, *Father of the Church: Homilies of Saint Jerome 1–59 on the Psalms* (Washington, DC: 1964), 1:255, 258–262.

108. Rosemary Radford Ruether, *Faith and Fratricide* (New York: 1965), 130.

109. *Homilies Against Judaizing Christians*, 6.2.10.

110. *8 Orations Against the Jews*, I:4.

111. Mary Stroll, *The Jewish Pope: Ideology and Politics in the Papal Schism of 1130* (Leiden, The Netherlands: 1987), 166.

112. Pope Leo XIII in *Aeterni Patris*, August 4, 1879.

113. Aquinas, *Summa Theologiae*, 1a 2ae, 102, 6.8.

114. Edward Synan, *The Popes and the Jews in the Middle Ages* (New York: 1965), 120, 134.

115. Riley-Smith, "The First Crusade and the Persecution of the Jews," 51–52.

116. Yosef Yerushalmi, *Assimilation and Racial Antisemitism* (New York: 1982).

117. Léon Poliakov, *The Aryan Myth: A History of Racial and Naturalist Ideas in Europe* (New York: Basic Books, 1974), 12–13; Albert Sicroff, *Les controverses des statuts de "pureté de sang" en Espagne du XVe au XVIIe siècle* (Paris: 1960); Michael Glatzer, "Pablo de Santa Maria on the Events of 1391," in *Antisemitism Through the Ages*, ed. Shmuel Almog, trans. Nathan H. Reiser (Oxford: 1988), 127–137.

118. James Reites, S.J., "St. Ignatius of Loyola and the Jews," *Studies in the Spirituality of Jesuits* (September 1981): 15, 16, 32.

119. Reites, "St. Ignatius of Loyola and the Jews."

120. Jerome Friedman, "Jewish Conversion, the Spanish Pure Blood Laws and Reformation." *The Sixteenth-Century Journal* (Spring 1987): 16–17.

121. Frank E. Manuel, *The Broken Staff: Judaism Through Christian Eyes* (Cambridge: 1992), 223–224; Yerushalmi, *Assimilation and Racial Antisemitism*, 16.

122. Martin Luther, "That Jesus Christ Was Born a Jew," in *Luther's Works*, ed. Walther Brandt (Philadelphia: 1967), 5:213.

123. Luther, "Jews," 137–138. See also Lewin, *Luthers Stellung zu den Juden*, 77.

124. Martin Luther, "The Jews and Their Lies," in *Luther's Works*, trans. Franklin Sherman (Philadelphia: 1971), 170, 216, 217, 253, 267, 268–269, 285, 286.

125. Sterling, *Judenhass*; Herman Greive, *Theologie und Ideologie: Katholizmus und Judentum in Deutschland und Osterreich* (Heidelberg, Germany: 1969). For a secular analysis of Hitler's racism, see Michael Burleigh and Wolfgang Wippermann, *The Racial State: Germany, 1933–1945* (Cambridge: 1991), 37–43.

126. Mosse, *Toward the Final Solution*, 119, 121, 127.

127. Christof Dipper, "Der Deutsche Widerstand und die Juden," in *Geschichte und Gesellschaft* 9 (1983): 372. See also Rose, *Revolutionary Antisemitism*, 14.

128. For Hitler's use of the church as a model for many elements of Nazism having nothing to do with his antisemitism, see Robert G.L. Waite, *The Psychopathic God: Adolf Hitler* (New York: 1977), 32–36.

129. Adolf Hitler, *Mein Kampf*, trans. Ralph Mannheim (Boston: 1962), 324.

130. Klaus Scholder, "Judentum und Christentum in der Ideologie und Politik des Nationalsozialismus, 1919–1945," in *Judaism and Christianity under the Impact of National Socialism, 1919–1945* (Jerusalem: 1982), 198.

131. Werner Masur, ed., *Hitler's Letters and Notes* (New York: 1976), 210.

132. Hitler, *Mein Kampf*, 312, 316, 327; see also 305.

133. Henry Picker, ed., *Hitler's Tischgespräche im Führerhauptquartier, 1941–1942* (Bonn: 1951), 321.

134. Alfred Rosenberg, *Race and Race History, and Other Essays* (New York: 1974), 68–70, 175–190, 198–199.

135. Robert Pois, ed., *Race and Race History and Other Essays by Alfred Rosenberg* (New York: 1970).

136. Peter Matheson, ed., *The Third Reich and the Christian Churches* (Grand Rapids, MI: 1981), 99–101.

137. Jonathan Wright, "The German Protestant Church and the Nazi Party in the Period of the Seizure of Power," in *Studies in Church History* 14 (1977): 398.

138. Alfred Rosenberg, *Unmoral im Talmud* (Munich: 1920).

139. Alfred Rosenberg, *Die Spur des Juden im Wandel der Zeiten* (Munich: 1920).

140. Alfred Rosenberg, *Judentum, Jesuitismus, Deutsches Christentum* (Munich: 1932).

141. Franz von Papen, *Memoirs* (London: 1952), 261.

142. Hitler, *Hitler's Secret Conversations*, 400. See also "The Story of Rosenberg's 'Mythus,'" *Wiener Library Bulletin* 7 (1953): 33.

143. Similarly, in December 1943 Benito Mussolini called the Fascist Race Manifesto "a piece of pseudo-scientific rubbish *(astruseria scientifica)*." See Renzo De Felice, *Storia degli ebrei italiani sotto il fascismo* (Turin, Italy: 1972), 541–542; Bruno Spampanato, "Contromemoriale," in *Mussolini and the Jews: German-Italian Relations and the Jewish Question in Italy, 1922–1945* (Oxford: 1978), 396–397.

144. "The Story of Rosenberg's 'Mythus,'" 33.

145. G.M. Gilbert, *Nuremberg Diary* (New York: 1961), 321.

146. Paul de Lagarde, *Die gegenwärtigen Aufgaben der deutschen Politik in deutsche Schriften* (Munich: 1924), 30.

147. Paul de Lagarde, *Juden und Indogermanen*, in Alex Bein, "Modern Antisemitism and Its Effect on the Jewish Question," *Yad Vashem Studies* 3 (1959): 14.

148. Robert Lougee, *Paul de Lagarde, 1827–1891: A Study of Radical Conservatism in Germany* (Cambridge: 1961), 151–154.

149. Fritz Stern, *The Politics of Cultural Despair* (Berkeley: 1974), 201.

150. Edouard-Adolphe Drumont, *La France Juive* (Paris: 1885), 2:572.

151. Steven Aschheim, "The Myth of 'Judaization' in Germany," in *The Jewish Response to German Culture: From the Enlightenment to the Second World War*, ed. Jehuda Reinharz and Walter Schatzberg (Hanover, NH: 1985), 230.

152. Peter G.J. Pulzer, *The Rise of Political Anti-Semitism in Germany and Austria* (Cambridge, MA: 1988), 312.

153. Hitler, *Mein Kampf*, 307.

154. Langmuir, *Toward a Definition of Antisemitism*, 348.

155. In the early 1920s, Hitler stated this idea to Dietrich Eckart (see Aschheim, "The Myth of 'Judaization' in Germany," 240).

156. Hermann Rauschning, *Hitler Speaks* (London: 1939), 229.

157. In his final Political Testament, after blaming the Jews for the war, Hitler would "call upon the government and the people scrupulously to uphold the racial laws and mercilessly to oppose the universal poisoner of all nations, international Jewry." Nuremberg Document PS-3569.

158. First published in French by Fayard as Martin Bormann, *Le Testament politique de Hitler: Notes Recueillies par Martin Bormann* (Paris: 1959), it contains an important monologue of February 13, 1945. Republished in English, as *The Testament of Adolf Hitler: The Hitler-Bormann Documents, February–April 1945*, ed. L. Craig Fraser (London: 1960).

159. Fraser, *The Testament of Adolf Hitler*, 55-56.

160. John Carroll, ed., *Language, Thought, and Reality* (Cambridge: 1956), 134. See also Haig A. Bosmajian, *The Language of Oppression* (Washington, DC: 1974).

161. Margaret Schlauch, *The Gift of Language* (New York: 1955), 13.

162. *Grosses Vollständiges Universal Lexicon*, published in 1735.

163. Manuel, *The Broken Staff*, 250–251.

164. Such usage is at least five centuries old, if not fifteen.

165. Rose, *Revolutionary Antisemitism*, 6; James Edward Young, *Writing and Rewriting the Holocaust: Narrative and the Consequences of Interpretation* (Bloomington, IN: 1988), 4.

166. From Hitler down to the average German there was an intimate relationship between their conscious and unconscious religious values and their perception of Jews. The

Nazis found that their antisemitic propaganda was most effective when it coincided with Christian defamations. See Marlis G. Steinert, *Hitler's War and the Germans: Public Mood and Attitude During the Second World War* (Columbus, OH: 1977), 334.

167. Hans Jacob, "An ihrer Sprache sollt Ihr sie erkennen: Die Gleichschaltung der deutschen Sprache," *Das Wort* 1 (1938): 81–86. Wolfgang Mieder has studied how the National Socialists began to change the German language. See Wolfgang Mieder, "'. . . as if I were the master of the situation': Proverbial Manipulation in Adolf Hitler's *Mein Kampf*," *DE PROVERBIO: An Electronic Journal of International Proverb Studies* 1(1) (1995). Many of the following citations derive from Professor Mieder's study.

168. Luther, "Jews," 265.

169. Karl Kraus, *Die dritte Walpurgisnacht*, ed. Heinrich Fischer (München: 1952), 8, 211.

170. Siegfried Bork, *Mißbrauch der Sprache: Tendenzen nationalsozialistischer Sprachregelung* (Munich: 1970), 50–51, 91–95; Walther Dieckmann, *Sprache in der Politik* (Heidelberg, Germany: 1969), 108; Sigrid Frind, "Die Sprache als Propagandainstrument in der Publizistik des Dritten Reiches, untersucht an Hitlers 'Mein Kampf' und den Kriegsjahrgängen des 'Völkischen Beobachters'" (Ph.D. diss., Free University of Berlin, 1964), 70–73; Sigrid Frind, "Die Sprache als Propagandainstrument des Nationalsozialismus," *Muttersprache* 76 (1966): 129–135; Jürgen Henningsen, *Bildsamkeit, Sprache und Nationalsozialismus* (Essen, Germany: 1963), 14–16; Gerhard Voigt, "Bericht vom Ende der 'Sprache des Nationalsozialismus,'" *Diskussion Deutsch* 19 (1974): 445–464. Mieder, "'. . . as if I were the master of the situation.'"

171. Katherine Powers, "When Finding the Words Is a Matter of Life, Death, and Sanity," *Boston Globe* (January 30, 2000): E4.

172. Cornelia Berning, *Vom Abstammungsnachweis zum Zuchtwort: Vokabular des Nationalsozialismus* (Berlin: 1964); Werner Betz, "The National-Socialist Vocabulary," in *The Third Reich*, ed. Maurice Baumont, John Fried, and Edmond Vermeil (New York: 1955), 784–796; Bork, *Mißbrauch der Sprache*; Rolf Glunk, "Erfolg und Mißerfolg der nationalsozialistischen Sprachlenkung," *Zeitschrift für deutsche Sprache* 22 (1966): 57–73, 146–153; 23 (1967): 83–113, 178–188; 24 (1968): 72–91, 184–191; 26 (1970): 84–97, 176–183; 27 (1971): 113–123, 177–187; Heinz Paechter, *Nazi-Deutsch: A Glossary of Contemporary German* (New York: 1944); Wolfgang Werner Sauer, *Der Sprachgebrauch von Nationalsozialisten vor 1933* (Hamburg, Germany: 1978); Eugen Seidel and Ingeborg Seidel-Slotty, *Sprachwandel im Dritten Reich: Eine kritische Untersuchung faschistischer Einflüsse* (Halle, Germany: 1961).

173. Aldo Enzi, *Il Lessico della violenza nella Germania nazista* (Bologna, Italy: 1971), 18.

174. Anna-Vera Sullam, "A Name for Extermination" (unpublished manuscript.)

175. All quotations of Hitler's speeches are cited from the standard edition by Max Domarus, *Hitler: Reden und Proklamationen 1932-1945*, trans. Wolgang Mieder (Neustadt an der Aisch, Germany: 1962), 1:244.

176. Waite, *The Psychopathic God*, 35–36. Adolf Hitler, *My New Order*, ed. Raoul de Roussy de Sales (New York: 1973), 26–27, 597; Hitler, *Mein Kampf*, 65, 307; Hitler's speech at Koblenz, in *The Speeches of Adolf Hitler*, ed. Norman Baynes (New York: 1969), 240, 386–387; Pinchas Lapide, *Three Popes and the Jews* (New York: 1967), 90, 239; Weiss, *Ideology of Death*, 390; Heer, *God's First Love*, 309; Kershaw, The "Hitler Myth," 107; George Bailey, *Germans: Biography of an Obsession* (New York: 1974), 196.

177. George Steiner, *Language and Silence: Essays on Language, Literature, and the Inhuman* (New York: 1967), 99.

178. Cornelia Berning, "Die Sprache der Nationalsozialisten," *Zeitschrift für deutsche Wortforschung* 18 (1962): 109.

179. This quotation is from the English translation of *Mein Kampf* by Ralph Manheim (Boston: 1962), 477. Professor Mieder has provided a more colloquial translation of the German proverbial language.

# Nazi-Deutsch: An Ideological Language of Exclusion, Domination, and Annihilation

Karin Doerr

Positive words, negative words, ambivalent words, words with warped meanings, words with narrowed meanings—together with catch-all expressions and the many compounds created out of words like *Rasse*, *Blut*, and *Volk*, they comprised a *weltanschaulich* vocabulary that set forth in emotionally charged idiom the Nazi outlook on life.[1]

German, as it changed during the Third Reich period, represents a deviation from human and humanistic language development and a violation of civil interaction and even the meaning of speech. It was so pervasive that it helped influence the thinking of a nation and had a devastating, irreparable effect on the victims. This important, if shameful, chapter in the history of the German language and culture demonstrates the opposite of what language could or should be, namely, in George Steiner's words, "the vessel of human grace and the prime carrier of civilization."[2]

Instead, Nazi Germany employed language as an instrument of coercion and indoctrination toward specific racial and spatial goals. The Third Reich language reveals to us these intentions even when they were meant to be concealed. Ironically, it was in democratic Weimar Germany, after World War I, that the right wing National-Socialist German Workers Party (*Nationalsozialistische Deutsche Arbeiterpartei*) began its ascent under Hitler. From his accession to power in 1933, the regime embarked on an elaborate program of bringing all levels of government, all institutions and all businesses into line with Nazi ideology. They used a term from electrotechnology for this endeavor: *Gleichschaltung* (coordination). Denying personal freedom of choice, everyone had to conform to the political framework of the state. The Nazi leadership employed efficient propaganda techniques in radio, in the press, and at official functions to promote their ideas and win public support for their long-ranging plans. What was heard, seen in print, and eventually used in all walks of German life was a language that was influenced by and infused with Nazi *Weltanschauung*. It has become known as Nazi-Deutsch (Nazi German) and is a true mirror of its time, as it lays bare all the nuances of German National Socialist thought and action and the impact on all levels of speech. This included the language in dictionaries, grammar books, and common literature.

In addition, the regime introduced specific language changes and controlled language usage by means of numerous binding regulations (*Sprachregelung*). In the beginning, they reflected the policy of political coordination and, later, helped to disguise aggressive military and murderous actions. From 1940, the propaganda ministry issued a twice-daily briefing at which the "daily word" (*Tagesparole*) of the Reich publishing chief was released. Another part of language interference by the state was "Germanization," which advocated reintroduction of archaic Germanic words and/or replacement of foreign words (*Fremdwörter*) with specially coined German ones.[3] Some of these new word creations bordered on the ridiculous in their forced attempt to circumvent the term of foreign origin. This included the well established words *Mikroskop* and *Maschine*, which were to be replaced with *Feinsehrohr* (fine-seeing tube) and *Gangwerk* (motion work), respectively. At the same time, Nazi officials retained the practice and privilege of using terms of non-German origin, such as *exekutieren* (to execute), *liquidieren* (to liquidate), or *Totalevakuierung* (complete evacuation), either as linguistic distancing devices, or for effect, as was the case with *gigantisch* (gigantic) and *total*.[4] The Nazis even Germanized script by requiring the employment of the angular German handwriting (*Deutsche Schrift*) in official communication until 1941. All government-controlled printed matter, textbooks, and newspapers were reset in gothic or "black" letters, which were considered to be a specifically "German" type, in contrast to the so-called "foreign" roman type.[5]

Familiarizing oneself with this language means recognizing how pervasive it was and how totalitarian German National Socialist ideology was. It shows without a doubt the passive or active acceptance of the regime's ways and goals in the areas of culture, economy, and education, as well as its political and military agencies. The many euphemisms, neologisms, names, codes, and Third Reich jargon in general open the door to a world of concepts, intricate institutions, and unique positions within German military and civilian life. Their names and functions reveal the state's influence on education, work, and leisure activities of German children and adults. There was the Hitler Youth (*Hitlerjugend* or *HJ*) with its hierarchy of youth leaders (*Jugendführer*), youth camps (*Jugendlager*), and organized activities, such as club night (*Heimabend*), which consisted of mandatory Wednesday evening courses for boys and girls.[6] The names of other organizations show further how the regime impacted the lives of German women by reinforcing traditional gender roles. Mother schooling (*Mütterschulung*), an ideological and practical training, prepared them for family and motherhood—all in the name of the state and its people (*Volksganze*). Not without the willingness of some women, the powerful National Socialist Women's Organization (*Nationalsozialistische Frauenschaft*) was, from 1936, exclusively responsible for training the female leaders and assigning official tasks and projects that involved all German women. It started with the association for young girls (*Jungmädelbund*). During the war, the women of the League of German Girls (*Bund Deutscher Mädchen*) had to give their services to the state (*Kriegshilfsdienst*). The notion of family had lost its traditional sense and had become instead an ideological interpretation of German blood ties defined with the archaic term *Sippe* (clan). Even the choice of a marriage partner was determined by the state as Germans had to provide the *Ariernachweis* (proof of Aryan descent), which was required after the racist 1935 Nuremberg Laws were enacted. Members of the SS elite needed the government's approval to get married and needed a proof of ancestry pass (*Ahnenpaß*).

Almost all Germans had to pledge their fealty to Hitler as leader in one form or another. This was verbalized in the different loyalty oaths (*Treueide*) that ranged from those of the young boys and girls of the Hitler Youth to the highest ranks of the SS. The personal bonding, like that expressed in the SS motto, "My honor is [synonymous with] loyalty" (*Meine Ehre heißt Treue*), relied on the notion of a common destiny.[7] Slogans, such as *Deutschland erwache!* (Wake up, Germany!) and *Führer befiehl, wir folgen!* (You, Führer, command and we will follow and obey!), were directed at the German public to attain an obedient national collective. An archaic Germanic mythology was revived and suffused the Third Reich discourse with a glorified heroism (*Heldentum*) and a willingness for self-sacrifice (*Opferwilligkeit*) and sacrificial death (*Opfertod*) of the individual. The verbalization of such concepts was intended to evoke sentiments of mystical blood ties and emotions to make Germans believe in the transcendental German nation (*Volk*). The exclusion of others from this racially perceived community (*Volksgemeinschaft*) was underscored in a heightened sense of belonging, by way of birth, to this privileged group. These few linguistic examples of life in Nazi Germany also attest to a tight government control and the connection and constant interaction of the leader, the party, and society, as well as the firm grip the state had on every aspect of an individual's life.

With their public Aryan grandiloquence, the National Socialists intended to affect collective thinking. The basic nationalistic concepts of *Volk* (people), *Blut* (blood), and *Rasse* (race) defined a system designed to exclude anything non-German as foreign (*artfremd*), as a "counter race" (*Gegenrasse*), and damaging (*Volksschädlinge*) to the entire German people.[8] The ideological discourse reflected Social Darwinist theory and contained the conviction of the superiority of the German race (*Herrenrasse*). This racial nationalism was concatenated with a particularly virulent form of antisemitism that filtered through to the language in the public and private spheres. Parallel to this pro-German agenda, the Nazis cultivated anti-Jewish beliefs already embedded into the cultures and languages of European Christendom.[9] Centuries-old hostile myths and powerful negative icons about Jews had long predisposed many Christians against the Jews and often resulted in alienation, exclusion, and death.[10] This stereotyping and prejudice resisted the humanitarianism that stemmed from the European Enlightenment and the French Revolution, so that the Nazis intertwined these old threads of religious Jew hatred (*Judenhaß*) with new, racial forms of antisemitism. They also continued the myth of a political and economic Jewish world conspiracy (*Weltjudentum*), a fiction that lay at the core of the nineteenth-century forgery *Protocols of the Elders of Zion*. There seemed to be no problem in describing Jews both as Judeo-Bolsheviks (i.e., Communists) and as the string pullers of world capitalism. Max Weinreich summed it up succinctly in 1946:

> The Jew could be represented as the embodiment of everything to be resented, feared, and despised. He was a carrier of bolshevism but, curiously enough, he simultaneously stood for the liberal spirit of rotten Western democracy. Economically, he was both capitalist and socialist. He was blamed as the indolent pacifist but, by strange coincidence, he was also the Western instigator to wars.[11]

The most noticeable reality expressed in Nazi German is the exclusionary nationalism that contained, even when not specifically stated, the will to gain more territory (*Lebensraum*) for Germans. The plan for this expansion process included military aggression and the use of or elimination of others. Had the Nazis won World War II, their barbarous utopia would have also targeted and murdered millions of Europe's Slavic peoples. Elimination was first an open-ended concept expressed in a variety of different words, such as *abwandern* (to make go), *Zwangsentjudungsverfahren* (forced removal of Jews), and *Abschub* (expulsion). It was also concealed with euphemisms and codes: *Abrechnung mit den Juden* (the settling of accounts with the Jews), expressed as a threat, and *Umsiedlung* (resettlement), the concrete plan of removal. Sometimes elimination meant incarceration or murder of political enemies, euthanasia of the institutionalized ill, and finally the expulsion and murder of peoples. Jews were singled out and, to a lesser degree, also the Sinti-Roma (*Zigeuner*). History and language both reveal that the Jews were not only a target but their global annihilation represented an important Nazi ideal. Numbering only about half of one percent of the German population, it was the Jews whom the German National Socialists perceived as the ultimate enemy of their country and people (*Volksfeinde*), and all Jews (*Gesamtjudentum*) as the enemy of the world (*Weltfeind*) or world plague (*Weltpest*).

According to the German racist principle of *Blut und Boden* (blood and soil), German Jews were described also as *volksfremd* (alien to the German *Volk*) and therefore understood to be outside the *Volksgemeinschaft* (the community of the German people). In a short period of time, the Nazi government paved the way for legalized persecution, then expulsion, and finally genocide. This process was accompanied by an antisemitic rhetoric that Germans heard on a regular basis as part of the constant public discourse. Its language contained old and familiar epithets as well as numerous neologisms directed against the Jews both as individuals and as a collective. Based on *Jude*, the already derogatory word throughout the centuries, the Nazis used many opprobrious propaganda concepts such as *Verjudung* (judaization and jewification), *Entjudung* (dejudaization), and *Alljuda* (all Judah). There were also the dehumanizing and blunt imperative slurs, some of them visible on public signs, directed against Jews: *Juda verrecke!* (Jews, drop dead!) and *Juden raus!* (Jews out!). Repetition of such venomous words and phrases certainly amounted to linguistic manipulation during the Third Reich. It is not surprising that this degrading vocabulary, replete with expletives, has remained prominent in survivors' memories.[12]

By using the German propensity to form compound words, the Nazi ideologues further produced etymological agglutination expressed or emphasized with terms such as *Blutschutz* (protection of [German] blood), *Istjude* (being Jewish according to the law), and *Rassenschande* ([sexual] violation of the [German] race). They, including many others, provided the terminology for the numerous anti-Jewish laws (*Judengesetze*). The latter were issued throughout the Third Reich period, each time becoming more restrictive for Jews. From the so-called *Judenboykott* (boycott of Jews) in 1933 to the infamous Nuremberg Race Laws for the "Protection of German Blood and Honour" (*Gesetz zum Schutze des deutschen Blutes und der deutschen Ehre*) in 1935, and those after 1938, they all manifest the vicious fight against the Jews from within the country. The various stages of this new legal and social reality, in turn, constructed word combinations such as *Judenhaus* (buildings designated for Jews), *Judenstern* (Jewish star), and *Sternträger* (bearer of the [Jewish] star), which were accepted and employed as a matter of course in daily speech. The result, clearly expressed in the language, is well-known: isolation of the Jews from the German community, exclusion from civil rights, deprivation of their livelihood, and expulsion and/or murder.

Nazi-Deutsch reveals also a "new [German] form" of *Judenhaß* that Saul Friedländer described: "this representation of evil was not merely religious, not merely racial, not merely political. It was a stage-by-stage aggregation of these successive waves of anti-Jewish hatred, of the successive layers of a tale of Jewish conspiracy against Aryan humanity."[13] Therefore, an admixture of medical and religious terms, in addition to the Darwinian phraseology, was present in the Nazi language. Based on a pseudo medical science, the Jews were perceived as scourge (*Seuche*) or bacteria (*Volksbazillen*) that needed to be excised from the body of the German nation (*Volkskörper*). These convenient analogies facilitated the acceptance by the general German public of the need for a healthy and pure German race, *judenrein* (literally, "clean" or "cleansed" of Jews), and, ultimately, a new super nation. The government's means to this end was the program of *Rassenhygiene* (race hygiene), a vague term that promoted the protection and cleansing (*Säuberung*) of German blood and society. Ideas of purification were already concretized when Nazi doctors started to kill thousands of German patients in institutions under the euthanasia program, coded "T-4," in the later 1930s. They made murder legitimate by calling the lives of the incurably sick "life unworthy of life" (*lebensunwertes Leben*). The subsequent planning of the murder of the Jews was the next step and expressed with existing words that underwent a shift of meaning or were given different metaphoric and ambiguous connotations. One poignant example is the term *Endziel* (final goal), a precursor to the infamous euphemism *Endlösung* (final solution) *der Judenfrage* (Jewish problem). The solution was the eradication or extinction (*Ausrottung* or *Ausmerze*) of this "Jewish world parasite" (*Weltparasit*).

In official communication, the Nazis favored noun phrases and the imperative and passive modes. Bureaucrats, in particular, employed German in this style and manner in order to render their statements and actions imprecise and impersonal. For instance, the passive voice "He was taken into protective custody (*Schutzhaft*)" served as a double veil in that it avoided mentioning the agent of this action and, at the same time, concealed the assigned or newly established meaning. The euphemism "protective custody" stood for forced incarceration and often torture and death in prisons and concentration camps situated mainly in Germany. *Schutzhaft* allowed those who issued the orders to act with impunity and often with unparalleled brutality and sadism.

Further, Hitler and his followers, in their aggressive propaganda speeches, misused and distorted well-known phrases and proverbs to appeal to the public. Wolfgang Mieder's extensive study on this "proverbial manipulation" shows how a nation's heritage of collective and common wisdom was tampered with during the Third Reich.[14] Proverbs and variations of them, such as *Arbeit macht frei* (Work will set you free), were displayed in the barracks and on gates of Nazi concentration camps. Today, few postwar Germans realize how colloquial German is still permeated with Nazi-popularized sayings, of which *Jedem das Seine* (To each his own) and *Leben und leben lassen* (Live and let live) are but two further examples.[15] For former inmates, they are a cruel reminder of their suffering, and many German-speaking survivors are reluctant or unable to use them.[16] Some old sayings had lost their symbolic meaning and returned to a literalness that often exceeded their graphic origin. "He who digs a hole for others will fall into it himself" (*Wer andern eine Grube gräbt, fällt selbst hinein*) became perversely real in a sadistic killing method called *Brunnenlaufen* (literally, running around the water well) in Dachau. Prisoners were forced to run around a deep water hole without moving their heads. Dizziness made them fall into it and drown. This and other realities created an immense, sustained fear for one's life, inside and outside concentration camps, for which German Jews coined the word *Judenangst*.[17] Gratuitous violence used in these constantly invented tortures also gave brutality to verbal expression. As George Steiner later concluded, if one uses a language "to conceive, organize, and justify" concentration camps (and genocide), "something perverse will happen to the language"[18] and of course to the users and recipients of this language.

Nazi bureaucrats often used abbreviations. They ranged from the common *RS* (meaning *Rundschreiben* [circulating memo]) to the macabre *S.B.* The latter was later a code, instead of *Sonderbehandlung* (special treatment), in official prisoners' files to conceal the fact of execution.[19] *RU* stood for *Rückkehr unerwünscht* (return not wanted) and signified a death sentence for inmates. Other single letters or combinations were used to simplify communication and perhaps to avoid spelling out the word in full and thus articulating its true meaning even to the perpetrators. For example, *A* stood for *Arbeitsjude* (a Jew deemed fit for forced labor and subsequent death) and *MKL* for *Männerkonzentrationslager* (concentration camp for men). Acronyms were popular as well as terrifying, of which *Gestapo* for *Geheime Staatspolizei* (secret state police) is one of the best known. Letters sometimes became intimidating symbols, such as SS written as two lightning bolts and situated prominently on officers' uniform collars and all correspondence. The government typewriters during the Nazi era were equipped with a special key bearing this symbol, which dates back to the origins of the Germanic *Sig-Rune* (sigrún, victory rune).

Linguistically, the steps toward war and genocide also meant the rapid devolution of German from a vocabulary of exclusionary nationalism to a language of persecution and murder. After the *Reichskristallnacht*, itself a Nazi euphemism for the vicious November 1938 pogrom that signaled the beginning of the intensified war against the Jews, the regime's official language became more opaque, distorted, and euphemistic. It culminated in what has been termed *Exekutionsvokabular* (execution vocabulary) and *Nazi-Tarnjargon* (Nazi camouflage language) as it hid military activities that went hand in hand with the plans for murder and annihilation.[20] One well-known euphemism for this plan was *Umsiedlung* (resettlement), which stood for expulsion of the Jews from Germany. The most infamous phrase of all was *Endlösung der Judenfrage* (Final Solution of the Jewish Problem), the unprecedented scheme for industrialized mass murder and genocide.[21] Berel Lang proposes, "quite simply, to call this new figure by an old name, one which more usually would not be associated with *figures* of speech at all—that is, the lie."[22]

These terms have been of special concern to many scholars who have dealt with the Nazi period and its language. Most of them were camouflage or code words (*Tarnwörter*) whose function was to conceal actions or facts. They differed from standard neologisms, for these terms generally consisted of old and familiar words that had been given new meanings, while the old meaning remained in use as well. Its new purpose and newly assigned context were camouflaged to render the word at best enigmatic or ambiguous. The Nazis employed these terms widely in official and unofficial documents, such as letters, memos, and (secret) reports. When the murderous connotation of a euphemism had become too well-known, sometimes an official would request another word be used instead. The old word became "a dysphemism, which meant that new euphemisms must be minted; and these in their turn . . . came to acquire all the horrific connotations of the word they replace[d]."[23] One example is the substitute *Evakuierung* (evacuation) for *Auswanderung* (emigration), both meaning, in addition to their original and still-valid usage, forced transportation of Jews to ghettos and concentration camps, as was recorded in the minutes of the Wannsee Conference in 1942.[24] Another term was *Sonderbehandlung*, to be replaced, on Himmler's order from 1943, by the innocuous participle *durchgeschleust*, meaning "funneled" or "flushed through," but used as a euphemism for "killed in a death camp."[25]

In examining such terms, non-German and German scholars have pondered the likelihood of the regime's apparent success in disguising completely Nazi crimes and mass murder. Historian Raul Hilberg, among others, has highlighted the major words and exposed their camouflage.[26] Other experts have studied their application. Several English-language publications, dating back to the 1950s and 1960s, look at Nazi use and misuse of language mainly from the Jewish, that is to say, the victims', viewpoint. Nachman Blumenthal and Saul Esh, in various issues of *Yad Vashem Studies*, between 1957 and 1967, are among the earliest recorders of the German vocabulary of genocide. Similarly, the annotated German compilations of Nazi terminology, notably, *Aus dem Wörterbuch des Unmenschen* (From the Dictionary of the Beasts) and *Aus dem Lexikon der Mörder* (From the Encyclopedia of Murderers),[27] reveal in their descriptive and accusatory titles a victim-oriented perspective. Both volumes explain with bitterness and emotion the use of the Nazi language as a weapon of destruction against the Jews. These were pioneering works by those who suffered, in addition to their ordeals, from Nazi speech acts.

For people who lived outside the Third Reich environment and were not familiar with Nazi-Deutsch and its context, it needed to be defined, explained, and translated. To this purpose, the U.S. War Department published its *Handbook on German Military Forces* in 1945. It provided English definitions of German military terms and those belonging to the Nazi war effort and its machinery.[28] One year earlier, the Office of European Economic Research had issued the German-English *Nazi-Deutsch: A Glossary of Contemporary German Usage*. Much smaller in scope, it contains mainly government and military terminology that was gleaned from, at that time, "current German newspapers and magazines, a list of Germanizations of foreign technical terms issued by the Reich Patent Office, the *Brockhaus* [a widely used German dictionary], and a number of German military dictionaries," among others.[29] During the Nuremberg war crimes trials in 1946, the Allied officials in charge of the proceedings had to rely on such glossaries, both to understand the Nazi abbreviations and codes and also to identify the Nazi government and military ranking systems. Although very useful tools, such compilations had and have their limitations, in part because they exclude the vocabulary of persecution and genocide. For example, the reader of the 1944 glossary does not find entries for the infamous Nazi euphemisms, such as *Aktion, Selektion, Sonderbehandlung*, and *Umsiedlung*. No references point to the large body of then-current antisemitic words, and the word *Jude* is defined only according to the Nazi Race Laws. Pejorative words referring to Jews, especially newly formed compounds, were also translated to express the Nazi perspective, so that *Judengenosse* became "philo-semite" or "Republican," and *judenrein*, matter of factly, "free from Jewish elements." Finally, these handbooks are not comprehensive.

German scholars, such as Cornelia Berning,[30] have researched the connection between language and ideology. They were followed, in 1964, by her important glossary of selected Nazi terms.[31] Her dictionary includes the numerous word combinations with *Volk, Blut*, and *Rasse* that provided the linguistic basis for the Nazi ideology of race. Konrad Ehlich wrote critical analyses on Nazi-Deutsch in the 1980s; Utz Maas published articles in 1983 and 1984 and wrote a book on the subject in 1984.[32]

A huge undertaking was the historic reference work, *Das Große Lexikon des Dritten Reiches* (The Great Encyclopedia of the Third Reich).[33] It documents the Hitler epoch and contains Nazi terminology. In 1988, Renate Birkenauer and Karl-Heinz

Brackmann contributed their extensive compilation *NS-DEUTSCH*. It has been a valuable German research tool for decades and the most detailed work on the major Nazi German terms to date. Cornelia Berning's 1998 *Vokabular des Nationalismus* is an extended version of her earlier publication; it is intended also for German researchers in this field. However, both volumes deal predominantly with Nazi ideology as expressed in the political theory of race and less with individual policies and actions against and impacts on the Jews and the Eastern European peoples.

This scholarly preoccupation over the decades with the phenomenon of Nazi German demonstrates both interest and the importance of this charged language. Basically the research can be divided into the two categories: glossaries of terms and sociolinguistic analyses. What is often neglected in these studies of the latter category is how the Nazi language affected society in general and how people used it and/or were victimized by its use. One such person, who was both observer and target during the Third Reich, was Victor Klemperer. His work on the German of the Nazi era differs from all other publications on the subject because he presents it as a living and evolving language. His is a revealing, professional eyewitness account and a testament to Nazi Germany's language use in political, public, and private discourse.

Klemperer's (only now) widely known and lauded *LTI: Notizbuch eines Philologen* (*Lingua Tertii Imperii:* Notebook of a Philologist) is based on his secretly written diaries throughout the Hitler period. He was a philologist and university professor of literature when the Nazis came to power. Although he had converted to Protestantism in his youth and belonged to Germany's highly educated intellectuals, he lost his post because the regime defined him as Jewish. He survived persecution and the Nazi extermination program because he was married to a German gentile. He called the German language he watched being transformed and deformed before his very eyes and ears *Lingua Tertii Imperii,* Latin for "language of the Third Reich."[34] One of Klemperer's notable observations was that it influenced the country's written and oral language, not just at the government level. For this reason, his firsthand analysis and his experiences as a persecuted Jew are vivid reminders of how exclusionary and targeting speech functioned in Nazi Germany's daily life.[35] For example, some surviving German Jews associate distinctly the Nazi adjective *judengelb* (Jew yellow) with an assault on their being.[36] Among other things, it refers to the yellow star that Jews (*Sternträger*) were ordered to wear publicly from September 19, 1941. Klemperer found this moment of degradation and stigmatization the heaviest day in "those twelve years of hell" and referred with rage to the "yellow rag with the black imprint: *Jude.*"[37] Other survivors recall the yellow park benches restricted to Jews as visual signs of segregation. They bore the painted phrase *Nur für Juden* (For Jews only). It is this open antisemitic vocabulary, attesting to a grim reality, that is generally missing from Nazi-Deutsch glossaries and Nazi language discussions.

Another recently published memoir, *Mein Leben* (My Life), by Germany's foremost literary critic Marcel Reich-Ranicki, deals with yet another aspect of language use and experience during the Third Reich.[38] The author and his parents belonged to those Jews who carried Polish passports and were expelled from Germany, precipitously, shortly before the *Reichskristallnacht* pogrom of 1938. He later became secretary of the translation and correspondence section (*Übersetzungs- und Korrespondenzbüro*) of the *Judenrat* (a Jewish council instituted by the Nazis) in the Warsaw Ghetto. In this capacity he encountered and had to employ the euphemistic language of the Nazi regime. He witnessed the deadly consequences as three terms spelled, in disguise, the destruction of the ghetto and the death of its inhabitants: *Erste Aktion* (first action), *Große Aktion* (great action), and *Umsiedlungsaktion* (resettlement action). They stood for the German order from Berlin to start transporting the majority of the ghetto's Jews (on July 22, 1942) to be murdered in the death camp of Treblinka. At the same time, Reich-Ranicki encountered the degrading behavior of German and Austrian officials, including common soldiers. Their language illustrated how the pervasive antisemitism in their countries had borne fruit when some of them forced the already terrified people to sing in a chorus: "We are Jewish pigs. We are dirty Jews. We are subhuman" (*Wir sind jüdische Schweine. Wir sind dreckige Juden. Wir sind Untermenschen.*[39] His frightening experience outside Germany was different from Klemperer's within the country. Unlike the latter, Reich-Ranicki came into too-close contact with what has been termed "the Nazi beast" whose speech was defined as "barking" rather than speaking. Therefore, many survivors are particularly sensitive to commands in German because they can activate memories and a chain of reactions.[40]

Such significant moral devolution also caused the German language to sink to its nadir. When the criminal regime was finally unmasked, some German journalists and writers declared the need for a new language. May 7, 1945, often called *Stunde Null* (Zero Hour) or *Nullpunkt* (Point Zero), referred to this distinct temporal reference point as a new linguistic beginning as well as a political and moral one.[41] This allowed ordinary Germans to focus on their lives, to rebuild their bombed-out country, and perhaps to forget. Their silence may reflect discomfort with the perpetrator's perspective because their recalling Nazi-Deutsch and what it signified may cut too close to personal knowledge. At the same time, those few thousand Jews who survived Nazi persecution and murder tried to recover their shattered lives. The aftermath of World War II and the war against them yielded the unfathomable reality of the virtual annihilation of their people in Central and Eastern Europe. As displaced persons and often stateless, they carried the *Churban* (Hebrew for destruction; later, Holocaust) with them internally, and a part of their indelible memories of Nazi terror related to things German, including the language. These individuals had suffered the impact of the crimes connected with that "dangerous" language, and they have had to deal with the psychological consequences ever since. These contrasting fields of recollecting and forgetting mirror the two parallel histories of the Nazi period—one for the self-declared Aryans and one for those defined by Nazi German law as Jews.[42] According to Dan Diner there will be no bridge to connect these contrasting memories of the German perpetrators and of their victims in the foreseeable future.[43]

This historical reality parallels the fact that Nazi-Deutsch was a living language that either influenced or impacted people. The examination of one particular word as a representative example of how it affected Germans and Jews differently will demonstrate how some euphemisms functioned at that crucial time and how they have persisted up to the present. The word *Umsiedlung* received, in addition to its denotative, original meaning of "resettlement," a euphemistic meaning that stood first and foremost for "the forceful removal of German Jews and left to die or to be murdered in the East of Europe." As we know, the Nazi regime's public explanation was "resettlement to an Eastern European country to work," implying of course, to live. Assuming that many German Jews at first did not know the Nazi government's true intentions behind that plan—simply because the plan was plausible—"resettlement" still represented for them being uprooted from their familiar geographical, professional, cultural, and linguistic environment and being transported to restart life in an unknown place with nothing certain. Further, it meant that they were stripped of their citizenship, were expelled from their country, and had to leave everything behind. But they could not imagine the degrading treatment and inhuman means of transportation that they actually faced—from coaches to freight cars once across the German border. Thus, in this context, *Umsiedlung* lost its original dictionary meaning and became expulsion. This word signified a nightmarish experience that was a prelude to an even more unimaginable reality: death to the Jews for the crime of existence.

But many Germans, even if they did not know of what was also called more precisely but still ambiguously after 1942 the "Jewish transports" (*Judentransporte*) to concentration camps, generally found *Umsiedlung* to be a proper solution to their problem of a Jewish presence in Germany. Despite the fact that they had to be aware of this legally and morally questionable procedure, the word "resettlement" was a perfect umbrella term for the entire project and process to eliminate the Jews from what they considered their own space. Marion Kaplan sums up the different German attitudes.

Some [Germans] wanted them [German Jews] to "disappear"; others were afraid to ask; still others hoped to exonerate themselves later by not "knowing" now. . . . Moreover, those Germans who chose ignorance had an easy time of it, since Jews had been so thoroughly ostracised and segregated before their deportation.[44]

If Germans did know more, it was still preferable for them to believe in or hide behind the government-provided meaning of resettlement, for they actually saw their Jewish citizens being deported. As Kaplan suggests correctly, to know only what the Nazi regime actually told them about resettlement, did not incriminate them morally in their minds and was, further, a respectable and civilized solution to Germany's "Jewish problem" (*die Judenfrage*). David Bankier argues similarly: "Knowledge generated guilt since it entailed responsibility, and many believed that they could preserve their dignity by avoiding the horrible truth."[45] Thus, until now, could so many Germans claim ignorance. When they do recollect the Nazi era they usually exclude the suffering of others during the war and all aspects of the Holocaust. Instead, they focus on their own war experiences.

Indeed, the language of that time attests to their hardship, their losses, and their sacrifices. Alone the many words refer euphemistically to emergency situations, such as the rationing of all goods (*Bewirtschaftung*), forced donations for the soldiers on the front (*Winterhilfe*), and compulsory labor for the war effort (*Arbeitsdienst*) by young and old, including women. The Nazi government expected these services and sacrifices from them for the sake of their country (*Vaterland*). The language also reveals mounting resentment with the regime as the war persisted and bombs fell on German civilians. The abbreviation *Bolona* (for "*Bombenlose Nacht!*"), "Have a bombless night," instead of "Good night," expressed their black humor. German army slang lays bare the soldiers' sarcastic attitude toward the losing war battles and their military superiors. "Frozen-meat medal" (*Gefrierfleischorden*) and "frost medal" (*Frostmedaille*) are but two of their many versions for decorations earned while fighting on the Eastern Front in the brutal Russian winter.

There is no doubt that war hardship for Germans was real and that many perceived the disastrous situation the country had reached under the Hitler regime. Yet, they may not realize how the Third Reich language reveals their lack of compassion for others, albeit very often dictated by the Nazi state. For example, during Allied air raids, Jews and foreign (slave) workers were not allowed to join Germans in the bomb shelters. The workers had to use a "splinter ditch" (*Splittergraben*) outside, which they had usually dug themselves. For this reason, all German suffering and expressions of discontent pale in comparison with the suffering inflicted upon those whom they had exposed to death by excluding them from their human community: first the German Jews and then all other Jews and non-Germans. The difference between historical experience and recollections is a known fact. Dan Diner distinguishes between the "banality on the side of the perpetrators" and the "monstrosity of the victims" who suffered the force of their deeds.[46] Heartlessness, indifference, open hostility and hatred expressed in word and deed against their fellow Jewish citizens may have facilitated the actions of Germans that finally led to the Holocaust. The revelations of the horrific crimes against civilians by the special task groups (*Einsatzgruppen*) in the Eastern territories, the mass murders by the Nazi death-head officers (*Totenkopf SS*) in concentration camps, and the questionable deeds by the German military (*Wehrmacht*) often relativize German suffering during the war. Unfortunately, this may make it even more difficult for some to feel empathy for a German woman who lost a son or husband in the war. In the back of our minds we wonder about a soldier's actions as the German troops advanced into foreign territory. Usually, Germans suppress these harsh realities of the past, some of which George Steiner highlights with these graphic words:

Most Germans probably did not know the actual details of liquidation. They may not have known about the mechanics of the gas/ovens. . . . But when the house next door was emptied overnight of its tenants, or when Jews, with their yellow star sewn on their coats, were barred from the air-raid shelters and made to cower in the open, burning streets, only a blind cretin could not have known.[47]

As the Third Reich reality vanished with the collapse of the Nazi regime and its elaborate ideologically influenced apparatus, a large part of its nomenclature disappeared as well. Germans remained in their cultural and linguistic environment and contributed to a renewal and change of their language. Some of the euphemistically used words took on either a different meaning or reverted back to their original form. Other important aspects of the Third Reich's language and life were simply silenced and, perhaps unwittingly, retained the mentality behind them.[48] As a nation's dictionaries reveal historical and other influences on its language, so do German reference works. Unless one consults a specialized dictionary or glossary, such as those mentioned previously, it is generally difficult to find Nazi-Deutsch terms.[49]

The standard contemporary German dictionaries are selective as to their inclusion and definitions of Nazi vocabulary, some of them signaling it with the abbreviation *ns* (National Socialist) and thus relegating it to the past. The most infamous code words for the policy of genocide reveal an unsettling tendency in their definitions or omissions. Entries often do not explain sufficiently their true Nazi meaning, or they use inappropriate terminology in their definitions as some words are replaced by other words (e.g., the equation of *Endlösung* with *Liquidierung* [liquidation]).[50] In fact, the continued use of Nazi German is also noticeable in scholarly publications and in German school textbooks.[51] Most of their authors have not yet found an acceptable contemporary language in their writings about Nazi atrocities. Walter F. Renn and Elisabeth Maxwell call this practice siding with the perpetrator.[52] They warn about the perpetuation of Nazi terminology in this way, particularly their crass terms, such as *Ausrottung der Juden* (extermination or eradication of Jews) or the coded *Endlösung* instead of "destruction, mass murder, or genocide of the European Jews." Renn explains:

The designation [of the Final Solution of the Jewish Problem] is so firmly entrenched in texts and scholarly literature that it will probably never entirely be replaced; but its use is no less objectionable since it renders harmless the unspeakable reality of the Holocaust and continues to use the terminology of the murderers. Perhaps, most important, it subtly perpetuates the idea that there was a *Jewish* problem—instead of an antisemitic problem—and conveys the obscene notion that genocide may be referred to legitimately as a "solution." Nothing could be less edifying than, in effect, making the killers the final judges for designating the terms of description for what they did to the Jews of Europe. The term was Hitler's, and its use is a posthumous victory.[53]

The title of Raul Hilberg's book *The Destruction* [rather than extermination] *of the European Jews* demonstrated early in Holocaust scholarship that Nazi German is not a valid language to be used today. Years later, Dominick LaCarpa still argues similarly and suggests:

Other terms such as "final solution" or "annihilation" repeat Nazi terminology, often of course with the use of square quotes as a distancing frame or alienation effect. . . . Still, the best option may be to use various terms with an awareness of their problematic nature and not to become riveted on one or another of them.[54]

Particularly in Germany, inappropriate usage may be symptomatic of a continued ambivalence about how the country deals with the fate of the Jews. Others may want to underscore Nazi cruelty by using their words.

Holocaust survivors also use Nazi German terms to express the circumstances of their people's genocide. This includes the heavily burdened term *Jude* that is forever linked to the fundamental denial of their existence by Nazi Germany. For survivors who do not speak German on a regular basis, Nazi-Deutsch has stayed frozen in time. They need not search dictionaries for the correct terms because they are etched into their memory, and they use them with a chilling familiarity. The potent meaning and force of German words, for example, *Judenrat* (Jewish council) and *Umschlagplatz* (official gathering point for Jews before deportation), would be diminished or lost in translation.

As Nazi-Deutsch shows without a doubt, sixty years ago the German language was distorted and misused to deceive or dehumanize those who were targeted, to conceal gross human rights violations, to shield citizens from the grim facts behind criminal state actions, and most likely to deceive the perpetrators themselves. The high-ranking Nazi officials who were present at the 1942 Wannsee Conference in Berlin discussed openly the unprecedented scheme for the systematic killing of Jews by means of hard labor under inhuman conditions and by industrialized mass murder. But the conference minutes that recorded the agenda for this large-scale, murderous operation provide a chilling example of concealing the criminal intentions of a government with veiled language. This document was skillfully honed to make it sound almost innocuous if one did not know the implicit meaning behind the terminology and the carefully chosen words. It has become a historic paradigm for the official *Nazi-Tarnjargon* (camouflage jargon) that Nazi leaders and military personnel used in discussions and written records to disguise, even from future readers, the scheme for and the execution of the physical destruction of Jewish life and culture. Camouflaging the genocide with language—even in the planning stages— was the first denial of it. Contemporary Holocaust deniers use these very documents as proof for their viewpoint, arguing that "any Nazi 'coded' document—that is, using euphemisms for practices associated with the extermination of Jews—is to be interpreted in its strictly literal meaning, whereas any document speaking plainly of the genocide is to be ignored or 'underinterpreted.'"[55] There was to be no record of the fate of the Jews, as the often-cited remark by Heinrich Himmler suggested: "In our history this is an unwritten, never-to-be-written page of glory."[56] The relevance of Nazi (euphemistic) language practices and, consequently, the accuracy in defining this usage has come to the fore again today during the libel trial of *David Irving v. Deborah Lipstadt*, in Britain.[57]

The opaque Third Reich terminology has provided a linguistic and psychological veil that has, over the years, protected many Germans from confronting the reality of the past. The old euphemisms have actually aided both onlookers and perpetrators, then and now, by neutralizing any guilt, and they have also prevented expressions of compassion and sorrow. Despite the fact that more than half of Germans alive today were born after World War II, what is still "needed is a genuine analysis of antisemitism, of prejudice based on cultural difference that expresses itself as the negation of the other [Jewish] identity."[58] Perhaps then we would come to a different conclusion than Eric A. Johnson did in his recent findings that also confirm those of other scholars.

[A]fter reading more than 1,000 Gestapo and Special Court case files and speaking with scores of people who spent their younger years in Nazi Germany, it is not clear to me whether in that older generation people feel compassion even now for the victims of the crimes perpetrated by their former country. Most older Germans do regret that these crimes were committed, if only because they placed a heavy and lasting burden on Germans. Many aging Germans, as they now face their own death, look back at their past not remembering that they were once perpetrators or bystanders but with the sense that they have been the real victims of Nazi terror.[59]

After a lengthy involvement with the language of the Nazi period and recognizing how it, together with the exclusionary policies and the murderous intentions of this regime, touched on every aspect of German society, one can only conclude that virtually all citizens had to be aware of some of the regime's human rights violations. Under the cloak of war, events were happening that were contrary to long-established ethical values. The numerous words of the Nazi-Deutsch vocabulary are the individual pieces to the large puzzle that, in the end, gives the complete picture of government control, aggression, persecution, and annihilation. Shortly after the Holocaust, Nachman Blumenthal wrote:

Comprehension of the Nazi terminology is largely dependent upon understanding of the period in which it was created. Thus research into Nazi terminology must constitute an introduction to historical research. This is necessary in order to avoid wholesale deception and confusion of the terms coined and used by the Nazis [and to endure that they] are taken at their face value.[60]

Nazi-Deutsch remains an indelible map of the intricate system under German National Socialism. This language has become an essential part of the academic discourse of Holocaust scholarship and it may even shed some light on the decades-old debate as to whether the Holocaust was an intentional Nazi objective or an evolving plan. As the twentieth century has passed into history, and its greatest catastrophe recedes further into the past, we need to assure that the next generation of scholars and students, especially in English-speaking milieux, has access to the specialized language of the Third Reich that reflects its horrific ideological *Weltanschauung*.

Historians may revise history and even distort meanings of events, but this language, embedded in its Nazi context, concretizes a world like few other elements can. It is impossible to deny that *Sturm* (storm), as an officer's rank, reflects the notion of conquest and attack. The language even lays bare the thread of antisemitism that was woven, at times seemingly invisible, into the entire fabric of National Socialist Germany and exposes the disguise of codes. Otherwise, who would guess that behind beautiful words like *Frühlingswind* (literally, spring breeze) and *Meerschaum* (literally, sea foam) lay hidden the crass reality of planned roundups and attacks against Jews in France. Who could have imagined that *Sternträger* (bearer of a star) and *Rosengarten* (rose garden) camouflaged discrimination, torture and murder, and that *Kristallnacht* (crystal night) was one of the key events in Germany's war against the Jews that culminated in the worst genocide of the twentieth century? The true meaning of these terms makes us recognize illegal and inhuman acts hidden beneath benign words and urges us to be vigilant in our own language use. Victor Klemperer expressed his observations of Third Reich language with his anti-proverb, "*In lingua veritas*" and, with this motto, underscored the irony that Nazi-Deutsch reveals the incontrovertible fact of a criminal regime that was thriving in the heart of a once-civilized Europe.

## Notes

1. John Wesley Young, *Totalitarian Language: Orwell's Newspeak and Its Nazi and Communist Predecessors* (Ann Arbor, MI: UMI Bell and Howell, 1994), 262.

2. George Steiner, *Language and Silence: Essays on Language, Literature, and the Inhuman* (New York: Athenaeum, 1982), 109.

3. For example, *Lichtbild* instead of *Photo; Fernsprecher* instead of *Telephon; Fernsehrohr* instead of *Teleskop*. However, not all of the official suggestions were accepted by the public and some of them never established themselves in the German vernacular. Others entered common usage and remained beyond the Nazi period. For instance, *Fernsprecher* has only recently been changed to the more international term Telefon on public phone booths in Germany.

4. Foreign words were preferred when using military terminology, such as *Front* and *mobilisieren*, and fashionable words, such as *dynamisch* and *garantieren*. See Eugen Seidel and Ingeborg Seidel-Slotty, *Sprachwandel im Dritten Reich: Eine kritische Untersuchung faschistischer Einflüsse* (Halle, Germany: VEB Verlag Sprache und Literatur, 1961), 123, 124.

5. Renate Birkenauer and Karl-Heinz Brackmann, *NS-DEUTSCH: "Selbstverständliche" Begriffe und Schlagwörter aus der Zeit des Nationalsozialismus* (Straelen/Niederrhein, Germany: Straelener Manuskripte Verlage, 1988), 50.

6. The latter were Nazi training camps for the obligatory German youth work service (*Jugenddienstpflicht*), decreed in 1939, for all Hitler Youth members from ages ten to eighteen. Their service was for the war effort and included harvesting crops, helping in air-raid shelters, and aiding war-injured combatants at train stations and sick barracks.

7. This may be one clue as to why Germans remained true to their people and leader for two more years, after it was clear the war was lost in 1943.

8. See, for example, the compilation of Nazi terms demonstrating the predominance of these words in compounds, in Cornelia Schmitz-Berning, *Vokabular des Nationalsozialismus* (New York: de Gruyter, 1998). Critical opposition to such nationalistic language came, in the beginning of the Hitler period, from well-known figures, such as Karl Kraus and Bertolt Brecht. For instance, Brecht would deliberately write *Bevölkerung* (population) instead of *Volk*.

9. Arthur Cohen, *The Myth of the Judeo-Christian Tradition* (New York: Harper and Row, 1970), 52; Jacob Katz, "Was the Holocaust Predictable?" in *The Holocaust in Historical Experience*, ed. Yehuda Bauer and Nathan Rotenstreich (New York: Holmes and Meier Publishers, 1981), 34, 36.

10. Ruth Mellinkoff, *Outcasts: Signs of Otherness in Northern European Art of the Late Middle Ages*, vols. 1 and 2. (Berkeley: University of California Press, 1993).

11. Max Weinreich, *Hitler's Professors: The Part of Scholarship in Germany's Crimes Against the Jewish People* (New York: Yiddish Scientific Institute—YIVO, 1946), 28.

12. For many of them, just hearing commands or a particular tone of voice from Germans today can trigger fear and reactions that mentally thrust them back into the Nazi era.

13. Saul Friedländer, "Extermination of Jews in Historiography," in *The Holocaust: Origins, Implementation, Aftermath*, ed. Omer Bartov (New York: Routledge, 2000), 83.

14. Wolfgang Mieder, "'As if I were the master of the situation': Proverbial Manipulation in Adolf Hitler's *Mein Kampf*," in *The Politics of Proverbs: From Traditional Wisdom to Proverbial Stereotypes* (Madison: University of Wisconsin Press, 1977), 9; and in *De Proverbio* 1, no. 1 (1995): 1; "Sprichwörter unter dem Hakenkreuz," in *Deutsche Sprichwörter in Literatur, Politik, Presse, und Werbung* (Hamburg, Germany: Buske, 1983), 181–201; "Proverbs in Nazi Germany," in *Proverbs Are Never Out of Season* (New York: Oxford University Press, 1993), 252–255; and "Language and Folklore of the Holocaust," in *The Holocaust: Introductory Essays*, ed. David Scrase and Wolfgang Mieder (Burlington: Center for Holocaust Studies, University of Vermont, 1996), 93–106.

15. Karin Doerr, "'To Each His Own' (*Jedem das Seine*): The (Mis-)Use of German Proverbs in Concentration Camps and Beyond," in *Proverbium* 17 (2000): 71–90; and Wolfgang Brückner, *"Arbeit macht frei": Herkunft und Hintergrund der KZ-Devise* (Opladen, Germany: Leske and Budrich, 1998).

16. Ruth Klüger (Auschwitz survivor) recalls with cynicism the German proverbs "Reden ist Silber, Schweigen ist Gold" ("Speech is silver, silence is gold") and "Leben und leben lassen" ("Live and let live"). See her *weiter leben: Eine Jugend* (Göttingen, Germany: Wallstein, 1992), 21.

17. Victor Klemperer, *Ich will Zeugnis ablegen bis zum letzten: Tagebücher 1933–1945*, vol. 2, ed. Walter Nowojski (Berlin: Aufbau-Verlag, 1995), 551.

18. Steiner, *Language and Silence*, 101.

19. Joseph Wulf, *Aus dem Lexikon der Mörder: "Sonderbehandlung" und Sinn verwandte Worte in nationalsozialistischen Dokumenten* (Gütersloh, Germany: Sigbert Mohn, 1963).

20. Siegfried Bork, *Mißrauch der Sprache: Tendenzen nationalsozialistischer Sprachregelung* (Bern: Francke, 1970), 88.

21. The term and concept *Endlösung* represents the entirety of the Nazi genocide of the Jews as understood by the perpetrator. For the general population during the Hitler period, *Endlösung* stood for the elimination of Jews from German society. Due to the intended vagueness of the language and the lack of more written documents, the historical debate continues today as to whether this originally meant the intention for deportation or mass murder. The eventual meaning of *Endlösung* was made fully known to the public only in 1946 with the Nuremberg War Crimes Trials. See Birkenauer and Brackmann, *NS-DEUTSCH*, 62.

22. Berel Lang, "Language and Genocide," in *Act and Idea in Nazi Genocide* (Chicago: 1990), 91. Many of these terms and certainly their real meanings were concealed from the public.

23. Young, *Totalitarian Language*, 459.

24. John Mendelsohn, ed., *The Holocaust: Selected Documents in Eighteen Volumes*. Vol. 11: *The Wannsee Protocol and a 1944 Report on Auschwitz by the Office of Strategic Services* (New York: Garland, 1982), 3–17.

25. Birkenauer and Brackmann, *NS-DEUTSCH*, 55.

26. Raul Hilberg, *The Destruction of the European Jews* (New York: Holmes and Meier, 1985), 1:328–334, 3:1007–1029; Henry Friedlander, "The Manipulation of Language," in *The Holocaust: Ideology, Bureaucracy, and Genocide*, ed. Henry Friedlander and Sybil Milton, (Millwood, NY: Kraus International, 1980), 103–113. If not otherwise noted, all translations into English are my own.

27. Dolf Sternberger, Gerhard Storz, and W. E. Süskind, *Aus dem Wörterbuch des Unmenschen* (Hamburg, Germany: 1957). Wulf, *Aus dem Lexikon der Mörder.*

28. U.S. War Department, *Handbook on German Military Forces* (1945; reprint, with an introduction by Stephen E. Ambrose, Baton Rouge: Louisiana State University Press, 1990).

29. Heinz Paechter *Nazi-Deutsch: A Glossary of Contemporary German Usage* (New York: Frederick Ungar, Spring 1944), n.p.

30. Cornelia Berning, "Die Sprache der Nationalsozialisten," *Zeitschrift für deutsche Wortforschung* 16–19 (1960–1963).

31. Cornelia Berning, *Vom Abstammungsnachweis zum Zuchwort: Vokabular des Nationalsozialismus* (Berlin: de Gruyter, 1964).

32. Konrad Ehlich, ed., *Sprache im Faschismus* (Frankfurt am Main, Germany: Suhrkamp, 1987); Utz Maas, "Sprache im Nationalsozialismus," *Diskussion Deutsch* 14 (1983): 499–517; Utz Maas, *Als der Geist der Gemeinschaft eine Sprache fand: Sprache im Nationalsozialismus: Versuch einer historischen Argumentationsanalyse* (Opladen, Germany: Westdeutscher Verlag, 1984). Maas limits his research to the linguistic analysis of fascism in Nazi youth texts (*Hitlerjugend*) between 1933 and 1938. For a Marxist perspective, see Seidel and Seidel-Slotty, *Sprachwandel im Dritten Reich*.

33. Christian Zentner and Friedemann Bedürftig, *Das Große Lexikon des Dritten Reichs* (Munich: Südwest Verlag, 1985). English translation: Amy Hackett, ed. and trans., *The Great Encyclopedia of the Third Reich* (New York: Macmillan, 1991).

34. Victor Klemperer, *LTI: Notizbuch eines Philologen* (Leipzig, Germany: Reclam, 1996). His diaries from that period were first printed in 1947 and reissued in Germany in 1996. In 1998, the first volume also became available to English-speaking readers under the title *I Will Bear Witness*, trans. Martin Chalmers (New York: Random House, 1998).

35. Wolfgang Mieder crystallizes the reality of the Jews in Germany by showing examples of proverbial speech in Klemperer's work. See Wolfgang Mieder, *"In lingua veritas:" Sprichwörtliche Rhetorik in Victor Klemperers Tägebüchern 1933–1945* (Vienna: 2000).

36. Karin Doerr, interview with Charlotte Lintzell, Montreal, July 10 and October 22, 1997.

37. "Von da an war der Judenstern zu tragen, der sechszackige Davidsstern, der Lappen in der gelben Farbe, die heute noch Pest und Quarantäne bedeutet und die im Mittelalter die Kennfarbe der Juden war, die Farbe des Neides und der ins Blut getretenen Galle, die Farbe des zu meidenden Bösen; der gelbe Lappen mit dem schwarzen Aufdruck: 'Jude.'" See Mieder, *"In lingua veritas,"* 213.

38. Marcel Reich-Ranicki, *Mein Leben* (Stuttgart, Germany: Deutsche Verlags-Anstalt, 1999).

39. Ibid., 184, 185.

40. For instance, "Los, los! Vorwärts!" ("Hurry up, move on!") signifies nothing threatening to "normal people," as one survivor writes, but it can trigger a panic attack in someone who remembers the past context of persecution. See Yaacov Ben-Chanan, "Weiterleben—weiter leben" oder "Vom rauhen Glück, heute Jude zu sein" (Open Letter, 1995), 10. Olga Sher confirms such occurrences with her experience when, on a tour bus, she heard a German guide shouting, "Alles raus!" ("Everybody out!") (Karin Doerr, interviews with Olga Sher, Montreal, June 5 and July 5, 1997).

41. Stephen Brockmann, "German Culture at the 'Zero Hour,'" in *Revisiting Zero Hour 1945: The Emergence of Postwar German Culture*, ed. Stephen Brockmann and Frank Trommler (Washington, DC: Johns Hopkins University, 1996), 23, 25.

42. Saul Friedländer calls this *Alltagsgeschichte* (history of everyday life). See Saul Friedländer, *Memory, History, and the Extermination of the Jews of Europe* (Bloomington: Indiana University Press, 1993), 93.

43. Dan Diner, "Der Holocaust als Geschichtsnarrativ—Über Variationen historischen Gedächtnisses," in *In der Sprache der Täter: Neue Lektüren deutschsprachiger Nachkriegs-*

*und Gegenwartsliteratur,* ed. Stephan Braese (Opladen, Germany: Westdeutscher Verlag, 1998), 23.

44. Marion Kaplan, *Between Dignity and Despair: Jewish Life in Nazi Germany* (New York: Oxford University Press, 1998), 199.

45. David Bankier, *The Germans and the Final Solution: Public Opinion Under Nazism* (Oxford: Blackwell, 1992), 130.

46. "Im großen und ganzen zerfällt die Tat der Massenvernichtung gleichsam notwendig in zwei unterschiedliche, ja gegensätzliche Erfahrungswelten: Banalität auf der Täterseite—hervorgerufen durch die verwaltungstechnischen Maßnahmen in der Durchführung; Monstrosität auf Seiten der die volle Wucht der Tathandlung erleidenden Opfer." See Diner, "Der Holocaust als Geschichtsnarrativ," 23.

47. Steiner, *Language and Silence,* 107, 108.

48. Horst Mahler, a 1960's German student activist and representative of the postwar generation, stated, "Only the political power of German fascism was broken in 1945; its ideological power [was broken] only in parts." Quote from Sabine von Dirke, " 'Where were you 1933–1945?' The Legacy of the Nazi Past Beyond the Zero Hour," in *Revisiting Zero Hour 1945: The Emergence of Postwar German Culture,* ed. Stephen Brockman and Frank Trommler (Washington, DC: Johns Hopkins University Press, 1996), 77.

49. At the Technische Universität of Braunschweig a team of language experts is presently working on the tenth edition of Hermann Paul's *Deutsches Wörterbuch.* Special consideration is being given to the vocabulary of National Socialism.

50. Karin Doerr and Kurt Jonassohn, "The Persistence of Nazi German," paper presented at the Genocide Scholars Conference, June 12–15, 1999, Madison, Wisconsin; and "In Search of the Vocabulary of Genocide in German Dictionaries," paper presented at the 30th Annual Scholars' Conference on the Holocaust and the Churches: The Century of Genocide, March 4–7, 2000, Saint Joseph's University, Philadelphia, Pennsylvania.

51. Randolph L. Braham, ed. *The Treatment of the Holocaust in Textbooks: The Federal Republic of Germany, Israel, The United States of America* (New York: Columbia University Press, 1987).

52. Walter F. Renn, "Textbooks: Treatment of the Holocaust and Related Themes," in *The Treatment of the Holocaust in Textbooks,* ed. Randolph L. Braham (New York: Columbia University Press, 1987). Elisabeth Maxwell argues similarly: "If we allow memory to tamper with the past, we are not only becoming partners in crime, helping to kill the dead a second time, but we are also allowing the ideologies of the repressors of memory to go unchallenged." See Elisabeth Maxwell, "The Crystal of Memory or the Smoke of Remembrance?" in *Confronting the Holocaust: A Mandate for the 21st Century. Studies in the Shoah,* ed. G. Jan Colin and Marcia Sachs Littell (New York: University Press of America, 1997), 19:152.

53. Renn, "Textbooks," 92.

54. Dominick LaCarpa, *History and Memory after Auschwitz* (Ithaca, NY: Cornell University Press, 1998), 53–54.

55. Richard J. Golsan, "Introduction," in *The Future of a Negation: Reflections on the Question of Genocide,* ed. Alain Finkielkraut, trans. Mary Byrd Kelly (Lincoln: University of Nebraska Press, 1998), xxvi.

56. English translation taken from Lucy Dawidowicz, ed., *A Holocaust Reader* (West Orange, NJ: Behrman House, 1976), 132–133.

57. The German word in question was *abschaffen,* which translates into "to do away with" or "to get rid of." The denial argument claimed that the meaning was not genocidal.

58. Friedmann J. Weidauer, "'Fighting for Defeat': Jewish Identity in Postwar Germany and Austria," *Seminar: A Journal of Germanic Studies* 34(3) (September 1998), 297.

59.  Eric A. Johnson, *Nazi Terror: The Gestapo, Jews, and Ordinary Germans* (New York: Basic Books, 1999), 486.

60.  Nachman Blumenthal, "On the Nazi Vocabulary," *Yad Vashem Studies: On the European Jewish Catastrophe and Resistance* 1 (1957), 65.

# LEXICON

# A

**A.** *See* Arbeitsjuden.

**AA.** *See* Auswärtiges Amt.

**Aal.** Eel. Naval torpedo.

**a.B.** *See* auf Befehl.

**AB-Aktion.** *See* außerordentliche Befriedigungs-Aktion.

**Abbau der rückstellenden Gruppen.** Dissolution of remaining groups. Order to identify and remove all Jews working in military and civil offices.

**Abbeförderung.** Dispatching, removal. Slang and euphemism for killing.

**abbuchen.** To deduct, to balance an account. To cross out the name of a murder victim from the concentration camp roster.

**abdirigieren.** To direct away. Bureaucratic euphemism for murdering someone or sending someone to a camp to be murdered because of an inability to work.

**Abendappell.** Evening roll call. *See also* Appell.

**Abfahrthalle.** Departure room of a station. Slang and euphemism for concentration camp crematorium room.

**abfangen.** To pull up. To pull an aircraft out of a dive.

**abfertigen.** To make ready for dispatch. Bureaucratic euphemism for preparing mass deportations to death camps in special trains.

**abflaken.** To shoot down with antiaircraft fire.

**Abgang.** Departure. Official bureaucratic reference to Jews deported from German companies to concentration camps in eastern Europe; also death or murder of concentration camp inmates.

**Abgänge.** Persons departed. Dead German soldiers, according to military accounts, and dead Jews and other murder victims.

**abgeräumt.** Cleared away. Euphemism for murdered. *See also* ausmerzen.

**abgewandert werden.** To be migrated. Bureaucratic slang for forceful removal or deportation of Jews to concentration camps. *See also* Absiedlung; Abwanderung.

**abgrundtief.** Deep as the abyss. Adjective used often in connection with Jews and opponents of the Nazi state; for example, "der abgrundtiefe Haß der Juden" (the deep hatred of the Jews).

**Abholer.** Fetchers. Those who identified Jews for the Germans and/or who came to take the Jews to the deportation center.

**Abhörverbrecher.** Radio-listening criminal. Germans and other people in the occupied countries who listened to foreign news broadcasts illegally.

**abimpfen.** *See* abspritzen.

**abkämmen.** To comb. To search an area, to destroy through bombing.

**AbKdo.** *See* Arbeitskommando.

**abladen.** To unload. Euphemism for to deport Jews.

**ablenken.** To distract, to shunt aside. Those the Nazis deemed unfit for their economic plan for eastern Europe were left to die without food or work.

**Ablieferungspflicht.** Delivery duty. Farm products, for example, had to be contributed to the state to be sold on the German market.

**Ablieferungsschlacht.** Delivery battle. Campaign for increased contributions of farm products during the war. *See also* Reichsnährstand.

**Ablösung.** Relief, replacement. Nazi dismissal of Jewish business owners. Also, in military vernacular, a casualty to replace.

**abmeiern.** To take away the right of management or ownership of a farm. Archaic. Third Reich meaning: dispossessing a farmer who was unable or unwilling to work his farm and/or to sign it over to his heirs or other capable person.

**Abmeierung.** *See* abmeiern.

**"Ab nach Dachau!"** "Away to Dachau!" (concentration camp). Signs in 1930s Germany referring to sending the Reich's so-called enemies to concentration camps.

**Abnahme.** Wehrmacht ordnance-testing station.

**Abnehmertausch.** Consumer exchange. *See also* Absatzkreis.

**Abordnungsgeld.** Relocation money. Bonus for workers who had to work outside of their place of residence.

**Abpfeifen.** Whistle. Curfew signal in a concentration camp, between 8 and 10 P.M., depending on the season, for all prisoners to move inside the barracks and, half an hour later, to be in bed. Exceptions only for those who were ordered to work.

**Abraham.** Name Jewish men were forced to take from 1939. *See also* Zusatzname.

**Abrechnung mit den Juden.** The settling of accounts with the Jews. The plan to eliminate Jews from the German economy and society and then murder them all.

**Absatzbewegung.** Disengagement. Military retreat. Flight.

**Absatzbezirk.** Sales area. *See also* Absatzkreis.

**Absatzkreis.** Sales Circle. Market restricted to one company. The exchange of customers saved companies transport time and costs.

**absaufen.** (Crude for) to drown. Slang for to make a forced landing, to lose altitude.

**abschaffen.** To do away with, to get rid of. Slang for to murder.

**Abschaum.** Scum. Political adversaries of the Nazis.

**Abschaum der Menschheit.** Scum of humanity. Invective for Jews, "enemies of the state," and, after 1941, Russians.

**abschieben.** To shunt off; to get rid of. To forcefully evacuate Jews. *See also* umsiedeln.

**(wilde) Abschiebungen.** Chaotic expulsions. Savage repression and removal of Jews from a location to a concentration camp or ghetto, with many killed in the process.

**abschlachten.** To butcher. To mass murder.

**Abschnitt.** Sector, section. Administrative subdistrict. Also, removable tab on ration card. Also section of the war front. Also, section of the SD and SS.

**Abschreckung.** Terror. The terroristic means of governing German-occupied territory in eastern Europe.

**abschreiben.** To write off (a debt). To work Jews to death to write off their imagined debt to Germany.

**Abschub.** Expulsion. Euphemism for forceful removal of Jews to eastern Europe to be killed. *See also* abschieben; (wilde) Abschiebungen.

**Abschußring.** Hit ring. White markings on the barrel of an antiaircraft gun indicating each enemy plane shot down.

**Abschußstock.** Shooting cane. A "hit cane" awarded as a trophy to pilots, with markings indicating each air victory.

**absetzen.** Clear out/get away. Euphemism decreed by German army regulation describing retreat of German troops during World War II. Equivalent to tactical withdrawal. *See* Absatzbewegung.

**(den Kurs) absetzen.** To compensate for a side wind so as not to move off course.

**(von der Lagerbelegung) absetzen.** To delete from the camp roster. SS jargon in concentration camps for recording deaths of prisoners.

**Absiedler.** Emigrants. *See also* Absiedlung.

**Absiedlung.** Resettlement. Forceful removal of people from German-occupied or annexed regions. *See* Umsiedlung.

**absondern.** To select, to separate. In the concentration camps, to decide who is to live, who is to die.

**Absperre.** Closing off. Dismissal following the evening roll call in the concentration camps.

**abspritzen.** To inject. Derogatory for to murder by injection.

**Abstammungsbescheid.** *See* Abstammungsnachweis.

**Abstammungsnachweis.** Genealogical certificate. To prove Aryan descent and the lack of alien (Jewish) blood.

**Abstammungszeugnis.** Genealogical certificate. *See also* Abstammungsnachweis.

**Abstich.** Germanization of Kontrast (contrast).

**Abstrebung.** Buttress, base. *See also* Geopolitik.

**Abt.** *See* Abteilung.

**Abteilung.** (Abt.) Battalion. A tactical unit consisting of a number of companies actively engaged in combat (500 to 1,000 men). The smallest self-contained and self-sufficent combat formation with enough firepower and support units to fight on its own.

**Abteilung.** (Abt.) Department, section, branch. Unit of Nazi Party and government of the Third Reich.

**(politische) Abteilung.** Political branch. Section of a concentration camp occupied by political prisoners. Also, concentration camp unit that registered prisoners and kept records on them and supervisory personnel; represented the Gestapo and was empowered to run internal investigations.

**Abteilung Allgemeines Kriegsgefangenenwesen.** General Branch for Prisoner-of-War Matters. Armed forces branch.

**Abteilung Bothmann.** Bothmann Branch. SS killing squad operating at the Chelmno death camp.

**Abteilung Entwesung und Entseuchung.** Extermination and Decontamination Unit. Shipments of Zyklon poison gas originated from the Deutsche Gesellschaft für Schädlingsbekämpfung (DEGESCH) in Frankfurt am Main and were addressed to the extermination and decontamination branches at Auschwitz and other concentration camps.

**Abteilung für Erb- und Rassenpflege.** Branch of hereditary and racial maintenance.

**Abteilung für Sonderhäftlinge.** Section for special prisoners. At Flossenbürg concentration camp, in particular, for those members of the military resistance against Hitler arrested late in the war.

**Abteilung für sowjetische Kriegsgefangene.** Section for Soviet war prisoners. At Flossenbürg concentration camp.

**Abteilung für Wehrmachtfachschulunterricht.** Armed Forces Technical-School Classes Branch. Wehrmacht educational system.

**Abteilung für Wehrmachtpropaganda.** Armed Forces Propaganda Branch.

**Abteilung Kriegsschulen.** Cadet school branch of the armed forces.

**Abteilung Landesverteidigung.** (Abt. L.) Defense Department.

**Abteilung Nachtigall.** Nightingale Unit. Ukrainian militia involved in mass murder of Jews in Lvov, Ukraine. *See also* Aktion Petliura.

**Abteilung Reinhard.** Reinhard Unit. Death camp organization. Heinrich Himmler selected Odilo Globocnik to organize mass murder in Poland, including the death camps and Einsatzgruppen. *See also* Aktion Reinhard.

**Abteilungsführer.** Branch Leader. Unit leader in the Reich workforce.

**Abteilung Umsiedlung.** Resettlement Branch. Ghetto administration department that oversaw the creation of the Warsaw-Ghetto.

**Abteilung Wehrmachtnachrichtenverbindungen Funkwesen.** Armed Forces Radio Communications Branch.

**Abteilung II.** Department II. *See* (politische) Abteilung.

**Abteilung II Raum.** Space Branch II. Headquarters in Riga, Latvia, whose role was to place German colonists in the Baltic states and western Belorussia.

**Abt. L.** *See* Abteilung Landesverteidigung.

**Abw.** *See* Abwehr.

**abwandern.** To make go. Euphemistic and derogatory for to deport. *See also* abgewandert; Abwanderung.

**Abwanderung.** Emigration, leaving one region for another. Population exchange. Also, forced emigration of Jews. Later, official euphemism for deportations of Jews to their deaths in the east. *See also* Absiedlung.

**Abwanderungsabgabe.** Emigration fee. Fee levied on Jews by the Reich security office toward their costs incurred by their deportation. *See also* Abwanderung.

**Abwehr.** (Abw.) Defense. Nazi Counterintelligence Agency established in 1933 and attached to the Wehrmacht's High Command. It took charge of espionage, sabotage, commando raids, and spying outside of Germany. Absorbed in 1944 into the Rasse und Siedlungshauptamt. Under the leadership of its head, Admiral Wilhelm Canaris, it came to oppose the Nazi regime. *See also* Schwarze Kapelle,

**Abwehrangelegenheiten.** Counterespionage issues.

**"(Der) Abwehrkampf hat begonnen."** "The defensive war has begun." 1933 Nazi antisemitic slogan.

**Abwehrpolizei.** Counterespionage Police detailed along the border. *See also* Gestapo.

**Abwehrschlacht.** Defense battle. The fight of the German army against the advancing Soviet enemy during the last years of World War II.

**Abwehrstelle.** (AST, ASt) Military Intelligence Center. Military intelligence department with subordinate groups: I—Geheimer Meldedienst; II—Sabotage und Zersetzung; III—Spionageabwehr.

**Abwehrstellenleiter.** Military Intelligence Center Leader. Official in German Military Intelligence.

**abweisen.** To repulse. To repel an attack.

**Abwesenheitspfleger.** Trustee during absence of owner. Foreign property custodian. *See also* Treuhänder.

**Abzeichen.** *See* Goldenes Parteiabzeichen.

**abziehen.** To leave, clear out. Euphemism for deporting and killing Jews.

**Achse.** Axis. 1939 alliance first between Germany and Italy (Stahlpakt, or Pact of Steel), joined in 1940 by Japan to become the Berlin-Rome-Tokyo Axis. Also code name for plan to disarm Italian army.

**Achse Berlin-Rom.** *See* Achse.

**Achsenmächte.** Axis powers. *See also* Achse.

**(die ersten) Acht.** The first eight. Respectful term for the first eight men of the SS who were responsible for Hitler's protection during rallies.

**"Achtung, Feind hört mit!"** "Watch out, the enemy is listening!" Nazi slogan. Repeated warning against spies published in newspapers, posted in shop windows and restaurants, printed on notepads and matchboxes, and so forth. *See also* Lauscher.

**Ackernahrung.** Smallest unit comprising a working farm. Law of 1933 defined the minimum farm size necessary for a family of four to be self-sufficient.

**Addresse unbekannt.** *See* "umgezogen, Addresse unbekannt."

**Adel.** Aristocracy, nobility. Unlike the old privilege by birth or talent, the Nazi version was determined by descent, by race, or by blood.

**ADEUST, ADEuRst.** *See* Amtliche Deutsche Ein- und Rückwandererstelle.

**ADFW.** *See* Ausfuhrbestimmungen über Dringlichkeit der Fertigungsprogramme der Wehrmacht.

**Adjutant.** Deputy commander of concentration camp. SS officer second in command.

**Adjutantur.** Armed Forces Personnel Section.

*(Der) Adler.* The Eagle. Luftwaffe magazine published from 1939 to 1944.

**Adlerangriffe.** Eagle Attack. Air war against Great Britain.

**Adler(s)horst.** Eagle's Nest. Hitler's headquarters between December 10, 1944, and January, 16, 1945, in Bad Nauheim, near the Ardennes.

**Adlerorden.** Eagle medal. *See also* Verdienstorden vom Deutschen Adler.

**Adlertag.** Eagle Day. Code name for the beginning of the air battle (August 8, 1940) to win command of the skies over Great Britain. The British fighter pilots inflicted heavy losses on the German bombers, postponing the German amphibious assault on Britain. Code for the attack on British Royal Air Force bases and aircraft manufacturing plants (September 15, 1940) as a prelude to Germany's planned invasion of Great Britain. *See also* Unternehmen Seelöwe.

**Adler und Falke.** Eagle and Falcon. Nazi youth group.

*Admiral Graf Spee.* Admiral Count Spee. German pocket battleship scuttled by its crew in Montevideo, Uruguay, harbor after raids on Allied shipping and naval battles involving the British ships *Ajax*, *Achilles*, and *Exeter*.

*Admiral Scheer.* Most successful of the German pocket battleship raiders. Throughout the war it sank or captured several Allied ships. Bombed and sank in April 1945.

**ADO.** *See* Allgemeine Dienstordung.

**Adolf-Hitler-Platz.** *See* Reichsparteitagsgelände.

**Adolf-Hitler-Schulen.** (AHS) Adolf Hitler Schools. Established in 1937 as political training schools for future Nazi leaders.

**Adolf-Hitler-Spende.** Adolf Hitler fund. Businessmen who profited from their association with the Nazi Party contributed to this fund controlled by Martin

Bormann. Also, funds coerced from Jewish businessmen.The fund spent money on a variety of Nazi Party activities.

**Adolf-Hitler-Straßen.** *See* Reichsautobahnen.

**Adolf Legalité.** Adolf the Legal One. Applied to Hitler by those who saw him as desiring to obtain political power only through legal means. Also used sarcastically by SA members who preferred violent means to overthrow the Weimar Republic.

**AEG.** *See* Alles echte Germanen.

**A-Fall.** Case A. Code in correspondence to and from the Reich Security Administration referring to a possible revolt in the Auschwitz death camp. *See also* Reichssicherheitshauptamt.

**Aferna.** *See* Armee-Fernsprech-Abteilung.

**Affenschaukel.** Monkey's swing. Military slang for shoulder cord on full-dress uniforms.

**Afrikakorps.** *See* Deutsches Afrikakorps.

**Afrikaner.** African. A former member of Field Marshal Erwin Rommel's Africa corps.

**Afterkultur.** Anus culture, spurious art. Derogatory Nazi label for so-called degenerate art. *See also* entartete Kunst.

**AfV.** *See* Amt für Volksgesundheit.

**Agenten.** Agents. SD operatives. *See also* A-Mann; Sicherheitsdienst.

**Aggregat 4.** (A4) Aggregate 4. Earlier code for V-2 rocket. *See also* Vergeltungsbombe.

**Aggressor.** Aggressor. The Allies during World War II.

**Agram.** Croatia's Zagreb.

**Agrarpolitik.** Agricultural Policy. Nazi Party department.

**agrarpolitischer Apparat.** (aA) Agrarian Policy Organization. 1930 Nazi organization dealing with agrarian issues. *See also* Reichsnährstand.

**Ahn(e).** Ancestor of German origin.

**Ahnenerbe.** *See* Ahnenerbe-Forschungs-, und Lehrgemeinschaft.

**Ahnenerbe-Forschungs- und Lehrgemeinschaft.** Society for Research into the Teaching of Ancestral Heritage. SS institution founded by Himmler in July 1935 for research into racial prehistory of the German Volk. Sponsored about forty research projects dealing with Germanic prehistory, race, lore, and ethnic, national, and cultural identity. Later involved in so-called medical experiments on concentration camp prisoners, especially those performed by August Hirt, Head of the Anatomy Institute at the University of Strasbourg, whose project was to decapitate Jews to study their skulls and brains in order to obtain scientific support for Himmler's racial theories.

**Ahnenforschung.** Ancestry research. Research into specifics about each family's racial background and history.

**(großer) Ahnennachweis.** Proof of ancestry. Proof that an SS member could trace his Aryan ancestry back to the year 1750.

**Ahnenpaß.** Proof of ancestry pass. Official card issued to SS and civilians identifying them as German after 1935 Nuremberg Laws.

**Ahnenprobe.** Ancestry proof. Proof of German descent.

**Ahnenschatzkästlein.** Ancestry treasure chest. Assortment of forms, such as genealogical tables and statistical cards, that needed to be completed, together with providing other personal information, in order to determine ancestry and family history of German citizens.

**Ahnenschein.** Genealogical document. Paper used to prove valid German descent.

**Ahnentafel.** Genealogical chart. List of German forbears.

**Ahnenverlust.** Loss of ancestry. Loss of racial status due to marriage between blood relatives.

**Ahnerbenbehörden.** Heritage authorities. Courts that adjudicated cases under the Reich farm inheritance law. *See also* Reichserbhofgesetz.

**AHS.** *See* Adolf-Hitler-Schulen.

**Aïda.** Code for German attack on Egypt.

**a.K.** *See* auf Kriegsdauer.

**AK.** *See* Armeekorps.

**Akademie für Deutsches Recht.** Academy for German Law. Founded by Hans Frank in 1933 for members of the German judiciary in the Reich political leadership who were to rewrite the entire corpus of German law. Except for the Nuremberg Laws, the Academy did not play its intended role.

**Akademie für Jugendführung.** Academy for Youth Education. Institution in Braunschweig for the education of Hitler Youth leaders.

**AKBF.** *See* Arbeitskreis für biozentrische Forschungen.

**Akdo.** *See* Außenkommando.

**Aktion.** Action, operation, measure, steps. Roundup, deportation, and murder of Jews. Also any nonmilitary campaign to further Nazi ideals of race. Military operations. *See also* Sonderaktion.

**(Die) Aktion.** The Action. Propaganda Ministry newspaper spreading pro-German, anti-Jewish, and anti-Allies propaganda.

**(direkte) Aktion.** (Direct) action. Immediate murder of Jews in eastern Europe.

**Aktion A.** Operation A. Registration of Jews in the Warsaw-Ghetto.

**Aktion Arbeitsscheue im Reich.** Operation Reich Laziness. In June 1938, Jews with previous convictions, even the most trivial, were deported to concentration camps where dozens were murdered. Also called Asozialen-Aktion.

**Aktion B.** Operation B. Collection, sorting, and listing of Jewish property from the Warsaw-Ghetto stored in SS warehouses.

**Aktion Brunner.** 1942 roundup of Berlin Jews sent to death camps in the east.

**Aktion Bürckel.** 1940 roundup of German Jews sent to camps in Vichy, France, and later deported to death camps in the east.

**Aktion 1005.** *See* Kommando 1005.

**Aktion Erlaßentwurf.** Operation Blueprint Release. 1942 roundup of Jews in Belgium sent to death camps in the east.

**Aktion Erntefest.** Operation Harvest Festival. Code name for the mass killings of Jews remaining in the Lublin area, November 3, 1943. An estimated 42,000 people were shot while loud music was played to drown out the sound of the shootings. Last operation of Aktion Reinhard.

**Aktion Fabrik.** Operation Factory. 1943 roundup of Berlin Jews working for the German war effort and who were married to Aryans.

**Aktion Frühlingswind.** Operation Spring Breeze. *See also* Aktion Meerschaum.

**Aktion Gitter.** Action (behind) Bars. 1939 operation soon after German occupation of Czechoslovakia that resulted in the arrest of Czechoslovakian public figures, German émigrés, and Jews, with the cooperation of pro-Nazi Czechs. Also, 1944 Gestapo operation that rounded up Catholic politicians to be sent to concentration camps.

**Aktion Heu.** *See* Heu-Aktion; Lebensborn.

**Aktion Heyde.** Operation Heyde. Identification and registration of mentally ill concentration camp inmates and those unable to work. They were to be deported to camps or sanitariums with gassing facilities. *See also* Aktion T-4; Sonderbehandlung 14f.13.

**Aktion Höss.** Operation Höss. The murderous SS response to the revolt of the Auschwitz Sonderkommando. Rudolf Höss was the Auschwitz commandant.

**Aktion Iltis.** Operation Iltis. 1943 operation deporting Belgian Jews to the east.

**Aktion Jecklin.** Operation Jecklin. 1941 operation in which 25,000 Jews were taken from the Riga-Ghetto in Latvia and murdered in the Rumbula Forest.

**Aktion Judenfrei.** Operation Jew-Free. Systematic mass murder of Jews in ghettos located in Soviet territories that marked the beginning, in 1941, of the German Wehrmacht's participation in the destruction of the Jews.

**Aktion Kaiserbaron.** Operation Gypsy Baron. Kidnapping of non-German children with Aryan features. *See also* Lebensborn.

**(Die) Aktion: Kampfblatt für das neue Europa.** The Action: Battle Pages for the New Europe. Nazi propaganda newsletter (1939–1945) aimed especially at readers in neutral nations, blaming the war on Jewish and British money.

**Aktion Kugel.** Operation Bullet. Roundup and murder of escaped Allied prisoners of war.

**Aktion Margarethe.** Operation Margaret. Code name for the German occupation of Hungary in 1944 resulting in the deportation and murder of nearly a half million Hungarian Jews.

**Aktion Meerschaum.** Operation Sea Foam. Roundup of Jews in France in 1943 and 1944 who were deported to concentration camps. Also called Aktion Frühlingswind.

**Aktion Möbel.** (M-Aktion) Operation Furniture. Systematic plundering of Jewish apartments in occupied Europe.

**Aktion nach Kriegsgebrauch.** Action according to the usage of war. Euphemism for shooting POWs as well as civilian men, women, and children.

**Aktion Petliura.** Operation Petliura. Named after Ukrainian antisemitic leader. 1941 Lvov operation in which thousands of Jews were slaughtered by the Ukrainian Militia of the Nachtigall Battalion.

**Aktion Reinhard.** Operation Reinhard. Code name for the Hitler-Göring-Himmler ordered expropriation, deportation, forced labor, and mass murder of European Jews located in German-occupied eastern territories and those deported there, beginning in 1941–1942. SS-Brigadeführer Odilo Globocnik was assigned to oversee these mass-murder operations in part as a memorial to the recently assassinated Reinhard Heydrich. Gassing specialist Christian Wirth, called the "Technocrat of Destruction," was appointed in 1942 to head the death camp Chelmno, and later became inspector of the Belzec, the Sobibor, and the Treblinka death camps (the four Aktion Reinhard camps) where the mass murderers first utilized carbon monoxide in mobile vans to kill Jews; later, closed gas chambers were used. The staff of T-4 subsequently provided the trained force of killers at the Operation Reinhard camps. In towns and villages of German-occupied eastern Europe, the Einsatzgruppen as well as units of the Order Police, the SS, the SD, the German armed forces, volunteers, and the Polish police carried out the killings. *See also* Aktion T-4; Einsatzgruppen; Hilfswillige; Ordnungspolizei; SD; SS; Wehrmacht.

**Aktion Ritterbusch.** Operation Ritterbusch. Initiated in 1940 by Paul Ritterbusch, rector of Kiel University, it was a published series of sixty-seven books attempting to prove German superiority in the humanities. Part of the struggle for Nazi ideological supremacy, these writings were based on a compilation of conference contributions in the different disciplines within the humanities, titled collectively *Deutsche Geisteswissenschaft.*

**Aktionsgruppe.** *See* Einsatzgruppen.

**Aktionsgruppe Frankreich.** Action Group for France. Himmler's operation to destroy the Jews living in France.

**Aktionshäftlinge.** Operation prisoners. Austrian, Czech, and German political activists arrested and jailed for their anti-Nazi political activities just before the outbreak of World War II.

**Aktionsjuden.** Operation Jews. The 26,000 German and Austrian Jews arrested during the November 1938 Pogrom called Reichskristallnacht, who were sent to Buchenwald and other camps and released weeks later.

**Aktion Sumpffieber.** Operation Swamp Fever. SS and Wehrmacht forces attempting to destroy Russian partisans, called Plünderer and Banditen (brigands and bandits).

**Aktion Tannenberg.** Operation Tannenberg. Shortly after the outbreak of World War II, in September and October 1939, SS special task forces murdered hundreds of Jews and the Polish intelligentsia, politicians, aristocrats, teachers, and Catholic clergy; destroyed dozens of synagogues; and waged of an all-out terror campaign against non-German, Polish civilians.

**Aktion T-4.** Operation T-4. Code name for the Nazi euthanasia program. Name taken from the Reich Chancellery's address at Tiergartenstraße 4. The program first murdered German incurables utilizing carbon monoxide in mobile vans to kill more than 100,000 adults and children; later, closed gas chambers were used. The staff of T-4 subsequently provided the trained force of killers at the Operation Reinhard camps in Poland: Belzec, Chelmno, Sobibor, and Treblinka. *See also* Aktion Reinhard; Aktion 14 f 13 KZ-Häftlinge; Euthanasie.

**Aktion 14 f. 13.** *See* Aktion 14 f. 13 KZ-Häftlinge.

**Aktion 14 f. 13 KZ-Häftlinge.** Operation 14f13 concentration camp prisoners. Murder of concentration camp inmates unable to work. Also called Invalidenaktion and Aktion Heyde. *See also* Euthanasie; Sonderbehandlung 14 f. 13.

**Aktion Walküre.** Operation Valkyrie. Plan for German home army to take control of cities if foreign workers in Germany revolted.

**Aktion Wolkenbrand.** Operation Cloud Fire. Plan to poison all Dachau inmates before Allied liberation, except for non-Jewish POWs.

**Aktion Wolke A I.** Operation Cloud A I. Code name for a planned order to the Luftwaffe to destroy the Jewish work camps Landsberg and Mühldorf in Bavaria by simulating an Allied air attack.

**Aktive.** Active. Soldier slang for store-bought cigarettes in contrast to those rolled by hand.

**aktivistisch.** Activistic. Goal-oriented training of willpower, deemed worthy of Germans under National Socialism.

**Alarich.** *See* Unternehmen Alarich.

**Allbuch.** Germanization of Konversationslexikon (encyclopedia).

**alldeutsch.** Completely German.

**"All-Deutschland gegen Alljuda!"** "All Germany against all Jewry." Antisemitic slogan.

**"Alle Juden bleiben nach!"** "All Jews remain behind." German command to Jews at camp roll calls. The result was often humiliation and torture.

**"Alle Juden herunter!"** "All Jews downstairs." German command to Jews during an Aktion—a virtual death sentence.

**"Alle Juden raus!"** "All Jews out."

**Allel.** Variation within a race. Nazi genetic/racial term.

**Alles echte Germanen.** (AEG) All genuine Germans. Right-wing term after Hitler's victory in 1933 applying to pro-German attitudes.

**"Alles für Deutschland!"** "Everything for Germany." Motto of the National-sozialistische Kraftfahrkorps and the Sturmabteilung.

**Alles in Ordnung.** All in order, all OK. Often used as a euphemism to indicate mass murders had proceeded well.

**"Alles raus!"** "Everyone out." *See also* "Juden raus!"

**"Alles was ich bin, bin ich nur durch euch; aber alles was ihr seid, seid ihr nur durch mich!"** "All that I am, I am only through you; but all that you are, you are only through me." Hitler slogan. *See also* "(Das) Volk der Führer ist, und der Führer das Volk ist."

**Allgemeine Dienstordung.** (ADO) General service order.

**Allgemeine Elektrizitäts-Gesellschaft.** (AEG) General Electric Corporation. Used slave labor.

**Allgemeine Krankentransportgesellschaft.** General Ambulance Service. Code name for the SS agency responsible for the deporting of euthanasia candidates to the sanatoriums where they were to be killed.

**Allgemeine SS.** General SS. All SS agencies not included in the Waffen-SS.

**Allgemeines Wehrmachtsamt.** (Aw, AWA) General Armed Forces Office. *See also* Wehrmachtsamt.

**Alliierte.** Allies. The World War II alliance consisting of Britain, the Free French, the Soviet Union, and the United States opposing Germany and the other Axis powers. *See* Feindmächte.

**Alljuda.** All Judah. All Jews, Jewishness, Judaism, Jews as enemy, and the imagined international Jewish conspiracy.

**Alljude.** Completely a Jew. According to race theorist Alfred Rosenberg, the German-born American Jew, Otto Hermann Kahn, was considered the archetypal example of a Jew. Often-used Nazi antisemitic propaganda word.

**Alljudenheit.** All Jewishness. International Jewish conspiracy.

**alljüdisch.** All Jewish. Devoted to high finance, the stock market, and narrow party politics.

**Allkett.** Berlin tank manufacturer. *See* Panzer.

**allnordisch.** Completely Nordic. Racial term.

**Allod Eigenheim und Kleinsiedlung GmbH, Berlin.** Allod Home Owner and Small Settlement Company, Ltd. Office created in 1938 to determine management and usage of property that was seized by the German army in occupied countries.

**allweltlich.** All world. Race theorist Alfred Rosenberg tried in vain to replace kosmisch (cosmic) with the German allweltlich.

**(das) Alm.** Germanization of Aluminium (aluminum).

**Alpenfestung.** Alpine fortress. Area of the Bavarian Alps where Hitler imagined his forces would make a last stand against the Allies. His mountain residence of Berchtesgaden was to serve as the command post. Also, camp for Jews located near the Austro-Hungarian border.

**Alpen- und Donauländer.** Alpine and Danube lands. Austria, previously Österreich.

**Alpenveilchen.** Alpine violet. Code name for invasion of Albania in January 1940 and for German aid to Italian forces in Albania.

**alpin.** *See* ostisch.

**Alte Garde.** Old Guard. Old-time Nazis, those in party ranks at the time of the Hitler Putsch in Munich on November 8–9, 1923. *See* Alte Kämpfer.

**Alte Kämpfer.** Veteran(s), old fighter(s). Members of the SA, the SS, and the Stahlhelm before January 30, 1933. Also Nazis who took part in the Hitler Putsch Munich on November 8–9, 1923.

**Alteltern.** Great-great-grandparents.

**Altersghetto.** Elders' ghetto. *See also* Theresienstadt.

**Altersraum.** Germanization of Generation (generation).

**Altes Führerkorps.** *See* Alte Kämpfer.

**Ältestenrat.** Elders' council. Jewish council at Theresienstadt and other ghettos. *See also* Judenrat.

**Ältestenrat der israelitischen Kultusgemeinde in Petraikau.** Elders' Council of the Israelite Community in Petraikau. Jewish council of the first ghetto in German-occupied Poland.

-ältester-. Senior. Prefix and suffix used in concentration camp service ranks for prisoners; for example, Ältesterführer (senior leader). *See also* Blockälteste.

**Ältester der Juden.** Senior Jew. Senior Jewish worker at the Treblinka death camp.

**Altgroßeltern.** Great-great-great-grandparents.

**Altmaterial.** Old material. Recyclable materials such as paper, cloth, cans, tubes, and so forth collected by the Hitler Youth.

**Altona.** Code name for cancellation of Barbarossa. *See also* Fall Barbarossa.

**Altreich.** Old Reich. Germany in 1937 before the Anschluß of Austria in 1938.

**Altstoff.** Old material. Recyclable scrap metal.

**A-Mann.** A-man. Agent of the Security Service, spy and informant; collected information on every individual in the Nazi Party, government, church, society, and so on. *See also* H-Mann; U-Mann; V-Mann; Z-Mann.

*Amerika.* America. Code name for Hitler's special armored train. *See* Atlas.

**Amerika.** *See* Projekt 1061, 1062.

**Amerikadeutsche.** American Germans. Germans living in America. Previously, Deutschamerikaner.

**Amerikadeutscher Volksbund.** German-America People's League. German-American association led by German Nazi Party member Fritz Kuhn, supported during the 1930s by Hitler.

**Amersfoort.** *See* Polizeiliches Durchgangslager Amersfoort.

**Amt.** Department, office. Calling, destiny.

**Amt Auslandsnachrichten und Abwehr.** *See* Amtsgruppe Auslandsnachrichten und Abwehr.

**Amt des Generalgouverneurs.** Office of the Governor General. *See also* Generalgouvernement.

**Amt für Ausrottung.** Extermination Department. SS department that directed mass murder operations against the Jews.

**Amt für die Umsiedlung von Polen und Juden.** Department for the Resettlement of Poles and Jews. In 1940 became the Umwandererzentralstelle.

**Amt für jüdische Auswanderung.** Department for Jewish Emigration. After the German annexation of Austria, Adolf Eichmann headed this office in Vienna and through extortion and other means forced 150,000 Jews to leave Austria.

**Amt für volksgermanische Führung.** *See* (Amt für) Volksgermanische Führung.

**Amt für Volksgesundheit.** (AfV) Department for Public Health.

**Amtliche Deutsche Ein- und Rückwandererstelle.** (ADEUST, ADEuRst) Official German Office for Immigration and Emigration.

**Amtliche Nachrichtenstelle.** (A.N.St.) Official news station.

**Amt Mil.** German Military Intelligence unit that succeeded the Abwehr. *See also* Abwehr.

**Amt Rosenberg.** Office Rosenberg. *See also* Beauftragter des Führers für die Berwachung der gesamten geistigen und weltanschaulichen Schulung und Erziehung der NSDAP.

**Amtsgruppe Auslandsnachtrichten und Abwehr.** Intelligence and Counterespionage Service of the German Armed Forces High Command. *See also* Abwehr; (Amt) Ausland-Abwehr.

**Amtsgruppe IVB.** Division 4B. Office of the RSHA headed by Adolf Eichmann to handle the emigration and evacuation of Jews. By 1943, Eichmann supervised Jewish matters, evacuation, seizure of assets of those hostile to the German people and state, revocation of German citizenship, and the roundup, ghettoization, deportation to concentration camps, and mass murder of Europe's Jews.

**Amtsleiter.** Commissioner. Nazi Party official on the staff of the District Leader. Also, German ghetto chief. *See also* Gauleiter.

**Amtsleiter für die Presse.** Press Commissioner. Position held by Max Amann.

**Amtsträger.** Authority holder. Reich or Nazi Party functionary.

**Amtswalter.** Department Manager. Official of the Deutsche Arbeitsfront. A functionary of the Nazi Party's associated organizations.

**Amtswaltung.** Department management. *See also* Amtswalter.

**Amtswart.** Office official. Party official or functionary.

**Amt IVB4.** *See* Amtsgruppe IVB; Dienststelle Eichmann.

**Amt Zentrale Planung.** Office of Central Planning. Headed by Hermann Göring.

**Anbauschlacht.** Building campaign. *See also* Arbeitsschlacht.

**(der) Andere.** The other. Foreign radio station broadcasting news in German, such as Radio Beromünster, the BBC, and Radio Moscow. It was forbidden, on pain of death, to listen to these stations.

**Andreas.** Code name for Nazi plan to counterfeit Allied money in order to ruin Allied economies. *See also* VI F, 4a.

**Anerbenbehörden.** Heritage authorities. Courts that adjudicated the Reich Farm-Inheritance Law. *See also* Reichserbhofgesetz.

**Anerbenrecht.** Heritage Law. Instituted to prevent division of land or indebtedness.

**"Anerkannt deutsch-christliches Unternehmen."** "(Officially) recognized German-Christian enterprise." Sign on red background in German stores during the boycott of Jewish stores in 1933. *See also* Judenboykott.

**anfallen.** To accrue, obtain. To confiscate the property of Jews after their deportation.

**angearbeitetes Eisen.** Worked iron. Scrap metal.

**angelernter Arbeiter.** Worker trained on the job. *See also* Anlehre.

**angeschlossene Verbände.** Associated federations. Associations attached to the Nazi Party.

**angliedern.** To annex, incorporate.

**(die) anglo-amerikanische Plutokratie.** Anglo-American plutocracy. Propaganda term for the alleged Anglo-American-Jewish alliance formed against Germany.

*(Der) Angriff.* The Assault/Attack. Nazi Party newspaper first published weekly then once or twice a day. Founded and under the control of Joseph Goebbels from 1927.

**Angstbrosche.** Badge of fear. Ironic for Nazi Party pin worn by latecomers to the Party in 1933.

**Anhaltelager.** (AnL) Temporary detention camp. From 1934 to 1938 in Austria, place to confine political opponents of the pre–Nazi Austrian government, including members of the Nationalsozialistische Deutsche Arbeiterpartei.

**Anhängekalkulation.** Appended calculation. Correction of a calculation.

**animalische Wärme.** Animal warmth. As part of a freezing torture, four women were used to attempt to revive Dachau prisoners who had undergone hypothermia experiments.

**ankratzen.** To scratch. Military slang: to damage.

**Anlehre.** Short-term on-the-job training. Six-month job training in a factory.

**Anleihestock.** Loan basis. Undistributed profits invested in Reich loans.

**Anlernberuf.** Job acquired after short-term on-the-job training. *See* Anlehre.

**Anlernling.** On-the-job trainee. *See* Anlehre.

**anpreisen.** To put price tags on merchandise.

**Anruf der rassischen Werte.** Appeal to racial values. Emotional appeal to racial background.

**Anruf des Blutes.** Call of the blood. Inner calling to follow Nazi ideology.

**Ansatz.** Basic approach, departure, starting point. Military expression from World War I, used in the language of National Socialism. Sometimes replaced by Einsatz. *See also* Einsatz.

**Anschluß.** Annexation. Integration to the Reich of Austria, Sudetenland, Danzig, Westpreussen, and Memelland.

**Anschluß an den deutschen Wirtschaftsraum.** Connection to the German economic area. Economic coordination of the countries neighboring the German Reich.

**Anschlußgedanke.** Annexation thought. The desire of many Austrians, from 1918 on, to be united with the German Reich.

**Anschluß Österreichs an das Deutsche Reich.** *See* Anschluß.

**ansetzen.** To implement, attack, start. To attack the enemy; to populate the German-occupied eastern regions with Germans.

**A.N.St.** *See* Amtliche Nachrichtenstelle.

**Anstalt A, B, C, D.** Institution A, B, C, D. Code names for those German medical institutions that were equipped with gas chambers to kill the mentally ill and handicapped. *See also* Aktion T-4.

**anständiger Jude.** Decent Jew. An exceptional Jew who was still to be destroyed along with all Jews.

**Ansteckungsgebiet.** Contagious zone. Nazi claim that the diseased Jewish ghettos in eastern Europe had to be sealed off to keep local non-Jewish inhabitants healthy.

**Ansturm.** Stampede. Condescending for the Russian defenses during the first half of World War II.

**Ansturm der Steppe.** Steppe offensive. The attack of the Soviet army after the battle of Stalingrad.

**ansumpfen.** To swamp. Slang for to conquer a country.

**Anteilszahl.** Ratio number. Quota. Germanization of Prozentsatz, *numerus clausus* (percentage, or restricted entry).

**Antijüdische Aktion.** Anti-Jewish Action. Goebbel's antisemitic research institute. Originally Antisemitische Aktion but changed to mollify pro–Nazi Arabs who considered themselves Semites.

**Antijüdischer Kongress.** Anti-Jewish Congress. Rosenberg's stillborn brainchild to hold a congress at Krakow among representatives of the Axis powers to order the removal of all the European Jews.

**Antikominternpakt.** Anti-Commintern (Communist International) Pact. 1936 agreement between Germany and Japan to defend themselves against the Communist International. Joined in 1938 by Italy and several other European states allied to, or occupied by, Germany, such as Hungary, Spain, Bulgaria, Croatia, Denmark, Finland, Rumania, and Slovakia, as well as Japanese satellite nations.

**Antisemit.** Antisemite. Roll-your-own cigarette tobacco introduced by the Nazis in 1920 to further their antisemitic propaganda campaign.

**Antisemitische Aktion.** Antisemitic Action. *See also* Antijüdische Aktion; Institut zum Studium der Judenfrage.

**Antisemitismus.** Antisemitism. Prejudice, discrimination, brutality, expulsion, murder, or mass murder against Jewish people. Also, hostility toward Judaism and/or Jewishness. Coined by the German Wilhelm Marr in the late nineteenth century to replace Judenhaß (Jew hatred). It is often associated with modern racism and violent political movements against Jews, although its history is almost as old as the Jews themselves.

**antisozial.** Antisocial. Deviating from the natural desire for community. *See also* asozial.

**Anton.** *See* Unternehmen Anton; Unternehmen Attila.

***anus mundi.*** "Asshole of the world." Latin phrase used widely for Poland in general and Auschwitz in particular. *See* "Arsch der Welt."

**Anweiserin.** Person in charge. Female concentration camp supervisor. *See also* Grüne; Kapo.

**AO.** *See* Auslandsorganisation der NSDAP.

**AOG.** *See* Arbeitsordungsgesetz.

**AOK.** *See* Armeeoberkommando.

**AP.** *See* Außenposten.

**APA.** *See* Außenpolitisches Amt.

**Appell.** Roll call. Within the camps, inmates were forced to stand at attention for hours at least twice a day while they were counted, no matter what the weather. Often accompanied by beatings, punishments, and collective torture.

**Appellmacher.** Roll caller. Inmate who counted assembled prisoners at roll call.

**Appellplatz.** Place for roll call in the camps. *See also* Appell.

**APWVO.** *See* Arbeitsplatzwechselverordnung.

**Arbeit.** Work. The Aryan concept of work was contrasted with the Jewish idea of work for purely economic motivation and exploitation. Aryan work was part of the mystical connection with the community, the Volk.

**"Arbeit adelt."** "Work ennobles." Ironic phrase placed above the entrance gates of some work camps. Also, motto of Reichsarbeitsdienst.

**Arbeiter am Recht.** Workers in the law. Lawyers.

**Arbeiter der Stirn und der Faust.** Workers of the forehead and the fist. Expression made popular by Hitler referring to the German workforce of intelligentsia and physical laborers.

*Arbeitertum.* The Workforce. Official newspaper, established in 1931, of the Nationalsozialistiche Deutsche Arbeitsfront und die Nationalsozialistiche Gemeinschaft Kraft durch Freude.

**"Arbeiter, wählt den Frontsoldaten Hitler!"** "Worker, choose the frontline soldier: Hitler" Pre-1933 Nazi campaign slogan attempting to lure workers from the Socialist and Communist Parties.

**Arbeiterwiderstand.** Worker resistance. Nazi opponents on the political Left.

**Arbeiterziehungslager.** (AEL) Worker education camp.

**"Arbeit macht das Leben süß."** "Work makes life sweet." Ironic concentration camp saying. Contained in Gottlieb Wilhelm Burmann's 1777 *Kleine Liedern für kleine Jünglinge.*

**"Arbeit macht frei."** "Work will set you free." SS General Theodor Eicke, so-called father of the concentration camp system, ordered this slogan posted over the entry gate at Dachau. It was placed also at Auschwitz and at other camps, giving the impression that the camp was a labor camp.

**Arbeitsamt.** Labor Department. Local labor office of the Nazi Party.

**Arbeitsarzt.** Work doctor. Physician member of Reich Labor Service. *See also* Reichsarbeitsdienst.

**Arbeitsbereiche.** Work areas. Nazi division of German-occupied Europe under the control of Martin Bormann.

**Arbeitsbeschaffung.** Job creation. Special employment program based on the 1933 law to reduce unemployment. *See also* Reinhardt-Programm.

**Arbeitsbuch.** Workbook. Employment record that a worker carried on his person at all times. *See also* Deutsche Arbeitsfront.

**Arbeitsbuchverordnung.** (ArbVO) Workbook Regulation. Law requiring a record book of a German's employment history.

**Arbeitsdank.** A department of the German Workers' Front. *See* Deutsche Arbeitsfront.

**Arbeitsdienst.** Labor service. Labor service in concentration camps that could classify prisoners as skilled, or not, and thereby held power of life and death over prisoners, for to work was to live, not to work was to be murdered. Also, conscription of German men, eighteen to twenty-five, for labor on public-works projects for half a year, 1935 to 1939. *See* Reichsarbeitsdienst.

**Arbeitsdienstführer.** Work detail leader. SS officer who had overall responsibility for slave-labor details in a given concentration camp and who submitted proposals for the recommendation of new Kapos. *See also* Arbeitsdienst.

**Arbeitsdienstlager.** Work camp. Training camp for labor service.

**Arbeitsdienstpflicht.** Work conscription. Young women in their twenties obligated to military training and service, many as auxiliaries at the front. *See also* Reichsarbeitsdienst.

**arbeitsdienstverpflichtet.** Obliged to do service in the Reichsarbeitsdienst. It included working for the military. *See also* Arbeitsdienstpflicht; Reichsarbeitsdienst.

**Arbeitseinsatz.** Work deployment. Concentration camp office responsible for the organization of labor details and use of camp and ghetto slave labor in the manufacture of arms. German worker deployment. Also, SS directive to the Jewish council in the ghetto holding them accountable for carrying out German orders that required Jews to report for forced labor. Also, deportation of foreign workers into German war industries.

**Arbeitseinsatzführer.** Work detail supervisor. Labor supervisor in concentration camps.

**Arbeitseinsatzingenieur.** Work detail engineer. Specialist for work assignment and labor efficiency; placed in factories by the Ministry of War.

**Arbeitseinsatzschreibstube.** Work detail office. Place where concentration camp prisoners were assigned work inside or outside the camp in accordance with SS orders. *See also* Arbeitsdienst.

**Arbeitseinsatzstab.** Work Service Unit. Specialized engineers who worked for the army in occupied territories.

**Arbeitserziehungshäftling.** Disciplinary work prisoner. *See also* Arbeitserziehungslager.

**Arbeitserziehungshäftlingslager.** Prisoner reeducation labor camp. Laborers within Germany who fled from their jobs were sent to special correctional work camps where their fugitive natures were to be "rectified."

**Arbeitserziehungslager.** Labor and disciplinary work camps. Police-run punishment work camps for those unwilling to work for the Reich and for recalcitrant foreign workers.

**arbeitsfähig.** Able to work. In the camps, those prisoners able to work were allowed to live, temporarily, although Jewish prisoners and others were meant in the long term to be worked to death or killed. *See also* Vernichtung durch Arbeit.

**Arbeitsfeldarzt.** Work doctor in the military. Reich Labor Service physician who served with the armed forces. *See also* Reichsarbeitsdienst.

**Arbeitsfront.** *See* Deutsche Arbeitsfront.

**Arbeitsführer.** Work Leader. High-ranking official in the Reich Labor Service. Also, concentration camp official in charge of labor. *See also* Reichsarbeitsdienst.

**Arbeitsgauführer.** District Work Leader. High-ranking official in the Reich Labor Service responsible for a district. *See also* Reichsarbeitsdienst.

**Arbeitsgemeinschaft.** Work community. Cartel of companies; also, army unit working in Nazi training schools.

**Arbeitsgemeinschaft für deutsche Volkskunde.** Working Community for German Folklore. National Socialist organization founded by Alfred Rosenberg, Agriculture Minister Richard Walther Darré, Reich Labor Leader Konstantin Hierl, Heinrich Himmler, and Baldur von Schirach that ensured cooperation between Nazi leaders and German folklorists. Fairy tales, legends, and proverbs, many of which already contained anti-Jewish themes, were used to enhance Nazi antisemitic ideology.

**Arbeitsgemeinschaftsleiter.** Work Community Leader. Leader of the National Socialist German Student Alliance. *See also* Nationalsozialistischer Deutscher Studentenbund.

**Arbeitsheer.** Workers' Army. *See also* Reichsarbeitsdienst.

**Arbeitsjuden.** (A) Work Jews. Jews capable of work for German war industry, ultimately to be worked to death.

**Arbeitskamerad.** Work colleague, buddy. *See also* Volksgemeinschaft.

**Arbeitskarte.** *See* Arbeitsschein.

**Arbeitskommando.** (AbKdo) Work detail. Concentration camp work detachment led by a Kapo, often with subordinate assistant Kapos. Also, engineers. *See* Unterkapo.

**Arbeitskommando aufgelöst.** Work detail liquidated. SS guard report to the Lagerführer accounting for the Jews murdered during the day.

**Arbeitskraft.** Workforce. *See also* wertvollstes Gut des Volkes.

**Arbeitskreis für biozentrische Forschungen.** (AKBF) Work Circle for Biocentric Research. Founded in 1933 by adherents of philosopher Ludwig Klages, whose critique of rationality and modernity they promoted and popularized. Officially dissolved in 1936.

**Arbeitslager.** (AL) Work camp. Slave labor camp.

**Arbeitsleiter.** Work Leader. Low-level Nazi Party official.

**Arbeitslenkung.** Control of work. Requirement to register for the labor force after completion of schooling. Also, forced placement of workers in the economy. *See also* Arbeitseinsatz.

**Arbeitsmaid.** Labor girl. Young woman in the Labor Service. *See also* Reichsarbeitsdienst.

**Arbeitsmann.** Workman, craftsman. Worker belonging to the Labor Service. *See also* Reichsarbeitsdienst.

**Arbeitsmaterial.** Work material, available workers. Also, Jews capable of performing productive work before being killed. *See also* Menschenmaterial.

**Arbeitsmensch.** Workperson. Belief in an ideal German member of the Volk who will effortlessly perform his/her tasks at an improved and elevated level, leading to freedom and beauty.

**Arbeitsopfer.** Work victims. From 1933, injured workers recuperating in a convalescent institution organized by the German Labor Front. *See also* Deutsche Arbeitsfront.

**Arbeitsordungsgesetz.** (AOG) *See* Gesetz zur Ordnung der nationalen Arbeit vom 20.1.34.

**Arbeitspaß.** Workers' identification card. For German workers aged seventeen to twenty-five.

**Arbeitspflicht.** Compulsory work. Nazi decree ordering Poles between the ages of eighteen and sixty to work for the Germans.

**Arbeitspflichtiger.** Individual with a sense of duty to work. Every German worker was expected to believe that the nation depended on his service.

**Arbeitsplatzaustausch.** Workplace exchange. Government program to integrate unemployed Germans into the workforce.

**Arbeitsplatzwechselverordnung.** (APWVO) Legal order to change jobs.

**Arbeitsrasse.** Race that works. Positive, applied to German workers in contrast to the slow and inefficient British.

**Arbeitsressorts.** Work departments. Ghetto workshops.

**Arbeitsschatzanweisungen.** Shares (issued in 1933) to finance employment program. *See also* Arbeitsbeschaffung.

**Arbeitsschein.** Work permit. This document allowed Jews to work and survive, at least temporarily.

**Arbeitsscheue.** Individuals avoiding work. Able-bodied Germans who rejected work offers. A category of inmates in protective custody (*see* Schutzhaft) considered slackers, reported to the Gestapo by the Employment Department (*see* Arbeitsamt), and interned for at least three months in the Buchenwald concentration camp.

**Arbeitsschlacht.** Work battle. From 1933 on, German government campaign to create jobs. Also, paramilitary German labor battalions funded by the sale of Aryanized Jewish property.

**Arbeitsspende.** Work donation. Based on a 1933 law, euphemism for financial donation required of Germans, aimed to finance public works and provide jobs.

**Arbeitsstatistik.** Work statistics. Concentration camp office that kept a work card on each prisoner and assigned prisoners to work details.

**arbeitsunfähig.** Unable to work. Concentration camp inmates who were no longer able to work were killed or transferred to death camps to be killed. This included the disabled and the old.

**(die) Arbeitsunwilligen.** Those unwilling to work. Euphemism for those condemned to death.

**Arbeitsversehrter.** Person injured in work-related accident.

**arbeitsverwendungsfähig.** (a.v.) Able to work. Germans able, but unfit, for full military service were drafted for light work. *See also* Diensttaugtlichkeitsgrade.

**Arbeitsvolk.** Worker people. The Slavic peoples were to serve the German master race. *See also* führerloses Arbeitsvolk; Herrenvolk.

**Arbeitszwang Reich.** (AZR) Forced labor in the Reich.

**ArbVO.** *See* Arbeitsbuchverordnung.

***Archiv für Judenfragen.*** Archive for Jewish Questions. Antisemitic publication of Goebbels' Institut zum Studium der Judenfrage, first appearing in 1943.

**Arier.** Aryan. The racial component seen as common to all true Germans and other people of German descent or similarity. Non-Aryans were those with foreign or alien blood, like Gypsies or Blacks, but especially Jews. The term was intended by its originator, the philologist Friedrich Müller, to be applied only to a group of Indo-European languages.

**Ariergesetz.** Aryan law.

**Ariergrundsatz.** Basic Aryan philosophy.

**Ariernachweis.** Proof of Aryan descent. Required after the Nuremberg Laws enacted in 1935.

**(großer) Ariernachweis.** Proof of Aryan descent including ancestors back to the year 1750.

**(kleiner) Ariernachweis.** Proof of Aryan descent including only one's grandparents.

**Arierparagraph.** Aryan clause. 1933 law banning Jews, considered non-Aryans, from the civil service and beginning their exclusion from German society, politics, and economic life.

**Arierschrift.** Aryan typeface. Gothic print considered of Germanic origin and preferred for school textbooks; supposed to be used only by Germans.

**Arierstatus.** Aryan status. At the beginning of the Nazi regime, Jews useful to the state were given special status and treated as if they were Germans. *See also* Ehrenarier.

**arisch.** Aryan. *See also* Arier.

**arische Abstammung.** Aryan stock. Germans free of foreign blood.

**arisieren.** Aryanize. *See also* Arisierung.

**Arisierung.** Aryanization. Expropriation of Jewish property by the Third Reich.

**Arisierungsspenden.** Contributions from aryanization. Money from the sale of expropriated Jewish property used to support the Nazi Party and pay the debts of prominent Nazis.

**Arisierungsverordnung.** Aryanization Law. The first law was passed in 1938 to expropriate Jews.

**Arko.** *See* Artilleriekommandeur; Artilleriekommando.

**Armee.** Army. Unit equivalent to one or more army corps and attached units amounting to 60,000 to 100,000 men. A strategic, not tactical, concept.

**Armeeabteilung.** Army unit. Army detachment, equivalent to a battalion.

**Armee-Fernsprech-Abteilung.** (Aferna) Army telephone detachment.

**Armeegruppe.** Army group. German collection of armies and attached units, ranging from 100,000 to 300,000 men.

**Armeekorps.** (AK) Army corps. Consisted of one or more divisions and attached units, amounting to 40,000 to 60,000 men.

**Armeeoberkommando.** (AOK) Army headquarters. German Army Field Command.

**Arrest.** Arrest. Incarceration with torture as a form of punishment for camp infractions. *See also* Disziplinar- und Strafverordnung.

**Arrestbunker.** Detention bunker. Gas chamber at Neuengamme used to kill Soviet POWs.

**Arsch. Ass.** Term of degradation applied to camp prisoners.

**"Arsch der Welt."** "Asshole of the world." Popular Nazi phrase for Poland in general and Auschwitz in particular. *See also anus mundi.*

**Art.** Type, kind. Biological type, racial nature, way of life. Also used as a prefix/adjective.

**Artaman-Bund.** Antisemitic, antiurban nationalist German youth group. Many of its members, like Heinrich Himmler, drifted away to Nazi Party in the early 1920s.

**Artamanen.** Utopian-type community founded by Willibald Hentschel in 1923. It pursued nature and group activities and Volkish-political objectives. After 1933 formally integrated into the Reichssiedlungsamt to promote pro-German culture in eastern Europe.

**artbestimmt.** Determined by race. Human qualities based on characteristic racial origins.

**artbewußt.** Race conscious. Positive for Germans' awareness of their racial origin.

**Artbewußtsein.** Race consciousness. *See also* artbewußt.

**artblütig.** Race blood. Racially pure; pure-blooded.

**artdeutsch.** Racially German. Characteristically German in being professional and following/obeying the leader.

**artecht.** Racially authentic. Typically, genuinely German.

**arteigen.** Racially specific. Authentic Germanness.

**arteigene Kultur.** Race-specific culture. Aryan-German-Nordic culture.

**Arteigenheit.** *See* arteigen.

**Arterhaltung.** Preservation of race. Maintaining the German race. *See also* Art.

**artfremd.** Alien. Un-German, non-Aryan, Jewish.

**artfremde Güter.** Foreign goods. Non-German imported products.

**artfremdes Blut.** Alien blood. Jewish and Gypsy blood in Europe.

**artfremdes Eiweiß.** Alien protein. Un-German (Jewish) sperm. *See* artfremd.

**Artfreude.** The joy of belonging to one's kind. The innate sense of belonging to the Nordic, Aryan, race.

**artgebunden.** Tied to the race. Bound by blood.

**artgemäß.** According to one's race. Typically (or characteristically) German.

**artgemäßes Christentum.** Christianity of one's kind. Religion appropriate to Germans. *See also Deutsche Gottschau.*

**artgeprägt.** Marked by race. Racial character.

**Artgeschichte.** History of race. The evolutionary history of the German people.

**Artgesetz.** Racial principle. Racial, biological imperative.

**artgestalten.** To create according to one's race. Writers and philosophers expressing themselves according to their racial origin and character.

**arthaft.** According to one's kind. Conscious of one's Germanness; proud.

**Artilleriekommandeur.** (Arko) Artillery Commander.

**Artilleriekommando.** (Arko) Artillery command.

**artlos.** Without race. Jewish.

**artnah.** Close to one's kind, race. *See also* artverbunden.

**arttreuer Glaube.** Authentic racial belief. National Socialist worldview and belief based on German race theory, in contrast to institutional Christianity.

**Artus-Plan.** (King) Arthur Plan. Code name for the planned invasion in the summer of 1940 of Ireland with the support of the IRA.

**artverbunden.** Bound spiritually through one's race. The German people's sense of belonging together.

**artvergessen.** Forgetting one's race. Losing one's German honor.

**artverwandt.** Racially related. Biologically connected to one's race; specifically, related to the German race.

**artverwandten Blutes.** Of genetically related blood. The Reich citizenship law defined German citizens as German nationals or as of genetically related blood; that is, those who proved by their conduct that they were willing and suitable to belong to the German people and nation. Only a Reichsbürger had full political rights. *See also* Reichsbürgergesetz.

**artverwandtes Volkstum.** German and related peoples.

**Artwille.** Racial will. German form of *élan vital*. A palpable force, signifying the renewal of the German people.

**Arztvormelder.** Person reporting to the doctor. Sick inmates of concentration camps obliged to consult an SS doctor who decided on their fate.

**Arztvorsteller.** Person going to the doctor. *See also* Arztvormelder.

**Asch(en)kolonne.** Ashes work detail. Inmates of death camps who had to collect the remaining human bones from the ashes and crush, sift, and spread them, or throw them into the river.

**asiatisch.** Asiatic. Insulting term, especially applied to Jews.

**(die) asiatische Rasse.** The Asiatic race. Pseudoscientific term for the Jews.

**ASKI.** *See* Ausländersonderkonten für Inlandszahlungen.

**ASKI-Mark.** German money blocked from being spent outside Germany. *See also* Ausländersonderkonten für Inlandszahlungen.

**asozial, Asoziale.** (Aso, aziol) Asocials. One of several categories of people in Germany targeted for, and prisoners in, concentration camps, including the biologically criminal, beggars, vagrants, thieves, habitual criminals, homosexuals, prostitutes, Gypsies (Romani and Sinti), and the unemployed. *See also* schwarzer-Winkel.

**asoziale Elemente.** Asocial elements. *See also* asozial.

**asoziale fremdrassige Elemente.** Asocial alien-racial elements. Jews and Gypsies.

**Asphalt.** Asphalt. Metaphor for city, in contrast to the countryside. Racial impurity, in contrast to German Blut und Boden (blood and soil). Also, the intellectual, Jewish-democratic civilization of the Weimar Republic.

*Asphaltblatt.* Asphalt newspaper. Asphalt rag, derogatory, for the Jewish newspaper *Telegraf am Mittag*.

**Asphaltdemokratie.** Asphalt democracy. Negative for the Weimar Republic.

**Asphaltkultur.** Asphalt culture. Negative for the cultural life in large cities that was deemed un-German, cosmopolitan, and Jewish. *See also* Asphalt.

**Asphaltliteraten.** Asphalt writers. Negative for writers who were deemed un-German and, predominantly, Jewish.

**Asphaltmensch.** Asphalt man. Person in German cities who was deemed without roots to the land, cosmopolitan, and thus un-German or Jewish.

**Asphaltmenschentum.** Asphalt humanity. Decadent city Jews. *See also* Asphalt.

**Asphaltpresse.** Asphalt press. Negative for publishing houses owned by Jews.

**Asphaltwüste.** Asphalt desert. Negative for big city, in contrast to the idealized countryside. *See also* Asphalt.

**AST, ASt.** *See* Abwehrstelle.

**Asylierung.** Asylum stay. Program to remove incurable tuberculosis patients from German society to institutions in order to be murdered.

**A.T.G.** *See* Automobil- und Flugtechnische Gesellschaft.

**Atlantikwall.** Atlantic wall. A line of fortifications constructed along the Atlantic coast and in the coastal waters of western Europe in 1942–1944 to repel an anticipated Anglo-American seaborne invasion. Fritz Todt employed thousands of forced laborers to construct underwater obstacles, pillboxes, and gun emplacements.

*Atlantis.* Atlantis. A German raiding ship disguised as a merchantman. After sinking twenty-two ships and 140,000 tons of British shipping in the South Atlantic, it was sunk by the heavy cruiser *Devonshire* while refueling a German submarine.

*Atlas.* Atlas. Code name for the special train used by Hitler and the Wehrmacht. *See Amerika.*

**Attila.** *See* Unternehmen Attila.

**Aucharbeiter.** Also-workers. Derogatory for Jews.

**"Auch Du gehörst dem Führer."** "You, too, belong to the Führer." A slogan of the League of German Girls. *See* Bund Deutscher Mädel in der Hitlerjugend.

**"Auch hier im fernen California. In Treue fest steht die S.A."** "Even here in faraway California. The SA stands strongly loyal." Slogan of California-based American Nazi sympathizers.

**Auert.** Berlin firm that manufactured gas chamber equipment.

**aufarten.** To racially improve. *See also* Aufartung.

**Aufartung.** Improving the race through racial-hygienic measures. Renewal and continuation of a so-called racially valuable people (i.e., Germans) by means of biological, societal, and political measures, including the elimination of people considered inferior.

**Aufbau.** Structuring, building up. Building up the German armed forces based on the Nazi Party model.

**Aufbau Ost.** Building up the east. Code name for the German plan to build up the Eastern Front for the anticipated invasion of the Soviet Union.

**Aufbaukommando.** Building squad. Jewish slave laborers who constructed Auschwitz and were later murdered.

**Aufbauschule.** Preparatory schools. One of the two new secondary school types after the 1938 school reform; placed more emphasis on physical education and practical subjects. Graduates could attend university and advance to civil-service positions. *See also* Oberschule.

**auf Befehl.** (aB) According to orders. To obey an order, often a justification/rationale for a murderous activity.

**(der) Aufbruch.** The uprising, awakening, change. The awakening of Germany, of the German people (to the Jewish menace). Also, uprising of Germans in the Sudetenland, leading to the Munich Conference.

**Aufbruch der Nation.** Awakening of the nation. Start of World War I. Later, Nazi revolution. *See also* (der) Aufbruch.

**"auf der Flucht erschossen."** "Shot while trying to escape." Often a justification for murder and mass murder of Jews and other people during roundups.

**Aufenthaltslager.** Detention camp. An addition to the Bergen-Belsen camp built in 1943 housing non-German European Jews who were held for exchange. They were treated better than other inmates and were not allowed contact with them. *See also* Protektionsjuden.

**Aufenthaltsverbot.** Forbidden to remain in parish. A Security Police order intended to harass church members and priests opposing the Reich.

**Auferstehung des Großdeutschen Reiches.** Resurrection of the greater German Reich. Reference to the German annexation of Austria in 1938.

**Auffang.** Catching. Military for reorganization of troops while retreating from the Eastern Front.

**Auffanglinie.** Catching line. Military for the formation of a new front line while retreating from the Eastern Front.

**Auffangsgesellschaft.** Holding company. Organization created to transfer to the Reich Jewish property in occupied nations.

**Auffangslager.** (AuL) Absorption camp, reception camp.

**Auffangstelle.** Catching point. Military for the place where German soldiers retreating or fleeing from the Eastern Front were collected and regrouped for combat.

**Auffangstellung.** Catching formation. Military for the prepared defensive line receiving retreating German soldiers and the stabilizing of the new front line.

**aufgelöst.** Demolished. *See also* auflösen.

**aufgezwungen.** Forced. What Germany's enemies did to Germany; for example, "der uns aufgezwungene Krieg" ("the war that was forced upon us").

*Auf gut Deutsch.* In plain German. Dietrich Eckart's newspaper published in Munich after World War I. Eckart, a poet and songwriter, participated in the Hitler Putsch.

**Aufklärungsfeldzug wider den undeutschen Geist.** Enlightenment campaign against the un-German spirit. *See also* Gesamtaktionen.

**Aufklärungsgruppen.** Reconnaisance groups. Luftwaffe unit.

**auf Kriegsdauer.** (a.K.) During wartime. Abbreviation used after one's signature in wartime military correspondence.

**Auflage.** Burden, taxation. Forced contribution as collective punishment, especially from cities in German-occupied areas.

**Auflockerung.** Thinning out. Genocidal killings.

**auflösen.** To dissolve. To dissolve existing organizations and businesses. Also, euphemism for murder.

**Aufmarsch.** Deployment, march. Prewar Nazi demonstrations by the SA and Nazi student organizations.

**aufnorden.** To Nordicize. To increase the proportion of the Nordic race in a nation; to improve the family tree or appearances. *See also* Aufartung.

**Aufnordung.** Nordicization. *See also* aufnorden.

**Aufpasserin.** Female monitor. Overseer of Ravensbrück women inmates working at the Siemens plant.

**Aufräumungskommando.** Cleanup unit. Squads of Jews, later murdered, assigned to pack up personal effects not taken by deported Jews.

**Aufruf.** Proclamation. Orders issued by Nazi occupation authorities and Jewish ghetto councils. Also, after the morning roll call in concentration camps, inmates called by number to their respective groups had to wait for hours outside, and often suffered abuse by the SS guards.

**Aufschwung.** Upward swing, revival. Glory and peaceful spirit of the Third Reich as a vision of Hitlerian Germany.

**(Frau) Aufseherin.** (Madame) matron, female guard. Female guard working for the SS in the concentration camps.

**Aufsichtsbehörde.** Supervisory authority. Gestapo and related departments.

**Aufsichtsverwaltung.** Supervisory administration. *See also* Schutzverwaltung.

**(im) Auftrag.** (i.A.) By order of.

**Auftragslenkung.** Order management. Allocation of business and government orders according to the Four-Year Plan. *See also* Vierjahresplan.

**Auftragsverlagerung.** Order shifting. Moving orders to German-occupied countries.

*Aufzeichnung über Gliederung und Tätigkeit der Kriegsgefangenenorganisation des Auswärtigen Amtes.* Guidelines for the Structure and Implementation of the Prisoners-of-War Organization of the Foreign Office. A fifteen-page document from 1944 advising concentration camp commanders on how to treat prisoners of war, how to increase their willingness to work, and how to indoctrinate them according to Nazi ideology and antisemitism.

**aufziehen.** To organize. Nazi Party organization of large-scale public events.

**Augsburg.** City in Germany. Code name for delaying the offensive in the west, November 1939.

**Ausbildungslager der Waffen-SS.** Training camp for the Waffen-SS (at Dachau) September 1939–February 1940.

**Ausbildungswesen.** (AW) Education Formation. Founded in 1933 and responsible for military education within the SA.

**ausbomben.** To bomb out. To force evacuation by bombing.

**Ausbürgerung.** Revocation of citizenship. Jews were stripped of their German citizenship.

**Auschwitz.** Located near the Polish town of Oswiecim. The largest forced labor/death camp, located on an important rail line in southwestern Poland near Krakow. Composed of three large camps: Auschwitz I, the main camp housing five crematoria and forty-five sub-camps; Auschwitz II (Birkenau, near the village of Brzezinka), the death center; and Auschwitz III (Monowitz), IG Farben (Buna) chemical factory slave-labor camp. Reichsführer SS Heinrich Himmler ordered its creation on April 27, 1940. It evolved from a camp to hold mainly Polish political prisoners to a forced- and slave-labor facility to a poison-gassing center for murder on an industrial scale. About 2 million people were killed here, approximately 80 percent of them Jews. The camp was organized around a men's camp, a women's camp from March 1942, a quarantine camp, a family camp from fall 1943, a Hungarian Jews camp from May 1944, a Gypsy camp, a prisoner medical building, a Mexiko camp, and a Kanada camp.

**Auschwitz-Buna.** *See* Bunawerke.

**aus dem Hebräischen.** From the Hebrew. Obligatory label in German books identifying the writer as a Jew.

**auserwähltes Volk.** Chosen People. Ironic for Jews.

**Ausfall.** Absence, loss. Casualties, death victims.

**ausfallen.** To lose, drop. To get killed.

**Ausfuhrbestimmungen über Dringlichkeit der Fertigungsprogramme der Wehrmacht.** (ADFW) Export Regulations for the Urgency of Army Industry Programs.

**ausgearbeitet.** Worked out, worn out. Ready to be scrapped.

**ausgebombt.** Bombed out. Homeless due to the air war against Germany during World War II.

**Ausgeburten morscher Intellektualität.** Abomination of rotten intellectualism. Nazi description of Jewish humor, culture, and philosophy. *See* Intellektuel, Intellektueller.

**ausgemerzt.** Extinguished. *See also* ausmerzen.

**ausgeräumt.** *See* ausräumen.

**ausgerottet.** Eradicated. *See also* ausrotten.

**ausgesiedelt.** Displaced. Poles forcibly evicted from their homes to make room for ethnic Germans as part of the Nazi racial resettlement program. These Poles were often resettled into houses belonging to Jews, who in turn were deported to ghettos.

**ausgesondert.** Selected. *See also* aussondern.

**ausgewandert.** Emigrated. Notation in deportation registers of Jews who had been deported to death camps in eastern Europe. According to Gestapo language regulation of 1942, the destination was not to be mentioned.

**(besonders) ausgezeichnet hat sich.** (Especially) distinct behavior of. Euphemism in army reports instead of "high casualties of" toward the end of World War II.

**ausgleichen.** To equal the value. The number of hostages killed for each German soldier killed by resistance: 5 Danes, 10 Italians, 50 Poles, 100 Jews.

**Ausgleichsstelle.** Contract-awarding center.

**Ausgliederung.** Separation, exclusion. Separating Jews out from German society.

**Ausgriff.** Expansion. Conquest, vision.

**auskämmen.** To comb out. To clear an area of Jews.

**auslagern.** To move to a different location. *See also* Verlagerung.

**Auslagerung.** Transfer. *See also* Verlagerung.

**(Amt) Ausland-Abwehr.** Office of Foreign Intelligence. Department of Wehrmacht High Command responsible for foreign intelligence.

**Ausländersonderkonten für Inlandszahlungen.** (ASKI) Special foreign accounts for payments within the country (Germany).

**ausländische Arbeiter.** Foreign workers. Non-German workers laboring in Germany during World War II. In 1944, there were nearly 8 million such workers, mostly from the USSR and Poland; and nearly half of those working the soil in Germany were foreign workers. Also, special desk at the Gestapo that oversaw foreign laborers working in Germany. *See also* Vierjahresplan.

**Auslandsabteilung der NSDAP.** Overseas Branch of the Nazi Party. A number of branches were founded in Latin America. *See also* Auslandsorganisation der NSDAP.

**Ausland-SD.** Overseas-SD. Department of SD dealing with intelligence in foreign countries.

**Auslandsdeutsche.** German nationals living abroad.

*Auslandsdeutsche Volksforschung.* People's Research of Germans Abroad. Original title of the periodical *Volksforschung. See* Deutsches Auslands-Institut.

**(SD-) Auslandsnachrichtendienst.** Overseas Communications Service. *See also* Reichssicherheitshauptamt.

**Auslandsorganisation der NSDAP.** (AO) Overseas Organization. Nazi Party agency founded in 1931; supervised Germans residing outside of Germany. Considered a district. *See also* Gau.

**Auslappung.** Spreading. Geopolitical term for spreading into and overlapping another territory.

**Ausleihzentrale für ungelernte Arbeiter.** Center for Lending Unskilled Workers. Office to place unskilled Polish workers drafted to work in Germany.

**(natürliche) Auslese.** (Natural) selection. The self-declared right of the Nazi state to choose the most racially perfect people and to implement laws to eliminate others.

**Auslieferung der Asozialen für die Vollstreckung ihrer Urteile.** Consignment of asocial elements for the execution of their appropriate sentences. Justification for sending all Jews and certain Gypsies, Russians, and Poles to concentration camps without judicial process.

**Auslöschen ewig feindlicher Elemente.** Extinction of eternal enemy elements. Euphemism for mass murder of Jews.

**Ausmerze.** *See* Ausmerzung.

**ausmerzen.** To eliminate, expunge. To extinguish all Jewish life.

**Ausmerzung.** Extinction. Complete extinction of the Jews.

**Auspeitschtisch.** Whipping table. Special table used in camps to tie prisoners to when they were whipped.

**ausradieren.** To wipe out, eradicate. To destroy English cities through mass bombing.

**ausräumen.** To clear out. Euphemism for to murder Jews.

**ausrichten.** To bring into line. *See also* Ausrichtung.

**Ausrichtung.** Bringing into line. Indoctrination and reeducation according to Nazi thinking; government pointers for the media about what to stress, avoid, or suppress regarding the military and the murder of Jews. *See also Deutscher Wochendienst.*

**ausrotten.** To tear out root and branch. To eradicate all Jewish life.

**Ausrottung.** Rooting out. *See also* ausrotten.

**(völkische) Ausrottung.** Extermination of a people. Genocide.

**Ausrottungslager.** (Permanent) death camp.

**Ausrottungsmaßnahmen.** Extermination measures. Actions taken to achieve genocide.

**ausrücken.** To leave. To leave the concentration camp daily to do forced labor.

**ausschalten.** To remove. To eliminate Jews from Germany and later from the world through murder.

**Ausschaltung der Juden aus dem Wirtschaftsleben.** Removal of the Jews from economic life. Nazi government policy from April 1933 on.

**Ausscheidung.** Elimination, removal. Deprivation of Jews' rights; expulsion of Jews from society; elimination of Jews from Nazi Germany.

**Ausschuß für wirtschaftliche Fertigung.** (AWF) National production committee.

**Ausschuß für wirtschaftliche Verwaltung.** (AWV) National management committee.

**Außenbrigaden.** Outside brigades. Jewish laborers allowed to work outside the concentration camp or ghetto.

**außenbürtig.** Born outside (the racial community).

**Außendienst.** Outside duty. Organized outside events held by HJ, SA, and SS members.

**Außendienststelle.** Outside Duty Office. Local office of the SD or the SIPO. Also applied to camp prisoner details working outside a concentration camp or ghetto.

**Außengeltung.** Outside worth status. Respect from abroad.

**Außenkommando.** (Akdo) Outside unit. Jewish laborers sent to work outside the concentration camp or ghetto.

**Außenlager.** (AusL) External camp. Forced-labor camp outside main concentration camp; satellite or sub-camp.

**Außenpolitisches Amt.** (APA) Foreign Policy Department. Alfred Rosenberg's racist organization with connections to fascist parties outside Germany.

**Außenposten.** (AP) Forward positions; military outpost.

**Außenstelle.** (Ast) Branch Office.

**Außenstelle Generalgouvernement.** Branch Office General Government. Provisional office at the former coffeehouse Bergfrieden in Josefsthal, Germany, after Hans Frank, the governor general of the occupied territories in the east, fled there in 1945. *See also* Generalgouvernement.

**Außerordentliche Befriedigungs-Aktion.** (AB-Aktion) Extraordinary Pacification Action. From May to June 1940 over 1,000 Polish politicians and intellectuals, many Jewish, were executed after a summary judicial trial along with approximately 3,000 criminals who received no trial.

**(das) außerwählte Volk.** Chosen people. Ironic for the Jews.

**aussiedeln.** To move. To tranport Jews to concentration camps.

**Aussiedlung.** Resettlement. Deportation of people, mostly Jews, to their deaths as articulated in the Wannsee Conference Protocol of January 20, 1942.

**Aussiedlungsaktion.** Resettlement operation. Moving Jews to death camps or killing them nearby.

**Aussiedlungskommandos.** Resettlement units. Death squads under the overall command of the SS, especially the chain of command of Reichsführer Heinrich Himmler, Reinhard Heydrich, and Adolf Eichmann.

**Aussiedlungslager.** Resettlement camp. Temporary camp for Jews who had escaped an initial roundup; from here they were sent off to death camps.

**Aussiedlungsstab der SS.** SS Emigration Staff. Special unit in Warsaw to organize the deportation of Jews from the ghetto to the death camp Treblinka; ordered the Jewish council, from 1942 on, to gather first 6,000 and then up to 10,000 Jews for daily deportation.

**aussondern.** To select. *See also* Aussonderung.

**Aussonderung.** Selection. Captured Communist officials segregated from Soviet POWs, then murdered. Also, exclusion of Jews from society.

**Austauschbier.** Substitute beer. Imitation beer sold under the traditional brand name.

**Austauschjuden.** Exchange Jews. Jews held by Nazis for possible bartering.

**Austauschstoff.** Exchange material. Substitute. *See also* Ersatz.

**Austauschware.** Exchange goods. *See also* Ersatz.

**Austilgung des Judentums.** Extermination of Jewry.

**Ausw. Amt.** *See* Auswärtiges Amt.

**auswählen.** To select. To choose for death.

**Auswanderungsdrang.** Emigration pressure. Nazi measures to coerce Jews to emigrate from Germany before the decision between 1939 and 1941 to murder them all.

**auswanderungslustige Juden.** Jews eager to leave. Ironic for Jews wanting to emigrate from Germany.

**Auswanderungs- und Räumungsangelegenheiten.** Emigration and evacuation matters. Supervised by Reinhard Heydrich, who was in charge of Adolf Eichmann's Reichssicherheitshauptamt.

**Auswärtiges Amt.** (AA, Ausw. Amt.) Ministry of Foreign Affairs.

**Ausweichlager.** Evaders' camp. Draft-dodger camp.

**Ausweichwaren.** Alternative goods. Unrationed luxury items whose purchase was supposed to ease the tight rationing during the war years.

**Ausweis.** Identification card. ID card that sometimes provided temporary safety from deportation to death camps for Jews working in the ghetto.

**Ausweisung.** Expulsion. Expulsion of Jews to ghettos and death camps.

**Ausweiszwang.** Obligation to identify oneself. In Germany, from September 10, 1939, every individual had to carry at all times identification papers, such as a passport, a workbook, a Nazi Party membership book, and/or a driver's license.

**Auswurf.** Sputum. *See also* Abschaum.

**Autarkie.** Autarchy, autarky, self-sufficiency. Geopolitical policy of economic self-sufficiency aimed at removing the need for imports by producing all economic requirements at home. Germany adopted such a policy in the 1930s to make itself blockade-proof (e.g., creating Ersatz rubber, oil, butter, and coffee and establishing an extensive recycling program).

**Autobahn.** Automobile route. *See also* Reichsautobahnen.

**Auto-car.** *See* Sonderwagen.

**Automobil- und Flugtechnische Gesellschaft.** (A.T.G.) Automobile and Aircraft Company.

**Automobil-Verkehrs- und Übungsstraße.** (Avus) Automobile traffic and training road. The first Autobahn. Opened in the Berlin-Wannsee district in 1921, later became part of the Reichsautobahn.

**Autostraße.** *See* Läusestrasse.

**a.v.** *See* arbeitsverwendungsfähig.

**A4.** *See* Aggregat 4.

**Aw, AWA.** *See* Allgemeines Wehrmachtsamt.

**AWF.** *See* Ausschuß für wirtschaftliche Fertigung.

**AWV.** *See* Ausschuß für wirtschaftliche Verwaltung.

**A-Zeit.** Time A. Period of front-line military service.

**aziol.** *See* asozial.

**AZR.** *See* Arbeitszwang Reich.

# B

**Babi Yar.** A ravine outside the Ukrainian city of Kiev where the Germans killed more than 33,000 Jews of Kiev on September 29 and 30, 1941. Later, Gypsies (Romani and Sinti) and Soviet prisoners of war were taken to the Babi Yar ravine and shot. An estimated 100,000 people were killed in total.

**Badeanstalten.** Bathhouses. Disguised gas chambers at death camps.

**Badeanstalt für Sonderaktionen.** Bathing establishment for special actions. Underground gas chambers and crematoria in death camps.

**"Badenweiler Marsch."** "Badenweiler March." One of Hitler's favorite marches and played by SS marching bands in his presence.

**Bade- und Inhalationsräume.** Bath and inhalation-therapy rooms. Lettering on gas chamber at Belzec and other death camps intended to deceive users into believing the gas chamber was a spa facility.

**Bahnbeauftragter.** Railroad coordinator in the military.

*Bahn frei.* Clear the Road. Nazi propaganda film praising the Autobahn.

**Bahnschutzpolizei.** Railroad Protection Police. Auxiliary police taken over by the SS in 1942.

**Bakterienkrieg.** War against bacteria. German armed forces warning to its troops about plague, cholera, and typhus in their war against the Soviet Union.

**bald deutsche Mutter.** Soon a German mother. Humorous for BDM (Bund Deutscher Mädel).

**Balder.** Nordic god of the sun. Son of Odin, the god of light, springtime, and hope. His birthday was celebrated on December 21 as the date of the ancient solstice; he held a very special place in children's literature.

**Balkonschwein.** Balcony pig/pork. Ironic for main course of a German meal during the final stages of World War II—in reality cat meat.

**Ballastexistenzen.** Ballast lives. Unnecessary, superfluous lives; rationale for mass murder.

**Balte.** *See* Deutschbalte.

**Bamberg-Konferenz.** Bamberg Conference. Nazi Party conference in February 1926 during which Hitler unsuccessfully tried to keep the left wing of the Party, the Straßer group, in line.

**Banden.** Gangs. Derogatory for resistance fighters, guerrilla bands, partisans in the German-occupied territories to diminish their importance. *See also* Banditen.

**Bandenbekämpfung.** Fight against gangs. Antipartisan operations.

**Bandenbildung.** Partisan units. Description of Jews condemned to death in Russia.

**Bandenjagdkommando.** Gang-hunting Commando. Army units that fought partisans and often murdered Jews in the east. *See* Banden; Jagdkommandos.

**Bandenkampfabzeichen.** Gang fighter medal. Three-category medal instituted in 1944 to reward fighting partisans and murdering Jews in the eastern war zone.

**Bandenkampfverbände.** (BKV) Antipartisan Units. Units composed of SS, Waffen-SS, Wehrmacht, police, and Russian collaborators who fought partisans and also liquidated Jewish communities.

**Bandenkinder.** Partisan children. Children captured when their partisan parents were killed. *See* Jugendverwahrlager.

**Bandfabrik Ewald Vorsteher.** (BEVo) Ewald Vorsteher Woven-Band Factory. Manufacturer of woven badges for the Wehrmacht.

**Banditenbekämpfung.** Bandit fighting. Antipartisan operations in the east. Often a cover for anti-Jewish operations of SS and Wehrmacht from 1942.

**Bank der Deutschen Arbeit.** German Labor Bank. Nazi bank devoted to loans intended for housing seized from the labor unions. *See also* Deutsche Arbeitsfront.

**Bank der Deutschen Arbeit AG.** German Work Bank Ltd. Created in 1933, it managed the savings of workers in order to purchase a Volkswagen. Through this bank, the German Labor Front controlled banks and industrial enterprises in German-occupied countries.

**Bann.** Area of authority. Unit of the Hitler Youth, numbering about 3,000 members, from fourteen years old.

**Bannerträger der Nation.** Standard-bearer of the nation. Example and guardian of the National Socialist idea.

**Bannführer.** High-ranking Hitler Youth leader. *See also* Bann.

**Banngut.** Germanization of Schmuggelgut (smuggled goods).

**Bannware.** Germanization of Schmuggelware (smuggled wares).

**barbarisch.** Barbaric. Used positively by the Nazis to express the ferocity needed to punish treason.

**Barbarossa.** Red beard. Twelfth-century German emperor Friedrich III. Code name for the Wehrmacht's ideological war to destroy the Soviet Union begun in June 1941.

**Barlow-Palais.** *See* Braunes Haus.

**Barmherzigkeit.** Mercy. Ghetto Jews killed as an act of mercy to save them from dying from epidemic disease.

**Barry.** Dog at Treblinka trained to attack the genitals of naked prisoners awaiting death in the gas chambers.

**BASt.** *See* Ablieferungspflicht; Bezirksabgabestelle.

**Bastarde.** Bastards, hybrids. Gypsies and others considered racially inferior.

**Bataillon.** (Batl., Btl.) Battalion. *See also* Abteilung.

**Batl.** *See* Bataillon.

**Bauarbeiter.** Construction worker. Concentration camp inmate used as construction worker.

**Baubrigaden.** Construction brigades. Slave laborers working at German-company-owned concentration camps. *See* Nebenlager.

**Bauchfreiheit.** Belly freedom. A tank's clearance over terrain.

**Baudienst.** Construction service. Compulsory labor service. Also, Poles used by Germans to help round up Jews.

**Bauer.** Peasant. In contrast to a Landwirt (farmer), the German peasant was perceived as mystically bound to the soil. *See also* Landwirt.

**Bauernadel.** Peasant nobility. *See also* Neuadel aus Blut und Boden.

**Bauern-Partei.** Farmers' Party. Splinter party during the Weimar Republic.

**Bauernfähigkeit.** Ability to be a peasant. To own a farm one had to be a proven, pure German (*see* Abstammungsnachweis), healthy and politically reliable. *See also* Reichserbhofgesetz.

**Bauernkultur.** Peasant Culture. A Nazi cultural office that operated within the Ministry of Agriculture.

**Bauernschaft.** Peasantry. Local and regional divisions of the Reich Agricultural Organization. *See also* Reichsnährstand.

**Bauernschule.** Farmers' School. Training center for young farmers and future farmer leaders.

**Bauerntum.** Pertaining to peasant and farming. Farmers were considered one of the three pillars of the nation, together with workers and soldiers.

**Bauhof.** Building yard, farm. Area of Auschwitz where labor units were assigned to construction and repair of the camp.

**Baukastensystem.** Building-kit system. Assembly of prefabricated machined parts.

**Baukommando.** *See* Aufbaukommando.

**Bauleitung SS.** SS Construction Management. SS unit coordinating construction of concentration camps, including gas chambers and crematoria.

**Baum.** Tree. In some camps the post where prisoners were bound and whipped.

**Baumhängen.** Tree hanging. A torture in which a prisoner's hands were tied behind his back and a line affixed to the hands and pulled over the limb of a tree until his feet were off the ground.

**Baumschütze.** Tree shooter. Sniper.

**Baustab.** Construction authority.

**Baustab Speer.** Speer Contruction Authority. Defense organization headed by Albert Speer until 1942, when he replaced Fritz Todt as Armaments Minister.

*Bausteine zum deutschen Nationaltheater.* Building Blocks of the German National Theater. Nazi theater periodical.

**Bauten des Führers.** Führer buildings. A building program that represented Hitler's ideas for a new Germany, under which the regime built the new Olympic stadium and new Reich Chancellery (Berlin), the museum of German culture and Party headquarters (Munich), and the Nazi Party rally areas (Nuremberg). The projects were built on a monumental scale in stone, implying the insignificance/intimidation/submission of the individual and the importance/permanence/dominance of the German community/state/race. Hitler spoke of the eternal character of the monumental and his worldview cast into stone, seeing politics as a work of art (Kunstwerk) in itself. *See also* Führerkanzlei; Haus der Deutschen Kunst; menschlicher Architektur; Parteibauten; Reichsparteitagsgelände.

**Bau X.** Building X. Gas chamber at Dachau.

**Bayerische Politische Polizei.** (BayPoPo) Bavarian Political Police. Established in 1933 under Himmler and his deputy Reinhard Heydrich; a precursor to the Gestapo. *See also* Geheime Staatspolizei.

**Bayerischer Josef.** Bavarian Joe. Homosexual acquaintance of General Werner von Fritsch, Commander in Chief of the Army in 1938. Von Fritsch's alleged relationship served as the pretext for Hitler's demand that von Fritsch resign, to be replaced by Hitler himself. Though later vindicated of all charges, Fritsch was killed in action near Warsaw in September 1939.

**Bayerische Volkspartei.** (BVP) Bavarian People's Party.

**BayPoPo.** *See* Bayerische Politische Polizei.

**BdE.** *See* Befehlshaber des Ersatzheeres.

**BDH.** *See* Befehlshaber des Heeres.

**B-Dienst.** *See* Beobachtungsdienst des feindlichen Funkverkehrs.

**BDM.** *See* Bund Deutscher Mädel in der Hitlerjugend.

**BDM-Werk.** *See* BDM-Werk Glaube und Schönheit.

**BDM-Werk Glaube und Schönheit.** League of German Girls Belief and Beauty. Activity program for German young women aged seventeen to twenty-one. *See also* Bund Deutscher Mädel in der Hitlerjugend; Glaube und Schönheit.

**BdS.** *See* Befehlshaber der Sicherheitspolizei und des Sicherheitsdienstes.

**BdU.** *See* Befehlshaber der U-Boote.

**Beamtenbund.** Civil Service League. *See also* Reichsbund deutscher Beamter.

**bearbeiten.** To process. To torture, to subject to medical experiments, to kill in gas chambers.

**Beauftragter.** Administrator, representative. Nazi administrator in occupied Europe.

**Beauftragter der NSDAP.** Representative of the NSDAP. Those who represented Hitler in oversees communities, appointing mayors and community councils, bestowing medals, and so forth.

**Beauftragter des Führers für die Überwachung der gesamten geistigen und weltanschaulichen Schulung und Erziehung der NSDAP.** Representative of the Führer for the Oversight of the Complete Spiritual and Ideological Training and Education of the Nazi Party. From 1934, Alfred Rosenberg held this administrative position. *See also* Germanisierung.

**Beauftragter des RFSS.** Representative of the Reichsführer-SS. Adolf Eichmann's title as Himmler's personal representative in all matters concerning the Jews.

**Beauftragter für die Durchführung des Vierjahresplans.** Administrator for the Implementation of the Four-Year Plan. One of Göring's roles. *See also* Reichsmarschall.

**Beauftragter für Vierjahresplan.** (BfVJP) Administrator for the Four-Year Plan. *See also* Beauftragter für die Durchführung des Vierjahresplans.

**Bedarfsschein.** Special voucher for scarce goods. During the war prerequisite for a special ration card. *See also* Bezugsschein.

**Bedingtheit.** Fateful causation.

**bedingt tauglich.** *See* tauglich 3.

**bedingungslos ausrottbar.** Unconditional eradication. Goebbels' proposal for treatment of Jews and Gypsies. *See also* Zigeuner.

**Beefsteak-Nazi.** Beefsteak Nazi. Former German Reds—Communists, Socialists—who joined the brown-shirted Nazis out of expedience. They were "red on the inside and brown on the outside."

**"Befehl ist Befehl."** "An order is an order." Germans generally considered following orders an obligation, and frequently used this common expression as a rationale for mass murder.

**Befehlshaber.** (Bfh) Commander.

**Befehlshaber der Sicherheitspolizei und des SD.** (BSipoSD) Commander of the Security Police and Security Service of the Reichsführer-SS.

**Befehlshaber der Sicherheitspolizei und des Sicherheitsdienstes.** (BdS) Chief of the Security Police and Security Service. In each German-occupied country.

**Befehlshaber der U-Boote.** (BdU) Commander in Chief of Submarines. From September 1939. *See* Führer der U-Boote.

**Befehlshaber des Ersatzheeres.** (BdE) Chief of the Army Reserve.

**Befehlshaber des Heeres.** (BDH) Army Chief.

**Befehlstand.** *See* Befehlstelle.

**Befehlstelle.** Command post. Military command post. Also, any agency with governmental authority.

**Befriedigung.** Satisfaction. Appeasement of German claims.

**Befriedigungsaktion.** Pacification action. Code name for the systematic killing of Jews, political undesirables, partisans and political opponents in German-occupied areas. *See* Säuberungsaktion.

**befristeter Vorbeugungshäftling.** (BV, BVer) Non-Jewish prisoner in limited-term preventive custody. Gestapo classification of hardened criminal in a concentration camp. Inmate in temporary custody. Later, abbreviation for Berufsverbrecher (habitual criminal). Such persons often held supervisory positions in concentration camps and were generally feared for their brutality.

**begasen.** To gas. To attack with gas.

**Begegnungsgefecht.** Encounter combat. Military combat that called for initiative, fighting spirit, imagination.

**Begeisterungstopf.** Enthusiasm pot. Slang for armed forces personnel's steel helmet.

**Begleitbataillon des Führers.** The Führer's bodyguard. Elite group of personal guards of Hitler and other Party leaders that developed into the SS in 1925.

**Begleitkommando-SS.** Bodyguard SS. SS guard protecting government buildings.

**Begleitpapier.** Accompanying documents. Bill of lading.

**begradigen.** To level, to straighten the line. To retreat.

**Begriffsfach.** Germanization of Kategorie (category).

**behandeln.** To treat. Euphemism for mistreat, torture, murder.

**(schlecht) behandeln.** To treat badly. Mistreatment of a German as a pretext to send a Jewish family to a concentration camp.

**Behandler.** A person who treats the sick. Official name for Jewish doctors and other caregivers who were not permitted to use proper professional titles, such as dentist.

**Behandlung.** Treatment. *See also* behandeln.

**Behelfsgeld.** Temporary or emergency money. Currency valid only at armed forces establishments. *See also* Kantinengeld.

**Behelfsheim.** Emergency home. Large barracks erected in 1943 across Germany for Germans who had lost their homes in Allied air raids.

**"(nicht endenwollender) Beifall."** "Unending applause." Phrase used by German radio and press to describe the success of Hitler's public speeches.

**Beileidsbrief.** Letter of condolence. Notification to relatives that a concentration camp prisoner had died despite medical care, whereas in reality he/she had been murdered.

**Beiwert.** Germanization of Koeffizient (coefficient).

**Beizahl.** *See* Beiwert.

**Bekanntmachungen.** Proclamations. In occupied Europe, German authorities posted decrees, the removal of which was punishable by death.

**(dritte) Bekanntmachung über den Kennkartenzwang.** Third Notice regarding the Identification Card Requirement. July 23, 1938, order requiring Jewish identity cards be stamped with the letter J.

**Bekennende Kirche.** Confessional Church. Protestant group under Pastors Martin Niemöller and Dietrich Bonhöffer, who opposed the Nazis. After taking an antisemitic position in the early and mid-1930s, by the late 1930s opposed the Reich on the Jewish issue as well.

**Bekenntniskirche.** *See* Bekennende Kirche.

**Bekleidung der Waffen-SS.** Clothing of the Waffen-SS. Clothing, other valuables, and women's hair (steamed and packed in bales) taken from prisoners killed in death camps and sent back to Germany as property of the SS.

**Bekleidungskammer.** Clothing room. Area where new camp prisoners received their striped uniforms.

**Belange.** Interests. German word preferred by the Nazis instead of the earlier Interessen.

**belastet.** Burdened. To be related to Jews by blood or to be suspected of such.

**Belastung.** Burden. Euphemism for defeat of German troops on the Eastern Front.

**Belsen.** *See* Bergen-Belsen.

**Belzec.** Small Polish town in the Lublin District. Death camp where more than 600,000 Jews were gassed between 1941 and 1943. Its first commandant was Christian Wirth and it was visited by Kurt Gerstein, the SS officer who unsuccessfully attempted to report the existence of the camp to Pope Pius XII. Because of its inefficiency as a death camp, late in 1943 Himmler ordered the camp razed and plowed under as had been done at the Sobibor and the Treblinka death camps.

**bemannter Torpedo.** Manned torpedo. One-man submarine.

**Bendlerstrasse.** Bendler Street. Location of the Ministry of War. Nickname for the German High Command.

**Beobachter-Offizier.** (B-Offizier) Submarine-observing Officer.

**Beobachtungsdienst.** Observation Service. German military's radio listening service.

**Beobachtungsdienst des feindlichen Funkverkehrs.** (B-Dienst) Observation Service for Enemy Radio Communication.

**berasen.** To fire on something.

**Berechtigungsschein.** Permit. Document that allowed Germans to qualify for a ration card to purchase a commodity (e.g., to obtain gasoline). *See* Bezugsschein.

**Bereich.** *See* Lenkung.

**Bereitschaft.** Readiness. *See also* politische Bereitschaften.

**Bereitschaftsdienst.** On-call duty. Shock troop.

**Bereitschaftsleiter.** Readiness Leader. Nazi official.

**Bereitstellungsraum.** Preparatory military position.

**Berg.** Mountain. Hitler's nickname for Berghof; also Norwegian concentration camp. *See also* Berghof.

**Bergen-Belsen.** Concentration camp located near the German village of Bergen, close to Hannover. Erected in 1943. As Germany's war effort collapsed in eastern Europe and other camps were closed, tens of thousands of Jews, political prisoners, and POWs were incarcerated and left to die there, including Anne Frank, who died in March 1945. Liberated by British troops in April 1945, it contained 60,000 prisoners, of whom 10,000 were corpses and 28,000 would soon die from typhus and starvation. It was also the site of an SS training school.

**Berghof.** Hitler's private estate on the Obersalzberg near Berchtesgaden in Bavaria. Famous political guests were Austrian Chancellor Kurt Schuschnigg before the Anschluß and British Premier Neville Chamberlain before the Munich Conference.

**Berlin.** Capital city of the Third Reich; name of Wehrmacht division.

*Berliner Arbeiterzeitung.* Berlin Workers' News. Otto Straßer's Nazi periodical, published in Berlin.

*Berliner Illustrierte Zeitung.* Illustrated Berlin News. Satirical Nazi weekly magazine.

**Berlin-Putsch.** September 1938 attempt to overthrow Hitler by politicians, military, future members of the Kreisau circle, and Dietrich Bonhöffer, stimulated by the Czech crisis. The putsch faded away once the British and French appeased Hitler and conceded Czechoslovakia's Sudetenland to Germany.

**Bernhard.** Code name for Nazi plan to counterfeit Allied money in order to ruin Allied economies. *See also* VI F, 4a.

**Beruf.** Profession. Position in the community to serve the nation according to one's inner calling.

**Berufsbeamtengesetz.** Act to establish the civil service with tenure. With the establishment of this January 26, 1937, law, the Nazi Party had control of the civil service. Those who were not of Aryan descent, in particular, Jews and Poles, were forced from their jobs.

**Berufskameradschaft.** *See* Kameradschaft.

**Berufsschule.** Vocational school. *See also* Fortbildungsschule.

**Berufsverbrecher.** Professional criminals. Elite of the concentration camps, often chosen as Kapos, because they could speak German and were street smart.

**Besatzungspolitik.** Occupation policy. Administration of German-occupied Europe.

**Besatzungsverwaltung.** Occupation administration. German-occupied country administered by the German army: Belgium, northern France, Serbia. *See also* Militärbefehlshaber.

**Beschaffungsamt.** Aquisitions Department. Acquired food and other material for the Lwów-Ghetto in Poland. Its Judenrat was forced to supply the houses of the German generals, and so it set up an office of provisions that confiscated items from the houses of well-to-do Jews, and imposed a tax to meet these needs.

**Beschäftigung von Zigeunern.** Employment of Gypsies. March 1942 race law defining Gypsies (Sinti-Romani).

**beseitigen.** To eliminate. To murder Jews.

**beseitigt.** *See* beseitigen.

**Beseitigung.** Elimination. Determination to murder all the Jews of Europe.

**Besetzte Gebiete.** Occupied districts. National Socialist plan for territories occupied by the German armed forces during World War II, involving the armed forces, the National Socialist Party, the SS, and police authorities. The goal was to exploit the areas to help the German war effort by raising industrial production, bringing foreign workers to the Reich, collecting forced labor, and, especially, carrying out the destruction of Jews.

**Besetzte Ostgebiete.** Occupied eastern districts. German-occupied Soviet territory, under the administration of Alfred Rosenberg. Location of mass murders of Jews by the Einsatzgruppen, the police, the Wehrmacht, and local volunteers. *See also* Kolonialverwaltung.

**Besitzbürgertum.** Propertied middle class. Enemy of Ernst Röhm faction of Nazi Party. After "Night of the Long Knives," with Röhm murdered, Hitler turned his attack on the educated middle class, the intellectuals, rather than German business and financial leaders.

**(zur) besonderen Verwendung.** (z.b.V.) For special use, purpose, task.

**Bestallung.** Approbation. To appoint or employ someone racially acceptable to the professions, in accordance with Nazi race laws.

**Bestallungsordnung für Apotheker.** Licensing Order for Pharmacists. October 8, 1937, decree excluding Jewish pharmacists from being approved for licenses.

**Bestellschein.** Order form. Part of a ration card used to order food items from a German grocer four weeks in advance.

**Bestgestaltung der Arbeit.** Best workplace arrangement. Each worker's workplace was to be kept as efficient and safe as possible.

**(die blonde) Bestie.** The Blond Beast. The ideal Nazi, sometimes applied to Reinhard Heydrich.

**(die schöne) Bestie.** The Beautiful Beast. Irma Grese, from nineteen, served at Ravensbrück, Auschwitz-Birkenau, and Bergen-Belsen, and was responsible for the torture and murder of thousands of women and some men. Reputed to be a bisexual sadist. *See also* Aufseherin.

**Bestie von Belsen.** Monster of Belsen. Josef Kramer, Commandant at Belsen at war's end, served also in camp administrations of Sachsenhausen, Mauthausen, Natzweiler-Struthof, and Auschwitz-Birkenau, where he supervised the murders of some 400,000 Hungarian Jews.

**Bestie von Buchenwald.** Bitch of Buchenwald. Ilse Koch, wife of Commandant Karl Koch of Buchenwald, notorious for her involvement in the torture and murder of camp prisoners, her collection of tatooed skin, her promiscuity with camp guards, and her financial corruption.

**bestimmen.** To decide, arrange. To preordain.

**Bestimmung.** Decision, arrangement. Destiny.

**bestimmungsgemäß behandelt.** Treated according to regulations. *See also* behandeln.

**Bestleistung.** Best performance. German word used in annual work competitions and sports events, instead of the un-German word Rekord (record).

**Bestrafung.** Punishment. Operational code name for German air attacks on Belgrade, April 1941.

**Bestverfahren.** Best method. Best way to achieve optimum production.

**Betätigungsverbot.** Forbidden occupation. All activities as a priest forbidden. A Security Police means to harass Roman Catholic priests opposing the Reich.

**Betreffnis.** Food ration.

**betreuen.** To take care of. Euphemism for murder of Jews; for example, "Die Gestapo betreut die Juden" ("the Gestapo takes care of the Jews.")

**Betreute Organisationen der NSDAP.** Supervised organizations of the Nazi Party. German Women's Work (Deutsches Frauenwerk), German Students' Society (Deutsche Studentenschaft), NS-Altherrenbund der Deutschen Studenten (League of Former German Students), Reich League of German Family (Reichsbund Deutsche Familie), German Communal Congress (Deutscher Gemeindetag), and NS-Reichsbund für Leibesübung (Association for Physical Exercise). *See also* Gliederungen und Angeschlossene Verbände der NSDAP.

**Betreuung.** *See* betreuen.

**Betreuungsausschuß.** Managing committee. All officials responsible for managing the war industry.

**Betreuungsstelle für Auslandsdeutsche.** Managing Office for Germans Living Outside Germany. *See also* Auslandsorganisation der NSDAP.

**Betreuungsvertrag.** Support Contract. German worker's front organization to preserve contact with German groups outside Germany.

**Betriebsappell.** Workplace roll call. Meeting of the leaders and staff of an industry or workplace for instruction on the ideological meaning of their work.

**Betriebsarbeiterin.** Female company worker. Women who trained female company workers according to Nazi ideology and maintained contact with Nazi officials.

**Betriebsblock.** Company unit. Lowest unit of the government workforce active in companies and businesses. *See also* Deutsche Arbeitsfront.

**Betriebsbuße.** Work penalty. Fine for employees who neglect regulations and safety measures at work.

**Betriebsführer.** Workplace leader. Manager of a firm responsible for all economic and political activities in the company.

**Betriebsgemeinschaft.** Community within a company. The cooperation between an employer and employees promoting the welfare of the German state and its people.

**Betriebsjugendwalter.** Young workplace adviser, leader. Young, Nazi-trained men who served as ideological spokespersons between German companies and German youth.

**Betriebsobmann.** Supervisor. Representative of the government workforce whose function was to instruct company workers according to Nazi ideology. *See also* Deutsche Arbeitsfront.

**Betriebszelle.** Company cell. Nazi unit at the workplace.

**Betrüger.** Swindlers. Gypsies, Jews, and others considered racially inferior.

**betrügerisch.** Deceptive. Adjective frequently used to describe Jews.

**Bettenbau.** Making one's bed. In the camps, not making up one's sleeping place correctly served as a pretext for severe punishment.

**(des) Beurlaubtenstandes.** (d.B.) On leave.

**Beutedeutsche.** Prized/booty Germans. Ironic for Volksdeutsche. *See also* Volksdeutscher.

**Bev.** *See* Bevollmächtigter.

**BEVo.** *See* Bandfabrik Ewald Vorsteher.

**Bevölkerungsballung.** Clustering of people. Massing of population.

**Bevölkerungsdruck.** Population pressure.

**Bevölkerungswesen.** Population division of the German administration.

**Bevollm.** *See* Bevollmächtigter.

**Bevollmächtigter.** (Bev, Bevollm) Official in charge, plenipotentiary. Government official from any area of state control. *See also* Lenkung.

**Bewachungsmannschaft.** Guard detail. SS guard unit at the camps.

**Bewaffnete SS.** Armed SS. Early term for Waffen-SS. *See also* Waffen-SS.

**bewährte Deutsche und Deutschstämmige.** Proven Germans and descendants of Germans.

**Bewährungsbataillon 999.** Rehabilitation Battalion 999. Following the high German casualties in Russia in 1941–1942, this army unit was formed. It was comprised of 40,000 criminals and political prisoners who could redeem themselves by fighting on the Eastern Front.

**bewegliche Kampfführung.** Elastic military tactics. Retreat.

**Bewegung.** Movement, motion, action. Nazi Party's self-image of dynamism and forward movement.

**Bewetterung.** Germanization of Klimaanlage (air conditioning).

**Bewirtschaftung.** Rationing, government control of economy. Starting in 1939, the Third Reich strictly regulated use of food, clothing, and other necessities by a system of ration cards, customer lists, order forms, and special ration allowances for different categories of people, such as children, workers performing hard labor, and Jews.

**Beziehung.** Relationship. Racial rootedness, integration, and dependence.

**Beziehungen.** Connections. *See also* Vitamin B.

**beziehungslos.** Without relationship. Racially uprooted, deracinated.

**Bezirk.** (Bez) District.

**Bezirksabgabestelle.** (BASt) District reception point. *See also* Ablieferungspflicht.

**Bezirksbombe.** District bomb. Blockbuster bomb.

**Bezirksgroßhändler.** District wholesaler. District wholesale dealer in German-occupied countries.

**Bezirkswalter.** District Supervisor. Service rank in the Deutsche Arbeitsfront.

**Bezirkswirtschaftsämter.** District economic offices. More than a dozen regional offices controlling the rationing of consumer goods, under the direction of Walther Funk, Minister of Economic Affairs.

**Bezogenheit.** Relatedness. *See also* Beziehung.

**Bezug.** Purchase, acquisition. Acquisition of rationed goods during World War II.

**Bezugsausweis.** *See* Bezugsschein.

**Bezugskarte.** Order card. Special, individualized ration card, valid only for a restricted time period during the war years to purchase household items and clothing; preference was given to the war injured.

**Bezugsschein.** Acquisition paper. Special voucher for scarce goods for the needy, especially those bombed out. *See also* Kriegsauflagenprogramm.

**BfVJP.** Representative for the Four-Year Plan. *See also* Beauftragter für Vierjahresplan.

**Bibel.** Bible. For the Nazis, a history of the reviled Chosen People: the Jews.

**Bibelforscher.** (Bifo) Bible researchers. International Union of Sincere Bible Researchers. Jehovah's Witnesses. *See also* Ernste Bibelforscher.

**Bifo.** *See* Bibelforscher.

**Bildberichterstatter.** Press photographer.

**Bildung.** Education. Sarcastic for learning, culture. Overeducation.

**Bildungsphilister.** Educated philistine, narrow-minded intellectual. Any intellectual.

**Bindenträger.** Armband carriers. Jewish security police in the ghettos and in some camps. *See also* jüdischer Ordnungsdienst.

**Bindung.** Connection. Organic relationship to destiny.

**biologische Anpassung.** Biological adjustment. Fitting into the (German) race.

**biologische Lebensgesetze.** Biological principle of life. Racial destiny.

**biologisches Reservat.** Biological reserve. Biological pool, race.

**biologische Weltanschauung.** Biological worldview. The view that life and fate are determined by racial principles.

**biologisch wertvolles Material.** Biologically valuable material. Adolf Eichmann's term for Jewish women who took part in the Warsaw-Ghetto revolt. An acknowledgment of their courage and reason for their destruction.

**Birkenau.** *See* Auschwitz.

**Birkenwald.** Birch forest. Brzezinka Forest on the grounds of Auschwitz where Jews and others were killed; the Jews were gassed and the others shot. Also, name for Buchenwald concentration camp.

**Birkenwäldchen.** Little birch-tree forest. *See also* Birkenwald.

*Bismarck.* German battleship. In 1941 engaged British navy in several sea battles, sinking the British battleship *Hood. Bismarck* was ultimately sunk by British navy and air force.

**BKV.** *See* Bandenkampfverbände.

**Blasangriff.** Blow, blister attack. Gas attack.

**Blasen.** Bubbles. Youth groups in Munich who opposed the Hitler Youth.

**Blaue Division.** Blue Division. Spanish volunteer division fighting alongside the Wehrmacht from 1941 on the Eastern Front.

**blaue Karte.** Blue card. Identification card for stateless students to attend university lectures in Germany.

**Blaue Polizei.** Blue Police. *See also* Junaks.

**blauer Winkel.** *See* Dreieckswinkel.

**Blaue Schwestern.** Blue Nurses. Members of the Reich Association of Independent Nurses. In 1938, it was combined into the Lebensborn association National Socialist People's Welfare Nurses Organization. *See also* Lebensborn; NSV-Schwesternschaft; Reichsbund freier Schwestern.

**blaue Zone.** Blue zone. The last thousand feet before reaching the enemy positions.

**Blauschein.** Blue identification papers. Work documents issued by the SS to Polish Jews that temporarily prevented deportation.

**Blechbüchse.** Tin can. Slang for destroyer.

**Blechkrankheit.** Tin or cough sickness. The bends.

**Blechkrawatte.** Tin tie. Soldier slang for the order of merit. *See also* Ritterkreuz.

**Blendbombe.** Blinding bomb. Flare.

**Blendflasche.** Blinding bottle. Molotov cocktail.

*Blick in die Zeit.* Look at the Times. Nazi political and cultural journal that published collections of anti-Jewish newspaper articles.

**blind.** Blind. Unconditional, automatic.

**Blitz.** Lightning. *See also* Blitzkrieg.

**Blitzableiter.** Lightning conductor. Code name for a study on the possibility of bacteriological warfare in early 1943.

**Blitz-FS.** Lightning telegram. Telegram.

**Blitzkrieg.** Lightning war. On a strategic level, Germany's rapid conquest of a nation. On a tactical level, Wehrmacht attack by means of aerial bombardment, massed armor, and motorized infantry, combined with speed, intensity, and efficiency. Like a lightning bolt, the Schwerpunkt (main line of attack) was unpredictable and disconcerting to the enemy forces.

**Blitzmädchen.** *See* Blitzmädel.

**Blitzmädel.** Lightning girl. Name for female communication helper working for the Wehrmacht. *See also* Nachrichtenhelferin.

**Blitzpogrom.** Lightning attack on Jews. SS atrocities, in cooperation with the Wehrmacht, against Polish Jews early in the war.

**Block.** Block. Smallest unit of the National Socialist Party, consisting of thirty to fifty families. Smallest unit of public opinion. Also, barracks in a concentration camp.

**Block 10.** Auschwitz area where medical experiments were carried out on women.

**Block 11.** Punishment area in Auschwitz where first experiments using Zyklon-B gas to poison hundreds of Soviet POWs and those deemed incurables were conducted.

**Block 20.** Punishment and murder area of Mauthausen.

**Block 25.** On October 25, 1943, at Birkenau, 2,500 Jewish girls from Salonica, Greece, were gassed. They sang the "Hatikvah" as they were marched to the gas chamber.

**Block 41.** Body-disposal area of Birkenau.

**(das) blockadefeste Europa.** Blockade-resistant Europe. *See also* Festung Europa.

**Blockälteste.** Senior block prisoners. Prisoners, often German or Austrian professional criminals, in charge of a barracks in the concentration camps.

**Blockarzt.** Block doctor. Prisoner doctor of a block in a concentration camp.

**Blockführer.** Block leader. SS sergeant in charge of a number of barracks in a camp.

**Blockführerstube.** Block leader's guardhouse.

**Blockhelfer.** Block helper. Person designated to be in charge of a building in emergencies and for government-controlled activities. He had to be of German origin and a member of the German workforce.

**Blockleiter.** Block Chief. Leader of a Party unit. *See also* Block.

**"(Im) Block Mützen ab!"** "Hats off in the block." Directive carved into rafters at Auschwitz-Birkenau.

**Blockobmann.** Block supervisor. Representative of the German workforce.

**Blockschreiber.** Prisoner block clerk. Inmate chosen by SS to keep records on block prisoners. Member of camp's prisoner administration.

**Blocksperre.** Block arrest. Prisoners were confined to their block except for work or roll call.

**Blockwalter.** Block Administrator. *See also* Blockwart.

**Blockwart.** Block Keeper. Low-level Nazi Party organizer, who on a local level kept Germans in line, often reporting remarks he considered hostile to the regime.

**Blondi.** Hitler's favorite dog. Put to death in Hitler's Berlin bunker on the day of Hitler's suicide.

**Blubo.** *See* Blut und Boden.

**Blücher.** Code name for German offensive in the Crimea in 1942.

**Blut.** Blood. The crucial element in the Third Reich's racial ideology.

**(gutes) Blut.** Good blood. In Nazi racial categories, the German Volk had the most racially pure and valid blood. A racial idea institutionalized as early as fifteenth-century Spain's Pure Blood Laws.

**blutbedingt.** Conditioned by blood. Based on the special quality of one's own race.

**Blutbewußtsein.** Blood consciousness. Pride in, and awareness of, one's (German) race.

**blutecht.** Of genuine blood. Used positively for Germans with Nazi-appropriate blood lines.

**Bluteinsatz.** Blood operation. Duty to sacrifice one's life during wartime.

**Blutfahne.** Blood flag. Bullet-ridden Nazi flag, supposedly soaked with the blood of so-called Nazi martyrs, initially in the Hitler Putsch of November 8–9, 1923. The flag shows a black swastika in a 45-degree tilt within a white circle centered on a red background. Hitler would consecrate Nazi flags by holding the Blutfahne with one hand and touching the new flags with his other hand, intoning, "Keine Fahne ist uns so heilig, wie die Blutfahne des 9. November" ("No flag is so holy to us as the Blood Flag of November 9 [1923]"). It was presented to the SS for safekeeping in November 1926 and was last seen publicly in April 1944.

**blutgebunden.** Bound by blood. Belonging to a particular race.

**blutige Brygida.** Bloody Bridget. An inmate term for the cruel Hildegard Lachert, SS Staff Leader of the women's camp at Lublin-Majdanek.

**Blutkitt.** Blood cement. Hitler's concept of Germans bonding through shared atrocities and horrible experiences.

**Blutkreis.** Circle of blood. The mythical community of Germans connected through blood ties.

**blutlich.** Blood related. A member of the racial community.

**Blutmärsche.** Blood marches. In 1944–1945, the SS and the Wehrmacht forced hundreds of thousands of concentration camp inmates on death marches toward Germany. Between 250,000 and 375,000, mostly Jews, perished.

**blutmäßig.** Blood-like. Concerned with race.

**Blutmischungen.** Blood mixings. Sexual relations between Jews and Christians.

**Blutopfer.** Blood sacrifice/victim. Those Germans who died for the cause of National Socialism, such as Horst Wessel.

**Blutorden.** Blood medal. Highest Nazi award, instituted in 1933, for those participating in the Hitler Putsch of November 8–9, 1923. From 1938, also used to honor severely wounded Nazi members and those who had been sentenced to a prison term in Germany, Austria, or the Sudetenland.

**Blutquell(e).** Source of blood. The Bauerntum was considered the source of pure German blood.

**Blutrache.** Blood vengeance. Germanic law-concept of eradicating "treasonable blood" throughout a whole clan, reborn in Nazi law and practice after the July 20, 1944, attempt on Hitler's life. *See also* 20. Juli.

**Blut(s)reinheit.** Blood purity. Pure race, German blood.

**Blutrichter.** Hanging judge. Description of Roland Freisler, Nazi Head of the People's Court. *See also* Volksgericht.

**Blutsbrüderschaft.** Blood brotherhood. Racial kinship.

**Blutschande.** Incest. Miscegenation, the mixture of races.

**Blutschranke.** Blood barrier. Biological differences among non-Aryan races.

**Blutschutz.** Blood protection. Protection of German racial purity from miscegenation.

**Blutschutzgesetz.** (BSG) Blood Protection Act. A Nuremberg law to "protect German blood and German honor." Marriages and sexual contact were forbidden between Jews and German nationals or those with "generically related blood."

**Blutseele.** Blood soul. The single common biological-ideological source of all Germans, particularly the great thinkers.

**blutsfremd.** Of foreign blood. Of foreign race.

**Blutsgefühl.** Blood feeling. The sense of mystical belonging that all Germans should have.

**Blutsgemeinschaft.** Blood community. The German people. *See also* Blutsbrüderschaft.

**Blutsgeschwister.** Blood siblings. Blood-related Germans who desired a mystical union with their own people.

**Blutsonntag.** Bloody Sunday. Name given to several massacres taking place on a Sunday, including the clash between German Communists and Nazis in July 1932 in Hamburg. Also mass murders of Jews in Prague and the Ukraine in 1941.

**"(Das im) Blut sprechende Gesetz."** "The law speaking through the blood." Nazi phrase indicating that the biological imperative expresses itself in the blood.

**Blutsreinheit.** *See* Blutsreinheit.

**Blutstolz.** Blood pride. A natural imperative to be proud of one's Nordic origin.

**Blutstraße.** Blood Street. Access road to the Buchenwald camp built by camp inmates in 1939; ran parallel to the railroad line.

**Blutsünde.** Blood sin. *See also* Blutschande.

**blutsverantwortlich.** Responsible for one's blood. The German soil was responsible for nourishing the country's pure blood and feeding the German population.

**blutsverfälscht.** Contaminated by blood. Polluted by racially alien blood.

**Blutsvergiftung.** Blood or race poisoning. *See also* Rassenvergiftung.

**blutsverwandt.** Related by blood. Racially connected.

**Blutswertigkeit.** Blood value. Belief in the value of Germanic blood ties.

**blutswertlich.** Valued by blood. *See also* Blutswertigkeit; Blutwert.

**Bluttaufe.** Baptism of blood. Because fifteen Nazis were shot during the Munich Putsch, it was referred to as a baptism of blood.

**Blutträger.** Blood carrier. Hitler's term for Germans who were killed in World War I.

**Blut und Boden.** (Blubo) Blood and soil. German peasants were considered the backbone of a pure Aryan-Nordic race. Only they had the right and duty to grow food on German soil to nourish healthy and strong Germans.

**blut- und bodenverwurzelt.** Tied to blood and soil. *See also* Blut und Boden.

**"Blut und Ehre."** "Blood and honor." Motto of the Hitler Youth.

**Blutvergiftung.** Poisoning of (German) blood. Destruction of the German people by admixture with an alien race.

**Blutwert.** Blood value. The value of German blood as part of the basic National Socialist philosophy.

**Blutzeuge.** Blood witness. Nazi racial-idealogical celebration of national solidarity, November 9, commemorating those early National Socialists who died for the cause during the 1923 Hitler Putsch. Also on this day each year all new SS candidates were first allowed to wear their black SS uniforms and took their personal oaths of loyalty to Adolf Hitler. *See also* Blutorden; Bluttaufe.

**BNSDJ.** *See* Bund Nationalsozialistischer Deutscher Juristen.

**Bock.** Vaulting horse. Wooden structure used to torture camp inmates by tying them to it and beating them on their buttocks. Also, navy slang for diesel engine.

**Bock von Babelsberg.** Whoremonger of Babelsberg. Nickname for Propaganda Minister Goebbels because of his affairs with actresses. Babelsberg was the film center of Berlin.

**Boden.** Soil. The sacred earth of Germany believed to stand in a mystical relationship to the roots of the Volk.

**bodenbedingt.** Determined by the soil. *See also* Boden.

**bodenbestimmt.** Related to the soil. *See also* Boden.

**bodenbezogen.** Related to the soil. *See also* Boden.

**bodenentstammte Volksart.** Specific race originated from the soil. Germans. *See also* Boden.

**Bodenfreiheit.** Ground clearance. Ground clearance of tank.

**bodengebunden.** Bound to the soil. *See also* Boden.

**bodenhaft.** According to the soil. *See also* Boden.

**Bodenplatte.** Base plate, slab. Code for last-ditch, all-out German air offensive against Allied airfields in northwestern Europe, December 1944; coordinated with the Ardennes ground offensive. *See also* Unternehmen Wacht am Rhein.

**Bodenpolitik.** Policy in regard to the conquered territories.

**Bodenraum.** Area, space.

**B-Offizier.** *See* Beobachter-Offizier.

**Bogerschaukel.** Boger's swing. Named after Oberscharführer Wilhelm Boger, a member of Auschwitz's camp security. The male or female prisoner would be stripped then made to sit with the legs drawn up toward the body. Next the prisoner would be told to clasp his or her hands in front of and below his or her knees. The hands would then be bound together and a rod would be slopped through the gap formed by the elbows and knees. *See* Schaukel.

**Böhmen.** Bohemia. Area, along with Moravia, of the traditional Czech lands. Also, German army division.

**Bolona.** *See* "Bombenlose Nacht!"

**Bolschewismus.** Bolshevism. Nazi ideology pictured Jews as fundamentally responsible for plotting to seize world power, warmongering, and theft of private property.

***Bolschewismus von Moses bis Lenin: Ein Zweigespräch zwischen Adolf Hitler und mir.*** Bolshevism from Moses to Lenin: A Dialogue between Adolf Hitler and Myself. Book published in 1923 by Dietrich Eckart shortly after his death, containing the ideological anti-Jewish ideas shared by him and Adolf Hitler.

**Bolschewist.** Bolshevik. Russians and enemies of National Socialism, especially Jews. *See also* Bolschewismus.

**(musikalische) Bolschewisten.** Musical Bolsheviks. Composers of modern, corrupt music, particularly Jews.

**Bolzano.** Area in Italy's Dolomite mountains near Austria and with a large German-speaking minority. Also, Italian concentration camp.

**Bombenflüchtling.** Bomb refugee. German city dweller sent to the countryside because of Allied bombing.

**Bombenfrischler.** Recently bombed. Slang for bombed-out evacuee removed to the countryside.

**"Bombenlose Nacht!"** (Bolona) Humorous, "bombless night" instead of "good night."

**Bombenteppich.** Carpet bombing. Massive aerial bombing of German cities by the Allies from 1942 on.

**Bombenterror.** Bomb terrorism. *See also* Terrorismus.

**Bonbon.** Candy. Ironic for Nazi Party pin.

**Bonze.** Party bigwig. Derogatory for politicians of the Weimar Republic.

**Bonzenblock.** Big-shot barracks. Privileged section at Ravensbrück for mainly political female prisoners.

**Bonzokratie.** Bonzo democracy. Derogatory for the Weimar Republic.

**Bonzopolis.** City of party bigwigs. The Berlin suburb of Dahlem, where many Nazi Party officials moved once Jews were evicted. Bonzo was a cartoon dog noted for his cowardice and greed.

**Bordell-Literatur.** Brothel literature. Jewish and modern literature.

**Börgermoor.** *See* Emsland-Lager.

**Boxheim-Dokumente.** Boxheim Documents. In 1931 plans were discovered belonging to the Nazi Party that contained a blueprint for a Nazi coup if the German Communists came to power. They described measures for expropriation, Nazi courts, forced labor, and the murder of all political opponents, those owning weapons, and Jews, including barring them from economic activities and starving them to death.

**"Boykottiert die Juden!"** "Boycott the Jews." March 1933 Nazi campaign for an economic boycott of German Jews, climaxing on April 1, 1933.

**BRABAG.** *See* Braunkohle-Benzin A.G.

**Bracksche Hilfsmittel.** Brack's remedy, Brack's device. Mobile gassing unit employing carbon monoxide, developed by euthanasia specialist Vicktor Brack. *See also* Gaswagen.

**Bramsig und Knöterich.** Two characters created by Goebbels to ridicule German grumblers.

**Brandenburger.** Person from Brandenberg. Also, name of a German army division. *See also* Regiment z.b.V. 800/Brandenburger.

**Brandflasche.** Fire bomb. *See also* Blendflasche.

**Brandmeister.** Burning master. Man in charge of cremating bodies in concentration camps.

**Bratkartoffelverhältnis.** Fried potatoes relationship. Soldier slang for relationship with a woman or family who fed the soldier well.

**brauchtümlich.** According to custom.

**"Brauch deutsche Mädchen."** "I need German girls." Humorous for BDM (Bund Deutscher Mädel).

**Braunau am Inn.** Austrian town near German border; Hitler's birthplace.

**braune Bataillone.** Brown battalions. SA units.

**braune Bibel.** Brown bible. Hitler's *Mein Kampf.*

**braune Hemden.** Brown shirts. Surplus World War I African compaign brown uniforms supplied to the SA by former Freikorps leader and SA man Gerhard Rossbach. *See also* Sturmabteilung.

**braune Husaren.** Brown hussars. Soldier slang for fleas.

**braune Karte.** Brown card. University identification card for German students.

**braune Mappe.** Brown folder. SS code name for Alfred Rosenberg's instructions to murder Jews in occupied Soviet territory.

**Braune Messe.** Brown fair. Markets and fairs held to demonstrate the economic boom under the National Socialists.

**Braune Schwestern.** Brown nurses. Wearing brown uniforms, some of these nurses were trained to kidnap healthy Aryan Polish children for the Lebensborn program. *See also* Lebensborn; Nationalsozialistische Volkswohlfahrt; NSV-Schwesternschaft.

**Braunes Haus.** Brown house. Nazi Party headquarters in any large city (originally Munich) where the party headquarters was bombed out during the war.

**Braunes Heer.** Brown army. The SA wore brown uniforms from 1926 on.

**Braunhemd.** Brown shirt. SA-man.

**Braunkohle-Benzin A.G.** (BRABAG) Lignite and Benzine Company. German mining company exploiting slave labor from Auschwitz and Buchenwald.

**Braunschweig.** German city. Code name for Caucasus offensive in 1942.

**Brause.** Shower. Disguise for gas chamber.

**Bräuteschule.** Brides' school. *See also* Mütterschulung.

**Brautkind.** Child of an unmarried but engaged couple. Legitimized child with the same rights as the child of a married couple. Racially accepted as member of the German Volk.

**BRB.** *See* Bund der Reichsdeutschen Buchhändler.

**Brechung der Zinsknechtschaft.** *See* (Brechung der) Zinsknechtschaft.

**Brenner.** *See* Brandmeister.

*Brennessel*. Stinging nettle. Nazi Party humor journal.

**Brennkommando.** Arson squad. German police squads that burned synagogues and other buildings in Poland during the German invasion.

**Brennmeister.** *See* Brandmeister.

**Breslau.** German name for Wroclaw, Poland. Also, German concentration camp; also German army division.

**Brezhinka.** Location where clothing taken from victims of Auschwitz was stored and sorted through to find items that could be sent back to Germany.

**Briefaktion.** Letter action. Nazis forced Jews, upon their arrival at the camps, to write letters/postcards to relatives complimenting conditions. Such epistles often deceived the ghetto Jews about their deadly future.

**Brigade.** Brigade. Tactical unit of 5,000 to 7,000 men, either independent or part of a division. Consisting of a number of regiments and associated units.

**Brigadeführer.** (Brigf) Major general.

**Brigf.** *See* Brigadeführer.

**Britisches Freikorps.** British Free Corps. Formerly Legion of St. George. British volunteers fighting with the SS against Jews and Bolsheviks.

**Bromberger Blutsonntag.** Bloody Sunday of Bromberg. Polish attack on Germans living in Bromberg, Poland, after Germany invaded Poland in 1939, where approximately 1,000 were killed; followed by revenge on Poles by German military.

**Brotfreiheit.** *See* Nahrungsfreiheit.

**Bruderschaftswerk.** Brotherhood organization. SS-financed escape organization. *See also* (die) Schleuse.

**Brunnenlaufen.** To run around the water well. In this brutal method of torture and murder at Dachau, prisoners had to run around a deep water hole looking straight ahead until dizziness made them fall into it and drown.

**Brunswick.** Code name for companion operation to Braunschweig, the 1942 Caucasus offensive.

**Brustschmerzen.** Pain in the chest. *See also* Halsschmerzen.

**brutal.** Brutal, cruel. Fanatical and ruthless, decided without compromise, positive connotation for Nazis.

**Brutpflege.** Cultivation of brood. Maintenance of the racial stock. *See also* Erbpflege; Züchtung.

**BSG.** *See* Blutschutzgesetz.

**BSipoSD.** *See* Befehlshaber der Sicherheitspolizei und des SD.

**B-Tag.** B Day. Opening day of the Barbarossa attack on the Soviet Union.

**Btl.** *See* Bataillon.

**"Bubi drück mich."** "Baby squeeze me." Humorous for BDM (Bund Deutscher Mädel).

**(Das) Buch der Jugend.** The Book of Youth. Authoritative bibliographical guide published jointly with the Hitler Youth and the National Socialist Teachers Association. Recommended German children's literature with National Socialist orientation and always contained a list of rejected books and a basic holdings list for school libraries.

**Buchenwald.** Concentration camp near Weimar, Germany. One of the three largest concentration camps in Germany, the others being Sachenhausen and Dachau. Built in 1937, it was not a major death camp, yet more than 100,000 civilian prisoners and British, Canadian, and Soviet POWs died or were killed there. The camp contained a department for medical research, the Division for Typhus and Virus Research of the Hygiene Institute of the Waffen-SS, whose doctors and technicians used inmates to test the effects of viral infections and vaccines. In April 1945 Jewish inmates were forced on a 100-mile death march to Flossenbürg; non-Jewish prisoners were left behind. *See* Hygiene-Institut der Waffen-SS.

**"(Das) Buchenwald-Lied."** "The Buchenwald Song." Composed by order of the then Buchenwald commander Karl Koch in 1938, the song was written by two Austrian Jews: Löhner-Beda and Leopoldi. Repeated singing of this song, especially outside and during bad weather, was a form of collective punishment or torture.

**Bücherverbrennung.** Book burning. The May 10, 1933, public burning at Berlin's Opernplatz (the square in front of the State Opera House) of 20,000 books (removed from public libraries) written by Jews, socialists, pacifists, and scientists considered anti-Nazi. The activities were performed by student leaders and units of the SA and the SS. Authors included were Sigmund Freud, Berthold Brecht, Karl Marx, Albert Einstein, Carl von Ossietzky, Erich Kästner, Heinrich and Thomas Mann, Franz Werfel, and Arnold and Stefan Zweig. The words of the mock ceremony: "Against the soul-destroying overemphasis on life drives, for the nobility of the human soul. I consign the writings of Sigmund Freud to the flame!" ("Gegen seelenzerfasernde Überschätzung des Trieblebens, für den Adel der menschlichen Seele. Ich übergebe der Flamme die Schriften des Sigmund Freud!)" It was the beginning of the Nazi campaign against Jewish and anti-government authors and teachers. Within two years, more than 1,000 university and high school instructors were dismissed.

**"(Das) Buch—unsere Waffe."** "The Book—Our Weapon." Slogan to promote especially in young Germans the spirit of the National Socialist idea through books.

**Bückeberg.** *See* Erntedanktag.

**Bückware.** Bending-down goods. Slang for scarce goods that were sold from under the counter. *See also* Ladenkiebitz.

**Bügeleisen.** Flat iron. Air force slang for antiaircraft shrapnel; also, navy slang for battleship.

**Buna-Suppe.** Buna soup. Extra ration for Auschwitz prisoners who worked at Buna, IG Farben's synthetic-rubber plant.

**Bunawerke.** Synthetic rubber factory. Buna was a sub-camp of Auschwitz where IG Farben made rubber. It was the only camp organized and built by a major German company in close consultation with the SS and the Deutsche Bank, which financed both Auschwitz and the construction of the IG Farben factory.

**Bund der deutschen Arbeiterjugend.** Alliance of German Worker Youth. One of many Nazi youth organizations; founded in 1926.

**Bund der Freunde der Hitler-Bewegung.** Association of the Friends of the Hitler Movement. A branch of the Nazi Party outside Germany.

**Bund der Reichsdeutschen Buchhändler.** (BRB) Alliance of Reich German Booksellers.

**Bund Deutscher Mädel in der Hitlerjugend.** (BDM) League of German Girls. Paralleled boys' Hitlerjugend. Established to urge young German women, aged fourteen to twenty-one, to serve the German people. "Your body belongs to the nation," "belief and beauty is the beautiful girl," and "carriers of the National Socialist ideological worldview" were slogans. Millions of German girls were expected to fit the model Aryan (blue eyes, blond hair) and be industrious, pure, healthy, and involved in sport. Their activities were camping, evenings at home, traveling, and marching in twin pigtails, white blouses, blue skirts, and brown jackets to prepare them for German motherhood. *See* Jungmädel; Glaube und Schönheit.

**Bund deutscher Milchkühe.** League of German Milk Cows. Derisive for BDM (Bund Deutscher Mädel).

**Bund für Deutsche Gotterkenntnis.** *See* Deutsche Gotterkenntnis.

**bündische Jugend.** Youth gangs. Members of the Free-Youth Movement (middle-class, all-boy groups) during the Weimar Republic.

**Bund Nationalsozialistischer Deutscher Juristen.** (BNSDJ) *See* NS-Juristenbund.

**Bund Nationalsozialistischer Juristen.** *See* NS-Juristenbund.

**Bündnisverwaltung.** Alliance administration. Nations allied to, and occupied by, the Reich: Bulgaria, Croatia, Finland, (Vichy) France, Hungary, Italy, Romania, and Slovakia.

**Bunker.** Bunker, air-raid shelter. Punishment block of Auschwitz I and other concentration camps where prisoners would be held until they starved to death or committed suicide. *See also* Block 11.

**bunte Räume.** Colored spaces. Gas-poisoned landscape.

**Buntmetall.** Colored metal. Nonferrous metal.

**bunt schießen.** To shoot with color. Army slang for to shell with gas.

**Bürger, bürgerlich, Bürgertum.** Town resident. Compliant person.

**Bürger-Arier.** Citizen-Aryans. Non-Jews.

**Bürgerbräukeller.** Munich beer hall. Hitler's Beer Hall Putsch began at this beer hall on November 8–9, 1923. *See also* Hitler-Putsch.

**Bürgerbräu-Keller-Attentat.** Unsuccessful attempt on Hitler's life in Munich in November 1939.

**Bürgerbräukeller-Putsch.** *See* Hitler-Putsch.

**Bürgerbräu-Keller-Putsch.** *See* Hitler-Putsch.

**Bürgertum.** Bourgeoisie, middle class. Social level rejected by the National Socialists, who attempted to replace it with a racially based völkisch culture only for those whom they perceived as authentically German. *See also* Mittelstand; Spießer.

**Burgfriede.** Public peace. Moratorium on political activity in Germany in 1923, because of the French invasion and massive inflation; agreed to by all political parties except the Nazis.

**Büro der Abgeordneten.** Office of Deputies. Used by Hitler to disguise the illegal activities of the Nazi Party during the period it was supposed to be dissolved, in the 1920s.

**Büro Ribbentrop.** Ribbentrop Office. Nazi Party foreign affairs office founded by Hitler and led by Joachim von Ribbentrop, Hitler's adviser on foreign affairs. Competed with the regular German Foreign Office until Ribbentrop became German Foreign Minister in 1938.

**-bürtig.** Born. Typical racial suffix. *See also* außenbürtig; echtbürtig; innerbürtig.

**Busch.** *See* Wilhelm-Busch-Gesellschaft.

**Buttarine.** Derisive for Margarine (margarine).

**Butter und Kanonen.** In January 1936, Propaganda Minister Joseph Goebbels explained that food shortages in the German Reich were unimportant because "if necessary, one could manage without butter but never without cannons."

**b.v. beschränkt verfügbar.** Limited availability.

**BV, BVer.** *See* befristeter Vorbeugungshäftling.

**B-Zeit.** Time B. Period of military service not spent in front lines.

# C

**C.** One-letter abbreviation for Reinhard Heydrich, standing for Capo or Chief (chief). *See also* Kapo; Chef.

**Canada.** *See* Kanada.

**Capo.** *See* Kapo.

**Carachoweg.** *See* Karacho-Weg.

**CdZ.** *See* Chef der Zivilverwaltung.

**Cellon.** Artificial material similar to cellophane.

**Charakter.** Character, personality. Racial and spiritual stamp of human beings.

**charakterlich.** According to character. Adjective coined by the Nazis meaning the German character. *See also* Charakter.

**Charakterwert.** Character value. Positive quality of German character.

**Charlemagne.** Name of Waffen-SS division.

**Chefbesprechungen.** Department head discussions. Meetings of Nazi ministers and/or state secretaries in an attempt to fill the executive gap and diffuse responsibility in the Third Reich during World War II.

**Chef der Auslands-Abteilung.** Chief of the Overseas Branch (of the Nazi Party). Position held by Ernst Wilhelm Bohle.

**Chef der Deutschen Polizei—Reichsinnenminister.** Chief of the German Police—Reich Interior Minister. Himmler's official government position.

**Chef der politischen Polizei in allen Ländern des Deutschen Reiches.** Chief of the Political Police in All Territories of the German Reich. One of Himmler's titles from 1934.

**Chef der Sicherheitspolizei und des SD.** (CSSD) Head of the Security Police and the SD. Title given to the Head of the Reichssicherheitshauptamt (RSHA) (Head of Reich Security Administration) in Berlin. He was subordinate only to Himmler as Head of the Gestapo and the SD, who in turn was subordinate only to Hitler. From 1939–1942, Reinhard Heydrich held the post; his successor was Dr. Ernst Kaltenbrunner.

**Chef der Zivilverwaltung.** (CdZ) Head of the Civilian Administration of a German-occupied territory.

**Chef des Generalstabs des Heeres.** (Chef GenStdH) Chief of the General Staff of the Army.

**Chef des Generalstabs der Luftwaffe.** (Chef GenStdL) Chief of the General Staff of the Air Force.

**Chef des Generalstabs einer höheren Dienststelle.** (Chef dGen.St., Chef GenSt.) Chief of the General Staff of a Higher Headquarters.

**Chef des Persönlichen Stabes der Reichsführer-SS.** Chief of the Personal Staff of the Reichsführer-SS. Founded in 1936, this position controlled the operations directly associated with Himmler and oversaw Hitler's bodyguards.

**Chef des Stabes des Stellvertreters des Führers.** Chief of Staff of the Deputy Führer. Martin Bormann's position. But once Hitler's deputy Rudolf Hess fled to Great Britain, Bormann became Acting Deputy Führer, directing Nazi Party affairs. *See also* Stellvertreter des Führers.

**Chef dGen.St.** *See* Chef des Generalstabs einer höheren Dienststelle.

**Chef GenSt.** *See* Chef des Generalstabs einer höheren Dienststelle.

**Chef GenStdH.** *See* Chef des Generalstabs des Heeres.

**Chef GenStdL.** *See* Chef des Generalstabs der Luftwaffe.

**Chef Oberaufseherin.** Chief senior overseer. Head of women guards in the employ of SS at concentration camps.

**Chefs.** *See* Chefsache.

**Chefsache.** Most important subject. The highest degree of secrecy in the armed forces.

**Chelmno (Kulmhof).** Near Polish village of the same name and close to city of Lodz. One of the six death camps, all located in Poland. The first death camp, located in western Poland. Altogether more than 600,000 Jews were gassed between

1941 and 1943, as well as 5,000 Gypsies. In comparison to the other death camps, Chelmno was technologically primitive, employing carbon-monoxide-gas vans as the main method of killing. The Nazis dismantled the camp in late 1944/early 1945.

**(Abteilung) Chiffrierwesen.** Coding Branch. Of the Oberkommando der Wehrmacht.

**Chopinlager.** Chopin camp. Lublin warehouse on Chopin Street used by the Lublin-Majdanek death camp.

**Christbäume.** Christmas trees. *See also* Laternenanzünder.

**Christbaum-Lager.** Christmas tree camp. Section of the Bergen-Belsen concentration camp.

**Christengemeinschaft.** Society of Christians. Group that took in members of the forbidden and dissolved anthroposophical society.

**(der wilde) Christian.** The Savage Christian. Christian Wirth, leader of the T-4 Euthanasia Program and later inspector of the Aktion Reinhard death camps. *See also* Aktion Reinhard.

**Christian der Grausame.** Christian the Terrible. Christian Wirth. *See also* (der wilde) Christian.

*Christlichsozialer Reichsbote.* Christian-Social Reich Messenger. Antisemitic publication closely associated with the Lutheran Church in Germany.

**C-Lager.** C Camp. Part of Birkenau's women's comcentration camp housing mostly Polish and Hungarian Jewish women, up to 30,000.

**Colditz.** Castle in Saxony, Germany, in which Allied officers from Australia, Belgium, Canada, Czechoslovakia, France, Great Britain, India, the Netherlands, New Zealand, Poland, Serbia, South Africa, and the United States were imprisoned. Built on rocks high above the town and overlooking the valley of the River Mulde, the high-security prison was subject to more than 300 escape attempts, though few were successful.

**Columbia-Haus.** Columbia house. Gestapo torture prison in Berlin.

**Condor.** Troop transport. *See also* Legion Condor.

**coventrieren.** To coventry, to completely destroy a city through bombing. Verb formed after the German bombing and destruction of the English city Coventry.

**C-Zeit.** Time C. Period of military service spent at rest.

# D

---

**DA.** *See* Deutsche Angestelltenschaft.

**DAA.** *See* Dienststelle im Auswärtigen Amt.

**Dachau.** The first concentration camp, established in March 1933 in southern Germany, at the edge of the town of Dachau, northeast of Munich under Theodor Eicke, chief of all concentration camps. In 1942 a gas chamber was established in connection with medical experiments in which a few experimental gassings took place. Used mainly to incarcerate German political prisoners until late 1938, whereupon large numbers of Jews, Gypsies, Jehovah's Witnesses, homosexuals, and other supposed enemies of the state and antisocial elements were sent. Nazi doctors and scientists, led by Sigmund Rascher, used many Dachau prisoners as guinea pigs for experiments determining the effects of sudden increases and decreases in atmospheric pressure on humans; studying the effects of freezing on humans; infecting prisoners with malaria; and testing prisoners for the effects of drinking seawater and starvation and more. During the war, construction began on a gas chamber, but it was never put into operation, although the crematoria were used. Dachau was the model and training center for SS-organized camps. During World War II the main camp was supplemented by more than 150 satellite camps using slave labor to manufacture military hardware for the German war effort. Dachau was liberated as a German military facility, not as a concentration camp, by American troops in April 1945.

**Dachhase/Dachkaninchen.** Roof rabbit. *See also* Balkonschwein.

**Dachorganisaton der Filmschaffenden Deutschlands e.V.** (DACHO) Umbrella Organization of German Filmmakers. Independent cinema association of German directors and actors disbanded by Goebbels in 1933, at which time many Jewish members and anti-Nazi members left Germany for Hollywood.

**DAD.** *See* Deutscher Arbeitsdienst.

**DAF.** *See* Deutsche Arbeitsfront.

**DAG.** *See* Deutsche Ansiedlungsgesellschaft.

**DAI.** *See* Deutsches Auslands-Institut.

**DAK.** *See* Deutsches Afrikakorps.

**Danzig.** Prussian city taken from Germany by the Versailles Treaty that ended World War I. The treaty awarded most of West Prussia, including Poznan (the Polish Corridor), as well as other territories, to Poland and established Danzig as a free city. Also, code word for the plan to proceed with a German offensive in the west in November 1939. *See also* Großdeutsches Reich; Weserübung.

**DAP.** *See* Deutsche Arbeiterpartei.

**Darbietungstyp.** *See Rasse und Seele.*

**darf in kein anderes Lager.** Must not be moved to another camp. *See also* DIKAL-Häftling.

**Dasein ohne Leben.** Being without Life. Nazi propaganda film made to gain German public-opinion support for the Euthanasia Program.

**Dauergemüse.** Dried vegetables.

**dauernd dienstuntauglich.** (d.u.) Permanently unable to work. *See also* Diensttauglichkeitsgrade.

**dauernd untauglich.** Permanently unfit (for military service). *See also* tauglich.

**Dauervernichtigungslager.** Permanent extermination camps. Death camps.

**Davidstern.** Star of David. Symbol of the Jewish enemy of Nazism.

**DAVO.** *See* Dividendenabgabe.

**DAW.** *See* Deutsche Ausrüstungswerke GmbH.

**d.B.** *See* (des) Beurlaubtenstandes.

**D-Banken.** D-Banks. The three largest German banks: Deutsche Bank, Diskonto-Gesellschaft, and Dresdner Bank.

**DC.** *See* Deutsche Christen.

**DDAC.** *See* (der) Deutsche Automobil-Club.

**DDP.** *See* Deutsche Demokratische Partei.

**d.E.** *See* des Ersatzheeres.

**Defaitismus.** Defeatism. Doubt as to victory in World War II.

**Defaitist.** Defeatist. Critic of Nazi Germany and its leaders.

**DEGESCH.** *See* Deutsche Gesellschaft für Schädlingsbekämpfung.

**Degusa.** Subsidiary of IG Farben, involved, along with the Prussian mint, in smelting gold taken from those murdered in concentration camps and elsewhere.

**Dehnsteife.** Stretching capacity. Germanization of Elastizität (elasticity).

**DEHOMAG.** *See* Deutsche Maschinen-Gesellschaft.

**DEHOMAG D-11.** Hollerith electric tabulating system. The first automatic sequence-controlled printing calculator. IBM electric punch card and printing device capable of processing millions of punch cards, enabling the Nazis to efficiently identify and mass murder Jews, Gypsies, Poles, and others. The machines were custom designed for the Third Reich, serviced monthly by IBM-trained Nazi personnel, and enhanced the entire commercial, industrial, and war-making capability of Nazi Germany, as well as enabling the Third Reich to mass murder Jews and others with unprecedented efficiency. *See also* Deutsche Maschinen-Gesellschaft; Lochkarten.

**Dekadenz.** Decadence. All modern and progressive expressions of art and philosophy that opposed Nazi ideology.

**Demarkationslinie.** Demarcation line. Borders between German-occupied territories and free nations not yet conquered by Germany.

**Demokratie.** Democracy. Liberal thinking as negative in contrast to positive National Socialism. *See also* demokratisch.

**demokratisch.** Democratic. Denigration of liberals, considered pro-Jewish and undermining National Socialism.

**demoplutokratisch.** Combination of democratic and plutocratic. Negative, presumably coined by Goebbels, against the Allies, especially Britain.

**Dentisten.** Dentists. Death camp inmates forced to extract gold from teeth of corpses and to check for other hidden valuables.

**Denunziatur.** Neologism combining the German words for informer (Denunziant) and pontifical-nuncio residence (Nunziatur). Central office of the Reichssicherheitshauptamt.

**Deportation.** *See* Abwanderung.

**Deportationszug.** Deportation train. Train carrying Jews and other people to their death in ghettos and/or concentration camps.

**Depothäftlinge.** Prisoner holding area. Location at Auschwitz where new prisoners were held until the gas chambers and ovens could be cleared and made ready for them to be murdered.

**Der.** The German article der, or "the," beginning with a capital letter. Used before a title in official correspondence to indicate, for example, by order of the Reichsführer-SS (Der Reichsführer-SS).

**Der Chef.** The Boss. Hitler's staff called him by this nickname.

**der Reserve.** (d. R.) Of/from the reserve (army).

**Der schöne Adolf.** Handsome Adolf. Nickname for Hitler used by millions of German and Austrian women and teenagers infatuated with him.

**Der stolze Jude.** The proud Jew. Nazi nickname for Jacob Gens of the Vilna Judenrat.

**des Ersatzheeres.** (d.E.) Of/from the reserve army.

**Deserteurrevolte.** Revolt of deserters. Nazi interpretation of the November 1918 revolution that led to the creation of the Weimar Republic.

**Desinfektion.** Disinfection. Prisoners in the concentration camps with cuts were forced to bathe their wounds in a disinfection solution that burned their skin. Prisoners' clothing was also disinfected instead of washed.

**Desinfektionsraum.** Disinfection room. Euphemism for gas chamber in concentration camps.

**"(zum) Desinfektionsraum."** "To the disinfection room." Sign at Auschwitz directing prisoners to the disguised gas chamber.

**DEST.** *See* Deutsche Erd- und Steinwerke GmbH.

**destruktiver Außenseiter.** Destructive outsider. A public enemy whose crimes fell under the war criminal laws and who was prosecuted by special courts: Germans who listened to foreign radio, ignored air-raid warnings, refused to perform civil duties, helped POWs, and committed other crimes against the German people. All were subject to the death penalty.

**deutsch.** German, belonging to the people. Aryan in contrast to foreign, of German blood and soil.

**Deutschamerikaner.** *See* Amerikadeutsche.

**Deutschbalte.** German living in the Baltic countries.

**deutschbestimmte Exterritorien.** Territories deemed German. Areas to be annexed to the Reich.

**deutschbewußt.** German conscious. Awareness of German blood or race.

**deutschblütig.** Of German blood.

**Deutschblütiger.** *See* deutschblütig.

**Deutsche Akademie der Dichtung.** Academy of German Poetry. Part of the Prussian Academy of Art after 1933 and under government control.

**Deutsche Angestelltenschaft.** (DA) Federation of German White Collar Workers. Subsection of the Deutsche Arbeitsfront.

**Deutsche Ansiedlungsgesellschaft.** (DAG) German Settlement Company. Nazi organization, headed by SS General Oswald Pohl, that managed land, forests, and property in areas in German-occupied eastern Europe that were to be resettled by Germans. The company also oversaw the forced expulsion of non-Germans, especially Poles.

**Deutsche Arbeiterpartei.** (DAP) German Workers' Party. Precursor of the Nationalsozialistische Deutsche Arbeiterpartei founded in Munich on January 5, 1919. In September 1919, Hitler, still in the German army, was assigned by his superiors to investigate the new party and to join the party as an undercover agent. He quickly became the DAP's chief of propaganda and most active member. On February 24, 1920, Hitler publicly announced the DAP's "Twenty-five Point Program" and, on August 8, 1920, received permission from its leadership to rename the party the National-Socialist German Workers' Party. *See also* politischer Arbeiterzirkel.

**Deutsche Arbeitsfront.** (DAF) German Labor Front. Established May 10, 1933. A massive Nazi organization replacing all former German labor unions and guilds and professional organizations. Its goal was to organize all German labor (mental and physical) and to train all authentic Germans into an effective work community. *See also* Nationalsozialistische Gemeinschaft Kraft durch Freude.

**Deutsche Ausrüstungswerke GmbH.** (DAW) German Armaments Works. One of many SS armaments enterprises using slave labor from concentration camps. *See also* Reinhardt-Programm.

**(der) Deutsche Automobil-Club.** (DDAC) German Automobile Club. From 1935, the only organization for private vehicle owners; controlled by the Third Reich.

**Deutsche Baugesellschaft.** German Construction Company. Nazi building conglomerate seized from the labor unions. *See also* Deutsche Arbeitsfront.

**"(Der) deutsche Christ liest das 'Evangelium im Dritten Reich.'"** "The German Christ Reads: Gospel in the Third Reich." Poster hung at meeting of German-Christians in Berlin in 1934.

**Deutsche Christen.** (DC) German Christians. Evangelical (Protestant) Church organization/members attempting a synthesis between Christianity and National Socialism. Their goal was to obey Hitler as Führer within the context of a National Socialist state. Their motto was "Ein Volk! Ein Gott! Ein Reich! Eine Kirche!" ("One people, one God, one Reich, one church"). *See* Nationalkirche deutscher Christen.

**Deutsche Demokratische Partei.** (DDP) German Democratic Party. Liberal political party (1918–1933) most closely identified with the Weimar Republic. Became the German State Party (Deutsche Staatspartei) in 1930 and dissolved in 1933 after Hitler came to power.

**Deutsche Erd- und Steinwerke GmbH.** (DEST) German Earth and Stone Works Ltd. SS enterprise exploiting slave labor in construction at concentration camps, especially Flossenbürg, Gross-Rosen, and the Wienergraben quarry at Mauthausen.

**deutsche Farben.** German colors. *See also* Reichsfarben.

*Deutsche Flugillustrierte.* German Illustrated Flight. Magazine of the Reichsluftschutzbund. *See also* Reichsluftschutzbund.

**Deutsche Forschungsgemeinschaft.** (DFG) From 1936, German Association for Scientific Research. *See also* Notgemeinschaft Deutscher Wissenschaft.

**Deutsche Frauenwehr.** German Women's Defense (League).

**"(Die) deutsche Frau raucht nicht."** "The German woman doesn't smoke." Government slogan to stop women from smoking.

**Deutsche Front.** German Front. Union of non-Marxist political parties in the Saar region from 1933 to 1935.

**Deutsche Gesellschaft für Schädlingsbekämpfung.** (DEGESCH) German Corporation for Vermin Control. After 1941, it was absorbed by IG Farben, the huge German chemical conglomerate. It manufactured Zyklon poison gas (that was used to murder millions) and other chemicals. Used Auschwitz slave labor. *See also* Zyklon.

**Deutsche Gesellschaft für Wehrpolitik und Wehrwissenschaft.** German Society for Defense Policy and Military Education. 1933 organization designed to propagandize and educate the German people for military readiness. Based on the ideas of Ewald Banse (i.e., nationalism, nordic racism, and geopolitics).

**Deutsche Glaubensbewegung.** German Faith Movement. Nordic-German Christianity. *See also* Deutscher Glaube Kampfring.

**Deutsche Gotterkenntnis.** German God Acknowledgment. German World War I Chief of General Staff Erich Ludendorff established this religious movement according to the principles of race and antisemitism. From 1937 on, it was officially recognized as a religion.

*Deutsche Gottschau.* German Way of Seeing God. Book by W. Hauer, published in 1935. *See also* artgemäßes Christentum.

**Deutsche Heeres-Werkstätten.** (DHW) German army workshops.

**Deutsche Heimschulen.** German native schools. Part of the SS attempt from 1942 to Germanize certain racially qualified Polish children. *See also* Eignungsprüfer; Heu-Aktion; Lebensborn; Ostkinder; Wiedereindeutschung.

**Deutsche Jägerschaft.** German Hunter's Group. Taken over by the Nazis in 1934, under the leadership of the chief hunter, Hermann Göring. It became the Reichsbund Deutsche Jägerschaft.

**(die) deutsche Kämpferin.** German fighting women. *See also* Nationalsozialistische Frauenschaft.

**Deutsche Kinderschar.** German Children's Group. Organization of six- to seven-year-old girls. Project of the Nationalsozialistische Frauenschaft.

**Deutsche Kulturbuchreihe.** German cultural book series. Nazi-sponsored public book club.

**Deutsche Kulturwacht.** *See* Kampfbund für deutsche Kultur.

**(Das) *deutsche Leben*.** German Life. *See also* Schriftenreihe biozentrischer Forschungen.

**(Das) deutsche Mädel.** The German girl. *See also* Bund Deutscher Mädel in der Hitlerjugend.

**"Deutsche Männer und Frauen, kauft nicht bei Juden!"** "German men and women, don't buy from Jews." Sturmabteilung slogan printed on placards and chanted by the SA while marching in the streets of Germany during the government-initiated boycott of Jewish businesses in April 1933 and on other occasions.

**Deutsche Maschinen-Gesellschaft.** (DEHOMAG) German Machine Company—International Business Machines Germany. IBM subsidiary that supplied indispensable technological assistance to the Third Reich for profit, enabling the Reich to automate the mass murder of Jews by identifying, expropriating, and deporting them from their homes to ghettos and from ghettos to death camps. Thomas J. Watson, president of IBM and friend of Franklin D. Roosevelt, supplied the DEHOMAG D-11 card-sorting system for the Third Reich to use at all major concentration camps.

**deutsche Menschlichkeit.** German humanity. Contrasted with (negative Jewish) human values that favored the individual rather than the collective. *See also* Humanität.

**(mit) deutschem Gruß.** With German greetings. Common concluding salutation of a semiformal letter, instead of writing Heil Hitler!

**Deutsche Nationalsozialistische Arbeiterpartei in der Tschechoslowakei.** (DNSAP) German National-Socialist Workers Party in Czechoslovakia.

**deutschen oder artverwandten Blutes.** Of German or racially related blood. A requirement of citizenship according to the Nuremberg Laws. *See also* artverwandten Blutes.

**Deutsche Normalschrift.** Normal German longhand. *See also* Normalschrift.

**Deutsche Ölschiefer-Forschungs GmbH.** German Shale Oil Research Company Ltd. SS corporation for fuel production, headquartered in the Natzweiler-Struthof concentration camp.

**Deutscher Adler-Orden.** German eagle medal. Great Golden Cross of the Order of the German Eagle. Award Hitler presented to foreign diplomats.

**Deutscher Arbeitsdienst.** (DAD) German Labor Service. Young citizens' obligatory work or training on behalf of the state. *See also* Reichsarbeitsdienst.

**deutsche Raumfrage.** German space question. *See also* Lebensraum.

**deutscher Blick.** German glance. Humorous for Germans looking in all directions before criticizing Hitler and the Nazi government.

**Deutsche Rechtsfront.** German Legal Front. Professional union of all lawyers, notaries, and associated professions.

**Deutsche Rechts-Partei.** (DRP) German Rights Party. Neo-Nazi political party under the Weimar Republic.

**Deutsche Reichsbahn.** German Reich Railway. Its efficiency and cooperation were crucial to the Third Reich's success in World War II and the Holocaust.

**Deutsche Reichsbank.** *See* Reichsbank.

**(die) Deutsche Revolution.** *See* Schwarze Front.

**Deutscher Fichte-Bund.** German Fichte Association. German propaganda organization established in 1914. Later became part of Nazi Reichsbund für Deutschtumsarbeit.

**Deutscher Frauenorden Rotes Hakenkreuz der NSDAP.** German Women's Order of the Red Swastika of the Nazi Party. Nazi women's organization founded in 1928.

**deutscher Freund.** German friend. Collaborator with the Nazis in occupied Europe.

**Deutscher Gemeindetag.** (DGT) German Community Day. Before 1933, German city day, national conference of German mayors.

**Deutscher Glaube Kampfring.** German belief battle ring. Developing from the Deutsche Glaubensbewegung, it was a Nazi church established to replace traditional Christian churches. This religious movement was rooted in German racial beliefs but soon lost significance under the Third Reich. *See also* deutschgläubig; Gottgläubig.

**Deutscher Gruß.** German greeting. Nazi greeting during the Third Reich was a raised-right-arm salute along with "Heil Hitler!" *See also* "Heil Hitler!"; Leitgedanken zur Schulordnung.

**Deutscher Handelsdienst.** (DHD) German Trade Service.

**Deutscher Hochschulring.** German University League. A racist, nationalist, and antisemitic organization to which most German university fraternities belonged during the early years of the Weimar Republic. It came to dominate student politics but in the mid-1920s it was replaced by the National-Socialist Students' Association. *See* Nationalsozialistischer Deutscher Studentenbund.

**"(Ein) deutscher Junge weint nicht!"** "A German youth doesn't cry." Nazi Youth slogan.

**(Bund) deutscher Juristen.** *See* NS-Juristenbund.

**Deutscher Kampfbund.** German Fighting Union. Association of nationalist and Free Corps organizations that participated with Hitler and the Nazi Party in the 1923 Munich Putsch.

**Deutscher Kolonialkriegerbund.** German Colonial Veteran League. *See also* Nationalsozialistches Reichskriegerbund.

**Deutscher Luftsportverband.** (DLV) German Air Sports Association. From 1937 part of the National Socialist Flyers' Corps. Forerunner of the German air force. *See also* NS-Fliegerkorps.

**Deutscher Männerorden.** German Men's Order. The SS.

**Deutsche Meisterwerkstätte.** German Master Workshop site. SS furniture factory.

**Deutscher Nationalpreis.** *See* Nationalpreis für Buch und Film.

**Deutscher Nationalpreis für Kunst und Wissenschaft.** German national prize for art and science. Nazi substitute prize for the Nobel Prize.

**Deutscher Orden.** German order. Order of German Knights, top hierarchy of National Socialists. Highest decoration/award.

**Deutscher Reichsbund für Leibesübungen.** (DRL) German Reich League for Physical Exercises.

**Deutschschädling.** German parasite. Anti-Nazi elements within the German people. *See also* Volksschädling.

**Deutscher Stil.** German style. Nazi Party style.

**Deutscher Verlag.** German Publishing House. Name of the former Jewish Ullstein Publishing House, which the Nazis seized in 1934. *See* Uli-Taschenbücher.

**Deutscher Volkssturm.** *See* Volkssturm.

**deutscher Wehrgeist.** German military spirit. Contrasted to Christian spirit.

*Deutscher Wochendienst.* (DW) German Weekly Service. Reich Propaganda Ministry's internal journal emphasizing race and Jewish conspiracy themes.

**deutsch erzogen.** Raised the German way. Children from mixed (i.e., German-Jewish) marriages who were not registered as Jewish.

**Deutsches Afrikakorps.** (DAK) German Africa Corps. Germany's elite, motorized forces fighting in North Africa (1941–1943). Led by General Erwin Rommel, who was called the Desert Fox.

**Deutsches Auslands-Institut.** (DAI) Institute for Germans Living Abroad. Located in Stuttgart and issued the periodical *Volksforschung*. *See also* Auslandsorganisation der NSDAP.

**Deutsche Schrift.** *See* Arierschrift.

**(die) deutsche Seele.** The German soul. The German racial-ideological essence, Goebbels' propaganda concept. *See* Idee; Weltanschauung.

**Deutsches Frauenwerk.** (DFW) German Women's Organization. Nazi women's organization that coordinated and unified all German women's associations under the leadership of the National Socialist Women's League. Responsible for women's education in child care, home economics, culture, and auxiliary services in Germany, border areas, and abroad on behalf of National Socialism. *See also* Mütterschulung; Nationalsozialistische Frauenschaft.

**Deutsche Siedlungsgesellschaft.** *See* Deutsche Ansiedlungsgesellschaft.

**Deutsches Jungvolk.** German Youth. Youth organization. *See also* Deutsches Jungvolk in der Hitlerjugend.

**Deutsches Jungvolk in der Hitlerjugend.** (DJ) German youth in the Hitler Youth. German youth between the ages of ten and fourteen, organization affiliated with the Hitler Youth. The boys' oath: "Befehle sind ohne Wenn und Aber durchzuführen. Disziplin und Ordnung sind nationsozialistische Grundtugenden" ("Orders are to be obeyed with no ifs, ands, or buts. Discipline and order are the National Socialist basic virtues"). *See also* Hitlerjugend.

**Deutsches Kreuz.** German cross. War medal in gold or silver introduced in 1941.

**Deutsches Künstlerhaus.** House of German Art. Nazi art gallery opened in Munich in 1937.

**Deutsches Nachrichtenbüro.** (DNB, dnb) German News Office. Official Nazi press agency founded in 1933 ideologically to coordinate the German press.

**deutsche Sprache.** German language. The National Socialists established new definitions and time periods for the German language.

**deutsches Recht.** (DR) Germanic law. Medieval German law contrasted to Roman law, which was seen as egalitarian. On the contrary, German law emanated from the Führer. Also, official National Socialist law journal. *See also* Akademie für Deutsches Recht; Führergesetz; Nationalsozialistischer Rechtswahrerbund.

*Deutsches Reichslesebuch.* German Reich reader. Uniform reader for elementary schools gradually introducing the ideological principles of (1) blood and soil, (2) leadership and fellowship, (3) honor and loyalty, (4) service and sacrifice; and, (5) struggle and work as established by Reich Education Minister Bernard Rust.

**deutsches Schicksal.** German destiny. *See also* Schicksal.

**Deutsches Schutzwallehrenzeichen.** German protective-wall medal. Medal introduced in 1939 to honor those who worked on building the western defense fortifications. *See also* Westwall.

**(das) Deutsche Stadion.** *See* Reichsparteitagsgelände.

**Deutsche Staatspartei.** (DStP) German State Party. *See also* Deutsche Demokratische Partei.

**Deutsche Studentenschaft.** *See* Nationalsozialistischer Deutscher Studentenbund.

**Deutsches Turn- und Sportabzeichen.** *See* Reichssportabzeichen.

**Deutsches Volksbildungswerk.** German National Education Project. Taught German language and culture to those who claimed German nationality in German-occupied Europe.

**"Deutsches Volk! Wehr dich! Kauf nicht beim Juden!"** "Germans. Defend yourselves. Don't buy from Jews." Nazi slogan during 1933 anti-Jewish boycott.

**"Deutsches Volk, werde hart!"** "German people, become hard!" "Hart wie Stahl" ("Hard as Steel"); "Hart wie Kruppstahl" ("Hard as Krupp steel")." Nazi slogans.

**Deutsche Umsiedlungs-Treuhand-GmbH.** (DUT, UTAG) German Resettlement Trust Ltd. Corporation transferring property seized from Jews to the Volksdeutsche Bank and also planning for colonies in the east.

**Deutsche Versuchsanstalt für Ernährung und Verpflegung.** German Experimental Institute Station for Nutrition and Food. Part of the SS economic empire.

**deutsche Volksgemeinschaft.** (Great) community of the German people.

**Deutsche Volkskirche.** German People's Church. Insignificant German pagan sect that rejected the Bible and claimed God was nordic-German. Ultimately abandoned by the Third Reich.

**Deutsche Volksliste.** (DVL) List of ethnic Germans. Ethnic Germans in Poland were divided into racial categories, from those in category one, who could prove their racial Germanness and warranted full Reich citizenship, to those in category four, that is, polonized racial Germans deserving only limited Reich protection.

**Deutsche Volkspartei.** (DVP) German People's Party. Right of center political party during the years of the Weimar Republic.

**deutsche Volkszugehörige.** Belonging to the German people. Individuals considered part of the German people both inside and outside Germany.

**deutsche Waisenkinder.** German orphans. Polish children Nazis considered worthy of being Germanized. *See also* Heu-Aktion; Lebensborn; Ostkinder; Wiedereindeutschung.

**"Deutsche, wehrt euch! Kauft nicht bei Juden!"** "Germans, defend yourselves. Don't buy from Jews." *See also* "Deutsche Männer und Frauen, kauft nicht bei Juden."

*Deutsche Weihnachten, Brauchtum und Feiergestaltung.* German Christmas, Customs, and Celebrations. Hitler Youth handbook that advised youth leaders to omit all stage decorations at the National Socialist winter solstice celebration referring to Christianity. Instead, images of Nordic Germanic and German folklore were to be used indicating loyalty, dedication to the Führer, the spirit of revenge, and the mission of war.

**Deutsche Wirtschaftsbetriebe GmbH.** (DWB) German Economic Enterprises Ltd. Corporation created by the SS Wirtschafts- und Verwaltungshauptamt to coordinate SS economic activities.

*(Die) Deutsche Wochenschau.* The German Weekly. Weekly newsreels produced by the Propaganda Ministry summarizing the events of the previous week for the German audience.

*Deutsche Wochenschau für Politik, Wirtschaft, Kultur und Technik.* German Weekly for Politics, Economy, Culture, and Technology. Published in Berlin from 1935 to 1940, published articles on the Jewish problem.

*Deutsche Zeitung.* German Newspaper. Periodical of the Reich Agricultural Organization. *See also* Reichsnährstand.

**Deutsche Zentrumspartei.** German (Catholic) Center Party. Political party during the Weimar Republic.

**deutschfeindliche Äußerung.** German hostile expression. Any comments made by Jews and Poles concerning Germany. *See also* Verordnung über Strafrechtspflege gegen Polen und Juden in den eingegliederten Ostgebieten.

**Deutschfremdheit.** Being un-German. Friendliness to Jews. *See* Judenfreundlichkeit.

**deutschgesinnt.** German minded. Race conscious.

**deutschgläubig.** Believing in the German (National Socialist) religion. *See also* Deutsche Glaubensbewegung; Deutscher Glaube Kampfring; Gottgläubiger.

**deutschgottgläubig.** *See* gottgläubig.

**Deutschisierung.** Germanization. In Poland and Soviet Russia, it meant removal and probable genocide of natives. In Scandanavia, believed to be already essentially Germanic, it meant a return to German racial identity.

**Deutschland.** Germany. Concept of a German community, a people united by a common blood, race, territory, and ideology.

*Deutschland.* Germany name of German pocket battleship launched in 1933. After the ship was bombed during the Spanish Civil War near Ibiza, it was refitted as a cruiser and renamed *Lützow* in 1939.

**"Deutschland, Deutschland über alles."** *See also* "Deutschlandlied."

**"Deutschland erwache!"** "Wake up, Germany." Nazi song and slogan.

**"Deutschland erwache! Juda verrecke!"** "Germany awake. Destroy the Jews." Antisemitic slogan.

**Deutschlandflug.** Plane ride over Germany. Hitler's sensational fourteen-day propaganda and campaign trip in a Ju52 airplane in 1932, when he visited sixty German cities.

**"Deutschland ist Hitler! Hitler ist Deutschland!"** "Germany is Hitler, Hitler is Germany." Rudolf Hess–led cheering of Hitler before and after his speeches.

**"Deutschlandlied."** Germany Song. Nazi Germany's national anthem, along with the "Horst-Wessel-Lied." "Deutschland, Deutschland über alles/Über alles in der Welt" ("Germany, Germany over everything/Over everything in the world") were its most renowned lyrics. Published in 1841, the words were written by August Heinrich Hoffmann von Fallersleben and set to music from Joseph Haydn's earlier *Emperor Quartet*.

**Deutschland-Pakt.** Germany Pact. Agreement between Hitler and the Reichswehr generals assuring their supremacy over the SA.

**Deutschlandsender.** Germany transmitter. German national radio station, alternative to local radio stations.

**"Deutschland über alles."** *See* "Deutschlandlied."

**Deutschnationaler Handlungsgehilfenverband.** (DHV) German National Trade-Helpers Association.

**Deutschnationale Volkspartei.** (DNVP) The National German People's Party. Rightest Weimar Republic party created from the union of several other political parties: Freikonservative Partei, Deutschkonservative Partei, Deutsche Vaterlandspartei, Alldeutscher Verband, Die Christlichsozialen, and Die Deutschvölkischen. It joined political coalitions with the Nazi Party.

**deutschrechtlich.** According to Germanic (Nazi-German) law. Natural law, right.

**(der) deutschrechtliche Gedanke.** The Germanic (Nazi-German) concept of law. Natural law, right, state structure.

**(der) deutschrechtliche Staatsaufbau.** The Germanic (Nazi-German) concept of the state structure.

**Deutschreligion.** *See* Deutscher Glaube Kampfring.

**Deutsch-Sowjetischer Nichtangriffspakt.** German-Soviet Nonaggression Treaty. August 1939 treaty between Germany and the Soviet Union declaring peace between the two powers, but a secret supplementary protocol divided Poland and other areas of eastern Europe between them.

**Deutsch-Soziale Partei.** German Social Party. Julius Streicher's political party that merged with the Nazi Party in 1922.

**(in das) Deutschtum hineinwachsen.** To grow into being German. Developing into Germans. Some children of mixed Jewish–Aryan German marriages whom the SS wanted to murder but the Ministries of Interior and Justice argued were developing into Germans.

**Deutsch-Vlämische Arbeitsgemeinschaft.** (Devlag) German-Flemish Labor Community. A Belgian collaborationist organization.

**Deutschvolk.** *See* Deutsche Volkskirche.

**Deutsch-Völkische Freiheitspartei.** (DVFP) German People's Freedom Party. Political party associated in the 1920s with the Nazi Party. Ernst Röhm ran for the Reichstag in 1924 representing this party.

**Deutschvölkischer Schutz- und Trutzbund.** German People's Defensive and Offensive Alliance. Largest of the post–World War I antisemitic German veterans' defense leagues of the radical right, engaging in political violence and assassination. They were the group responsible for the murder of the Weimar Republic's Jewish Foreign Minister Walther Rathenau in 1922. Rathenau had headed the War Resources Department of the War Ministry during World War I and although a solidly patriotic German, like the rest of Germany's Jews, was regarded by the Nazis and their allies as part of the so-called Jewish world conspiracy and scapegoated for Germany's defeat.

**Devisengesetze.** Foreign exchange law. Permitted the Nazi authorities to seize Jewish property and give it over to a trust. *See* Grundstücks-Verwaltungsgesellschaft.

**Devlag.** *See* Deutsch-Vlämische Arbeitsgemeinschaft.

**DF.** *See* (Der) Führer.

**DFG.** *See* Deutsche Forschungsgemeinschaft.

**DFW.** *See* Deutsches Frauenwerk.

**DGT.** *See* Deutscher Gemeindetag.

**DHD.** *See* Deutscher Handelsdienst.

**DHL.** *See* Durchgangshaftlager.

**DHV.** *See* Deutschnationaler Handlungsgehilfenverband.

**DHW.** *See* Deutsche Heeres-Werkstätten.

**dicker Paul.** Fat Paul. Nickname for Russian T-32 tank.

**Diebe.** Thieves. Gypsies, Jews, and others considered racially inferior.

**Dienst.** Duty. Obligation to share in the meetings and obey the orders of the Nazi Party.

**"Dienst am Volk tun."** "To serve the nation." Motto and project of the Hitler Youth introduced in 1934 by Reich youth leader Baldur von Schirach to educate the young according to National Socialist ideology. *See also* Heimabend; Staatsjugendtag.

**Dienstanzug.** Service uniform. Uniforms prescribed by army and Party organizations to be worn on different occasions.

**Dienstauszeichnung.** Duty decoration. *See also* Eisernes Kreuz.

**Dienstbücher der Hitlerjugend.** Duty books of the Hitler Youth. Manuals to train the mind and body of the Hitler Youth according to Nazi ideology.

**Dienstdolch.** Service dagger. An accoutrement to the uniform of the SA, SS, NSKK, and the NSFK.

**Dienstrang.** Duty rank. Nazi Party rank.

**Dienststelle.** Government department/office. Bureau, command headquarters, administrative center, office.

**Dienststelle Eichmann.** Eichmann Headquarters. SS agency established March 19, 1944, to expedite the mass murder of the Hungarian Jews.

**Dienststelle Heißmeyer.** Administrative Office Heißmeyer. Serviced SS school system and members of the SS and their families.

**Dienststelle im Auswärtigen Amt.** (DAA) Department in the Foreign Office.

**Dienststelle Ribbentrop.** Ribbentrop Headquarters. *See also* Büro Ribbentrop.

**Diensttauglichkeitsgrade.** Serviceability grading. Individuals divided into five categories for army work.

**dienstverpflichtet, Dienstverpflichtung.** Forced mobilization of workers for the war effort.

**Diet.** Middle-high-German for Volk. Used to create new word formations to emphasize Germanness.

**Dietarbeit.** Maintaining German traditions. Organizing German dances, national celebrations, and so forth. *See also* Diet.

**Dietwart.** Volk guardian. Official responsible for the ideological training of sportsmen. *See also* Diet.

**Dietwesen.** Pertaining to the Volk. Race science, research into German cultural values. *See also* Diet.

**DIKAL-Häftling.** Must-not-be-moved-to-another-camp prisoner. Abbreviation for "darf in kein anderes Lager" posted in the file of a prisoner suspected of having broken out of a camp.

**Diktat.** Ultimatum, demand. Versailles Treaty.

**Diktatfriede.** Dictated peace. Versailles Treaty.

**dinarisch.** One of the six races that allegedly comprise the Germans. Characteristics are large nose, high small face, dark hair, and slender, as well as loving the homeland and being heroic. *See* fälisch; nordisch; ostbaltisch; ostische Rasse; westisch.

**Dirlewanger Sonderbataillon.** Dirlewanger Special Battalion. A troop of German criminals recruited by, and under the command of, SS-Oberführer Oskar Dirlewanger who were assigned to murder Russian civilians claimed to be bandits. Often a code word for Jews, Gypsies, and other civilians.

**Distriktschef.** District Chief. Official in the German General Government.

**Disziplinar- und Strafverordnung.** Disciplining and punishing order. Regulations for severe and brutal punishment of prisoners instituted and supervised at Dachau by camp commandant Theodor Eicke. Prisoners were punished after violating the imposed rules of the camp, such as failing to salute an SS officer; those committing major infractions (e.g., refusing to work) were killed. Such regulations and punishments spread to other camps.

**DIV.** *See* Division.

**Dividendenabgabe.** Surrender of excess profit. *See also* Reichskommissar für die Preisbildung.

**Division.** (DIV) Division. Consisted of one to four regiments and attached units, with 10,000 to 20,000 men. A combat and tactical unit.

**DJ.** *See* Deutsches Jungvolk in der Hitlerjugend.

**D-Lager.** *See* Durchgangslager.

**DLV.** *See* Deutscher Luftsportsverband.

**DNB, dnb.** *See* Deutsches Nachrichtenbüro.

**DNSAP.** *See* Deutsche Nationalsozialistische Arbeiterpartei in der Tschechoslowakei.

**DNVP.** *See* Deutschnationale Volkspartei.

**(der) Doktor.** (The) doctor. Ironic for the chief stoker assigned to the crematoria to smash with an iron pipe the skulls of the near-dead unloaded from a newly arrived trainload of prisoners.

**Dolchstoß.** Stab in the back. Myth that claimed the German military had not been defeated by the western Allies in World War I, but that the Germans had been betrayed by Jews, socialists, and liberals who forced them to surrender.

**Dolchstoßlegende.** The stab-in-the-back myth. *See also* Dolchstoß.

**dolmetscher.** Interpreter. Prisoner interpretation of SS orders, or slang for the club the SS applied to the prisoners' bodies.

**Donau.** Danube (River). German army division.

**Donau- und Monte-Rosa-Aktion.** The Danube and Mount Rose Operation. Norwegian Jewish women and children arrested and sent aboard two ships, the *Donau* and the *Monte Rosa*, to slave labor or death at Auschwitz.

**Doppelverdiener.** Double-income earners. Negative description of German working couples until women were needed in the workforce for the war effort.

**Dora.** Dora. Code name for the collection of art works hidden in a salt mine near Salzburg.

**Dora-Mittelbau.** A satellite camp of Buchenwald located near Nordhausen, Germany, housing inmates used as slave laborers who assembled rockets. Other satellite camps were Dora, Laura, and S III. *See* Nordhausen.

**Dora/Nordhausen.** *See* Nordhausen.

**Dorfdreieck.** Village triangle. Consisted of the mayor, the local Nazi Party representative, and the Ortsbauernführer.

**Dorfsippenbuch.** Village clan book. From 1938, family registry in a village to establish ancestry.

**Dozentenschaftsleiter.** Director of University Professors and Assistants. Responsible to the university rector and often university leader of the National Socialist Association for University Professors.

**d. R.** *See* (der) Reserve.

**DR.** *See* Deutsches Recht.

**Draht.** Wire. Referring to the electrified wire surrounding the camps. "Sprung in den Draht" ("jumped on the wire") meant committed suicide.

**Drahtamsel.** Blackbird on a wire. Derogatory for female communication help. *See also* Nachrichtenhelferin.

**Drahtfunk.** Wire transmission. Radio broadcast via telephone cable to warn against air raids. *See* Luftmeldungen.

**Drahtglas.** Glass reinforced with wire. *See* Kölner Glas.

**Drahtgemeinschaft.** Wire cartel. *See also* Reichsvereinigung.

**Drahtverhau.** Wire barrier. Barbed wire around concentration camps.

**Drancy.** The largest camp for the deportation of Jews from France, located near Paris. Between July 1942 and August 1944, 61,000 Jews passed through on their way to Auschwitz.

**dränen.** To drain.

**Drang nach Osten.** Drive toward the east. Traditional German notion that conquest and expansion lies to the east.

**Dreckjude.** Filthy (shit) Jew. Common antisemitic insult.

**Dreckschwein.** Filthy (shit) pig. Swearword applied to men and women imprisoned at the camps.

**(gelbes) Dreieck.** Yellow triangle. Patch indicating Jewish prisoner. *See also* Dreieckswinkel.

**Dreiecksgeschäft.** Triangle business. Advantageous business exchange via a third party.

**Dreieckswinkel.** Triangle. Patch located on the left side of the chest of prisoners in the concentration camps. Identification was indicated by color, numbers, and letters. The lower the number, the more senior the prisoner. Letters printed in the center of the triangles indicated: T for Czech, N for Dutch, I for Italian, A for Aktionshäftlinge (political activists), K for Kriegsverbrecher (war criminal), S for Schwerverbrecher (serious offender), D for German, F for French, and so on. Political opponents wore a red triangle pointing downward, German emigrants a blue triangle, and race defilers who were Jews wore a black stripe above their yellow triangle. Prisoners under special surveillance wore a red circle badge with a dot in the middle. Wehrmacht prisoners wore a red triangle pointing upward. Common criminals wore green triangles; homosexuals pink; asocials, or prostitutes, perverts, and Gypsies black or brown; priests and Jehovah's Witnesses violet; and Jews yellow. The Jewish yellow triangle pointed upward.

**Dreierausschuß.** Committee of Three. Short-lived attempt to coordinate decision making in the Third Reich in 1943. A committee comprised of the heads of the three main executive arms of Hitler's authority: Field Marshal Wilhelm Keitel, Head of the Wehrmacht's High Command; Hans Lammers, Head of the Reich Chancellery; and Martin Bormann, Head of the Nazi Party Chancellery.

**Dreierkollegium.** Three-Man Collective. An executive committee that failed to speed up the cumbersome legislative process of the Third Reich: Wilhelm Frick, Minister of the Interior; Walther Funk, Plenipotentiary for the War Economy; and Wilhelm Keitel, Chief of the High Command of the Wehrmacht.

**Dreierpakt.** Tripartite Pact. Alliance of Germany, Italy, and Japan.

**Dreimächtepakt.** Three-Power Pact. *See also* Dreierpakt.

**Drei-Säulen-Theorie.** Three-Prong Theory. Nazi plan to educate German youth through the collaboration of three institutions: parents, schools, and Hitler Youth, the latter the most important.

**Dreißigjähriger Krieg.** Thirty-Years War. German language period from 1618 to 1648. *See also* Deutsche Sprache.

**Dresden.** German city. German Army division.

**(Von) Drinnen und Draußen.** From Inside and Outside. 1936 school primer containing traditional material of folk songs, tales, and so forth, and from 1939, more images of Hitler Youth, May Day parades, solstice celebrations, and so forth related to everyday Third Reich experience of children. *See* Appendix.

**Drittelsbrot.** Three-part bread. Bread made of wheat, rye, and barley.

**(das) Dritte Reich.** *See* Drittes Reich.

**drittes Lager im Ausland.** Third camp outside (of Germany). Kovno, Lithuania, fortresses where thousands of European Jews were murdered.

**Drittes Reich.** Third Reich. Nazi designation of Germany and its regime from 1933 to 1945. Historically, the First Reich was the medieval Holy Roman Empire of the German nation which lasted from 962 until 1806. The Second Reich, led by the Hohenzollern, was the German Reich from 1871 to 1918. The Weimar Republic was considered an In-Between Reich (1918–1933).

**DRL.** *See* Deutscher Reichsbund für Leibesübungen.

**Drückebergerbasis der Totenkopf-Elite.** Shirker base of the death's-head elite. Ironic, base of the elite Death's-Head Units.

**Drückebergergäßchen.** Shirker street. Viscardi Street in Munich where people avoided offering the Hitler salute to two SS guards flanking the monument for those who died during the November revolt. *See also* Ehrentempel; Hitler-Putsch.

**Druckfallkrankheit.** Compression-dive sickness. Military slang for the bends.

**DStP.** *See* Deutsche Staatspartei.

**d.u.** *See* dauernd dienstuntauglich.

**"Du bist nichts, dein Volk ist alles!"** "You are nothing; your people is everything." Propaganda slogan to convince people to believe in the community rather than the individual. Especially directed at schoolgirls.

**(der) Duce.** The Leader. Name for Italian dictator Benito Mussolini.

**Duellieren.** Dueling. From 1935, Himmler declared that every SS man had the right and duty to defend himself and his honor.

**Dulag.** (Durchgangslager) Transit camps.

**Dünger aus ihnen machen.** To make manure, fertilizer, out of them. Sarcastic threat to murder Jews.

**Düppel.** Chaff. Metal strips dumped by Allied war planes to interfere with German radar signals; first used over Hamburg in 1943. *See also* Lametta.

**Durchbruch.** Breakthrough. Euphoric for each turn of the war for the better for Germany.

**durchführen.** To execute, to bring to an end, to follow through, to enforce. A favorite bureaucratic word meaning to see that something is done.

**(zur) Durchführung bringen.** To take to a conclusion. *See also* durchführen.

**Durchgangshaftlager.** (DHL) Transit prison camp.

**Durchgangsjuden.** Jews in transit. Jews not listed in the Auschwitz camp registry. Generally they were murdered upon arrival.

**Durchgangslager.** (D-Lager, DL, Dulag) Transit camp.

**Durchgangslager für Juden.** Transit camp for Jews. Hitler saw all of Poland as a Jewish transit camp (i.e., Jews only temporarily residing there, alive).

**durchgeschleust.** Funneled or flushed through. New euphemism used on Himmler's orders from 1943 to replace getötet, abgeschossen, and euphemisms for murdered. *See* Sonderbehandlung.

**durchgreifen.** To act with rigor. To take drastic steps, for example, September 1941 order of OKW Chef Field Marshal Wilhelm Keitel to murder Jews as the main carriers of Bolshevism.

**Durchhalteappelle.** Appeals to hold out. Propaganda campaign toward the end of the war asking the German people to stick it out, not to give up fighting for Hitler and Germany.

**durchleuchten.** To x-ray, to floodlight. To round up Jews in order to murder them.

**Durchstoß.** Break through. Piercing of enemy lines.

**Dusche.** Shower. Disguised gas chamber.

**DUT.** *See* Deutsche Umsiedlungs-Treuhand-GmbH.

**DVFP.** *See* Deutsch-Völkische Freiheitspartei.

**DVP.** *See* Deutsche Volkspartei.

**DVL.** *See* Deutsche Volksliste.

**DW.** *See Deutscher Wochendienst.*

**DWB.** *See* Deutsche Wirtschaftsbetriebe GmbH.

**Dynamik, dynamisch, Dynamismus.** Dynamic. In National Socialism, ultra-forceful. According to Alfred Rosenberg, a positive characteristic of Germans.

**D II.** Auschwitz medical office overseeing camp doctors, who selected prisoners for experiments and murder.

# E

**E.** *See* Elt.

**E.** *See* exekutiert.

**ebenbürtig.** Of equal birth. Racially equal; that is, German; prerequisite for a German couple to marry.

**echtbürtig.** Pure from birth. Of truly German stock.

**Edelweißpiraten.** Edelweiß (mountain flower) pirates. German working-class youth gangs who, in the 1930s, refused to join the Hitlerjugend and rejected National Socialism. In 1944 they were joined by deserters, some foreign workers, and German Communists especially in Cologne to form a short-lived resistance that attacked Nazi Party and Hitler Youth members as well as police. The Gestapo and Wehrmacht soon destroyed this insurrection.

**Edul.** Military term for counterclockwise.

**Effektenkammer.** Movable properties room. The warehouse in a concentration camp where precious metals, jewelry, foreign currency, and other valuables taken from the inmates were kept.

**Effektenkammerkommando.** Movable-properties room unit. *See also* Effektenkammer.

**Effektenlager.** Properties camp. Lager Kanada at Auschwitz II. *See also* Kanada.

**Ehe.** Marriage. From 1938, this basis of German family life and legal institution was devoted to the perpetuation of a healthy nation. *See also* Gesetz zum Schutze der Erbgesundheit des deutschen Volkes.

**Ehegesundheitsgesetz.** Marriage-health law. *See also* Ehetauglichkeitszeugnis; Gesetz zum Schutze der Erbgesundheit des deutschen Volkes.

**Ehehindernis.** Impediment to marriage. The Nuremberg Laws forbade marriages between Christians and Jews.

**Eheordnung.** Marriage regulation. SS marital code.

**Eherne Romantik.** Iron romanticism. Concept of Alfred Rosenberg describing archaic foundations of culture and obsolete forms of community.

**Eher-Verlag.** Eher Publishers. Nazi publishing house (1925–1945).

**Ehestandsdarlehen.** Marriage loans. State-supported loans for marriage between German-blooded pairs free from hereditary diseases.

**Ehestandshilfe.** Marriage help. From 1933, money collected for and from un-married working Germans that was applied to a marriage credit for engaged cou-ples to encourage their marriage and to assist them in establishing a household.

**ehetauglich.** Suited for marriage. Having the legal right to marry after obtaining an official document. *See also* Ehetauglichkeitszeugnis.

**Ehetauglichkeitszeugnis.** Certificate attesting to the suitability of a marriage. Document stating that, according to the Ehegesundheitsgesetz, two Germans en-tering marriage had no hereditary disease and no Jewish, Black, or Gypsy blood that would prevent a union between them.

**Eheweihe.** Marriage sanctification. SS ceremony instead of a church wedding. *See also* Heiratsbefehl.

**EHFV.** *See* Erbhoffortbildungsverordnung.

**Ehre.** Honor, glory. National honor, glory. *See also* "Meine Ehre heißt (meine) Treue."

**"Ehre kann nur mit Blut gewaschen werden."** "Honor can only be redeemed with blood." 1937 Hitler statement after German aerial bombing during the Span-ish Civil War.

**Ehrenarier.** Honorary Aryan. Early Nazi Party Jewish members. Later, individual Jews protected by high SS officials.

**Ehrenbuch für die deutsche kinderreiche Familie.** Honor book for the Ger-man multiple-child family. Identification card used by families with several chil-dren to obtain subsistance privileges.

**Ehrendegen des Reichsführer SS.** Honorary épée. SS dagger bestowed by Himmler on SS individuals from the rank of Untersturmführer on, to elevate them above those privileged to wear the SS ring with the deaths-head insignia.

**Ehrendienst am deutschen Volk.** Honorary service for the German people. Obligatory civil and military duty for Germans.

**Ehrenführer.** Honorary Leader. Title granted by Himmler to leading Nazis, equivalent to an SS general.

**Ehrengericht.** Honor Court. Military court of senior generals. Hitler ordered this court to try those military officers involved in the July 1944 plot to kill him and to expel them in disgrace from the armed forces before being handed over to the People's Court for trial. *See also* 20. Juli.

**Ehrenkarte für kinderreiche deutsche Mütter.** Honor card for multiple-child German mothers. Restricted to families with German blood, mental competence, and hereditary health.

**Ehrenkreuz.** Honorary cross. Award established in 1934 for front-line soldiers, participants in World War I, and family members of those who had been killed in World War I.

**Ehrenkreuz der deutschen Mutter.** Honorary cross of the German mother. Medal established in 1938 that encouraged German women to have children. The medal went to women with four or more children and was gold, silver, or bronze depending on the number of children. These mothers were considered as important to the war effort as a soldier in battle, as guardians of the future of the German people.

**Ehrenkreuz für Hinterbliebene deutscher Spanienkämpfer.** Honorary cross for surviving dependants of German fighters in Spain. Medal instituted in 1939 to honor relatives of German soldiers who lost their lives in the Spanish Civil War of 1936–1939.

**Ehrenliste.** Honor list. List of those murdered by political opponents of the Third Reich.

**Ehrensold.** Honor pay. Pensions for German war widows, war wounded, and those crippled by industrial accident under the Thrid Reich.

**Ehrentempel.** Honor temple. Two memorials built at the Königsplatz in Munich commemorating the Hitler Putsch of 1923 and annually drawing thousands of visitors for ceremonies on November 9. *See also* Ewige Wache.

**Ehrenunterstützung.** Honorary support. From 1935, financial support for those Party members who had been disabled while struggling for the cause of National Socialism.

**ehrenvolle Erwähnung des Totenkopfrings der SS.** Citation accompanying the SS death's head ring. *See also* SS-Totenkopfring.

**ehrenwürdiger Kontinent.** Honorable continent. Respectful term for Europe.

**Ehrenzeichen des 9. November 1923.** Medal of November 9, 1923. *See also* Blutorden.

**Ehrenzeichen für deutsche Volkspflege.** Medal for German care of the Volk. Instituted in 1939 and substitute for the Red Cross medal.

**"Ehrlich währt am längsten."** "Honesty is the best policy." German saying carved into the cross beams of barracks at Auschwitz.

**EHRV.** *See* Erbhofrechtsverfahrensordnung; Erbhofrechtsverordnung.

**EHW.** *See* Ernährungshilfswerk.

**Eiche.** Oak. Code name for operation that freed Italian Dictator Benito Mussolini in September 1943, performed by SS paratroopers led by Otto Skorzeny.

**Eichenlaubträger.** Oak leaves dignitary. Person with the Knight's Cross with oak leaves. *See also* Ritterkreuz.

**Eif-Rune.** Rune that symbolized eagerness and enthusiasm. Early on, it represented Hitler's aides.

**Eigenfinanzierung.** Personal financing. War credit with company money.

**Eigengesetzlichkeit.** Determined by inner law. Germanization of Autarchie (autonomy).

**Eigenleben.** Life of one's own. Early Nazi promise that Jews could live in Germany outside of society.

**eigenständig.** Independent. Standing on one's own feet, independent. Old German word that the Nazis used to describe the self-reliance of the German people.

**Eignungsauslese.** Suitability selection. Selection in the military on the basis of aptitude testing.

**Eignungsprüfer.** Suitability testers. Specialists from the Main Office for Race and Settlement of the SS and/or health department doctors who tested Polish children to determine their racial worthiness for Germanization. They checked dozens of points as to the child's physique, shape, eye color, type of hair, and so on. Then, it was determined whether the child was desirable for natural reproduction, tolerable, or undesirable. The first two categories were psychologically and morally tested and, if passed, the child was Germanized. The undesirable children were often sterilized if one parent was Jewish or sent to concentration camps. *See* Wiedereindeutschung.

**Eilbeck-Kamaraden.** Comrades of Eilbeck. Anti-Nazi underground group formed by Social Democrats at Eilbeck, Hamburg. Active in the mid-1930s.

**Eimer.** Bucket. Navy slang for ship.

**einbauen.** To insert, build in. A form of military defense by means of circular attack.

**Einbaum.** (From a) single tree. Colloquial for a coastal submarine.

**Einbruch.** Break through. Enemy offensive breaking through the German Front.

**Eindeutschung.** Germanization. The incorporation of Slavs, who the Nazis believed possessed Aryan racial characteristics, into Germany. Those deemed unfit to belong were expelled and/or murdered. *See also* Deutsche Heimschulen; Eignungs-prüfer; Heu-Aktion; Lebensborn; Ostkinder; Wiedereindeutschung.

**eindeutschungsfähige Kinder.** Children suitable for Germanization. *See also* Deutsche Heimschulen; Heu-Aktion; Lebensborn; Ostkinder; Wiedereindeutschung.

**Eindeutschungsfähigkeit.** Germanization worthiness. Race appraisal of foreign-ers as a prerequisite for Eindeutschung.

**"Eine Laus, dein Tod!"** "One louse, your death." Antisemitic slogan referring to the Nazi-fostered filthy conditions in the ghettos and concentration camps. Lice spread deadly typhus.

**"Einer für alle, alle für einen."** "One for all, all for one." Nazi slogan to strengthen the German nation. Also, an inscription on several concentration camp entrance gates.

**eingegliederte Ostgebiete.** Incorporated eastern territories. The westernmost part of Poland absorbed into the Third Reich in October 1939.

**Eingliederung.** Integration. Partial annexation to the Reich: Alsace, Lorraine, Luxembourg, and so forth.

**Eingreiftruppen.** Reserve troops.

**Einheit.** Unit. Engineers' troop. *See also* Organisation Todt.

**Einheitserzeugung.** Unified production. Standardized production.

**Einheitsfront.** Unified front. Unity of all Germans according to Nazi ideology.

**Einheitsgericht.** Standard meal. *See also* Stammgericht.

**Einheitsmunition.** Standard ammunition. Standard ammunition supplied in magazines to the Wehrmacht.

**Einheitspreisgeschäft.** Department store that sold merchandise at regulated prices. A 1933 law disallowed this practice in favor of small business.

**Einheitsstaat.** Unified state. Germany under Nazi Party centralized control after the elimination of parliament and the rights of the German states in 1933.

**Einheit von Partei und Staat.** Unity of (Nazi) Party and state. Dissolution of all parties except the NSDAP as the single legal party in Germany.

**175er.** A male homosexual. Homosexual inmate. Called after the paragraph in the German law that made (male) homosexuality criminal. The law remained in effect from the late nineteenth century to the late twentieth century. Also, concentration camp inmate identified as homosexual.

**186.** The number of stairs in the Wienergraben quarry at Mauthausen concentra-tion camp in Austria.

**einmalig.** Unique. Applied to German government and military achievements instead of "great."

**Einmannloch.** One-man hole. Individual foxholes, spread apart, to protect a single soldier from air raids.

**Einmann-U-Boot.** One-man submarine. Miniature submarines operated by one man that carried only one torpedo and had a limited firing range.

**Einmischung.** Intervention. Racial proportion, mixture.

**Einrichtungsdarlehen.** Start-up credit. *See also* Ehestandshilfe.

**einrücken.** To move in. Return to the labor camp.

**Eins A.** A one. *See also* Stabsoffizier.

**Eins-A Abteilung.** Branch 1-A. Prussian police department for special investigations transformed into the Gestapo in 1933.

**Eins B.** B one. *See also* Versorgungsoffizier.

**Eins-C Dienst.** Office 1-C. Early name for the SD, which came from its office number.

**Einsager.** Germanized for Sauffluer (theater prompter).

**Einsatz.** Commitment, employment. Operation, deployment, action, mission, attack, mobilization, effort, cooperation, initiative.

**(besonderer) Einsatz.** Special commitment. Active duty, special task mass murder.

**Einsatzbereitschaft.** Readiness for service. The courage and willpower the individual German needed to develop obedience and sacrifice for people and country.

**Einsatz Bernhard.** Operation Bernhard. Operation of RSHA Office 6F4a to forge English banknotes.

**einsatzfähig/einsatzunfähig.** Fit/unfit for service. Jews in ghettos were listed as fit or unfit for work. The unfit were to be murdered on the spot or sent to a death camp.

**Einsatzgruppen.** (EG) Special Task Groups. Mobile SS killing units that accompanied German troops when they invaded Poland in 1939 and Russia in 1941. Their operations continued throughout the war. These battalion-size units, subdivided into Sonderkommandos and Einsatzkommandos, consisted of Sicherheitspolizei or SIPO (KRIPO or Kriminalpolizei, and Gestapo) and Sicherheitsdienst or SS agents to attack and murder Nazi enemies in conquered territories. Their charge was to kill all officials of the Commintern and Communist politicians; Jews in party and state employment; and radical elements, such as saboteurs, propagandists, snipers, assassins, inciters, and so forth. A follow-up order of October 12, 1941, indicated the principal targets of execution would be political functionaries, Jews mistakenly released from POW camps, Jewish "sadists and avengers," and "Jews in general." Many German army units, German Order Police, and auxiliaries

(Ukrainian, Latvian, Lithuanian, and Estonian Hiwis) collaborated in these mass murders. Many German army units had also collaborated to mistreat and murder Poles and Jews in the 1939 campaign, a prelude and training ground for the mass murder of Russians and genocide of Jews in the Russian campaign. The military war in the east and the Holocaust of Jews were inextricably mixed, as was the relationship between the Einsatzgruppen and the Wehrmacht.

The victims were executed by mass shootings and buried in unmarked mass graves; later, the bodies were dug up and burned to cover the evidence of what had occurred (*see* Kommando 1005.) Between one and two million Jews were killed in this manner. There were six Einsatzgruppen (I–VI) at work in the Polish campaign. In Russia there were four (A–D). Einsatzgruppe A, commanded by Franz Stahlecker, operated in the Baltic area and murdered approximately 250,000 men, women, and children. Einsatzgruppe B, commanded by Arthur Nebe, operated in Belorussia and Russia and murdered 70,000. Einsatzgruppe C, commanded by Emil Rausch, operated in northern and central Ukraine and murdered 150,000. Einsatzgruppe D, commanded by Otto Ohlendorf, operated in the southern Ukraine and Crimea and murdered 90,000. The leadership consisted of men who had been well-educated professionals in their civilian lives.

Later, more Einsatzgruppen were formed to murder Jews in Greece, Rumania, Slovakia, and especially Hungary (*see* Sondereinsatzkommando Eichmann).

Each Einsatzgruppe was approximately battalion strength and was comprised of a variety of personnel. In October 1941, for example, Einsatzgruppe A was made up as follows: Administration, 18; Auxiliary Police, 87; Female Aids, 13; Gestapo, 89; Interpreters, 51; Kriminalpolizei, 41; Motorcyclists, 172; Ordnungspolizei, 133; Radio Operators, 8; Sicherheitsdienst, 35; Teletype Operators, 3; and Waffen-SS, 340. A slightly different analysis of Einsatzgruppe A indicates that 9 percent were Gestapo men, 3.5 percent SD, 4.1 percent Kripo, 13.4 percent Ordnungspolizei, 8.8 percent foreign auxiliary police, and 34 percent Waffen-SS, the rest were technical personnel and clerks. In 1941, at the start of Operation Barbarossa, the total strength of the Einsatzgruppen was approximately 3,000. The number of personnel in each Einsatzgruppe varied (e.g., Einsatzgruppe A, 990; Einsatzgruppe D, 500). Each Einsatzgruppe was divided into Einsatzkommandos or Sonderkommandos of about 70–120 men, each attached to an army unit, and further divided into subcommandos of about twenty to thirty. But as the war progressed Eisatzgruppen numbers grew considerably.

**Einsatzgruppen der Sicherheitspolizei und des SD.** Special operations groups of the security police and of the security service of the SS. *See also* Einsatzgruppen.

**Einsatzgruppe z.b.V.** *See* Einsatzgruppe z.b.V. für das oberschlesische Industrialgebiet.

**Einsatzgruppe z.b.V. für das oberschlesische Industrialgebiet.** (Einsatzgruppe z.b.V.) Special-Purpose Operational Group in the Upper Silesian Industrial Area. Established by order of Hitler on September 3, 1939, SS and police unit headed by Lieutenant General (Obergruppenführer) Udo von Woyrsch operating in Silesia and Galicia under Himmler's special orders. In September and October 1939, this unit murdered unknown numbers of Jewish men, women, and children and Polish hostages. *See* Aktion Tannenberg; Sonderfahndungsbuch.

**Einsatzgruppe zur besonderen Verwendung.** *See* Einsatzgruppe z.b.V. für das oberschlesische Industrialgebiet.

**"Einsatz ist Leistung."** "Application makes for efficiency." Slogan.

**Einsatzkommando.** (EK) Task Force. Company-size component of the Einsatzgruppen. *See also* Einsatzgruppen.

**Einsatzkommando der Sicherheitspolizei und des SD.** Special Operations Detachment of the Security Police and of the Security Service of the SS. *See also* Einsatzkommando.

**Einsatz Otto.** Operation Otto. Improving rail lines using mostly Jews as slave workers in the Generalgouvernement in anticipation of the attack on the Soviet Union.

**Einsatz Reinhard.** *See* Aktion Reinhard.

**Einsatzstab Reichsleiter Rosenberg für die Besetzten Gebiete.** (ERR) Special Operation Staff of Reich Leader Rosenberg for the Occupied Areas. Organization created by Alfred Rosenberg to plunder the cultural and artistic treasures in occupied nations, especially from Jews.

**Einsatzstab Rosenberg.** *See* Einsatzstab Reichsleiter Rosenberg für die Besetzten Gebiete.

**Einsatztrupp.** Special Squad. Smallest unit of the Einsatzgruppen.

**einschalten.** To insert. To include Jews as slaves/forced laborers in the German workforce.

**Einschlag.** Mixture. Mixed race, coming from impure blood.

**einschrecken.** To silence by terror.

**einsiedeln.** To settle in. To force Jews to live in a ghetto.

**Eintopf.** One-pot meal. *See also* Eintopfessen.

**"Eintopf, das Opferessen des Reiches."** "A one-pot meal, the sacrificial meal for the Reich." Slogan on propaganda posters. *See also* Eintopfsonntag.

**Eintopfessen.** One-pot meal. A one-course dish consisting of a thick vegetable stew or soup with little or no meat to conserve food, and especially meat. Became the meal of individual sacrifice for the country. *See also* Eintopfsonntag.

**Eintopfsonntag.** One-pot meal Sunday. To show solidarity with the poor, from 1933, every second Sunday of the months of October through March was reserved for these types of meals in German homes and restaurants. A one-pot meal implied a simple, inexpensive meal. A neighborhood warden, Blockwart, came to homes to check that families upheld this practice. Money thus saved was collected and donated to the Winterhilfswerk. House inspectors ensured compliance. *See* Eintopfspende.

**Eintopfspende.** One-pot meal collection. Door-to-door money collection on the Sundays of the one-pot meal. *See also* Nationalsozialistische Volksfahrt; Winterhilfswerk des deutschen Volkes.

**"Ein Volk, ein Reich, ein Führer."** *See* "(Ein) Volk, ein Reich, ein Führer."

**einwaggonieren.** To put into railroad cars. To load Jews into cattle cars and/or freight trains for deportation to concentration camps.

**Einwandererzentralstelle.** *See* Einwanderungszentralstelle.

**Einwanderungszentralstelle.** (EWZ) Central Immigration Office. Established in 1939 and directed by Reinhard Heydrich, this organization dealt with dispossessing and murdering Jews and non-Jewish Poles and using their property for Volksdeutsche. *See also* "Heim ins Reich"; Umwandererzentralstelle.

**Einweisungslager.** Holding camp. Bergen-Belsen concentration camp for Polish and Hungarian Jewish women.

**Einwohnerwehr.** Civil guards. Anti-Bolshevik civilian volunteer paramilitary forces active in German cities after World War I.

**Einzelaktionen.** Individual actions. Arbitary individual attacks on German Jews in the 1930s. Nazi leadership feared the outside world would react negatively.

**Einzeldienst.** Individual service. Order police in precinct duty.

**Einziehung.** Confiscation. Property of Polish Jews was subject to confiscation.

**Eisbeinorden.** Frozen-bone (pig-knuckle) medal. One of thirty-two army slang words for military decorations earned while fighting on the Eastern Front in Russia in freezing temperatures in 1941–1942. *See also* Ost-Medaille.

**Eisengeld.** Iron money. *See also* Scheck.

**Eisenschein.** Iron bill, certificate. *See also* Scheck.

**(der) Eiserne.** The Iron One. Reference to Göring and his iron will.

**Eiserne Faust.** Iron Fist. Munich right-wing political association where Hitler met Ernst Röhm.

**Eiserne Front.** Iron Front. Socialist-led anti-Nazi coalition consisting of the Socialist Party, trade unions, and Reichsbann. *See* Reichsbanner Schwarz-Rot-Gold.

**Eisernes Kreuz.** (EK) Iron Cross. Traditional German military decoration for heroism. Three levels: second class, first class, and grand class.

**eisernes Sparen.** Iron saving. Compulsory saving for all workers from 1941 on to control buying power. The money thus collected by the government was to be repaid with interest after the war.

**(auf) Eis legen.** To keep on ice. Hold Jews for possible exchange.

**Eiterbeule des Deutschen Reiches.** Abscess of the German Reich. Name for Berlin during the time of Hitler's struggle (i.e., before his coming to power). *See also* Kampfzeit.

**EK.** *See* Einsatzkommando; Eisernes Kreuz.

**elastisch.** Elastic. Euphemism for retreat of the German army in Russia after the defeat at Stalingrad. *See also* Einbruch.

**Elbe.** German river. Code name for delay of offensive in the west during the early months of World War II. *See also* Augsburg.

**Elemente.** Elements. Derisive for Hitler's enemies.

**Elt.** (E) Electricity.

**Eltwerk, Elektrizitätswerk.** Power station.

**Emigranten.** Émigrés, emigrants. Concentration camp inmates consisting of Germans who had left Germany and then returned. Identified by a blue triangle. *See also* Dreieckswinkel.

**Emil.** Air force slang for pilot.

**Emsland-Lager.** Moor camps. A chain of fifteen concentration camps opened in 1933 and closed in 1936, located close to the Dutch border, initially containing about 4,000 political prisoners. The best-known camps were Börgermoor and Esterwegen. From 1939 to 1945, these camps were used for prisoners of war from the Soviet Union, Italy, and France; in 1944–1945, the Emsland camps became satellites of Neuengamme concentration camp, with a total of 80,000 prisoners.

**Endausleselager.** Final selection camps. *See also* Adolf-Hitler-Schulen.

**Endausleselehrgang.** Final selection course. Selection camp course for candidates for Adolf Hitler schools. *See also* Adolf-Hitler-Schulen.

**endgültige Lösung der Judenfrage.** Ultimate solution of the Jewish problem. *See also* Endlösung der Judenfrage.

**Endkampf.** Final battle. In Nazi ideology, climactic battle between Aryans and Jews late in the Holocaust.

**Endlager.** Final camp. False Nazi propaganda that from Theresienstadt there would be no further deportation of prisoners to Polish death camps.

**Endlösung der Judenfrage.** Final solution of the Jewish (question) problem. As discussed and recorded in the minutes of the Wannsee Conference of January 20,

1942, and elsewhere, the Nazi program to kill every Jew in Europe, even if risking losing World War II. From 1941, the Reich government euphemism for systematic mass murders in eastern Europe by special-action squads and systematic deportation of Jews to ghettos (where hundreds of thousands died) and to concentration camps (where millions were killed through forced labor, mistreatment, torture, and poison gassings). The destruction of the European Jews has similarities with earlier pogroms and mass murders of Jews and others, and the Nazi program to "solve" the Jewish problem paralleled the suggestions of Martin Luther in 1543. But the "Final Solution" is the only example in history in which every single individual (Jew) was sentenced to death for the crime of having been born; in which all (Jews) were to be murdered wherever German influence was decisive, ultimately across the entire world; in which (Jewish) prisoners were murdered even when it damaged the German war effort. *See also* Einsatzgruppen; judenrein; Konzentrationslager; Wannsee-Konferenz.

**(der) Endlösung zuführen.** To lead to the "Final Solution." To transport Jews from ghettos to death camps. *See* Transport; Umsiedlung.

**Endsieg.** Final victory. The objective of fighting World War II and committing the mass murder of Jews. Especially in the last year of the war, the word was used as a propaganda tool to stir the German people to resistance.

**Endziel.** Final objective. The National Socialist goal of eliminating the Jewish people by all means at their disposal. *See also* Endlösung.

**England-Hilfe.** England help. United States lend-lease program.

**Engpaß.** Bottleneck, shortage, squeeze. Economic crisis or depression; also used to describe military setbacks during World War II.

**Engpaß-Kommissionen.** (Labor) shortage commissions. Groups established by Fritz Todt, Reich Minister of Armaments and Munitions, in each armed forces district to allocate labor to war industry and the armed forces.

**ENIGMA.** Code machine adopted by the German armed forces in the 1920s and 1930s. The system encrypted and decrypted messages, but the code was broken by the Allies during the war.

**entarten.** *See* entartet.

**entartet.** Degenerate, alien. Racially corrupted. Anything and anybody not in accord with the Nordic ideal of culture and morals.

**entartete Kunst.** Degenerate, alien art. Art that Hitler determined was decadent and subversive, and he did not like. Modern, avant-garde, so-called Jewish art. Among the artists categorized here were Picasso, Chagall, Otto Dix, Franz Marc, Klee, Beckmann, Grosz, and Kollwitz. In the broadest sense, this forbidden category also included works of art in music, literature, theater, film, and architecture.

**entartete Musik.** Degenerate, alien music. Music that was considered non-German (e.g., Jazz, modern music, and music composed by Jews). *See* artfremd.

**(geschlechtlich) Entartete.** Sexual deviants. Persons accused of a sexual crime (e.g., homosexuals, individuals violating the German race laws).

**Entartung.** Deviation, degeneration. Cultural corruption of peoples and individuals and art due to racial mixing and ethical and moral decay, in particular, applied to Germany.

**Entdeutschung.** Degermanization. Elimination of Germanic elements. According to Hitler, the Habsburgs were responsible for this negative development in Austria.

**Ente.** Duck. Army slang for dud shell.

**Enteignung.** Expropriation. Confiscation of property of enemies of the German state and people, based on laws passed against Communists and Social Democrats in 1933. By contrast, the takeover of Jewish property was considered Aryanization.

**Enterdungsaktion.** Disinterment operation. *See also* Kommando 1005; Sonderkommando 1005.

**Enterdungskommando.** *See* Kommando 1005.

**Entetauchen.** Duck dive. Navy slang for emergency submarine dive.

**Entfallgebiet.** Designated area. Locations in which recyclable materials were collected.

**Entfeinerung.** Decreased finishing. From 1943, elimination of the last step in the finishing process of a product to save on manufacturing time.

**Entgiftung.** Decontamination.

**Enthebungstyp.** *See Rasse und Seele.*

**Entjudung.** Dejudaization, freeing from Jewish influence, removal of Jews. The goal of Nazi antisemitism in the short term was the removal of Jews and so-called Jewish influence from German social, professional, and economic life, and the seizure, sale, and removal from Jews of their businesses and assets. In the long term, it was the removal of Jews from Europe and from life itself.

**entlassen.** To dismiss. To murder Jews.

**entlaust.** Deloused. An area permanently free of Jews.

**Entlausungsaktion.** Disinfection operation. To transfer prisoners to the gas chambers.

**Entlausungsstation.** Disinfection station. Special barracks designated to disinfect prisoner clothing in order to combat typhus epidemics, since such epidemics could potentially also spread to SS guard personnel.

**entnorden, Entnordung.** To de-Nordify. To decrease the Nordic element through negative impact of alien blood. *See also* Entrassung.

**Entpflichtung.** Discharge from civil or military duty.

**Entpolnisierung.** Depolonization. Clearing Poland of racially alien Poles and Jews by all means, including slave labor and mass murder.

**entrahmte Frischmilch.** Skim milk. On the market from 1939; purchaser had to be on a customer list.

**entrasst.** *See* Entrassung.

**Entrassung.** Degeneration, diminishment of the Nordic race. Decline in personal performance due to the loss or dissolution of racial characteristics.

**Entrümpelung.** Cleaning out. To free the attic of every house of unwanted and useless items to prepare for shelter for the homeless after air raids. Program implemented and supervised by the Nazi Party from 1933.

**Entschachtelung.** Disentanglement. To dissolve industry trusts.

**Entschuldung.** Freeing from debt. Legal liberation of rural property from debts.

**entsprechend behandelt.** Appropriately dealt with. Cover term for the murder of the Jews.

**Entstädterung.** Deurbanization. The fight against urban culture and values. *See also* Asphalt; Verstädterung.

**Entvolkung.** Degermanization. Loss of Germanness in German groups that lived outside of Germany. *See* Volkstumskampf.

**Entwarnung.** *See* Luftalarm.

**entwehrt.** Germanized for wehrlos (defenseless).

**entwelschen.** To de-gallicize, de-French, de-latinize. To rid the German language of French and other foreign words.

**Entwesung.** To exterminate vermin, to disinfect. Code for death by gassing. *See also* Abteilung Entwesung und Entseuchung.

**Entwesungstruppe.** Destruction-of-pests unit. Search and destroy unit; partisan hunters; mass murderers of civilians.

**entwurzelt.** Uprooted. Opposed to German nationalism.

**Erbbauer.** Farmer inheriting a farm. *See also* Reichserbhofgesetz.

**Erbe.** Heritage. *See* Blut und Boden.

**Erbgeprägtheit.** Characterization through genes. Description of the positive genetic characteristics of the Nordic (hero) type.

**erbgesund.** Free of hereditary illness.

**Erbgesundheit.** Healthy hereditary factors. Medically and racially documented.

**Erbgesundheitsgerichte.** Hereditary-health courts. Often decided on the sterilization of individuals.

**Erbgesundheitsgesetz.** Hereditary-health law. *See also* Gesetz zum Schutze der Erbgesundheit des deutschen Volkes; Gesetz zur Verhütung erbkranken Nachwuchses.

**Erbgesundheitspflege.** Hereditary-health care. Eugenics.

**Erbgesundheitszeugnis.** Hereditary-health certificate.

**Erbhof.** Farm inheritance. *See also* Reichserbhofgesetz.

**Erbhöferrolle.** Farm inheritor's list. *See also* Reichserbhofgesetz.

**Erbhoffortbildungsverordnung.** (EHFV) Decree for Hereditary Farm Education. *See also* Reichserbhofgesetz.

**Erbhofgesetz.** *See* Reichserbhofgesetz.

**Erbhofrechtsverfahrensordnung.** (EHRV) Decree for Farm Heredity Procedure. *See also* Reichserbhofgesetz.

**Erbhofrechtsverordnung.** (EHRV) Farm Heredity Law Decree. *See also* Reichserbhofgesetz.

*Erbkrank.* Hereditarily Ill. One of five silent films produced by the Race and Political Office (1935–1937) to convince Germans of the need to stop wasting German resources on useless lives. *See also* Euthanasie.

**erbkranker Nachwuchs.** Offspring with hereditary disease. During the Third Reich era, nearly half a million men and women were sterilized. *See also* Gesetz zur Verhütung erbkranken Nachwuchses.

**Erbkrankheiten.** Hereditary diseases. *See also* Gesetz zur Verhütung erbkranken Nachwuchses.

**erblich kriminell belastete Kinder und Jugendliche.** Hereditary-criminal-polluted children and youth. The children of Gypsies, alcoholics, the homeless, prostitutes, and Communists categorized in this manner were sent to concentration camps.

**Erbmeister.** Inheritance master. From 1935, any German worker who succeeded in securing a small plot of land for his family as an inheritance.

**Erbpflege.** Hereditary care, maintenance. State encourgement of racially pure marriages. In 1934, suggested as replacement word for eugenics. *See also* Eugenik; Rassenpflege.

**erbpflegerische Gesetze.** Hereditary laws. Race laws.

**Erbsünde.** Original sin. Race defilement.

**Erbtauglichkeit.** Ability to reproduce. Good health and pure German blood were considered factors in the right to reproduce and were prerequisites for Bauernfähigkeit.

**Erbtüchtigkeit.** Visual proof of the ability to reproduce. Numerous healthy off-spring confirmed this condition. It was a criterion in the selection of honorary godchildren.

**Erbwert.** Racial value. Hereditary factors of individual Germans and families as leading to the racial improvement of the German people.

**erbwertlich.** Pertaining to the value of genetic inheritance. The inherent value of Germanic forefathers.

**Erdabwehr.** Ground defense. Antiaircraft fire.

**Erdtruppen.** Ground troops.

**Ereignismeldung.** (ERM) Operational report. Account of the Einsatzgruppen commanders to the Reichssicherheitshauptamt in Berlin. This report listed their daily murder activities in code in the occupied areas of the Soviet Union.

**erfassen.** To register; catch. To keep perfect and bureaucratic lists of individuals considered antigovernment. To seize Jews and other people to send them off to concentration camps and murder. To intern people in order to sterilize or murder them as part of the Euthanasia Program.

**Erfassungsaktion.** Seizure operation. SS and local fascists roundup of Jews to be sent to death camps in German-occupied Europe.

**Erfassungsamt.** Information Department. SS bureau that advertised and facili-tated German population resettlement in the east.

**Erfassungs-GmbH.** Registration/Information Company Ltd. Cooperative for commerce in eastern occupied Europe. *See also* Ostraum.

**Erfinderbetreuer.** Inventions Supervisor. German Labor Front official supervis-ing inventions made by workers. *See also* Deutsche Arbeitsfront.

**Erfüllungspolitik.** Fulfillment policy. Sarcastic for those in the Weimar Republic who were willing to meet French demands on Germany and follow the obligations of the Versailles Treaty.

**Ergänzungsamt.** (SS) Recruiting Office. With priority over armed forces recruit-ing. *See also* Wehrersatzdienststelle.

**Ergänzungs-Instandsetzungs-Dienst.** Supplementary Repair Service. Nazi Party service helping those Germans whose homes were bombed out.

**Ergänzungsstelle.** (SS) Recruiting Office. In German-occupied countries.

**Ergänzungsraum.** Replenishment space. *See also* Raumordnung.

**Erhebung.** Uprising. *See also* nationale Erhebung.

**Erholungslager.** Recuperation camp. Ironic description of the camps where sick inmates were sent to die (e.g., at Bergen-Belsen).

**"Er ist in der Prinz-Albrecht-Straße."** "He is in the Prince Albert Street." "He is arrested by the Gestapo." *See also* Prinz-Albrecht-Straße.

**Erklärung.** Declaration, avowal. Papers SS men had to sign, in which they swore that they had no Jewish Blood.

**Erlaß des Führers und Reichskanzlers über den weiteren Kriegseinsatz des Reichsarbeitsdienstes für die weibliche Jugend.** Decree of the Führer and Reich Chancellor concerning the Extention of War Service of the Reich Labor Service for Female Youth. Decree of July 1941. *See also* Kriegshilfsdienst.

**Erlaß des Führers und Reichskanzlers über die Konzentration der Kriegswirtschaft.** Ordinance of the Führer and Reich Chancellor regarding the Concentration of the War Economy. Führer decrees of September 2 and 21, 1943, delegating extensive economic powers to Albert Speer.

**Erlaß des Führers und Reichskanzlers über die Verwertung des eingezogenen Vermögens von Reichsfeinden.** Ordinance of the Führer and Reich Chancellor regarding the Utilization of the Seized Property of Enemies of the State (May 29, 1941).

**Erlaß des Führers und Reichskanzlers zur Festigung deutschen Volkstums.** Decree of the Führer and Reich Chancellor concerning the Strengthening of German Nationality. *See* Festigung deutschen Volkstums.

**Erlaß des Reichsführers SS und Chefs der deutschen Polizei.** Decree of the Reichsführer-SS and Chiefs of the German Police. March 1938 decree prohibiting Jews from attending theaters, cinemas, cabarets, public concerts, libraries, museums, and other places of entertainment.

**Erlaß über die Zusammenfaßung der Zuständigkeiten des Reichs und Preussens in Kirchenangelegenheiten.** Decree to Unite the Jurisdictions of the Reich and Prussia in Church Affairs. Transferring to Hans Kerrl, the new Reich Minister for Church Affairs, the church administration previously handled by Reich and Prussian Ministers of the Interior and of Science, Education, and Training.

**Erlaß zur Bekämpfung der Zigeunerplage.** Decree on Combatting the Gypsy Plague. June 1936 law regulating the movement of German Gypsies in connection with the Summer Olympics. Later, Gypsy property was confiscated and many Gypsies sent to concentration camps where hundreds of thousands ultimately were murdered.

**erledigt.** Finished. Code for murdered ghetto Jews.

**erleichtert.** Relieved. Euphemism for mass murder of all or part of a ghetto's population.

**Erlösungsmensch.** (In need of) redemption man. A person outside of German tradition, a Jew.

**Erlösungstyp.** *See Rasse und Seele.*

**ERM.** *See* Ereignismeldung.

**Ermächtigungsgesetz.** Enabling Act. An act passed by the Reichstag on March 24, 1933, enabling Hitler to rule by decree and suspend the Weimar Constitution, thereby establishing Hitler's dictatorship. *See also* Gesetz zur Behebung der Not von Volk und Reich; Reichstagsbrandverordnung.

**Ernährungsamt.** Food Supply Department. Allocated food to Germans under rationing; also, allocated food to the Jews in the ghettos.

**Ernährungshilfswerk.** (EHW) Food Welfare Organization. Collected food refuse for animal feed; part of the German self-sufficiency program. *See also* Autarkie.

**Ernährungsopfer.** Donation/sacrifice for food. Collection of food that was to facilitate Germany's achieving an independent food supply and self-sufficiency. *See also* Autarkie.

**Ernährungsschlacht.** Battle for food supply. Element of autarky.

**Ernste Bibelforscher.** Serious bible researchers. Jehovah's Witnesses who refused to swear a loyalty oath to Hitler and were sent to concentration camps.

**Erntedanktag.** Thanksgiving. From 1933, the Nazis ordered their version of a traditional Nordic holiday as a secular national harvest holiday with ceremonies on the Bückeberg mountain near Hameln.

**(zum) Erntedienst abkommandiert.** Received orders for harvest duty. Euphemism for transfer to SS guard duty in concentration camps.

**Erntefest.** Harvest festival. *See also* Aktion Erntefest.

**Erntehelfer.** Harvest helper. *See also* Landhelfer(in).

**Erntekindergarten.** Harvest nursery. Nurseries in farming areas to aid farming families during harvest time.

**Ernting.** Month of August.

**Eroberer der Reichshauptstadt.** Conqueror of the Capital City of the Reich. Nickname for Goebbels because of his many affairs in Berlin.

**ERR.** *See* Einsatzstab Reichsleiter Rosenberg für die Besetzten Gebiete.

**Errichtungsverbot.** Prohibition against investments in private enterprises.

**Ersatz.** Replacement. Synthetic substitutes for traditional products. *See also* Autarkie.

**Ersatzhandlungen.** Substitute acts. False accusations by the Peoples' Tribunals (e.g., that Jews within the Reich engaged in sexual acts with German women, which was a pretext for their arrest as violators of race laws). *See also* Rassenschande.

**Ersatzheer.** Reserve army.

**Ersatzstoffe.** Substitutes. Products made of local raw materials or newly developed chemical combinations as substitutes for products that were scarce or no longer available due to lack of foreign exchange or the war economy.

**Erschießungsgang.** Shooting corridor. Execution area at Ravensbrück.

**Erschießungsaktion.** Shooting action.

**Erschießungskommando.** Firing squad.

**Erste Aktion.** First Operation. Beginning of the clearing of the Warsaw Ghetto, on July 22, 1942, and transporting of the majority of the ghetto's Jews to the death camp of Treblinka. *See* Umsiedlungsaktion; Warschau-Ghetto.

**(die) ersten Opfer der Partei.** The (Nazi) Party's first victims. The sixteen people (Nazis) who were shot during the 1923 Hitler Putsch. *See also* nationale Erhebung.

**Esterwegen.** *See* Emsland-Lager.

**Erste Verordnung zur Durchführung des Gesetzes über das Beschlußverfahren in Rechtsangelegenheiten der Evangelischen Kirche.** First Ordinance for Execution of the Law concerning Procedure for Decisions in Legal Affairs of the Evangelical (Protestant) Church. Setting up detailed organization and procedures under the law of June, 21 1935.

**"Erst wenn der letzte Jude ist verschwunden, / Hat das Volk seine Erlösung gefunden!"** "Only when the last Jew has disappeared, / Will the German people have found its salvation." Antisemitic slogan Nazis disguised as a proverb.

**Ertüchtigung.** Attainment of physical discipline and fitness. *See also* Wehrertüchtigung.

**erweiterte Polizeigefängnisse.** Extended police prisons. *See* Lager der Gestapo.

**erwünschter Bevölkerungszuwachs.** Desirable population increase. *See also* Eignungsprüfer.

**Erzeugungsschlacht.** Battle for food, for agricultural production. Attempts to make Germany independent of foreign sources for food. *See also* Arbeitsschlacht.

**erziehen.** To educate. To educate everyone, especially the young in the ideas of National Socialism.

**Erzieherin.** Female educator. Overseer at the youth camp near Ravensbrück.

**Erziehungshäftling.** Reeducation prisoner. Non-Jewish political prisoners sent temporarily to concentration camps.

**Erzpolen.** Arch Poles. Complete Poles, individuals of Polish origin with a Polish national outlook.

**Esak.** *See* evangelische Sündenabwehrkanone.

**Esel Isidor.** Isidor the Jackass. *See also* Isidor.

**Etappendienst.** Rear-Area Service. German Naval Intelligence Communications.

**etappenverwendungsfähig.** *See* tauglich 2.

**Eugenik.** Eugenics. Measures promoting reproduction of healthy hereditary stock of the German people. Often resulting in the murder of the supposedly unfit. *See also* lebensunwertes Leben; Rassenhygiene.

**Europäische Neuordnung.** The New European Order. The Third Reich's racial and eugenic program to rule all of Europe, including the forced conversion of the Slavs into slaves and mass murder of all Europeon Jews.

**europäischer Einigungs- und Freiheitskrieg.** European Unity and Freedom War. Propagandistic description of World War II.

**Europa-Plan.** Europe Plan. Rabbi Michael Ber Weissmandl's failed plan to pay the Nazis $2 million in order to ranson up to a million Jews to prevent their being sent to concentration camps in Poland.

**Euthanasie.** Euthanasia. Greek for good death. Euphemism for the deliberate killing of institutionalized physically, mentally, and emotionally handicapped people. The Euthanasia Program began in 1939, with German non-Jews as the first victims and was later extended to Jews. This program culminated in the murder of the incurably insane, permanently disabled, deformed, and other people the Third Reich deemed superfluous. There were three major classifications: euthanasia for incurables, immediate killing of camp prisoners unable to work, and experiments in mass sterilization. In August 1941 Bishop von Galen of Münster protested the program on behalf of the Christian community of Germany. Although as a result Hitler publicly shut down the program, it continued surreptitiously. *See also* Aktion T-4; Gesetz zur Verhütung erbkranken Nachwuchses; lebensunwertes Leben.

**Euthanasie-Aktion.** *See* Euthanasie.

**Euthanasiebefehl.** Euthanasia Order. Secret written order of Adolf Hitler in fall 1939 that empowered physicians to review the health status of patients with incurable diseases and grant these patients a graceful death, or mercy killing. This opened the door to the murder of more than 100,000 adults and children. *See also* Euthanasie.

**evakuieren.** To evacuate. To move German bombing or war victims, especially women and children, to another location. Also, to move Jews to another location to murder them.

**Evakuierung.** Evacuation. *See also* evakuieren.

**evakuiert.** Evacuated. *See also* evakuieren.

**Evakuierungslager.** Evacuation camp. Holding camp for Jews before they were sent to concentration camps.

**Evakuierungsnummer.** (EvNr., Ev. Nr.) Evacuation number. Identification number issued to Jews for forced transports to death camps. *See also* evakuieren.

**(der) evangelische Kirchenkampf im Dritten Reich.** (KK) The Evangelical (Protestant) Church battle in the Third Reich. The relationship between the Lutheran churches and membership and the Nazi Regime. Most Lutherans collaborated with the regime, actively or passively, with a few standing up to Hitler. Such Lutheran pastors as Martin Niemöller and Dietrich Bonhöffer felt that God was their leader, not Hitler. After initial sympathy with the regime's antisemitism, both men opposed it and they ended up in concentration camps.

**evangelische Sündenabwehrkanone.** (Esak) Evangelical sin defense artillery. Soldier slang for Protestant chaplain at the front.

**Evipannatrium.** Evipan anesthetic. Experimental overdose injections killed more than 100 Buchenwald prisoners.

**EvNr., Ev. Nr.** *See* Evakuierungsnummer.

**ewig.** Eternal. Adjective used often by the Nazis, as in das ewige Deutschland (eternal Germany).

**(der) Ewige Jude.** (The) eternal Jew. The concept of the ever-present absolutely-evil Jew whom only National Socialism can eradicate. Also, the pre-Nazi myth of the Wandering Jew. *See also Der Ewige Jude.*

**"(Der) Ewige Jude."** "(The) Eternal Jew." Antisemitic exhibition in the building of the Munich public library, opened on November 8, 1937, and called a "great political exhibition."

*(Der) Ewige Jude.* The Eternal Jew. Nazi hate-propaganda film of 1940 that summarized the whole Nazi rationale for the mass murder of the Jews. According to distorted Nazi ideology and the script of this film, Jews were the ultimate mixed race, an oriental pre-Asiatic racial mixture, with a hint of the negroid, foreign to Europeans, born from totally different kinds of racial elements, different from Germans in body and above all in soul. Through distorted images and false propaganda techniques, the Nazis compared the Jews to rats, spreading disease, plague, leprosy, typhoid, cholera, and dysentery. The Nazis claimed Jews were cunning, cowardly, and cruel and found mostly in large packs. Like the rats among other animals, Jews represented the rudiment of an insidious and underground destruction. Nazis hysterically maintained that Jewry was most dangerous when it was allowed to meddle in the most sacred things of a people—its culture, religion, and art, and the Jew was interested instinctively only in the abnormal and depraved. The politics of this race of parasites must be carried out in secret. According to the film, each Jew was exposed to these ideas from early childhood, implying the only solution was complete mass murder of these Jews, from the baby at the breast to the aged about to die naturally. Under the leadership of Hitler, the film proclaims, Germany has raised the battle flag of war against the eternal Jew, "Die Vernichtung der jüdischen Rasse in Europa!" ("the annihilation of the Jewish race in Europe!").

**ewiger Jude.** *See* (der) Ewige Jude.

**Ewige Wache.** Eternal Watch. Two "honor temples" erected in 1933 in Munich containing two sarcophagi of Nazi Party members killed during the Hitler Putsch on November 9, 1923, with SS standing guard. *See* Ehrentempel.

**EWZ.** *See* Einwandererzentralstelle.

**exekutiert.** (E) Executed. Murdered.

# F

**F.** Abbreviation for Franzose (Frenchman) on French prisoners' triangles. *See also* Dreieckswinkel.

**Fabrikaktion.** Operation Factory. SS seizure of Jewish men working in Berlin factories in February 1943. Their Aryan wives and German-Jewish children, numbering about 6,000 people, successfully protested their arrest. *See also* Rosenstraße.

**Fabrik-Medizin.** Factory medicine. Derogatory for Jewish medical practices.

**Fachkräfte.** Special Task Forces. Units of the Technical Emergency Help and Todt Organization. *See also* Organisation Todt; Technische Nothilfe.

**Fachschaft.** Specialty organization. Group of all students studying the same subject, meeting twice a week for ideological and physical training.

**FAD.** *See* Freiwilliger Arbeitsdienst.

**Fahndung Funk.** (F. Fu.) Radio Search. Branch of Military Intelligence that located forbidden radio transmitters in France.

**"(die) Fahne hoch!"** "Raise the flag high." *See also* "Horst-Wessel-Lied."

**"(die) Fahne ist mehr als der Tod."** "The flag is more than death." Line from the Hitler Youth anthem.

**Fahneneid.** Flag oath. The oath of allegiance to Hitler sworn by the German armed forces. *See also* Appendix: Treueid.

**Fahnenheid.** *See* Fahneneid.

**Fahnenweihe.** Consecration of the flag. Annul ritual during which Hitler consecrated the new Party flags by touching them with the blood flag. *See also* Blutfahne.

**Fähnlein.** Squad. Unit of the Deutsches Jungvolk in der Hitlerjugend.

**Fähnrich.** Ensign, cadet. Wehrmacht and SS rank of noncommissioned officer.

**fahrbare Gaskammer.** Mobile gas chamber. Truck with a hermetically sealed compartment serving as a mobile gas chamber; invented by Walter Rauf and used especially at Chelmno, where the first mass murders by gas were done. Each van accommodated about 100 people, who were supposed to be killed by exhaust from the van engine and then their bodies removed from the van and buried in mass graves. *See also* Sonderwagen.

**Fahrbereitschaftsleiter.** Coordinator for driving readiness. Freight car official acting as local trucking coordinator.

**Fahrnis.** Germanization of Möbel (furniture).

**Fahrtenmesser.** Sheath knife. An inscribed dagger, as part of Hitler Youth uniform. *See* "Blut und Ehre."

**Fahrt ins Blaue.** Mystery tour. Entertainment excursion by bus or train to an undisclosed destination as part of the Nazi Party organized leisure program. *See* Freizeitgestaltung.

**fälisch.** One of the six races that allegedly comprise the Germans. Characteristics were large nose, small face, dark hair, and slender, as well as loving the homeland and being heroic. *See* dinarisch; nordisch; ostbaltisch; ostische Rasse; westisch.

**Fall Barbarossa.** Case Barbarossa. The code name for the German invasion of the Soviet Union, which began on June 22, 1941. It refers to the Holy Roman Emperor Friedrich Barbarossa, so called because of his red beard, who drowned while leading the Third Crusade.

**Fall Bernard.** Case Bernard. SD secret operation at Sachsenhausen using Jewish prisoners to forge Allied money.

**Fall Blau.** Case blue. In 1938 code name for a study from the Luftwaffe about aerial warfare against England. Also, in 1942, the code name for the operations of German Army Group South targeting Woronesh, Stalingrad, and Baku.

**Fall Braun.** Case brown. Code name for the German plan to attack the French army on the Western Front in June 1940.

**Fall Gelb.** Case yellow. Code name for the attack on France and the Low Countries in May 1940.

**Fallgleiter.** Parachute glider. Paraplane.

**Fall Grün.** Case green. *See also* Grün.

**Fall Madagaskar.** Case Madagascar. A Nazi proposal and plan for the expulsion of east European Jews to Madagascar Island off southeast Africa. British, Dutch, and Polish antisemites all supported the plan, and the Polish government sent a commission to examine the feasibility of a mass Jewish emigration. Ultimately, the plan was considered impractical and was abandoned.

**Fall Otto.** Case Otto. *See also* Otto.

**Fall Rot.** Case red. *See also* Rot.

**Fallschirm.** Parachute, airborne.

**Fallschirmjäger.** (Fschjg) Paratrooper.

**Fallschirmspringer.** Parachutists. Prisoners who jumped from the top of the Wienergraben quarry. *See also* Wienergraben.

**Fallschirmtruppen.** (FST.) Airborne troops.

**Fall Weiß.** Case white. Code name for the attack on Poland.

**Fall-X.** Case X. 1930s code name for Germany and its allies to attack Czechoslovakia, Lithuania, and Russia.

**Familienlager.** Family camp at Auschwitz. Camp B II b for Jews from Theresienstadt; B II e for Gypsies.

**Familienunterhalt.** (FU) Family support. Financial help from the state during the war years for families whose provider was serving in the German army. *See also* Wirtschaftsbeihilfe.

**Fanal.** Beacon, torch, signal. Nazi propaganda term applied to historical events, (e.g., German cities burning as a result of Allied bombing raids were seen as part of a national suffering that would lead to utopia).

**Fanatiker.** Fanatic. *See also* fanatisch.

**fanatisch.** Fanatical. Used positively as devoted to the Nazi cause. In *Mein Kampf*, Hitler wrote: "Ich war in kurzer Zeit zu einem fanatischen Deutschnationalen geworden" ("I had in a short time become a fanatical/devoted German nationalist").

**Fanatismus.** Fanaticisim. *See also* fanatisch.

**Faschismus.** Fascism. Used exclusively for the political movement and state theory under Mussolini in Italy.

**Faserstoff.** Fiber material. Germanization of Textilien (textiles).

**Fäulniserscheinung.** Occurrence of putrefaction. Antisemitic collective term for Jews.

**FBK.** *See* Führerbegleitungskommando.

**F-Boot.** F boat. Escort vessel.

**FdU.** *See* Führer der U-Boote.

**fedrig.** Bouncy. Germanization of elastisch (elastic).

**Feger.** Sweeper. Navy jargon for a destroyer.

**Fehlschicht.** Missed shift.

**Feierabendgestaltung.** After-work activities. Government-organized leisure-time activities for all Germans. *See also* Heimabend.

**Feiertag der nationalen Arbeit.** National work holiday. In an attempt to recruit a higher percentage of the workforce to the Nazi Party—it stood at only about 5 percent—Hitler declared a national labor day in April 1933 to be celebrated with Nazi Party events and rallies on the first day of every May.

**Feiertage.** Holidays. *See also* nationale Feiertage.

**feig(e).** Cowardly. Applied to Jews and enemies of the Nazi Party and the Reich.

**Feindbegünstigung.** To the advantage of the enemy. Dissemination of news, especially those of foreign broadcasts.

**Feindeinflug.** Enemy air attack. Enemy raid.

**Feindeinsatz.** Enemy action.

**Feindfahrt.** Enemy journey. U-boat raid.

**Feindflug.** Enemy flight. Combat mission.

**Feindhörer.** Listeners to the enemy. Germans who listened to Allied radio.

**"Feind hört mit!"** "The enemy is listening." *See also* "Achtung, Feind hört mit!"

**Feindmächte.** Enemy powers. Nazi enemies during World War II (i.e., the Allies).

**Feindnachrichtenabteilung.** Intelligence Branch. *See also* Sicherheitsdienst des Reichsführers SS.

**Feindseite.** Enemy side. All individuals and organizations opposed to World War II.

**Feindsender.** Enemy radio station. Any Allied radio station broadcasting in German; also, a station broadcasting behind enemy lines.

**Feindwirkung.** Enemy effect. Damage caused by enemy military action.

**feiner Maxe.** (FM) Elegant Max. Colloquialism for special SS pin awarded to those who supported the SS financially. *See also* Schutzstaffel Fördernde Mitglieder.

**Feinfrostgemüse.** (Delicately) frozen vegetables.

**Feingemüse.** Delicate vegetables. Collective term for all vegetables except cabbage during the war-ration period.

**Feinsehrohr.** Germanization of Mikroskop (microscope).

**Feinwaschmittel.** Mild detergent. No-name brand detergent of poor quality during World War II.

**Felddegenkorps.** Field Dagger Corps. Early SA shock formation dissolved in 1935 and absorbed by the German police.

**Feldgendarmerie.** Field Police. Military police who served on all fronts during World War II performing traffic control and crime investigation; maintaining order and discipline; disarming, searching, collecting, and escorting POWs and stragglers; seeking saboteurs; searching for downed enemy airmen; supervising civilians in occupied areas; checking papers of soldiers on leave and in transit and apprehending deserters; preventing the distribution of air-dropped enemy propaganda leaflets; carrying out street patrols in occupied areas; controlling evacuees and refugees during retreats; border control; and antipartisan executions. Toward the end of the war, they were often employed as regular troops on the front line.

**Feldgerichtsabteilung.** (FGA) Court-martial Branch. Military courts that worked behind the front line and ordered executions of German soldiers accused and convicted of desertion or treason. *See also* Feldgendarmerie.

**Feldhaubitze.** Field howitzer.

**Feldherrnhalle.** Military memorials. Hero halls located in Munich—in front of which the Hitler Putsch was defeated—Berlin, and other German cities. Later, name of the elite SA-sponsored unit (motorized SA-Guard Regiment) and the Wehrmacht (Panzergrenadier-Division). Units bearing this name were encircled and annihilated in Byelorussia in the summer of 1944, then in Budapest in early 1945.

**Feldjägerkorps.** (FJK) Sharpshooter Corps. SA formation that was later incorporated into the police and even later developed into military police units. *See also* Feldgendarmerie.

**Feldkanone.** Field gun.

**Feldkommando SS.** Field Command SS. Himmler's field headquarters.

**Feldm.** *See* Feldmarschall.

**Feldmarschall.** (Feldm) Field Marshal.

**Feldpolizei.** Battlefield Police. SS military police.

**Feldpostausgaben.** Outpost editions. Books in notebook format especially printed for soldiers at the front and often containing antisemitic material. *See* Richthefte des Oberkommandos der Wehrmacht.

**Feldpostliteratur.** *See* Feldpostausgaben.

**Feldpostmarder.** Field-post-office marten. An individual who stole mail going to or coming from German soldiers.

**Felix.** *See* Unternehmen Felix.

**Felsennest.** Cliff Nest. One of Hitler's command posts, near the Belgian border.

**Fememord.** Political murder. Killing ordered by an emergency court. *See* Fem(e)grichte.

**Fem(e)gerichte.** Secret courts. Post–World War I secret courts of the Black Reichswehr who handed down death sentences to those revealing the existence of this secret army to the Allies. Also, emergency courts during the Third Reich. *See also* Schwarze Reichswehr.

**Fernbild.** Picture from afar. Telephoto, target photography.

**Fernkampfbatterie.** Long-distance fighting battery. Long-range artillery along the coast of the English Channel.

**Fernleit.** Remote control.

**Fernmeldewesen.** Long-distance communication. SS control service.

**fernmündlich.** Germanization of telephonisch (by telephone).

**Fernrakete V-2.** Remote-controlled rocket V-2. *See also* Vergeltungswaffen; Wunderwaffen.

**Fernschreiben.** (FS) Telegram.

**Fernschreiber.** Teletype, teletype operator.

**Fernsehrohr.** Germanized for Periskop (periscope).

**Fernsprecher.** Germanized word for telephone.

**Ferntrauung.** Marriage by proxy. During World War II, German proxy marriages were allowed with only the bride present, the groom unavailable because he was at the front or in some kind of military service. Based on the Personenstandsverordnung der Wehrmacht (Family Status Order of the Armed Forces) of October 1942.

**fertigmachen.** To make ready. To finish someone off. Slang, to kill. To assign someone to a work party at the concentration camp. Because of the harsh conditions, this became synonymous with ordering death for a prisoner.

**fertig werden.** To deal (with someone). Euphemistic for murder.

**Festigung deutschen Volkstums.** Strengthening of the German nationality. The deportation and mass murder of Jews and Poles from occupied Poland to make room for people of authentic German blood. To bring not only German language and law to eastern Europe but also to clear out that area of all but those people who were German and of Germanized blood.

**Festpreise.** Frozen prices.

**Festung.** Fortress. Military term for places that Hitler wanted to be defended at all costs.

**Festung Europa.** Fortress Europe. The territory of German-occupied Europe and that of Germany's allies. *See also* Europäische Neuordnung.

**Fettlücke.** Fat gap. Scarcity in cooking fat and oil supply in Germany during the war.

**Feuerglocke.** Fire bell. Pattern of artillery fire.

**Feuerpatsche.** Fire beater. Leather or cloth patch on a wooden stick meant to extinguish flames from fire bombs.

**Feuerschlag.** Fire hit. Short, heavy bombardment to prepare way for shock troops.

**Feuerschutzpolizei.** Fire-Protection Police. Founded in 1938 as a component of the Order Police. *See also* Ordnungspolizei.

**Feuerwehr.** Fire defense. Prisoner fire brigade in concentration camp.

**Feuerzauber.** *See* Unternehmen Feuerzauber.

**F. Fu.** *See* Fahndung Funk.

**FGA.** *See* Feldgerichtsabteilung.

**FH.** *See* Fremde Heere.

**FHO.** *See* Fremde Heere Ost.

**FHQ, F.H.Qu.** *See* Führerhauptquartier.

**FHW.** *See* Fremde Heere West.

*Fichtebundblatt.* Fichte-Association Newsletter. Periodical of the Deutscher Fichte-Bund.

**"Ficken für Volk und Führer."** "Fuck for the (German) people and leader." Obscene, to be a full National Socialist and produce children.

**Fideikommissariat.** Estate Commission. In charge of the Aryanization of Jewish property and businesses in occupied Poland.

**"(Er) fiel für seinen geliebten Führer."** "He fell (was killed) for his beloved Führer." Nazi propaganda phrase for German soldiers killed in action.

**"(Er) fiel im festen Glauben an seinen Führer."** "He fell (was killed) in the unshakable faith in his Führer." Nazi propaganda. *See* "(Er) fiel für seinen geliebten Füuhrer."

**Figuren.** Figures. Corpses dug up and burned by members of the Sonderkommando 1005. Also, derogatory for Jews and other people chosen for deadly medical experiments.

**Filmberichter.** Film reporter. *See also* Propaganda-Kompanien.

**Filmschaffen.** Filmmaking. Filmmaking in Nazi Germany.

**Filtricht.** Germanization of Filtrat (filtrate).

**Finanzjude.** Jew working in the financial market. Often-used Nazi antisemitic propaganda word.

**Finanzkapital.** Finance capital. International lending capital allegedly in few Jewish hands and supposedly used to counteract Germany's goals. *See also* (Brechung der) Zinsknechtschaft.

**Firmenlager.** (FL) Company camp. One of many camps organized by German companies involved in the war effort, like Siemens, Messerschmidt, Mittelwerk, Saurer. Incorporated into the SS camp system in 1943. *See* Judenlager.

**Fischen.** Fishing. Code name for German attack on Polish fortress Westerplatte near Danzig.

**Fischfang.** Fish catch. Code name for the German counterattack on the Allied beachhead at Anzio in February 1944.

**Fischreiher.** Heron. Code name for attack on Stalingrad in 1942.

**F.i.SD.** *See* Führer im Sicherheitsdienst der SS.

**FJK.** *See* Feldjägerkorps.

**FKL.** Frauenkonzentrationslager. *See* Frauenlager.

**FKM.** *See* Fremde Kriegsmarine.

**FL.** *See* Firmenlager; Fremde Luftwaffe.

**Fladdermine.** Self-activating land mine. Booby trap.

**Flaggenerlass.** Flags Order. Decree to set up Nazi flags in churches. A Security Police means to harass church members opposing the Reich.

**Flak.** *See* Fliegerabwehr; Flugabwehrkanone.

**Flakhelfer.** Antiaircraft gun helper. Students about sixteen years old trained to operate air defense artillery during the war. *See* Luftwaffenhelfer.

**Flakwaffenhelferin.** Young women in uniform who were employed in the service of air defense. They handled ground searchlights to spot enemy planes and operated measuring instruments and listening devices.

**Flasche.** Flask. Code name for assassination attempt on Hitler (March 1943) when a bomb was placed on his aircraft. *See also* Schwarze Kapelle.

**Flaschenbiergustav.** Bottled beer Gustav. Contemptuous for 1920s Weimar Chancellor and later Foreign Minister Gustav Stresemann, who had written about Germany's bottled-beer industry and survived Hitler's Beer Hall Putsch. Seeking closer ties to the west and married to a Jewish woman, the Nazis saw him as a major foe.

**Fleckfieber.** Spotted fever. Nazi signs posted on Jewish ghettos to warn off Aryans.

**Fleckfieberversuchsstation.** Station for typhus experiments. Typhoid research station at the Buchenwald camp in Block 46 that conducted experiments on humans from 1942 to 1945. *See also* Hygiene-Institut der Waffen-SS.

**Fleischmarkt.** Meat market. Slang for location of execution by shooting, or site of Roland Freisler's People's Court. *See also* Volksgericht.

**fliegender Bleistift.** Flying pencil. Slang for Dormier-17 bomber aircraft.

**fliegende Truppe.** Parachute troops, shock troops. Paratroopers.

**Fliegerabwehr.** Flak. (Anti-)aircraft defense.

**Fliegeralarm.** Flyer alarm. *See also* Luftalarm.

**Flieger-Division.** Luftwaffe division.

**Fliegerführer.** Flight Leader, Air Commander. German air force operational rank and command area.

**Fliegergeschädigte.** Flyer damaged. Bureaucratic word for bombed out; individuals whose property was destroyed or damaged by air raids and therefore eligible for extra ration cards for clothing and food. *See* ausgebombt; Fliegerschäden.

**Flieger-Hitlerjugend.** Flyer Hitler Youth. German youth trained to serve in the air force.

**Fliegerkorps.** *See* Luftwaffe.

**Fliegerschäden.** Damage from air raids. Destruction of German cities through Allied bombing; compensation (from property of deported Jews) for Germans whose household articles had been destroyed.

**Fliegerversuchstation.** Flyer research area. Location of German air force–sponsored cold-water experiments on Jewish prisoners at Dachau. *See also* Unterkühlungsversuche.

**Fliegerwart.** Plane spotter.

**"Flink wie die Windhunde, zäh wie Leder, und hart wie Kruppstahl."** "Fast as hound dogs, tough as leather, and hard as Krupp steel." Hitler's ideal image of German youth. An often-quoted propaganda slogan and part of the Hitler Youth swearing-in ceremony. *See also* Schwertworte.

**Flintenweib.** Shotgun woman. Derogatory for female soldiers of the Soviet army or female partisans in the German-occupied territories.

**Flossenbürg.** Concentration camp at edge of German town of Floss, in Bavaria near Czech border. Thousands of prisoners were worked to death at Messerschmidt and DEST. *See also* Deutsche Erd- und Steinwerke GmbH.

**Flotte.** *See* Kriegsmarine.

**"(auf der) Flucht erschossen."** "Shot in the attempt to escape." Often a pretext for murder of prisoners in the camps. *See also* Todesfallsaufnahmen; (gefälschte) Todesursachen.

**flüchtige Kampfstoffe.** Fleeing combat materials. Easily dispersible war chemicals.

**Fluchtokrat.** Flight-ocrat. One who fled to the country from urban bombing raids.

**Fluchtversuch.** Attempt to flee. SS rationale for shooting prisoners.

**Flugabwehrkanone.** Flak. Antiaircraft gun.

**Flugbombe V-1.** Flying bomb V-1. Pilotless flying bomb powered by a pulse-jet engine, carried a 1,875 lb high-explosive warhead, and had a range of up to 200 km (125 mi). *See also* Vergeltungswaffen; Wunderwaffen.

**Flugmelder.** Flight dispatcher.

**Flugordnung.** Flying order. Formation.

**Flugwaffenkommando.** (Fluko) Air defense unit.

**Flugzeugmutterschiff.** Aircraft mother ship. Air carrier. Also, reference to Czechoslovakia as a serious threat to Germany in the 1930s.

**Fluh.** Concrete.

**Fluko.** *See* Flugwaffenkommando.

**Flurbereinigung.** Land distribution. Cleaning up, purging, combing out an area of enemies and Jews.

**Flüssiggas.** Liquid gas. Liquid bottled motor fuel, propane, butane.

**Flüsterparole.** Whispering campaign. Goebbels' propaganda technique. Also, antifascist campaign.

**Flüsterpropaganda.** Whisper propaganda. The dissemination of news heard via Allied radio broadcasts.

**FM.** *See* feiner Maxe.

**FM, fMSS.** *See* förderndes Mitglied der SS.

*foetor judaicus.* Latin for Jew stink. Nazi theorist Alfred Rosenberg updated this medieval Christian fantasy that Jews had a peculiar odor that indicated their evil nature. He wrote about how this so-called Jew stink corrupted modern drama, theater, and music in Europe and New York.

**förderndes Mitglied der SS.** (FM, fMSS) Promoting members of the SS. Paid monthly contributions. *See also* Schutzstaffel Fördernde Mitglieder.

**Förderungsdienst.** Assistance Service. Founded in 1941 to provide funding for loans to small businessmen to purchase and run businesses expropriated from Jews and others regarded as enemies of the Third Reich.

**Formular 14 f. 13.** Form or schedule 14 f. 13. *See also* Aktion 14 f. 13 KZ-Häftlinge; Sonderbehandlung 14 f. 13.

**form- und charakterloses Lumpenproletariat.** Formless and spineless tramps, beggars, transients. Gypsies and others considered racially inferior.

*Forschungen der Judenfrage.* Research on the Jewish Problem. Publication of Reichsinstitut für Geschichte des Neuen Deutschlands (Reich Institute for the History of the New Germany).

**Forschungsabteilung.** Research Branch. Göring's intelligence office responsible for tapping telephones in Berlin.

**Forschungsabteilung Judenfrage.** Research Branch for the Jewish Problem.

**Forschungsamt.** Research Department. The intelligence service of the Luftwaffe.

**Forschungsamt Hermann Görings.** Research Department of Hermann Göring. *See* Forschungsamt.

**Fortbildungsschule.** Continuing-education school. Trade and technical schools.

**Frankenführer.** Leader of Franconia. Nickname for Franconian district leader and editor of the antisemitic periodical *Der Stürmer*, Julius Streicher. *See also (Der) Stürmer.*

*Frankfurter Zeitung.* Frankfurt News. One of Germany's oldest and most prestigious newspapers. Closed down in 1943 on Hitler's orders because of its liberal and Jewish past and criticism of the Nazi regime.

**Franz.** Air force and army slang for observer.

**franzen.** Air force and army slang for to reconnoiter.

*(Die) Frau.* The Woman. A journal, edited by feminist leader and politician Gertrud Bäumer, first during the Weimar years and then in collaboration with the Nazi regime.

**Frauenabteilung.** Women's labor branches.

**Frauenamt der Deutschen Arbeitsfront.** Women's Department of the German Labor Front. *See also* Deutsche Arbeitsfront; Reichsfrauenführerin.

**Frauenfront.** *See* Nationalsozialistische Frauenschaft.

**Frauenhilfsdienst für Wohlfahrts- und Krankenpflege.** Women's Aid Service for Welfare and Health Care. Two-year voluntary service for women instituted in 1938.

**Frauenkonzentrationslager.** (FKL) Women's concentration camp. *See also* Frauenlager.

**Frauen-KZ.** *See* Frauenkonzentrationslager.

**Frauenlager.** (FrL) Women's camp. Concentration camp whose inmates and guards were exclusively women; for example, at Ravensbrück.

**Frauenschaft.** Women's League. *See also* Nationalsozialistische Frauenschaft.

**Frauen-Warte.** Women's Watch-Tower. Nazi Party's illustrated biweekly magazine for women.

**Frauenwerk.** Women's Work. National Socialist Women's Organization that combined all former women's associations with one woman as its leader. *See* Reichsfrauenführerin.

**Freiheit.** Freedom. Free reign for the Reich government, no individual freedom.

**Freiheitsberaubungen.** Freedom deprivation, false imprisonments. After the 1933 Reichstag fire, the new Nazi government arrested its opponents and sent them to concentration camps to be tortured and/or killed.

**Freiheitskämper.** Freedom fighter. Participants in Hitler's unsuccessful attempt at a coup in 1923. *See also* Hitler-Putsch.

**(Der) Freiheitskampf.** The freedom fight. Increased antisemitic campaign in 1935.

**Freikorps.** Free Corps. Paramilitary World War I veteran groups. Although dissolved in 1921 after crushing German Bolshevik uprising in Munich and the Spartacists in Berlin, many members joined the Nazi Party.

**freiwillig.** Voluntary. Under the Third Reich, volunteerism was often coerced.

**Freiwillige.** Volunteers. Collaborators with the Germans, or those forced to cooperate with the Germans.

**Freiwillige Legion Niederlande.** Dutch Volunteer Legion. Dutch volunteers attached to the SS, fighting in the Soviet Union.

**Freiwilliger Arbeitsdienst.** (FAD) Voluntary Work Service. From 1931, a Nazi program of voluntary community work for all young Germans of all social levels. In 1935 this program became law. *See also* Arbeitsdienstpflicht.

**freiwilliger Selbstschutz.** (FS) Voluntary self-defense.

**Freiwillige Schutzstaffel.** Volunteer SS. Volksdeutsche living in Slovakia.

**Freizeitgestaltung.** Leisure activities. Part of the Nationalsozialistische Gemeinschaft Kraft durch Freude. *See also* Fahrt ins Blaue.

**Fremdarbeiter.** Foreign laborers. About 12 million voluntary or forced laborers brought during World War II to the Reich from Nazi-occupied Europe, especially Belgium, France, the Netherlands, Poland, and Russia.

**fremdblütig.** Foreign blooded. In contrast to deutschblütig.

**Fremde Heere.** (FH) Foreign armies. German Army Intelligence Evaluation Service. Branch of the German intelligence community. *See also* militärischer Geheimdienst.

**Fremde Heere Ost.** (FHO) Foreign armies east. German Army Intelligence Evaluation Service, Eastern Section.

**Fremde Heere West.** (FHW) Foreign armies west. German Army Intelligence Evaluation Service, Western Section.

**Fremde Kriegsmarine.** (FKM) Foreign naval forces. German Naval Intelligence.

**Fremde Luftwaffe.** (FL) Foreign air force. German Air Force Military Intelligence.

**Fremdenrecht.** Alien (legal) status. Pan-German League's antisemitic plan even before World War I to remove the rights of German citizenship from German Jews.

**Fremdmoral.** Foreign morality. Individual or alien (non-German) morality.

**fremdrassig, fremdrassisch.** Of alien race. Of non-German origin.

**Fremdstämmige.** People of alien descent. Non-Germans.

**Fremdstämmigenkartei.** File of aliens. Card-index list of persons of alien race supplied by the German churches to the SS.

**Fremdvölker, fremdvölkisch.** Foreign peoples, alien. Non-Aryan and racially alien to the German people.

**fressen.** To eat like an animal. "Na, gib ihnen zu fressen" ("Well, give these animals something to eat"). Sarcastic joke by SS personnel as they introduced poison gas crystals into the gas chamber in the death camps.

**Freundeskreis Adolf Hitler.** Friendship Circle Adolf Hitler. Wealthy contributors to Hitler's Nazi Party.

**Freundeskreis der Wirtschaft.** Friendship Circle for the Economy. *See also* Freundeskreis Reichsführer SS.

**Freundeskreis Heinrich Himmler.** *See* Freundeskreis Reichsführer SS.

**Freundeskreis Reichsführer SS.** Friendship Circle, Reichsführer-SS. A group of people from industry and business who collaborated with the SS and linked the top business and political leaders of the Third Reich. They financed Nazi election campaigns in the early 1930s and later helped supply the Waffen-SS with arms. Their contributions paid for SS activities from culture to medical experiments in the camps. Contributors received high honorary rank in the SS and priority for using slave labor from the camps.

**Friede.** Peace. The state of affairs that would occur when all of Germany's racial and spatial requirements were satisfied.

**(deutscher) Friede.** German peace. A future peace without Jews. *See also* Friede.

**FrL.** *See* Frauenlager.

**Front.** Military front.

**Front.** Political organization, body. Activities of organized and informal Nazi groups (e.g., to fight against political enemies).

**Frontarbeiter.** Front worker. *See also* Organisation Todt.

**Frontaufklärungstruppe.** Front reconnaissance (spy) troop.

**Frontbann.** Nazi paramilitary organization formed by Ernst Röhm and temporarily replacing the Sturmabteilung when it was banned in the 1920s after Hitler's Munich Putsch.

**Frontbauer.** Front farmer. German farmers settled in the newly conquered eastern regions.

**(die) Front begradigen.** To straighten the front line. Euphemism for German loss of territory or military positions during World War II.

**Frontberichter.** Front reporter. *See also* Kriegsberichter.

**Frontbücherei.** Front library. Mobile library run by the German army for front-line soldiers.

**Frontbuchhandlung.** Front bookstore. Mobile bookstore run by the German Labor Service for front soldiers.

**Front der Heimat.** *See* Heimatfront.

**Fronterlebnis.** Front experience. Writing style emphasizing World War I as a unifying experience of camaraderie and nationalism preparing German people to die for Germany.

**Frontflugspange.** Front flying (clasp) medal. A three-level award established in 1941 for German air force pilots.

**Frontführung.** Front management. *See also* Organisation Todt.

**Frontgeist.** Front spirit. *See also* Fronterlebnis.

**Frontgemeinschaft.** United-front community. 1936 expression of a genuine and united German community. *See also* Fronterlebnis.

**Frontismus.** Frontism. Semi-fascist movement in Belgium, Switzerland, and France.

**Frontkämpfer.** Front fighters. World War I veterans who had fought on the front for the German Reich or its allies during World War I. Also, men whose fathers or sons had died fighting in World War I. Jewish Frontkämpfer were exempt from anti-Jewish laws and regulations during the first year of the Nazi regime.

**Frontsoldat.** Front soldier. Hitler's self-description.

**Frontsozialismus.** Front socialism. German community connected by blood and destiny having nothing to do with Marxist socialism.

**Front-Todt.** *See* Organisation Todt.

**Frostmedaille.** Frost medal. Soldier slang for military decorations earned while fighting on the Eastern Front. *See also* Eisbeinorden.

**Frühlingserwachen.** Spring awakening. Code name for German counterattack against Soviet forces in Hungary (March 5, 1945).

**FS.** *See* Fernschreiben.

**FS.** *See* freiwilliger Selbstschutz.

**Fschjg.** *See* Fallschirmjäger.

**FST.** Fallschirmtruppen. Airborne troops.

**FU.** *See* Familienunterhalt.

**Fuchsloch.** Foxhole. Covered hole in a trench. *See also* Schützenloch.

**Fuhlsbüttel.** (Kola-Fu) Satellite concentration camp of Neuengamme, punishment camp, and prison in Hamburg.

**(Der) Führer.** (DF) The Leader. One of Hitler's official titles in Nazi Germany. The Nazi Führer had a mystical, magical, mysterious relationship to the German people. Hitler had five roles in Nazi Germany: Head of State (Der Führer, or Staatsoberhaupt des Großdeutschen Reiches), Head of the Government (Reichskanzler, or Regierungschef), Head of the Party (Führer der NSDAP), Supreme Commander in Chief of the Armed Forces (Der Führer und oberste Befehlshaber der Wehrmacht), and Acting Commander in Chief of the Army (Oberbefehlshaber des Heeres). From the spring of 1939, Hitler ordered that he wanted only the designation Der Führer to be used.

**Führeradel.** Führer aristocracy. The highest level of National Socialist leadership. Also, the German people (Volk), destined to lead other nations.

**Führer aller Germanen.** Führer of all the German Peoples. Hitler title. *See also* Oberster Gerichtsherr.

**Führerbau.** Führer Building. A major Party office building in Munich from the late 1930s, with a large office for Hitler.

**Führerbefehl.** Führer Order. The highest-level directive from Hitler. It did not tolerate contradiction.

**Führerbefehl für die Endlösung.** Führer Order for the "Final Solution." Most likely oral directives from Hitler to his underlings.

**Führerbefehl vom 17.9.1940.** Führer Order of September 17, 1940. Hitler's order that Jewish art in German-occupied western Europe be confiscated.

**"Führer befiehl, wir folgen!"** "You, Führer, command, and we will follow and obey." Slogan stressing the absolute loyalty of the German people to Adolf Hitler.

**Führer-Begleit-Bataillon.** Führer Escort Battalion. Hitler's security convey.

**Führer-Begleit-Kommando.** Führer Escort Unit.

**Führerbegleitungskommando.** (FBK) The Führer's Escort Squad. Personal security troops of the Waffen-SS who protected Hitler during the war.

**Führerbild.** Picture of the Führer. Hitler's photo, ordered to be hung in German public places and homes.

**Führerbunker.** Führer's Bunker. Hitler's underground and camouflaged Berlin headquarters made of concrete and steel.

**"(Dem) Führer das germanische Reich zu bauen."** "To build the Germanic Reich for the Führer." A goal of the SS.

**Führer der Nation.** Führer of the Nation. Another of Hitler's titles. *See also* Oberster Gerichtsherr.

**Führer der NSDAP.** Führer of the Nazi Party. Hitler's title from 1921 on.

**Führer der U-Boote.** (FdU) Führer of the Submarines. Position held by Admiral Karl Dönitz. *See also* Befehlshaber der U-Boote.

**Führererlaß.** *See* Führerbefehl.

**Führergesetz.** Führer Law. The supreme basis for all law was the Führer's will, which expressed race law.

**"(Das) Führergesetz ist der unantastbare und verbindliche, unmittelbare Ausdruck, des völkischen Rechts."** "The Führer Law is the uncontestable, binding, and direct expression of the law of the German people."

**Führergrundsatz.** *See* Führerprinzip.

**"(Der) Führer hat immer recht."** "The Führer is always right." Nazi phrase.

**Führerhauptquartier.** (FHQ., F.H.Qu.) Führer Headquarters. Hitler's central command post for military operations.

**Führer im Sicherheitsdienst der SS.** (F.i.SD) Führer in the Security Service of the SS. *See* Sicherheitsdienst des Reichsführers SS.

**Führer-Informationen.** Führer information. Bulletins sent by Goebbels to Hitler late in the war indicating progress of the propaganda campaign on the home front.

**Führerinnenschule.** Girls' leadership school. Schools in German-occupied Europe where potential Aryan girls were to be converted into real German Aryans.

**"(Der) Führer ist das Reich."** "The Führer is the Nation." Nazi slogan.

**"(Der) Führer ist das Volk, und das Volk ist der Führer!"** "The Führer is the people and the people is the Führer." Nazi slogan.

**Führerkanzlei.** The Führer Chancellery. Berlin buildings where Hitler's private office was located and his affairs were conducted. It was headed by Reich Leader Philipp Bouhler. *See also* Bauten des Führers.

**"(Dem) Führer Kinder schenken!"** "To give one's children to the Führer." Motto of the BDM. *See also* Bund Deutscher Mädel in der Hitlerjugend.

**Führerkorps.** Führer Corps. *See* (Das) Führerkorps der Sicherheitspolizei und des Sicherheitsdienst; (Das) Führerkorps der NSDAP.

**(Das) Führerkorps der NSDAP.** Führer Corps of the Nazi Party. The elite of Nazi Party officials. Ran Germany's side of World War II along with the Reichskabinett, SS und SD, SA, Gestapo and Generalstab und Oberkommando der Wehrmacht.

**(Das) Führerkorps der Sicherheitspolizei und des Sicherheitsdienst.** Führer Corps of the Security Police and the Security Service. In twenty-five troop schools and in three Reichsführer schools of the SA, 22,000 to 25,000 officers and noncommissioned officers were trained yearly from 1934 as an elite officer corps. The training was physical, military, and ideological.

**Führerlexikon.** Führer Dictionary. A who's who of Nazi Party leaders and other important members published in 1934.

**führerloses Arbeitsvolk.** Leaderless workpeople. The Polish people who needed to be led by Germany. *See also* Arbeitsvolk.

**Führer-Maschine.** Hitler machine. Large four-engined Focke-Wulff aircraft used to fly Hitler to various locations during the war. Also, special typewriter that printed in large letters readable by Hitler, whose failing eyesight required it late in the war.

**Führermaterial.** *See* Menschenmaterial.

**Führerpaket.** Führer parcel. Food packet that German soldiers on the Eastern Front going on furlough received as gifts for their families at home. The contents came from confiscated goods of the occupied territories.

**Führerprinzip.** Leadership principle. Nazi principle outlined in *Mein Kampf* that created an authoritarian system with power emanating from the top. When Hitler ordered something it was as if God had spoken. At each level of the hierarchy, those below owed absolute allegiance to those above. In effect, all were to obey Hitler without question. The Führer controlled the state, the Party, Hitler Youth, the economy, society, communications in the broadest sense, coercion/force/concentration camps, and the armed forces. General of Artillery Wilhelm Ulex reported that Himmler told him: "Ich tue nichts, was der Führer nicht weiss" ("I don't do anything that the Führer doesn't know about").

**Führerrede.** Führer speech. Hitler's important speeches were broadcast on all German radio stations simultaneously.

**Führerschulen.** Leader schools. Nazi schools that trained future Nazi leaders. *See also* Ordensburgen; Reichsschule.

**Führers Geburtstag.** Führer's Birthday. Official name for April 20, Hitler's birthday, analogous to the formerly celebrated Kaisers Geburtstag.

**Führerstaat.** Führer state. The German Reich consisted of Hitler's authoritarian leadership, the elimination of parliament and non-Nazi political parties, and the existence of a relationship of absolute trust between the people and their Führer. *See also* Führerprinzip.

**Führer-Städte.** Führer cities. Cities in Germany and Austria important to Hitler: Berlin (capital city of the Reich), Hamburg (city of commerce), Linz (Hitler's hometown), München (Munich, capital of the Nazi movement), and Nürnberg (Nuremberg, city of the Reich Nazi Party rallies).

**Führersonderzug.** Führer's special train. Hitler's railroad train.

**führertreu.** Loyal to the Führer. Those who remained absolutely faithful to Hitler; they were regarded as the highest level of humanity.

**(Der) Führer und oberste Befehlshaber der Wehrmacht.** *See* (Der) Führer.

**(Der) Führer und Reichskanzler.** The Führer and Chancellor. Hitler's official title and position after the death of President Paul von Hindenburg in August 1934, whose office of president was combined with the chancellorship. *See also* Oberster Gerichtsherr.

**Führerverrat.** Führer treason. Breech of the oath of loyalty to Hitler. High treason, betrayal of the Führer.

**Führerweisung.** Führer directive. Hitler order.

**Führerwille.** Führer will, intention. *See also* Führerprinzip.

**Führungshauptamt.** *See* SS-Führungshauptamt.

**Führungsstäbe der Wirtschaft.** Coordinating Staffs of the Economy. Under the direction of Walther Funk, Minister of Economic Affairs.

**Führung und Gefecht der verbundenen Waffen.** Management and Engagement of Combined Arms. Military service and combat command.

**Füllpulver 31.** Charged powder 31. TNT.

**Fu.M.B.** *See* Funkmeß-Beobachtungsgerät.

**Fünfte Verordnung zur Durchführung des Gesetzes zur Sicherung der Deutschen Evangelischen Kirche.** Fifth Decree for Execution of the Law for the Safeguarding of the German Evangelical (Protestant) Church. Prohibiting the churches from filling their pastorates, ordaining ministers, visiting, publishing of bans, and collecting dues and assessments.

**Fünfundzwanzig am Arsch.** Twenty-five on the arse. Whipping punishment for concentration camp prisoner who violated any rule. Bent over a table or trestle, the prisoner would be whipped while hearing the SS chant: "Fünfundzwanzig am Arsch."

**Fünfundzwanzig Punkte des nationalsozialistischen Programms.** The Twenty-five Points of the National Socialist Program. *See also* Appendix: Parteiprogramm: Fünfundzwanzig Punkte des nationalsozialistischen Programms.

**Fünfzehnte Verordnung zur Durchführung des Gesetzes zur Sicherung der Deutschen Evangelischen Kirche.** Fifteenth Decree for the Execution of the Law for Security of the German Evangelical (Protestant) Church. Reich Ministry for Church Affairs finance department to supervise the administration of the church property budget, tax assessment, and use of budget funds.

**Funkaufklärung.** Radio Intelligence. Branch of German military intelligence.

**Funkberichter.** Radio reporter. *See also* Propaganda-Kompanie.

**Funker.** Radioman. In Wehrmacht.

**Funklenk.** Radio controlled. Remote-controlled high-explosive-bearing tanks.

**Funkmeß-Beobachtungsgerät.** (Fu.M.B.) Instrument detecting the location of Allied radio signals.

**funkpeilen.** To locate by means of a radio. To fix a location by means of a direction finder.

**Funkraum.** Radio room.

**Funkspruch.** Radio message.

**Funktionshäftlinge.** Special assignment prisoners. Camp inmates of German nationality who ran the internal administration of the camps.

**Furcht.** Fear. *See* Weltfurcht.

**"Für Führer, Volk, und Vaterland."** "For the Führer, the People, and the Fatherland." Standard phrase used from the beginning of the war to announce the death of soldiers.

**Fürsorgeoffizier.** Welfare officer. Officer in charge of soldiers' welfare.

**Füße.** Feet. Air force slang for landing gear.

**Fußmarsch.** Foot march. Death march. *See also* Todesmärsche.

**Futtermittelschein.** Ration card for pet food. *See also* Reichskleiderkarten.

# G

g., G. *See* geheim.

**Galizien-Division.** Galicia Division. Ukrainian volunteer military formation recruited by the Germans largely in the district of Galicia, Poland. One of many non-German units in the Waffen-SS.

**Gangwerk.** Germanization of Maschine (machine).

**Ganzheit.** *See* Gemeinschaft.

**Ganzheitsbild.** View of the whole situation. Total appreciation of the whole situation.

**Garant, garantieren.** Guarantor, to guarantee. National Socialist keywords, especially Hitler as guarantor of a new order, European peace, new future for the world.

**"Garant der deutschen Freiheit."** "Guarantor of German Liberty." Hitler.

**"Garant des Friedens."** "Guarantor of Peace." Hitler.

**"(die) Garanten der Zukunft."** "The Guarantors of the Future." German youth. Expression was discouraged after 1940.

**"(die lebenden) Garanten Deutschland."** "The living Guarantors of Germany." German youth. Expression was discouraged after 1940.

**garnisonsverwendungsfähig.** (g.v.) Suitable for garrison duty. Soldiers who were not able to remain at the front due to injuries or illness. They were placed behind the front line or sent home.

**Gasauto.** Gassing car. Mobile gas chamber. *See also* Gaswagen.

**Gaskammer.** Gas chamber. The method of mass murder of Jews, Gypsies, Poles, Soviets, and others most often used by the Nazis. *See also* Endlösung der Judenfrage.

**(fahrbare) Gaskammer.** Mobile gas-chamber. *See also* Gaswagen.

**Gaslager.** (Poison-) gas camp. *See also* Chelmno (Kulmhof).

**Gastarbeiter.** Foreign worker. Hundreds of thousands or more foreign workers were forced into Germany to work for the German war effort.

**Gaswagen.** Mobile gas chamber. Sealed five-ton trucks employed by Einsatzgruppen in 1942 to murder people using poisonous exhaust from the diesel engines, during the German attack on the Soviet Union. Such mass-murder devices were also used at the death camp Chelmno from 1941 to 1944, where more than 150,000 human beings (the vast majority Jews) were killed.

**Gau.** District, province. Highest territorial and organizational unit of the Nazi Party under the Third Reich.

**Gauführer.** *See* Gauleiter.

**Gauleiter.** Heads of Regional Administrative Districts. Supreme territorial or regional Nazi Party authority. The Nazi Party divided Germany and some annexed territories into geographical units called Gaue, headed by a Gauleiter. Superior to an Ortsgruppenleiter and a Kreisleiter. In 1939, there were more than forty Gaue.

**Gauleiter von Wien.** Regional Nazi Party Leader of Vienna. Baldur von Schirach's appointment in 1940 for Hitler's express purpose of driving Jews and Czechs out of Vienna to make it once again a so-called German city.

**Gaupropagandaleitung.** District Propaganda Leadership. Those responsible for propaganda in the district.

**Gauredner.** Regional Speaker. Nazi Party propaganda officer in the Gau.

**Gaustudentenführung.** District Student Leadership. *See also* Nationalsozialistischer Deutscher Studentenbund.

**Gautag.** District Day. Annual official celebration with rallies and parades.

**Gauvertrauensschwester.** Official District Nurse. Head nurse of the National Socialist Nurses Association responsible for health matters in a district.

**Gauwirtschaftskammer.** District Economic Chamber. In 1942 Albert Speer created an economic council in each Gau, bypassing the Gauleiter.

**GBA.** *See* Generalbevollmächtigter für den Arbeitseinsatz.

**GDVG.** *See* Großdeutsche Volksgemeinschaft.

**Gebiet.** District. Major unit of Hitlerjugend and Deutsches Jungvolk in der Hitlerjugend.

**Gebietskommissar.** (Geb.K.) Territorial commissioner.

**Gebinde.** Germanized for container, barrel.

**Gebirgskanone.** Mountain gun.

**Gebirgskorps.** (Geb.K.) Mountain Corps.

**Geb.K.** *See* Gebietskommissar; Gebirgskorps.

**"Gebt mir vier Jahre Zeit!"** "Give me four years." Referring to the duration of the new Nazi government administration beginning in 1933. *See also* Ermächtigungsgesetz.

**Gebührnis.** Germanization of Sold (soldier's pay).

**Geburtenkrieg.** Birth war. 1936 description of the campaign to increase the German birthrate.

**Geburtenschlacht.** Birth battle. Fight to increase the German population.

**Geburtensieg.** Birth victory. Aryans outpopulating other races.

**Geburtenträgheit.** Birth sluggishness. Reluctance to bear (German) children.

**Gedankenführungen.** Thought guides. Antisemitic educational material supplied to the armed forces personnel by the Wehrmacht.

**Gedob.** *See* Generaldirektion der Ostbahn in Krakau.

**gef.** *See* gefährlich; gefangen.

**Gefahrengeld.** *See* Gefahrenzulage.

**Gefahrenzulage.** Indemnity for risk. SS who rounded up Jews for death in the Polish ghettos were awarded extra pay in consideration of their risk of infection from the Jews. Also, four Reichsmark daily for paratroopers.

**gefährlich.** (gef) Dangerous.

**Gefälle.** Gradient, slope. Differential, as a geopolitical term. Also supply.

**Gefallene des Marsches auf die Feldherrnhalle.** Fallen in the march on the Feldherrnhalle. So-called martyrs who died in the 1923 Hitler Putsch.

**(die) Gefallenenehrungsfeiern der NSDAP.** Ceremonies to honor the dead of the National-Socialist German Workers' Party. The Nazis developed an elaborate system of rituals and ceremonies for birth, marriage, and death. During the war, they were particularly distressed to find that the vast majority of Germans chose church ceremonies rather than Party ceremonies.

**"Gefallen im Glauben an Adolf Hitler."** "Died in battle, believing in Adolf Hitler." Common phrase in death announcements from the front.

**gefangen.** (gef) Captured.

**Gefangenen-Stärkemeldung.** Prisoner-strength reports. Statistics about numbers and categories of prison and concentration camp inmates.

**Gefechtsstreifen.** Combat zone.

**Gefolgschaft.** Entourage. Followers loyal to Hitler; community that followed the Führer's will. Also, subsection of Hitlerjugend with about 150 members.

**Gefolgschaftsappell.** Roll call of the entourage. Weekly (Hitler's) staff roll call.

**Gefolgschaftsführer.** Leader of the followers. Hitler Youth leader.

**Gefolgschaftssparen.** Saving by the followers. Community savings in German factories.

**Gefolgsherr.** Vassal lord. Feudal term used for the person who educated Nordic youth; a mentor rather than a drillmaster.

**Gefolgsmann.** Entourage man. Unconditionally faithful follower.

**Gefolgsnation.** A nation that follows. Nazi goal that Germany follow Hitler unconditionally.

**Gefrierfleischorden.** Frozen-meat medal. Soldier slang, military decorations earned while fighting on the Eastern Front in winter. *See also* Eisbeinorden.

**Gefrisch.** Germanization of Regenerierung (regeneration). Recycling of material (e.g., rubber, oil).

**GEFU.** *See* Gesellschaft zur Förderung gesellschaftlicher Unternehmungen.

**GEG.** *See* Großeinkaufs-Gesellschaft Deutscher Konsumvereine mbH.

**Gegenauslese.** Opposed to selection. Establishing good hereditary lineage by bogus means.

**Gegennation.** Opposition nation. An anti-Nazi country.

**Gegenrasse.** Anti-race. Not of the Nordic race, especially Jews, Blacks.

**Gegenreich.** Anti-Nazi Reich. Jewish nation.

**Gegenschlag.** Counterattack. German military offense presaged by Goebbels toward the end of the war and supposed to effect a German reversal of fortune.

**Gegenseitigkeitsgeschäft.** Reciprocal business. Bartering in foreign trade, requiring no exchange of currencies.

**Gegenterror.** Counter terror. Goebbel's intention to counter Allied air attacks on German cities with German attacks on Allied cities. *See also* Terror; Vergeltungsaktion.

**Gegentyp(us).** Anti-type. Enemies of the Third Reich, especially the Jew.

**Gegenvolk.** Anti-people. Jews as subhuman.

**Gehag.** *See* Gemeinnützige Heimstätten- Spar- und Bau-AG.

**geheim.** (g., G.) Secret, confidential. Abbreviation stamped on certain documents.

**Geheime Feldpolizei.** (GFP) Secret Field Police. In charge of security tasks in the Wehrmacht, including counterintelligence. Most of their functions were taken over by the RSHA in 1942. *See* Sicherheitsdienst.

**Geheime Kommandosache.** (GKdoS) Top-secret level. Second highest level of secret orders, used especially for military documents.

**Geheime Reichssache.** (geh.R., GRS, ghs) State secret. Highest level of confidentiality for official and military documents. The most important Reich secret was the Endlösung der Judenfrage.

**Geheimer Kabinettsrat.** Secret Cabinet Council. Hitler's 1938 secret foreign affairs advisory council. Functioned only to allow Hitler to replace Foreign Minister Konstantin von Neurath with Joachim von Ribbentrop.

**Geheimer Meldedienst.** Secret Reporting Service. An office of the German intelligence community.

**Geheimes Polizeiamt.** (GPA) Secret Police Department.

**Geheime Staatspolizei.** (Gestapo) Secret State Police. Powerful political police of the Third Reich. It grew out of Göring's Prussian Political Police and Himmler's Bavarian Political Police. Chief of the Gestapo was Heinrich Müller, called Gestapo-Müller, and above him Himmler as head of all police. Prior to the outbreak of war, the Gestapo used brutal methods to investigate and suppress resistance to Nazi rule within Germany. After 1939, the Gestapo expanded its operations into Nazi-occupied Europe. Its role was counterespionage and to arrest enemies of the Third Reich, including leftist and church opponents, Jews, Freemasons, political enemies, rightist opponents, and male homosexuals. Gestapo operatives also participated in the deportation of Jews to death camps and the Einsatzgruppen's mass murder of Jews in German-occupied eastern Europe. *See also* Einsatzgruppen.

**Geheimes Staatspolizei-Amt.** (Gestapa) Secret State Police Office. Established under the authority of Himmler, who appointed Reinhard Heydrich to head it up, coordinated all Gestapo business. Gestapo headquarters in Berlin.

**Geheimnis.** Secret. Synonymous with terror in the Third Reich. A crucial element in all political, social, and military organizations of Hitler's regime.

**geh.R.** *See* Geheime Reichssache.

**Gehsperre.** Curfew. Strict regulation for people living in ghettos not to go outside after a certain hour. The SS ordered Jewish leaders to impose a curfew in order to facilitate roundups of Jewish ghetto inhabitants and their deportation to the death camps.

**Geisellager.** (GIL) Hostage camp.

**Geiselmord.** Hostage murder. *See also* Sühnemaßnahmen.

**Geistesjuden.** Jews in spirit. Sympathizers of Jews.

**Geistliches Ministerium.** Spiritual ministry. Highest level of the German Protestant Church. Under the Third Reich, appointed by the Reich bishop.

**Gekados.** (GKdos) *See* Geheime Kommandosache.

**gekonnt.** Capable. In 1933, sports terminology for admirable personal capability.

**Gekrat.** *See* Gemeinnützige Krankentransport GmbH.

**Geländedienst.** Outdoor Service. Pre-military training of the Hitler Youth, the SA, and the SS.

**geländegängig.** (All-) terrain driving. (Car) suitable for cross-country driving.

**Geländesport.** Terrain sport. Training in the military use of terrain.

**Geländewagen.** Car comparable to a jeep.

**gelbe Armbinden.** Yellow arm bands. Stigmatic emblem that the German Armed Forces Command ordered Yugoslavian Jews to wear from 1941.

**gelbe Flecke.** Yellow stains. One of many stigmatic emblems identifying Jews in German-occupied Europe. Sometimes a yellow Star of David, other times, as in Poland, a white armband with a blue star of David. *See also* Judengelb.

**gelbe Judenkarte.** Yellow card for Jews. 1933 identification card that permitted Jewish students to attend university lectures and seminars. *See also* blaue Karte; braune Karte.

**gelbe Plakate.** Yellow posters. Antisemitic posters calling for the boycott of Jewish businesses and professionals in 1933.

**gelber Raum.** Yellow room. Any area containing poison gas.

**Geleitzug.** Convoy. *See also* Geleitzugkrieg.

**Geleitzugkrieg.** Convoy war. The mostly U-boat war against Allied shipping in the Atlantic (1939–1945).

**Geltungsjuden.** Jews worth something, valid Jews. Early on, Jews who served in World War I. Later, offspring who practiced Judaism and were the product of mixed marriages with two fully Jewish grandparents and two Aryan grandparents.

**gemäß Sonderanweisung.** According to special instructions. Euphemism for actions such as mistreating, torturing, and murdering Jews and others, carried out on special orders.

**gemäß Sonderanweisung behandelt.** Treated according to special instructions. *See also* behandeln; gemäß Sonderanweisung.

**Gemeindepolizei.** Local Police. Founded in 1936 and later fought together with the Order Police. *See also* Gendarmerie; Ordnungspolizei.

**"Gemeinnutz geht über Eigennutz!"** "The welfare of the community over the welfare of the individual." Slogan and rationale used to justify taking possession of Jewish property.

**Gemeinnutz geht vor Eigennutz.** *See* "Germeinnutz geht über Eigennutz."

**Gemeinnützige Heimstätten- Spar- und Bau-AG.** (Gehag) Community Home Savings and Building Company Ltd. One of its responsibilities was the building of workers' housing.

**Gemeinnützige Krankentransport GmbH.** (Gekrat) Non-profit Patient Transport Ltd. SS agency that in gray buses transported victims to euthanasia sites to be murdered. *See also* Allgemeine Krankentransportgesellschaft.

**Gemeinnützige Krankentransportgesellschaft GmbH.** (Gekrt) Non-profit Patient Transport Company Ltd. *See also* Allgemeine Krankentransportgesellschaft.

**Gemeinnützige Stiftung für Anstaltspflege.** Charitable foundation for institutional care. Code name for the Nazi Party's euthanasia branch that provided the funds to operate the Foundation for Institutional Care.

**Gemeinschaft.** Community. Mystical relationship among the German race, destiny, contrasted with mere society, or Geselschaft. Also, economic cartel. *See also* Volksgemeinschaft.

**Gemeinschaft Hohlglas.** Cartel of glassware. *See also* Reichsvereinigung.

**Gemeinschaftsbauten.** *See* Bauten des Führers.

**Gemeinschaft Schuhe.** Cartel of shoes. Shoe cartel. *See also* Reichsvereinigung.

**Gemeinschaftsempfang.** Collective reception. Obligatory listening at home, at work, and in public places to radio broadcasts of Hitler speeches. *See* Führerrede.

**gemeinschaftsfeindlich.** Inimical to the German national-racial community. Individualism.

**Gemeinschaftsfremde.** Strangers to the community. Any person who did not fit into the concept of Volksgemeinschaft. *See also* Volksgemeinschaft.

**gemeinschaftsgebundene Wirtschaft.** Collective economy. Planned economy.

**Gemeinschaftslager.** (GL) Communal camps. Jewish slave-labor camps owned by private German companies who rented Jews, paying the SS almost nothing. Also, training areas for lawyers and teachers.

**Gemeinschaftsschädling.** Community pest, disgrace of the community. Nazis portrayed their enemies as sources of illness to the body politic.

**Gemeinschaftssiedlung.** Community settlement. According to the National Socialist idea of space, a harmoniously designed housing complex with its own center that visually reflected the notion of a community of people.

**gemeinschaftsunfähig.** Community unsuitable. *See also* Gemeinschaftsunfähige.

**Gemeinschaftsunfähige.** Individuals deemed unable to live in the community. Germans not deemed worthy to live in the German community. Any person who was considered asocial and did not contribute to Germany (e.g., alcoholics, prostitutes, drug addicts, racial violators, people charged with abortions, the chronically unemployed, etc.). *See also* asozial.

**Gemeinschaftsverpflegung.** Common meals. Government-organized community kitchens to feed German children.

**Gemeinschaftswerk.** Cooperative company. Combined businesses; commonly managed factories.

**Gemeinschaftswerkstätte.** Cooperative workshops. *See also* Gemeinschaftswerk.

**gemischtvölkische Ehe.** Mixed marriage.

**Gendarmerie.** Rural Police. As part of the Ordnungspolizei, some units were involved in roundups, deportation, and mass murder.

**Gendarmerie-Station.** (GS) Police station.

**Gen.d.Artl.** *See* General der Artillerie.

**Generalbevollmächtigten für den Arbeitseinsatz.** Plenipotentiaries-General for Labor Mobilization. Führer decree of March 1942. *See also* Generalbevollmächtigter für den Arbeitseinsatz.

**Generalbevollmächtigter für den Arbeitseinsatz.** (GBA) Plenipotentiary-General for Labor Mobilization. Title of Fritz Sauckel, who was responsible for the exploitation of millions of foreign workers and POWs and the deaths of tens of thousands of Jewish workers in Poland under German auspices.

**Generalbevollmächtigter für den totalen Kriegseinsatz.** Plenipotentiary-General for Total War Deployment. Hitler-appointed position for Goebbels after July 1944 Putsch. It awarded Goebbels extensive power in most areas of the German war effort, however, it was too near the end of the war to achieve much.

**Generalbevollmächtigter für die Reichsverwaltung.** Plenipotentiary-General for the Reich Administration. One of many positions held by Himmler.

**Generalbevollmächtigter für die Wirtschaft.** Plenipotentiary-General for the Economy. Position first held by Hjalmar Schacht, then Walther Funk.

**Generalbevollmächtigter für Rüstungsaufgaben und Kriegsproduktion.** *See* Reichsminister(ium) für Rüstungs (aufgaben) und Kriegsproduktion.

**General der Artillerie.** (Gen.d.Artl.) Artillery General.

**Generaldirektion der Ostbahn in Krakau.** (Gedob) Directorate-General for Eastern Railways in Cracow. Responsible for the schedules of deportation trains to the concentration camps.

**Generalfeldmarschall.** (Gen.Feldm.) General Fieldmarshal. Highest rank in the German armed forces.

**Generalgouvernement.** (GG) General Government. A civilian administrative unit established by the Germans in October 1939, consisting of eastern Poland occupied by Germany but not incorporated into the Third Reich. It included the districts of Warsaw, Krakow, Radom, Lublin, and Lwów. Hans Frank was appointed Governor General, and he oversaw the mass murder of millions of Jews and thousands of intellectuals, professionals, and politicians, and the enslavement of millions more. The Germans destroyed Polish cultural and scientific institutions and viewed the Polish population as a potential workforce. The portions of western Poland not included in the Generalgouvernement, but incorporated into the Reich, were Danzig, East Prussia, the Wartheland, and the administrative districts of Zeichenau and Upper Silesia; Galicia was added on August 1, 1941.

**Generalgouverneur.** Governor General of Generalgouvernement.

**Generalinspekteur.** (Gisass) General Inspector of the SA and SS.

**Generalinspektor für das deutsche Straßenwesen.** General Inspector of the German Road System. Another of Alfred Speer's titles.

**Generalinspektor Wasser und Energie.** General Inspector of Water and Energy. Another of Alfred Speer's titles.

**Generalkommando.** (GK) General command.

**Generalplan Ost.** (GPO) Master Plan East. Commissioned by Himmler in June 1941 and completed in July 1941 from the Reich Commission for Germanization. Nazi plan to deport 31 million eastern Europeans (Poles, Russians, Baltics) and enslave and/or murder 14 million eastern Europeans, including 5 to 6 million Jews, replacing them with 10 million Germanic people. *See* Reichskommissar für die Festigung des deutschen Volkstums.

**Generalplan Ost, rechtliche, wirtschaftliche und räumliche Grundlagen des Ostaufbaues.** Master Plan East, legal, economic, and spatial bases of the construction of the east. In May 1942, Himmler received this memorandum from Professor Konrad Meyer-Hetling. *See* Generalplan.

**Generalquartiermeister.** (GenQu) General Quartermaster. Staff officers responsible for supply in both the High Command of the army and the air force.

**Generalrat der Wirtschaft.** General Economic Council. Committee of experts formed in 1933 to advise the German government on the economy.

**Generalspeisezettel.** General menu. Example menu established by the Institute for Economic Research.

**Generalstab des Heeres.** (GenStdH) Army General Staff. Top administrators of the army.

**Gen.Feldm.** *See* Generalfeldmarschall.

**Genickschuß.** Shot in the nape of the neck. Rapid SS executions.

**Genickschußanlage.** Neck-shooting facility. Specially designed and disguised facilities at Buchenwald, Dachau, and Mauthausen concentration camps where more than 100,000 Soviet POWs were murdered.

**GenQu.** *See* Generalquartiermeister.

**Geopolitik.** Geopolitics. The theory of Halford Mackinder about the importance of geography's impact on politics and world history. Through Karl Ernst Haushofer, a German army officer and geographer, Mackinder's ideas influenced the geopolitical basis for Nazi plans of world domination. Director of the Institute of Geopolitics at the University of Munich, Haushofer had great influence on the German army and on Hitler, especially through Rudolf Hess. Hitler's demands for more space in the east at the expense of the Slavic nations was encouraged by Haushofer's theories, even though it was a twentieth-century formulation of the traditional Drang nach Osten (*see* Autarkie). Geopoliticians saw boundaries merely as a temporary halt of a nation in its march toward world domination. The nature of Germany's Herrenvolk precluded other states from their rights to "natural frontiers." *See also* Herzland; Lebensraum.

**George-Kreis.** (Stefan) George Circle. Late nineteenth-century and early twentieth-century nationalistic and antisemitic cult that may have influenced Hitler just after World War I.

**Gepäckmarschmeisterschaft.** Route march competition with full kit. Competition between different NSDAP formations to test endurance, toughness, and energy level during a fast twenty-mile march carrying a thirty-pound pack.

**gepanzert.** Armored. Widely used Wehrmacht term describing German armored vehicles.

**Gerichtseingesessener.** Archaic, person under the competency of an assigned court.

**Germanenorder.** Germanic Order. Racist, nationalist, antisemitic German society. *See also* Thule-Gesellschaft.

**Germania.** *See* Welthauptstadt Germania.

**Germanisation.** *See* Germanisierung.

**germanische Demokratie.** Germanic Democracy. According to Hitler, Germanic democracy is unlike Jewish parliamentary democracy that responds to lobbying. Germanic democracy occurs when Germans place their trust in a leader, who publicly takes responsibility for making political decisions.

**germanische Freiwillige.** Germanic volunteers. Norwegian, Swedish, Danish, and Dutch volunteers in the Waffen-SS.

**Germanische Freiwilligenverbände.** Germanic Volunteer Units. From 1940 on, Norwegian, Danish, and Dutch SS divisions.

**Germanische Glaubensbewegung.** Germanic Belief Movement. Insignificant German pagan sect that rejected the Bible and claimed God was Nordic-German. Ultimately abandoned by the Third Reich.

**Germanische Leitstelle.** *See* Germanische Freiwilligen-Leitstelle.

**Germanische Freiwilligen-Leitstelle.** (GFL) German Volunteer Bureau. Section of SS headquarters that recruited volunteers from northern and western Europe for the Waffen-SS as well as for the General SS abroad.

**germanische NN.-Häftlinge.** Germanic Nacht-und-Nebel (Night and Fog) prisoner. These were often sent to Natzweiler-Struthof concentration camp. *See also* Nacht-und-Nebel-Häftlinge.

**Germanische SS.** Germanic SS. *See also* Germanische Freiwillingenverbände.

**Germanische Sturmbanne.** Germanic Storm Battalions. SS recruits from Denmark, the Netherlands, Norway, and Switzerland.

**Germanisierung.** Germanization. Converting to the German way. In eastern Europe, this consisted of removal and mass murder of un-German races, especially Jews, and opening the eastern territory to German settlers.

**Ger-Rune.** Symbolic of the spirit of community.

**Geruchsspürer.** Scent tracer. Scout recognizing gas by smell.

**Gesamtaktionen.** Collective action. A four-week period at all German universities in preparation for the burning of blacklisted books on May 5, 1933. *See also* Aufklärungsfeldzug wider den undeutschen Geist.

**gesamtdeutsch.** Fully German. German in blood, race, spirit, and politics.

**Gesamtheit.** Totality, wholeness, type. Sometimes replaced the old concept of Gestalt.

**Gesamtjudentum.** Total Jewry. All Jews of the world.

**Gesamtlösung der Judenfrage.** Complete solution of the Jewish problem. Euphemism preceding Endlösung for the methodical and systematic destruction of Jews, Judaism, and Jewishness in Europe. In 1941, Reinhard Heydrich had Adolf Eichmann prepare a draft of an authorization to effect "the complete solution of the Jewish problem in the German sphere of influence in Europe," the document to be signed by Göring, who was then still nominally in charge of Germany's anti-Jewish policies.

**Gesamtorganisation der gewerblichen Wirtschaft.** (OGW) Organization of all industrial and commercial firms by trades. The trades being industry, commerce, banks, insurance, power, tourism, transportation, and crafts.

**Gesamtsiedlungsplan.** Complete resettlement plan. Himmler's inclusive plan for population transfers and deportations in Europe, especially depolonization and dejudaization of German-occupied eastern Europe. The war ended before the plan could be fully actualized.

**Gesamt-SS.** Total SS. All SS branches.

**Gesamtwille.** Combined will. The will of the community; the German will.

**(gute) Geschäfte.** Good business. Concentration camp Kapos confiscated and sold goods found on new prisoners.

**Geschehen.** Happening. History perceived as developing as an organic process according to its own inescapable laws.

**Geschichte.** History. German history from a Nazi-racial point of view.

**geschichtlich.** Historical. Political, from a Nazi-ideological point of view.

**Geschichtlichkeit.** Historicity. Relevant to politics.

**geschichtslos.** Nonpolitical. Apolitical.

**geschlechtlich gebraucht.** Sexually used. Justification for charges against, and convictions of, Polish and other foreign prisoners for having had sexual relations with a German woman. Convictions carried the death penalty.

**geschütztes Haus.** Protected house. In Budapest, houses set up by Raoul Wallenberg and other people where Jews were temporarily safe from deportation.

**Geschwader.** Groups. Luftwaffe squadrons.

**Gesellschaft.** *See* Gemeinschaft.

**Gesellschaft Das Ahnenerbe e.V.** *See* Ahnenerbe Forschungs- und Lehrgemeinschaft.

**Gesellschaft für Textil- und Lederverwertung, GmbH.** Association for Textile and Leather Utilization, Ltd. Company created in 1940 and owned by the SS. By 1943, 3,000 Ravensbrück prisoners worked there in two shifts of eleven hours each producing or altering uniforms and other items of clothing for the Waffen-SS.

**Gesellschaft zur Förderung gesellschaftlicher Unternehmungen.** (GEFU) Organization to promote corporations.

**Gesetz.** Law. Racial and individual destiny.

**Gesetz gegen die Neubildung von Parteien.** Law Prohibiting the New Formation of (political) Parties. Law of July 14, 1933, it meant the end of democracy and the ascension of the Nazi Party as the only political party in Germany. *See also* Gleichschaltung.

**Gesetz gegen die Überfüllung von deutschen Schulen und Hochschulen vom 25.4.33.** Law Prohibiting the Overcrowding of German Schools and Universities of April 25, 1933. In effect, restricting Jewish attendance at schools.

**Gesetz gegen heimtückische Angriffe auf Staat und Partei und zum Schutz der Parteiuniformen.** Law against Malicious Attacks on the State and Party and for the Protection of the Party Uniform. This December 1934 law, along with another in March 1933, provided prison sentences for critics and opponents of National Socialism. *See also* Verordnung zur Abwehr heimtückischer Angriffe gegen die Regierung der nationalen Erhebung.

**gesetzloses Treiben.** Lawless activities. Unofficial SA acts against Jews.

**Gesetz über das Beschlußverfahren in Rechtsangelegenheiten der Evangelischen Kirche.** Law concerning Procedure for Decisions in Legal Affairs of the Evangelical (Protestant) Church. Giving the Reich Ministry of the Interior sole authority to determine the validity of measures taken in the churches since May 1, 1933, when raised in a civil lawsuit.

**Gesetz über das Schlachten von Tieren.** Law regarding the (ritual) Slaughter of Animals. April 22, 1933, law prohibited Jewish kosher slaughter.

**Gesetz über das Staatsoberhaupt des Deutschen Reiches.** Law concerning the Head of State of the German Reich. August 1, 1934, law that united the titles and functions of German chancellor and president, political chief and chief of state, and conferred them on Hitler, who was also Führer. *See also* (Der) Führer; Treueid.

**Gesetz über den Neuaufbau des Reiches vom 30.1.1934.** *See* Neuaufbaugesetz vom 30.1.1934.

**Gesetz über den organischen Aufbau der deutschen Wirtschaft.** Law concerning the Organizational Structure of the German Economy. February 27, 1934, law that organized the German economy into trade and into regional groups.

**Gesetz über den Widerruf von Einbürgerungen und die Aberkennung der deutschen Staatsangehörigkeit.** Law concerning the Revocation of Naturalization and the Loss of German Nationality.

**Gesetz über die Änderung von Familien- und Vornamen.** Law regarding the Changing of Family and First Names. January 5, 1938, law that restricted first names of Jews to obviously Jewish names. *See also* jüdische Vornamen.

**Gesetz über die Einziehung volks- und staatsfeindlichen Vermögens vom 14.7.33.** Law concerning the Confiscation of the Property of Enemies of the People and the State of July 14, 1933.

**Gesetz über die Herstellung von Waffen.** Law regarding the Manufacture of Firearms (March 18, 1938).

**Gesetz über die Hitlerjugend.** *See* Hitlerjugend.

**Gesetz über die Neuwahl von Schöffen, Geschworenen, und Handelsrichten.** Law regarding New election of Assessors, Jurors, and Commercial Judges. One of the April 7, 1933, laws excluding Jewish professionals from German public life.

**Gesetz über die Rechtsverhältnisse der jüdischen Kultusvereinigungen.** Law on the Legal Status of Jewish Religious Organizations. March 28, 1938, law making Jewish religious organizations illegal.

**Gesetz über die Überfüllung von deutschen Schulen und Hochschulen.** Law concerning the Overcrowding of German Public Schools and Schools of Higher Education. This April 25, 1933, law drastically limited the number of Jewish students.

**Gesetz über die Verfassung der Deutschen Evangelischen Kirche.** Law concerning the Constitution of the German Evangelical (Protestant) Church. Establishing among other things the new post of Reich Bishop.

**Gesetz über die Zulassung zur Rechtsanwaltschaft.** Law concerning Admissions to the Bar Association. This April 7, 1933, law removed Jews from the German Bar Association.

**Gesetz über Einziehung von Erzeugnissen entarteter Kunst.** (May 1938) Law concerning the Confiscation of Works of Degenerate Art. *See also* entartete Kunst.

**Gesetz zum Schutz der Erbgesundheit des deutschen Volkes.** Law for the Protection of the Hereditary Health of the German People. Required that marriages were subject to certificate of hereditary health.

**Gesetz zum Schutz des deutschen Blutes und der deutschen Ehre.** (Nuremberg) Law for the Protection of German Blood and German Honor. It defined who was an Aryan, who a Jew, who was of mixed blood. Some Nazis, like Wilhelm Stuckart and Hans Globke, interpreted this law as applying to Gypsies as well as Jews. *See also* Blutschutzgesetz; Nürnberger Judengesetze; Zigeuner.

**Gesetz zum Schutze des Einzelhandels vom 12.5.33.** Law for the Protection of Retail Business of May 12, 1933.

**Gesetz zum Schutze von Volk und Staat.** Law for the Protection of the (German) People and State.

**Gesetz zur Behebung der Not von Volk und Reich.** Law to Remove the Distress of the People and the State. Reichstag law of March 24, 1933, which authorized Hitler to rule by decree and suspend civil liberties, essentially destroying the Weimar Republic. *See also* Ermächtigungsgesetz.

**Gesetz zur Gleichschaltung der Länder mit dem Reich.** Law for the Consolidation of the Provinces with the Reich. Created national Reich law as supreme in Germany.

**Gesetz zur Ordnung der nationalen Arbeit vom 20.1.34.** Law for the Regulation of National Labor of January 20, 1934. Banned Jews from participating in the German Labor Front.

**Gesetz zur Sicherung der Deutschen Evangelischen Kirche.** Law for the Safeguarding of the German Evangelical (Protestant) Church. Empowering the Reich Minister of Church Affairs (Hans Kerrl) to issue ordinances with binding legal force.

**Gesetz zur Sicherung der Einheit von Partei und Staat vom 1.12.33.** Law for the Safeguarding of the Unification of (Nazi) Party and State of December 1, 1933. Law suppressing all political parties except the Nazi Party.

**Gesetz zur Verhütung erbkranken Nachwuchses.** Law for the Prevention of Children with Hereditary Diseases. People were to be sterilized against their will for the following conditions: angeborener Schwachsinn (congenital feeblemindedness), Epilepsie (hereditary epilepsy), Veitstanz (St. Vitus' Dance, hereditary chorea), Blindheit (hereditary blindness), Taubheit (hereditary deafness), Schizophrenie (schizophrenia), manische Depression (manic-depressive psychosis), schwere körperliche Mißbildungen (severe bodily deformities), schwerer Alkoholismus (severe alcoholism). *See also* Euthanasie.

**Gesetz zur Wiederherstellung des Berufsbeamtentums.** Law for the Reconstitution of the Civil Service. This law of April 1933 mandated the dismissal of non-Aryan, especially Jewish, government workers (with the temporary exception of Jewish World War I veterans). In essence, the law defined a Jew as a person who was descended from Jewish parents or grandparents, even if only one parent or grandparent adhered to the Jewish religion. At Nuremberg, the law was later extended to politically suspicious persons and to those who were descended from at least three racially fully-Jewish grandparents (November 14, 1935). In an earlier law, a grandparent was defined as without question fully Jewish if he or she belonged to the Jewish religious community. Moreover, a half-Jew descended from two fully-Jewish grandparents was also regarded as a Jew if, at the time of the promulgation of the law, he or she belonged to the Jewish religious community or afterward joined it. In other words, the basic definition of Jew in the Third Reich depended on religion, not race. *See also* Berufsbeamtengesetz.

**Gesinnungsakrobaten.** Attitude acrobats. Derisive for critics and opponents of the Nazi regime.

**Gesinnungsunterricht.** Character training. The teaching of Nazi ideology.

**gesonderte Unterbringung.** Separate accommodation. Euphemism for mass murder of Jews. *See also* Sonderbehandlung.

**gesondert untergebracht.** Placed separately. *See also* gesonderte Unterbringung; Sonderbehandlung.

**Gestalt.** Form, shape. Image, type, concept, structure, destiny.

**Gestapa.** *See* Geheimes Staatspolizei-Amt.

**Gestapo.** *See* Geheime Staatspolizei.

**Gestapohaftlager.** (GHL) Gestapo prison camp.

**Gestapo-Müller.** Gestapo Müller. Nickname for Heinrich Müller, Head of the Gestapo under Himmler and Reinhard Heydrich. *See* Geheime Staatspolizei.

**Gestellungsaufruf.** Roll call. *See also* Gestellungsbefehl.

**Gestellungsbefehl.** Muster order, call-up. Military term applied to civilian life during World War II, requiring the individual to report for war-industry work.

**Gestrauchelter.** Staggerer. Sneak thief; considered a curable and educable criminal.

**gesund.** Healthy. The goal of Nazi life and community was racial health.

**gesundes rassisches Empfinden.** Proper racial sense. German way of feeling.

**gesundes Volksempfinden.** (Healthy) proper Volk feeling. To be and act in accordance with the will of the Führer.

**Gesundheitsamt.** Health Office. Government Health Office with branches all across Germany whose goal was to keep Aryans healthy.

**Gesundheitsbogen.** Health form. Health questionnaire; compulsory form filled out for every German newborn.

**Gesundheitsdienstmädel.** Health services girl. Nurse's aide/receptionist working for Hitler Youth doctors.

**Gesundheitsmädel.** Health girls. Trained in first aid and health care by the League of German Girls and used to care for children and wounded soldiers.

**Gesundung.** Healing. Healing of the Aryan race after the destruction of Europe's Jews.

**Get(t)o.** *See* Ghetto.

**Gewalteinwirkung.** Impact of violence. Mass murder in the camps.

**Gewaltverbrecher-Verordnung.** Decree against Violent Criminals.

**Gewinnbeteiligung.** Profit sharing. Unrealized Nazi Party program of profit sharing as a solution to labor problems.

**Gewinnstop.** Profit ceiling. Part of Price-Control Commissar authority. *See also* Reichskommissar für die Preisbildung.

**Gewitteraktion.** Operation lightning storm. Code name for Himmler's August 1944 roundup of 5,000 Germans believed to be directly or indirectly involved in the July 20, 1944, plot to kill Hitler.

**GF.** Gruppenführer. Group leader.

**GFL.** *See* Germanische Freiwilligen-Leitstelle.

**GFP.** *See* Geheime Feldpolizei.

**GG.** *See* Generalgouvernement.

**ggl.** *See* gottgläubig.

**Ghetto.** The Nazis revived the medieval term ghetto to describe their compulsory Jewish Quarter. Medieval ghettos were usually established in the unhealthy sections of a city, where Jews from the city and surrounding areas were forced to reside. The area was surrounded by a wall and its gates guarded. These areas remained until the eighteenth and nineteenth centuries. The Nazis also sealed off their ghettos, which were established mostly in eastern Europe (e.g., Lodz, Warsaw, Vilna, Riga, Minsk) and characterized by overcrowding, malnutrition, and heavy labor. All were eventually dissolved, and the Jews were murdered there or in nearby death camps.

**Ghettogeld.** Ghetto money. Money issued in ghettos to enable the economy to run efficiently. Also, coins and notes introduced in 1942 in the Lodz-Ghetto in Poland. Also, money used at Theresienstadt called *Theresienstädter Kronen* (Th-Kr), which depicted Moses with long sideburns and a crooked nose. *See also* Theresienstädter Kronen.

**Ghetto ohne Mauern.** Ghetto without walls. Restricted and discriminated status of Jews in Germany.

**Ghetto Ost.** Ghetto East. Part of the Rzeszow-Ghetto. Transformed in 1942 into a forced labor camp; ultimately most in the ghetto were murdered in the camps.

**Ghettoverwaltung.** Ghetto Administration. German agency that oversaw the whole ghetto system of eastern Europe and especially the Jewish councils. *See* Judenrat.

**Ghettowache.** (GW) Ghetto guard. Formed in 1941 from inmates at Theresienstadt who had to guard the ghetto/concentration camp and its perimeter. Under the threat of death, they also had to perform executions.

**GHL.** *See* Gestapohaftlager.

**"Giftige Gase! Lebensgefahr!"** "Poison gases. Life endangering." Sign on the gas chamber door at Auschwitz.

**Giftgas.** Ironic in English, the German word for poison gas. *See also* Zyklon-B.

*(Der) Giftpilz.* The Toadstool (or poison mushroom). Antisemitic children's book published by *Der Stürmer* in 1938.

**gigantisch.** Enormous. Aspect of National Socialist propaganda wherein important issues were seen as huge.

**GIL.** *See* Geisellager.

**(die) Giovenezza singen.** To sing the Giovenezza. To sing the anthem of the Italian fascists, giovenezza meaning youth. German youth doing something that was forbidden while outwardly adhering to the rules.

**Gipfelwert.** Peak value. Germanization for maximum value.

**Gisass.** *See* Generalinspekteur.

**GK.** *See* Generalkommando.

**GKdoS.** *See* Geheime Kommandosache.

**GL.** *See* Gemeinschaftslager.

**G-Ladung.** G load, G charge. Explosives for the destruction of tanks.

**Glanzstoff.** Glitter material. Germanization of Zellophan (cellophane).

**Glashaut.** Glass skin. *See also* Glanzstoff.

**Glaube.** Faith. Political and quasi-religious faith in National Socialism and the Führer and in the supremacy and worth of the Nordic race and blood.

**(blinder) Glaube.** Blind faith. Fanatical belief in Hitler and the Nazi point of view. Belief in the Nazi trinity (Dreieinigkeit) of blood, faith, and nation.

**"Glauben, gehorchen, kämpfen!"** "Believe, obey, fight." Motto in Hitler schools for boys.

**Glaubensbewegung deutscher Christen.** Movement of German Christian Believers. Nazi-oriented religious organization that advocated the Aryanization of German Christianity and the removal of Jewish influences.

**Glaubensjude.** Religious Jew.

**Glaubenslehre.** Faith education. School subject replacing the Christian religion with a religion based on Norse mythology and exclusive to the German nation.

**glaubensverschiedene Ehen.** Religiously mixed marriages. Marriages between Germans and Jews.

*Glauben und kämpfen.* To Believe and to Fight. Instructional manual for Hitler Youth training, including chapters on the war, Germany's enemies, the German people and race, the Führer, and Nazi ideology.

**Glaube und Schönheit.** Faith and Beauty. Special branch of the Bund Deutscher Mädel in der Hitlerjugend of young women between the ages of seventeen and twenty-one for spiritual and physical training for marriage and motherhood in the German Reich.

**Gleichberechtigung.** Equality. *See also* "Rüstungsgleichberechtigung Deutschlands."

**Gleichschaltung.** Consolidation. All of the German Volk's social, political, and cultural organizations to be controlled and run according to Nazi ideology and policy. All opposition to be eliminated.

*Gleichschaltungsgesetz. See* Ermächtigungsgesetz; Gesetz zur Gleichschaltung der Länder mit dem Reich.

**gleichstoffen.** Germanization of homogenisieren (to homogenize).

**Gleiskette.** Track chain, caterpillar. *See* Gliederkette.

**Gleiwitz.** *See* Unternehmen Himmler.

**Glied.** Military ranks. The Nazis created new forms for the Waffen-SS hierarchy.

**Gliederkette.** Chain. Caterpillar track.

**Gliederung.** Hierarchy. The organizational structure of the Nazi Party.

**Gliederungen und Ausgeschlossene Verbände der NSDAP.** Organizations and affiliated associations of the Nazi Party. Those organizations actually part of the Nazi Party were the SS, SA, NSKK (motor corps), Hitlerjugend, NS-Studentenbund, NS-Frauenschaft, and the NS-Dozentenbund (university teachers). The most prominent organizations affiliated with the Nazi Party were the NS-Ärztebund (medical association), NS-Juristenbund, NS-Rechtswahrerbund (lawyers' association), Lehrerbund (teachers' association), NSV, NS-Volkswohlfahrt (Public Welfare Organization), Kriegsopferversorgung (war victims), Reichsbund der deutschen Beamten (civil service), Deutscher Technik (German technology group), Deutsche Arbeitsfront (German Labor Front), and Nationalsozialistische Gemeinschaft Kraft durch Freude. For a third group, *see* Betreute Organisationen der NSDAP.

**Gliedstellung.** Position of members. In German society the community may have come before the individual, but under Nazism every individual had a place in the hierarchy established within the community.

**Globalkontingent.** Global contingent. Wholesale quota of raw materials at the disposal of planning organizations. *See also* Lenkungsbereiche.

**Globus.** Globe. Code name of Odilo Globocnik. *See also* Aktion Reinhard.

**Glocke.** Bell. Torture cell where the prisoner was alternatingly overheated and frozen.

**Glockenaktion.** Operation Bells. With the exception of one church bell per community and those bells that were specially valuable, all church bells had to be delivered to authorities between November 1941 and April 1942 to be melted down for the war effort.

**Gnadentod.** Mercy killing. Murder of the incapacitated including severely wounded German soldiers. *See also* Euthanasie.

*Gneisenau.* German cruiser. Along with the *Scharnhorst*, the backbone of German surface naval forces at the start of World War II. It was sunk later in the war.

**Goering.** *See* (Hermann) Göring.

**Goethezeit.** Goethe era. Classical German language period (1772–1832), that ended with Goethe's death.

**Goldene internationale.** Golden international. Alleged international conspiracy between Jews and capitalists.

**Goldenes Kreuz des Deutschen Ordens.** Golden Cross of the German Order. One category of the German Order. *See also* Deutscher Orden.

**Goldenes Parteiabzeichen.** Golden party pin. Lapel decoration awarded by Hitler to Party members of distinction.

**Goldfasan.** Gold pheasant. A derisive allusion to the gold-brown color of the Nazi Party uniform with red insignia; to the Nazi eagle that decorated Nazi Party officials' gold-embroidered badges; and to the recipients of the gold Nazi Party badge. *See* goldenes Parteiabzeichen.

**Goldhansi.** Golden Jackie. Nickname for an Austrian woman criminal and long-time block senior, because of her gold teeth and her habit of stealing gold and jewelry from newcomers to Ravensbrück.

**Goldjuden.** Gold Jews. Small detachments of Jews in death camps consisting of jewelers and watchmakers whose job was to sort, pack, and ship to the SS treasury all valuables (such as gold, silver, and currency) taken from the victims murdered in the camps.

**(Hermann) Göring.** At one time or another during the Third Reich, Göring was President of the Reichstag, Commander in Chief of the Luftwaffe, Plenipotentiary for the Four-Year Plan, Prime Minister and Minister of the Interior of Prussia, Chairman of the Reich Council for National Defense, and Commander in Chief of the Police and Gestapo.

**Göring-Werke.** Göring Works. *See also* Reichswerke Hermann Göring.

**Goslar.** Official Nazi Reich farmers' town from 1936 on.

**Gotenhafen.** Polish harbor city of Gdingen (Gdynia), Poland. From 1939 to 1945.

**gottgläubig.** (ggl) God believing. Nazi religious category for those Germans who withdrew from the Christian churches but were not atheists. Jews who withdrew from their religious community were not allowed to classify themselves as gottgläubig.

**Gottgläubiger.** *See* gottgläubig.

**"Gott mit uns!"** "God's on our side." Wehrmacht motto.

**Gottschedzeit.** Gottsched era. German language period (1720–1760), named after Johann Christoph Gottsched.

**Gouvernement-Générale.** *See* Generalgouvernement.

**GPA.** *See* Geheimes Polizeiamt.

**GPO.** *See* Generalplan Ost.

**GPP.** *See* Grenzpolizeiposten.

**G.P.U.** *See* Politische Geheimpolizei der Sowjetunion.

**Graf Zeppelin.** Count Zeppelin. Theoretician and soldier (d. 1917) who created the first dirigible (Luftfahrzug). Also, name of first dirigible. Zeppelins had both military and civilian uses.

**Graz.** The first city in Austria declared free of Jews by the Nazis. Called City of the Rebellion of the Volk.

**Greif.** Griffin. Code name for the dropping of English-speaking German troops wearing American uniforms behind the Allied lines during the Battle of the Bulge.

**Greifer.** Catcher. Jewish collaborator used by the Gestapo to discover Jews in hiding.

**Grenadier.** Infantryman, rifleman.

**Grenadier Division.** (Gren.D.) Infantry Division.

**Gren.D.** *See* Grenadier Division.

**Grenze.** Frontier. Combat zone, sphere of influence, expansion.

**(blutende) Grenze.** Bleeding border. Germany's borders with Poland, especially in the areas where the Versailles Treaty took German territory and awarded it to Poland.

**Grenzlanddeutsche.** Frontier-area Germans. German settlements adjacent to the Reich and struggling for existence.

**Grenzler.** Frontiersman. *See also* Grenzlanddeutsche.

**Grenzmark.** Border area. German border province.

**Grenzpolizei.** (Grepo) Border Police. Criminal police unit of the Sicherheitspolizei. From 1936, combined with Gestapo and criminal police; from 1939 absorbed into the SD.

**Grenzpolizeiposten.** GPP. Border Police post.

**Grepo.** *See* Grenzpolizei.

**Greuelhetze.** Atrocity mongering. Nazi declaration that foreign news reporting German atrocities was only propaganda. *See also* Greuelmärchen; Greuelmeldungen; Greuelpropaganda.

**Greuelhetzer.** Atrocity monger. *See also* Greuelhetze.

**Greuelmärchen.** Atrocity fairy tales. Atrocity stories about the new Germany told by Jews and others inside and outside of Germany.

**Greuelmeldungen.** Atrocity reports. Nazi broadcasts denying reports of German atrocities.

**Greuelpropaganda.** Atrocity propaganda. Nazi dismissal of the validity of foreign press reports about anything negative concerning the Reich, especially atrocities and concentration camps.

**"(Die) Greuelpropaganda ist eine Lügenpropaganda" sagen die deutschen Juden selbst.** "Atrocity propaganda is false propaganda" say the German Jews themselves. 1933 book title concocted by Goebbels and broadcast to the foreign press as evidence that the Nazis were not targeting Jews.

**GRF.** *See* Gruppenführer.

**Gröfaz.** *See* größter Feldherr aller Zeiten.

**Groschengrab.** Penny grave. Image on posters to warn of thoughtless wastage of food during the period of scarcity of raw materials.

**Großaktion.** Massive roundup. Extensive operations against Jews. *See* Erste Aktion; Umsiedlungsaktion.

**Großbetrieb.** Massive operation, large company. Euphemism for mass-murder program.

**großdeutsch.** Great German. Involving all Germans in the world.

**großdeutscher Freiheitskrieg.** *See* Großdeutschlands Freiheitskrieg.

**Großdeutsches Reich.** Greater German Reich. Expanded Germany that was intended to include all German-speaking peoples, in particular Austria and those territories lost to Germany and Austria in France and eastern Europe because of the treaties concluding World War I. Re-creating the greater Reich was one of Hitler's most important war aims. It included Germany and territory taken from Germany under the Versailles Treaty: parts of Poland (Danzig, West Prussia, Upper Silesia, Warthegau), Austria, Sudetenland, the Saar and Rhineland, as well as Memel (from Lithuania), North Schleswig (from Denmark), Alsace-Lorraine (from France), and Eupen-Malmédy (from Belgium). After the conquest of most of western Europe during World War II, it became a brief reality. *See also* Anschluß.

**Großdeutsche Volksgemeinschaft.** (GDVG) Greater German People's Community. Political party ally of Nazi Party.

**Großdeutsche Zeitung.** Greater German Times. Early Nazi newspaper, replaced by *Völkischer Beobachter.*

**Großdeutschland.** Greater Germany. Bringing together all Germans. A centuries-old concept finally brought briefly to fruition after the Anschluß of Austria in 1938.

**Großdeutschlands Freiheitskrieg.** Greater Germany's war for freedom. World War II.

**Große Aktion.** *See* Großaktion.

**Große deutsche Kunstausstellung.** The grand German art exhibition. 1937 Nazi art exhibition demonstrating the superiority of Aryan art over degenerate art. *See also* entartete Kunst.

**Großeinkaufs-Gesellschaft Deutscher Konsumvereine mbH.** (GEG) Purchasing body for the German Consumer Association Ltd. It was completely revamped and renamed Deutsche Großeinkaufs-Gesellschaft mbH. (German Purchasing Company Ltd.) in 1934.

**(am) Großen Wannsee.** *See* Wannsee-Konferenz.

**(das) größere Deutschland.** (The) greater Germany. The Reich and German settlements beyond the frontier. *See also* Großdeutsches Reich.

**(das) größere Reich.** The greater Reich. Included German settlements outside Germany's borders. *See also* Großdeutsches Reich.

**Große Staße.** *See* Reichsparteitagsgelände.

**Großexekution.** Mass execution. Mass murder.

**Großfahndung.** Mass tracing. Code word for secret response plan to possible mass breakouts from POW camps. *See also* Unternehman Walküre.

**Großfamilie.** Large family. Family of Nazi-defined asocials containing more than three children and considered unsuited for reproduction.

**Großkampftag.** Great day of struggle. Ironic colloquialism for a day of hard work.

**Großlazarett.** Large military hospital. Location in Ukraine where fatal medical experiments on contagious diseases and infections were performed on Soviet prisoners.

**(die) Großmutter begießen.** To water the grandmother. Colloquial for to baptize the dead Jewish grandmother posthumously in order to qualify for a certificate of Aryan status. *See also* jüdische Großmutter.

**Großoffensive.** Great offensive. Near the end of World War II, Goebbels' term meant to inspire hope for a successful German counterattack.

**Großraum.** Large space. Area that the Nazis claimed Germans required to exist self-sufficiently. *See* Autarkie; Lebensraum.

**Großraumhandel.** Large-scale trading.

**Großraumpolitik.** Large-area politics. Government politics of conquest and self-sufficiency.

**Großraumverwaltung.** Large-area management, administration. *See* Großraum.

**Großraumvolk.** Large-space people. Members of the German co-prosperity sphere. *See* Großraum.

**Großraumwirtschaft.** Greater economic sphere of interest. European economic integration under Nazi Germany.

**Großreich.** *See* Großdeutsches Reich.

**Groß-Rosen.** Concentration camp located in Lower Silesia. Important euthanasia camp, where tens of thousands of Soviet POWs were murdered, and thousands of Jewish and night-and-fog prisoners were worked to death in the DEST quarries. *See also* Deutsche Erd- und Steinwerke GmbH; Nacht-und-Nebel-Häftlinge.

**größter Feldherr aller Zeiten.** (Gröfaz) The greatest commander in chief of all times. Ironic for Hitler, stated by Field Marshal Wilhelm Keitel after the attack on France in 1940.

**Großverbraucher.** Large-scale consumer. German industry and large companies.

**Großvolk.** A people large in number and geographical distribution. Germany of the future. *See* Großraum.

**Großwirtschaftsraum.** Large-economy area. Co-prosperity sphere, economic empire dominated by Germany.

**GRS, gRs.** *See* Geheime Reichssache.

**Gruf.** *See* Gruppenführer.

**Grün.** Green. Plan for attack on Czechoslovakia, September 1938. Plan was canceled as a result of the Munich Agreement. Executed without resistance in the spring of 1939. Also, in 1940 code name for the plan for a frontal attack on the Maginot line. Later renamed Fall Braun.

**Grundbefehl.** Basic Order. Hitler issued his "Basic Order No. 1" on security in January 1940 and stipulated that it be displayed on posters in every military headquarters. Henceforth, no one was to be given any classified information that was not directly relevant to his job, and even then, he was not to be told earlier, or more, than was absolutely necessary.

**Grunderlaß.** Basic decree. *See also* Grundbefehl.

**Grundlehre.** Basic teaching. Germanization of Theorie (theory).

**Grundrechte.** Bill of Rights. Weimar Republic's constitutional protection of individual rights, suspended by the Reichstag fire decree. *See also* Reichstagsbrandverordnung; subjektive öffentliche Rechte des Einzelnen.

**Grundsätze der inneren Staatssicherheit während des Krieges.** Bases of Internal State Security during the War. A decree sent out on September 3, 1939 (at the start of World War II) to regulate foreign workers, initially Poles. Circulated by the SD chiefs, along with Göring as Administrator of the Four-Year Plan and Himmler as Reichsführer-SS and Head of the German Police.

**Grundsätze für die Neuordnung in Deutschland.** Principles for the New Order in Germany. Document outlining goals of the Kreisau Circle: a nation ruled by Christian principles of justice and human rights and responsibilities. *See* Kreisauer Kreis.

**Grundschule.** Elementary school. Grades 1–4 in the Nazi educational system.

**Grundstücks-Verwaltungsgesellschaft.** (GVG) Real Estate Management Association. Society established in 1938 that handled the disposition of expropriated Jewish property in Hamburg.

**Grüne.** The green one. Female prisoner wearing the green triangle of a habitual criminal often in important position in women's concentration camps. *See also* Anweiserin; Kapo.

**Grüneberg-Metallwerk.** Grüneberg Metal Works. Munitions factory employing female slave labor from Ravensbrück.

*(Der) grüne Otto.* Green Otto. Publication of the Social Democratic anti-Nazi movement. *See also* Neu Beginnen.

**Grüne Polizei.** Green police. Dutch police aiding the Germans in rounding up Jews.

**Grünspan-Affäre.** Grünspan Affair. *See also* Reichskristallnacht.

**Gruppe.** Group. Component of a platoon; also, Luftwaffe wing.

**Gruppe Herbert Baum.** A Communist and Jewish resistance group that in 1942 set fire to a Goebbels' anti-Soviet exhibition, das sowjetische Paradies (The Soviet Paradise). Most members were caught by the Gestapo and executed.

**Gruppen.** Groups. Three to four Luftwaffe groups comprised a squadron. See *also* Geschwader.

**Gruppenführer.** (GRF, Gruf) Lieutenant general in the SS.

**Gruppenleiter.** Group leader. Nazi Party official.

**Gruppenmord.** Murder of large groups.

**Gruppenpreis.** Group price. Standard cost of certain goods by factories divided into industry groups.

**Gruppenstab.** Group staff.

**Gruppenverteiler.** Group distributor. Official in charge of distributing ordnance orders.

**Gruppe Seelsorge.** (Armed Forces) Chaplains' Section.

**GS.** *See* Gendarmerie-Station.

**G-Schreiber.** G writer. Code for telex machine.

**Gustav-Linie.** Code name for German defense line in Italy, centered on Monte Casino.

*Gutachtenanzeiger.* Good review indicator. White list containing book reviews of works in accordance with National Socialist ideology; published periodically as a supplement to the journal *Die Bücherkunde* (book news) and more comprehensive than the National Socialist bibliography. *See Nationalsozialistische Bibliographie.*

**gutrassige Kinder.** (Polish) children of good racial stock; racially valuable.

**gutrassige Polen.** Poles of good racial stock; racially valuable Poles. Poles in German-occupied areas the Nazis deemed suitable to be Germanized.

**g.v.** *See* garnisonsverwendungsfähig.

**GVG.** *See* Grundstücks-Verwaltungsgesellschaft.

**GW.** *See* Ghettowache.

**G-Wagen.** *See* Gaswagen; S-Wagen.

# H

**H.** *See* Heer.

**HA.** *See* Hauptamt.

**Haavarah.** *See* Palestina-Treuhandstelle zur Beratung deutscher Juden GmbH.

**Hackenholtstiftung.** Hackenholt Foundation. Cynical term of the SS for the gassing building at the death camp Belzec. SS Oberscharführer Lorenz Hackenholt was responsible for the operation of the gassing facility.

**Hadamar.** A psychiatric hospital founded in 1906 in the town of Hadamar, Germany. In 1933 it was renamed State Psychiatric Hospital and Sanitarium. From 1941 to 1945, it was rented to T-4 as a euthanasia killing center where more than 11,000 people were murdered.

**Hafthohlladung.** Clamp hollow charge. Magnetic antitank mine.

**Haftlager der Werbestelle.** (HW) Enlisted man's prison camp.

**Häftlingsakte.** Prisoner's file. Data—accurate or not, and in any case inaccessible to the prisoner—on a concentration camp inmate, collected in a dossier, containing personal information, photo, protective custody order, Gestapo interrogation report, and so forth.

**Häftlingsarzt.** Prisoner doctor. Often Jewish doctors were used to treat some Jewish prisoners in a concentration camp because SS doctors refused.

**Häftlingskrankenbau.** (HKB) Ill-prisoner barracks. In prisons and concentration camps.

**Häftlingslager.** Detention camp. Concentration camp.

**Häftlingspersonalbogen.** Prisoner registration forms at the camps. *See also* Häftlings-Personal-Karte.

**Häftlings-Personal-Karte.** Prisoner's personal information card. File card at concentration camps containing personal data, including physical description of each registered inmate. *See* Häftlingspersonalbogen; hollerith erfaßt.

**Häftlingsselbstverwaltung.** Prisoner self-administration. Hierarchy of prisoners, beneath the SS, who ran the concentrations camps on a day-to-day basis. Subdivided into those prisoners who administered the quarters and those who organized the work parties. For quarters, *see* Blockälteste; Lagerälteste; Stubemälteste. For work parties, *see* Kapo; Oberkapo; Vorarbeiter.

**Häftlingsverzeichnis.** Prisoner list. List of names of prisoners belonging to various camp labor units.

**Haftmine.** Clamp mine. Depth charge.

**Hagal-Rune.** *See* Hagel-Rune.

**Hagel-Rune.** Nordic symbol roughly resembling an H. It meant destruction of the old and making way for the new, belief and loyalty. Waffen-SS division emblem.

**Hakenkreuz.** Hooked cross. Swastika, most important Nazi emblem. A Germanic symbol of the god of thunder, Thor. In ancient India, sign of purity. Nazis employed it to symbolize Aryan blood and destiny. First used as political symbol by antisemitic organizations in 1918, including the Heimwehr and Freikorps.

*Hakenkreuz.* Swastika. Nazi propaganda film.

**Hakenkreuzfahne.** Swastika flag. Nazi Party flag, red with black swastika on a white circle. The colors were said to mean blood, earth, and nature. Designed by Dr. Friedrich Krohn and adopted by Hitler as a symbol of the supremacy of the Aryan man and victory over the Jews. On all national holidays, the flag had to be displayed on all German buildings, or else the Gestapo paid a visit. On the battlefields of Europe and in the concentration camps, the swastika flag meant suffering and death.

**Halbarier.** Half Aryan.

**halben.** To halve. Germanization of halbieren (to cut in half).

**Halbjude.** Half Jew. Male person with two Jewish grandparents. *See also* Mischlinge.

**Halbjüdin.** Half Jew. Female person with two Jewish grandparents. *See also* Mischlinge.

**Halbweltmarschall.** Half-world marshal. Derisive for Goebbels, who was supposed to become world marshal after the war.

**Halb-Zug.** Half platoon. *See also* Zug.

**hälften.** To halve. *See also* halben.

**Halseisen.** Neck iron. Soldier slang for the Knight's Cross. *See also* Ritterkreuz.

**Halsschmerzen.** Sore throat. Soldier slang for especially zealous officers who coveted the Knight's Cross medal, which hung around the neck, usually at the expense of their subordinate soldiers. *See also* Brustschmerzen; Ritterkreuz.

**Haltegurt.** Holding belt. Parachute harness.

**"Halte Ordnung!"** "Keep order." Directive carved into the cross beams of the barracks at Auschwitz.

**Haltung.** Attitude, demeanor. German character, dignity, honor.

**Haltungslyrik.** Heroic lyric. Legendary Germanic poetry.

**Hamburger Plan.** The Gestapo plan to establish a Jewish self-ruling state in Poland.

**Hamsterfahrten.** Hamster trips. During the war, movement of German civilians into the countryside seeking food.

**"Hände hoch!"** "Hands Up." Nazi film celebrating the ideal National Socialist community spirit.

**Handelsstörer.** Trade harasser. Navy raider.

**Handmädel.** Handmaiden. Girl doing her obligatory service year. *See also* Pflichtjahr.

**Handwerksbetriebe.** Workshops. Small and inefficient German craftsmen's shops; they were discouraged by the Nazis.

**Handwerksrolle.** Trade, craft list. List of licensed craftsmen.

**Hans Bauer und Karl Schranz AG.** Hans Bauer and Karl Schranz Ltd. Company situated in Czestochowa, Poland. It used 13,000 Jews for forced labor.

**Hanseatische Vermögensverwaltungs- und Treuhand-Gesellschaft.** (Treuhansa) Hanseatic Property Administration and Trust Society. A front organization covering the illegal expropriation of Jewish property in Hamburg in 1938. *See* Grundstücks-Verwaltungsgesellschaft.

*Hans Westmar.* Nazi propaganda film based on the life of Horst Wessel.

**hart.** Hard. To be hard was the Nazi ideal. *See* "Deutsches Volk, werde hart!"

**"Harte Zeiten Harte Pflichten Harte Herzen."** "Hard times, hard tasks, hard hearts." Slogan from 1943 on a war propaganda poster depicting men with guns and tools.

**"Hart gebeugt durch Versailles, aber nicht gebrochen!"** "Badly bent because of Versailles, but not broken." *See also* (blutende) Grenze.

**Hartheim.** Largest of euthanasia murder facilities with more than 30,000 victims. Also location of Mauthausen gas chambers.

**Hartmut.** Code name for German invasion of Norway in April 1940. *See* Weserübung.

**Hartung.** January.

**Harzburger Front.** Harzburger Front. Short-lived 1931 alliance among the Nationalists, Pan-Germans, Nazis, Stahlhelm, and other rightist German political parties and industrialists opposing the Weimar Republic.

**HASAG.** *See* Hugo Schneider Aktiengesellschaft.

**Hasenjagd.** Rabbit hunt. Hunting down and killing Jews. *See also* auf der Flucht erschossen.

**Hasenkurve.** Rabbit curve. Evasive air maneuver.

**Haß.** Hatred. For Nazi ideology, in combination with heroic, a positive for the Nordic race; in combination with Jewish, a negative.

**Hauptabteilung.** Main department. *See also* Reichsnährstand.

**Hauptamt.** (HA) Administration, headquarters.

**Hauptamt Ordnungspolizei.** Order Police Headquarters. There were twelve such offices organized by the SS.

**Hauptamt SS-Gericht.** Headquarters SS Legal Department. Responsible for internal SS legal affairs.

**Hauptamt Volksdeutsche Mittelstelle.** Center for the Welfare of Ethnic Germans. VOMI Office assigned to aid and nazify Volksdeutsche. *See also* Volksdeutsche Mittelstelle.

**Hauptgruppe.** Office. Exception being the Foreign Office, or Auswärtiges Amt.

**Hauptkampffeld.** (H.K.F.) Main combat zone.

**Hauptlager.** (HL) Main camp.

**Hauptscharführer.** (Hschf, HSCHF) Master Sergeant. Waffen-SS Master Sergeant.

**Hauptschriftleiter.** Germanization of Chefredakteur (editor in chief of a newspaper or journal).

**Hauptschule.** Middle school. Established in 1941–1942, these schools selected the most talented among the ten-year-old graduates of the elementary school to attend special training for jobs ranging from technical and artistic to home economics.

**Hauptstadt der Bewegung.** Capital City of the Movement. Munich, where Hitler's ascension toward ruling Germany began.

**Hauptsturmführer.** (HSTF) Captain. Waffen-SS Captain.

**Haupttreuhandstelle Ost.** (HTO) Main Trust Center East. Göring established a public corporation whose sole purpose was to seize and administer confiscated Jewish and Polish properties.

**Haus der deutschen Erziehung.** House of German Education. Headquarters of the Reich management of the teachers' federation in Bayreuth.

**Haus der deutschen Kunst.** House of German Art. Large neoclassical building in Munich housing Nazi-approved art exhibitions, of which there were eight, from 1937 on. It was the first public building dedicated by the Third Reich. The cornerstone was laid in 1933 by Hitler himself, indicating his interest in making art a central concern for the new Reich and Volk. *See also* Bauten des Führers; entartete Kunst; Palazzo Kitschi.

**Hausfahne.** House flag. Swastika flag owned by an individual.

**Hausgemeinschaft.** Building-group committee. The German government demanded the formation of units consisting of the inhabitants of a building to provide reciprocal assistance during Allied air raids. Jews were excluded by law. *See also* Luftschutzgemeinschaft.

**Hauskapellen.** House chapels. Secret service within Admiral Wilhelm Canaris' Abwehr.

**Haus Ludendorff.** *See* Deutsche Gotterkenntnis.

**Hausratserfassungsstelle.** Registration Office for Household Goods. Office in Amsterdam for the registration of property seized from Jewish households following confiscation of life insurance, pension documents, and securities.

**Haus Wewelsburg.** Wewelsburg House. Training school for SS, transformed into a castle for Himmler, where SS members studied advanced SS ideology, consisting of the Nordic race and runes, ancestor cult, medieval history, and genealogy.

**Hauswirtschaftsjahr.** Home economics year. *See also* Pflichtjahr.

**H.Bau-A.** *See* Heeresbauamt.

**H.Bekl.-A.** *See* Heeresbekleidungsamt.

**HBL.** *See* Heeresbetriebsstofflager.

**HCN.** Hydrogen cyanide gas or hydrocyanic acid. The chemical components of the poison gas Zyklon.

**HDV.** *See* Heeresdienstvorschrift.

**H.Dv.g.** *See* Heeres-Dienstvorschrift geheim.

**"(aus dem) Hebräischen."** "From the Hebrew." Obligatory notice in books written by Jews in German.

**hebräische Volksverderber.** Hebrew corruptors of the (German) people. Referring to the allegedly evil racial, economic, social, and political impact of Jews on the German people.

**Heckenholt-Stiftung.** *See* Hackenholtstiftung.

**Heckenschütze.** Bush shooter. Enemy sniper; partisan.

**Heer.** (H) Army.

**Heeresabnahmestelle.** Army Acceptance Organization. Subsidiary of the Army Weapons Office, overseeing German rearmament. *See also* Waffenamt.

**Heeresbauamt.** (H.Bau-A.) Army Housing and Construction Department.

**Heeresbekleidungsamt.** (H.Bekl.-A.) Army Uniforms Department.

**Heeresbetriebsstofflager.** (HBL) Army supplies depot.

**Heeresdienstvorschrift.** (HDV) Army service regulation.

**Heeres-Dienstvorschrift geheim.** (H. Dv.g.) Secret army service regulation.

**Heeresgruppe.** (Hgr.) Army group.

**Heeresküstenartillerie.** (HKA.) Coastal Army Artillery.

**Heeresmunitionslager.** (HML) Army ammunition storage.

**Heeresnachrichtenwesen.** (HNW) Army Intelligence and Communications.

**Heeresunterkunftsverwaltung.** (HUV) Administration for Army Quartermaster.

**Heeresverpflegungslager.** (HVL) Army provisions and supplies storage.

**Heereswaffenamt.** Army Weapons Office. *See also* Waffenamt.

**Hegehof.** Nursery manor. Houses where SS men and Aryan women were to procreate a new German racial nobility. Supervised by the Rasse- und Siedlungshauptamt.

**Hehlergut.** Stolen goods. From September 1942, all Jewish property.

**"Heil Hitler!"** "Long live Hitler." The centuries-old German greeting "Heil" as adopted by the Nazis to replace "Guten Tag!" The accompanying raised-arm salute probably in imitation of the Italian fascist salute. Nazi Party greeting from mid-1920s; 1933 to 1945, the official German greeting. Other meanings of "Heil" are hail, health, salvation, safety, long life, and God save. *See* Deutscher Gruß.

**"Heil Hitler Dir!"** "Long live Hitler to you." SA marching song: Germany, awaken from your bad dream/Kick the alien Jews out of the Reich/we're fighting for your resurrection/Aryan blood must not perish/ . . . Jews get out of our German house/ . . ./Hail to the Führer, Hail Hitler to you!

**"Heil Hitler! Juda verrecke!"** *See* "Heil Hitler! Jude verrecke!"

**"Heil Hitler! Jude verrecke!"** "Long live Hitler. May the Jews croak (die like animals)."

**Heiliger Grund und Boden.** Holy ground and soil. Propaganda phrase referring to Germany.

**"Heil, mein Führer!"** "Long live my Führer." Personal salute to Hitler.

**Heilszeichen.** Salvation badge. Symbol on the collars of the those SS Totenkopf who had received a Totenkopfring. *See also* SS-Totenkopfring.

**Heimabend.** Club night. Mandatory Wednesday-evening courses for Hitlerjugend and Bund deutscher Mädel. Typical subjects for ten- to fourteen-year-olds: Germanic Gods and Heros, Hitler Youth in the Time of War, and Adolf Hitler and his Comrades in Arms. For fourteen- to eighteen-year-olds: The Racial Blood-Community, We Need Living Space, and The Creation of the Movement Is the Work of the Führer. Members also listened to the weekly radio program "Hour of the Young Nation" and learned songs such as "Bombs on England" and "The Rotten Bones of the World Tremble When Faced with War." *See also* Kameradschaftsabend; "Stunde der jungen Nation."

**Heimatfront.** Home front. Propaganda term for solidarity between civilians and soldiers. Hitler stated in October 1941: "[A] whole people is now at war, some at the front, others at home."

**Heimatroman.** Homeland novel. These sentimental novels were promoted by the state to build nationalism.

**Heimeinkaufvertrag.** Home-buyer agreement. Forced contract for the sale of Jewish homes confiscated by the Third Reich.

**"Heim ins Reich!"** "Home to the Reich." Slogan and policy of moving ethnic Germans into the greater Reich.

**heimlicher Adel.** Secret nobility. The leaders of the Nazi underground during the period of struggle for power. *See also* Kampfzeit.

**Heimschulen.** *See* Deutsche Heimschulen.

**Heimtücke.** Treachery, malice. Slander of Hitler or other Reich leaders.

**Heimtückegesetz.** Malice Law. *See also* Gesetz gegen heimtückische Angriffe auf Staat und Partei und zum Schutz der Parteiuniformen.

**Heimwehr.** Home guard. Austrian ultraconservative militia.

**Heinkel-Flugzeugwerke.** Heinkel Airplane Factory. Located at Krakow-Plaszow, building airplanes for the German air force, using forced Jewish labor.

**Heinrich I, der Vogelfänger.** Henry I the Fowler. Uncrowned Holy Roman Emperor 916–936. Founder of the first German Reich, he built castles and valiantly defended German territories against many enemies. Himmler believed himself to be a reincarnation of Henry I.

**Heiratsbefehl.** Marriage order. Himmler's order subjecting marriages of members of the SS to strict racial requirements.

**"Heiß Flagge!"** "Hoist the flag." Command for the morning ritual of the daily hoisting of the flag at German schools and youth camps. *See also* "Hol nieder die Flagge!"

**Heißgetränk.** Hot beverage. Hot water with artificial flavoring as a substitute for mulled wine, coffee, or tea.

**Heldenehrungfeier.** Hero-distinction celebration. Military commemoration for Nazi Party war dead, rejecting traditional Christian church services.

**Heldengedenktag.** Heroes Memorial Day. From 1934, memorial day for World War I dead and for those who died in the 1923 Munich Putsch. From March 1940, those who died in World War II were also honored.

**Heldengedenktag-Attentat.** Heroes Memorial Day assassination attempt. Planned German resistance attempt on Hitler's life on March 21, 1943.

**(in) heldenhaftem Kampf untergegangen.** Perished while fighting heroically. Official death announcement of German soldiers killed while retreating from the Eastern Front after 1942.

**heldenhaft kämpfende Truppe.** Heroically fighting troops. After 1942 euphemism for the desperate retreat of German troops along with heavy losses on all fronts.

**Heldenklau.** Hero theft. Nickname for General Walter von Unruh, the Wehrmacht general in charge of replacing key German workers being drafted into the Wehrmacht. He also combed the behind-the-lines staffs of military units during World War II for able-bodied soldiers.

**Heldentum.** Heroism. Glorified German and Germanic heroism.

**heldisch.** Heroic. Self-controlled, stoic quality of the racially-pure Nordic human being.

**Helfer.** Helper. Low-level Nazi Party rank.

**Helferin(nen).** Female helper(s). Women who worked for the German military. Also, women guards working for the SS at Ravensbrück.

**Helfershelfer.** (H-Mann) Secondary informants. Special unit of the SD. *See also* A-Mann; U-Mann; V-Mann; Z-Mann.

**Henlein Freikorps.** Henlein Free-Corps. Nazi organization in the (Czech) Sudetenland.

**Herbergswarte.** Youth-hostel wardens. From 1933, replacing Herbergseltern.

**Herbstnebel.** *See* Unternehmen Herbstnebel.

**Herbstreise.** Autumn journey. Plan to deceive the British into believing Germany was planning an attack on Great Britain two days before the planned actual attack. *See* Seelöwe.

**Herkules.** Hercules. Code name for German attack on the island of Malta in 1942.

**Hermann.** Herman. 1,000 kg bomb nicknamed after the sizable Head of the Luftwaffe, Hermann Göring.

**Hermann Meier.** A derisive reference to Göring, who had stated in August 1939, just before the outbreak of World War II, that if enemy aircraft appeared over German skies, people could call him Meier, sometimes a German-Jewish name.

**heroisch, Heroismus.** *See* heldisch.

**heroischer Stil.** Heroic style. The Nazi art form of monumentalism.

**Herrenmensch.** Master man. Individual member of the Herrenvolk who is destined to rule others.

**Herrenrasse.** Master race. *See* Herrenvolk.

**Herrenvolk.** Master race. Germans or Aryans seen as a racially superior aristocracy based on traditional values of honor, obedience, courage, and loyalty, and the instrument of a vast experiment in modern racial engineering. *See* Arbeitsvolk; Übermenschen; Volk.

**Herrgott.** Lord God. Term used by Hitler; replaced later by Providence. *See also* Vorsehung.

**Herr Rolf.** Mr. Rolf. At Plaszow concentration camp, Commandant Amon Göth's dog who was trained to attack, especially naked Jewish women prisoners being beaten by the SS.

**Herzland.** Heartland. A geopolitical theory that states that the nation controlling the Eurasian/African landmass—considered the center of human life—would control the world.

**Herzschwäche bei Lungenentzündung.** Heart weakness with pulmonary complications. A frequently used official explanation for concentration camp deaths.

**(akutes) Herzversagen.** Acute cardiac deficiency. A frequently used official explanation for concentration camp deaths.

**Heuaktion, Heu-Aktion.** Hay action. Code name for the displacement and transport of 40,000–50,000 ten- to fourteen-year-old Polish boys and girls with Aryan features to Germany. Organized by the administrators of the occupied eastern countries to reduce their next generation and to gain work hands for Germany. *See also* Eignungsprüfer; Lebensborn; Ostkinder; Wiedereindeutschung.

**Heulturm.** Howling tower. Tower with siren.

**Heumond.** Hay month. July.

**"Heute (erobern wir) Deutschland, morgen die (ganze) Welt!"** "Today (we are conquering) Germany, tomorrow the (whole) world." Nazi slogan and song.

**Hexe.** Witch. Nickname of Ilse Koch. *See also* Bestie von Buchenwald.

**Hgr.** *See* Heeresgruppe.

**Hib.** *See* Hib-Aktion.

**Hib-Aktion.** *See* "Hinein in die Betriebe!"

**"Hier ist der Jude XY."** "Here is the Jew XY (so-and-so)." Prescribed introduction of a Jewish prisoner before the Gestapo.

**Higa.** *See* Hilfsgrenzangestellte.

**"Hilf auch Du mit!"** "You can help, too." Poster slogan from 1943 encouraging women to help in the war effort.

**Hilflinge.** Helpers. Synonym for Sonderkommando at Auschwitz. *See also* Sonderkommando.

*Hilf—Mit: Illustrierte deutsche Kinderzeitung.* Pitch In: Illustrated German Children's Journal. Published as a regular supplement to the journal *Die Volksschule* by the National Socialist Teachers' Association. Used as additional reading text in the elementary schools; contained ideological and antisemitic material.

**Hilfsaufseherin.** Overseer's helper. Female assistant to the female guards at women's concentration camps. *See* Aufseherin.

**Hilfsgrenzangestellte.** (Higa) Border patrol helpers. Reinforcement of customs border control to 2,400 SS members, ordered by Hitler in 1933.

**Hilfskasse.** Relief fund. Martin Bormann fund created in 1930 to help Nazis injured in street fighting.

**Hilfsmittel.** Auxiliary equipment. Gas vans used in the Soviet Union and Yugoslavia as a means of speeding up the mass murder of Jews by the Einsatzgruppen. *See* Gaswagen.

**Hilfspolizei.** (Hipo) Auxiliary police recruited from other Nazi agencies to assist the order police. Also, auxiliary police recruited from the native populations in German-occupied Europe who helped murder Jews. *See also* Ordnungspolizei; Schutzmannschaft der Ordnungspolizei.

**Hilfsvölker.** Helper peoples. Inferior peoples fit only to help and serve the German Volk.

**Hilfswerk Mutter und Kind.** Organization Assisting Mother and Child. Core social assistance organization of the NSDAP concerned with family welfare, instituted in 1934. *See* Volkswohlfahrt.

**Hilfswillige.** (HiWi, Hiwi, HiWis) Volunteers, helpers. Russians and other people drafted into the Wehrmacht primarily to guard ghettos and concentration camps. east European POW volunteers for noncombat service with the German army.

**Hilfszug Bayern.** Help convoy Bavaria. Truck convoy equipped with medical help, food supply, and tents for emergency situations and mass rallies. *See also* Technische Nothilfe.

**Himmelbett.** Canopy bed. From early 1941 code name for the Central Organization of German Air Force Nightfighters using the radars Freya and Würzburg.

**Himmelfahrt.** Ascension, journey to heaven. Ironic for a 90-meter-long fenced path between Treblinka Camp I (where prisoners arrived) to Treblinka Camp II (where gas chambers and crematoria were located). Also, mass murder by poison gas of Jews at Treblinka; also mass murder of Czech civilians during the German occupation. *See also* Schlauch.

**Himmelfahrtbetten.** Journey-to-heaven beds. Air force slang for the empty barracks beds of German flyers killed in action.

**Himmelfahrtskommando.** Heaven-journey command, suicide squad. Military jargon for paratrooper. Also, title of a book by Franz Carl Weiskopf.

**Himmelfahrtsstraße.** *See* Himmelstraße.

**Himmelstraße.** Road to heaven. The narrow pathway between two walls of entangled barbed wire trod by Jews selected for death in the gas chambers.

**Himmelweg.** *See* Himmelstraße.

**Himmlerpfunde.** Himmler pounds. Counterfeit English pound notes produced in a counterfeit workshop within Sachsenhausen concentration camp by order of Himmler 1942–1943. They were distributed abroad in neutral countries via their German embassies. *See* VI F, 4a.

**Himmlerstadt.** Himmler city. Planned Nazi expansion of Auschwitz, housing three-quarters of a million prisoners and with the capacity of murdering 40,000 a day.

**"Hinein in die Betriebe!"** (Hib, Hib-Aktion) "Into the workshops." Goebbels' antiunion slogan in 1931. Nazi worker organization using propaganda and terror against non-Nazi workers. *See also* NS-Betriebszellen-Organisatian.

**hingerichtet.** Executed. Einsatzgruppen's daily toll of murdered Jews.

**Hipo.** *See* Hilfspolizei.

**historisch.** Historic. Used to describe Hitler's speeches, Party rallies, special holidays, dedications, inaugurations, and so forth.

*Historische Zeitschrift.* Historical Journal. Publication of Reichsinstitut für Geschichte des Neuen Deutschlands (Reich Institute for the History of the New Germany), concerning Aryan studies.

**Hitler-Gruß.** Hitler greeting, salute. *See also* Deutscher Gruß.

**"Hitler ist der Sieg!"** "Hitler is victory itself." Goebbels' most popular slogan.

**Hitlerjugend.** (HJ) Hitler Youth. Branch of Nazi Party founded in 1922 by Adolf Lenk to train the young as Nazis, reformed in 1926 when the Party was refounded. Ultimately, an umbrella organization of almost ten million members, including other German youth groups such as Deutsches Jungvolk in der Hitlerjugend, Bund deutscher Mädel in der Hitlerjugend, Jungmädelbund, and BDM-Werk Glaube und Schönheit. On April 20, Hitler's birthday, of the year they became ten years old, all children entered a Hitler Youth organization after passing an initiation test called Pimfemprobe. The oath sworn to by members: "I promise as a member of the Hitler Youth always to do my duty with love and loyalty to Führer and flag." The organization's goal was ideological education, sports, premilitary training, travel, and professional competitions. The Hitler Youth wore uniforms with black stockings, brown shirts with epaulettes, a shoulder belt, and a dagger.

**Hitlerjugend-Flieger.** Hitler Youth flyers. Air force glider training for Hitler Youth, from late 1930s.

**Hitler-Jugend-Gesetz.** Hitler-Youth Law. 1936 law stipulating that the entire German youth be educated in the spirit of National Socialism to serve the German nation. *See also* Hitlerjugend.

**Hitlerjugend-Marine.** Hitler Youth Navy. Provided naval courses to Hitler Youth, from late 1930s.

**Hitlerjugend-Motor.** Hitler Youth Motor. Hitler Youth training in vehicle maintenance and motorcycling for ultimate service in the German army, from late 1930s.

*Hitlerjugend Zeitung.* Hitler Youth Times. Periodical of the Hitler Youth.

**Hitlerjunge.** Hitler boy. Hitler Youth boy, largest and lowest rank of the Hitler Youth. *See also* Hitlerjugend.

*Hitlerjunge Quex.* Hitler Youth Quex. Nazi propaganda film, biography of Hitler Youth "martyr" Heinz Norkus.

**Hitlermädel.** Hitler girl. Girl of the Hitler Youth. *See* Bund Deutscher Mädel in der Hitlerjugend.

**Hitler-Putsch.** Hitler's unsuccessful attempt at coup. On November 8–9, 1923, Hitler attempted to seize leaders of the Bavarian government, who escaped. Seeking ultimately to seize power in Berlin, Hitler and several Nazis (Hermann Göring and Julius Streicher), along with General Erich Ludendorff, began by attempting to capture the government of Bavaria. Also called Bürgerbräu-Keller-Putsch, Munich Putsch, and November Putsch.

**Hitler-Stalin-Pakt.** *See* Deutsch-Sowjetischer Nichtangriffspakt.

**HiWi, Hiwi.** *See* Hilfswillige.

**HiWis.** *See* Hilfswillige.

**HJ.** *See* Hitlerjugend.

**HJ-Ehrenzeichen.** Hitler Youth honor badge. Insignia for members of the Hitler Youth, the League of German Girls, and the National Socialist German Student Federation.

**HJ-Landdienst.** *See* Landdienst.

**HJ-Leistungsabzeichen.** Hitler Youth achievement badge. Badge earned for passing a test in Nazi ideology and sports.

**HJ-Streifendienst.** Hitler Youth Patrol Service. After 1934, an internal Hitler Youth police, during the war, cooperated with the SS, Gestapo, and German police. Regarded as future SS and the SS-Totenkopfverbände.

**HKA.** *See* Heeresküstenartillerie.

**HKB.** *See* Häftlingskrankenbau.

**H.K.F.** *See* Hauptkampffeld.

**HL.** *See* Hauptlager.

**H-Mann.** *See* Helfershelfer.

**HML.** *See* Heeresmunitionslager.

**HN.** *See* Hundenation.

**HNW.** *See* Heeresnachrichtenwesen.

**Hochlinden.** German-Polish frontier post where SS men, dressed as Poles, mounted a simulated attack. *See also* Unternehmen Himmler.

**hochrassig.** Racially superior.

**Hochschulsport.** University sports. From 1934, sports became an obligatory university subject during the first three years; voluntary in the fourth year. Continued studies required a sports test.

**Höchstwert.** Highest value. Germanization of Maximum (maximum).

**hoffnungslos aber nicht ernst.** Hopeless but not serious. Ironic-sarcastic description of the situation in Germany toward the end of the war.

**Hofjuden.** Court Jews. Ironic for Jewish inmates at Treblinka who worked for guards.

**Hofkarte.** Farm card. Farmers' document about their production and deliveries; contained information about farm size, location, and estimated harvest.

**Höflichkeitswettbewerb.** Politeness competition. Established in 1942 by Goebbels to offset the belief of the German people that an easy victory in World War II was possible.

**hohe Frau.** Women in high position. Term for the wives of Hermann Göring and Baldur von Schirach.

**Hoheitsabzeichen.** *See* Hoheitszeichen.

**Hoheitsadler.** National eagle. *See also* Hoheitszeichen.

**Hoheitsgebiete.** National areas. Regional governing areas within Germany.

**Hoheitsträger.** Sovereignty holders. Nazi Party leaders with sovereign power.

**Hoheitszeichen.** National emblem. Eagle and swastika as insignia for Nazi Party and Wehrmacht. Nazi eagle faced left; Wehrmacht faced right.

**Höhenflugversuche.** High-flying experiments. Medical experiments on prisoners at Dachau to study the body's reaction to pressure changes at high altitudes. German non-Jewish survivors were granted clemency, but others were sent back to the camp population.

**"Höher als jede andere Treue steht dies zum Artgesetz; Recht der Art bricht jedes andere Recht."** "Higher than every other loyalty stands the principle of race; the right of race breaks every other right." Nazi legal principle.

**Höhere Lehranstalten.** Secondary schools. Eight grades, equivalent to American high school and junior college.

**Höherer SS- und Polizeiführer.** (HSSPF) Higher SS and Police Leader. Local chief SS and police officer in areas of occupied Europe as Himmler's personal representatives.

**Hohe Schule.** Advanced school, university. Nazi institute for advanced research and education.

**Hohe Schule für Nazi Kultur und Weltanschauung.** Advanced School for Nazi Culture and Ideology. Institute located in Frankfurt am Main and intended to assemble the largest and greatest library on world Jewry.

**Hollerith D-11.** IBM sorting machine. *See also* DEHOMAG D-11.

**hollerith erfaßt.** Entered into the IBM sorting machine. Stamp on concentration camp registration forms. *See also* DEHOMAG D-11; Häftlings-Personal-Karte.

**"Hol nieder die Flagge!"** "Take the flag in." Command for the evening ritual of lowering the flag at Nazi schools and youth camps. *See also* "Heiß Flagge!"

**Holocaust.** *See* Endlösung der Judenfrage.

**Holzvergaser.** Wood combustion. Car using burning wood as energy source.

**Homosexualität.** Homosexuality. Homosexuality was a criminal offense according to the 2d Reich Penal Code of 1871, and even under the liberal Constitution of the Weimar Republic, although it was not widely enforced. Beginning in 1934, Nazi authorities sent approximately 10,000 homosexuals to concentration camps to work, to suffer, and to die. Only gay men were considered dangerous to the Third

Reich, not gay women. As a result, the Reich's persecution of lesbians was rare, although some did end up in Ravensbrück. Though officially condemned, homosexuality itself was tolerated among certain Nazi circles. *See also* 175er.

**Horchraum.** Sound-detection room. On a German naval vessel.

**Hordenführer.** Group leader. Rank in a Hitler Youth group.

**Hörgoi.** Hearing goy. German who allowed Jews to listen to his radio.

**Hornung.** February.

**"Horst-Wessel-Lied."** "Horst Wessel Song." A Nazi song composed in 1927. Second in importance only to "Deutschland über alles" as German national anthem as of Hitler's takeover in 1933. *See also* Appendix: Horst-Wessel-Lied.

**Hörverbot.** Forbidden to listen. *See also* Schwarzhörer.

**Hoßbach-Niederschrift.** Hoßbach memorandum. *See also* Hoßbach-Protokoll.

**Hoßbach-Protokoll.** Hoßbach Protocol. Record of the November 5, 1937, conference held in the Reich Chancellery, during which Hitler expounded his vision of Germany to his top military officials. Hitler's Wehrmacht adjutant, Friedrich Hoßbach, wrote the minutes, recording Hitler's talk on Germany's racial-geopolitical need for space and the use of force to achieve this goal.

**Hottmusik.** Jitterbug, jazz. *See also* Swing.

**Hschf, HSCHF.** *See* Hauptscharführer.

**HSSPF.** *See* Höherer SS- und Polizeiführer.

**HSTF.** *See* Hauptsturmführer.

**HTO.** *See* Haupttreuhandstelle Ost.

**Hugo Schneider Aktiengesellschaft.** (HASAG) Hugo Schneider Joint-Stock Company. Used slaves; major armaments manufacturer for the Third Reich.

**humanistisch.** Humanistic. Un-German, Jewish. *See also* Asphaltmensch.

**Humanität.** Humanity. According to Nazi ideology, a degenerate belief fostered by Jews to place the interests of the individual above the people and the nation.

**Humanversuch.** Experiment on human beings. Experiments on Jews and others were carried out by German university professors and concentration camp doctors.

**Hund.** Dog. Camp prisoner.

**Hundenation.** (HN) Nation of dogs. Epithet for French deportees to a special German camp at Hinzert, near Trier, who were ordered to wear HN in large letters on their jackets.

**"Hunden und Juden verboten."** "Forbidden to dogs and Jews." Signs in stores of German-occupied Poland.

**Hundertprozentiger.** Hundred-percenter. A convinced National Socialist.

**Hundertschaften.** Hundreds. SA action squads in early 1920s.

**Hundestaffel.** Trained dogs. German dogs trained to herd prisoners at concentration camps and transfer points.

**Hundestart.** Dog start. *See also* Meuten.

**Hundezellen.** Dog cells. Tiny space at Dachau concentration camp used to punish or torture prisoners. Here inmates were treated like dogs and had to bark when they wanted food.

**Hündin von Buchenwald.** Bitch of Buchenwald. *See also* Bestie von Buchenwald.

**Hungerhäuser.** Starvation houses. Places where the Nazis planned to starve German elderly to death as part of the Euthanasia Program from 1943.

**HUV.** *See* Heeresunterkunftsverwaltung.

**HVL.** *See* Heeresverpflegungslager.

**HW.** *See* Haftlager der Werbestelle.

**Hygiene-Institut der Waffen-SS.** Hygiene Institute of the Armed SS. Research center in Buchenwald concentration camp. The main focus of the research was the pathology and serology of typhus fever, resulting in the deaths of its human subjects.

**Hygiene-Institut SS und Polizei Auschwitz.** SS and Police Institute for Hygiene at Auschwitz. Euphemism for Barrack No. 10 at Auschwitz where experiments on humans were conducted.

# I

**Ia-Zug.** *See* Sonderzug.

**IBV.** Internationale Bibelforscher-Vereinigung. International Bible Researcher Association. Also, Internationale Vereinigung Ernste Bibelforscher. International Association of Serious Bible Researchers. *See also* Internationale Vereinigung für Bibelforschung.

**Ic-Dienst.** *See* Sicherheitsdienst.

***Ich klage an!*** I Accuse. Nazi propaganda film made to gain German public-opinion support for the Euthanasia Program.

**ID.** Infanterie Division. Infantry division.

**Idee.** Idea, notion. German propaganda concept referring to National Socialist ideology. *See also* Weltanschauung; weltgeschichtliche Mission.

**Igel.** Porcupine. Antitank device.

**Igelit.** Artificial leather produced by IG Farben.

**IG Farben.** (IGF) I.G. Farben. Powerful German industrial conglomerate, comprising eight leading German chemical manufacturers. Benefited enormously under Hitler's Four-Year Plan to revitalize Germany's economy for war by producing most of Germany's synthetic oil and rubber, gasoline, explosives, poison gas, and more. Thousands of the company's slave laborers, Jews and others, were worked to death. *See also* DEGESCH; Auschwitz.

**IL.** *See* Internierungslager.

**Ilag.** *See* Internierungslager für Zivilisten.

**illegale Bewegung.** Illegal movement. Underground resistance.

*Illustrierter Beobachter.* Illustrated Observer. Weekly NSDAP journal established in 1926.

**Immelmann I, II, III.** Hitler's special airplanes. Named after World War I German ace Max Immelmann, who invented the Immelmann turn, a half turn at the top of a loop so that the aircraft would come out of the loop right side up.

**"Im Westen liegt Frankreich, im Osten wird Frank reich."** "In the west lies France, in the east, [Hans] Frank is getting rich." Pun referring to the alleged greed of Hans Frank, Governor General of the occupied territories in the east.

**Ina.** *See* Nachrichtenmittelabteilung eines Infanterieregiments.

**Indianer.** Indians, redskins. Air force slang for enemy aircraft.

**"In diesem Ort sind Juden nicht erwünscht."** "Jews are not wanted in this place." Sign placed at outskirts of German towns.

**"(Das) Individuum hat weder das Recht, noch die Pflicht zu existieren."** "The individual has neither the right nor the duty to exist." Nazi legal principle.

**Industrieabteilung.** Industry Branch. *See also* Wirtschaftskammer.

**Industrieklub.** Industry Club. Organization of wealthy and influential industrialists in Düsseldorf who were impressed by Hitler in 1932.

**Infanterieregiment Großdeutschland.** Infantry Regiment Greater Germany. Wehrmacht Panzer brigade with a twelve-year term of service. Modeled on the SS and specially trained for urban warfare.

**Infanteriesturmabzeichen.** Infantry assault medal. Award established in 1939 for members of an infantry division who had fought valiantly three times within three days.

**Inf III.** *See* Informationsabteilung III.

**Informationsabteilung III.** (Inf III) Information Branch III. Spy branch of the German Foreign Office.

**Inländer.** Native. Those protected as Reich citizens but with limited rights.

**Inl II g.** *See* Inland II geheim.

**Inland II geheim.** (Inl II g) Secret Domestic (Office) II. German Foreign Office Branch.

**innerbürtig.** Born within the (German) race.

**innerbürtige Kräfte.** Inborn forces. Characteristically German; inner strength and calling.

**innere Emigration.** Internal emigration. Euphemism for murder. Also applied to Germans who silently opposed the Nazis.

**innere Front.** Internal Front. Fight against defeatists and underground within Germany.

**Inschutzhaftnahme.** Taken into protective custody. Deported to a prison or concentration camp.

**Inspekteur und Befehlshaber der Sicherheitspolizei.** (IuB Sipo) Inspector and Commander of Security Police.

**Inspektor der Sicherheitspolizei und des SD.** (InspSipoSD) Inspector of Security Police and Security Service.

**InspSipoSD.** *See* Inspektor der Sicherheitspolizei und des SD.

**Instinkt.** Instinct. Natural, positive (German) feelings in contrast to the intellect, which Nazis deemed diabolical. *See also* Intellekt.

**Institut der NSDAP zur Erforschung der Judenfrage.** National-Socialist German Workers Party Institute for Research on the Jewish Problem. Frankfurt am Mein institute founded in 1939 sponsored by Alfred Rosenberg. In separate decrees between 1940 and 1942, Hitler empowered Rosenberg to "search out, safeguard, and ship to Germany materials found in libraries, archives, . . . or owned by Jews," and confiscate them to serve the ideological purposes of the NSDAP for the scholarly research of the Hohe Schule für Nazi Kultur und Weltanschauung.

**Institut für deutsche Ostarbeit.** Institute for German Work in the East. 1940 Krakow organization to study Polish Jews to prove Nazi racial theories.

**Institut für Erbbiologie und Rassenforschung.** Institute for Hereditary Biology and Race Research. Founded in 1934 by Dr. Otmar von Verschuer at the University of Frankfurt am Mein. This organization, which sponsored research on race and heredity (including Dr. Josef Mengele's experiments on twins) later transferred to Auschwitz.

**Institut für wehrwissenschaftliche Zweckforschung.** (IWZ) Institute for the Scientific Research and Design of Weapons.

**Institut zum Studium der Judenfrage.** Institute for the Study of the Jewish Problem. Goebbels' creation in 1936 as part of the Ministry of Propaganda. Dedicated to publishing on Jewish issues seen through the lens of Nazi ideology. In December 1939, the Institut changed its name to Antisemitische Aktion.

**Institut zur Erforschung der Judenfrage.** *See* Institut der NSDAP zur Erforschung der Judenfrage.

**Institut zur Erforschung des jüdischen Einflusses auf das deutsche kirchliche Leben.** Institute for Research into the Jewish Influence on German Church Life.

**"Insuffizienz des Herzmuskels."** "Heart-muscle failure." Entry on death certificates and in registries to conceal the murder of Jews and others in concentration camps. *See also* Todesfallsaufnahmen; (gefälschte) Todesursachen.

**integrieren.** To integrate. *See also* Integrierung.

**Integrierung.** Integration. Any political arrangement that increased the power of the Nazi state.

**Intellekt.** Intellect. Rootless, hypercritical, sterile, Jewish. *See also* Intelligenz.

**Intellektbestie.** Intellect beast. *See also* Intelligenzbestie.

**Intellektualismus.** Intellectualism. Perverted western intellectualism.

**intellektuel, Intellektueller.** Intellectual. *See also* Intellekt; Intelligenz.

**Intelligenz, Intelligentsia.** A destructive, educated, (Jewish) bourgeois group undermining German society.

**Intelligenzaktion.** Intellectual Operation. 1942 roundup and murder of Jewish intelligentsia in the Krakow-Ghetto in Poland.

**Intelligenzbestie.** Intelligence beast. Intellectual. *See also* Intelligenz.

**Interessen.** Interests. *See also* Belange.

**Interessenentenhaufen.** Interested pack. Pressure group.

**Interessengrenze.** Border of interests. Border dividing defeated Poland into German and Soviet spheres in 1939.

**international.** International. Un-German, foreign, repugnant, alien, non-Aryan, Jewish.

**(das) internationale Judentum.** International Jewry. Collective perception of National Socialism's archenemy.

**internationale Mörderbande.** Band of international murderers. Nazi name for Jews.

**Internationale Vereinigung Ernster Bibelforscher.** *See* Internationale Vereinigung für Bibelforschung.

**Internationale Vereinigung für Bibelforschung.** International Association for Bible Research. Jehovah's Witnesses. Recognizing that their early attempts to ingratiate themselves with Hitler were impossible, the Witnesses resisted the Third Reich and were sent to concentration camps.

**Internierungslager.** (IL) Internment camp. *See also* Konzentrationslager.

**Internierungslager für Prominente.** Internment camp for VIPs. At Buchenwald.

**Internierungslager für Zivilisten.** Internment camp for noncombatants.

**Invalidenblock.** Barrack (at some concentration camps) housing the sick. There was none at Auschwitz because the sick were murdered.

**Invalidenaktion.** Operation against the sick. Murder of sick concentration camp inmates.

**Isabella.** Code name for planned invasion of Portugal.

**Isidor.** In 1930, nickname that Goebbels used to attack a Jewish enemy of his and the SA's, Berlin's Deputy Police Chief, Dr. Bernhard Weiß. *See* Esel Isidor.

**Isolierblock.** Isolation ward. Concentration camp location where experiments on prisoners and other atrocities were committed.

**Israel.** Israel. Name Jewish men were forced to take from 1939. *See also* Zusatzname.

**israelitisch.** Of Israel, Jewish. *See also* mosaisch.

**Istjude.** Being Jewish. According to the Reichsbürgergesetz of November 1935, a person was deemed Jewish who had three Jewish grandparents, regardless of his or her confession of faith or nationality.

**Italienisches Militärinterniertenlager.** Italian military internment camp. At Buchenwald.

**IuB Sipo.** *See* Inspekteur und Befehlshaber der Sicherheitspolizei.

**I.V.** (in Vertretung) By proxy, deputy, representative.

**IWZ.** *See* Institut für wehrwissenschaftliche Zweckforschung.

# J

**J.** *See* Jude.

**Jabo.** *See* Jagdbomber.

**Jafü.** *See* Jagdfliegerführer.

**Jagdbomber.** (Jabo) Fighter bomber.

**Jagdfliegerführer.** (Jafü) Fighter Leader. Chief Luftwaffe field commander.

**Jagdführer.** Fighter Leader. Commander of the fighter defense in an air defense zone.

**Jagdgeschwader.** (JG) Fighter squadron.

**Jagdkommandos.** Hunter units. SS units that operated in Poland against partisan units and committed mass murders of Jews.

**Jagdverbände.** Hunter units. SS sabotage units operating in Russia.

**Jäger.** Hunters. Light infantry.

**Jägerleitoffizier.** Leading hunters officer (Luftwaffe). Controlled the dispatch of night fighters via radio on the ground.

**Jahresbestleistung.** Highest annual achievement. Sports term used for the highest achievements in annual work competitions. *See also* Bestleistung.

**Jahrweiser.** Year indicator. Germanization of Kalender (calendar).

**JAL.** *See* Judenarbeitslager.

**JÄR.** *See* jüdischer Ältestenrat.

**J.A. Topf und Söhne.** *See* Topf und Söhne.

**JAuL.** *See* Judenauffangslager.

**"Jedem das Seine."** "To each his own." On the main gate of Buchenwald concentration camp and at several other locations at concentration camps.

**Jehovas Pleite.** Jehovah's crash. Destruction of Jewish holy objects. *See also* Reichskristallnacht.

**Jena.** German city. Site of a 1932 Nazi conference during which Hitler decided against joining a General Kurt von Schleicher government in a subordinate capacity.

**Jenische.** Footlose swindlers. Word coined by Himmler applying to Germans who mixed with Gypsies.

**JG.** *See* Jagdgeschwader; Jüdische Gemeinde.

**JKG.** *See* Jüdische Kultusgemeinde.

**JL.** *See* Judenlager.

**JM.** *See* Jungmädelbund.

**Joint-Juden.** Joint Jews. Jews representing the American Jewish Joint Distribution Committee.

**"Jordansplantscher unerwünscht!"** "Splashers from the Jordan River not wanted." Text of a sign forbidding Jews to swim in the lake at Wannsee, Berlin.

**Journaille.** Journalism. Yellow journalism. Dirty-dog journalism. Anti-Nazi journalism. Jewish, Marxist, lying press.

**Jud.** Yid, Jew. More contemptuous name for Jew than Jude.

**Juda.** Jewry, Jews. Negative collective term for all Jews.

**Judas-Jude.** Judas Jew. Nazi enemy, traitor.

**"Juda verrecke!"** "Croak, Jews!" Motto of the SA and the SS beginning with the April 1933 anti-Jewish boycott.

**Jude.** (J) Jew. The "J" was stamped on German-Jewish passports from 1938 onward, based on a request by the Swiss police. *See also* Jud; Reichsbürgergesetz.

**(der) Jude.** The Jew. Singular form used as collective term for all Jews in ideological contrast to "der Deutsche" (the German). Also, form used to refer to an individual Jewish scientist, artist, writer (e.g., der Jude Einstein, the Jew Einstein). Also, every enemy of the Nazi regime, even when they were not Jews; for example, "der Jude Kiepure" (the Jew Kiepure) was a non-Jewish Polish singer. *See also* (Der) Ewige Jude.

**(Der) Jude als Weltparasit.** The Jew as World Parasite. Title of one of the instructional booklets given to German soldiers. *See also* Richthefte des Oberkommandos der Wehrmacht.

"(Wenn der) Jude deutsch schreibt, lügt er!" "When the Jew writes German, he lies." Hate phrase written on German high school blackboards in 1933.

*(Der) Jude im Sprichwort der Völker*. The Jew in Peoples' Proverbs. Collection of antisemitic proverbs by the publisher of *Der Stürmer* in 1942.

Juden-. Jewish, Jew. Used in compound words.

Juden! Jews! Signs posted on rooms such as toilets restricting their use to Jews and Jews only.

"(Für) Juden." "For Jews." Sign posted on the gas chamber at Sobibor concentration camp.

(wilde) Juden. Wild or untamed Jews. Unregistered Jews of the Warsaw-Ghetto not working in factories.

Judenaktion. Jew operation. Attack on Jews.

Judenältester. Chief Jew. Head of the Jewish Council in the ghetto. The most notable: Adam Czerniakow in Warsaw; Jacob Gens in Vilna; and Mordechai Rumkowski in Lodz.

Judenarbeitslager. (JAL) Jew work camp. In 1941 Alfred Rosenberg proposed labor camps for the Jews living in the Warthegau. At Poznan University, he said, "The Jews will have to pay with blood for the twenty-five years of suffering they have inflicted on the Germans and Poles here." In May 1941, the first Jewish work camp was established in the Sport-Stadium in Poznan, Poland, with 1,000 Jewish men brought there from the Lodz-Ghetto.

Judenauffangslager. (JAuL) Jew reception camp

Judenausrottung. Extermination of Jews.

Judenausrottungslager. Jew extermination camp.

Judenbann. Ban on Jews. Police ordinance forbidding Jews to enter off-limits section of a German city. For example, on December 6, 1938, Berlin Jews were banned from museums, sports arenas, ice-skating rinks, and public swimming pools.

Judenbegünstigung. Favoring Jews. Non-Jews who disobeyed Nazi law and risked much to help Jews.

Judenberater. Jew adviser. Member of the German Foreign Office sent as an adviser on Jewish affairs to the foreign ministries of Germany's allies.

judenblind. Jew-blind. Individual who did not agree with Nazi antisemitic politics.

Judenbörse. Jewish stock market. Ironic, Jewish street trading in German towns.

Judenboykott. Boycott of Jews. The boycott of Jewish stores, doctors, and lawyers began on April 1, 1933.

Judenbuße. Jewish fine, penance. A billion-Reichsmark fine demanded of Jews as "reparations" after the November 1938 Pogrom. *See also* Reichskristallnacht.

**Juden-Christen.** Jew-Christians. Germans who could not prove Aryan ancestry.

**Judendelikt.** Jew-crime. Racial offense commited by a Jew in violation of Nazi race laws.

**Judeneinsatz.** Jew-operation. Jewish labor section of cities in German-occupied Europe.

**Judenevakuierung.** Evacuation of Jews. Deportation and mass murder of Jews.

**Judenfeindschaft.** Jew-hostility. Antisemitism.

**Judenfrage.** Jewish problem, Jewish question. The Nazis saw this as a racial-survival issue: how to deal with the Jews and Jewishness in Germany, in Europe, in the world. *See also* Endlösung der Judenfrage.

*(Die) Judenfrage.* The Jewish Problem. Publication of the Institut zum Studium der Judenfrage, issued from Berlin (1937–1943). *See also* Antijüdische Aktion; Antisemitische Aktion.

*(Die) Judenfrage in Geschichte und Gegenwart.* The Jewish Problem in History and in Our Time. Publication of the Institut zum Studium der Judenfrage.

**Judenfrage ist A und O.** The Jewish problem is the alpha and omega. From 1943, putting the Jews at the core of Germany's concerns. Alpha and omega refer to the first and last letters of the Greek alphabet.

**judenfrei.** Free of Jews. Posted on signs outside German cities and towns that were free of Jews, who had emigrated or been deported. *See also* judenrein.

**Judenfresser.** Jew-eater. Nickname of Julius Streicher, a violent antisemite.

**Judenfreund.** Jew-friend. Those non-Jews who sympathized with Jews. Those caught helping Jews were forced to wear an armband marked Judenfreund.

**judenfreundliches Verhalten.** Friendly behavior toward Jews. Absolutely forbidden by Nazi law and practice.

**Judenfreundlichkeit.** Friendliness to Jews. Un-German. *See* Deutschfremdheit; judenfreundliches Verhalten.

**Judengegner.** Opponent of Jews. Antisemite.

**Judengelb.** Jew-yellow. Derogatory for the color of the yellow Star-of-David badge identifying German Jews, from September 1941.

**Judengenosse.** Philosemite.

**Judengesetze.** Jew-laws. All laws against the Jews.

**Judengesetzgebung.** Jew-laws legislation. Civil Service Act. *See also* Gesetz zur Wiederherstellung des Berufsbeamtentums.

**Judengut.** Jew-estate. German estate/farm near Gross-Breesen vandalized during November 1938 Pogrom. Used to train Jewish boys and girls as farmers so that they could emigrate from Germany to a country other than Palestine, as part of the Nazi policy of emigration of Jews to make Germany judenrein. Many were ultimately deported to Theresienstadt and/or Auschwitz.

**Judenhaß.** Jew-hate. Often-used antisemitic word.

**Judenhäuser.** Jew-houses. Gestapo term for buildings managed or administered by the Jüdischer Religionsverband (Jewish Religious Federation). From the beginning of 1941, with the growing serious housing shortage following Allied bombing raids, Jewish home owners and tenants were forced to move to crowded accommodations in Germany and occupied eastern Europe before being deported to concentration camps.

**Judenhure.** Jew-whore. German woman who had sexual relations with a Jewish man.

**Judenjagd.** Jew-hunt. The hunting of Jews during the deportations from smaller ghettos in Russia and Poland. If Jews escaped, the Einsatzgruppen and Wehrmacht would organize a hunt in order to capture and kill the Jewish fugitives.

**Juden, Jesuiten, und Freimaurer.** Jews, Jesuits, and Freemasons. *See also* Juden- und Jesuitenverlage.

**Judenkarte.** Card for Jews. Temporary ration card for Jews for severely reduced food allowance with the letter "J" stamped on it; later Jude printed across it.

*(Der) Judenkenner.* The Jew-Knower. Nazi Julius Streicher's antisemitic youth journal.

**Judenknecht.** Jew-lackey. Epithet for Germans who continued to maintain contact with Jews.

**Judenlager.** (JL, Julag) Jew-camp. *See also* jüdisches Arbeitslager.

**Judenlauser.** Jew-rascal. Lousy Jew.

**Judenleihgebühr.** Fee for the loan of Jews. Fee (Reichmark 0.70 per day per head) paid for the renting of Jewish slave laborers paid by German corporations to the SS. The fees paid went into the SS-Ghettoverwaltung bank account. *See also* Ghettoverwaltung.

**Judenliberalismus.** Jew-liberalism. Nazi belief in the spiritual decomposition of the German people caused by the Jews.

**Judenmassaker.** Massacre of Jews.

**Judenmehl.** Jew-flour. Moldy flour allowed into the ghettos to bake bread.

**Judenmischlinge.** *See* Mischlinge.

**"(Wer den) Juden nicht kennt, kennt den Teufel nicht!"** "He who doesn't know the Jew, doesn't know the devil." Hate slogan on *Der Stürmer* newspaper bins.

**Judenquartier.** Jew-quarter. Predominantly Jewish section of a town or city, often later to become a ghetto.

**Judenrat.** Jewish council. Often, influential Jews whom the Nazis appointed to administer Jewish ghettos and assist in deportations.

**"Juden raus!"** "Jews out." A slogan demanding that Jews leave Germany; the name of an antisemitic board game; later, a dreaded phrase shouted by the Nazis throughout the ghettos when they were trying to force Jews from their hiding places.

**Judenreferat.** Jew department. *See also* Judenreferent.

**Judenreferate.** Jew desks. Officials in local Gestapo headquarters that specialized in Jewish matters.

**Judenreferent.** Expert on Jewish affairs. Working in Department IVB4 of the RSHA under Adolf Eichmann.

**judenrein.** Free of Jews. Clearing all Jews out of a specific German area or European community, the overriding goal of the "Final Solution." *See also* judenfrei.

**Judenreinigungsaktion.** Jew-cleaning operation. Mass murder of entire Jewish populations of small towns.

**Judenrepublik.** Jew-republic. Derogatory for the Weimar Republic, which many Germans believed was preparing for a Bolshevik takeover that would destroy traditional German values.

**Judenreservat.** Jew-reservation. Cluster of Jewish ghettos. *See also* Fall Madagaskar.

**Judensau.** Jew-pig, Jew-sow. Traditional German defamation, accusing Jews of learning their Talmudic religion from kissing, sucking the teats, and eating the feces of a sow. Graphic illustrations appeared in woodcuts and as sculptures on public bridges and in churches. Martin Luther was the first to describe this pictorial defamation, and he did so approvingly. Saujud was a common German invective.

**Judenschwein.** Jew-pig. Derogatory term often used by the SS when addressing Jews.

**Judensechser.** Jew-six. In the antisemitic children's book in German schools, *Der Giftpilz*, the allegedly typical Jewish nose was shaped like the number 6 reversed.

**"(Die) Juden sind an allem schuld."** "The Jews are guilty of everything." Propaganda theme claiming Jewish responsibility for World War II.

**"Juden sind hier nicht erwünscht."** "Jews not wanted here." Signs on Nazi-German businesses after 1933. Also, similar to signs on German businesses even before World War I.

**"Juden sind hier unerwünscht."** "Jews are unwanted here." *See also* "Juden sind hier nicht erwünscht."

**"(Die) Juden sind unser Unglück!"** "The Jews are our misfortune." A line from Martin Luther's *Von den Juden und ihren Luegen*. In 1879, the German historian and antisemite Heinrich von Treitschke used the phrase in his *Preussische Jahrbücher*. It also appeared at the bottom of the front page of each issue of the Nazi weekly newspaper *Der Stürmer*, on *Der Stürmer* display cases, on banners at Nazi rallies, and other locations in Germany during the 1930s.

**Judensöldling.** Jew-mercenary, Jew-hireling. Epithet for liberals, democrats, and other Germans who were in favor of the Weimar Republic.

**Judensprung.** Jew-jump. To escape the murderous work in the quarries, many Jews committed suicide by jumping from the quarry surface.

**Judenstaat.** Jew-state. In Treblinka, name given to the gas chambers.

**Judenstämmling.** Jewish descendent. Baptized descendent of a Jewish/non-Jewish marriage.

**Judenstern.** Jewish star. A stigmatic emblem originating in the Middle Ages, an identification badge that the Jews were forced to wear in order to distinguish them from non-Jews. It consisted of a yellow six-pointed star on which two opposite-facing black triangles were printed, along with the word JUDE in black. From November 1939, all Jews residing in German-occupied Poland from sixteen years old and older had to wear a star. In 1941 a police decree ordered Jews in the Reich and the Protectorat of Bohemia and Moravia to wear a star. In 1942 the order was extended to all of German-occupied Europe. During World War II, the Nazis used various signs, including an armband stamped with a blue six-pointed Star of David in eastern European ghettos and a yellow six-pointed star with the letter J in western Europe. In many concentration camps Jews were marked with a red triangle (political opponent) overlapped by a yellow triangle (Jew) to form a Judenstern.

**Judentransport.** Jew-transport. Segregated public transportation for Jews in Nazi Germany. Also, trains deporting Jews to concentration camps.

**Juden- und Jesuitenverlage.** Jews and Jesuits publishing houses. Nazi version of traditional German hostility to Jews, Jesuits, and Freemasons.

**"Juden und Judengenossen."** "Jews and their associates." An antisemitic phrase long before Alfred Rosenberg used it.

**"Juden unerwünscht."** "Jews (are) not wanted." Common German slogan during the Hitler years posted on German businesses and at the outskirts of cities and towns.

**"(Für) Juden verboten."** "For Jews forbidden." Signs posted on inns and businesses before the Nazi era. From 1933, posted on entrances of seaside resorts. *See also* "Juden unerwünscht."

**Judenvermögensabgabe.** Handing over of Jewish property. *See also* Kontribution.

**Judenvernichtungsbrigade.** Jew-destruction brigade. Nickname of the Einsatzgruppen.

**Judenvolk.** Jew-rabble. Pejorative term for all Jews as a group.

**Judenzählung.** Jewish census. Census that confirmed that Jewish participation in World War I was proportionately equivalent to that of non-Jews but was intentionally misinterpreted and used by antisemitic officials and groups to support their false accusations that the German Jews did not fight for Germany but instead used the war to exploit the nation economically.

**Judenzug.** Jew-train. A train deporting Jews from other parts of Europe to the ghettos and death camps of Poland. After 1943, even German troop trains had to give precedence to these trains.

**"(Der) Jude zerstört das deutsche Wesen!"** "(The) Jew destroys Germanness, the German being." Nazi slogan during the Weimar Republic.

**jüdisch.** Jewish. Standard adjective meaning Jewish. Also, antisemitic term, meaning dirty corrupt Jew. Often used in combination with other adjectives; for example, jüdisch-marxistische Weltanschauung (Jew-Marxist worldview).

**jüdische Elemente.** Jew-elements. Those to be murdered by the SD and the Wehrmacht were verbrecherische, bolschewistische, meist jüdische Elemente; that is, criminal, bolshevik, and most of them Jewish elements.

**jüdische Erfindung.** Jew-invention. That is, the conscience, or humanitarian feelings.

**jüdische Geistesüberfremdung.** Jewish alienating influence on (German) thought or spirit. Before 1933, the alleged dominating Jewish influence on German culture.

**Jüdische Gemeinde.** (JG) Jewish community.

**jüdische Greuelhetze.** Jew horror propaganda. Alleged Jewish-influenced propaganda from abroad; a pretext for the boycott against Jews in 1933.

**jüdische Großmutter.** Jewish grandmother. Macabre joke referring to the hushed-up revelation of a Jewish relative in a German family history. *See also* (die) Großmutter begießen.

**jüdische Intelligenz.** Jewish-cleverness. Derogatory for everyone out of favor with the Nazi regime.

**(der) jüdische Krieg.** The Jewish-war. Accusation that the Jews caused World War II.

**Jüdische Kultusgemeinde.** (JKG) Jewish community for religious, educational, and cultural affairs.

**jüdische Morde.** Jewish-murders. Murders the Nazis alleged the Jews committed.

**jüdische Pressetaktik.** Jewish press tactic. Nazi criticism of those elements of the press who opposed them, prior to Hitler's rise to power.

**jüdischer Ältestenrat.** (JÄR) Jewish Elder Council. Early designation of Judenrat. *See also* Judenrat.

**jüdischer Angeklagter.** Jew-accused. All who were accused of being Jewish and/or anti-Nazi.

**Jüdischer Arbeitseinsatz.** Mobilization of Jewish labor. Organization of Jewish forced labor during the war.

**jüdische Rasse.** Jewish-race. Summary of everything Jewish in contrast to what was German. Near the end of his life, Hitler admitted to Martin Bormann, "[W]e use the term Jewish race as a matter of convenience, for in reality and from the genetic point of view there is no such thing as the Jewish race. There does, however, exist a community. . . . It is [a] spiritually homogeneous group [to] which all Jews throughout the world deliberately adhere . . . and it is this group of human beings to which we give the title Jew race. [Jews are] an abstract race of the mind [that] has its origins, admittedly, in the Hebrew religion. . . . A race of the mind is something more solid, more durable than just a [biological] race, pure and simple."

**jüdischer Feuilletonismus.** Jewish factual sloppiness (in newspapers). Accusation against Jews and middle-class leftists of being unscientific.

**Jüdischer Kulturbund.** Jewish Cultural Federation. In 1935 all Jewish cultural and artistic organizations were disbanded and amalgamated into the Reichsverband jüdischer Kulturbund by the President of the Reichskulturkammer (Reich Chamber of Culture).

**jüdischer Mischling.** Jewish progeny of a mixed Jewish/non-Jewish marriage. Someone who racially descends from one or two fully-Jewish grandparents, according to the Reichsbürgergesetz of November 14, 1935.

**jüdischer Napoleon.** Jew Napoleon. Jakob Lejkin, Assistant Head of the Jewish Ordnungsdienst of the Warsaw-Ghetto, was killed by Jewish resisters as a Nazi collaborator.

**jüdischer Ordnungsdienst.** Jewish Order Service. The Jewish ghetto police. These units were established by the Nazis in the larger ghettos and served the Judenrat as a means to control the Jewish ghetto population. *See also* Bindenträger; Judenrat.

**jüdischer Wohnbezirk.** Jewish residental district. Slang name for a Jewish ghetto. These districts were strictly off limits to the Aryan population.

**jüdisches Arbeitslager.** (Julag) Jewish labor camp. Camps under the control of German companies, not incorporated into the SS camp system until 1943.

*Jüdisches Nachrichtenblatt.* Jewish Newsletter. Publication of Die Reichsvereinigung der Juden in Deutschland (the Reich Jewish Union in Germany). Publicizing Nazi Jewish regulations.

**jüdisches Problem.** Jewish problem. *See also* Judenfrage.

**jüdisches Siedlungsgebiet.** Jewish settlement region. The Theresienstadt ghetto/camp outside of Prague. *See also* Theresienstadt.

**jüdische Stunde.** Jewish hour. Refers to the limited time German Jews were permitted to be on the street to shop in late 1930s and early 1940s.

**"Jüdisches Wohnviertel."** "Jewish quarter." Inscription in Hebrew letters on the main gate of the Jewish ghetto of Krakau, erected in 1941 on German orders.

**jüdische Vornamen.** Jewish forenames. Long list of Jewish-sounding first names permitted under German law in 1938. Those Jews without such names as Abel, Zevi, Abigail, or Zorthel had to use Abraham, Israel, or Sara.

**Jüdische Winterhilfe.** Jewish Winter Relief (Program). Jewish self-help organization that paralleled the German Winterhilfswerk der NSV. *See also* Winterhilfswerk des deutschen Volkes.

**jüdische Zwangsarbeitslager.** Jewish forced-labor camps. Hundreds of these slave-labor camps were established in Germany and occupied Europe, as well as Bulgaria and Libya.

**jüdisch versippt.** Jew-tainted. Related to, married to Jews.

**"Jud kaputt!"** "Jew finished." Grammatically incorrect phrase, especially Ukrainian, heard when German armed forces arrived.

**Jüdlein.** Little Yid. Contemptuous name for Jews used by their murderers.

*Jud Süß.* Jew Süß (sweet). Antisemitic propaganda film in 1940. A historical melodrama picturing an evil Jewish businessman, Süß Oppenheimer, treasurer to the corrupt Duke of Wurttemburg. The Jew sees to it that the local Jews are tolerated, but when the Duke dies, the Assembly of Elders tries him and sentences him to death for having "carnal knowledge of a Christian woman." Himmler ordered all members of the SS and the German Police to view this very popular film.

**Jud XY.** Jew XY. Derogatory Nazi phrase for Jews.

**Jugenddienstpflicht.** Youth service obligation. Obligatory work, decreed in 1939, for all Hitler Youth members from ages ten to eighteen, to perform work for the war effort, such as harvesting, helping in air-raid shelters, and helping war-injured combatants at train stations and sick barracks.

**Jugenddienstverordnung.** Youth service order. Law establishing Hitler Youth. *See also* Hitlerjugend.

**Jugendführer.** Youth leader. Ranking member of the leadership corps in the Hitler Youth.

**Jugendführer des Deutschen Reiches.** Youth Führer of the German Reich. Baldur von Schirach's official government position until 1940, when he was replaced by Artur Axmann. *See also* Reichsjugendführer.

**Jugendlager.** Youth camp. Nazi training camp for German youth.

**jugendliche Cliquen.** Youth cliques. *See also* Edelweißpiraten.

**Jugendlicher Hilfsdienst.** Youth Help Service. Auxiliary service of German youth between the ages of ten and sixteen.

**Jugendmädelbund in der Hitlerjugend.** *See* Bund Deutscher Mädel in der Hitlerjugend.

**Jugendmusik.** Youth music. Folk songs, marching songs, and Nazi fighting songs were organized and promoted by the Hitler Youth to enhance the sense of mutual belonging and being part of the German people.

**Jugendorganisation der NSDAP.** Youth Organization of the Nazi Party. Precursor of Hitler Youth, initially subordinate to the SA. *See also* Hitlerjugend.

*Jugendschriften-Warte.* Youth Literature Guardian. The first professional children's literature journal established in 1893 and taken over by the National Socialists in 1933; served to promote their ideology and to censure books deemed un-German or written by Jews.

**Jugendschutzkammer.** Youth Protection Chamber. Court hearing cases concerning German youth.

**Jugendschutzlager.** Youth protection camp. Concentration camp for young offenders and politically undesirable youths at Moringen/Solling and Uckermark/Mecklenburg.

**Jugendverwahrlager.** Youth custody camp. Concentration camp for children captured from non-Jewish partisans.

**Jugendwalter.** Youth counselors. Advisers to the school principal and the Schulgemeinde; composed of parents, teachers, and/or Hitler Youth members.

**jugendwert.** Valuable for youth. Label applied to films and books deemed of educational value according to the judgment of the official educational body, Reichsjugendführung.

**Jugendwohnheim.** Youth residence. Company hostel for apprentices.

**Ju(h)l.** December.

**Julag.** *See* jüdisches Arbeitslager.

**Junaks.** Rowdies, daredevils. "Junak," Polish for daring. German-speaking Polish police helpers (Blaue Polizei) recruited to assist the SS with roundups of, and attacks against, Jews in Poland. *See* Judenaktionen.

**Jungbann.** Largest unit of Deutsches Jungvolk in der Hitlerjugend.

**Jungdeutscher Orden.** Young-Germans Order. Liberal middle-class young people who opposed the Nazis.

*Die Junge Front.* The Youth Front. Hitler Youth periodical.

**Jungfernhof.** Virgin manor. Location where Jews were murdered at Riga, Latvia.

**Jungmädel.** Young girl. Ten- to fourteen-year-old girl member of the Jungmädel-bund. Almost all German ten-year-old girls became Jungmädel on Hitler's birthday, April 20. Also, synonymous with Jungmädelbund.

**Jungmädelbund.** (JM) League of German Girls. Association of German girls (aged 10–14) affiliated with the Bund Deutscher Mädel and Hitlerjugend. Oath of the Jungmädelbund: "Over the whole course of the service to the German Girls, our obligation is to the Führer, who is our model and raison d'etre in his battles and labors." *See also* Bund Deutscher Mädel in der Hitlerjugend.

**Jungmänner.** Young men. Students of the National Socialist Educational Organizations. *See also* Nationalpolitische Erziehungsanstalten.

**Jungstahlhelm.** Young Steel Helmet. Youth division of Stahlhelm. Incorporated into the Hitler Youth in 1933.

**Jungsturm Adolf Hitler.** Young-Storm Adolf Hitler. Youth section of the Sturmabteilung founded in 1922, then became Hitler Youth.

**Jungvolk.** *See* Deutsches Jungvolk in der Hitlerjugend.

**Jungwerker.** Apprentice.

**Junker.** SS cadet. *See also* Junkerschule.

**Junkerschule.** Elite officers' school. Training schools for SS cadets at Ordensburgen, Braunschweig, and Bad Tölz. *See also* Ordensburgen.

# K

**Ka-Be.** (KB) Krankenbau. Camp infirmary.

**Kadavergehorsam.** Corpse-like obedience. Total obeisance to authority, the goal of the Third Reich for the German population in general and the SS in particular.

**Kaderheer.** Skeleton army.

**Kaffeemittel.** Coffee substitute.

**Kaffeemühle.** Coffee mill. Air force slang for aerial dogfight.

**Kaiser-Wilhelm-Gedächtnisrock.** Emperor Wilhelm remembrance tunic. Army slang for the colorful jacket of full-dress German army uniform that apparently was based on a design by the German emperor. *See* Sarassanirock; Waffenrock.

**Kaleu.** *See* Kapitänleutnant.

**Kälteversuche im Freien.** Outside hypothermia experiments. Medical experiments on prisoners at Dachau to study the body's reaction to cold temperatures. Poorly-clad prisoners, sometimes without shoes, were left standing outside up to fourteen hours in 6° C (42.8° F) weather.

**Kamerad.** Comrade. Form of address among Party members.

**Kameradendiebstahl.** Stealing from a comrade. Robbing a fellow German, Nazi, SS, or member of the armed forces; punished severely.

**Kameradenwerk.** Work on behalf of comrades. ODESSA, the organization assisting Nazi criminals to escape from justice.

**"Kamerad, reich mir die Hände!"** "Comrade, Give Me Your Hand." 1923 SA song.

**Kameradschaft.** Comradeship. New spirit of national solidarity in the German Volk community; also the name for a small unit of the Hitler Youth.

**Kameradschaftsabend.** Comradeship evening. *See also* Heimabend.

**Kameradschaftsdienst.** Comrade service. Sending parcels to the front to soldiers without relatives.

**Kameradschaftsführer.** Comradeship leader. Officer in the Nazi student organization. *See also* Nationalsozialistischer Deutscher Studentenbund.

**Kameradschaftshaus.** Comradeship house. Residence for students. *See also* Nationalsozialistischer Deutscher Studentenbund.

**Kameradschaftswerke.** Comrade organizations. SS-financed escape organization. *See also* (die) Schleuse.

**(durch den) Kamin.** Through the chimney. Referred to people murdered by gas and their bodies cremated, with the smoke rising from the chimneys.

**Kammhuber-Linie.** Kammhuber line. North-south line of German air defenses from Denmark to the south of France set up in 1940–1941, consisting of radar, aircraft, and searchlights.

**Kampf.** Fight, struggle, battle. Favorite National Socialist word; military word used in ideological context for propaganda purposes. *See also Mein Kampf.*

**Kampfabzeichen.** Honor medal for distinguished fighting. Award instituted between 1939 and 1941 to honor any soldier displaying distinguished military courage in battle.

**Kampfbinde.** Fighter armband. Hitler Youth and Sturmabteilung armband featuring a prominent black swastika on a red and white background.

**Kampfbund.** Fighting Association. League of Bavarian rightist groups that helped plan the Hitler Putsch.

**Kampfbund für den gewerblichen Mittelstand.** Fighting Association for the Commercial Middle Class. Nazi organization founded in 1932.

**Kampfbund für Deutsche Kultur.** Fighting Association for German Culture. Nazi organization founded in 1929 by Alfred Rosenberg to attack modern culture, especially the arts and literature, and to promote Nazi culture.

**Kampf dem Verderb.** Fight against spoilage. Campaign against the wasting of food and consumer items and for the collection of recyclable goods; part of the second Vierjahresplan.

**Kämpfer.** Fighter(s). *See also* Alte Kämpfer.

**kämpferisch.** Battling. Heroic. One of the chracteristics of the ideal German type.

**Kampfflugzeug.** Fighter plane. Air force fighter plane that also bombed land and sea targets.

**"Kampf gegen die verjazzte und verjudete Tanzmusik der Systemzeit."** "Battle against the jazzed and 'Jewed' dance music of the constitutional system" of the Weimar Republic. Nazi propaganda attempt to eliminate jazz music, assumed to be Jewish, as an alien, non-German element.

**Kampfgemeinschaft revolutionärer Nationalsozialisten.** Revolutionary Combat Community of National Socialists. Otto and Gregor Straßer organization that favored Marxist revolutionary principles and the workers. In 1930 Otto walked out of the Nazi Party with 200 of his followers.

**Kampfgeschwader.** Luftwaffe bomber squadrons.

**Kampfgruppe.** Battle group. Closest in concept to an American task force. It could range in size from a corps to a battalion or company. It was essentially an ad-hoc organization of different arms (e.g., armor, artillery, infantry, assault boats, antitank guns, etc.) organized temporarily for a specific operational task. Kampf-gruppen were usually named after the person choosen to command the formation.

**Kampfgruppe zur besonderer Verwendung.** Battle Group for Special Purpose. Air force transport group.

**Kampfpartei.** Combat Party. Early 1920s term for the Nazi Party, emphasizing its militancy and World War I veterans in its leadership. The term was dropped after the Hitler Putsch. *See also* Hitler-Putsch.

**Kampf-Rune.** *See* Tyr-Rune.

**Kampfverlag.** Battle Publishers. Nazi publishing house controlled by Otto Straßer. *See also* Kampfgemeinschaft revolutionärer Nationalsozialisten.

**Kampfzeit.** Battle time, time of struggle. Period of early years of the Nazi Party in Munich; also, period of the Weimar Republic and ascent of the Nazi Party (1918–1933); also wartime period when Germans favored national spirit over factionalism.

**Kanada.** Canada. Slang name used by the guards and inmates for the warehouses in Auschwitz II where the personal property taken from the thousands of victims heading for the gas chambers was sorted, collected, and stored. Most likely a Polish term used before the war.

**Kanalkampf.** Channel battle. First part of the Battle of Britain when the German air force bombed British shipping in the English Channel.

**Kaninchen-Orden.** Bunny medal. *See also* Karnickel-Orden.

**Kanister.** Canister. Container of phosphorous dropped from British and American planes during bombing runs over Germany to increase the destructive effect of firebombs.

**"Kanonen statt Butter!"** "Cannons instead of Butter." Nazi slogan discouraging the use of butter in favor of margarine. And in October 1936, Göring, as head of the Four-Year Plan, announced it as a nutritional principle related to security material: "Guns not butter. First, create a strong nation. Too much fat—too big a belly. I myself have eaten less butter, and I've lost twenty pounds." *See also* Butter und Kanonen.

**Kanonen und Butter.** *See* Butter und Kanonen.

**Kantinengeld.** Canteen money. PX (post-exchange) voucher system, valid only in the military. Soldiers were partially paid in this mode.

**Kanzlei des Führers.** *See* Führerkanzlei.

**Kanzlei des Führers der NSDAP.** Chancellery of the Führer of the National Socialist Party. Hitler chancellery for contact with Nazi organizations.

**Kanzler.** Chancellor. German prime minister under the Weimar Constitution. *See also* (Der) Führer und Reichskanzler.

**"Das Kapital ist für die Wirtschaft da und die Wirtschaft für das Volk."** "Capital serves the economy and the economy serves the people." Hitler dictum.

**Kapitänleutnant.** (Kaleu) Lieutenant captain.

**Kapo.** Foreman. A camp inmate appointed by the SS to head a unit of other prisoners. Many Kapos were brutal toward other prisoners and were sometimes feared more than the SS.

**Kapp-Putsch.** 1920 rightist conspiracy and putsch against the Weimar Republic.

**Karacho-Weg.** Fast Street (from Spanish *carracho*, from *carrera*, a run). Street at KZ Buchenwald where prisoners were beaten into running so that they would understand the rapid pace of the camp.

**Karbowanez.** Ukrainian money worth 100 kopeks. Currency used in German-occupied Soviet Union.

**Karinhall.** Göring's official residence near Berlin. A large country house named after his deceased first wife, Karin von Kantzow. He filled it with artworks and other material looted from Europe.

**Karl-Liebknecht-Haus.** Karl Liebknecht House. German Communist Party headquarters in Berlin targeted by the Nazis. In February 1933, the SA attacked the house and seized documents.

**Karnickel-Orden.** Rabbit medal. Derogatory name for the medal of German mothers, alluding to the tendency of rabbits to have several offspring. *See also* Ehrenkreuz der deutschen Mutter.

**Karrete.** Vehicle using caterpillar tracks. Light tank.

**Kartoffelflocker.** Potato flaker. Worker employed in the production of dried potatoes (potato chips).

**Kartothek.** Card catalogue. File cards of concentration camp inmates for quick access to information from the prisoner file, such as number, name, and other personal data. *See* Häftlingsakte.

**Kaseinwolle.** Artificial wool.

**kaserniert.** Kept in barracks. Jewish workers were kept in barracks within liquidated ghettos, temporarily employed by Nazis, but in the end murdered.

**kasernierte Hundertschaften.** Barrack hundreds. Early SS units.

**Kategorien der KL-Gefangenen.** Categories of concentration camp prisoners. German and non-German political adversaries of the Nazi regime, so-called racial inferiors or enemies, criminals, asocials, Gypsies, Jews.

**Kathleen.** *See* Artus-Plan.

**Kaufering.** Sub-camp of Dachau. *See also* Landsberg am Lech.

**"Kauft nicht bei Juden! Kauft in deutschen Geschäften!"** "Don't buy from Jews. Shop in German stores." Nazi slogan to boycott Jewish businesses in the early 1930s.

**Kazett.** (KZ; pronounced Ka-tset). *See* Kazettlager; Konzentrationszuchthaus.

**Kazet(t)lager.** (KL, KZ) Abbreviations for Konzentrationslager (concentration camp).

**Kazet(t)ler.** Concentration camp prisoner. From abbreviation KZ for concentration camp (Konzentrationslager). One of the most famous prisoners was the writer renamed Yehiel de-Nur, a brilliant poet, who called himself Katzetnik 135633.

**Katzmann-Erlaß.** Katzmann Decree. Order to transfer to the east all the Jews of Galicia, Umsiedlung nach dem Osten. Transfer of all Jews to the death camps of the Generalgouvernement in Poland.

**KB.** *See* Krankenbau.

**KdF.** *See* Nationalsozialistische Gemeinschaft Kraft durch Freude.

**Kdf-Wagen.** *See* Kübelwagen; Volkswagen.

**Kdf-Wart.** Party worker. *See also* Nationalsozialistische Gemeinschaft Kraft durch Freude.

**KDL.** *See* Kinderlandverschickung.

**KdS.** *See* Kommandeur der Sicherheitzpolizei und des Sicherheitsdienstes; Kommandeur der Sipo und des SD.

**"Kein Deutscher kauft noch bei einem Juden."** *See* "Deutsche Männer und Frauen, kauft nicht bei Juden."

**"Kein November!"** "No November." Goebbels' World War II slogan to convince Germans not to repeat the armistice of November 1918 (i.e., not to surrender but to fight on).

**Keitel-Erlaß.** Keitel Decree. Order signed by Chief of Staff of the Armed Forces Field Marshal Wilhelm Keitel. *See also* Nacht-und-Nebel-Erlaß.

**Kennkarte.** (KK) Identification card. Official personal identification card for Germans within Germany to replace the regular passport and to curb traveling abroad. Also used in occupied Poland by Jews working for the Germans.

**Kennkartenzwang.** Obligation to obtain identification cards. According to the third public notice of July 23, 1938, every Jew had to register at the local police station for an identification card by December 31, 1938. Their identification as Jews was marked on these cards as well as entered into the people's card file. *See also* Volkskartei.

**Keppler-Kreis.** Keppler Circle. Wealthy, conservative businessmen who contributed to the Nazi Party and who expected to be able to use Hitler to their economic purposes.

**Kern.** Core. Full-fledged member of the Hitler Youth, ages fourteen to eighteen. *See* Pimpf.

**Kette.** Chain. Three-aircraft combat formation.

**Kettenhunde.** Chain-dogs. Military police so-called because of the chain and breastplate, or duty gorget, they wore around their necks. *See also* Feldgendarmerie.

**Kettenkrad.** Half-track. Motor vehicle with two caterpillar tracks instead of rear wheels.

**KGL.** *See* Kriegsgefangenenlager.

**K-Häftling.** *See* Kugelhäftling.

**Kinderaktion.** Operation Children. Murder of nearly 5,000 disabled children as part of the Euthanasia Program in 1938–1939. Also, specific roundups of Jewish children in Lodz-Ghetto and other ghettos (e.g., November 5, 1943, roundups in Lithuania, during which the Nazis seized 574 children plus 249 old and disabled people and deported them all to concentration camps).

**Kinderblock.** Children's barracks. Fall 1943 to summer 1944, area of Auschwitz housing those children subject to brutal experiments.

**Kinder deutscher Abstammung.** Children of German descent. Polish children Nazis considered worthy of being Germanized. *See also* Lebensborn; Ostkinder; Wiedereindeutschung.

**"Kinder, Kirche, Küche."** "Children, church, kitchen." Pre-Nazi and Nazi slogan applied to German women.

**Kinderlager.** Children's camp. Several concentration camps contained special areas for children, including Auschwitz and Buchenwald.

**Kinderlandverschickung.** (KDL, KLV) Children send-away to the country. Before World War II, program to send German children from big cities to healthier areas. With the war, program to transfer schoolchildren away from areas likely to be bombed. From 1943, often forced evacuation of children. Between 1940 and 1944, almost a million German boys and girls were sent away to safer locations.

**Kinderlandverschickungslager.** (KLV-Lager) Country camp where children were sent. *See also* Kinderlandverschickung.

**(der) Kindermord bei Ypern.** The massacre of the innocents at Ypres. *See also* Langemarck.

**Kinder polnischer Familien.** Children of Polish families. Polish children Nazis considered worthy of being Germanized. *See also* Lebensborn; Ostkinder; Wiedereindeutschung.

**"Kindersegen!"** "Blessed with children." Slogan attempting to increase the German birthrate.

**Kindertagesstätte.** Nursery school. Government nursery school.

**Kindertransporte.** Children's transports. Convoys or trains made up solely of Jewish children caught during Nazi roundups and deported to death camps. Also, transports of Jewish children out of Germany and Austria to England and other countries, organized by Jewish communities in Germany and relief organizations abroad, such as the World Movement for the Care of Children from Germany.

**Kinder-und-Halbwüchsigen-Sammellager.** Children and adolescent camp. At Majdanek. *See also* Kinderlager.

**Kinobesuch.** Going to the cinema. Ironic for being selected to go to the gas chamber.

**Kirchenbewegung deutscher Christen.** *See* Nationalkische deutscher Christen.

**Kirchenkampf.** (KK) Church battle. Nazi attempt to control the German churches was opposed by a minority of Germans.

**Kittelbachpiraten.** (K.P.) Kittelbach Pirates. Düsseldorf anti-Nazi youth group. *See also* Edelweißpiraten.

**KK.** *See* (Der) Evangelische Kirchenkampf im Dritten Reich; Kennkarte; Kirchenkampf; Kohlenklau; Kreiskommandantur.

**KL.** Official abbreviation for Konzentrationslager in Nazi documents. *See also* Konzentrationslager.

**Klages-Kreis.** Klages Circle. Group of German academics founded in the 1920s by philosopher Ludwig Klages. After 1933 it criticized scientific rationality, technological control of nature, mass culture, and economic capitalism. Although anti-semitic, it opposed theories of race as well as class. In 1938 restricted by the Amt Rosenberg.

**Klages-Weiber.** Klages women. Term used by Thomas Mann in 1939 to criticize the Klages Circle who promoted a "German bio-centric science of life." *See also* Arbeitskreis für biozentrische Forschungen; Klages-Kreis.

**Klappbuch.** Clatter book. A Morse code signal light.

**Klassenführer.** Class leader. Classroom representative appointed by the Hitler Youth.

**KLB.** Konzentrationslager Buchenwald. *See* Buchenwald.

**Kleiderkarte.** *See* Reichskleiderkarte.

**Kleiderweste.** Vest. Small long-sleeved jacket with leather buttons; part of the BDM uniform.

**(die) kleine Festung.** The small fortress. Part of the Czech fortress town of Theresienstadt, which the Nazis converted into a ghetto/camp. The Prague Gestapo converted the building into a political prison that housed prisoners before they were sent to forced-labor or death camps.

**kleine Häuser.** Small houses. Euphemism for crematoria at Auschwitz.

**(das) kleine Lager.** (The) small camp. Special section of a concentration camp surrounded by barbed wire either to house extra prisoners or to perform special tortures and murders; also, part of Buchenwald where Reichkristallnacht Jewish prisoners were kept; also, quarantine area for new prisoners.

**Kleinempfänger.** Small receiver. Small radio built in 1938 and available to Germans for only 35.00 Reichmark.

**kleine Volksgenossen.** Little fellow countrymen. Hitler's description of his early Nazi followers.

**Kleinkampfmittel.** Small battle device. *See also* Einmann-U-Boot.

**Kleinkind.** Small child. German child between age two and six; category for ration cards.

**Kleinstkind.** Very small child. German child under the age of two; category for ration cards.

**Kleinst-U-Boot.** Smallest submarine. *See also* Einmann-U-Boot.

**Kleinterror.** Small terror. The first stage of the mass-murder process against European Jews. In occupied Poland, this referred to uprooting smaller Jewish communities by ordering them to move into certain areas, or by moving larger Jewish communities into overcrowded ghettos where adequate sanitary facilities were not available.

**Kluft.** Clothes. Uniform of the Jungmädel.

**KLV.** *See* Kinderlandverschickung.

**KLV-Lager.** *See* Kinderlandverschickungslager.

**Knappenschaft.** Young Apprentices. Youth group of 1920s, opposed Versailles Treaty, Jews, and Communists. *See also* Wandervögel.

**(Frau) Knätscherich.** (Mrs.) Grump. Female figure used to ridicule German women who refused to donate from their wardrobes to the public clothing collection.

**Knickebein.** Knock-knees. Slang for German navigational system using radio beams to guide bombers.

**Knochenmühle.** Bone-crushing machine. A machine specially built by Schriever AG of Hanover for use in the Chelmno death camp to crush the bones of the already gassed victims.

**Knopffabrik.** Button factory. Sobibor death camp, where Nazi officials told their victims that once they arrived at the camp, they were going to produce buttons.

**Ko.** *See* Kommandeur.

**KOB.** *See* Kriegsoffiziersbewerber.

**Koffer.** Suitcase. Military lingo for bomb.

**Kofferpatrioten.** Suitcase patriots. Skeptics among the German border population (1938–1939).

**Kohlenklau.** (KK) Coal thief. Figure of half-man, half-animal monster with crooked face and claws, clad in black, carrying a bag of coal. Widely distributed propaganda poster, warning against the waste of state resources. Also, nickname of a German military vehicle and the Ju 290 A-5 bomber.

**Kohlenverbände.** Coal organizations. German cartel of carbon-chemical industry.

**Kohlenwertstoff.** Coal product. Refined coal product such as synthetic oil or synthetic gasoline.

**Kohntinent.** Cohen's continent. Derisive for continent of North America and alluding to Jewish influence on the United States.

**Kokarde.** Cockade. Double encirclement battle.

**Kokszaun.** Coke fence. Demarcation line between zones supplied by eastern and western coke trusts.

**Kola-Fu.** *See* Fuhlsbüttel.

*Kolberg.* Nationalistic Nazi propaganda film concerning the defense of Kolberg against Napoleon. In late 1944, Hitler, convinced that the propaganda film would be more useful to him than a military victory, allowed almost 200,000 German soldiers to be used as extras.

**Kolibri.** Hummingbird. Code name for "Night of the Long Knives." *See also* Nacht der langen Messer.

**Kölner Glas.** Cologne glass. After 1942, windowpane reinforced with wire to limit shattering in air raids.

**Kolonialpolitisches Amt.** Colonial-Policy Department. Nazi Party division headed by Franz Ritter von Epp.

**Kolonialverwaltung.** Colonial administration. Area of German-occupied Europe with no autonomous organization of any kind. *See also* Besetzte Ostgebiete; Europäische Neuordnung.

**Kolonisation.** Colonization (Germanization). Nineteenth-century German political goal of achieving parity in colonies with other nations. Later, Nazi ideology called for German colonization of the eastern European heartland.

**Kolonisation nach Osten.** Colonization (Germanization) of the east. *See also* Kolonisation; Lebensraum.

**Kolonne.** Crew, column. An independent transportation unit, varying from company to platoon size, transporting equipment or supplies. Also, latrine cleaning unit at the concentration camps.

**Kombi.** Abbreviation for Kombination (combination). Air force flying suit.

**Komite für die russische Befreiungsarmee.** (RONA). Committee of the Russian National Liberation Army. *See* Russische Befreiungsarmee.

**Komitee zur Befreiung der Völker Rußlands.** (KONR) Committee for the Liberation of the Russian Peoples. Russian National Liberation Army (RONA), a Russian army formation that collaborated with the German army from 1941 in antipartisan warfare. Another formation, the ROA (the Russian Liberation Army) under anti-Stalinist Russian General A.A. Vlasov (Wlassow), also collaborated with the German army. *See* Osttruppen.

**Kommandant rückwärtiges Armeegebiet.** (Korück) Commandant of Army Rear-Area Security.

**Kommandeur.** (Ko) Commander.

**Kommandeur der Sicherheitspolizei und des Sicherheitsdienstes.** (KdS) Commander of the Security Police and the Security Service.

**Kommandeur der Sipo und des SD.** (KdS) *See* SD; Sipo.

**Kommandeurwagen.** Commander car. Manufactured in limited quantities by Volkswagen for the war effort, a kind of jacked-up Volkswagen bug, 4-wheel drive in first gear only.

**Kommandeuse.** [Female] commandant. *See also* Bestie von Buchenwald.

**Kommando.** Labor squads made up of camp prisoners. Also, command, unit.

**Kommandoamt der Waffen-SS.** Headquarters of the Waffen-SS.

**Kommando Berta.** SS slave-labor unit at Buchenwald working at the Rhein-metall Munitions Factory and at the Hohenzollern Lokomotivfabrik.

**Kommandobefehl.** Commando Order. Führer order allowing the execution of captured Allied Special Operations personnel.

**Kommando Blau.** Blue detachment. *See also* Arbeitsjuden.

**Kommando Bothmann.** Bothmann detachment. Chelmno euthanasia unit.

**Kommando 1005.** Unit 1005. Adolf Eichmann's Department IVb of the RSHA. From 1942, Eichmann directed a unit of 335 Jewish prisoners and Soviet POWs who were forced to destroy the evidence of the Nazi mass murders by digging up and burning the corpses of those murdered by the Einsatzgruppen. Members of the unit were themselves murdered after their grisly task was completed. *See also* Einsatzgruppen.

**Kommandoführer.** Supervisor of Labor Groups.

**Kommando 99—Pferdestall.** Order 99—Horse Stable. Execution facility disguised as showers with loud music playing at Buchenwald concentration camp.

**Kommandostab Reichsführung-SS.** (KRFSS) Command Staff of the Head-quarters of the Reichsführer-SS. An executive administrative staff located at Himmler's personal headquarters. During the war, it acted on a mobile basis under the title Feldkommadostelle Reichsführung-SS and was organized like a military headquarters. In effect, it was the Waffen-SS High Command, in the way the Oberkommandos were the high commands for the other arms of the military.

**Kommissarbefehl.** Commissar order. *See also* Kommissar-Erlaß.

**Kommissar-Erlaß.** Commissar decree. Hitler and Wehrmacht order in 1941 to murder all Soviet officials.

**kommissarische Landräte.** Commissar subprefects. Politically reliable, but professionally incompetent, local Nazi officials sent to German-occupied Poland. *See also* Landrat.

**kommissarische Verwaltung.** Provisional administration by a commissioner. Nazi administration of German-occupied Denmark, The Netherlands, and Norway.

**Kommißbrot.** Commissioned bread. Hardtack; hard black bread of the German navy.

**Kommunist.** Communist. Often synonymous with Jew, degenerate, anti-German, and partisan.

**Kommunistische Partei Deutschlands.** (KPD) Communist Party of Germany. Communist Party during the Weimar Republic.

**Kompanie.** Company in the German army.

**Kondor.** German espionage operation based in Egypt.

**Kondorlegionen.** Condor Legion. German Wehrmacht forces fighting in Spain on behalf of General Francisco Franco during the Spanish Civil War (1936–1939).

**Kongreßhalle.** *See* Reichsparteitagsgelände.

**König des Ghettos.** King of the Ghetto. Mordechai Haim Rumkowski, the Elder of Lodz-Ghetto.

**Königsgraben.** King's ditch. Name for draining channel from the concentration camp Birkenau to the river Weichsel. Infamous work site at Auschwitz-Birkenau.

**Königstiger.** King tiger. Tiger II, a top-notch German tank introduced in 1943.

**KONR.** *See* Komitee zur Befreiung der Völker Rußlands.

**Konstantin.** Code name for the German occupation of the Balkan areas previously occupied by Italian forces, September 1943.

**Konsummargarine.** Margarine for people on special rations.

**Kontingentquote.** Contingent quota. Allotment.

**Kontingentträger.** Claimant. Claimant of quota or allotment.

**(Konto) Max Heiliger.** (The Account of) Max(imilian) (the) Holy. Pseudonym of Heinrich Himmler. The SS Office for Economy and Administration, which oversaw the concentration camp economy, deposited currency and the proceeds of jewelry and gold (including gold teeth) confiscated from the Jews murdered in the camps into the Reichsbank account of Max Heiliger.

**Kontribution.** Contribution. Euphemism for the reparation sum levied on the Jews after the November 1938 Pogrom. Also, compulsory payments to a conquering power by the occupied nation after defeat. *See also* Reichskristallnacht.

**Kontrollabschnitt.** Stub. Coupon for a clothing item on a ration card.

**Konversionskasse.** Conversion bank. Foreign-exchange clearing office. *See also* Verrechnungsabkommen.

**Konzentrationär.** Concentrationaire. A prisoner whose behavior demonstrated concentration camp experience.

**Konzentrationslager.** (KL, KZ) Concentration camp. The SS preferred the unofficial abbreviation KZ instead of KL because it sounded more threatening. Any internment camp for holding enemies of the Third Reich. The construction of concentration camps began almost immediately after Hitler gained power in Germany. There were several kinds: labor camps, prison camps (without regard to accepted norms of arrest and detention), and death camps. Initially (1933–1936), camps were used primarily for political prisoners. Later (1936–1942), camps were expanded and nonpolitical prisoners—Jews, Gypsies, homosexuals, and Poles—were also incarcerated. In the last period of the Nazi regime (1942–1945), prisoners of concentration camps were forced to work in the armament industry as more and more Germans were fighting in the war and production was increased. Living conditions varied considerably from camp to camp and over time. The worst conditions existed after the war broke out, when death, disease, starvation, overcrowding and unsanitary conditions, and torture were all part of daily life at the camps. Notable German camps were Dachau, Sachsenhausen, Buchenwald, Flossenbürg, Ravensbrück, and Mauthausen in Austria.

The concentration camps were organized into five departments: (1) the Administration, consisting of commandant, adjutant, and postal censorship office; (2) Political and Detective Branch, always led by a Gestapo official; (3) Camp Security; (4) Prisoner Property Administration, responsible for turning a profit from the prisoners' possessions, labor, and their bodies; and (5) Camp Doctor, not involved in prisoner health but often in sadistic medical experiments and mass murder.

**Konzentrationslager der Waffen-SS Lublin.** Concentration camp of the armed SS at Lublin. Better know as Majdanek, one of the six death factories.

**Konzentrationszuchthaus.** (KZ) Concentration maximum security prison.

**Konzentrierungspunkte.** Concentration points. Certain areas where Jews were to be sent and confined until the Nazis decided their fate.

**Konzertlager.** Concert camp. Ironic for concentration camp, used only in the 1930s.

**Konzertschar.** Concert group. *See also* Spielschar.

**Kopfjäger.** Headhunters. *See also* Feldgendarmerie.

**Kopplungsverkäufe.** Coupled sales. Illegal method of selling scarce goods to those who also bought large amounts of another, more easily available commodity. Such a businessman could be charged as a Volksschädling.

**Koralle.** Coral. Code name for Admiral Karl Dönitz headquarters near Berlin from December 1943.

**Korherr-Bericht.** Korherr Report. 1943 report written by SS statistician Richard Korherr, giving the first reliable figures concerning the numbers of Jews murdered by the Third Reich.

**körperliche Ertüchtigung.** Physical training. Basic principle of Hitler Youth education.

**Korps.** *See* Armeekorps.

**Korpstruppen.** Corps Troops. Special formation attached to an army corps.

**Korsettstangen.** Corset supports. Army slang for German soldiers sent to support the Italian army in World War II.

**kosmopolitisch.** Cosmopolitan. Un-German, Jewish. *See also* Asphaltmensch.

**Kostentzug.** *See* Nebenstrafen.

**Kovno-Aktion.** Kovno Operation. More than 30,000 Jews of the Kovno-Ghetto in Lithuania were rounded up in this operation and murdered by Germans with the help of Ukrainian, Lithuanian, and Latvian volunteers.

**K.P.** *See* Kittelbachpiraten.

**KPD.** *See* Kommunistische Partei Deutschlands.

**Krad.** Military abbreviation used in combination with other words to describe motorization. *See also* Kradschützen.

**Kradmelder.** Military motorcycle messenger.

**Kradschützen.** Motorized infantry. Infantry on motorcycles with sidecar; part of the tank corps.

**Kraft durch Freude.** *See* Nationalsozialistische Gemeinschaft Kraft durch Freude.

**Krafteier.** Power eggs. Slang for rockets.

**Kraftfahrzeugstaffel.** (K-Staffel) Military motorized unit.

**Kraftlinien.** Lines of power. Geopolitical term for humans as agents of abstract forces. *See also* Geopolitik.

**Krampfadergeschwader.** Varicose-veins squadron. Derogatory for Nazi women's organization. *See also* Nationalsozialistische Frauenschaft.

**Krampfhenne.** Excitable hen. Hitler's term for Alfred Duff-Cooper, British Secretary of State for War (1935–1937), then Lord of the Admiralty from which he resigned in 1938 in protest over the Munich Pact. Later, he served Prime Minister Winston Churchill as Minister of Far Eastern Affairs and then Ambassador to France.

**Krankenauslese.** Selection of the sick. In the concentration camps doctors chose the sick to be murdered.

**Krankenbau.** (KB) Hospital barracks. Auschwitz hospital where many were sent and few returned.

**Krankenbehandler.** Healer of the sick. From 1938, Jewish doctors and dentists who were allowed to practice only on their fellow Jews.

**Krankenhospital.** Invalid hospital. At Neuengamme, where tuberculosis experiments on Jewish children were carried out.

**Krankenlager.** (KrL) Hospital camp. Main hospital at Mauthausen.

**Krankenrevier.** Hospital. Medical facilities of the concentration camps where sick prisoners were often killed by phenol injection if they could not work. Also, location of deadly experiments performed on prisoners.

**Kräuselfaser.** Curly fiber. A fiber that served as a wool substitute.

**Krawatte.** Man's tie. Air force slang for bombsight.

**Kreis.** District. Nazi Party administrative area whose borders were congruent with national administrative districts.

**Kreisauer Kreis.** Kreisau Circle. Group of conservative opponents of Hitler, both military and civilian, Protestant, Catholic, Socialist, led by Count Helmuth von Moltke and named after his Silesian estate. Other members: Horst von Einsiedel, Peter Graf Yorck von Wartenburg, Theodor Haubach, Carl Dietrich von Trotha, Eugen Gerstenmaier, Hans-Bernd von Haeften, Adolf Reichwein, Adam von Trott zu Solz. Despite their courage in opposing Hitler, most were traditional antisemites who wanted the Jews to disappear from Germany but at a slower rate and less violently than the Nazis did. Only a few, like Jesuit father Alfred Delp, were not hostile to Jews. Most circle members were not directly involved in the July 20, 1944, attempt on Hitler's life. *See also* 20. Juli.

**Kreisbauernführer.** District Leader of Farmers. *See also* Landesbauernschaft.

**Kreishauptmann.** District Governor. *See also* Generalgouvernement.

**Kreiskommandantur.** (KK) District Command Office.

**Kreisleiter.** District Leader. Party official superior to an Ortsgruppenleiter but subordinate to a Gauleiter.

**Kreistag.** District Day. Official annual district celebration.

**Krematorium.** Crematory. Camp building that housed ovens to burn the bodies of the murdered; also, the gas chambers–crematoria complex.

**Kreuz.** Cross. *See also* Orden.

**Kreuzelschreiber.** Cross makers. Unofficial for the decision makers of the T-4 Euthanasia Program. On institutional forms they entered a red + for a patient to be killed and a blue − for a deferred case.

**KRFSS.** *See* Kommandostab Reichsführung-SS.

**KrGf, Krgef.** *See* Kriegsgefangener.

**Krieg.** War. To the Nazis, the word implied the positive values of freedom, conquest, and liberation.

**"(Wer im) Krieg irgendwelche Rücksichten nach innen oder außen nimmt, verdient, daß er ihn verliert!"** "In war, whoever fails to be utterly ruthless at home and abroad deserves to lose." Nazi phrase.

**Kriegsabzeichen.** War badges. A unique German phenomenon of World War II, war badges allowed an observer to determine the level of experience of a particular soldier at first glance. Though they were in existence before 1918, the number of German war badges dramatically increased during World War II and by 1945 there were over forty different patterns. These were often subdivided into classes, distinguished by the metal type (gold, silver, and bronze). All branches of the Wehrmacht were awarded war badges, including the Waffen-SS. They were generally composed of a wreath of oak or laurel leaves surrounding a symbol that represented the branch and service, with a German Eagle clutching a swastika surmounting the award.

**Kriegsauflagenprogramm.** War supply program. Wartime program to supply the German population with household goods marked with the letter Z, for zivil, meaning for civilian use. These goods could be obtained with ration cards (*see* Bezugsschein) only at special distribution centers (*see* Leithändler).

**Kriegsausbildungsschein.** (K-Schein) Wartime training certificate. Certificate issued upon completion of a Hitler Youth wartime training program. *See also* Wehrertüchtigungslager.

**Kriegsausgleichsverfahren.** Wartime method of compensation. 1939 regulation arranging compensation to Germans for property damaged during the war and assuring that Jews would not receive such compensation if they suffered such damages.

**Kriegsberichter.** War reporter. War correspondent who was also a member of an army unit. *See also* Propaganda-Kompanie.n

**Kriegsberichterkompanie.** *See* Propaganda-Kompanien.

**Kriegsbesoldung.** War pay. Increase in the pay of German armed forces conscripts to equal that of the professional soldiers.

**Kriegsdiensthilfsmaid.** War-service help-maiden. *See also* Kriegshilfsdienst.

**Kriegseinsatz.** War duty. Work assigned by the state, primarily for the war effort. Especially directed toward the Hitler Youth and the Bund Deutscher Mädel in der Hitlerjugend. *See also* Kriegseinsatzdienst der Hitlerjugend.

**Kriegseinsatzdienst der Hitlerjugend.** War Service of Hitler Youth. Work included transport, news service, and collection of goods to be recycled. During the last weeks of the war, many fought in the antiaircraft artillery and in the home guard and were killed in action. Girls of the BDM served in hospitals, in the Red Cross, and in youth camps, and worked as armed forces secretaries and telephone operators and as helpers in antiaircraft batteries.

**kriegsentpflichtet.** Relieved of war duties. Dismissed.

**Kriegsfischkutter.** Wartime fish cutter. Merchant mariner reassigned to work for the navy.

**(nach) Kriegsgebrauch (behandelt).** (Treated according to) war practices. Euphemism for mistreating, torturing, murdering Jews, political prisoners, and other individuals considered German enemies. *See also* behandeln.

**Kriegsgefangener.** (KrGf, Krgef) Prisoner of war. POW.

**Kriegsgefangenenlager.** (KGL) Prisoner of war camp. German POW camps for Allied prisoners all across Europe. *See also* Stammlager.

**Kriegsgefangenenlager der SS.** Prisoner-of-war-camp of the SS.

**Kriegshetzer.** Warmonger. Nazi expression for foreign statesmen accused of having forced the war on the allegedly peaceful National Socialist state.

**Kriegshilfeeinsatz.** *See* Kriegshilfseinsatz der deutschen Jugend.

**Kriegshilfsdienst.** War-Help Service. From 1941, extension by another six months of the compulsory half-year female work service, spent roughly half in the countryside and half in war work in companies, hospitals, and offices. *See also* Arbeitsmaid.

**Kriegshilfseinsatz der deutschen Jugend.** War-Help Duty of the German Youth. 1943 decree to place German boys born in 1926 and 1927 as Flakhelfer to relieve soldiers at the front.

**Kriegsmarine.** German naval forces.

**Kriegsmarine-Artillerie.** German naval artillery. Coastal artillery.

**Kriegsmoral.** Morale during war. *See also* Heimatfront.

**Kriegsmusterbetrieb.** Model war company. From 1942, award for exemplary German companies bestowed by Robert Ley and Albert Speer.

**Kriegsoffizier.** War officer. *See also* Volksoffizier.

**Kriegsoffiziersbewerber.** (KOB) Applicant for Kriegsoffizier/Volksoffizier.

**Kriegsopfer.** War victims/sacrifice for the war effort. All German citizens had the obligation to do their utmost to establish solidarity with front-line troops by acts of personal sacrifice in deeds and in donations to the war effort. *See also* Opfer.

**Kriegsopferversorgung.** National Socialist distribution of citizens' war-effort contributions. *See also* Nationalsozialistische Kriegsopferversorgung.

**"Kriegsräson geht vor Kriegsmanier."** "The necessity of war supersedes the customs of war." Rationalization for atrocities.

**Kriegs(sach)schädenverordnung.** (KSSchVO) (1940) ordinance dealing with wartime damages.

**Kriegsschauplatz Innerdeutschland.** Theater of war inside Germany. War against internal enemies.

**Kriegsschuldlüge.** Lie about war guilt. Perceived Allied lie about Germany's responsibility for starting World War I; Article 231 of the Versailles Treaty, the War-Guilt Clause. *See also* Versailler Diktat.

**Kriegssonderabteilung.** Wartime special branch. Euphemism for the navy's disciplinary unit, formerly Sonderabteilung der Kriegsmarine.

**Kriegssonderstrafrecht(s)verordnung.** (KSSVO) Special Ordinance dealing with War Crimes (of August 1939). Gave additional power to Nazi special courts. *See also* Sondergerichte; Wehrkraftzersetzung.

**Kriegsstärkenachweisung.** War footing table of organization.

**Kriegstagebuch.** (KTB) Official war diary.

**Kriegsverbrecher.** War criminal. Germans associated with the Versailles Treaty ending German participation in World War I.

**Kriegsverdienstkreuz.** (KVK) War-merit service cross. War decoration, from 1939 on, for military service deemed less meritorious than deserving the Iron Cross.

**kriegsverpflichtet.** Obliged to do service during wartime. Civilian work for the duration of the war; also to swear an oath to give one's best effort for the war.

**kriegsverwendungsfähig.** (k.v.) Ready and able to be sent to the front. Status for a soldier about to serve on active duty.

**kriegswichtig.** War essential. Qualification required for priorities and allocations.

**kriegswichtige Sonderaufgaben.** Special duties important to the war. Murders, mass murders. *See also* Großexekution; Sonderaktion.

**Kriegswirtschaftsstab.** War-economy staff. District agencies for labor, housing, economics, and prices.

**Kriegswirtschaftsverbrechen.** Business crimes during wartime. Wartime criminal offenses like black-marketeering or hoarding. *See also* Wirtschaftsparasit.

**Kriegswirtschaftsverordnung.** (KWVO) War-Economy Ordinance. 1939 measure to increase taxes to enable the Reich to pay for the upcoming war. *See also* Wehrwirtschaft.

**Kriminalbiologisches Instituts.** Biological Criminal Institute. Supported by the Reich Main Security Administration and performing research on Gypsies, among others. *See also* Reichssicherheitshauptamt.

**Kriminalpolizei.** (KRIPO) Criminal Police. Headed by Arthur Nebe, under Heinrich Himmler.

**Kriminalpolizei Sonderkommissariat Ghetto.** Special Criminal-Police Ghetto Commissariat. SS unit in the Lodz-Ghetto whose main role was to confiscate Jewish possessions.

**KRIPO.** *See* Kriminalpolizei.

**Krise.** Crisis. Temporarily unfavorable, but not hopeless, situation. Camouflage for defeats at the Eastern Front.

**Kristallnacht.** *See* Reichskristallnacht.

**Kritik.** Criticism. Criticism of National Socialist or Germany's enemies was regarded as positive; criticism of National Socialism or Germany was regarded as negative. *See also* (negative) Kritik.

**(negative) Kritik.** Negative criticism. Criticism of National Socialism or Germany considered destructive and therefore forbidden.

**Kritikaster.** Carping critic. Grumbling German defeatist.

**KrL.** *See* Krankenlager.

**Kru.** Navy slang for crew.

**krummnasig.** Crooked-nosed. Pejorative adjective used for Jews.

**K-Schein.** *See* Kriegsausbildungsschein.

**KSSchVO.** *See* Kriegssachschädenverordnung.

**KSSVO.** *See* Kriegssonderstrafrechtverordnung.

**K-Staffel.** *See* Kraftfahrzeugstaffel.

**KTB.** *See* Kriegstagebuch.

**Kübelwagen.** Bucket car. Army jeep. A military variation of Porsche's KdF-Wagen. Volkswagen made approximately 52,000 for the German army in the 1930s and during World War II. It was rear-engined and rear-wheel-driven. As such, its off-road performance was no match for the 4-wheel-drive American Jeep. From 1944 to 1945, they were 4-wheel-drive in first gear only. *See also* Volkswagen.

**Kugel.** Bullet. German technique of murdering Jews and others by means of a single shot to the back of the neck.

**Kugelerlaß.** Bullet decree. Gestapo's order for the execution of escaped Allied POWs by a bullet to the back of the neck.

**Kugelhäftling.** (K-Häftling) Bullet inmate. *See also* Kugelerlaß.

**Kühlungsborn.** Refreshing spring. From 1939, archaic name of the Baltic Sea spa Brunshaupten.

**Küken.** Chicks. Girls between the ages of six and ten, members of the Küken-Gruppe. *See also* Deutsche Kinderschar; Nationalsozialistische Frauenschaft.

**Küken-Gruppe.** Chicks group. *See also* Küken.

**Kulmhof.** *See* Chelmno (Kulmhof).

**Kulturabend.** Cultural evening. Party-approved local cultural events held during the Third Reich.

**Kulturbegründer.** Founders of culture. According to Hitler, only people of Aryan origin were capable of worthy cultural creativity and development. *See also* Kulturträger.

**Kulturbereich.** The (German) ethnic and cultural sphere.

**Kulturboden.** Cultural soil. Culture area; soil from which (German) culture springs. The territory between the Baltic and Black Seas that Nazis saw as forming an integral part of Greater Germany.

**Kulturbolschewismus.** Cultural or intellectual bolshevism. Modern art and literature condemned as un-German, too-Jewish, and degenerate. *See also* entartete Kunst.

**Kulturdünger.** Culture fertilizer. A culturally and racially superior people, who mixed with inferior cultures and races, becomes inferior itself. A people fulfilling its cultural mission but who were cheated out of their deserved political benefits.

**Kulturförderung.** Promotion of culture. National Socialist cultural politics.

**Kulturführung.** Cultural Leadership. Control and direction of the spiritual nature of the nation through art, under the direction of the Reichsministeriums für Volksaufklärung und Propaganda and Alfred Rosenberg.

**Kulturgründer.** Culture creators. Nordic/Aryan races that created culture.

**Kulturjuden.** Culture Jews. Jewish authors, artists, and composers and other people who did not fit into National Socialist Weltanschauung.

**Kulturkammer.** *See* Reichskulturkammer.

**Kulturlenkung.** Cultural steering. Government control over German cultural development according to Nazi ideology and racial exclusiveness.

**Kulturschaffen.** To create (German) culture. *See also* Reichskulturkammer.

**Kulturschaffende.** Cultural creators/workers. All German freelance cultural creative-arts professionals (artists, writers, actors) whose cultural output was equated with the productivity of German workers, reflecting the Nazi belief in a classless (and racially homogeneous) society. *See also* Reichskulturkammer.

**Kultursendung.** Culture mission. German mission to impose its culture, bring German civilization, to the rest of the world.

**Kulturträger.** Culture bearer. Nordic/Aryan races that sustained culture.

**Kulturzerstörer.** Culture destroyers. Non-German/Nordic races that destroyed culture, such as the Jews, who would, according to Hitler, themselves be destroyed.

**Kultusgemeinde.** Religious community. Negative for Jewish religious community.

**Kundenkarten.** Customer cards. Cards identifying a German customer as eligible for rationed goods.

**Kundenliste.** Customer list. List of German customers eligible for rationed consumer goods. *See also* Kundenkarten.

**Kundentausch.** Client exchange. *See also* Abnehmertausch.

**Kunstbericht.** Art report. Tactful appreciation of (mainly German) art in contrast to the hostile, allegedly Jewish, criticism that was forbidden by Goebbels in 1936.

**Kunstbetrachter, Kunstbetrachtung.** Art inspection. *See also* Kunstbericht.

**Kunstbolschewismus.** Artistic bolshevism. Degenerate, modern, un-German-Jewish art. Hitler was quoted as saying, "Kunst, die nicht aus unserer Seele kam" ("Art that does not emanate from our [German, Aryan] soul").

*Kunst der Nation.* Art of the Nation. A radical Nazi art periodical from 1935.

**Kunstfront.** Art front. Battle against degenerate art. *See also* entartete Kunst.

*(Die) Kunst im Dritten Reich.* Art in the Third Reich. A monthly published by the Central Publishing House of the Nazi Party, Zentralverlag der NSDAP.

**Kunstschriftleiter.** Art editor. Critic in favor of Nazi ideology.

**Kunstwerk.** Works of art. *See also* Bauten des Führers.

**Kurzbehandlung.** Short treatment. Brutal beatings of concentration camp inmates and foreign laborers, often ending in death.

**kurzfristige Festnahme.** Short-term arrest. Security Police measure taken against members of the church opposition to the Reich.

**k.v.** *See* kriegsverwendungsfähig.

**K44.** Code name for the International Anti-Jewish Congress that opened in Berlin in the fall of 1944.

**KVK.** *See* Kriegsverdienstkreuz.

**KWVO.** *See* Kriegswirtschaftsverordnung.

**Kyffhäuserbund.** *See* NS-Reichskriegerbund Kyffhäuser.

**KZ** (pronounced Ka-tset). Unofficial abbreviation for Konzentrationslager. The official abbreviation, KL, seemed too soft to the SS, who preferred KZ, which stood for Konzentrationszuchthaus (concentration prison). *See also* Konzentrationslager.

**KZ der Gestapo.** Gestapo concentration camps. Camps established as part of the National Socialist police system in collaboration with city administrations and industry. Between 1939 and 1945, 30,000 incarcerated men and women consisting of prisoners of war, political opponents, Jews, and Germans of mixed origin were forced to work in German war industry. *See also* Arbeitserziehungslager; Auffangslager; erweiterte Polizeigefängnisse.

# L

---

**L.** *See* Leichen; Liquidierung.

**LA.** *See* Lagerälteste.

**Lachsfang.** Salmon trap. Code name for planned seizure of the Murmansk railway to cut the Soviet supply line with the Allies.

**Ladenkiebitz.** Store kibitzer. Person who would remain in a store until they found out which goods could be purchased under the counter.

**LA-Führer.** *See* Landwirtschaftsführer.

**Lagebericht.** Situation report. Surveillance report of Gestapo, SD, and others.

**Lageno.** *See* Landeslieferungsgenossenschaft.

**Lagenwert.** Location value. Geopolitical term for the suitability of an area as a combat zone.

**Lager.** Camp. A location favored by the Nazis to educate and indoctrinate the young. Often an abbreviation or suffix for concentration camp. *See also* Konzentrationslager.

**Lager A.** The Gypsy camp at Auschwitz.

**Lager 1.** Camp 1. Part of Bergen-Belsen concentration camp. A typhus epidemic killed 40,000 of its inmates toward the end of the war.

**Lager 2.** Camp 2. Part of Bergen-Belsen concentration camp consisting of several different and separately administered smaller camps. Inmates lived under slightly better conditions and were used for prisoner exchanges.

**Lagerälteste.** (LA) Senior camp prisoners. In charge of the prisoners' internal camp administration under the SS.

**Lagerarzt.** Camp doctor. SS head of medical personnel at a concentration camp.

**Lagerbrauchtum.** Camp customs. Ways of living and acting in concentration camps.

**Lager der Gestapo.** (LdG) Gestapo (concentration) camp.

**Lagerevidenz.** Concentration camp evidence. System of documentation in the camps containing inmate personal information and identification number.

**Lagerführer.** Camp leader. SS concentration camp executive and operations officer.

**Lager für ausländische Juden.** (LAJ) Camp for foreign Jews.

**Lager für kriegsgefangene Offiziere.** *See* Offizierlager.

**Lagergeld.** Camp money. Money printed in a concentration camp or prisoner-of-war camp in order to allow the camp economy to run.

**Lagerkommandant.** (Concentration) camp commander. Chief SS concentration camp officer.

**Lagerleiter.** (Lalei) Camp administrator. Usually for a German children's camp. *See also* Kinderlandverschickungslager.

**Lagermutter.** Camp mother. Surrogate mother for orphaned children at women's camps.

**Lagerordnung.** Camp regulations. Enforced and supervised by block leaders.

**Lagerpolizei.** Prisoner camp police.

**Lagerschutz.** Camp guards. Police units organized in the 1940s by the Nazis to guard the concentration camps in Poland. These units were composed mostly of Ukrainians and Belorussians, with some Poles, and were exceptionally cruel toward the prisoners.

**Lagersprache.** Language of the (concentration) camps. A combination of words from prisoners all across Europe comprising a specially developed camp jargon.

**Lager-SS.** Concentration camp-SS. SS who operated concentration camps. *See also* SS-Totenkopfverbände.

**Lagerstraße.** Camp street. Main street in concentration camps.

**Lagersystem.** The system of (concentration) camps. The economy of the concentration camp organization, including the 2,500 German civilian firms that made use of forced labor from the camps, from Abeking & Rasmussen to Zündholzfabrik Lauenburg. Among the most prominent firms were Allianz, Audi, BASF, Bayer, BMW, Bosch, Daimler-Benz, Degussa-Huels, Dresdner Bank, IG Farben, Hoechst, Krupp, Leica, Siemens, Volkswagen—almost every firm in Germany—and German subsidiaries of American firms such as Ford and International Harvester. They classified prisoners, employed forced labor to terrorize prisoners and profit from their labor, instituted a system of formal and informal punishment, imposed the death penalty for mutiny and attempted escape, and justified arbitrary murder of prisoners. The SS camps were administered in five sections: Lagerführer, or camp director; Kommandantur, or headquarters office; Kommandanturstab, or headquarters staff; the SS-Truppen, or guards; and in some camps, the Gestapo (i.e., politische Abteilung, or political branch). *See also* Wirtschafts- und Verwaltungshauptamt; Zivilarbeitslager.

**Lagerverwaltung.** (Concentration) camp administration.

**LAH.** *See* Leibstandarte-SS Adolf Hitler.

**Lahmer Heinrich.** Crippled Henry. Air force slang for lame duck, a damaged aircraft. *See also* Nähmaschine.

**LAJ.** *See* Lager für ausländische Juden.

**Lakeitel.** (La Keitel, the Keitel.) Nickname of Field Marshal Wilhelm Keitel, Chief of the Armed Forces Department in the Reichs Ministry of War, then Chief of the Supreme Command of the Armed Forces (Chief of OKW), equal in rank to a Reichsminister. Also, allusion to Lakai (flunky); that is, Keitel's subservient relationship to Hitler.

**Lalei.** *See* Lagerleiter.

**Lametta.** Tinsel. German colloquialism for strips of tinfoil called "window" that the Allied planes dropped during air raids to deceive German radar. Also, ironic for military decorations and for the expansive number of medals that Göring planned to institute.

**Landarbeiterbrief.** Land-worker certificate. After successful completion of a training program and a two-year practical-service period, German men were issued a certificate as a farm hand.

**Landbund.** Land Association. German farmers' federation during the Third Reich.

**Landdienst.** Farm service. From 1934, work without pay on farms, especially in the eastern border regions, performed by German university students. Also Hitler Youth program to prevent young Germans from leaving the countryside (*see* Landarbeiterbrief). Accepted as prerequisite for Wehrbauern of the Waffen-SS. *See also* Mädellanddienst.

**Landdiensteinsatz.** Farm service. *See also* Landdienst.

**Länder.** States. German states before, during, and after the Nazi Reich.

**Landes-.** Provincial, regional, or national.

**Landesbauernschaft.** Farmers' Organization. Regional agricultural organization as part of the state agricultural union, called Reichsnährstand.

**Landeseigene (Freiwilligen-) Verbände.** Indigenous volunteer units. German auxiliary-troop units during World War II consisting of recruits from the occupied countries. *See also* freiwillig; Freiwillige Legion Niederlande.

**Landesinspekteur.** Provincial inspector. Nazi Party official.

**Landeslieferungsgenossenschaft.** (Lageno) District pool of subcontracting craftsmen.

**Landespolizeigruppe General Göring.** *See* Landespolizeigruppe Hermann Göring.

**Landespolizeigruppe Hermann Göring.** Regional Police Group Hermann Göring. Police unit under Hermann Göring, active in "Night of the Long Knives," redesignated Regiment General Göring in 1935. *See also* Nacht der langen Messer.

**Landesschützen.** Regional shooters. Volunteer units of former soldiers; also older veterans who were forced, often as a form of punishment, to serve the Wehrmacht.

**Landeswirtschaftsämter.** *See* Bezirkswirtschaftsämter.

**Landgänger.** Country roamers. *See also* Hamsterfahrten.

**Landhelfer(in).** Country help. Boys or girls serving on farms in the country. *See also* Landjahr.

**Landhilfe.** Country help. Girl serving in the country. *See also* Landjahr.

**Landjahr.** Year in the country. From 1934, German youth had to work for eight months on a farm after completion of schooling.

**Landjude.** Jews living in the countryside.

**Landnahme.** Acquisition of territory. Conquering land of eastern nations by means of war to utilize it for Germans.

**Landrat.** Subprefect. Nazi Party official, equivalent to Kreisleiter.

**Landsberg.** Prison fortress where, after his 1923 Munich Putsch, a pampered Hitler served his five-year sentence in nine months and dictated his political-racial autobiography *Mein Kampf.*

**Landsberg am Lech.** One of the subsidiary camps of the Kaufering sub-camp complex attached to the Dachau concentration camp, where nearly 30,000 prisoners—mostly Hungarian, Lithuanian, and Polish Jews—worked as slave laborers to build underground airplane factories and other military hardware. *See also* Dachau.

**Landschaft.** Landscape. Structure, coexistent events. *See also* Geopolitik.

**Landscharen.** Rural Squads. SS units.

**Landser.** Countryman. Ordinary German soldier. Equivalent to the American term, GI. Many Wehrmacht Landser participated in mass murders of civilians in German-occupied Europe.

**Landsturm.** Land Force. Wehrmacht reserves of men older than forty-five. *See also* Volkssturm.

**Landtag.** Provincial assembly.

**Landvolk.** Country people, farmers. Administrative unit of the Reich Agricultural Organization. Also, an agrarian political party. *See also* Reichsnährstand.

**Landwacht.** Country Guards. Former SA members drafted into this rural militia.

**Landwehr.** Land Forces. Military reserves (35–45 years old).

**Landwirt.** Farmer. Not admitted to farm-inheritance status. *See also* Bauer; Erbhof.

**Landwirtschaftsführer.** (LA-Führer) Local German agricultural supervisor in the Reichskommissariat.

**Langemarck.** Flanders village near where the German army took heavy casualties, some of whom were university students at the first Battle of Ypres in the fall of 1914. Also, on April 22, 1915, Langemarck was the scene of the first gas attack of World War I in which the Germans used chlorine gas against the French Colonial Corps (Turcos and Zouaves). The 1914 event took on mythic proportions with the German units supposedly composed only of youthful patriots charging the British and French with unloaded weapons and fixed bayonets while singing "Deutschland über alles." After Hitler claimed in *Mein Kampf* to have heard the singing, it developed into a Nazi propaganda campaign, signifying a love for Germany and readiness to die for it. As a party publicist put it, "National Socialism and Langemarck are one and the same." Also, name of SS Regiment with Flemish volunteers. Also, British-German battle (August 16, 1917) in the second Ypres campaign.

**Langemarckfeiern.** Langemarck celebrations. Celebrations held during the Third Reich on November 10, during which time the Nazi Party inducted students, and Hitler Youth units honored German heros. *See also* Langemarck.

**Langemarck-Pfennig.** Langemarck penny. From 1938, every member of the Hitler Youth had to pay this compulsory fee.

**Langemarck-Studium.** Langemarck scholarship. Grants for Germans without the means to complete the preparatory university program in order to begin university studies.

**Langsamflug.** Flying slowly. *See also* Storch.

**Lastensegler.** Transport glider. Glider plane used to supply the army when on campaign.

**Lastkraftwagen.** Heavy truck. The supposed offer made by Adolf Eichmann to exchange the lives of the Hungarian Jews for 10,000 heavy trucks in 1944. The so-called Joel Brand Plan, now considered an SS ploy.

**Lastverteiler.** Load distributor. Electricity-rationing authority.

**Laternenanzünder.** Lantern lighter. Nickname for Allied Pathfinder planes that dropped flares to locate and mark targets in air raids. Also called Christbäume (Christmas trees).

**Latte.** Slat. Air force slang for propeller.

**Läufer.** Runner. Some prisoners in concentration camps were used as runners to communicate information among the prisoner hierarchy.

**Laus.** Louse. Derogatory for Jew.

**Lauscher.** Listener. Figure of a man, positioned at an angle, in hat and high collar on propaganda poster with the text "The Enemy is Listening." *See also* "Feind hört mit!"

**Läusekontrolle.** Lice check. Concentration camp prisoners were checked for lice.

**Läuse-Promenade.** Lice promenade. The strip of hair left on a prisoner's head after all other hair was removed in order to mark potential escapees.

**Läusestraße.** Lice street. Shaved stripe on concentration camp inmate's head to be used as a means to identify him if he escaped.

**Lautscher Werkstätte.** Lautscher workshop. SS created this shop at Theresienstadt-Ghetto to make toys and other craft projects.

**Lautschwinger.** Sound oscillator. Germanized for membrane; that is, loudspeaker membrane.

**Lazarett.** Infirmary. Concentration camp infirmary. At death camp Treblinka, it was a fenced-off area where prisoners entered through a hut with a Red Cross flag on it. Thence through a plush waiting room to an outdoor pit where a Ukrainian or SS man shot the victim through the back of the head with a pistol. It was designed to murder those prisoners unable to easily walk to the gas chambers, especially the old, the sick, and young children. Also, military hospital.

**LdG.** *See* Lager der Gestapo.

**Lebensborn.** Fountain of life. SS program to improve the German race by means of selective breeding and euthanasia. Himmler formed a Lebensborn association in 1935, which later became an agency of his personal staff, and from 1940 led to systematic kidnapping of tens of thousands of foreign non-Jewish (especially Polish) children with German racial features or one German parent in order to raise them as Germans. *See also* Eignungsprüfer; Euthanasie; Heu-Aktion; Ostkinder; Wiedereindeutschung.

**Lebensfaden.** Life thread. Two-colored wool thread worn on the wrist of German youth during maneuver-like games; the thread of the opposing team had to be taken and counted as a dead person.

**Lebensfeier.** Life celebration. Wedding, birth, and death rituals designed by the Nazi Party.

**Lebensgefühl.** Feeling of life. The irrational, natural, and simple feeling of National Socialist existence, in contrast to complex rational thinking and intellect.

**lebensgesetzlich.** According to the law of life. Nazi synonym for biologisch (biological). *See also* volksbiologisch.

**Lebensmittel.** Food. Provisions the Wehrmacht confiscated from the Ukraine and sent back to Germany, resulting in death from starvation of millions of Ukrainians.

**Lebensmittelkarte.** Food ration cards. Ration cards issued in Germany from August 1939. Food allotments decreased by racial category. Germans were given the largest ration, Gypsies smaller, and Jews the smallest ration possible. Also, ghetto term for food ration cards that were specially stamped and distributed to a select group of Jews whom the Germans allowed to live to work for them. *See* Wochenabschnitte.

**Lebensraum.** Living space. German expansionist demand for more territory and colonies before World War I. An essential element of Hitler's ideology; namely, that living space was needed for Germany because it was overpopulated and lacked the natural resources to maintain its population. This living space was to be gained by a war and genocide in the east.

**Lebensrechtsmittel-Karten.** Right-to-live cards. Ghetto term for a card that was specially stamped and distributed to a select group of people whom the Germans allowed to live, at least temporarily.

**Lebens-Rune.** Life rune. Norse symbol (a capital Y with a vertical line) used by Nazi women's organizations, printed on SS documents and SS gravestones next to date of birth. Also placed on stickpins of SS Lebensborn. *See also* Toten-Rune.

**Lebensscheine.** Life certificates. A very important possession to European Jews because its power was to buy additional time from immediate deportation to the death camps. *See* Lebensrechtsmittle-kurten.

**"Leben und leben lassen."** "Live and let live." German saying, ironically placed in concentration camps.

**lebensunwert.** *See* lebensunwertes Leben.

**lebensunwertes Leben.** Life unworthy of life. *Die Freigabe der Vernichtung lebensunwerten Lebens* (The Permission to Destroy Life Unworthy of Life) by Karl Binding and Alfred Hoche was published in 1920. This work advocated the murder of the mentally and physically handicapped. Bills were introduced in the 1920s and 1930s into the Weimar parliament for the prevention of the birth of those with mental and physical handicaps (unwertes Leben und lebensunwerte Menschen). In 1940, Hitler ordered the systematic murder of those with fatal and hereditary diseases, the mentally ill, and the disabled. Euthanasia centers were established in order to rid the country of these so-called undesirable people. All Jews fell into this category and were to be euthanized. *See also* Euthanasie.

**Lebenswendefeier.** Celebration at a turning point in one's life. Public school graduation ceremony organized by the Nazi Party.

**(das) Leerwohnen.** Living (until) empty. Beginning in 1942 with the deportation of German Jews, their houses and apartments were gradually emptied and then sold or rented to Germans.

**Legalitäts-Eid.** Legality Oath. Hitler's promise after the failure of his 1923 putsch to reject force and use only legal means to win political power in Germany.

**Legion.** Legion. Military formation composed of foreigners serving in the German armed forces.

**Legion Condor.** Condor Legion. German auxiliary troop unit fighting for General Francisco Franco during the Spanish Civil War from 1936 to 1939. Consisted of German "volunteers" particularly from the air force and tank units.

**Lehrerbund.** *See* NS-Lehrerbund.

**Lehrwerkstätten.** Training workshops. Trained German labor to serve the economy of the Third Reich.

**Leibeserziehung.** Physical education. Physical training supervised by the state according to a well-developed plan and regarded as of equal importance with school education.

**Leibregiment des deutschen Volkes.** Bodyguard regiment of the German people. Additional name for the infantry regiment that was specially trained for urban war. *See* Infanterieregiment Großdeutschland.

**Leibstandarte Adolf Hitler.** (LSSAH) *See* Leibstandarte-SS Adolf Hitler.

**Leibstandarte-SS Adolf Hitler.** (LAH) SS Bodyguard Regiment Adolf Hitler. Used in the "Night of the Long Knives" against the SA, the unit later served as a Waffen-SS division. *See also* Nacht der langen Messer.

**Leibwache.** Bodyguard. Hitler's orginal bodyguard unit. *See also* Leibstandarte-SS Adolf Hitler; SS-Verfügungstruppen; Stabwache; Stoßtrupp Adolf Hitler.

**Leichen.** (L) Corpses. An "L" was marked on the jackets or tattooed on the arms of those prisoners unfit for work and to be killed or deported and killed (*see* Muselmann). Also, prisoners of Sonderkommando 1005 (*see* Kommando 1005).

**Leichenhalle.** Mortuary. Also a hall adjacent to the Auschwitz crematorium where the Nazis experimented with killing by using Zyklon.

**Leichenjuden.** Corpse Jews. *See also* Arbeitsjuden.

**Leichenkeller.** Corpse cellar. One of the many terms used by the Nazis when referring to the gas chambers and crematoria at Auschwitz-Birkenau.

**Leichenkommando.** Corpse unit. Detachment of prisoners forced to remove the corpses from the gas chambers to the crematoria and to collect the bodies of those who had died in the camp overnight.

**Leichenträger.** Corpse bearer. *See also* Sonderkommando.

**Leichenverbrennungsofen.** Crematory oven.

**leicht-.** Light. Used as military prefix.

**Leichtbauweise.** Light construction method. Building with a minimum of steel.

**leichtes Maschinengewehr.** (LMG) Light machine gun.

**Leichtgeschütz.** Light gun. Recoilless gun.

**Leipziger Abkommen.** Leipzig Agreement. Concluded in 1935 between the Minister of Economy and the German Labor Front. *See also* Deutsche Arbeitsfront.

**leisten.** To achieve, perform. To accomplish efficiently, to succeed well; Nazi ideal.

**Leistung.** Achievement, performance. One of the tenets of National Socialism was that individuals were judged by their output-production-performance, not by class. Measures taken to increase production in terms of the Nazi Four-Year Plan for the sake of the German people.

**Leistungsabzeichen.** Achievement (sports) badge. Awards also given to exemplary achievements in work-training programs.

**Leistungsaustausch.** Exchange of services. Barter.

**Leistungsbuch.** Achievement book. Work record that female university students had to obtain during a six-week work period in a large German household.

**Leistungseinsatz.** Achievement service. Required work from every German for the war effort.

**Leistungsertüchtigung.** Output enhancement. Anything that helped enhance the productivity of each German individual.

**Leistungsertüchtigungswerk.** Practical demonstrations to increase the productivity of each worker in the armaments industry. Also, the integration of war veterans back into the civilian workforce. *See also* Leistungsertüchtigung.

**Leistungsgemeinschaft.** Achievement society. German society oriented to achieve productivity for the common good of the German people.

**Leistungsgenossenschaft.** Achievement cooperative. Contract cooperative.

**Leistungsgrundsatz.** Achievement principle. *See* Leistungsprinzip.

**Leistungskampf.** Achievement competition. From 1936, an annual event for German companies competing to create the best work environment.

**Leistungslohn.** Performance wages. Incentive wages applied in most German war industries.

**Leistungsmensch.** Achieving man. The Nordic man.

**leistungsmenschliche Haltung.** Attitude of the achieving man. Nordic attitude towards achievement.

**Leistungspolen.** Achieving Poles. Those Poles working well for Germany were to be spared from death.

**Leistungsprinzip.** The principle of achievement. *See also* Leistung; Leistungsgrundsatz.

**Leistungsprüfung.** Achievement examination. First used to determine which farm animals were most useful for breeding. National Socialists applied it to humans in order to find the best Germanic types for procreation; also used in sporting competitions.

**Leistungsschau.** Performance show. Sports rally.

**Leistungstyp.** Achievement type. *See also Rasse und Seele.*

**Leistungswettbewerb.** Achievement competition. Annual Nazi event with speeches and ceremonies. *See also* Leistungsgemeinschaft.

**Leiter.** Leaders. Responsible leaders within the NSDAP hierarchy; political leaders. *See* politischer Leiter.

**Leiter der Organisation Todt.** Leader of the Todt Organization. *See also* Organisation Todt.

**Leiter des Amtes für Agrarpolitik.** Leader of the Department of Agricultural Policy. Nazi Party role of Richard Walther Darré, until 1942.

**Leiter des Parteikanzlei mit den Befugnissen eines Reichsministers.** Leader of the Nazi Party Chancellery with the authority of a Reichminister. One of Martin Bormann's titles.

**Leiter des Reichsberufswettkampfes.** Reich Athletic Profession Leader. Official of the German Student Alliance. *See also* Nationalsozialistischer Deutscher Studentenbund.

**Leitgedanken zur Schulordnung.** Guiding ideas for school regulations. Regulation of December 1934 ordering all German schoolteachers and students to stand at the beginning and conclusion of every hour and offer each other the Hitler salute. *See also* Deutscher Gruß.

**Leithändler.** Dealer, merchant, with special privileges. Regional businessman with special distribution rights. *See also* Kriegsauflagenprogramm.

**Leitsätze.** Guiding mottoes. Directives that the girls of the National Girls' League had to say in unison during their induction ceremony, for example, "Wahre deine Ehre!" ("Keep your honor!"). *See also* Jungmädelbund.

**Leitstelle.** Routing station. Army post office; also, traffic and freight-hauling control office.

**(die) Leitung.** Leadership. Leading position at any level of political and social life. Also, Jewish committee appointed by the SS to administer Theresienstadt-Ghetto. *See* Judenrat.

**Leitwerk.** Steering gear. Airplane rudders, controls.

**Lemberg.** Lwów. City in Poland.

**Lenkstelle.** Planning, control office.

**Lenkung.** Planning, control. State planning and control of German life, economics, culture, media, and so forth. *See also* Arbeitslenkung.

**Lenkungsbereiche.** Planning/control sectors (of the German economy). For utilization of equipment and manpower.

**Lenzing.** Month of March.

**"(Die) Letzten ziehen ab."** "The last ones (Jews) are moving out." Nazi slogan celebrating the emigration of Jews.

**Letztverbraucher.** Consumer at the end of the chain. The individual consumer who received food and other important commodities by means of stamps or ration cards.

**L.G.L.** *See* Lilienthal-Gesellschaft für Luftfahrtforschung.

**Liberalismus.** Liberalism. According to Nazi thinking, undesirable attitude held by Jews and other people that contributed to imperialism, World War I, and the fragmentation of parties in the Weimar Republic.

**Lichtbild.** Light picture. Germanized for photograph.

**Lichtdom.** Light cathedral. Theatrical lighting effects during Nazi Party mass rallies.

**Lichtenstein.** German airborne radar used for Luftwaffe nightfighting.

**Lidice.** Czech town near the site of the assassination of Reinhold Heydrich. The town was completely destroyed, all the men murdered, the women taken to concentration camps, and the children absorbed into Nazi homes and reeducated.

**"(In) Liebe und Treue zum Führer, allzeit ihre Pflicht zu tun."** "To always do one's duty in love and loyalty to the Führer." Slogan of League of German Girls.

**"(Das) Lied der Deutschen."** *See* "Deutschlandlied."

**"(Das) Lied der Getreuen."** "(The) Song of the Faithful." Collection of poetry edited by Baldur von Schirach, entitled *Verse ungenannter österreicher Hitlerjugend aus den Jahren der Verfolgung 1933 bis 1937* (Verses of Anonymous Austrian Hitler Youth During the Years of Persecution, 1933–1937).

**Lila.** Purple, violet. Code name for proposed German seizure of Toulon and the French fleet in 1942.

**Lilienthal-Gesellschaft für Luftfahrtforschung.** (L.G.L.) Lilienthal Society for Aviation Research. Aviation research company established in 1936.

**Lille.** *See* Meuten.

**Linienführung.** Flow of lines. Bureaucratic for Autobahnen. *See also* Reichsautobahnen.

**Links.** Left. *See also* Recht.

**links absondern.** Send to the left. Selection of who was to live, who to die among concentration camp prisoners. Usually, to be sent to the left meant to live for the time being in the camp; to be sent to the right meant fast death in the gas chambers.

**Linz.** Hitler and his family lived in and around Linz, Austria, until the end of his teens.

**Liquidationsanstalt.** Destruction center. Under the control of T-4, a number of institutions were created or designated for killing adult patients during the Euthanasia Program. In general, German children were killed in other institutions although there was some overlap. *See also* Aktion T-4; Reichsausschuß zur wissenschaftlichen Erfassung von erb- und anlagebedingten schweren Leiden.

**Liquidationskommando.** Liquidation unit. Special unit in death camps. *See also* Sonderkommando.

**liquidieren.** To liquidate, to settle, to dissolve. To shoot, to do away with, to murder Jews, political opponents, and partisans.

**Liquidierung.** (L) Liquidation. Mass murder.

**Liquidierungsbefehl.** Liquidation order. Murder decree.

**listig.** Cunning, sly, crafty. Adjective often applied to Jews.

**Literaturbolschewismus.** Literary bolshevism. Negative for literary direction of the Weimar Republic, aimed mainly at German writers considered Jewish.

**Litzmannstadt.** Litzmann's city. *See also* Lodz; Löwenstadt.

***Litzmannstädter Zeitung.*** Litzmannstadt Times. Official newspaper of Germans in Lodz.

**LKPA.** Landeskriminalpolizeiamt. Provincial Criminal Investigation Department.

**LMG.** *See* leichtes Maschinengewehr.

**Ln.** *See* Luftnachrichten.

**Lochkarten.** Punch cards. Cards used in their billions, supplied to the Nazis by the American corporation IBM during the period of the Holocaust and World War II. Each Jew and other concentration camp prisoner was recorded in a punch card, then processed by IBM's DEHOMAG D-11 sorting machine. Each prisoner was identified by holes punched in his or her card: by category of imprisonment (Jew, Gypsy, homosexual, antisocial), by nationality, date of birth, marital status, number of children, reason for incarceration, physical characteristics, and work skills. Columns 3 and 4, hole 8 indicated Jew. Reason for departure column, hole 4 indicated murdered, hole 6, to be murdered. Names were not used, just identification numbers. *See also* Deutsche Maschinen-Gesellschaft; DEHOMAG D-11; Sonderbehandlung.

**Lodz.** A western Polish city that was home to the first major ghetto in April 1940. 144,000 people lived in 1.6 square miles in September 1941. After growing in size with immigrants from conquered lands, many were sent to Chelmno, and in 1944 the ghetto was liquidated and the remaining Jews sent to Auschwitz. Germans referred to Lodz as Litzmannstadt or Löwenstadt.

**Lohnamnestie.** Wage amnesty. Legalization of wage increases in 1942.

**Lohnstopordnung.** Wage-freeze order.

**Losantin.** Anti-gas tablet. To be used against gas attacks during the war.

**"Los, los! Vorwärts!"** "Hurry up, move on." Directives often used in camps demanding faster movement or work, including during the mass-murder process.

**(der) Löwe.** Nickname of Admiral Karl Dönitz, Germany's submarine leader. Also, nickname of World War I German General Karl Litzmann. *See also* Löwenstadt.

**Löwenstadt.** Lion city. From 1939 to 1945, German name of the Polish city of Lodz. Named after German General Karl Litzmann, who had been killed attempting to take Lodz during World War I. During World War II, General Karl Sigismund Litzmann was German Governor-General for Estonia, part of the Ostland province of the Reich.

**LS.** *See* Luftschutz.

**LSSAH.** *See* Leibstandarte Adolf Hitler.

**LS-Spähdienst.** *See* Luftwarn-und Spähdienst.

**Lublin-Majdanek.** Nazi camp and killing center opened for men and women less than three miles from Lublin in eastern Poland in late 1941. At first a labor camp for Poles and a POW camp for Soviets, it was later classified as a death camp and intended to be the most important camp in the general government. A major killing center, Lublin-Majdanek was also the scene of freezing experiments on inmates conducted by Sigmund Rascher. *See also* Generalgouvernement.

**Lublin Reservat.** Lublinland. Lublin Reservation. The aborted Nazi plan to concentrate all European Jews in one locale.

**Lücke.** Gap. Bottleneck in food and military supplies during World War II.

**Luftalarm.** Air alarm. Air-raid warning. Three stages: early alarm (Voralarm of three long blasts of the sirens indicating people should head for the air-raid shelters, starting with familes with small children and the elderly); full alarm (Vollalarm of high tones alternating with low tones indicating enemy bombers less than 100 km away); and the all-clear (Entwarnung, consisting of a long drawn-out tone).

**Luftaufklärung.** Air reconnaisance. Military intelligence gathered by airplanes.

**Luftbarbaren.** *See* Lufthunnen.

**Lüfter.** Ventilator. Germanized for fan.

**Luftflotte.** Air fleet. Largest subunit of the German air force.

**Luftgangster.** Air gangster. *See* Lufthunnen.

**Luftgaukommandos.** District Air Headquarters. Administrative offices of the German air force during the Third Reich.

**Luftgefahr.** Air danger. *See also* Luftalarm.

**Luftgeltung.** Air power.

**Lufthansa.** German civilian air transportation company that camouflaged the creation of the German air force during the Third Reich.

**Luftherrschaft.** Mastery of the air. Control of the air space above a country by German or enemy planes.

**Lufthunnen.** Air barbarians. Derogatory for Allied bomber crews, coined by Joseph Goebbels in 1944 after the massive air raids.

**Luftkutscher.** Air coachman. Slang for pilots of army transport planes.

**Luftlage.** Air situation. Status of enemy planes over Germany.

**Luftlandetruppen.** Combat units that were parachuted into enemy territory or landed by plane.

**Luftmarschall.** Air marshal. Reichsmarschall Hermann Göring, Commander in Chief of Germany's Air Force. *See* Luftwaffe.

**Luftmeldungen.** Air messages. Radio broadcast via telephone cable warning Germans against air raids.

**Luftnachrichten.** (Ln) News, intelligence, or communication about the air war.

**Luftnachrichtenhelferin.** Women's Air Force Auxiliary. *See also* Luftwaffenhelferin.

**Luftpiraten.** *See* Lufthunnen.

**Luftschutzdienstpflicht.** Air-raid duty.

**Luftschutzgemeinschaft.** Air-Raid Protection Group. Smallest unit of civilian self-defense, consisting of the inhabitants of a building. *See also* Hausgemeinschaft.

**Luftschutzgerät.** Air-raid protection tools. Government-prescribed items, such as water buckets, axes, shovels, hand-held fire extinguishers, and so forth to fight fires and to save people buried under the rubble.

**Luftschutzgesetz.** Air-Raid Protection Law. This 1935 law obliged all Germans to train for, and perform, civil duties such as building air-raid shelters, following blackout guidelines during air raids, removing rubble, and related tasks.

**Luftschutzkeller.** Air-raid protection cellar. Reinforced room in the basements of all buildings to provide shelter during air raids. Jews were excluded from such protection by law. *See* Luftschutzraum.

**Luftschutzraum.** Air-raid protection room. *See also* Luftschutzkeller.

**Luftschutzraumgepäck.** Air-raid protection bag. An individual's small suitcase with prepared essentials to be taken to the shelter during air raids.

**Luftschutzsünder.** Air-raid protection sinner. Noncooperating individual. *See also* Destruktiver Außenseiter.

**Luftschutzwart.** Air-raid protection warden. Trained leader of the air-raid protection group who supervised preparatory work, evacuation, and rescue efforts.

**Luftterror.** Air terror. *See also* Terror.

**Luftverteidigungszone.** Air-defense zone. Security area with antiaircraft artillery, floodlights, airports for fighter planes, and so on to intercept enemy planes.

**Luftwache.** Air watch. During the war, night watchmen in residential and business buildings that stood empty at night.

**Luftwaffe.** (Luwa) German air force under Hermann Göring.

**Luftwaffenfelddivision.** Air Force Field Division. Infantry unit under direct command of Göring, practically his own private army.

**Luftwaffenhelfer.** Air force helper. *See also* Flakhelfer.

**Luftwaffenhelferin.** Female air force helper. Women's Air Force Auxiliary. Acted as aircraft observers, manned searchlights, and served in antiaircraft posts.

**Luftwaffenkommando Österreich.** Air Force Command Austria. Located in Vienna.

**Luftwarn- und Spähdienst.** Air-raid warning and reconnaissance service.

**Luftzellwolle.** Artificial wool.

**Lügenabwehr im In- und Ausland.** Defense against lies inside and outside the country. Official name of Department VII of the Ministry of Public Enlightenment and Propaganda. *See also* Propaganda.

***Lügen und Geld, die Waffen des Judentums.*** Lies and Money are the Jews' Weapons. The title of an elementary school curriculum fostering antisemitism among German children.

**"Lug und Trug."** "Lies and perfidy." Hitler's phrase used against the Jews.

**Luitpoldarena.** *See* Reichsparteitagsgelände.

**Luitpoldhain.** *See* Reichsparteitagsgelände.

**Luther-Deutsche.** Luther Germans. *See also* Deutsche Christen.

**Luwa.** *See* Luftwaffe.

**luziferisch.** Lucifer-like. Characteristic of all Jews. An age-old antisemitic term exploited by the Nazis.

# M

**Machtergreifung.** Seizure of power. The legal assumption of power by Hitler and the Nazis on January 30, 1933, when he was appointed chancellor. Other early steps were the laws that destroyed the civil liberties of the Weimar Republic and gave arbitrary powers to Hitler. *See also* Ermächtigungsgesetz; Machtübernahme; Reichstagsbrandverordnung.

**Machtübernahme.** Taking power. Hitler's appointment as Reichskanzler of the Weimar Republic on January 30, 1933. This takeover led to years of profound changes in German government, society, economy, legal system, communications, education, and the military, resulting in a totalitarian dictatorship: The Third Reich mandated one leader, or Führer; one recognized political party, the Nazi Party; Reich government and Nazi Party monopolies by means of law and propaganda, coercion and persuasion, on all forms of communication—including education and the media—on terror and violence, including concentration camps and the military; on the economy—especially dominating labor but essentially maintaining a capitalist system for management and ownership. *See also* Ermächtigungsgesetz; Gleichschaltung; Machtergreifung.

**Madagaskar-Plan.** *See* Fall Madagaskar.

**Mädel.** Girl. The ideal German girl; replaced Mädchen. Also, youngest members of the Bund Deutscher Mädel in der Hitlerjugend.

**Mädelführerin.** Girls' leader. Female leader of the ten- to twenty-one-year-old girls in the BDM; responsible for administration, training of the leaders, preparation for cultural and celebratory events, outings, gatherings, and public collections.

**Mädelgruppe.** Girls' Group. Unit within the BDM consisting of four Mädelscharen; that is, about 160 girls and one group leader.

**Mädel im Landjahr.** Girls in Their Service Year. Nazi film about women as militarized workers.

**Mädellanddienst.** Girls' service in the countryside. One-year work program in the Hitler Youth for fourteen- to twenty-five-year-old women on a farm, to alleviate the shortage of farm help and to familiarize city girls with country living. *See also* Landdienst.

**Mädelring.** Girls' Circle. Unit within the BDM consisting of three to five Mädelgruppen (i.e., between 600 and 800 girls).

**Mädelschaft.** Girls' Group. Smallest unit within the BDM consisting of approximately ten fourteen- to seventeen-year-old girls and one leader. *See also* Mädelschar.

**Mädelschar.** Girls' Group. Unit within the BDM consisting of approximately four Mädelschaften (i.e., forty girls and one leader).

**Mädeltanzkleid.** Girls' dance dress. Together with the girls' national ceremonial dress, part of the uniform of the BDM-Werk Glaube und Schönheit. *See also* BDM-Werk Glaube und Schönheit.

**Mädeluntergau.** *See* Bann.

**Magenbeton.** Stomach cement. Colloquialism for artificial honey.

**Magen David.** *See* Mogen David.

**Magermilch.** Skim milk. Obtainable without ration cards in the beginning of the war-rationing period.

**Maid, Maiden.** Girl, maid. *See also* Arbeitsmaid.

**Maifeier.** May celebration. May Day holiday, on May 1. *See* Feiertag der nationalen Arbeit.

**Maikäfer.** May bug, May beetle. Nickname for those Germans who rushed to join the Nazi Party in the spring of 1933 shortly after it came to power, like mayflies who at night move toward the light but who live only one day.

**Maiveilchen.** May violets. *See also* Maikäfer.

**M-Aktion.** *See* Aktion Möbel.

**Malariastation.** Malaria area. Location at Dachau where experiments with malaria were committed on Jewish prisoners.

**Mal- und Zeichen-Werkstätte.** Graphics and art workshops. Kovno-Ghetto studios creating signs and proclamations for Germans.

**Mangelware.** Scarce goods. Non-rationed goods that were scarce or unavailable during the war.

**Männerlager.** Men's camp. Concentration camp for men.

**Männer(konzentrations)lager.** (MK) Concentration camp for men.

**"Männer machen Geschichte, wir machen die Männer!"** "Men make history, we make men." Slogan of NPEA. *See also* Nationalpolitische Erziehungsanstalten.

**Mannschutzbunker.** Man's protection bunker. Dugout.

**Marcks-Plan.** (General Erich) Marcks' plan. Subset of Operation Barbarossa that made Moscow the key initial objective.

**Margarethe I.** 1944 German plan to occupy Hungary if that nation defected from its alliance with Germany.

**Margarethe II.** 1944 German plan to occupy Romania if that nation defected from its alliance with Germany.

**Margival.** Location of temporary Führer headquarters north of Soissons, France, in 1944.

**"(die) Marine fährt auf Räder."** "The navy rolls on wheels." Sarcastic for the inactivity and lack of success of German warships with the exception of submarines during World War II. Allusion to German Admiral Erich Raeder, the Chief of the German Navy until 1943.

**Marinehelferin.** Marine helper. *See also* Nachrichtenhelferin.

**Marine Hitlerjugend.** (MHJ) Naval Hitler Youth. Special formation that came to be associated with the German navy.

**Marine-Küstenpolizei.** Naval Coastal Police.

**Marinelager.** (Marlag) Prisoner-of-war camp for Allied naval personnel.

**Marine SA.** Naval Sturmabteilung. Naval force organization.

**Marita.** *See* Unternehmen Marita.

**Marken.** Stamps. Popular term for ration-card stubs.

**Marktaufsichtsverordnung.** Market-Control Decree. Cartel law of 1942.

**Marktbereinigung.** Market standardization. Purge of high-cost producers.

**Markteinzugsgebiet.** Market-feeder district. District assigned to a town as supplier of local foodstuffs.

**Marktordung.** Market control. *See also* Marktverband Reichsvereinigung.

**Marktverband Reichsvereinigung.** Market Cartel of Reich Union. Compulsory cartel fixing prices and quotas; marketing board of producers, processors, and distributors of goods. *See also* Reichsnährstand.

**Marlag.** *See* Marinelager.

**Mars.** In August 1943 Himmler ordered the gathering of dozens of soothsayers, fortune-tellers, and astrologers from prison and concentration camps to divine the whereabouts of Mussolini.

**Marsch auf die Feldherrnhalle.** March on the Feldherrnhalle. *See also* Marsch zur Feldherrnhalle.

**marschieren.** To march. In Nazi Party and Wehrmacht, to march on. To move in step with the future, to act in harmony with Nazi ideology, to shape the future.

**Marschketten.** Expeditionary force. Ukrainian militia collaborating with Germans in Generalgouvernement to round up, rob, murder Jews.

**Marsch zur Feldherrnhalle.** March to the Feldherrnhalle. Hitler's proposed 1923 Nazi march from the military memorial in Munich to the military memorial in Berlin. *See also* Bürgerbräukeller.

**Märzfeld.** *See* Reichsparteitagsgelände.

**Märzgefallene.** Those who joined in March. Germans who opportunistically joined the Nazi Party in March 1933.

**Märzveilchen.** Sweet violets. *See* Märzgefallene.

**(das) Maschinelle Berichtswesen.** (MB) The Mechanized Information Office. Central government agency established in 1937 to collect statistical information on the availability of raw material and all materials and machinery necessary for war.

**(das) Maschinelle Zentralinstitut für optimale Menschenerfassung und Auswertung.** The Mechanized Central Institute for Optimal People's Registration and Utilization. Attempt at an automated system to facilitate persecution and destruction of Jews and others.

**Maschinen-Fabrik Augsburg-Nürnberg.** (MAN) Machine Factory Augsburg-Nuremberg. Diesel works at Augsburg in Bavaria that produced a large proportion of the engines for U-boats. A large Social Democratic resistance formed there led by Bebo Wager. They planned organized resistance but were arrested by the Gestapo in 1942.

**Maschinengrundsätze.** Mechanism principles. Order forbidding the financing of industrial investments with government subsidies.

**Maschinenkanone.** (MK) Machine gun.

**Massen-.** Mass. Prefix to words describing the Nazi assault on, and murder of, Jews and other people (1939–1945); for example, Massenausrottung, Massenliquidierung, Massenmörder, Massentötungen, Massenvergasung, Massenvernichtung.

**Massenfeuer.** Massive fire. Concentrated fire.

**Massengemüse.** Mass vegetables. Staple vegetables.

**Material.** Material. People as material to be used or processed. *See also* Menschenmaterial.

**Material für die Judenumsiedlung.** Material for the resettlement of Jews. Euphemism for the poison gas Zyklon.

**mauscheln.** To speak German with a Jewish accent, gestures, and syntax. Although exploited by the Nazis, concept predated Third Reich by centuries.

**Mauthausen.** A concentration camp for men opened in August 1938 near Linz, Austria. It was established to exploit nearby stone quarries and was classified by the SS as a camp of utmost severity. Prisoners included Italian, French, Yugoslavian, and Spanish political prisoners; Jews from Czechoslovakia and the Netherlands (1941); Gypsies from Austria (1938–1940); nearly 30,000 Polish prisoners; and thousands of Soviet prisoners of war. The total number of prisoners who passed through Mauthausen was about 200,000, of whom 119,000 perished, including 38,000 Jews.

**Max.** Slang for 2,500 kg bomb. (About three tons.)

**Max Heiliger.** *See* Konto Max Heiliger.

**MB.** *See* (das) Maschinelle Berichtswesen.

**Mbfh.** *See* Militärbefehlshaber.

**m.d.F.b.** *See* mit der Führung beauftragt.

**M.d.R.** *See* Mitglied des Reichstag.

**Mebu.** *See* MG-Eisenbetonunterstand.

**Meckerer und Miesmacher.** Grumblers and defeatists. Terms used to attack critics of the war effort.

**Medaille zur Erinnerung an den 13. März 1938.** Medal to commemorate the 13th of March 1938. Decoration to honor those who distinguished themselves during the annexation of Austria. *See also* Anschluß.

**Mediterran.** Mediterranean. Racial type. *See also* westisch.

**medizinische Experimente.** Medical experiments. Nazi Germany sponsored more than seventy medical research projects on humans involving thousands of concentration camp inmates.

**Mefo-Wechsel.** Mefo check. Drafts drawn by war industries against the fictitious company Metallurgische Forschungsgesellschft GmbH and guaranteed by the Deutsche Reichsbank. Financial scheme of Hjalmar Schacht to divert billions of marks to underwrite the production of arms.

**Mehrarbeitsvergütung.** Remuneration for extra work. Air-raid duty bonus for foreign workers. *See also* Gastarbeiter.

**"Mehr sein als scheinen!"** "Be more than you appear to be." Motto of Nationalpolitische Erziehungsanstalten.

**Meier.** Nickname for Air Force Chief Hermann Göring, who boasted that if a single enemy plane ever penetrated German airspace, people could call him Meier.

**"Meine Ehre heißt (meine) Treue!"** "My honor is (my) loyalty." Waffen-SS motto.

*Mein Kampf.* My Struggle. Title of Adolf Hitler's autobiography. Written in Landsberg prison in 1924 after the Hitler Putsch. Hitler's political-ideological autobiography. During the Third Reich, millions of copies were sold or given away, often as a wedding gift, though no one knows how many Germans actually read the book.

*Mein politisches Erwachen.* My Political Awakening. Book by Anton Drexler, a nationalist, antisemite, and founder of the German Workers' Party. After reading the book, Hitler claimed he saw that Germany needed a nationalist solution to its problems. *See also* Deutsche Arbeiterpartei.

**Meintat.** Archaic for crime.

**Meister des weiblichen Schamhaares.** Master of the female pubic hair. Nickname for the president of the Reich Chamber of the Arts and Hitler's favorite painter, Adolf Ziegler, because of his detailed paintings of female nudes.

**Meldebezirk.** Registration area. District for army registration.

**Meldebogen.** Registration forms. 1939 forms sent to asylums and clinics concerning every patient hospitalized for five years or longer. Thereafter, the forms sent to referees who decided which patients would be murdered. *See also* Aktion T-4; Euthanasie.

**melden.** To register. In eastern Europe during the war, all Jews were ordered to register with the Gestapo or be shot.

**Meldequadrat.** Reporting square. Place for army registration.

**Meldung.** Notice. Official form that contained personal information on concentration camp inmates, their alleged infractions, and their punishment.

**Melmer.** Temporary Reichsbank account named after SS officer Bruno Melmer who delivered gold and currency stolen from concentration camp victims to the Reichsbank for the SS. *See also* Konto Max Heiliger.

**Memeldeutscher Ordnungsdienst.** (MOD) Order Service in the Memel area. *See also* jüdischer Ordnungsdienst.

**Memelland-Medaille.** Memel medal. Decoration to honor those who distinguished themselves during the annexation of Memel on March 22, 1939.

**Mensch.** Human being. In some concentration camps, the SS called their guard dog Mensch (human being) and let it loose to attack the prisoners, especially the Jewish prisoners, considered animals.

**Menscheneinsatz.** Human deployment. *See also* Reichskommissar für die Festigung des deutschen Volkstums.

**Menschenführung.** People management. Political-psychological guidance, control of public opinion.

**Menschenklau.** People theft. Ironic analogy with Heldenklau (hero theft) for the recruitment of experts from companies to work for the armaments industry.

**Menschenmaterial.** Human material. The function of a human being to follow the directives of the Führer and the Nazi Party, not personal goals. Nazis would say: "Wir sind alle Stahl und Eisen. Wir sind alle prima Material" ("We are steel and iron. All of us are first-rate material").

**Menschenökonomie.** Human economics. Nazi concept that no one sector of business should be favored over another. It led to the closing down of small and inefficient businesses in favor of larger and more efficient concerns. *See also* Handwerksbetriebe.

**Menschentum.** Humanity. German race.

**Mensch(en)tümelei.** Humanism. Derogatory for old, pre-Nazi humanism. *See also* Menschentum.

**menschliche Architektur.** Human architecture. At Nuremberg rallies, the celebrants were organized and shaped into regularized block formations. *See also* Bauten des Führers; Reichsparteitagsgelände.

**Menschlichkeit.** Humanity. *See* Menschentum.

**Mensur.** Duel. Student dueling forbidden by the Weimar Republic but reinstituted by the Third Reich.

**Merkers.** German village. Location of Kaiseroda potassium mine. A huge cache of gold and currency from the Reichsbank and other loot stolen from Nazi victims was stored here and nearby. In April 1945, the Allies discovered thousands of containers of gold and silver items ranging from dental work to cigarette cases, rings and gold teeth, diamonds, gold and silver coins, foreign currencies, and gold and silver bars. Also, hundreds of tons of artworks were stored. *See also* Konto Max Heiliger.

**Merkur.** *See* Unternehmen Merkur.

**Meschuggismus.** Cult of craziness. Modern art. Borrowed from the Yiddish meschugge (crazy). *See also* entartete Kunst.

**Messerschmidt ME 262.** First two-engine jet fighter developed by the Germans.

**Metallblock.** Metal Block. Economic organization of the electrical, motor vehicle, precision tool, and engineering industries.

**Metallurgische Forschungsgesellschft mbH.** *See* Mefo-Wechsel.

**Meuten.** Packs, mobs. Left-wing youth groups opposed to the Hitler Youth.

**Mexiko.** Mexico. Uncompleted camp at Birkenau for slave laborers arriving late in the war. Prisoners wore blankets that made them seem like Mexicans wearing ponchos.

**MG-Eisenbetonunterstand.** (Mebu) Reinforced-concrete machine-gun protection area. Pillbox.

**MG-42.** German light machine gun.

**MHJ.** *See* Marine-Hitlerjugend.

**Miefmobil.** Stale-air mobile. Slang for poison-gas truck.

**Miesmacher.** Defeatist. Critic of the basic work of National Socialism.

**Milag.** Merchant-marine internment camp.

**Milag-Inder.** Merchant marine internment camp accommodating Indian seamen.

**Milchkarte.** Milk card. Ration card for whole milk for pregnant German women, nursing mothers, children under fourteen, the sick, and designated groups during the war.

**Milchkuh.** Milk cow. Slang for U-boat supply ship.

**Milei.** Artificial egg powder.

**Militärbefehlshaber.** (Mbfh) Military commander; for example, General Otto von Stülpnagel was German Military Commander of France. *See also* Besatzungsverwaltung.

**militärischer Geheimdienst.** Military Secret Service. German offices dealing with military intelligence. Intelligence community.

**Militärkommandantur.** (MK) Military command post.

**Millionär.** Millionaire. Ironic nickname for a new concentration camp inmate with a high identification number.

**minderrassig.** Racially inferior. Of non-German, non-Aryan race.

**minderwertig.** Inferior. Related to a human being's biologically determined physical and mental health, performance, and morality.

**Minister der Reichsregierung mit Mitspracherecht in allen Bereichen.** Minister of the Reich Government with Authority in All Areas. Rudolf Hess's official government position as the Führer's secretary and plenipotentiary.

**Ministerpräsident.** German state president or prime minister.

**Ministerpräsident des Landes Preußen.** State President of Prussia. Another of Göring's titles. *See also* Reichsmarschall.

**Ministerrat für die Reichsverteidigung.** Ministry Council for Reich Defense. Hitler created this organization led by Göring, the highest authority below Hitler himself. Like many Nazi organizations, it had the power to operate independently but met only a few times in 1939 and promulgated only a few inconsequential laws.

**Mischehen.** Mixed marriages. Marriages between Jews and German Christians. Some marriages were privilegierte (privileged) when the husband was German and the wife Jewish, childless or with children brought up as non-Jews. Nicht-privilegierte (not privileged) occurred when the husband was Jewish and the wife non-Jewish, childless or children brought up as Jews. Officially forbidden after 1935.

**Mischlinge.** Hybrids, mixed blood. Defining the degree of Jewishness. Mischlinge of the first degree (Mischling ersten Grades) were defined as Germans who had two Jewish grandparents, were not Jewish by religion, and were not married to a Jew as of September 15, 1935 (Halbjude). Mischlinge of the second degree (Mischling zweiten Grades) were those individuals with only one Jewish grandparent (Vierteljude) and raised as a Christian. Generally, second-degree Mischlinge were accepted as Germans, whereas first-degree mischlinge were treated as Jews. The Wannsee Conference planned to murder or sterilize Mischlinge but generally this did not occur. *See also* Endlösung der Judenfrage; Wannsee-Konferenz.

**Mischlinge soundsovielten Grades.** Racially mixed of such and such a kind. First-class Mischlinge were half-Jews. Second-class were quarter-Jews. *See also* Mischlinge.

**Mischlingssiedlung.** Mixed-race colony or settlement. Special ghetto for Jews married to non-Jews and their children.

**Mischlingstum.** Mixing. Negative term for the genetic mixing of Germans with non-Germans.

**Mischrasse.** Mixed race. Poles and other people, who were not viewed as worthy to be Aryans.

**mischrassig.** Racially mixed.

**mischvölkisch.** Racially mixed population.

**Mission.** Mission. Ideological sense of the "religious" mission of the National Socialist movement.

**Mitarbeiter in der Studentenführung.** Associate Leader of Students. Official in the German Student Association. *See also* Nationalsozialistischer Deutscher Studentenbund.

**mit der Führung beauftragt.** (m.d.F.b.) Person authorized to lead or command.

**Mitgabegeld.** Money brought along. The money Jews were allowed to bring with them on being deported. Usually 50 Reichsmarks, but in Poland the equivalent in Zloty were allowed. Upon being interviewed at the receiving desk at the railroad station, each Jew had to hand over his or her Mitgabegeld.

**Mitglied des Ministerrats für Reichsverteidigung.** Member of the Ministry Council for Reich Defense. Permanent members were Hermann Göring (president), Rudolf Hess, Hans Lammers, Wilhem Frick, Minister of Economics Walther Funk, and General Wilhelm Keitel, Head of the Oberkommando der Wehrmacht.

**Mitglied des Reichstag.** (M.d.R.) Member of Reichstag (parliament).

**Mitglieder.** Members. Individual Nazi Party members.

**Mitläufer.** Fellow traveler. Individuals who supported Nazi policies but chose not to join the Party.

**Mitmacher.** Collaborator. Opportunist, yes sayer.

**Mittelbau.** *See* Dora-Mittelbau.

**Mittelinstanz.** Middle-level authority. Organization on the level of the Gau; most important executive and policy-shaping body linking the central authorities with the local offices.

**Mittelstand.** (Lower) middle class. Hurt by inflation and the depression of the 1920s and early 1930s, this group of factory foremen, clerks, and small shopkeepers were especially prone to Nazi propaganda.

**Mittelstelle.** *See* Volksdeutsche Mittelstelle.

**Mittelwerk GmbH.** Central Works Ltd. SS company in the Dora-Mittelbau concentration camp that used slaves to construct V-2 rockets and jet planes. *See also* Vergeltungsbombe; Volksjäger.

**Mittwoch-Gesellschaft.** Wednesday Society. Elite intellectual society in opposition to the Nazi regime.

**MK.** *See* Maschinenkanone; Militärkommandantur.

**MKL.** *See* Männerkonzentrationslager.

**Mob-Beauftragte.** Mobilization deputies. German officials administering mobilization of home front.

**Möbelwagen.** Moving truck. Slang for bomber.

**mobilisieren.** To mobilize. Prepare for war. Preferred military term (despite being of non-German origin).

**Mob-Kreditbank.** Mobilization credit bank. Ordnance financing corporation such as the Heeres- und Rüstungskreditbank.

**Mobstelle.** Place of mobilization. Economic mobilization of the home front.

**MOD.** *See* Memeldeutscher Ordnungsdienst.

**Mogen David.** Star of David. A six-pointed star as a symbol of Judaism. During the Holocaust, Jews throughout Europe under German hegemony were required to wear Stars of David on their sleeves or on their shirts, jackets, or dresses usually in yellow or on white armbands in blue.

**Molotov-Ribbentrop-Pakte.** Molotov-Ribbentrop Pacts. Pacts negotiated by the Foreign Ministers of the Soviet Union and Nazi Germany. *See also* Deutsch-Sowjetischer Nichtangriffspakt.

**Monatsnamen.** Month names. The traditional names were to be replaced with either old Germanic or new names (*see* Appendix).

***Monatsschrift für Blut und Boden.*** (*Odal*) Monthly Journal for Blood and Soil. From 1934, name for the German journal *Deutsche Agrarpolitik* (German Agricultural Policy), originally founded by Richard Walther Darré in 1932. From the Germanic "Odal," meaning "a clan's inherited site."

***Monatsschrift für die Judenfrage aller Länder.*** Monthly publication devoted to the Jewish problem in all countries. Subtitle for (*Der*) *Weltkampf.*

**Monsunboote.** Monsoon boat. U-boats operating in the Indian and Pacific Oceans.

**Montoire-sur-le-Loir.** City in France, site of meeting on October 24, 1940, between Hitler and Maréchal Pétain, head of the Vichy French government. Pétain agreed that France would help Germany but would not declare war on Great Britain.

**monumentaler Ewigkeitscharakter.** The eternal character of the monumental. Hitler's vision of the role of his building projects. *See also* Bauten des Führers.

**Moorexpress.** Bog express. Ironic for an old heavy cart at Dachau that was used as a transport vehicle. Prisoners were put in harnesses like horses, and beaten.

**"(Die) Moorsoldaten."** "The Bog Soldiers." Song composed in a German concentration camp depicting the work situation of the inmates. Prisoners were forced to sing this song, especially outdoors and in bad weather, as a form of collective punishment or torture.

**Mordbrenner.** Incendiary. Code name for wartime German submarine operations off the East Coast of the United States.

**Mordkisten.** Murder boxes. Name given by the pupils of the town of Hadamar, Hesse, for the gray buses with covered windows that deported the institutionally disabled to be murdered in the T-4 Euthanasia Program. *See also* Gemeinnützige Krankentransport GmbH.

**Mordkommando.** Murder Unit. SS Odilo Globocnik's murder squad.

**Morgenappell.** Morning roll call. *See also* Appell.

**Moringen.** Located between Göttingen and Hanover, it was the first central concentration camp for women from October 1933 to March 1938. It became a concentration camp for juveniles from August 1940, holding nearly 3,000 male and female juvenile prisoners aged sixteen to nineteen and sometimes younger, arrested for refusing to serve in the Hitler Youth or League of German Girls, for sabotage or refusing to work, criminality, membership in the Swing youth movements, homosexuality or prostitution, violation of race laws, or political resistance.

**mosaisch.** Mosaic. Of the same religion as Moses. Used on German official forms in addition to category of Jew. *See also* israelitisch.

**Mot.I.D.** *See* motorisierte Infanteriedivision.

**Motor.** Engine. Used metaphorically to express great activity; the NSDAP was called the powerful motor of Germany.

**Motor-Hitlerjugend.** Hitler Youth Motorized Unit.

**motorisiert.** (mot) Motorized.

**motorisierte Infanteriedivision.** (Mot.I.D.) Motorized Infantry Division.

**motorisierte Panzer und leichte Kräfte.** (Motpulk) Motorized tanks and light vehicles.

**Motorsportabzeichen.** Motor-sport medal. Three-level award instituted in 1938 to honor militarized motor-sport achievements.

**Motorsportschule.** Motor-sport school. Twenty-four training institutions for the Motor Corps (*see* NS-Kraftfahrkorps). The four-week obligatory course was for uniformed recruits assigned to a motorized Wehrmacht unit.

**Motor-Transport.** (MT) Motor transport.

**Motorwehrman.** Motorized soldier. Participant in a Motorsportschule.

**Motpulk.** *See* motorisierte Panzer und leichte Kräfte.

**Motti.** Finnish military technique for encircling the Soviets.

**Mottispezialisten.** Motti specialists. Finnish generals and officers working with the German army. *See also* Motti.

**MSG.** *See* Mutterschutzgesetz.

**MT.** *See* Motor-Transport.

**Mühldorf.** *See* Landsberg am Lech.

**Mühle.** Mill. Slang for airplane.

**"Mühlen arbeiten lassen."** "To let the mills work." To put the death machinery into action (i.e., to murder Jews).

**Müllabfuhrkommando.** Rubbish unit. Concentration camp detail in charge of rubbish removal. At Auschwitz and other camps, this unit was much sought after, as the rubbish provided material prisoners could use as food or barter.

**Mülltonnen.** Garbage cans. Slang for naval depth charges.

**Münchener Abkommen.** Munich Pact. September 1938 agreement between Germany, Italy, France, and Great Britain (Hitler, Mussolini, Daladier, and Chamberlain) conceding to Germany's demands for the Sudetenland of Czechoslovakia.

A diplomatic victory for Hitler, the agreement represented the nadir of the Allied policy of appeasement, as Member of Parliament Eleanor Rathbone defined it, "selling out one's friends to please one's enemies." Though Europe breathed a sigh of relief, the pact alienated the Soviet Union from the Allies and became, in retrospect, a major step toward war.

**Münchener Putsch.** *See* Hitler-Putsch.

**München, Hauptstadt der Bewegung.** Munich, Capital City of the Movement. Honorary title for the city of Munich as the birthplace of National Socialism.

**Mundfunk.** Word of mouth. Source of questionable news that circulated among concentration camp inmates; such news by itself.

**Muselmanische SS-Freiwillige.** Muslim SS volunteers from Bosnia and Herzegovina in the Balkans.

**Muselmann.** Muslim. Slang referring to a concentration camp inmate on his way to death by means of starvation, exhaustion, and despair. Living corpse ready to be chosen to be sent to the gas chambers to be murdered. *See* Schmuckstück.

**Musterbetrieb.** *See* Nationalsozialistischer Musterbetrieb.

**Muster-Ghetto.** Model ghetto. *See also* Theresienstadt.

**Musterlager.** Model camp. Concentration camps such as Dachau and Westerbork.

**Musterprotektorat.** Model protectorate. Denmark, treated gently by German military authorities for racial, political, and economic reasons.

**Musterung.** Examination. Preinduction examination for German army and labor services.

**Mütterdienst.** Mother service. Part of the German National Socialist Women's Organization, which trained women for motherhood. *See also* Mütterschulung; Nationalsozialistische Frauenschaft.

**Mutterehrenkreuz.** Mother's honor cross. *See also* Ehrenkreuz der deutschen Mutter.

**Mütterkarte.** Mother card. Ration card for German mothers. *See also* Lebensmittelkarte; Milchkarte.

**Mutterkreuz.** Mother's cross. *See also* Ehrenkreuz der deutschen Mutter.

**Mütterschulung.** Mother schooling. Ideological and practical training to convince German women of the importance of mothering.

**Mutterschutzgesetz.** (MSG) Mother-Protection Law. Instituted in 1942 to protect German working mothers.

**Mutter und Hausfrau.** Mother and housewife. According to National Socialist beliefs, the highest duty and the actual profession of the German woman was in the service of the German family and people.

**Mutter und Kind.** Mother and child. *See also* Hilfswerk Mutter und Kind.

**"Mützen ab, Mützen auf!"** "Hat on, hat off." Concentration camp inmates had to greet every passing SS officer and, after the morning and evening roll calls, the camp commander, with this ritual show of obeisance.

**Mützenschießen.** To shoot at hats. Shooting at allegedly fleeing concentration camp inmates. *See* "(auf der) Flucht erschossen."

**Mylius-Gruppe.** Mylius Group. Radical rightist anti-Hitler group led by Dr. Helmuth Mylius in the 1930s. Their plan to kill Hitler and seize the government failed when the Gestapo intervened.

*(Der) Mythus des 20 Jahrhunderts.* The Myth of the 20th Century. A book by Nazi racist ideologue Alfred Rosenberg that some considered the bible of neopaganism and regarded with an official awe second only to that of Hitler's *Mein Kampf*. But Hitler himself insisted it "was not to be regarded as an expression of the official doctrine of the party." Göring called it "junk" and Goebbels described it as "weltanschauliches Gerülpse" (philosophical belching). It was read mostly by Nazi ideologues and Nazi opponents.

# N

**Nachersatz.** Secondary (military) reserve.

**Nachfolger des Führers.** The Führer's Successor. One of Göring's many titles. *See also* Reichsmarschall.

**nachgeordnete Dienststellen.** Junior offices. Reich branch offices at the local level.

**Nachrichten.** News. Wartime intelligence, communications.

**Nachrichtendienst des Außenpolitischen Amt der NSDAP.** Intelligence Service of the Foreign-Policy Department of the Nazi Party. Early Nazi Party Overseas Intelligence Department under Alfred Rosenberg. *See* Sicherheitsdienst.

**Nachrichtenhelferin.** Female communication helper. German women who worked as telephone, radio, and teletype operators for the Wehrmacht staff offices both in Germany and the occupied countries. They wore uniforms and lived in barracks.

**Nachrichten-Hitlerjugend.** Communcations (Group) Hitler Youth.

**Nachrichtenmaid.** News girl. German girls from the age of seventeen who were asked to volunteer to work as telephone, radio, and teletype operators for the Waffen-SS and the police, both in Germany and in the occupied countries. *See also* Nachrichtenhelferin.

**Nachrichtenmittelabteilung eines Infanterieregiments.** (Ina.) News and Communication Bureau of an infantry regiment.

**Nachrichtensturm Unna.** Signal and Intelligence Unit Unna. SS signal and intelligence company stationed in Unna, Germany.

**Nachrichtenwesen.** Communications. SS Office of Communications Control.

**Nächsttreffer.** Near hit.

**Nacht der Feuer.** Night of Fire. *See also* Bücherverbrennung.

**Nacht der langen Messer.** Night of the Long Knives. June 30, 1934 wave of more than 100 SS assassinations of SA leadership to crush its power.

**Nachtjagdgeschwader.** Night-fighter squadrons.

**Nachtjäger.** Night hunters. Fighter planes that attacked enemy bombers during night raids.

**Nacht-und-Nebel-Erlaß.** Night-and-Fog Decree. 1941 Wehrmacht decree issued by General Wilhelm Keitel but instigated by Hitler, allowing the Gestapo and the SD to arrest all those found guilty of "undermining the effectiveness of the German Armed Forces" or seen as threats to the Reich and its occupied western territories; no information was to be offered to relatives of those arrested. The decree's purpose was to deter anti-Nazi resistance in France, Belgium, the Netherlands, Denmark, and Norway. Courts in the occupied areas of these countries that would not decree the death penalty for offenses against the Reich were superseded by German military courts that imposed death sentences, or deportation to concentration camps, on resisters and/or their families.

**Nacht-und-Nebel-Häftlinge.** (NN) Night-and-Fog prisoners. Those prisoners who were not executed often disappeared without a trace into the night and fog of the Third Reich. Police terror was such that even those found not guilty were turned over to the Gestapo.

**Nachwuchsplan.** Replacement plan. Labor supply scheme.

**Nachzügler.** Straggler, latecomer. During the concentration camp evacuations in spring 1945, the SS shot stragglers, individuals who were too weak and sick to walk.

**"Na, gib ihnen zu fressen."** *See* fressen.

**Nahkampfbunker.** Hand-to-hand combat shelter. Soldier lingo during the war for second-rate dance halls. *See* Nahkampfdiele; Nahkampfschuppen.

**Nahkampfdiele.** Hand-to-hand combat dance floor. *See* Nahkampfbunker; Nahkampfschupper.

**Nahkampfmittel.** Close combat devices. Pistols, flamethrowers, hand grenades, machine guns, and shovels.

**Nahkampfschuppen.** Hand-to-hand combat shack. *See* Nahkampfbunker; Nahkampfdiele.

**Nahkampfspange.** Close-combat medal. Three-category medal for hand-to-hand fighting, instituted December 1, 1942.

**Nähmaschine.** Sewing machine. Air force slang for damaged aircraft.

**Nähmittel.** Sewing material. Darning and mending material available through special ration coupons.

**Nährmittel.** Nutritious food. Term coined in 1939 for legumes.

**Nährstand.** *See* Reichsnährstand.

**Nährung.** Supply. German neologism; for example, supply of information or ammunition.

**Nahrungsfreiheit.** Food independence. The goal of making Germany's food supply completely self-sufficient.

**Namensträger.** Name bearer. Last son of a German family whose other sons or father had been killed in action; he would not be assigned to combat duty at the front.

**Namensweihe.** Naming ceremony. Replacing Christian baptism, this SS ceremony recognized a newborn's induction into the Aryan kinship community of the SS. An SS godfather was nominated as well.

**Napola.** *See* Nationalpolitische Erziehungsanstalten.

**Nardony Komissariat Wnutrennich Djel.** (NKWD) The secret service of the USSR, also known as the NKVD (Narodnyi Komissariat Vnutriennikh Del [National Committee of Interior Affairs]).

**Narvik-Schild.** Narvik shield. Badge worn on the German uniform on the upper left arm to commemorate soldiers of the battle of Narvik, Norway, in 1940.

**Nase.** Nose. The nose was either Jewish or not. *See also* Judensechser.

**Nation.** Nation. The German nation, Reich, Volk.

**nationale Arbeit.** *See* Feiertag der nationalen Arbeit.

**nationale Ehre.** National honor. *See* Ehre.

**nationale Erhebung.** National uprising. The Hitler Putsch of 1923. Later, the period between the Nazi accession to power on January 30, 1933, and the reopening of the German Reichstag on March 21, 1933.

**Nationale Fahne.** National flag. Under the Third Reich, a red background, white circle in the center, containing a tilted black swastika.

**nationale Feiertage.** National holidays. Official holidays with organized celebratory or commemorative events: January 30, Seizure of Power Day; February 24, Nazi Party Foundation Day; March 16, Hero Remembrance Day, Heldengedenktag (used to be Memorial Day); April 20, Hitler's Birthday; May 1, National Labor Day; second Sunday in May, (prolific) Mothers' Day; in June, Summer Solstice Day, commemorating Nazi martyrs and war heroes; September, Nazi Party Rally Day at Nuremberg; the first Sunday after St. Michael's Day in September, Harvest Thanksgiving Day (Erntedanktag); November 9, Hitler-Putsch Day; December, Winter Solstice Day, designed unsuccessfully to replace Christmas.

**Nationaler Buchpreis.** National book prize. *See also* Nationalpreis für Buch und Film.

**nationale Revolution.** National revolution. *See also* nationale Erhebung.

**Nationaler Musikpreis.** National music prize. Prize of 10,000 Reichsmarks, instituted by Goebbels for the best young German violinist or pianist.

**nationale Solidarität.** *See* Tag der nationalen Solidarität.

*(Der) Nationale Sozialist für Mitteldeutschland.* The National Socialist for Central Germany. Nazi newspaper of Gregor and Otto Strasser. The Strassers published several other such National Socialist newspapers for different sections of Germany, such as Norddeutschland, Die Ostmark, Rhein und Ruhr, Sachsen, Westdeutschland, and Württemberg.

**Nationalisierung.** Nationalization. Government seizure of private property making it state property (*see also* Arisierung). Also, making people more race-conscious or patriotic.

**Nationalkirche deutscher Christen.** National German Christian Church. Nazi Christians adhering to the ideology of the Third Reich.

**Nationalkirchliche Einigung.** National Church Agreement. From 1938 name of splinter group of Deutsche Christen in the province of Thüringen. *See also* Nationalkirche deutscher Christen.

**Nationalpolitische Erziehungsanstalten.** (NPEA) National political-educational organizations. Training schools for Hitler Youth as future civil service or SS officers.

**Nationalpolitische Lehranstalt.** (Napola) National Political-Institute. *See* Nationalpolitische Erziehungsanstalten.

**Nationalpreis.** *See* Nationalpreis für Buch und Film.

**Nationalpreis für Buch und Film.** National prize for book and film. Annual prize for books and films that best demonstrated the National Socialist spirit.

**Nationalsozialismus.** National Socialism. Ideology based on the leader principle, Adolf Hitler, and the Nazi Party. From January 1933, the determining factor in Germany's political, social, and economic system and cultural life. Ironically, the term was invented around 1860 by Moses Hess, father of Zionism. *See also* Nationalsozialistische Deutsche Arbeiterpartei.

*Nationalsozialistische Beamten-Zeitung.* (NSBZ) National Socialist Civil Servants' Newspaper. Only a few issues were published from 1931 to 1932.

*Nationalsozialistische Bibliographie.* (NSB) National Socialist Bibliography. Monthly publication of the Nazi Party listing new National Socialist literature. *See Gutachtenanzeiger.*

*Nationalsozialistische Briefe.* National Socialist Letters. Periodical published by Goebbels and Gregor Strasser.

**Nationalsozialistische Deutsche Arbeiterpartei.** (NSDAP) Nazi Party. Officially, the National-Socialist German Workers' Party. Founded in Germany on January 5, 1919, it was characterized by a centralist and authoritarian pyramidal-hierarchical structure from the Führer at the top to the Mitglieder, or mass of ordinary Nazi Party members, at the base. Its platform was based on militaristic, racial, antisemitic, and nationalistic policies. The Party membership and political power grew dramatically in the 1930s. Their oath of allegiance stated: "I pledge loyalty to my Führer Hitler. I promise always, to him and to the leaders whom he appoints above me, my respect and obedience." Hitler joined the Party on September 12, 1919, becoming its leader in 1921. As a result of his failed putsch in Munich on November 8–9, 1923, the Party was banned, with the ban lasting until February 27, 1925. Refounded on that day, it remained in existence until after Germany's defeat in World War II, when it was declared illegal by the Allies on September 20, 1945. Also written as Nationalsozialistische deutsche Arbeiter-Partei, Nationalsozialistische Deutsche Arbeiterpartei. *See also* politischer Arbeiterzirkel.

**Nationalsozialistische Frauenschaft.** National Socialist Women's Organization. Founded in 1931. From 1936, exclusively responsible for training the female leaders of the German Women's Organization. *See also* Deutsches Frauenwerk; Reichsfrauenführerin.

**Nationalsozialistische Freiheitsbewegung.** (NSFB) National Socialist Freedom Movement. Gregor Straßer and Ernst Röhm created this political party while the Nazi Party was forbidden after Hitler's Munich Putsch.

**Nationalsozialistische Gemeinschaft Kraft durch Freude.** (KdF) National Socialist Association of Strength through Joy. Nazi recreation program for organized sports, cultural activities, outings, travel, and so forth. An important part of the reorganization of German society. By 1936, it owned campgrounds, theaters, and ships and consisted of several departments: management, administration, agricultural liaison, soldiers and seamen's homes, leisure time, emergency food provision, art, theater, concerts, film, dances, fine arts, entertainment, folklore, celebrations and holidays, picnics, leisure activities, clubs, publishing and propaganda, individual and group travel and vacation, sports, beauty of labor, health, workhouses, planning, and guidance and education.

**Nationalsozialistische Handwerks-, Handels- und Gewerbeorganisation.** (NSHAGO, NS-Hago) National Socialist Workers' Commerce and Trade Organization. Dissolved in 1936 and integrated into the Hauptamt für Handwerk und Gewerbe.

**Nationalsozialistische Kampfbewegung Deutschlands.** *See* Schwarze Front.

*Nationalsozialistische Korrespondenz.* National Socialist Correspondence. Nazi periodical.

**Nationalsozialistische Kriegsopferversorgung.** (NSKOV) National Socialist War Victims Welfare Service. Charitable organization for German war veterans.

**Nationalsozialistische Kulturgemeinde.** (NSKG) National Socialist Cultural Community. Founded in 1934 and fused in 1937 with the NS-Gemeinschaft Kraft durch Freude.

*Nationalsozialistische Monatshefte.* National Socialist Monthly Notebooks. Chief Nazi theory periodical, edited by Alfred Rosenberg.

**Nationalsozialistischer Ärztebund.** National Socialist Doctors' Association. Founded in 1929; one of several Nazi organizations.

**Nationalsozialistischer Deutscher Frontkämpferbund.** (NSDFB) National Socialist German Veteran's League.

**Nationalsozialistischer Deutscher Marinebund.** (NSDMB). National Socialist German Navy League.

**Nationalsozialistischer Deutscher Studentenbund.** (NSDSt.B.) National Socialist German Student Alliance. One of many Nazi organizations, founded in 1926. All German university students were obliged to be members of this organization.

**Nationalsozialistische Revolution.** National Socialist Revolution. Hitler's legal assumption of power in January 1933 and the use of this power to make changes in Germany's economic, social, and political life. More specifically, the period from March, 1933, the subordination of all institutions to the Nazi Party by July 1933, and the prohibition of all political parties in Germany except the Nazi Party. *See also* Gleichschaltung.

**Nationalsozialistischer Führungsstab des Heeres.** (NSF St d H.) National Socialist Guidance Staff of the Army.

**Nationalsozialistischer Führungsstab des OKW.** (NSF/OKW) National Socialist Guidance Staff of the OKW.

**Nationalsozialistischer Musterbetrieb.** Model National Socialist company. Businesses with exemplary Nazi organization and attitude were given awards.

**Nationalsozialistischer Rechtswahrerbund.** (NS-RKB) National Socialist Lawyers' Association. Established in 1928 as NS-Juristenbund.

**Nationalsozialistcher Reichskriegerbund.** (NS-RKB) National Socialist Reich Veterans' League.

**Nationalsozialistischer Reichskriegerbund Kyffhäuser.** *See* NS-Reichs-kriegerbund Kyffhäuser.

**Nationalsozialistischer Schülerbund.** National Socialist Pupil Alliance. Founded in 1929 as one of many Nazi youth organizations.

**Nationalsozialistisches Automobil-Korps.** *See* Nationalsozialistisches Kraft-fahrkorps.

**Nationalsozialistische Schwestern.** National Socialist Nurses. *See also* Braune Schwestern; Lebensborn; Nationalsozialistische Volkswohlfahrt; NSV-Schwesternschaft.

**Nationalsozialistisches Kraftfahrkorps.** (NSKF, NSKK) National Socialist Motor Transport Corps. Originally, motorized Sturmabteilung unit. Until 1939, surreptitious training organization for recruits to military armored and transport units.

**Nationalsozialistisches Kulturwollen.** National Socialist activity promoting German culture. *See* Kulturförderung.

**Nationalsozialistisches Reichs-Symphonieorchester.** National Socialist Reich Symphony Orchestra. Nazi Party orchestra founded in 1931. It often played before audiences of the German Labor Front and Nationalsozialistische Gemeinschaft Kraft durch Freude.

**Nationalsozialistische Volkswohlfahrt.** (NSV) National Socialist Peoples' Welfare. This charitable organization reflected Nazi racial doctrine, discriminating against so-called asocials, inferior races, genetic defectives, and Jews. It aided German mothers and children by fighting serious diseases, by promoting school health and welfare, and by sending to Germans the valuables of people murdered by the Third Reich. *See also* Winterhilfswerk des deutschen Volkes.

**Natzweiler-Struthof.** Concentration camp established in 1941 near Strasbourg in Alsace after its annexation to Germany. The camp housed a wide variety of inmates, including Night-and-Fog prisoners, and was the scene of mustard-gas, castration, and other gruesome anatomical experiments conducted by Strasbourg University Professors August Hirt and Otto Bickenbach. *See also* Nacht-und-Nebel-Häftlinge.

**Navajos.** Navajos. Nonconformist youth group, similar to the Edelweißpiraten.

**Nazi.** *See* Nationalsozialistische Deutsche Arbeiterpartei.

**Nazi-Aufmarsch.** *See* Aufmarsch.

**Naziege.** Nazi/Ziege (goat). Cynical for a fanatically Nazi woman or wife.

**Nazismus.** Short for Nationalsozialismus.

**Nazisse.** Play on words with Narzisse (narcissus). *See also* Naziege.

**NDV.** *See* Notdienstverpflichtung.

**NDW.** *See* Notgemeinschaft Deutscher Wissenschaft.

**Nebelkerze.** Fog candle. Smoke bomb.

**(Inspekteur der) Nebeltruppen.** Inspector of chemical troops.

**Nebelung.** November.

**Nebenlager.** (NL) Sub-camp. *See also* Zweiglager.

**Nebenland.** Borderland. Poland.

**Nebenland des Reiches.** Dependency of the Reich. Status of the Generalgouvernement.

**Nebenstrafen.** Additional punishment. In addition to the standard punishments for camp infractions at Dachau and later other camps, prisoners were also beaten (Prügel), starved (Kostentzug), forced to do punishment drills (Strafexerzieren), and so forth.

**negative Kritik.** Negative criticism. Criticism of National Socialism considered destructive and therefore forbidden.

**Neger.** Nigger. Slang for one-man torpedo.

**Negerbastarde.** Nigger bastards. Derogatory. Racially mixed children of Black fathers and German/Aryan mothers.

**negerisch.** Nigger-like. Derogatory racial term also used for Jews.

**Negerkultur.** Nigger culture. Derogatory. Inferior culture of Blacks.

**Negermusik.** Nigger music. Derogatory. Hostile for modern music, especially jazz.

**Neidingswerk.** Jealous action. Behavior based on avarice or jealousy.

**Nero-Befehl.** *See* Nero-Erlaß.

**Nero-Erlaß.** Nero Decree. Hitler's 1945 scorched-earth policy punishing the German Volk for having allowed itself to be defeated by the Allies.

**Nerother Wandervögel.** The Hikers of Neroth. Nonconformist youth group. *See also* Edelweißpiraten.

**Netzsäge.** Net saw. Slang for U-boat.

**Neuadel aus Blut und Boden.** New nobility of blood and soil. German peasants/farmers as seen by the Nazis.

**Neuankömmling.** Newly arrived. Concentration camp prisoner in his or her first year.

**(der) Neuaufbau der seelischen Zellen der nordisch bestimmten Völker.** The rearrangement of the spiritual cells of the Nordic peoples. Alfred Rosenberg's racial goal.

**Neuaufbaugesetz vom 30.1.1934.** Reconstruction Law of January 30, 1934. This law helped destroy the Weimar Republic by awarding German provincial legislative power and authority to the Reichstag, subordinating the authority of the Reich governors to the Ministry of the Interior, and allowing the Reich government to create new constitutional law.

**Neubauer.** New builder. German settlers, especially in eastern European areas, under the direction of the SS.

**neu Beginnen.** New Undertaking. Social Democratic anti-Nazi organization in Ruhr and Berlin after Nazis came to power. Finally broken in 1944.

**neue deutsche Heilkunde.** New German healing practice. Non-Jewish German medical practice.

*(Die) neue Gemeinschaft: Das Parteiarchiv für nationalsozialistische Feier- und Freizeitgestaltung.* The New Community: The Party Source for National Socialist Celebrations and Leisure Activities. A Nazi periodical that provided material to help organize ceremonies on Nazi holidays, especially November 9 (the date of Hitler's Munich Putsch), the holiest day on the Nazi calendar.

**Neue Heimat.** New home. Nazi real estate conglomerate seized from the labor unions. *See also* Deutsche Arbeitsfront.

**(der) neue Mensch.** (The) new man. According to Nazi race specifications, a racially valuable person.

**Neuengamme.** Concentration camp near Hamburg, opened in December 1938, initially as a satellite of Sachsenhausen concentration camp producing bricks for the SS company DEST. It became an independent camp in June 1940. Later, medical experiments with tuberculosis were performed on prisoners. *See also* Deutsche Erd- und Steinwerke GmbH.

**neuer Nationalismus.** New nationalism. Militaristic ideology; total mobilization of the entire German nation.

**Neuer Plan.** New plan. Hjalmar Schacht's autarky plan.

**neue Waffe.** New weapon. *See also* Wunderwaffen.

*Neugestaltung von Staat und Wirtschaft.* Reconfiguration of State and Economy. German university outlines on the Nazi ideology.

**Neuland.** New (undeveloped) territory. Land conquered for settlement by Germans.

**Neuordnung.** New Order. Hitler's national revolution. Hitler's concept of the rearrangement of German society in accordance with Nazi ideology. *See also* Gleichschaltung.

**Neuordnung Europas.** New European Order. Nazi plan to conquer, control, and exploit all of Europe.

**Neustadt-Glewe.** A sub-camp of Ravensbrück concentration camp, where female prisoners were forced to work in an airplane parts factory. They included Polish political prisoners deported from Warsaw in September 1944, Jewish women evacuated from Auschwitz in December 1944 and January 1945, and Dutch, French, Greek, German, Hungarian, Russian, and Ukrainian female political prisoners.

**neutral.** Neutral, impartial. Unreliable.

**Neutralenlager.** Neutral camp. Camp for Jewish prisoners from neutral countries at Bergen-Belsen.

**neutralisieren.** To neutralize. To kill, to totally eliminate.

**Nichtangriffspakt zwischen Deutschland und der Union der Sozialistischen Sowjetrepubliken.** *See* Deutsch-Sowjetischer Nichtangriffspakt.

**Nichtarier.** Non-Aryan. A Jew and/or not of the Nordic-Germanic race.

**nichtarisch.** Non-Aryan. *See also* Nichtarier.

**nichtarische Christen.** Non-Aryan Christians. Baptized Jews.

**nichteinsatzfähig.** Unfit to serve. Those Jews who were not useful for slave work including the elderly, the sick, and many women and children. Often not included with those deported to death camps, they were the first to be killed, on the spot, on the grounds of Jewish cemeteries or in prepared pits.

**Nichtjude.** Non-Jew. Aryan, German, Nordic.

**Nichtprivilegierte.** The unprivileged. *See also* Mischehen.

**nichtslebensfähig.** Incapable of life. Those prisoners in concentraton camps who were condemned to die.

**"Nicht weg von der Arbeit, sondern hin zur Arbeit!"** "Not away from work, but to work." Slogan of the Nationalsozialistische Gemeinschaft Kraft durch Freude.

**Nichtzigeuner.** (NZ) Non-Gypsy. Code word used in people's card file distinguishing non-Gypsies from Gypsies. *See also* Volkskartei.

**Niederdonau.** The lower Danube region. In 1939, new name for Lower Austria.

**Niederrasse.** Inferior race.

**niederrassig.** Of inferior race.

**niederrassisch.** *See* niederrassig.

**Niederschlag.** Knockout, defeat. Germany would knock England out.

**Nisko.** A plan devised by Adolf Eichmann in the fall of 1939 to set up a temporary Jewish reservation in the Radom district of central Poland prior to deportation of the Jews to death camps.

**Nisko.** A Polish town on the San river in the Radom district of the Generalgouvernement.

**NKWD.** *See* Nardony Komissariat Wnutrennich Djel.

**NL.** *See* Nebenlager.

**NN.** *See* Nacht-und-Nebel-Häftlinge.

**NN-Transporte.** Nacht-und-Nebel-Transporte. *See* Nacht-und-Nebel-Häftlinge.

**nomadisch.** Nomadic. Pejorative adjective used for Jews.

**Norde.** Nordic man.

**nordfremd.** Foreign to the Nordic race. Alien, hostile.

**Nordhausen.** Town in Germany in the Hartz Mountains where an underground factory was built by slave labor from the concentration camp Dora-Mittelbau, which later assembled V-2 rockets.

**nordisch.** Nordic. Aryan, in opposition to everything Jewish. One of the six races that allegedly comprised the Germans. Characteristics were large nose, small face, dark hair, and slender, as well as loving the homeland and being heroic. *See* dinarisch; fälisch; ostbaltisch; ostische Rasse; westisch.

**Nordische Aktion.** Nordic action. Insignificant German pagan sect that rejected the Bible and claimed God was Nordic-German. Ultimately abandoned by the Third Reich.

**Nordische Glaubensbewegung.** Nordic Belief Movement. *See* Nordische Aktion.

**nordische Rasse.** Nordic race. A supposedly superior race of tall blonds with the most creative culture of all, speaking the Germanic languages, originally located in northern and central Europe, and consisting of more than 50 percent German racial stock and culture. Nordic individuals were believed to be light-skinned, tall and slim, and blue eyed.

**nordischer Bluteinschlag.** Nordic blood impact. *See also* Rasse.

**Nordischer Christus.** Nordic Christ. The Aryan Jesus.

**nordischer Einschlag.** Nordic component. *See also* nordische Rasse.

**nordisch-germanisch.** *See* nordische Rasse.

**nordisch-herrisch.** Nordic man-like. *See also* Rasse.

**nordisches Sittengesetz.** Nordic moral law. German law as opposed to the formalism of Roman law.

**Nordlicht.** *See* Unternehmen Nordlicht.

**Nordmark.** Northern border region. German neologism for the province of Schleswig-Holstein, considered the (temporary) northern border of Germany.

**Nordrasse.** The Nordic race. *See also* nordische Rasse.

**nordrassisch.** Of the Nordic race.

**Nordwind.** *See* Unternehmen Nordwind.

**normale Tagesquote.** Normal daily quota. Average number of concentration camp prisoners murdered each day.

**Normalschrift.** Normal longhand. Longhand used in all German schools from 1941 on, replacing the traditional German longhand, or Deutsche Schrift.

**Normalverbraucher.** Average consumer. German who had no connections during the war and had to make due without extra or special ration cards.

**Normung.** Standardization.

**Notabitur.** Emergency graduation examination. When a young German was called to serve in the armed forces or other war-related activity before graduation, he could graduate by taking this examination.

**Notdienstverordung.** Emergency Service Order. Decree of 1938 instituting compulsory military service other than in the army.

**Notdienstverpflichtung.** (NDV) The obligation of every German to perform emergency service.

**Notgemeinschaft Deutscher Wissenschaft.** (NDW) Association for the Emergency Funding of German Science. *See also* Deutsche Forschungsgemeinschaft.

**Nothelfer.** Emergency helper. Member of an emergency unit. *See also* Technische Nothilfe.

**notleidender Volksgenosse.** Fellow German in distress. Term used to gloss over poverty.

**Notstandarbeit.** Emergency work. Nazi program to create labor-intensive public works projects to help pull Germany out of the Depression.

**Notverordnung.** Emergency decree.

**Notwurf.** Emergency throw. Jettison.

**November-.** November. Derogatory prefix applied to the November 1918 revolution, the Weimar Republic, the politicians who accepted the Versailles Treaty, and the democratic politicians and parties of the Weimar Republic. *See* Novemberverbrecher.

**Novemberdemokratie.** November democracy. Derogatory for the Weimar Republic.

**November-Größen.** The great (men) of November. Ironic. *See also* Novemberverbrecher.

**Novemberjuden.** November Jews. The 30,000 male Jews temporarily arrested and sent to the Buchenwald, Dachau, and Sachsenhausen concentration camps in connection with the November 1938 Pogrom. *See also* Reichskristallnacht.

**Novemberlinge.** November men. Derogatory for the German revolutionaries of 1918.

**Novemberparteien.** November parties. Negative for the political parties of the Weimar Republic.

**November-Putsch.** *See* Hitler-Putsch.

**Novemberregime.** November regime.

**Novemberrepublik.** November republic.

**Novemberrevolte.** November uprising. The November 1918 revolution.

**Novemberstaat.** November state.

**Novemberverbrecher.** November criminals. Derogatory for the political leaders of the Weimar Republic, those who accepted the Versailles Treaty, especially German Jews.

**NPEA.** *See* Nationalpolitische Erziehungsanstalten.

**N-Referent.** N desk. From 1941, every state police office included an official who coordinated police undercover agents and coordinated work between other such offices.

**NS.** (N/nationalsozialistisch). National Socialist. Abbreviation used in combination with almost all government and other associations and organizations to indicate National Socialist affiliation. *See also* N/nationalsozialistisch [as prefix] entries.

**NS-Ärztebund.** *See Nationalsozialistischer Ärztebund.*

**NSB.** *See* Nationalsozialistische Bibliographie.

**NS-Betriebszellen-Organisation.** (NSBO) National Socialist Organization of Individual Cells. National Socialist factory organization operating in German companies founded in 1930. During the Weimar Republic, a right-wing radical workers' organization led by the SA. After the Nazis came to power, this organization attacked all unions and supported the dissolution of unions nationally in July 1933. From 1935, integrated into the German Workers Front. *See also* Deutsche Arbeitsfront.

**NSBO.** *See* NS-Betriebszellen-Organisation.

**NSBZ.** *See Nationalsozialistische Beamten-Zeitung.*

**NSDAB.** *See* Nationalsozialistischer Deutscher Ärztebund.

**NSDAP.** *See* Nationalsozialistische Deutsche Arbeiterpartei.

**"NSDAP Volksgemeinschaft. Volksgenossen braucht ihr Rat und Hilfe, so wendet euch an die Ortsgruppe."** "NSDAP (racial) community; comrades, if you need advice and help, turn to the local (Nazi) Party organizations." Nazi slogan.

**NSD-Ärtzebund.** National Socialist German Doctors' Alliance.

**NSD-Dozentenbund.** *See* NS-Dozentenbund.

**NSDFB.** *See* Nationalsozialistischer Deutscher Frontkämpferbund.

**NSDMB.** *See* Nationalsozialistischer Deutscher Marinebund

**NSD-Oberschule.** National Socialist High School. Elite school for Hitler Youth.

**NS-Dozentenbund.** National Socialist Teachers' Union. Teachers' organization, part of the Nazi Party. *See also* Gliederungen und Ausgeschlossene Verbände der NSDAP; NS-Lehrerbund.

**NSDSt.B.** *See* Nationalsozialistischer Deutscher Studentenbund.

**NSFB.** *See* Nationalsozialistische Freiheitsbewegung.

**NS-Fliegerkorps.** (NSFK) National Socialist Flyers' Corps. Volunteer organization, established in 1937, to train German youth—as future Luftwaffe pilots—to fly gliders and motorized planes. Its leader was under the direct supervision of the High Command of the German air force.

**NSFK.** *See* NS-Fliegerkorps.

**NSFO.** *See* NS-Führungsoffizier.

**NSF/OKW.** *See* Nationalsozialistischer Führungsstab des OKW.

**NS-Frauenschaft.** *See* Nationalsozialistische Frauenschaft.

**NS-Freiwilliger Arbeitsdienst.** National Socialist Volunteer Labor Service. Established in 1931 and forerunner of Reichsarbeitsdienst. *See* Reichsarbeitsdienst.

**NS-Führungsoffizier.** (NSFO) National Socialist Leadership Officers. On Hitler's order in 1943, the party assigned officers to educate the troops according to Nazi ideology.

**NS-Gemeinschaft Kraft durch Freude.** *See* Nationalsozialistische Gemeinschaft Kraft durch Freude.

**NSHAGO.** *See* Nationalsozialistische Handwerks-, Handels- und Gewerbeorganisation.

**NS-Hago.** *See* Nationalsozialistische Handwerks-, Handels- und Gewerbeorganisation.

**NS-Hilfskasse.** *See* Hilfskasse.

**NS-Jubel dritte Stufe.** National Socialist jubilation third stage. Highest volume of prearranged applause at Nazi Party meetings.

**NS-Juristenbund.** National Socialist Lawyers' Association, established in 1928. In 1936 the name changed to Rechtswahrerbund. Compulsory membership for all German lawyers.

**NS-Kampfspiele.** National Socialist sports competitions. Sports and military competitions with participation by all Party organizations, the police, and the army.

**NSKBK.** *See* NS-Kraftbootkorps.

**NSKF.** *See* Nationalsozialistisches Kraftfahrkorps.

**NSKG.** *See* Nationalsozialistische Kulturgemeinde.

**NSKK.** *See* Nationalsozialistisches Kraftfahrkorps.

**NSKOV.** *See* Nationalsozialistiche Kriegsopferversorgung; NS-Kriegsopferversorgung.

**NS-Kraftbootkorps.** (NSKBK) National-Socialist Motorboat Corps.

**NS-Kraftfahrkorps.** *See* Nationalsozialistisches Kraftfahrkorps.

**NS-Kriegsopferversorgung.** (NSKOV) National Socialist distribution of citizens' war-effort contributions. *See also* Kriegsopfer.

**NSLB.** *See* NS-Lehrerbund.

**NS-Lehrerbund.** (NSLB) National Socialist Teachers' Association. From 1933, compulsory professional organization of teachers in all German schools that framed teachers' political and ideological guidelines.

**NS-Musterbetrieb.** *See* Nationalsozialistischer Musterbetrieb.

**NS-Parteimitglieder.** Nazi Party members. *See* Mitglieder.

**NS-Rasse- und politisches Amt.** *See* Rassenpolitisches Amt der NSDAP.

**NSRB.** *See* Nationalsozialistischer Rechtswahrerbund.

**NS-Rechtswahrerbund.** *See* Nationalsozialistischer Rechtswahrerbund; NS-Juristenbund.

**NS-Reichsbund für Leibesübungen.** (NSRL) National Socialist Reich Sports League.

**NS-Reichskriegerbund Kyffhäuser.** (NSRKBK) National Socialist Reich League for War Veterans. Originally for World War I veterans; in 1934 it became an SA reserve.

**NS-Reiterkorps.** (NSRK) National Socialist Riding Corps. Sponsored equestrian events, then trained Wehrmacht and Waffen-SS cavalry units.

**NSRK.** *See* NS-Reiterkorps.

**NS-RKB.** *See* Nationalsozialistcher Reichskriegerbund.

**NSRKBK.** *See* NS-Reichskriegerbund Kyffhäuser.

**NSRL.** *See* NS-Reichsbund für Leibesübungen.

**NS-Schwesternschaft.** *See* Braune Schwestern; Lebensborn; Nationalsozialistische Schwesternschaft; Nationalsozialistische Volkswohlfahrt; NSV-Schwesternschaft.

**NS-Studentenbund.** *See* Nationalsozialistischer Deutscher Studentenbund.

**NSV.** *See* Nationalsozialistische Volkswohlfahrt.

**NS-Volkswohlfahrt.** *See* Nationalsozialistische Volkswohlfahrt.

**NSV-Schweinchen.** Piglet of the National Socialist pig-slop collection. Image on propaganda poster naming kitchen waste as suitable pig fodder to be collected as a public welfare measure. Printed on the poster were the words: "I eat potato peels, vegetables, salad and fruit, but not chemicals, cleansers, and spices."

**NSV-Schwesternschaft.** National Socialist Public Welfare Nurses Organization. *See also* Braune Schwestern; Lebensborn; Nationalsozialistische Volkswohlfahrt.

***numerus clausus.*** Closed number. Latin phrase indicating quota of Jewish students allowed to attend university in prewar Germany, and other nations.

***numerus relativus.*** Relative number. Latin phrase indicating quota of Jews allowed to work in government offices and professions before the exclusionary race laws; could not exceed the relative number of Jews in the population.

**"Nur für Juden."** "For Jews only." Sign painted on park benches and other designated areas for Jews before the forced deportations.

**Nürnberg.** Nuremberg. City in Germany, the spiritual home of the Nazi movement. The city was awarded the honoring epithet "die Stadt der Reichsparteitage" (the city of the Reich Party rallies). Nuremberg was also one of five Führer cities (Führer-Städte). *See also* Parteitagsgelände; Reichsparteitag.

**Nürnberger Gesetze.** Nuremberg laws. *See also* Nürnberger Judengesetze.

**Nürnberger Judengesetze.** The Nuremberg Jew Laws. The racial laws of autumn 1935. Three laws promulgated at the Nuremberg Nazi rallies were the Reichsbürgergesetz (Reich Citizenship Act), defining citizenship and excluding Jews; the Blutschutzgesetz (Blood Protection Act), forbidding marriage and other contact between Jews and Germans; and the Reichsflaggengesetz (Reich Flag Law), forbidding Jews to fly the German flag. Jews and Gypsies had no longer legally protected status in the Third Reich, and could not become German citizens under any circumstances and could not employ as housemaids German women younger than forty-five.

**Nürnberger Rassengesetze.** Nuremberg Race Laws. *See also* Nürnberger Judengesetze.

**NZ.** *See* Nichtzigeuner.

# O

---

**obdachlos durch Luftangriff.** *See* ausgebombt.

**Oberabschnitt.** Upper sector. Major regional division of the SS. Equivalent to a military district of the armed forces. *See* Wehrkreis.

**Oberaufseherin.** Female overseer. In administrative offices and at the camps.

**Oberbefehlshaber der Luftwaffe.** Commander in Chief of the Air Force. Position held by Göring. *See also* Reichsmarschall.

**Oberbefehlshaber des Heeres.** (OBH, OdH) Commander in Chief of the Army. One of Hitler's titles. *See also* Oberster Gerichtsherr.

**Oberdienstleiter.** A title indicating high rank in the central hierarchy of the Nazi Party in Berlin.

**Oberdonau.** Upper Danube. Name for the region formed in 1939, belonging to Austria.

**Oberfehlshaber West.** (OB West) General headquarters for the Western Front.

**Oberfeldkommandantur.** (OFK) High command in the field.

**Obergau.** Upper district. Largest organizational unit of the Bund Deutscher Mädel and Jungmädelbund.

**Obergebiet.** Upper district. Largest organizational unit of the Hitler Youth, comprising several geographic areas.

**Obergericht.** Appellate court. Court system Germans established in the Generalgouvernement.

**Obergruppenführer.** (OGruf) General of the Infantry, Artillery, and so on. Called lieutenant general in the United States Army.

**Obergruppenführer-SS.** (OGruf-SS) SS general.

**Oberhäftling.** Chief prisoner. Inmate with special functions in the concentration camps.

**Oberjude.** Head Jew. The Head of the Jewish Council. *See* Judenrat.

**Oberkapo.** Chief overseer. Head Kapo and usually most brutal of all prisoner Kapos at a concentration camp.

**Oberkommando der Kriegsmarine.** (OKM) Navy High Command.

**Oberkommando der Luftwaffe.** (OKL) Air Force High Command.

**Oberkommando der Wehrmacht.** (OKW) Armed Forces High Command.

**Oberkommando des Heeres.** (OKH) Army High Command.

**Obermajdan.** The railway station at the Treblinka death camp, disguised as a sleepy little village.

**Oberschule.** High school. One of the two new secondary school types after the 1938 German school reform that made schools nationally and ideologically uniform and replaced the former Realgymnasium. *See also* Aufbauschule; Grundschule; Hauptschule; Höhere Lehranstalten; Oberschule (für Mädchen); Oberstufe der Volksschule.

**Oberschule (für Mädchen).** High school (for girls).

**Oberschütze.** Private first class. In the SS.

**Oberschwester.** Chief nurse, nun. Title of the commandant of the women's camp at Ravensbrück.

**Oberste Nationale Sportbehörde für die deutsche Kraftfahrt.** (ONS) Highest authority in German national motor sports.

**Oberster Befehlshaber der Wehrmacht.** (Oberst. Bef. Wehrm.) Supreme Commander of the Armed Forces. Hitler's title during World War II. *See also* Oberster Gerichtsherr.

**Oberste Reichsbehörden.** Supreme Reich authorities. Different governmental authorities each with a specific mandate who operated largely independent of each other and often in competition. Order of authority following Hitler: Hermann Göring, Heinrich Himmler, Rudolf Hess (until his flight to Scotland in 1941), and Martin Bormann.

**Oberste Reichsleitung der NSDAP.** (OK) Highest leadership in the Party.

**Oberster Gerichtsherr.** Supreme Legal Authority. On April 26, 1942, the last session of the German Reichstag affirmed Hitler as supreme legal authority. He was already the leader of the nation, of all the German peoples, Commander in Chief of the Armed Forces, Supreme War Lord, Leader of the Nazi Party, Supreme Leader of the SA, and Commander in Chief of the Army.

**Oberster Kriegsherr.** Supreme War Lord. Another of Hitler's titles. *See also* Oberster Gerichtsherr.

**Oberster Prüfungshof für Volkszugehörigkeitsfragen.** (O.P.) Highest examination court for questions of national (German) belonging.

**Oberster SA-Führer.** (Osaf) Supreme SA Leader. In 1926, Hitler was established thus in Munich. *See also* Oberster Gerichtsherr.

**Oberstes Parteigericht.** Supreme Nazi Party Court.

**Oberstufe der Volksschule.** People's middle school. Grades 5–8 in the Nazi education system.

**Obersturmführer.** (OstF) First Lieutenant.

**OBH.** *See* Oberbefehlshaber des Heeres.

**Objektivität.** Objectivity. Seen negatively as an attitude, identifying with intellectualism and liberalism, that aims at unbiased appraisal instead of orienting itself only in regard to the interest of the German nation.

**Obmann.** Chairman, head man. Head of the Jewish Council in the ghettos. Also, appointed representative, supervisor. Used in combination with other words; for example, Kreisobmann (district leader).

**OBW.** *See* Ostdeutsche Bautischlerei-Werkstätte.

**OB West.** *See* Oberfehlshaber West.

**Ochsenkopf.** Ox head. Code name for German 1943 offensive in Tunisia.

**Odal.** *See Monatsschrift für Blut und Boden.*

**Odal-Rune.** Norse rune standing for family, togetherness of the same race, same blood. Placed on Nazi badges of ethnic Germans and used by volunteer mountain division Prince Eugen and the SS reconnaissance units.

**oder Vertreter im Amt.** (o.V.i.A.) Or office deputy/representative. Salutation in official correspondence.

**Odessa.** *See* Organisation der ehemaligen SS-Angehörigen.

**OdH.** *See* Oberbefehlshaber des Heeres.

**Odin.** The god of light in Norse mythology. Also seen as the leader of warriors. Parallel figure used in Nazi propaganda for Hitler in his position as the leader of the German people.

**Offenbarungsmensch.** Negative racial type. Associated with Asians, one of six racial types according to Ludwig Ferdinand Clauss, Head of the Rasseamt. *See also Rasse und Seele.*

**Offenbarungstyp.** *See Rasse und Seele.*

**öffentliche Luftwarnung.** (öLW) Public air-raid warning.

**öffentlicher Luftalarm.** Public air alarm. *See* öffentliche Luftwarnung.

**Offizierlager.** (Oflag, Offlag) Officer camp. Prisoner-of-war camp for officers.

**Of(f)lag.** *See* Offizierlager.

**Oflag IV c.** Officer Camp IV c. *See also* Colditz.

**OFK.** *See* Oberfeldkommandantur.

**OGruf.** *See* Obergruppenführer.

**OGruf-SS.** *See* Obergruppenführer-SS.

**OGW.** *See* Gesamtorganisation der gewerblichen Wirtschaft.

**ohne jede Trübung.** Without any trouble. SS relationship with the Wehrmacht in regard to murdering Jews in eastern Europe.

**OKH.** *See* Oberkommando des Heeres.

**Okkupationskommando.** Occupation Command. German occupation authorities.

**OKL.** *See* Oberkommando der Luftwaffe.

**OKM.** *See* Oberkommando der Kriegsmarine.

**OKW.** *See* Oberkommando der Wehrmacht.

**Olga.** Code name for the Communications Office at the Supreme Command of Armed Forces Headquarters in Ohrdruf.

**Ölsardinenmanier.** Sardine method. Slang for Einsatzkommando technique for mass murder of Jews. The first victims were forced to lie down in a pit and were shot. Then the next layer of victims would be forced to lie on top of the earlier victims with their heads at the latter's feet. This method would be repeated until the entire pit was filled with corpses.

**öLW.** *See* öffentliche Luftwarnung.

**Olympia.** Leni Riefenstahl propaganda documentary film of the 1936 Berlin Olympics.

**Omakaitse.** Estonian nationalist and antisemitic group who collaborated with the Wehrmacht in the German conquest of Estonia. Beginning in 1941, under SS-Obersturmbannführer Martin Sandberger, Sonderkommando 1a of Einsatzgruppe A and Omakaitse units murdered hundreds of Estonian Jews. Starting in the fall of 1942, tens of thousands of Jews were sent to Estonian slave-labor camps from other areas under Nazi rule. When they could no longer work, these Jews were killed; others died of disease, hunger, and torture.

**OMI.** *See* Ostministerium.

**ONS.** *See* Oberste Nationale Sportbehörde für die deutsche Kraftfahrt.

**O.P.** *See* Oberster Prüfungshof für Volkszugehörigkeitsfragen.

**Operation Himmler.** *See* Unternehmen Himmler.

**Opfer.** Victim, sacrifice. Voluntary sacrifice, later coerced, by each German on behalf of Germany; in 1941 and 1943, any fallen German soldier; in 1942 expressly limited to German soldiers who died on the Eastern Front.

**Opfer der Arbeit.** Victim of work. National Socialist benefit fund for injured workers.

*Opfer der Vergangenheit.* Victims of the Past. Sound sequel to the documentary film *Erbkrank*. *See also* Erbkrank.

*Opferdienst der deutschen Frau.* Sacrificial Service of the German Woman. National Socialist publication for German woman edited by Elsbeth Zander. Contained guidelines for how women could best serve their family and their country.

**Opferessen.** Sacrificial meal. *See* Eintopf.

**Opferring.** Sacrificial Circle. Organization of NSDAP candidates in Alsace; later, those who were not Party members, as well as inactive Party members, who could do honorary Party duties by paying money.

**Opfer-Rune.** Sacrifice rune. Symbolic of self-sacrifice. Associated with Nazi Party members who died in the 1923 Munich Putsch.

**Opfersonntag.** Sacrifice Sunday. *See* Eintopfsonntag.

**Opferwilligkeit.** Self-sacrifice, devotion. The government made repeated wartime appeals for self-sacrifice of all Germans.

**Oppositionsgeist.** Spirit of opposition. Rationale for condemning Russian Jews to death.

**Optik der Preise.** Price perspective. The apparent level of prices.

**Optik des Krieges.** Aspect of war. Term used to conceal the war labor draft.

**OR.** *See* Oberste Reichsleitung der NSDAP.

**Oradour-sur-Glane.** French town where, in June 1944 at the time of the Normandy invasion, the French Resistance killed several German soldiers and blew up a railway bridge ten kilometers distant in an attempt to slow the movement of an SS armored division toward the front. On June 10, elements of the SS regiment Der Führer, a unit of Das Reich Second Panzer Division, entered the village and ordered the residents to assemble on the fairground. Men were herded into barns and garages, the women and children into the church; 642 men, women, and children were machine-gunned, and then the Germans burned the whole village. *See also* Sperrle-Befehl.

**Orchester des Führers.** Führer's orchestra. *See also* Nationalsozialistisches Reichs-Symphonieorchester.

**Orden.** Order, designation. Nazis, as part of the faith community believing in the leader (Führer), and the SS as the Order of Good Blood (Orden guten Blutes).

**Orden Pour le Mérite.** Order for merit. The Prussian army's award for bravery from 1740; also German army award for bravery through World War I.

**Ordensburgen.** Order castles. Advanced school for Adolf Hitler school graduates. Three institutions (in Krössinsee, Vogelsang, Sonthofen) for the education of the Nazi elite, formed in 1936 using the ancient model of the German Order of Knights. *See also* Adolf-Hitler-Schulen; Nationalpolitische Erziehungsanstalten.

**Ordensjunker.** Order Junkers (lords). Graduates of the Adolf Hitler schools. *See also* Ordensburgen.

**Ordensstaat.** Order state. Alfred Rosenberg's political model of the state.

**Ordnertruppen.** Control Troops. Hitler's Nazi strong-arm squads used in the 1920s to protect Nazi meetings. Absorbed into the SA in 1921.

**Ordnungsdienst.** Order service. *See also* jüdischer Ordnungsdienst.

**Ordnungsmacht.** Order Force. The German Reich as the ruling power of Europe. *See also* Europäische Neuordnung.

**Ordnungspolizei.** (Orpo) Order Police. Regular police, consisted of Schutz-polizei (uniformed police) and Gendarmerie (rural police). Some units were involved in the deportation of Jews to the death camps and in mass murders. *See also* Aktion Reinhard; Polizei.

**Ordnungsschaffer.** One who establishes order. Euphemism for SS.

**Organisation der ehemaligen SS-Angehörigen.** (Odessa) Organization of Former SS Officers. A secret organization that aided SS members in their escape from justice after World War II.

**Organisation der SS Angehörige.** *See* Organisation der ehemaligen SS-Ange-hörigen.

**Organisation Escherisch.** (Orgesch) Rightist paramilitary organization during the Weimar Republic organized by Dr. Georg Escherisch. Acted as a military reserve for Weimar's armed forces.

**Organisation Schmelt.** An organization led by SS officer Albrecht Schmelt to co-ordinate Jewish forced labor in Polish ghettos and forced-labor camps, involving more than 50,000 prisoners. In 1943 Himmler decided to deport these prisoners to Auschwitz.

**Organisation Standartenführer Blobel.** Colonel Blobel Organization. Unit established by Reinhard Heydrich to eradicate all traces of mass murders, under the command of Paul Blobel, head of Einsatzkommando 4A, Einsatzgruppe C.

**Organisation Todt.** (OT) Todt Organization. Vast public works and slave labor agency established in 1938 by Fritz Todt (in February 1940 he was appointed Minister for Weapons and Munitions) to build strategic highways, military installations, and rear-area security. The organization used more than 1.4 million men, about 80 percent non-Germans, forced laborers, prisoners of war, and Jewish and non-Jewish slave labor. In February 1942, Todt was killed in an air accident and was succeeded by Albert Speer, who increased the size and activities of the organization, which was renamed Front-Todt in the fall of 1944.

**Organisation tot.** Dead organization. Soldiers' slang during the final war years, referring to the increasing disorganization and red tape in the German army.

**Organisation Ukrainischer Nationalisten.** (OUN) Organization of Ukrainian Nationalists.

**organisch.** Organic. Synonymous with the worldview of National Socialism, belonging biologically to the German nation.

**organisieren.** To organize. During the war, meaning to procure items that were only available through connections. In soldiers' slang, to steal; in concentration camps, to find or trade for material to survive.

**Organschaft.** Germanization for Kartell (cartel).

**Orgesch.** *See* Organisation Escherisch.

**Orpo.** *See* Ordnungspolizei.

**Orter.** Observer. Military tactical observer.

**Ortsbauernführer.** Local leader of the Farmers' Organization. *See also* Reichsnährstand.

**Ortsgruppe.** Local group. Subdivision of a district; consisting of 1,500 to 3,000 families.

**Ortsgruppenleiter.** District Party Group Leader. Nazi Party official subordinate to a Kreisleiter, itself subordinate to a Gauleiter.

**Ortsheimstättenverwalter.** Local supervisor of housing. Representative or officer in charge of housing for those Germans who had been evacuated or bombed out.

**Ortskommandant.** Local commander. Officer in charge of public security and management of an area occupied by German army troops.

**Ortsstützpunkt.** Local concentration point. Military combat base.

**Ortsunterkunft.** Local lodgings. Billeting of troops during war; also for security purposes, a heading on field correspondence purposely avoiding reference to the place of origin.

**Osaf.** *See* Oberster SA-Führer.

**OST.** *See* Ostabzeichen.

**Ostabzeichen.** (OST) East badge. The emroidered square that Soviets were forced to display when performing forced labor in Germany during the war.

*Ostara.* A series of antisemitic pamphlets published by Lanz von Liebenfels between 1907 and 1910. Hitler bought these regularly, and in 1909 he sought out Lanz and asked for back copies.

**Ostarbeiter.** East worker. Polish and Soviet forced laborers, mostly Ukrainian, working in German companies during the war. They wore a badge (*see* Ostabzeichen) on their clothing.

**Ostaufbau.** Constuction of the east. Himmler plan for the ultimate solution of the Jewish problem. *See also* Generalplan Ost.

**Ostbahn.** East railroad. Polish railway system widely used by the Germans to deport Jews and other people to death camps for mass murder.

**ostbaltisch.** East Baltic. One of the six races that allegedly comprised the Germans. Characteristics were large nose, small face, dark hair, and slender, as well as loving the homeland and being heroic. *See* dinarisch; fälisch; nordisch; ostische Rasse; westisch.

**Ostbataillone.** East battalions. *See also* Ost-Hiwis.

**Ostdeutsche Bau-Gesellschaft.** East German Construction Company. Company using forced labor to build concentration camps in Germany and Poland.

**Ostdeutsche Baustoffwerke.** East German Construction Material Factory. Provided construction material for concentration camps, including Auschwitz. Part of the SS economic empire involved in slave labor of Jews, Poles, and others.

**Ostdeutsche Bautischlerei-Werkstätte.** (OBW) East German Workshops for Carpentry Construction. Warsaw-Ghetto factory.

**Ostdeutscher Befreiungskampf.** East German struggle for liberty. Justification for Germany's attack on Poland in September 1939, setting off World War II. *See also* Krieg.

**Osteinsatz.** Support for the east. Service obligation of German youth to work in the German-occupied zones. It included tens of thousands of Hitler Youth boys who helped with the harvest, instructed racial Germans in the German language, and in close collaboration with the SS helped expel Poles from their farms. It also included BDM girls over sixteen, who were placed as school assistants to help teachers and to promote ideological training for Germans outside of Germany. *See also* Volksdeutscher.

**Ostermond.** April.

**Ostfeldzug.** Eastern campaign. Propaganda for the war of conquest and destruction of the Soviet Union.

**Osthilfe.** Help for the east. German subsidies granted, between 1928 and 1937, to areas east of the Elbe River.

**Ost-Hiwis.** Eastern volunteers. Ukrainians, Estonians, Latvians, and Lithuanians who volunteered to help the SS. *See also* Hilfswillige.

**Osti.** *See* Ostindustrie GmbH.

**Ostindustrie GmbH.** (Osti) East Industry Ltd. SS organization ran factories in Generalgouvernement, exploiting mostly Jewish labor. Under the direction of Odilo Globocnik.

**ostische Rasse.** Alpine race. One of the six races that allegedly comprised the Germans. Characteristics were large nose, small face, dark hair, and slender, as well as loving the homeland and being heroic. *See* dinarisch; fälisch; nordisch; ostbaltisch; westisch.

**Ostjuden.** Eastern Jews; Jews of eastern Europe; Jewish immigrants from eastern Europe.

**Ostkinder.** Children from the east. Polish children who, after testing, were deemed racially suitable to be raised German. They were taken after their parents were killed or stolen from the homes of parents or guardians, from orphanages, and, late in the war, from public schools in German-occupied Poland and brought to Germany for Germanization. Those who did not pass the racial tests were sent to Auschwitz to be killed. *See also* Deutsche Heimschulen; Eignungsprüfer; Lebensborn; Ostkinder; Wiedereindeutschung.

**Ostkolonisation.** East colonization. German policy to transform Poland into a nation of slaves.

**Ostkrieg.** Eastern war. *See also* Ostfeldzug.

**Ostland.** East land. German civilian administrative unit controlling the Baltic countries and parts of Poland and Belorussia.

**Ostlandnot.** Eastern territories (of Germany) privation. *See also* (blutende) Grenze.

**Ostmark.** Eastern frontier. From Bavarian "Ostmark." Name for Austria from 1938. Previously Österreich (eastern Reich).

**Ostmärkische Reichsgaue.** Eastern frontier Reich districts. Austrian districts annexed by Germany in 1938. *See* Ostmark.

**Ostmedaille.** East medal. Medal for service in the German winter campaign of 1941–1942 in Russia. Soldiers used dozens of different slang words for this medal.

**Ostmensch.** Eastern man. Eastern European Slavs who were seen as inferior. Nazi racial policy divided all European nationalities into superior and inferior groups.

**Ostministerium.** (OMI) (Reich) Ministry for the (Occupied) Eastern Territories. Created in 1941 under Alfred Rosenberg.

**Ostpolitik.** Eastern policy. Part of German foreign policy to obtain extra territory for the German people by any means.

**Ostraum.** Eastern space. Areas of Poland and the Soviet Union where the residents would be deported in order to make room for Germans who would settle and Germanize the territory.

**Ostraumlösung.** Eastern space solution. *See also* Ostraum.

**Ostsiedler.** Eastern settler. German colonists in eastern Europe.

**Ostsiedlung.** Eastern settlement. The German colonization of eastern Europe.

**Osttruppen.** East troops. Low-level German military units comprised of eastern Europeans.

**O'Stubaf.** *See* SS-Obersturmbannführer in Appendix: Waffen-SS Ranks.

**Ostvölker.** Eastern peoples.

**Ostwall.** East wall. Hitler proposed that even after a German victory in Europe, a defensive wall along the Urals would have to be built to stop any invasion of Asiatics. It would consist of German soldier-farmers inhabiting the area and engaged in a permanent border struggle.

**Ostwinter.** Eastern winter. The harsh winter during the German campaign against the Soviet Union.

**ostwürdig.** East-worthy. Those certified as racially of good Aryan stock and fit to settle in the east.

**Ostzeit.** Eastern era. *See also* Osteinsatz.

**OT.** *See* Organisation Todt.

**OT-Mann.** Organisation Todt man. *See also* Organisation Todt.

**Ottergerät.** Otter machine. Minesweeper device that cuts mines loose and, when they surface, allows their destruction. *See* Räumboot.

**Otto.** Code name for invasion of Austria.

**Otto-Programme.** Otto programs. Wehrmacht program to develop railroads and roads from Germany and eastern Europe to the Soviet border, completed in May 1941.

**OUN.** *See* Organisation Ukrainischer Nationalisten.

**o.V.i.A.** *See* oder Vertreter im Amt.

# P

P. *See* Polen.

Pak. *See* Panzerabwehrkanone.

P-akte. *See* Personalakte.

Paladin des Führers. Protector of the Führer. Honorary name for Göring.

Palast-Barlow. *See* Braunes Haus.

Palazzo Kitschi. Kitsch palace. Derisive name for the Museum of German Art in Munich.

Palestina-Treuhandstelle zur Beratung deutscher Juden GmbH. (PAL-TREU.) The Palestine Trust Society for Advice to German Jews, Inc. Organization set up after a 1933 agreement between the Reich Ministry of the Economy and German and Palestinian Zionists that encouraged German Jews to emigrate to Palestine by permitting the export of some of their assets. This transfer agreement, also called in Hebrew, Haavarah Agreement, enabled more than 60,000 German Jews to survive in Palestine. The Nazis hated the Jewish Zionists but exploited their one point of agreement, that is, the removal of Jews from Germany.

PALTREU. *See* Palestina-Treuhandstelle zur Beratung deutscher Juden GmbH.

Panzer. (Pz) Armor, armored, tank, mechanized.

Panzerabwehrkanone. (Pak) Antitank cannon. Antitank gun.

*(Der) Panzerbär.* The Armored Bear. Propaganda magazine of the German military. The last Berlin newspaper to publish as Berlin fell to the Soviets in April 1945.

**Panzerbefehlwagen.** (Pz-Bef) Command tank.

**Panzerbrecher.** Tank buster. Aircraft specializing in destroying tanks.

**Panzerbüchse.** Bazooka. Antitank gun.

**Panzerbunker.** Tank bunker. Dug-in tank.

**Panzerdivision.** (PzD) Armored division.

**Panzerfaust.** Tank fist. Bazooka. Simple, mass-produced antitank weapon, introduced in 1944.

**Panzergrenadier.** Motorized infantry, armored infantry.

**Panzerkampfabzeichen.** Tank-battle medal. Medal for members of the tank troops introduced in 1940.

**Panzerkampfwagen.** (PzKpfW) Armored war vehicle. Tank.

**Panzerknacker.** *See* Panzerbrecher.

**Panzerkorps.** (PzK) Armored Corps.

**Panzerkraftwagen.** (Pkw, Pzkw) Armored cars, tank.

**Panzerkreuzer.** Pocket battleship. The most notable: *Lützow, Admiral Scheer,* and *Admiral Graf Spee.*

**Panzer-Nachrichten.** Armored communications. Signal troops assigned to armored units.

**Panzerschiff.** *See* Panzerkreuzer.

**Panzerschreck.** Tank shock. Psychological impact of being attacked by tanks.

**Panzersperre.** Tank stopper.

**Panzervernichtungsabzeichen.** Medal for destroying a tank. Introduced in 1942 and awarded after destruction of an enemy tank in close combat. When five enemy tanks were destroyed, a gold medal was awarded.

**Parasit.** Parasite. Dehumanizing concept applied to Jews that helped lead, emotionally and pragmatically, to the use of insecticide in the form of Zyklon gas on Jewish human beings. The same analogy was made in France and the United States but without the same results. In the eighteenth and nineteenth centuries, Johann Gottfried von Herder and Paul de Lagarde also compared Jews to parasites.

*Parole der Woche.* Slogan of the Week. Weekly publication of the Nazi Party, including antisemitism and propaganda.

**Parteiabzeichen der NSDAP.** Party pin. Badge for all members of the NSDAP.

**Parteiamtliche Prüfungskommission zum Schutze des NS-Schrifttums.** (PPK) Official Party Department to Protect Nazi Writing. Established in 1934, this body was to monitor German publications to ensure their adherence to Nazi ideology. Its director had the power to confiscate or seize books directly through the Gestapo. Issued the NS-Bibliographie.

**Parteibauten.** Party Building. Nazi Party headquarters in Munich. *See also* Bauten des Führers.

**Parteigau.** (Nazi) Party district.

**Parteigenosse.** (Pg) Party comrade. Member of the Nazi Party.

**Parteigerichte.** Nazi Party courts.

**Parteigerichtsbarkeit.** Party Law Court. Disciplinary court for members of the NSDAP.

**Parteigeschäftsführer.** (Nazi) Party Business Manager. Philipp Bouhler held this position and later was head of Hitler's Chancellery and helped direct the Nazi Euthanasia Program.

**Parteikanzlei.** Party Chancellery. From 1941, the Nazi Party bureaucracy was directed by Martin Bormann who in effect controlled the Party and helped direct and effect the radical racist, antisemitic, and anti-church policies of the regime. *See also* (Der) Führer.

**Parteiprogramm.** *See* Appendix: Parteiprogramm: Fünfundzwanzig Punkte des nationalsozialistischen Programms.

**Parteistaat.** Party state. Weimar Republic. Once the Enabling Act was passed in March 1933, Hitler dissolved political parties and destroyed civil liberties. On July 14, 1933, a one-party state was ordained in a statement that forbade the formation of any other party: "The National-Socialist German Workers' Party constitutes Germany's only political party."

**Parteitag.** *See* Reichsparteitag.

**Parteitagsgelände.** *See* Reichsparteitagsgelände.

**Partisanen.** Partisans. Under the pretext of fighting partisans, the German army in the east killed civilians, many of them Jews. Real partisans were called gangs. *See also* Banden.

**Partisanenbekämpfung.** War against the partisans. *See also* Partisanen.

**Partisanjäger.** Partisan hunters. Wehrmacht units created to combat partisans and kill Jews and non-Jews in eastern Europe.

**Passierschein.** Safe-conduct pass. Document issued to ghetto Jews whom Nazis determined had to conduct business valuable to the Third Reich outside of the ghetto.

**Passo Romano.** Roman step. German goose step introduced into the Italian army by Mussolini in the 1930s.

**Pastorius.** Code name for Germany's first attempt to land spies in the United States in 1942, in Long Island and Florida to block American airplane production by sabotaging aluminum production. American Intelligence had been forewarned.

**Paukenschlag.** Drumbeat. Code name of German naval attack against Allied shipping in U.S. waters and the Caribbean in 1942.

**(dicker) Paul.** Fat Paul. Army slang for Russian 32-ton tank.

**Paulusbund.** (St.) Paul Union. Organization of Jewish converts to Protestantism.

**Pawiak-Juden.** Pawiak Jews. Jews imprisoned in the Pawiak jail in Warsaw where they were arrested and held to be used in prisoner exchanges. *See also* Austauschjuden.

**Pazifist.** Pacifist. Name for Germans who were opposed to Hitler's war policies.

**P.B.** *See* politische Beurteilung.

**PDL.** *See* Provisorisches DuLag.

**PeCe.** *See* Polyvinylchloride.

**Peenemünde.** Location of the Third Reich's Rocket Research and Development Center under the direction of Dr. Wernher von Braun. Also, sub-camp of Ravensbrück concentration camp.

**Peitsche und Zucker.** Whip and sugar. Reinhard Heydrich's policy toward Czechs of reward for cooperation and punishment for lack thereof.

**Pelle.** Peel. Figure on propaganda poster who encouraged the German population to eat unpeeled boiled potatoes for more efficient food consumption.

**Perbunan.** Form of synthetic rubber. *See also* Bunawerke.

**Personalakte.** (P-akte) Personal file.

**Personenstandsverordnung der Wehrmacht.** *See* Ferntrauung.

**Persönlichkeit.** Personality. Germans of the same blood; replacing Individuum (individual), a word deemed un-German and Jewish.

**Peter.** Code name for German naval operation to mine the Arctic Sea in 1942.

**Pfahlbinden.** Tie to a pole. Form of punishment at Dachau and other camps where a prisoner would be tied by the wrist to a pole for hours and in some cases up to two days.

**Pfarrenbund.** *See* Pfarrernotbund.

**Pfarrernotbund.** Pastors' Emergency League. This organization, led by Martin Niemöller and Dietrich Bonhöffer, developed into the minority German Protestant Church (Bekennende Kirche, or Professing Church). Its members opposed Hitler but suffered from a high degree of antisemitism no less than the pro-Nazi churches.

**Pfeilkreuzlerpartei.** Arrow-Cross Party. Hungarian fascist party (Nyilaskeresztes Part) that collaborated with the German occupation forces.

**Pfleger.** Male nurse. Prisoner medical attendant at a concentration camp.

**Pflichtarbeit.** Service duty. Conscript labor.

**Pflichtausleseschule.** Obligatory selection school. *See also* Hauptschule.

**Pflichterfüllung.** Fulfillment of duty. Not to be self-sufficient, but to serve the German community.

**Pflichtgemeinschaft.** Compulsory syndicate.

**Pflichtjahr.** Obligatory-service year. From 1938, after their schooling, all German girls/young women under twenty-five years of age were required to serve for one year in homes or on farms (e.g., placed as au pair helpers in families with many children).

**Pfundspende.** Pound collection. Solicited contribution of money or one-pound food items. Part of the program Winterhilfswerk. *See also* Winterhilfswerk des deutschen Volkes.

**Pg.** *See* Parteigenosse.

**Pharaonengräber.** Pharaoh's tomb. Graves at concentration camp mass-murder sites.

**PHD.** *See* Polizeihilfsdienst.

**Phenolinjektion.** Phenol injection. Nazi means of killing by phenol injection into the heart.

**PHL.** *See* Polizeihaftlager.

**Physiognomie-Brigade.** Physiognomy Brigade. Gestapo unit in France whose role was to identify Jews.

**Pi.** *See* Pionier.

**PID.** *See* Presse- und Informationsdienst.

**Piepel.** Male concentration camp helper and prostitute.

**Pimpf.** Lad. Youngest member of the Deutsches Jungvolk of the Hitler Youth.

**Pimpfenprobe.** Test of German boys and girls before their swearing-in ceremony as members of Hitler Youth.

**Pionier.** (Pi) Pioneer. Wehrmacht engineer.

**Pionier der Arbeit.** Pioneer of work. Award for successful managing of a business or company; first given to munitions maker Gustav Krupp von Bohlen in 1940.

**Pionierschutzmannschaft.** Pioneer Security. Unit of the Technische Nothilfe in German-occupied regions comprised of volunteers recruited by the Germans from the local population.

**Piraten- und Gangstertum.** Pirates and gangsters. Nazi name for enemy nations; also for those who conducted bombing raids over Germany. *See also* Lufthunnen.

**Pitschen.** German-Polish frontier post where SS men, dressed as Poles, mounted a simulated attack. *See also* Unternehmen Himmler.

**PJ.** *See* politische Juden; polnische Juden.

**PK.** *See* Propaganda-Kompanien.

**Pkw.** *See* Panzerkraftwagen.

**PL.** *See* politische Leiter.

**Planamt.** *See* Planungsamt.

**planmäßig.** According to plan. Euphemism for brutal; also military euphemism for retreat.

**Planstudie 1939.** Preparatory study 1939. *See also* Fall Blau.

**Plantage.** Plantation. Area of Dachau reclaimed from swamp at the cost of many prisoner lives.

**Planungsamt.** Planning Office. Of the Rüstungsministerium, headed by Hans Kehrl. It prepared the plans for the Central Planning Office under Göring. *See also* Amt Zentrale Planung; Reichsminister(ium) für Rüstungs(aufgaben) und Kriegsproduktion.

**Plan Z.** *See* Z-Plan.

**plattfüßig.** Flat-footed. Derisive for Jews.

**Plattfußindianer.** Flatfoot Indians. Derisive for Jews, often used by Hans Frank, Governor-General of German-occupied Poland.

**Platzschutz.** Site protection. Airport defense.

**Plötzensee.** Berlin prison where between 1933 and 1945 more than 3,000 people were executed, including Communist resistance groups, members of the Kreisau Circle, participants of the July 20, 1944, plot to assassinate Hitler, and numerous foreign prisoners from German-occupied European countries.

**Plünderer.** Pillager, looter. SS and Wehrmacht term for Jews. Pretext for their murder.

**Plutobolschewismus.** Plutocratic bolshevism. The United Nations assembled to oppose Germany during World War II.

**Plutodemokratie.** Plutocratic democracy. Derogatory for western Allies: England and the United States

**Plutokraten.** Plutocrats. Capitalist enemies of Germany.

**Plutokratie.** Plutocracy. *See also* Plutodemokratie.

**P Null.** P zero. Derogatory term that SA members used before July 1934 for the Political Organization of the Nazi Party, abbreviated PO, which resembled P0. *See also* politische Organisation.

**PO.** *See* politische Organisation.

**PoFu.** *See* politischer Funktionär.

**Polarisierung.** Polarization. Propaganda technique creating a many-headed enemy threatening the German people; a plot led by Jews, democracies, and capitalists.

**Polen.** (P) Poles. The abbreviation P was placed on Polish prisoners' triangles. Also, P marked the badge worn by Poles working in Germany during World War II. *See also* Dreieckswinkel; Fremdarbeiter.

**Polenaktion.** Operation Poland. 1938 deportation of Polish Jews residing in Germany to Poland. Precipitated events leading to November 1938 Pogrom. *See also* Reichskristallnacht.

**Polenerlaß.** Polish decree. March 1940 regulation that marked Polish forced workers with a P.

**Polenfeldzug.** Campaign against Poland. The war against Poland in September 1939. *See* Krieg.

**polenisierte deutsche Kinder.** Polonized German children. Term for Polish children Nazis considered worthy of being Germanized. *See also* Eignungsprüfer; Lebensborn; Ostkinder; Wiedereindeutschung.

**Polenkinder.** Polish children. Polish children whom Nazis considered worthy of being Germanized. *See also* Lebensborn; Ostkinder; Wiedereindeutschung.

**Polen-Reservat Generalgouvernement.** Polish-Reserve General Government. Area in German-occupied Poland that the Third Reich used as a temporary reserve for unassimilated Poles.

**Polensonderlager.** Special camp for Poles. At Buchenwald concentration camp.

**Polentum.** Polish nation. Seen as a source of forced labor for Germany.

**Politikaster.** Derogatory for irresponsible politicians, especially during the Weimar Republic.

***Politische Aussprache: Führungsunterlagen Folge 3.*** Political Discussion: Educational Basis No. 3. The most outspoken issue of indoctrination literature issued by the German army, in 1944, stressing the importance of the German race and species. *See also* Richthefte des Oberkommandos der Wehrmacht.

**politische Bereitschaften.** Political Squads. Organization of Nazi thugs that developed into the SS. *See also* SS-Verfügungstruppen.

**politische Beurteilung.** (PB) Political assessment. Reports written about SS candidates.

**politische Gefangene.** Political prisoners. Political enemies of the Third Reich kept in camps, consisting of opposition-party members, former members of the Nazi Party, soldiers who deserted, soldiers who refused to serve, soldiers charged with theft, Foreign Legionnaires, political opponents, operators of hidden radios, those denounced to the Gestapo.

**politische Geheimpolizei der Sowjetunion.** (G.P.U.) Soviet Political Secret Police.

**politische Juden.** (PJ) Political Jews. Dutch Jews deported to camps.

**politische Organisation.** (PO) Political Organization. Political administration of the Nazi Party. *See also* politische Leiter.

**politischer Arbeiterzirkel.** Political Workers' Circle. Founding organization of the German Workers' Party that became the Nazi Party. Founded in November 1918 by Anton Drexler and Karl Harrer. In 1919, became the Deutsche Arbeiterpartei (German Workers' Party). In early 1920, it was renamed the Nationalsozialistische Deutsche Arbeiterpartei. *See also* Deutsche Arbeiterpartei; Nationalsozialistische Deutsche Arbeiterpartei.

**politischer Funktionär.** (PoFu) Political functionary.

**politische Leiter.** (PL) Political Leaders. Leaders of the thirty levels of the Nazi hierarchy.

**PVH.** *See* Politischer Vorbeugungshäftling. (PVH) Political prisoner incarcerated to prevent infractions or crimes against the German state.

**politischer Soldat.** Political soldier. The ideal new German man.

**politisches Abteilungsamt.** Political Branch. Gestapo unit within the concentration camps that crushed attempts at escape.

**Politisches Amt und Ministeramt.** Political Department and Ministerial Department. Sturmabteilung's management disbanded after the "Night of the Long Knives."

**politisch unzuverlässig.** (PU) Politically unreliable. Based on the law of March 7, 1933, the Reorganization of the Civil Service, Jewish government employees were removed from office. Next to be removed were politically suspicious government workers. *See also* Gesetz zur Wiederherstellung des Berufsbeamtentums.

**politsai.** Slang for detachments of Order Police. *See* Schutzmannschaft der Ordnungspolizei.

**Polizei.** Police. From 1936, a unified national police force was commanded by Himmler. This helped transform the SS into the power that ruled Germany. *See also* Ordungspolizei; Sicherheitspolizei.

**Polizeiattachés und Polizeiverbindungsführer der Sicherheitspolizei und des SD.** Police Attachés and Police Liaison Leaders of the Security Police and the SD. SD officials attached to German embassies around the world.

**Polizeigefängnis.** Police prison. One definition of Theresienstadt concentration camp. *See also* Theresienstadt.

**Polizeihaftlager.** (PHL) Police detention camp. Transit camps for Jews (e.g., Compiègne and Drancy in France).

**Polizeihauptamt.** Police Main Headquarters. Founded in 1936 under Himmler; responsible for the coordination of all common police, fire, coast guard, and civil-defense functions. *See also* Reichssicherheitshauptamt.

**Polizeihilfsdienst.** (PHD) Auxiliary Police.

**polizeiliches Durchgangslager Amersfoort.** Police transit camp at Amersfoort in the Netherlands.

**Polizeiliches Durchgangslager Hertogenbosch.** Police transit camp at Hertogenbosch in the Netherlands.

**Polizeiverordnung über das Auftreten der Juden in der Öffentlichkeit.** Police Decree regarding the Appearance of Jews in Public. November 28, 1938, order forcing Jews to register their place of residence and restricting freedom of movement in public.

**Polizeiverordnung über die Kennzeichnung der Juden.** Police Decree regarding the Marking of Jews. Of September 1, 1941. The obligatory wearing of the Star of David as identifying badges for Jews residing in the greater Reich.

**polnische Juden.** (PJ) Polish Jews. RSHA code name for the trains headed for death camps. *See also* politische Juden.

**polnische Wirtschaft.** Polish business. Poland and Poles seen as Germany's enemies.

**Polyvinylchloride.** (PeCe) Synthetic textile fiber.

**Posen-Konferenzen.** Posen (Poznan) Conferences. Himmler's October 4, 1943, talk before SS officers in which he described the situation in the fifth year of the war. After a brief history of the prior years of war, he indicated that a major German goal and proudest success was the extermination of the Jews.

**positive Kritik.** Positive criticism. Permitted and desired acknowledgment of achievements in all Third Reich cultural areas. Honest criticism was suppressed.

**positives Christentum.** Positive Christianity. Antisemitic Christianity, Nazi Christianity. According to Nazi ideology, positive Christians were Christians who supported Nazi ideology (i.e., purity of the Nordic race, the old pagan virtues, and the spirit of the hero). Point 24 of the 25 Points in the Nazi Program indicated that the Party was Christian but did not bind itself to any one particular Christian confession; that the Party fought against the "Jewish materialist spirit" and advocated "common good before individual good."

**Postschutz.** Postal Security. Force that protected post offices and communications. Absorbed into the Waffen-SS in 1942.

**Potsdam-Putsch.** Unsuccessful plan by some Reichswehr generals opposed to Hitler to seize the German government in 1932–1933.

**Pour le Mérite.** For merit. The German army's highest award for bravery.

**Pour le sémite.** For the semite. Ironic reference to the Jewish star.

**PPK.** *See* Parteiamtliche Prüfungskommission zum Schutze des nationalsozialistischen Schriftums.

**Präsident des Amtes Zentrale Planung.** President of the Office(s) of Central Planning. Another of Göring's titles. *See also* Reichsmarschall.

**Präsident des deutschen Reichstags.** President of the German Reichstag. Another of Göring's titles. *See also* Reichsmarschall.

**Präsident des Ministerrates für Reichsverteidigung.** President of the Ministry Council for Reich Defense. Another of Göring's titles. *See also* Reichsmarschall.

**Präsidialkabinett.** President's Cabinet. Hitler Chancellery for Chief of State.

**Präsidialkanzlei.** President's Chancellery. From August 1934, Hitler's office as President of Germany headed by State Secretary Otto Meissner.

**Preisprüfer.** Price checkers. Field examiners studying the costs of producers. *See* Reichskommissar für die Preisbildung.

**Preisstopverordnung.** (Preisst.V.O.) Price-Freeze Decree. Issued in the mid-1930s to prevent Germany's prices from rising.

**Preisst.V.O.** *See* Preisstopverordnung.

**Pressburg.** German for the Polish town Bratislava.

**Pressechef der Reichsregierung.** Publication Chief of the Reich Administration. Otto Dietrich's official government position.

**Presse- und Informationsdienst.** (PID) Press and Information Service. Published monthly information outlining important daily events of the past month.

**Preßstoff.** Pressed (plastic) material.

**Priesterblock.** Priest block. At Dachau, prisoner Block 26, where ministers and priests were housed.

**Primitivbauweise.** Primitive construction technique. Albert Speer recommended that concentration camp forced workers use inferior material and manual labor for construction.

**Prinz-Albrecht-Straße.** Prince Albert Street. From 1934 to 1945, name of the most feared street in Berlin. Headquarters of the Gestapo, the SS Reich Leadership, and the SS Security Service (SD, or Sicherheitsdienst des Reichsführers SS).

*Prinz Eugen.* Prince Eugen. German heavy cruiser.

**Prinz-Regentenstraße.** Prince-Regent Street. Location of Hitler's Munich apartment.

**Privilegierte.** (The) privileged. *See also* Mischehen.

**privilegierte Gefangene.** Privileged prisoners. British- and American-Jewish POWs were not treated well but were treated better than Russian-Jewish and Pol-ish-Jewish POWs and Jewish civilians.

**privilegierte Juden.** Privileged Jews. German Jews with Aryan German spouses or parents whose murder was postponed.

**pro forma sterben.** Regular death. Concentration camp prisoner who died while being held.

**Projekt 1061, 1062.** German plan to build long-range reconnaissance planes and bombers that could reach New York City. Several prototypes were built, the most notable, the Messerschmitt ME 264.

**proletarisch.** Proletarian. Nazi Germany was seen as fighting the plutocratic democracies and capitalist exploitation and therefore was proletarian.

**Promi.** Unofficial abbreviation for Reichsminister(ium) für Volksaufklärung und Propaganda. *See also* Reichsminister(ium) für Volksaufklärung und Propaganda.

**Prominente.** Celebrities. Notable individuals—because of their international rep-utation—who were privileged German and foreign prisoners in the concentration camps; for example, Kurt Schuschnigg, former Chancellor of Austria; Martin Niemöller, former submarine captain and German pastor; and Léon Blum, former Premier of France. Himmler planned to use them as bargaining chips near the end of World War II.

**Prominenten-Bunker.** Prominents' bunker. Location of privileged prisoners at Dachau. *See also* Prominente.

**Propaganda.** Propaganda. Measures to align public opinion in terms of political questions and National Socialist ideology.

**Propaganda-Kompanien.** (PK) Propaganda companies. Units of servicemen, formed in 1939, consisting of journalists, radio announcers, cameramen, and so forth, sent to the front to report optimistically on the war back to Germany for the press, radio, and weekly newsreels in movie theaters.

**Propaganda-Lager.** Propaganda camp. One of the many names for the (model) transit camp Theresienstadt.

**Propaganda-Ministerium.** Propaganda ministry. Popular expression for Reichs-minister(ium) für Volksaufklärung und Propaganda.

**Protektionsjuden.** Protected Jews. *See also* Aufenthaltslager.

**Protektorat Böhmen und Mähren.** Protectorate of Bohemia and Moravia. After 1939, German-occupied Czech lands of Bohemia and Moravia.

*Protokolle der Weisen von Zion.* The Protocols of the Elders of Zion. Infamous antisemitic forgery produced by the czarist secret police and first published in 1911.

**Provisorisches DuLag.** (PDL) Provisional transit camp.

**Provinz.** Province. Nazi administrative area.

**Prügel.** Beatings. *See also* Nebenstrafen.

**Prügelblatt.** Caning page. Form that recorded each beating in a concentration camp, with medical report on the inmate and name of the person in charge.

**Prügelbock.** *See* Bock.

**Prügelraum.** Caning room. Special room in the punishment bunker at Ravensbrück.

**Prügelregiment.** Caning regiment. The brutal administration of the Többens factory in the Warsaw-Ghetto.

**PU.** *See* politisch unzuverlässig.

**Punkte.** Points. Part of the ration card for wartime German clothing allowance.

**PVH.** *See* Politischer Vorbeugunshäftling.

**Pz.** *See* Panzer.

**PzD.** *See* Panzerdivision.

**PzK.** *See* Panzerkorps.

**PzKpfW.** *See* Panzerkampfwagen.

**Pzkw.** *See* Panzerkraftwagen.

# Q

**Quasselbude.** Prattle hangout. Derogatory for the parliament of the Weimar Republic.

**Quatschbude.** Rubbish den. *See also* Quasselbude.

**Querbeet.** Cross(garden) bed. Army slang for cross-country.

**Querschlag.** Slanting strike, offset blow. Element of a non-German race.

**Querschnittaufgabe.** Cross-sectional task. Related to several fields under the jurisdiction of different offices.

# R

**RAB.** *See* Reichsautobahnen.

**Rabulistik.** Sophistic linguistic cunning. Derogatory, ascribed to Jewish intellectuals.

**Rächer Röhms.** (RR) Röhm's avenger. Sign left on the bodies of SS leaders murdered in revenge killings in 1934 and 1935 by SA in reprisal for the "Night of the Long Knives." *See also* Nacht der langen Messer.

**RAD.** *See* Reichsarbeitsdienst.

**Radau-Antisemitismus.** Hooligan antisemitism. Jewish persecution in the tradition of east European pogroms with disorganized street violence.

**Rädelsführer.** Youth leaders. Negative for vociferous leaders of non-Nazi and anti-Nazi youth groups. They risked corporal punishment, forced labor, and concentration camp for youth.

**(der Kleine) Rädelsführer.** (The Little) Leader. Endearing term for the young Hitler depicted in school readers as a role model for young German children.

**"Räder müssen rollen für den Sieg!"** "Wheels have to turn for victory." From 1942, propaganda slogan of the Reich railway to discourage personal travel in favor of war transports. The slogan also applied to keeping the trains rolling that were used to deport thousands of Jews and other people to their deaths in concentration camps. *See also* Endlösung der Judenfrage; Generaldirektion der Ostbahn in Krakau.

**Radieschen.** Radishes. Air force slang for signal flares.

**Radikalinski.** Derisive for radical or leftist Nazi. *See also* Nacht der langen Messer.

**RADwJ.** *See* Reichsarbeitsdienst der weiblichen Jugend.

**raffendes Kapital.** Grabbing capital. Non-creative capital; finance as opposed to industrial capital. *See also* schaffendes Kapital.

**RAG.** *See* Reichsarbeitsgemeinschaft Heil- und Pflegeanstalten.

**Raisko.** IG Farben's forced-labor camp where female prisoners worked on agricultural projects to create artificial rubber. *See also* Auschwitz.

**Rajsko.** *See* Raisko.

**RAM.** *See* Reichsaußenminister.

**Rampe.** Ramp. Disembarkation platform at the death camp of Auschwitz-Birkenau, where deportees were unloaded and selection for life or death occurred. *See also* Selektion; Sonderzüge.

**Rand-Germane.** Border Teuton. Baltic-Germans.

**Randstaaten.** (Rd) Border states. States bordering on Germany (i.e, from 1918–1939).

**Rangfolgeliste.** Ranking list. Priority list for construction orders.

**Rangklassen und Dienstgrade.** Hierarchy. In the German armed forces and SS, ranks from Schütze or SS-Mann at the bottom to Generalfeldmarschall and Reichsführer at the top.

**Rano.** *See* Reichsarbeitsnachweis für Offiziere.

**Raphaelsverein.** Catholic League of St. Raphael. Organization of non-German Catholics.

**Rapportführer.** Reporting officer. SS official who reported directly to the concentration camp Lagerführer.

**RArM.** *See* Reichsarbeitsminister.

**RA.S., R.a.s.** *See* Rassenschänder.

**RASS.** *See* Reichsarzt SS.

**Rasse.** Race, kind, genus. A biological-mythical sense of a group with its own soul and will. The ambiguous concept of race was considered a positive for the Germans and a negative for all non-Germans. The Aryan-Nordic race consisted of Übermenschen, superior to all other races, and Untermenschen, the worst of whom were the Jews. They, among others, had to be killed off because they were a threat to the Nordic race.

**Rasse(n)amt.** Race Department. An agency of the SS, the Rasse(n)amt decided on the Aryan qualities of individuals belonging to conquered nations and their potential for Germanization. It was headed by Ludwig Ferdinand Clauss. *See also* Rasse und Seele; Rasse- und Siedlungshauptamt.

**rasse(n)bewußt.** Race conscious. Conscious of the value of one's own (German) race.

**rasseecht.** Of genuine race. Positive adjective for everything that was in accord with the Nazi ideal of the Nordic racial type.

**rasseeigen.** Typical for a race. Used positively (for Germans) or negatively (for others, particularly Jews) to describe racially common characteristics.

**Rasse(n)feind.** Race enemy. Individual or group opposed to the racial hierarchy according to National Socialism.

**rassefremd.** Race foreign, race alien. Incompatible with the German race. Jewish.

**rasse(n)gebunden.** Shaped by, bound to, race. *See also* rasseeigen.

**Rasse(n)gedanke.** Racial thought, race idea. Basic Nazi belief that a people's culture was determined by race and genetic inheritance. Also, the absolute priority of the biologically determined, culturally valuable, pure Aryan-Nordic-German race and the Reich's programs leading to this situation.

**Rassegefühl.** Race feeling. To understand the innate superiority and value of the German race.

**Rass(en)genosse.** Racial comrade. Of the same race. Applied negatively and almost exclusively to Jews in contrast to Germans.

**rassegesund.** Racially healthy. National Socialist racial way of thinking, in opposition to a Jewish-individualist way of thinking.

**Rasseinstinkt.** Race instinct. Special feeling for the unique aspects of one's own (German) race.

**Rassejude und Bekenntnisjude.** Jew by race and religion.

**Rassekern.** Race core. The pure-race (German) proportion in a racially mixed people.

**Rassekreis.** Race circle. According to National Socialist thinking, the Darwinian concept of racial rise and decline to be altered to achieve a perfect (German) race through controlled genetic selection and breeding.

**rasselos.** Raceless. Not of pure race, without race consciousness. Non-German/non-Nordic.

**Rasse(n)mensch.** Person of good race. A person of pure and healthy racial stock, a Germanic or Nordic person, in contrast to an Untermensch (subhuman person).

**Rassenangst.** Race fear. Fear of the pollution of one's race by miscegenation or by genetically flawed persons.

**Rassenaufbau.** *See* Volksaufbau.

**Rassenbewußtsein.** Race consciousness. Pride in one's own race. Awareness of and willingness to act on behalf of the German race.

**rassenbezogenes Denken.** Racial thinking.

**Rassenbrei.** Racial stew. Hybrid or mixture. Derogatory for the mixing of German blood with non-German or Jewish blood.

**Rassenchaos.** Race chaos. Death of the master (German) race, the disastrous result of the mixing of races.

**Rassencharakter.** Race character. The unique characteristics of (the German) race.

**Rasseneinschlag.** Racial element/blood.

**Rassenempfinden.** Racial feeling. Shaped by one's (German) race and therefore never faultfinding.

**Rassenerbblut.** Racial/genetic blood.

**Rassenforschung.** Race research. Study of race in schools and universities of the Third Reich.

**Rassenfrage.** Race question. The problems National Socialism associated predominantly with the Jews.

**rassengebunden.** Determined by race. Characteristics as determined by race.

**Rassengeschichte.** Race history. National Socialist history of the world according to race.

**Rassengesetze.** Race laws. *See also* Nürnberger Judengesetze.

**Rassenhaß.** Race hatred. Fabrications created by the opponents of racial thought in order to embarrass National Socialism.

**Rassenhygiene.** Race hygiene. Eugenics. *See also* Rassenpflege.

**rassenhygienische und bevölkerungsbiologiche Forschungsstelle.** Department for Research on Race Hygiene and Population Biology. Agency of the Reich Department of Health (Ministry of the Interior) supported to a large extent by the Reich Ministry of Science. It identified and classified six tribes of Gypsies: Sinti (German), Rom (Hungarian), Gelderari, Lowari, Lalleri (Bohemia-Moravia), and Balkan. Its director was Dr. Robert Ritter. *See* Deutsche Forschungsgemeinschaft; Notgemeinschaft Deutscher Wissenschaft.

**rassenhygienische und erbbiologische Forschungsstelle im Reichsgesundheitsamt.** Race Hygiene and Hereditary Biological Department of the Reich Public Health Office. *See also* rassenhygienische und bevölkerungsbiologische Forschungsstelle.

**Rassenideologie.** Racial ideology. *See also* Rasse.

**Rassenkampf.** Race war.

**Rassenkörper.** Racial body. The German people as one body defined by race.

**Rassenkunde.** Racial studies. Subject taught in German schools. Lessons from *Mein Kampf* that Aryan-Nordic Germans were the master race and that Jews were the personification of the devil; furthermore, that Blacks, Gypsies, and all Slavic peoples were subhuman and to be treated as slaves of the German people. *See also* Juden; Rasse; Untermenschen.

**Rassenlehre.** Racial doctrine. *See also* Rassenkunde.

**rassenmäßig.** According to race.

**Rassenmischung.** Race mixing. The combining of foreign racial blood, especially Jewish blood, with German-Aryan-Nordic blood.

**Rassenpest.** Race plague. Severe contamination of the German race.

**Rassenpflege.** Race maintenance. Nazi program to maintain and enhance the purity of the German race. *See also* Aufartung; Aufnordung.

*Rassenpflege im Sprichwort.* Race Maintenance through Proverbs. Title of proverb collection about race by the medical doctor Julius Schwab in 1937.

**Rassenpolitik.** Race politics. National Socialist foreign and domestic policy based on racial principles.

**Rassenpolitisches Amt der NSDAP.** Race Policy Department of the National-Socialist German Workers' Party. Established on May 1, 1934, by Rudolf Hess to establish guidelines for racial legislation and eugenics.

**Rassenregister.** Racial register. Himmler ordered the following residents of Poland to be registered: racial Germans, descendents of racial Germans, those married to racial Germans, and those of German origin but Polish citizens who could be reeducated as Germans (i.e., re-Germanized). The rest ultimately to disappear.

**rassenrein.** Of pure race. Of German blood without the intermixture of foreign (mainly Jewish) blood.

**Rassenschande.** Race defilement. Sexual activity between Jews and Aryans, Jews and German citizens, and Jews and those related by blood to German citizens was considered a crime as defined in the September 1935 Blood Protection Law. *See also* Blutschutzgesetz.

**Rassenschänder.** (RA.S., R.a.s.) Race violator. Person who violated the German race laws and shamed the Aryan race. *See also* Rassenschande.

**Rassenschranke.** Race barrier. According to National Socialist thinking, the so-called barrier existing between Germans and non-Germans (especially Jews) to prevent racial mixing.

**Rasse(n)schutz.** Race protection. Government legal protection of the German race from alien (Jewish) influences. *See also* Nürnberger Rassengesetze.

**Rassenschutzgesetze.** Laws to protect (the German) race. *See also* Blutschutzgesetz; Nürnberger Judengesetze; Rassengesetze.

**Rassenseele.** Race soul. Mystical racial psyche greater than any individual member of the German race. *See also Rasse und Seele.*

**Rassenseelenkunde.** Race psychology. *See also Rasse und Seele.*

**rassenseelisch.** Pertaining to the race soul. *See also* Rassenseele.

**Rassenstolz.** Racial pride. German attempt to maintain and renew the German race, its characteristics and culture.

**Rassentod.** Racial death. Fear that without protection from alien races, the German race would be corrupted and die. Also, the Nazi idea that those of mixed race were already dead.

**Rassenträger.** Race bearers. German/Aryan youth to continue the battle to keep the Aryan race pure.

**Rasse(n)tum.** Pertaining to race, race nature. Race essence.

**Rassenunterschied.** Race difference. A measure of inequality under National Socialism.

**Rassenvergiftung.** Race poisoning. Miscegenation, the mixing of German blood with non-German or Jewish blood. *See also* Blut(s)vergiftung.

**Rassenzucht.** Race breeding. *See* Rassenhygiene.

**rassestark.** Strong characteristics of a race. Of good racial stock (i.e., German).

*Rasse und Seele.* Race and Soul. An introduction to "racial science" published in 1938 by Nazi race–psychologist Ludwig Ferdinand Clauss. A pseudoscientific ideologically tainted ethnology. Clauss divided races by psychological traits. Four Aryan racial varieties: Leistungstyp, achievement type, Nordic; Verharrungstyp, persistent type, Phalic; Darbietungstyp, self-sacrificing type, Western; Enthebungstyp, relaxed type, Alpine. Two non-Aryan types: Erlösungstyp, need of redemption type, Near Eastern; and Offenbarungstyp, revelation type, Oriental.

**Rasse- und Siedlungshauptamt.** (RuSHA) Race and Settlement Department. SS organization that oversaw racial purity in the SS and in conquered nations in the east.

**Rasseverrat.** Race treason, race crime. Sexual or social contact between Germans and Jews. *See* Rassenschande.

**Rassewert.** Race value. All Germans had to be conscious of the importance and value of their racial origin.

**rassisch.** Racial.

**rassische Gegner.** Racial enemies. Were supposed to be eliminated.

**Rastenburg-Konferenz.** Rastenburg Conference. Meeting of Hitler and top military at Wolfsschanze on July 20, 1944, where attempt was made on his life. *See also* Flash; Schwarze Kapelle; Walküre; 20. Juli.

**Rath-Aktion.** Operation Rath. *See also* Reichskristallnacht.

**Rationalisierung.** Rationalization. In the concentration camps, the system developed to achieve the most efficient murder of prisoners.

**Rationierung.** Rationing. Of consumer goods.

**Räuberbanden.** Gangs of thieves, of robbers. Pretextual terms used to justify the German murder of Jews in eastern Europe.

**Raucherkarte.** Smoker's card. Ration cards for cigarettes and tobacco; used often as trade and payment.

**Rauchfahne.** Column of smoke. Smoke exiting from the crematory ovens was often the first clue to newly arrived concentration camp prisoners that something was terribly wrong.

**Raum.** Room, space. Geopolitical necessity for the German/Aryan race. *See also* Lebensraum.

**"(Der) Raum an sich ist politische Kraft."** "Space in itself is political power." Dictum of Karl Haushofer, founder of German geopolitics. *See also* Geopolitik; Lebensraum.

**Räumboot.** (R-Boot) Clearing boat. Minesweeper.

**räumen.** To clear out. To clear the ghettos of Jews by mass murder and/or deportation to death camps; to murder camp prisoners in the infirmary or other locations to make room for new patients/prisoners.

**Raumforschung.** *See* Reichsarbeitsgemeinschaft für Raumforschung.

**raumfremd.** Alien to an area. Un-German nations occupying eastern Europe; the German army fought to claim this land for Germans.

**raumfremde Mächte.** Alien powers. Nations not belonging in an area. *See also* raumfremd.

**Raumgewinn.** Gaining space. Slavery or mass murder of non-Germans in order to gain more territory for Nazi Germany.

**Raumordnung.** Structure of space. Geopolitical nature of territory.

**(neue) Raumordnung.** New structure of space. Plans for investments and migration in Europe.

**Raumstrahler.** Area transmitter. Nondirectional radio transmitter. *See also* Richtstrahler.

**Raumüberdehnung.** Overextension of space. Inorganic expansion.

**raumüberwindende Mächte.** Conquering powers. Powers of geopolitical expansion.

**Raumüberwindung.** Space conquest. *See also* Lebensraum.

**Räumung.** Evacuation. *See also* räumen.

**Räumungsbefehl.** Evacuation order. Himmler's order to evacuate eastern concentration camps and bring prisoners into the Reich. Also used to justify the 1944–1945 death marches.

**Raumwert.** Value of an area. Strategic importance of a location for the Wehrmacht.

**raupengängig.** Caterpillar-tracked (military vehicle).

**Raupenschlepper Ost.** (RSO) Caterpillar transporter. Ammunition transport vehicle designed especially for the Eastern Front. Also, slang for staff officer.

**(lila) Raute mit gelbem P.** Violet diamond with yellow P. Diamond-shape identification patch for Polish forced laborers; worn on the chest. *See also* Ostarbeiter.

**Ravensbrück.** One of the major concentration camps in Germany, established in 1939 near Fürstenberg, fifty-five miles from Berlin. The only major concentration camp intended just for women, it eventually held more than 120,000 women and children from twenty-three nations, of whom more than 90,000 were killed. Commandants were SS Hauptsturmführer Max Koegel and from 1942 Fritz Suhren. The guards, nearly 600, were all female (one of the best known was Irma Grese) and were recruited mostly from prisoners who were trained at Ravensbrück for service there and at other camps. The chief overseers were women; and the prisoner's internal camp administration was conducted by Polish non-Jewish women. The camp was notable for its female forced labor, medical experiments, individual and mass executions, murder of the sick, and torture, especially of Jewish women. The prisoners included female political prisoners, Roma and Sinti, Jews, and Jehovah's Witnesses. There was also a separate men's camp, a children's camp, and a Soviet POW camp, with a contingent of Waffen-SS. *See also* (die schöne) Bestie; Oberaufseherin.

**Razzia, Razzien.** Raids and roundups. German assaults on Jewish and other communities sometimes preliminary to deportations to concentration camps in both eastern and southern Europe.

**RBG.** *See* Reichsbürgergesetz.

**R-Boot.** *See* Räumboot.

**RBWK.** *See* Reichsberufswettkampf.

**RD.** *See* Randstaaten; Reichsdeutscher.

**RDB.** *See* Reichsbund deutscher Beamter.

**RDF.** *See* Reichsbund deutsche Familie.

**RDO.** *See* Reichsverband deutscher Offiziere.

**RDS.** *See* Reichsverband deutscher Schriftsteller.

**RDT.** *See* Reichsbund deutscher Technik.

**Recht.** Right. The Third Reich's inherent right to act according to National Socialist Weltanschauung.

**Recht auf Arbeit.** The right to work. Declared National Socialist economic principle concerned more with the common good than with the individual.

**"Recht ist was dem deutschen Volke nützt."** "Right is what benefits the German nation." Basis of German justice during the Third Reich.

**Rechtsberater.** Legal consultant. Jewish lawyers representing and advising Jewish clients out of court after the September 1938 regulation disbarring Jewish lawyers and preventing them from appearing in court. Based on the Citizenship Law of 1935. Such restrictions were placed on Jewish lawyers in the nineteenth century as well. *See also* Nürnberger Judengesetze.

**Rechtsbetreuung.** Legal Aid. Official Nazi Party law offices available to those Germans who were unable to pay lawyer fees.

**Rechtserneuerung.** Law renewal. Legal reform. From 1933, measures to change German law according to National Socialist ideology.

**Rechtsfront.** *See* Deutsche Rechtsfront.

**Rechtsgenosse.** Comrade in law. German citizen enjoying equality under a law preferential to Aryans.

**Rechtskonsultent.** *See* Rechtsberater.

**rechts oder links.** Right or left. At death camps, the division of new arrivals into those heading for immediate murder or temporary survival. During roundups of Jews, the division into those to survive for the moment or killed on the spot versus those sent to death camps.

**Rechtsstand.** Legal position. Every German worker was protected by Nazi law.

**Rechtswahrer.** Keeper of the law. Used instead of standard terms for lawyer, such as Rechtsanwalt, Rechtsbeistand, and Rechtsgelehrter. Individuals of the legal profession in Nazi Germany. Lawyers under the Third Reich were to safeguard the German community of the people (Volksgemeinschaft) rather than apply the law.

**Rechtswahrerbund.** *See* NS-Juristenbund.

**"Reden ist Silber, Schweigen ist Gold!"** "Speech is silver, silence is gold." German proverb used as ironic slogan in Auschwitz barracks.

**Redeverbot.** Forbidden to preach. A Security Police order to fight church pastors and priests opposing the Reich.

**Rednerschule der NSDAP.** Public Speaker School of the Nazi Party. Training institute for Nazi Party orators.

**Reeperbahn.** Rope road. The Reeperbahn, originally where ships' ropes were wound, runs through the red-light district of St. Pauli in Hamburg. From the early nineteenth century, an entertainment district was established here, and it was where left-wing anti-Nazi youth groups congregated. *See also* Meuten.

**Referent für Judenfragen.** Office for Jewish issues. Headed by Adolf Eichmann.

**Regelung der Zigeunerfrage aus dem Wesen der Rasse heraus in Angriff zu nehmen.** Regulation of the Gypsy Problem from the Standpoint of Race. Himmler order of December 8, 1938, which further restricted the Gypsies. *See also* Erlaß zur Bekämpfung der Zigeunerplage; Zigeuner.

**Regenbogen.** *See* Unternehmen Regenbogen.

**Regenerat.** Recycled material (i.e., synthetic rubber and oil).

**Regierungsbezirk.** Nazi administrative district.

**Regierungschef.** Head of the Government. One of Hitler's titles, equivalent to Reichskanzler. *See also* (Der) Führer.

**Regierungsrat.** Government Councilor. A senior Nazi government offical sometimes sent on secret missions.

**Regierungs- und Kriminalrat.** (RuKR) Executive Council and Council for Criminal Affairs.

**Regierungsverwaltung.** Government Administration. German-occupied nation ruled by a German administrator and administration; local self-government by Volksdeutsche was encouraged. *See also* Generalgouvernement.

**Regiment.** Regiment. Tactical unit consisting of 2,000 to 6,000 men divided into battalions.

**Regiment Brandenburg.** *See* Brandenburger; Regiment zbV. 800/Brandenburger.

**Regiment General Göring.** *See* Landespolizeigruppe Hermann Göring.

**Regiment zbV. 800/Brandenburger.** Regiment 800 for Special Duties/Brandenburger. Wehrmacht Special Operations Commando/Ranger Unit trained in Brandenburg, consisting of men of non-German origin or multilingual Germans who operated, in civilian clothing or uniform, behind the front lines to misinform or confuse the enemy and to demolish bridges and fortifications; in Russia, operated as antipartisan units.

**Reibaktion.** Scouring action. The forcing of elderly Jews to clean roads with toothbrushes in Germany and German-occupied countries.

**Reich.** Empire. *See also* Drittes Reich. [Note: we retain the use of *Reich* and *Reichs* instead of translating them as "empire" or "imperial."]

***(Das) Reich.*** The Reich. Issued from 1940 to 1945, a supposedly sophisticated German weekly founded by Goebbels and directed toward a German-speaking readership outside of Germany.

**"(Das) Reich ist der Führer."** "(The) Reich is the Führer." Nazi slogan.

**Reichsaltersheim.** Reich home for the elderly. *See also* Theresienstadt.

**Reichsamt.** Reich Department. Nazi Party office.

**Reichsangehörige.** Belonging to the Reich. Full citizens (Germans only) of the Reich.

**Reichsappell.** Reich call. Nationwide holiday in which all Hitler Youth celebrated their membership in ceremonies, parades, and so forth.

**Reichsarbeitsdienst.** (RAD) Reich Labor Service. Compulsory national labor service for young men and women beginning at the age of eighteen. When many of the young German men served in the Wehrmacht and a labor shortage developed, the young women were obliged, until twenty-five years of age, to live in barracks and work in health services and in agriculture. As the war progressed, young German women began to work in factories and as helpers in antiaircraft batteries and military messengers. Some were wounded, killed, or made prisoner.

**Reichsarbeitsdienst der weiblichen Jugend.** (RADwJ) Reich Labor Service for Female Youth. *See also* Reichsarbeitsdienst.

**Reichsarbeitsführer.** Leader of the Reich Labor Service. Chief official in the Reichsarbeitsdienst.

**Reichsarbeitsgemeinschaft für Raumforschung.** Reich Task Force to Study the Geopolitical Situation of Space for Germany. *See also* Lebensraum; Raum.

**Reichsarbeitsgemeinschaft Heil- und Pflegeanstalten.** (RAG) Reich Cartel of Institutions for the Sick. Established in 1939, camouflage organization of doctors and lawyers responsible for the T-4 Euthanasia Program. *See also* Euthanasie.

**Reichsarbeitsminister.** (RArM) Reich Employment Minister.

**Reichsarbeitsnachweis für Offiziere.** (Rano) Reich officers' work records.

**Reichsarzt SS.** (RASS) Reich doctor SS.

**Reichsaufbaugesetz.** *See* Neuaufbaugesetz vom 30.1.1934.

**Reichsausleselager.** Reich selection camp. Retraining camp for wounded German civilians and military.

**Reichsausschuß zur wissenschaftlichen Erfassung von erb- und anlagebedingten schweren Leiden.** Reich Commission for the Scientific Registration of

Hereditary and Constitutionally Severe Disorders. Created in 1939, this commission consisted of pediatricians and a child psychiatrist directly responsible to the Hitler Chancellery. Midwives were required to report all cases of handicapped and malformed live-born infants, and all physicians were required to report children under the age of four with the same defects to the commission, which then decided whether the infant should be killed as part of the Euthanasia Program. Later, the commission also made decisions about the killing of older children and decided on requests by Gypsies for voluntary sterilization as an alternative to commitment to a concentration camp.

**Reichsaußenminister.** (RAM) Reich Foreign Minister.

**Reichsautobahnen.** (RAB) State highways. Restricted highways built by Organisation Todt. Also called Adolf-Hitler-Straßen and Straßen des Führers.

**Reichsautozug Deutschland.** Reich auto-carrying train. Transportation of the most advanced technological means necessary for all important national rallies, under the direction of Goebbels' chief of staff.

**Reichsbahnschutz.** National Railway Security Service. Transferred to the Waffen-SS in 1942.

**Reichsbank.** Reich Bank. German government's national bank. In 1942, Walther Funk, Minister of Economic Affairs and President of the Reichsbank, came to an agreement with Heinrich Himmler, Head of the SS, to deposit currency and launder gold and jewels taken from the murdered Jews and deposit the funds into a secret SS Reichsbank account under the name of Max Heiliger. The Reichsbank kept the coins and banknotes and sent the jewels, watches, and personal belongings to Berlin municipal pawnshops. The gold from eyeglasses and gold teeth and fillings were stored in the Reichsbank vaults. *See also* Konto Max Heiliger.

**Reichsbanner Schwarz-Rot-Gold.** Reich flag black, red, gold. Unarmed, uniformed World War I veterans' and trade-unionists' organization supporting the Social Democrats during the Weimar Republic until 1933.

**Reichsbauern.** Reich farmers. *See also* Reichsnährstand.

**Reichsbauernführer.** Reich Farmers' Leader. Official title of Richard Walther Darré who was Reich Minister of Food and Agriculture from 1933 and saw peasants as the backbone of the German race.

**Reichsbauernstadt.** Reich Farmers' City. Name for the town of Goslar.

**Reichsbauerntag.** Reich farmer's day. Annual meeting of the Reichsnährstand in Goslar.

**Reichsbeauftragter.** Reich Administrator. Head of the rationing office. *See* Reichswirtschaftsminister(ium).

**Reichsbehörden.** Reich offices. *See also* (oberste) Reichsbehörden.

**(oberste) Reichsbehörden.** Top-level Reich offices. The various governing ministries of the Third Reich.

**Reichsberufswettkampf.** (RBWK) Reich professional competition. Annual state-supported competitions within professions, along with a test of physical and ideological capabilities.

**Reichsbevollmächtigte für den totalen Kriegseinsatz.** *See* Generalbevollmächtigter für den totalen Kriegseinsatz.

**Reichsbewegung Deutsche Christen.** German Christians' Reich Movement. *See also* Deutsche Christen.

**Reichsbischof.** Reich Bishop. From 1933, the Nazi-appointed Head of the Lutheran Church; that is, the chief religious official of the German Evangelical Church.

**Reichsbräuteschule.** Reich bride school. School for young German women where they were trained in homemaking, child rearing, and race policies.

**Reichsbrotkarte.** Reich bread card. Ration card for bread and flour.

**Reichsbund der deutschen Freilicht- und Volksschauspiele.** Reich Union of German Open-Air and Popular Theater. Founded in 1934 by the Nazi Propaganda Ministry.

**Reichsbund der Kinderreichen.** Reich Association for Large Families. Alliance of German multiple-child families from 1920 as part of the Race-Politics Department of the Nazi Party. *See also* Ehrenbuch für die deutsche kinderreiche Familie; Ehrenkarte für kinderreiche deutsche Mütter.

**Reichsbund deutsche Familie.** (RDF) Reich League (of the) German Family.

**Reichsbund deutscher Beamter.** (RDB) Reich League of German Civil Servants. Civil servants group of more than one million members, allied to Nazi Party and under its control. Followed orders of Nazi government to the letter. *See also* Gleichschaltung.

**Reichsbund deutscher Technik.** (RDT) Reich League of German Technology.

**Reichsbund freier Schwestern.** Reich Association of Independent Nurses. *See also* Blaue Schwestern.

**Reichsbund für Deutschtumsarbeit.** Reich Association for the Work of Germanness. German propaganda organization.

**Reichsbund für Leibesübungen.** Reich Gymnastics League.

**Reichsbürger.** Reich citizen. Full German citizen of the Third Reich. *See also* Reichsbürgergesetz.

**Reichsbürgergesetz.** (RBG) Reich-Citizen Law. A 1935 Nuremberg law that declared only those with German or related blood were citizens with full political rights in the Third Reich. German Jews, although subjects of the Reich, were declared noncitizens and discriminated against.

**Reichsdeutsche im Ausland.** Reich German abroad.

**Reichsdeutscher.** (RD) (Any) German in and from Germany.

**Reichsdramaturg.** Reich Drama Expert. Position created in 1933 for the ideological supervision and control of all theater programs in Germany.

**Reichseinheit.** Uniformity within the Reich. The forced coordination of all institutions according to Nazi ideology. *See also* Gleichschaltung.

**Reichserbhofgesetz.** (RErbhG) Reich Farm-Inheritance Law. 1933 law stipulating that medium-size farms could not be divided and must be passed on to a single German heir in order to preserve the so-called inalienable rights of landowning farmers who were regarded as the racial wellspring of the German people. *See also* Bauer; Blut und Boden.

**Reichs-Erlaß des Reichsministers für Erziehung und Unterricht über den Schulbesuch jüdischer Kinder.** Decree of the Reich Minister of Education concerning the School Attendance of Jewish Children. This decree of November 1938 excluded all Jewish children from German schools.

**Reichsfarben.** The colors of the Reich. Black, white, and red. *See also* Reichsflaggengesetz.

**Reichsfettkarte.** Reich card for fats. Ration card for butter, margarine, artificial fat, oil, and so on. *See also* Bewirtschaftung.

**Reichsfilmkammer.** Chamber of Reich Films. *See also* Reichskulturkammer.

**Reichsfinanzminister(ium).** (RFM) Reich Finance Minister or Ministry.

**Reichsflagge.** *See* Reichskriegsflagge.

**Reichsflaggengesetz.** Reich-Flag Law. Third Nuremberg law of 1935 declared the swastika flag as the only national flag and excluded Jews from flying it.

**Reichsfleischkarte.** Reich card for meat. Ration card for meat. *See also* Bewirtschaftung.

**Reichsfluchtsteuer.** Reich flight tax. From 1933, special departure tax of 25 percent of the total value of possessions for those Germans who wanted to emigrate; levied especially on Jews.

**Reichsforstmeister.** Reich Forest Master. Another of Göring's titles. *See also* Reichsmarschall.

**Reichsfrauenführerin.** Reich Women's Leader. Leader of the National Socialist Women's Organization. From 1934, the position was held by Gertrud Scholtz-Klink. *See also* Nationalsozialistische Frauenschaft.

**Reichsführerschule.** (RFS) School for Reich leaders. *See also* Reichsschulungsburg der NSDAP.

**Reichsführer-SS und Chef der deutschen Polizei.** (RFSSuChdDtPl, RFSSuCHdDtPol) Reich Leader and Chief of German Police. Himmler's title starting in June 1936.

**Reichsführung-SS.** (RFSS) Reich Leadership, SS. Reich High Command of the SS. Himmler and his personal SS staff.

**Reichsgaue.** Reich districts or provinces. National administrative zones outside of Germany (e.g., Sudetenland) and the new Austrian provinces. *See also* Gau.

*Reichsgesetzblatt.* Reich Law Gazette. Official law journal of the German government.

**Reichsgesundheitsführer.** Reich Health Leader. Head of the Reichsärztekammer for all doctors in Germany.

**Reichsgewitterziege.** Reich sour old hag. Nagging woman; derogatory for the Reichsfrauenführerin Gertrud Scholtz-Klink.

**Reichsgletscherspalte.** Reich glacier crevasse. Derogatory name for the celebrated Reich filmmaker Leni Riefenstahl; an allusion to her films on the Alps.

**Reichsgruppe.** (Rgr) Reich group. Trade and industry organization.

**Reichsgruppe Industrie.** *See* Reichsgruppe.

**Reichsgruppen Handel und Handwerk.** Reich Groups of Trade and Craft. Organization and lobby for the economic interests of the German middle class during the Third Reich.

**Reichsheer.** Reich army. Part of the Weimar Republic's Reichswehr (armed forces). In 1935, changed simply to Heer (army). *See also* Reichswehr.

**Reichsheini.** Reich Ass. Heinrich Himmler's nickname; a pun on Heinrich/Heini, or dumb ass.

**Reichsindustrie für die Fettversorgung.** (RIF) Reich industry for the supply of fats.

**Reichsinstitut für Geschichte des neuen Deutschlands.** Reich Institute for the History of the New Germany. Founded by Walter Frank on July 1, 1935, to shed light on modern German history, taking into account Nazi ideology and focusing on the German Jews.

**Reichsjägermeister.** Reich Hunting Master. Title of Göring as Plenipotentiary of Forestry and Hunting.

**Reichsjugendamt.** Reich Youth Office. Office responsible for administering and training Nazi youth. *See* Reichsjugendführung.

**Reichsjugendführer.** (RJF) Reich Youth Leader. Baldur von Schirach, followed by Artur Axmann, held this highest Nazi Party position in the Hitlerjugend, Deutsches

Jungvolk, Bund deutscher Mädel, and Jungmädel, overseeing the physical, intellectual, moral, and ideological education of youth in the spirit of National Socialism.

**Reichsjugendführung.** Reich Youth-Education Leadership. Highest administrative body for the education of the Hitler Youth.

**Reichsjugendleiter.** Reich Youth Leader. *See also* Reichsjugendführer.

**Reichsjugendtag.** Reich Youth Day. Second of October, induction of ten-year-old boys and girls into the Hitler Youth; by 1939 the Hitler Youth numbered almost 9 million.

**Reichsjugendweihe.** Reich youth consecration. Pre-Christian ceremony sponsored by the German Faith Movement. *See also* Deutsche Glaubensbewegung.

**Reichsjustizminister(ium).** (RJM) Reich Justice Ministry.

**Reichskammer der bildenden Künste.** Reich Chamber of Visual Art. *See also* Reichskulturkammer.

**Reichskanzlei.** Reich Chancellery. Hitler chancellery as chief executive.

**Reichskanzler.** Reich Chancellor. Hitler was appointed German premier on January 30, 1933.

**Reichskarte für Marmelade und Zucker.** Reich ration card for jam and sugar. Ration card during the war to obtain jam, jelly, sugar-beet syrup, and other sweeteners.

**Reichskartei der deutschen Juden.** Reich card-file on German Jews. Established in 1939, each card contained a German Jew's family name (maiden name), given name, residence, sex, birth date, religion, mother tongue, profession, number of children under fourteen, and a declaration as to whether the person was cultivating land. This card system facilitated persecutions and roundups.

**Reichskirche.** Reich church. German Christians intended to unify all Germans into a Reich church. *See also* Nationalkirche deutscher Christen.

**Reichsklavier-Oma.** Reich Piano Grandmother. Derogatory nickname for the German woman pianist Elly Ney.

**Reichskleiderkarte.** Reich clothing card. Ration card for clothing, textiles, and shoes for all German women and children and men not in military service. Even pets had a form of this card. From 1940, Jews were denied it.

**Reichskommissar(e).** (RK) Reich Commissioner. Nazi Chief of Civilian Administration in the German-occupied areas of Europe.

**Reichskommissar für die Festigung des deutschen Volkstums.** (RKFDV, RFdV) Reich Commissioner for the Strengthening of German Nationhood. One of Himmler's offices.

**Reichskommissar für die Preisbildung.** (RfPr) Reich Commissar for Prices. *See also* Vierjahresplan.

**Reichskommissar für die Stärkung des deutschen Volkstums.** *See* Reichskommissar für die Festigung des deutschen Volkstums.

**Reichskommissar für die Überwachung der öffentlichen Meinung.** Reich Commissioner for the Monitoring of Public Opinion. Nazi official reponsible for detecting and suppressing open dissent within the Reich.

**Reichskommissariate.** Reich Administrative Offices. Chief unit of Reich Civil Administration of German-occupied eastern Europe.

**Reichskommissariate Ukraine.** Reich Civil Administration for the Ukraine. Reichskommissar was Erich Koch.

**Reichskommissariat für das Ostland.** (RKO) Reich Commission for the Eastern Territories. Government of occupied Soviet territory nominally under Alfred Rosenberg.

**Reichskommissariat für die besetzten niederländischen Gebiete.** Reich Commission for the Occupied Dutch Territories. Because of the absence of Dutch Queen Wilhelmina, the gap in the Dutch bureaucracy was filled by German administration. This in turn led to greater German control of Dutch government and society and made victimization of resident Jews among the highest in Europe. Reichskommissar was Artur Seyss-Inquart.

**Reichskommissariat Ostland.** Reich Commission for Eastern Territories. Civil administration of occupied Soviet territories including the Baltic States, Belorussia, and eastern Poland, under the supervision of Heinrich Lohse.

**Reichskonkordat.** Reich Agreement. A treaty signed on July 20, 1933, between the German Reich and the Vatican. In response to the Reich agreement to protect Catholic rights in Germany, the Holy See recognized Hitler's Third Reich, the first such political state to do so. The prelate who negotiated the agreement for Pope Pius XI was papal nuncio Eugenio Pacelli, in 1939 to become Pope Pius XII. The pact gave Hitler international prestige and weakened Catholic resistance to the Third Reich.

**Reichskreditkassenscheine.** Reich bill of credit. Means of payment used in German-occupied countries during World War II.

**Reichskriegsflagge.** Reich War Flag. Ernst Röhm's fascist organization that supported the Hitler Munich Putsch.

**Reichskriegsführer.** Reich Veterans Leader. Head of the NS-Reichskriegerbund Veterans Organization, formed in 1934 from the Reichskriegerbund Kyffhäuser.

**Reichskriegsgericht.** (RKG) Reich War Court.

**Reichskriegsministerium.** (RKM) Reich War Ministry.

**Reichskriegsschädenamt.** Reich War Damages Department. Instituted in 1941; highest decision-making office to determine damage caused by war in Germany.

**Reichskriminalpolizeiamt.** (RKPA) Reich Criminal Police Department. Internal security, including Gestapo, Kripo, Secret Information Service.

**Reichskristallnacht.** Reich "Night of Broken Glass." The November 1938 Pogrom in Germany and Austria. On November 9-10, 1938, the Nazis initiated a pogrom against Jews based on the pretext of retaliation for the assassination of Ernst vom Rath. Thousands of Jewish stores and apartments were damaged. With few exceptions, all the synagogues were desecrated and burned, thousands of Jews temporarily arrested, and at least 100 killed.

**Reichskükenschar.** *See* Deutsche Kinderschar.

**Reichskulturkammer.** (RKK) Reich Chamber of Culture. An instrument to control the entire cultural life in Germany as every cultural activity demanded membership in one of the RKK's subordinate associations for art, film, music, publishing, theater, and writers. *See* Reichskammer der bildenden Künste; Reichsfilmkammer; Reichsmusikkammer; Reichspressekammer; Reichsschrifttumskammer; Reichstheaterkammer.

**Reichskulturkammergesetz.** Reich Chamber of Culture Law. November 22, 1933, law. *See also* Reichskulturkammer.

**Reichskultursenat.** (RKS) Reich Culture Senate. Established in 1935 and responsible to the Reichskulturkammer.

**Reichskulturwalter.** Guardian of Reich Culture. Official in charge of German theater and similar enterprises.

**Reichskuratorium für Wirtschaftlichkeit.** (RKW) Reich Governing Board for the Economy. Concerned, among other things, with the efficient running of the ghettos.

**Reichslager.** *See* Reichsschule.

**Reichslehrerbund.** Reich Teachers' Association. *See also* NS-Lehrerbund.

**Reichsleistungsgesetz.** (RLG) Reich Law for Obligatory Payments and Confiscation of Property. Mobilization of the economy for war. *See also* Enteignung.

**Reichsleiter.** Reich Leader. Reich leader under direct command of Hitler, responsible for NSDAP affairs; also Hitler gave this title to those whom he wanted to give a privileged and independent position, the highest-ranking Nazi Party officials: Martin Bormann, Party Chancellery; Hans Frank, Party Legal Division; Heinrich Himmler, SS; Joseph Goebbels, Propaganda; Alfred Rosenberg, Party Foreign Affairs; and Robert Ley, Party Organization.

**Reichsleitung der NSDAP.** NSDAP Reich Leadership. Highest Nazi Party leadership, consisting of Hitler and Reich leaders, with headquarters in Munich.

*Reichslesebuch.* Reich Reader. From 1935, National Socialist primary school reader consisting of a unified central core and chapters dedicated to the twenty-two regions of the country.

**Reichsluftfahrtminister(ium).** (RLM) Reich Aviation Ministry.

**Reichsluftschutzbund.** (RLB) Reich Air-Raid Protection League. Göring's organization to educate the public about air defense and about protecting themselves against air attacks. Originally under the Sturmabteilung, later trained able-bodied males to help against air attacks.

**Reichsluftsportführer.** (RLF) Reich Sports Flying Leader.

**Reichsmarine.** Reich navy. *See also* Reichswehr.

**Reichsmark.** (RM) Reich mark. Money of the Third Reich.

**Reichsmarschall.** Reich Marshal. Göring's title as second in command to Hitler. Göring's other titles: Reichsminister der Luftfahrt, Oberbefehlshaber des Luftwaffe, Beauftragter für die Durchführung des Vierjaresplans, Präsident des Amtes Zentrale Planung, Reichsforstmeister, Präsident des deutschen Reichstags, Ministerpräsident des Landes Preussen, Nachfolger des Führers, and Präsident des Ministerrates für Reichsverteidigung.

**Reichsmarschall des Großdeutschen Reiches.** Reich Marshal of the Greater German Reich. *See also* Reichsmarschall.

**Reichsmessestadt.** Reich Convention City. Name for Leipzig.

**Reichsmilchkarte.** *See* Milchkarte.

**Reichsmilitärgericht.** (RMG) Reich Military Court.

**Reichsminister(ium).** (RM) Reich Minister or Ministry (for).

**Reichsminister der Luftfahrt.** Reich Minister of Aviation. *See also* Reichsmarschall.

**Reichsminister(ium) des Inner(e)n.** (RMdI) Reich Ministry of the Interior. Minister for Internal Affairs, a position held by Himmler.

**Reichsminister(ium) für Arbeit.** (RMfA) Reich Labor Ministry.

**Reichsminister(ium) für Bewaffnung und Munitionen.** (RMfBuM) Reich Ministry for Armaments and Munitions. See Reichsminister(ium) für Rüstungs- und Kriegsproduktion.

**Reichsminister(ium) für die besetzten Ostgebiete.** (RMbO) Reich Ministry for the Occupied Eastern Territories. *See also* Besetzte Ostgebiete; Ostministerium.

**Reichsminister(ium) für Ernährung und Landwirtschaft.** (RMEuL) Reich Minister for Nutrition and Agriculture. Richard Walther Darré's official government position.

**Reichsminister(ium) für Rüstungs(aufgaben)- und Kriegsproduktion.** (Ruk) Reich Minister (Ministry) for Armaments and War Production. Albert Speer's most important position. Subordinated to this ministry were agencies that handled defense orders, efficiency, electric power, transportation and shipping priorities, construction, and procurement.

**Reichsminister(ium) für Volksaufklärung und Propaganda.** (RMVP, RMVAP, RPM, RMfVuP [official abbreviation], Promi [unofficial abbreviation]). Reich Ministry for Public Enlightenment and Propaganda. Goebbel's official government post in the Propaganda Ministry.

**Reichsminister(ium) für Wissenschaft, Erziehung, und Volksbildung.** (REM) Reich Ministry for Science, Education, and National Training.

**Reichsmusikkammer.** Reich Music Chamber. *See also* Reichskulturkammer.

**Reichs-Mütterdienst.** *See* Mütterdienst.

**Reichsnährstand.** (RNSt) Reich Agricultural Organization. A compulsory cartel dealing with agricultural affairs that planned and carried out an independent food supply for Germany. From 1933 to 1942, it was headed by Richard Walther Darré.

**Reichsnovemberpogrom.** The Reich's November 1938 Pogrom. *See also* Reichskristallnacht.

**Reichsorganisationsleiter.** Reich Organization Leader. Title of the leader of Nazi Party organizations, Robert Ley.

**Reichsparlament.** Reich Parliament. Weimar Republic's parliament, consisting of a lower house and an upper house. *See also* Reichsrat; Reichstag.

**Reichsparteitag.** Reich political-party rally. Annual September holiday celebrating the National Socialist Party with mass rallies, marches, military ceremonies and maneuvers, games, commemorations, prizes, conferences, exhibitions, concerts, sports, and fairs. These gigantic theatrical performances developed into symbolic rituals of the Third Reich and were most often celebrated at Nuremberg.

**Reichsparteitagsgelände.** Reich Party rally grounds. Areas of Nuremberg where annual Nazi Party rallies were held accommodating up to one million celebrants and covering 25 square kilometers. The main areas were the old city (Nürnberger Altstadt), where the marketplace was renamed Adolf-Hitler-Platz; the parade grounds (Märzfeld), where the building project remained unfinished; the zeppelin field stadium (Zeppelinfel-Stadion), accommodating 160,000 and containing the huge reviewing stand (Zeppelintribüne), and the scene of the dome of searchlights, military reviews, aerial displays, and field maneuvers; Luitpold grove (Luitpoldhain), holding 150,000 for mass parades by the SA and the SS; Luitpold arena (Luitpoldarena), holding 16,000 for Party congresses; the unfinished Congress Hall (Kongreßhalle); the unfinished German Stadium (Deutsches Stadion), with a planned capacity of more than 400,000; and the city stadium (Städtisches Stadion) for swearing-in of Hitler Youth. The main street (Große Straße), paved with 60,000 huge stone blocks, was a central axis of the Party rally grounds, running from the Luitpold arena to the parade grounds.

**Reichspräsident.** Reich President. When Reichspräsident Paul von Hindenburg died, Hitler assumed his office in August 1934. *See also* Gesetz über das Staatsoberhaupt des Deutschen Reiches.

**Reichspressechef.** Head of Reich Publication. Nazi Party official Otto Dietrich. *See also* Pressechef der Reichsregierung.

**Reichspressekammer.** (RPK). Reich Press Office. *See also* Reichskulturkammer.

**Reichspressekonferenz.** Reich press conference. Daily conference chaired by the Propaganda Minister, Goebbels, to which every German paper was obliged to send a representative. Decisions were made on which stories would be covered, where they would be placed in the newspaper, and how they should be written. Violators received severe fines. *See also* Sprachregelung.

**Reichspropagandaamt.** (RPA) Reich Propaganda Office. Office reponsible for overseeing cultural activities in the Reich. *See* Reichsminister(ium) für Volksaufklärung und Propaganda.

**Reichspropagandaleiter.** Reich Propaganda Leader. 1925–1928, Gregor Strasser; from 1929 on, Goebbels title.

**Reichspropagandaleitung.** Reich propaganda leadership, direction. The Nazi Party's Central Propaganda Office, a subunit of the Propaganda Ministry. *See* Reichsminister(ium) für Volksaufklärung und Propaganda.

**Reichsprotektor.** Reich Protector. Of Bohemia and Moravia (German-occupied Czech territory). Konstantin Baron von Neurath, Reinhard Heydrich, and Kurt Daluege.

**Reichsrat.** Reich Council. Under the Weimar Republic, the Reichsrat was the upper house of the bicameral Weimar Parlament. From 1919, it represented the governments of the German states, or Länder. Under the Weimar Constitution, a strong central government was created that controlled all taxation, and its laws overrode those of the seventeen Länder. The Reichsrat's only power was to veto legislation passed by the powerful Reichstag for four years, unless the Reichstag overrode the Reichsrat's decision by a two-thirds majority. The Reichsrat was subordinate to the Reichstag, to which alone the chancellor and his government were responsible, and when the traditional states were overthrown by the Nazis in 1934, the Reichsrat disappeared, leaving a rubber-stamp Reichstag and Reich cabinet. *See also* Reichsparlament.

**Reichsrechtführer.** Reich Law Leader. From 1936, the government-appointed head of German lawyers.

**Reichsredner.** Reich orator. NSDAP propagandist who organized Party rallies.

**Reichsreform.** Reich reform. *See also* Neuaufbaugesetz vom 30.1.1934.

**Reichsregierung.** Reich government, administration.

**Reichsring für Propaganda.** Reich Circle for Propaganda. Nazi Party office under Goebbels.

**Reichs-Rundfunk-Gesellschaft m.b.H.** (RRG) *See* Reichssender.

**Reichsrundfunkkammer.** Reich Radio Chamber. Section of Reichskulturkammer.

**Reichsschaft.** All Reich organizations.

**Reichsschatzmeister.** Reich Treasurer Franz Schwarz, plenipotentiary appointed by Hitler and responsible for Nazi Party finances.

**Reichsschrifttumskammer.** (RSK) Reich Writers' Chamber. *See also* Reichskulturkammer.

**Reichsschrifttumskammergesetz.** Reich Writers' Chamber Law. Law of April 10, 1933.

**Reichsschule.** Reich School. Elite Nazi leader school at Chiemsee.

**Reichsschulungsburg der NSDAP.** Reich Nazi Party Fortress School. Elite school for potential Nazi political leaders.

**Reichsschulungslager.** Reich training camp. Training center for all Nazi organizations.

**Reichssendeleiter.** Reich Radio Chief. Director of the Reichs-Rundfunk-Gesellschaft m.b.H. Eugen Hadamovsky held the position until differences with Goebbels caused him to resign in 1942.

**Reichssender.** Reich radio broadcasting. From 1933, the formerly independent radio stations became centralized and stood under the direct command of the Reichsminister(ium) für Volksaufklärung und Propaganda headed by Goebbels.

**Reichssicherheitshauptamt.** (RSHA) Reich Main Security Administration. In charge of all security, SS, and police operations, headed by Reinhard Heydrich and later Dr. Ernst Kaltenbrunner. Included Domestic and Overseas Intelligence Departments, Ideological Research, Criminal Police, the SD, espionage, and Heinrich Müller's Gestapo (Department IV). Adolf Eichmann's desk (IV B 4) was located in the Gestapo department, where he was in charge of the mass murder of the European Jews.

**Reichssippenamt.** Reich Clan Office. Genealogical Department instituted in 1933, investigated Aryan background to discover Jewish blood and determine mixed-blood status. From 1935 to 1940 called Reichsstelle für Sippenforschung.

**Reichssportfeld.** Reich sports field. Location of the 1936 Olympic games in Berlin.

**Reichssportführer.** Reich Sports Leader. Leader of German physical education.

**Reichssportabzeichen.** Reich sports medal. New name, from 1934 to 1945, for the German sports medal established in 1913, Deutsches Turn- und Sportabzeichen.

**Reichsstatthalter.** Reich Governor, President. From 1933, governors of the Reich provinces (Länder), later including governors of annexed territories, who oversaw the implementation of Hitler's orders and recommended suitable leaders.

**Reichsstatthaltergesetz.** Reich Governor Law. Law of January 10, 1934, creating the positions of Reich governors.

**Reichsstatthalter—Oberpräsident.** *See* Reichsstatthalter.

**(Höhere) Reichsstellen.** Higher Reich centers. Branches of the highest government offices. *See* (oberste) Reichsbehörden.

**Reichsstelle für.** (Rf) Reich Center for. Abbreviation used in combination with many different offices. *See* Reichsbehörden.

**Reichsstelle für Musikbearbeitungen.** Reich Center for Music Arrangements. Authority founded in 1941 to ensure that all music and lyrics published or presented contained the appropriate German content and were composed by Aryans.

**Reichsstelle für Raum.** Reich Center for Space. Office of industrial planning; planning office for long-term investments. *See also* Absatzkreis; Neuordnung.

**Reichsstelle für Sippenforschung.** Reich Center for (Clan) Genealogical Research. *See also* Reichssippenamt.

**Reichsstelle für technische Erzeugnisse.** (RTE) Reich Office Overseeing Technical Products.

**Reichsstellen für Rohstoffbewirtschaftung.** Reich Centers for Raw-Material Imports and Allocation. Under the Minister for Economic Affairs, Walther Funk.

**Reichsstock für Arbeitseinsatz.** Reich employment fund. Fund built up from contributions to unemployment insurance.

**Reichsstraßenverkehrsordnung.** (RStrVO) Decree for the regulation of all road traffic in Germany.

**Reichsstudentenführung.** (RSF) Reich Student Leadership.

**Reichsstudentenwerk.** Reich Student Organization. Devoted to supporting the most ideologically oriented German students.

**Reichsstunde.** Reich hour. Hour provided and reserved for public celebrations of Nazi organizations.

**Reichstag.** Lower house of the Reich Parliament. A rubber stamp for Hitler after the March 1933 Enabling Act. *See also* Ermächtigungsgesetz; Reichsparlament.

**Reichstag-Beschluß.** Reichstag Resolution. Unanimously approved April 1942 declaration that Hitler was the law in Germany. As Führer of the nation, Supreme Commander of the Wehrmacht, Supreme Executive Officer of the German Government, Supreme Law Lord, and Führer of the Nazi Party, he was "empowered without being bound to existing legal precepts" arbitrarily to remove from office and punish anyone.

**Reichstagsbrandverordnung.** Reichtstag-Fire Decree. Originally, an anti-Communist decree of February 28, 1933, following the Reichstag fire, curbing basic civil rights, permitting arbitrary searches and seizure of property, and empowering the central government to assume functions of local authorities. *See also* Ermächtigungsgesetz; Schutzhaft.

**Reichstheaterkammer.** (RTK) Reich Theater Chamber. *See also* Reichskulturkammer.

**Reichstreuhänder der Arbeit.** Reich Trustees of Labor. Thirteen Reich officials, one for each economic region of the Reich, under the Minister of Labor who established working conditions, tariffs, and disciplinary courts. *See also* Deutsche Arbeitsfront.

**Reichstrunkenbold.** Reich drunkard. Allusion to the alcoholism among the Nazis and specifically to Hitler's personal photographer and art expert, Heinrich Hoffmann, and to Robert Ley, founder of the Deutsche Arbeitsfront.

**Reichsverband deutscher Offiziere.** (RDO) Reich League of German Officers. Formed in 1934 from the Deutscher Offiziersbund and the Nationalverband Deutscher Offiziere.

**Reichsverband Deutscher Schriftsteller.** (RDS) Reich League of German Writers. From 1933, compulsory membership for German writers, excluding Jews and political opponents of the Nazi government. *See also* Reichsschrifttumskammer.

**Reichsvereinigung.** (RV) Reich Association. Compulsory cartel in certain industries.

**Reichsvereinigung der Juden in Deutschland.** (RVJD) Reich Association of Jews in Germany. Primary organization of German Jews, all of whom were required to belong. Set up by the 10th Regulation of the Reich Citizenship Act of July 4, 1939, it was taken over by the Reichsicherheitshauptamt. It first encouraged Jewish emigration but was coerced into collaboration with the Reich government in identifying German Jews for their later deportations. *See also* Reichssicherheitshauptamt.

**Reichsvereinigung Eisen.** Reich Association Iron. Iron and steel cartel.

**Reichsvereinigung Kohle.** Reich Association Coal. Coal cartel.

**Reichsverkehrsminister.** (RVM) Reich Traffic Minister.

**Reichsverteidigungsausschuß.** (RVA) Reich Defense Committee.

**Reichsverteidigungsbezirke.** Reich Defense Districts. Divisions of the Reich corresponding to the Nazi Party areas (Gaue).

**Reichsverteidigungsgesetz.** (RVGes) Reich Defense Law.

**Reichsverteidigungskommissar.** (RVK) Reich Defense Commissar. Representative of the government, appointed at the beginning of World War II, to coordinate civil defense measures.

**Reichsverteidigungsrat.** (RVR) Reich Defense Council.

**Reichsvertretung der deutschen Juden.** *See* Reichsvertretung der Juden in Deutschland.

**Reichsvertretung der Juden in Deutschland.** Reich Representative Council of German Jews in Germany. Headed by Rabbi Leo Baeck, founded in 1933 by German-Jewish community leaders to create a central coordinating defense administrative agency.

*Reichsverwaltungsblatt.* (RVBL) Reich Administration Newspaper.

**Reichsverwaltungsgericht.** Reich Administrative Court.

**Reichsvollkornbrotausschuß.** Reich Committee for Whole-Grain Bread. Attested to high quality whole-grain bread.

**Reichswalter.** Reich Leader. Title for an official unit leader in the chain of command at the Party head office.

**Reichswasserleiche.** Reich Water Corpse. Nickname for the actress Kristina Söderbaum, whose films often ended in a watery suicide. She was one of the stars in the Nazi 1940 antisemitic film *Jud Süß.*

**Reichswehr.** (RW) Reich Defense Forces. German armed forces under the Weimar Republic, comprised of Reichsheer and Reichsmarine, limited by the Versailles Treaty. In 1935 became the Wehrmacht.

**Reichswehrminister.** Reich Minister of War.

**Reichswerke Hermann Göring.** Hermann Göring Reich Works. Huge, nationwide, then international, industrial trust owned by the Nazi Party. Its role was to absorb and administer industry in German-occupied Europe to contribute to Germany's war effort. It became the world's largest industrial corporation.

**Reichswerkscharführer.** Reich Work Squad Leader. Title of a leader of the German Labor Front. *See also* Deutsche Arbeitsfront.

**Reichswetterdienst.** (R.W.D.) Reich Weather Service.

**Reichswirtschaftskammer.** (RWK/R.W.K.) Reich Economics Authority. Main supervisory body for the economy.

**Reichswirtschaftsminister(ium).** (RWiM/RW) Reich Minister (Ministry) of Economics.

**Reichszentralstelle für jüdische Auswanderung.** Reich Central Office for Jewish Emigration. SS and Finance Ministry set this office up in January 1939 with Adolf Eichmann in charge, to get more Jews to move out of Germany and Austria. From October 1941 the office was used to organize mass murder because Jews were no longer able to leave.

**Reichszivilprozeßordnung.** (RZPO) Reich Law for Civil Litigation.

**Reifenkarte.** Tire card. Ration card to obtain tires for motorbikes and cars. During the war, only vehicles deemed important for the war effort were eligible and were issued a red triangle for their license plate.

**Reifevermerk.** High school leaving paper. German pupils in their last two years of high school, who could not complete their finals due to military conscription or working for the war effort, received a special permit that allowed them university entrance.

**Reihenwurf.** Row throw. Shooting stick bombs, or shaped artillery ammunition used to pierce armor. *See also* Steilgranate.

**"rein arisches Geschäft."** "Pure Aryan business." Notice on Jewish businesses confiscated by the Nazi government.

**Reinhardt-Programm.** Reinhardt Program. 1933 government program to fight unemployment by encouraging projects economically and militarily valuable to Germany. Named after Secretary of State Fritz Reinhardt. *See also* Arbeitsbeschaffung.

**reinigen.** To cleanse. To clear out and murder all Jews in an area. *See also* judenrein.

**Reinigung.** Cleansing. Wiping out Jews by mass murder. *See also* judenrein.

**Reinigungskommando.** Cleaning unit. Jewish forced labor detachments.

**"Rein ist fein."** "Clean is nice." Auschwitz sign.

**Reisemarken.** Travel stamps. Stamps issued to Germans who had to travel and to soldiers on leave, to obtain food and cigarettes.

**Reisepaß.** Passport. Based on a request by the Swiss authorities, the Reich government marked Jewish passports with the letter J. *See also* Jude.

**Reißwolf.** Shredder. Code name for wartime German submarine operations off the East Coast of the United States.

**Reißwolle.** Recycled wool.

**Reiter-Hitlerjugend.** Hitler Youth Mounted Unit.

**Reiter-SS.** Mounted SS. SS cavalry units.

**Reitersturm.** Rider Storm. Mounted units of the SA and SS.

**(der) Relativitätsjude.** The Relativity Jew. Pejorative for Albert Einstein.

**REM.** *See* Reichsminister(ium) für Wissenschaft, Erziehung, und Volksbildung.

**Renegaten.** Renegades. Poles and Czechs descended from Germans who refused to adopt German citizenship. *See also* Eindeutschung.

**Renk.** Bayonet lock.

**RErbhG.** *See* Reichserbhofgesetz.

**Restghetto.** (RG) Remainder ghetto. Special camps for Jews who had survived Aktion Reinhard. Most of them were killed there or sent to other death camps to be killed.

**Restjuden.** Remaining Jews.

**"Restlose Beseitigung jedes passiven oder aktiven Widerstandes."** "Elimination of all passive or active resistance." Wehrmacht directive to destroy resistance in the Soviet Union by all means possible. Also, justification for mass murder. *See* Kommissarbefehl.

**Rest-Polen.** Remaining Poles. *See also* Generalgouvernement.

**Resttschechei.** The rest of Czechoslovakia. Hitler's term for what remained of Czechoslovakia after the annexation of the Sudetenland in 1938.

**Retter Deutschlands.** The Savior of Germany. Hitler's nickname shortly after coming to power in 1933.

**Rettungsring.** Life preserver. Nickname for Nazi Party badge because of its round shape.

**Reusch-Kreis.** Reusch Circle. Anti-Nazi group of industrialists and businessmen.

**Revier.** *See* Krankenrevier.

**Rf.** *See* Reichsstelle für; Rottenführer.

**RFdV.** *See* Reichskommissar für die Festigung des deutschen Volkstums.

**RF-Fragebogen.** Reich office questionnaire. Document for the SS Reich leader with decisive personal information on German women to determine their genetic and ideological suitability for the program to create perfect children. *See also* Eignungsprüfer; Lebensborn; Ostkinder; Wiedereindeutschung.

**RFM.** *See* Reichsfinanzminister(ium).

**RfPr.** *See* Reichskommissar für die Preisbildung.

**RFS.** *See* Reichsführerschule.

**RFSS.** *See* Reichsführer-SS.

**RFSSuChdDtPl, RFSSuCHdDtPol.** *See* Reichsführer-SS und Chef der deutchen Polizei.

**RG.** *See* Restghetto.

**Rgr.** *See* Reichsgruppe.

**Rhein.** Rhine. German river and code name for 1939 offensive in the west. *See also* Danzig.

**Rheinland.** Rhineland. An area of western Germany bordering on France. The Versailles Treaty declared it forever demilitarized as a buffer between Germany and western Europe. However, in violation of the Versailles and Locarno Treaties, Hitler ordered it remilitarized in March 1936.

**Rheinlandbastarde.** Rhineland bastards. Racist for hundreds of mixed-blood children from unions of German women and Black soldiers during the French occupation of the Rhineland after World War I. *See also* Schwarze Schmach.

**Rheinmetall Düsseldorf.** Rhine Metal Düsseldorf. Munitions manufacturer using Buchenwald prisoners for forced labor.

**Rheinübung.** Rhine exercise. 1941 German plan to send a naval battlegroup into the Atlantic to attack Allied shipping.

**Richard.** Code name for secret underground slave-labor factory near Theresienstadt at the Litomerice concentration camp in Czechoslovakia.

**Richterbriefe.** Law letters. Letters from the Reichsjustizminister criticizing or praising legal decisions in regard to their appropriateness for National Socialism.

**Richthefte des Oberkommanos der Wehrmacht.** Instructional booklets issued by the (German) Defense Forces High Command. Mainly pro-German and antisemitic. An example is *Der Jude als Weltparasit*.

**Richtlinien für das Verhalten der Truppe Rußland.** Guidelines for the Behavior of the Troops (in) Russia. Principles formulated by the Supreme High Command of the Wehrmacht for the campaign against the Soviet Union: "[T]his fight requires relentless, energetic, and drastic measures against Bolshevik agitators, partisans, saboteurs, Jews." *See* Barbarossa; Oberkommando der Wehrmacht.

**Richtlinien für die Beurteilung der Erbgesundheit.** Guidelines for the Assessment of Genetic Health. *See also* rassenhygienische und bevölkerungsbiologische Forschungsstelle.

**Richtschütze.** Machine gunner.

**Richtstrahler.** Directional transmitter. Beamed shortwave radio transmitter. *See also* Raumstrahler.

**Ring.** Circle. Administrative level of Bund deutscher Mädel in der Hitlerjugend. Also, industrial planning and efficiency committee in the Armaments Ministry; merger in the fiber industry.

**Ringsendung.** Ring broadcasting. National radio network connection with transmissions from several stations.

**Ripkens.** SS radio transmitter in Berlin.

**Ritterkreuz.** Knight's Cross. The most honored medal for military bravery, higher than the Iron Cross Second or First Class, which replaced the Grand Cross in 1939. *See* Eisernes Kreuz.

**Ritterkreuz des Kriegsverdienstkreuzes.** Knight's Cross of the War Service Cross. Medal for civilians whose service could not be honored with the Iron Cross.

**RJF.** *See* Reichsjugendführer.

**RJM.** *See* Reichsjustizminister(ium).

**RK.** *See* Reichskommissar(-e).

**RKF, RKFdV.** *See* Reichskommissar für die Festigung des deutschen Volkstums.

**RKG.** *See* Reichskriegsgericht.

**RKK.** *See* Reichskulturkammer.

**RKM.** *See* Reichskriegsministerium.

**RKO.** *See* Reichskommissariat für das Ostland.

**RKPA.** *See* Reichskriminalpolizeiamt.

**RKS.** *See* Reichskultursenat.

**RKW.** *See* Reichskuratorium für Wirtschaftlichkeit.

**RLB.** *See* Reichsluftschutzbund.

**RLF.** *See* Reichsluftsportführer.

**RLG.** *See* Reichsleistungsgesetz.

**R-Liste.** *See* Rückstellungsliste.

**RLM.** *See* Reichsluftfahrtminister(ium).

**RM.** *See* Reichsmark; Reichsminister(ium).

**RMbO.** *See* Reichsminister(ium) für die besetzten Ostgebiete.

**RMdI.** *See* Reichsminister(ium) des Inner(e)n.

**RMEuL.** *See* Reichsminister(ium) für Ernährung und Landwirtschaft.

**RMfA.** *See* Reichsminister(ium) für Arbeit.

**RMfBuM.** *See* Reichsminister(ium) für Bewaffnung und Munitionen.

**RMfVuP.** *See* Reichsminister(ium) für Volksaufklärung und Propaganda.

**RMG.** *See* Reichsmilitärgericht.

**RMVAP.** *See* Reichsminister(ium) für Volksaufklärung und Propaganda.

**RMVP.** *See* Reichsminister(ium) für Volksaufklärung und Propaganda.

**RMWEV.** *See* Reichsminister(ium) für Wissenschaft, Erziehung, und Volksbildung.

**RNSt.** *See* Reichsnährstand.

**ROA.** *See* Russische Befreiungsarmee.

**Robby-Gruppe.** Anti-Hitler Communist Group founded by Robert Uhrig. Headquartered in Berlin's Osram Works in the 1930s and 1940s.

**Roges.** *See* Rohstoffhandelgesellschaft.

**Röhm-Putsch.** *See* Nacht der langen Messer.

**Rohstoff.** Raw material. Term for Soviet prisoners of war from 1943; worked to death because of labor shortage.

**Rohstofffreiheit.** Independence vis-à-vis raw materials. Goal of the Third Reich was autarky, to become self-sufficient and free from importing crucial resources by producing substitutes or synthetic goods. *See also* Autarkie; Ersatz.

**rohstoffgedeckter Auftrag.** Contract to which an allotment of raw material was attached.

**Rohstoffhandelgesellschaft.** (Roges) Company for raw material commerce.

**rollender Angriff.** Attack in (rolling) waves.

**Rollkommando.** Mobile squad. Strong-arm squad protecting mass meetings of the Nazi Party.

**Roma.** *See* Zigeuner.

**Romani.** Gypsies. *See also* Zigeuner.

**Römer-Gruppe.** Anti-Hitler resistance group led by Dr. Josef Römer in the 1930s and 1940s.

**römisch.** Roman. Used negatively with references to Roman Catholicism and the law if they stood in opposition to Nazi ideology and law.

**Rommelspargel.** Rommel asparagus. Based on an idea of General Erwin Rommel, millions of underwater obstacles were placed along the Atlantic coast of France and the Low Countries to strengthen beach defenses against the anticipated Allied invasion. *See* Atlantikwall.

**RONA.** *See* Kommite für die russische Befreiungsarmee.

**rosa Winkel.** Pink triangle. *See also* Appendix: Winkel.

**Rosengarten.** Rose garden. Named derisively after the frozen red heads of inmates whom the SS battered and were then left to die of exposure and starvation in a barbed-wire enclosure just in front of the gas chambers at Majdanek and at Buchenwald. *See* Stacheldraht-Haus.

**Rosenkranz.** Rosary. Air force slang for antiaircraft tracer bullets.

**Rosenstraße.** Berlin street where Gestapo headquarters was located. Scene of 1943 protest of non-Jewish spouses, along with their children, of Jews arrested in roundup. Goebbels soon ordered the Jews released, a decision later confirmed by Hitler himself. *See also* Fabrikaktion.

**Rot.** Red. The 1935 study to defend against a surprise attack by France while defending the German borders against Czechoslovakia and Poland. In 1937 code name for offensive operations against Czechoslovakia with the aim of preventing a prolonged two-front war. In 1938 code name for the German invasion of France during the Czech crisis. In 1940 code name for part of the attack on France.

**Rote.** Reds. Political prisoners in the concentration camps, especially Communists, Socialists, and captured resistance fighters. Marked with red triangles. *See also* Appendix: Winkel.

**Rote Front Kämpferbund.** Red-Front Fighter's League. German Communist Party's equivalent to the Nazi SA. Though their worst enemies were the Nazis, they often collaborated with the latter to break up Social Democrat meetings in the 1920s and 1930s.

**rote Hakenkreuzschwestern.** *See* Deutscher Frauenorden Rotes Hakenkreuz der NSDAP.

**rote Kapelle.** Red Orchestra. Pro-Soviet Germans organized by Harro Schulze-Boysen and Arvid Harnack. Provided the Soviet Union with information on German political, military, economic, and arms production in the late 1930s until discovered in 1942 and its membership murdered.

**roter Winkel.** Red triangle. Sign on the number plates of German private motorbikes and cars that were allowed to operate during the war. *See also* Reifenkarte.

**Rotfrontkämpferbund.** Paramilitary German Communist Party units.

*die Rothschilds.* The Rothschilds. 1940 antisemitic Nazi propaganda film about the eminent Jewish banking family. First Nazi film attempting to show the British as mere Jewish puppets.

**Rotte.** Squad. Smallest subdivision of the Hitlerjugend.

**Rottenführer.** (Rf) Squad leader. SS lance corporal.

**RPA.** *See* Reichspropagandaamt.

**RPK.** *See* Reichspressekammer.

**RPM.** *See* Reichsminister(ium) für Volksaufklärung und Propaganda.

**RR.** *See* Rächer Röhms.

**RRG.** *See* Reichs-Rundfunk-Gesellschaft m.b.H.

**RSF.** *See* Reichsstudentenführung.

**RSHA.** *See* Reichssicherheitshauptamt.

**RSHA VI.** Department VI of RSHA. Foreign intelligence department of the RSHA. *See also* Reichssicherheitshauptamt.

**RSHA-Transporte.** Reich Main Security Administration transport. Organized deportations, primarily of Jews, from collection areas in German-occupied countries to death camps. *See also* Reichssicherheitshauptamt.

**RSK.** *See* Reichsschrifttumskammer.

**RSO.** *See* Raupenschlepper Ost.

**RStrVO.** *See* Reichsstraßenverkehrsordnung.

**RTE.** *See* Reichsstelle für technische Erzeugnisse.

**RTK.** *See* Reichstheaterkammer.

**RU.** *See* Rückkehr unerwünscht.

**rückdeutschungsfähig.** Able to become German again. *See also* Eindeutschung; Eindeutschungsfähigkeit.

**Rückgabe der deutschen Kolonien.** Return of the German colonies. Nazi demand that all German colonies taken from Germany after World War I under the Versailles Treaty be returned.

**Rückgeführte.** Those brought back. German and foreign people brought to Germany from German-occupied territories.

**Rückgliederung.** Reintegration. *See also* Anschluß.

**Rückkehr unerwünscht.** (RU) Return not wanted. Euphemistic indication on the documents of non-Jewish concentration camp prisoners to be murdered after their term of imprisonment.

**Rückkreuzung.** Breed reappearance. Reemergence of pure-blooded types after many generations of crossbreeding.

**Rückschlag.** Backlash. Diminishment of the impact or denial of the importance of German military defeat or stalemate, especially in Russia in 1942 and 1943.

**rücksichtslos.** Without consideration. Efficient, effective in the interests of National Socialism.

**rücksichtslos durchsetzen.** To push through without mercy. To succeed at all costs in the interests of National Socialism.

**rücksichtsloses Vorgehen.** Ruthless advance (in the interests of National Socialism).

**Rücksiedlung.** Resettlement. The Nazi plan to resettle Germans living outside Germany back into the German nation. *See also* Volksdeutscher.

**Rückstellungsliste.** (R-Liste) List of those kept back. List of names of Jews who were temporarily spared deportation.

**Rückstoßmotor.** Back-thrust motor. Jet propulsion.

**Rückwanderer.** *See* Umsiedler.

**Rudel.** Wolf Pack. A submarine group.

**Ruk.** *See* Reichsminister(ium) für Rüstungs(aufgaben) und Kriegsproduktion.

**Ruko.** *See* Russenkoller.

**Rüko.** *See* Rüstungskommando.

**RuKR.** *See* Regierungs- und Kriminalrat.

**Rundfunk.** Radio. German radio system controlled by the Nazi government during the Third Reich.

**Rundfunkspielschar.** Radio Youth Group. Institution of the Hitler Youth to promote music for the young. *See also* Jugendmusik.

**Rundfunkverbrechen.** Radio crime. Listening to enemy broadcasts; also, broadcasting against Gemany.

*Rundschau.* Panorama. The German Communist Party's newspaper during the Weimar Republic.

**Runen.** Runes. Ancient Germanic letters. Under the Nazis, some Runic letters were introduced in an attempt to establish authentic Germanic symbols. A single runic S was considered a symbol of victory, the double S a symbol of battle. *See also* Schutzstaffel; Sig-Rune.

**RuSHA.** *See* Rasse- und Siedlungshauptamt.

**Russenkoller.** (Ruko) Russian dizzies. Slang for nervous breakdown of German soldiers fighting on the Eastern Front in the USSR.

**Russische Befreiungsarmee.** (ROA) Russian Liberation Army. Formed in 1944 under General Andrej Wlassow; consisted of Russian workers, prisoners of war, and battalions of Russian volunteers.

**russisches Kriegsgefangenenarbeitslager.** Russian POW work camp. Area of Auschwitz designated for Soviet prisoners of war, most of whom were killed, some in early Zyklon-B tests.

**Rußlandfreiwillige.** Volunteers to fight against Russia. Men from German-occupied countries and from those sympathetic to Germany, such as Spain and Italy, fought alongside the German army on the Eastern Front.

**Rüst.** *See* Rüstungsministerium.

**Rüster.** Assembly-line worker.

**Rüsthalle.** Assembly hall.

**Rüstmann.** *See* Rüster.

**Rüstungseinsatz.** Armament service. Voluntary labor in armaments industries.

**"Rüstungsgleichberechtigung Deutschlands."** "Armaments equality for Germany." Propaganda slogan at home and abroad among non-Nazis and Nazis demanding Germany's international equality in armaments.

**Rüstungsinspektor.** Armament Inspector. General in charge of all issues related to the war economy in a specific region.

**Rüstungskommando.** (Rüko) Armament and War Production Authority. One of its main objectives was to ensure sufficient labor to reach the Reich's munitions goals.

**Rüstungsministerium.** (Rüst) *See* Reichsminister(ium) für Rüstungs(aufgaben) und Kriegsproduktion.

**RV.** *See* Reichsvereinigung.

**RVA.** *See* Reichsverteidigungsausschuß.

**RVBL.** *See Reichsverwaltungsblatt.*

**RVGes.** *See* Reichsverteidigungsgesetz.

**RVJD.** *See* Reichsvereinigung der Juden in Deutschland.

**RVK.** *See* Reichsverteidigungskommissar.

**RVM.** *See* Reichsverkehrsminister.

**RVR.** *See* Reichsverteidigungsrat.

**RW.** *See* Reichswehr.

**R.W.D.** *See* Reichswetterdienst.

**RWiM/RW.** *See* Reichswirtschaftsminister(ium).

**RWK/ R.W.K.** *See* Reichswirtschaftskammer.

**RZPO.** *See* Reichszivilprozeßordnung.

# S

**S.** *See* Schwerverbrecher; Sonderstufe SS.

**S-3.** Buchenwald Little Camp.

**SA.** *See* Schutzabteilung; Sportabteilung; Sturmabteilung

**Saalschlachten.** Hall battles. SA attacks on meetings of political parties, especially Communists and Socialists, hostile to the Nazi Party in the 1920s.

**Saalschutz.** Hall security. Nazi Party members designated to protect Party meetings and break up meetings of other political parties before the Nazi takeover of power in 1933. Developed into the SA.

**Saalschutz und Propagandatruppe.** *See* Sturmabteilung.

**Sabotagetrupp.** Sabotage troop. Propaganda term for British commandos.

**Sabotage und Zersetzung.** Sabotage and disruption. Office of German intelligence community, dissolved 1941.

**Sachbearbeiter für Judenangelegenheiten.** (German) official in charge of Jewish matters.

**Sachherrschaft.** (Economic) ownership.

**Sachsengruß.** Saxons' salute. A form of torture inflicted on new arrivals at concentration camps in Germany. After initial physical ill-treatment, the inmate had to remain, sometimes for hours in any weather and without food or drink, with his hands behind his head, often kneeling, while guards abused him.

**Sachsenhausen.** Located in town of Orienburg near Berlin. Concentration camp housing political prisoners, criminals, Jehovah's Witnesses, asocials, German homosexuals, AWOL soldiers from the Wehrmacht and the Waffen-SS, Polish and Soviet POWs, nationals from several occupied nations, Gypsies, and Jews, including those sent there after the Nazi November 1938 Pogrom. Prisoners enslaved for Deutsche Machinenfabrik and Heinkel, two of 2,500 German firms using forced labor. Thousands of Soviet POWs were shot or gassed to death. Of the 200,000 prisoners held there, about half survived. Painted in huge letters on each of the barracks at Sachsenhausen was the camp slogan: "Es gibt einen Weg zur Freiheit; seine Meilensteine heißen: Gehorsam, Fleiß, Ehrlichkeit, Ordnung, Sauberkeit, Nüchtenheit, Wahrhaftigkeit, Opfersinn, und Liebe zum Vaterland" ("There is one road to freedom; its milestones are obedience, diligence, honesty, order, cleanliness, sobriety, truthfulness, self-sacrifice, and love for the Fatherland").

**Sacklandung.** Sack landing. Pancake landing of airplane not using landing gear.

**"SA-Dienst erzieht zur Kameradschaft, Zähigkeit, Kraft!"** "SA service raises one to comradeship, toughness, and strength." SA slogan.

**SA-Feldpolizei.** Sturmabteilung Field Police. *See also* Feldjägerkorps.

**Saisonstaat.** Seasonal state. Derogatory term for Poland and Czechoslovakia, two states founded after World War I, in 1919.

**SA Jesu Christi.** Storm Battalion Jesus Christ. Church organization founded in 1932 by German National Socialist theologians.

**säkular, säkulär.** Secular. Something immense, extraordinary.

**Sal.** *See* Sammellager.

**Salamander.** Code name for German jet fighter. *See also* Volksjäger.

**Salami.** Derogatory for Hungarian Jews arriving at Auschwitz in 1944 to be killed.

**SA-Liederbuch.** SA Songbook. Published in 1933 and introduced by SA Chief of Staff Ernst Röhm.

**Salon Kitty.** Kitty's salon. Luxurious Berlin house of prostitution run by Kitty Schmidt for the Nazi SD, where important foreign visitors were offered food, drink, and sex while their conversations were recorded on tape. According to German spy chief Walter Schellenberg, "quite a few ladies from the upper crust of German society were only too willing to serve their country in this manner." Occasionally Kitty's services were used by Nazi leaders, particularly Reinhard Heydrich.

**Salzwedel.** Satellite camp of Neuengamme concentration camp where female prisoners were used to manufacture land mines.

**SA-Mann.** Member of the SA.

*(Der) SA-Mann.* The SA Man. Sturmabteilung periodical.

**SA-mäßig.** In the style of the SA.

**Sammellager.** (SaL) Assembly camp.

**Sammellager für Zigeuner.** Assembly camp for Gypsies. Concentration camps established in late 1930s for German Gypsies. On January 30, 1940, 30,000 Gypsies were deported to such camps along with tens of thousands of Poles and Jews.

**Sammellager für Nacht-und-Nebel-Häftlinge.** Assembly camp for Night-and-Fog prisoners. At Natzweiler-Struthof concentration camp. *See also* Nacht-und-Nebel-Erlaß.

**Sammellehre.** Cumulative teachings. Doctrine of German collectivism.

**Sammelplatz.** Assembly center. Location of mandatory roll call in concentration camps.

**Sammelstelle.** *See* Sammelplatz.

**Sammlungsgesetz.** Collection law. Order to force church members to contribute to (Nazi) Party projects. A Security Police means to fight church members opposing the Reich.

**Sanitätsdienstgrad.** (SDG) A rank in the Ambulance Service. *See also* Allgemeine Krankentransportgesellschaft.

**Sanitätsdienstgefreiter.** Health Service Officer. Official responsible for killing prisoners in the gas chamber. He and an SS officer administered the Zyklon-B gas.

**Sanitätsführerkorps im SA-Sanitätsdienst.** (SFK) Leadership body in the SA Ambulance Service.

**Sardinen.** Sardines. SS slang for French Jews arriving at Auschwitz.

**SA-Reserve.** (SAR) SA Reserve.

**SA-Standarte.** SA Regiment.

**SAR.** *See* SA-Reserve.

**Sara, Sarah.** Hebrew name that all German-Jewish women had to use in their identification papers and in all official correspondence from 1938, in addition to their given names if the latter were not expressly Jewish. *See also* Abraham; Israel.

**Sarassanirock.** Sarassani tunic. Army slang for the colorful jacket of the full-dress German army uniform after the popular circus Sarassani. *See also* Kaiser-Wilhelm-Gedächtnisrock; Waffenrock.

**Sargmobil.** Coffin-mobile. Army slang for scouting tank.

**SA-Stabswache Göring.** SA Bodyguard Göring. *See also* Landespolizeigruppe Hermann Göring.

**SA-Standarte Feldherrnhalle.** SA-Regiment Ferrnhalle. Elite SA Motorized Division. *See also* Feldherrnhalle.

**Satan.** Army slang for 1,800-kilogram bomb.

***Sätze zur Arierfrage.*** Principles on the Aryan Question. Book containing Pastor Martin Niemöller's "burdensome" defense of baptized Jews against Nazi racial criteria. During his concentration camp internment, he dropped his traditional Christian antisemitism.

**"Sauberkeit ist Gesundheit."** "Cleanliness is health." Sign on gas chambers disguised as showers in several death camps and on barracks rafters.

**Säuberung.** Cleansing. Cleaning Jews out of education, as teachers and students. Also, whole communities of Jews being taken from their neighborhoods and sent to death camps.

**Säuberungsaktion.** Cleansing Operation. Forced removal of Jews and other people in German-occupied Europe to be sent to concentration camps.

**Säuberungsaktion gegen die homosexuelle Subkultur.** Cleansing activity against the homosexual subculture. *See also* Homosexualität.

**Säuberungs- und Sicherheitsmaßnahmen.** Cleansing and security measures. Special Einsatzgruppen that murdered Jewish and Catholic Poles during the early months of World War II. A useful by-product of the murders was to ensure terror and fear of German occupation forces.

**Säuberungsziel.** Cleansing goal. Einsatzkommando goal in eastern Europe to murder Jews as soon as possible.

**Sauckel-Mädchen.** Sauckel girls. Late in the war, Fritz Sauckel, Chief of Labor Mobilization, recruited young women for forced labor from German-occupied eastern Europe. *See also* Generalbevollmächtigter für den Arbeitseinsatz.

**Sauckel-Mädel.** *See* Sauckel-Mädchen.

**Saurer.** German company that designed and built poison-gas vans. *See also* Sonderwagen.

**Saurerwagen.** (S-Wagen) Saurer vehicle. Poison-gas van. *See also* Sonderwagen.

**Saujud.** Jew pig. *See also* Judensau.

**SA-Wehrabzeichen.** SA defense badge. Awarded to SA candidates after first pre-military training.

**SA-Wehrmannschaften.** *See* Wehrmannschaften.

**SB./S.B.** *See* sonderbehandelt; strengstens bestraft.

**S-Boot.** *See* Schnellboot.

**Schachmeister.** Chess champion. Ironic for chief foreman at a concentration camp. *See* Oberkapo.

**Schädlinge.** Vermin, parasites. People, in particular Jews and Gypsies, whom the Nazis saw as damaging their national community—politically, racially, socially, ideologically. *See also* Volksgemeinschaft; Volksschädlinge.

**Schädlingsbekämpfung.** War against vermin. Code name for killing Jews with Zyklon-B gas in concentration camps.

**schaffendes Kapital.** Creative capital. Industrial capital. *See also* raffendes Kapital.

**Schafstall.** Sheep barn. Part of Buchenwald concentration camp without beds, tables, and benches; the ground covered with pine branches. Jews were housed there in 1938 with next to no food and daily tortures. Many died soon after incarceration or they committed suicide.

**Schaft.** League. Abbreviation for Jungenschaft (boys' league) or Mädelschaft (girls' league). Also the smallest unit of the Deutsche Jungvolk.

**Schamil.** Code name for airborne attack on Soviet oil installations at Maikop.

**Schande von Nürnberg.** Shame of Nuremberg. Derogatory for Nuremberg's synagogue.

**Schandfleck.** Stain, blot, disgrace. Badge of shame. Yellow Star of David that German Jews were forced to wear, from 1941.

**Schandpfahl.** Post of shame. Erected by students before the book burning in 1933 denouncing Jews and those not in favor of National Socialism. *See also* Bücherverbrennung.

**Schandvertrag.** Treaty of shame. Disdainful Nazi term for the 1919 Treaty of Versailles.

**Schanzzeug.** Entrenching junk. Soldier slang for shovel.

**Schar.** Troop. Hitler Youth unit of about fifty.

**Scharführer.** (SchF) Troop Leader. SS Staff Sergeant.

*Scharnhorst.* German cruiser. Along with the *Gneisenau*, the backbone of the German surface fleet at the start of World War II. It was sunk later in the war.

**Schaukel.** Swing. Auschwitz torture device.

**Scheck.** Check, cheque. Raw material bill transferable under certain conditions.

**Scheinvolk.** Phony people. Jews as dangerous and corruptive anti-people; a deadly threat to all that must be destroyed.

**Scheißkommando.** Shit unit. A punishment unit for inmates who had to clean the latrines in the concentration camps.

**Scheißkopf.** Shithead. Derogatory for Jews in camps, often accompanied by a blow to the head.

**Scheißmeister.** Shit master. The camp inmate whose job was to time how long and how many times prisoners of the camps used the toilets.

**"Schenk dem Führer ein Kind!"** "Give a baby to the Führer as a present." Propaganda phrase appealing to all German women to produce children. *See also* "Ficken für Volk und Führer."

**Scheunenviertel.** Barns quarter. Berlin Jewish section.

**scheußliche Gestalten.** Vile figures. Goebbels' phrase for Jews, who had to be killed.

**SchF.** *See* Scharführer.

**SchHL.** *See* Schutzhaftlager.

**Schich(te).** Level. Word used by Hitler and others to avoid the appearance of class distinctions, referring to racial levels instead of classes within the social hierarchy; for example, the leading group within the German race was called Herrenschicht.

**Schicksal.** Fate. Nazi belief that the Aryan race had an inevitable destiny. Ideological rationale for their actions.

**schicksalhaft.** Fateful. Favorite adjective used by the German media referring to historical uniqueness and the destiny of Nazi Germany.

**schicksalhaft hineingeboren in den Typ.** Born into the destined racial type.

**schicksalsbezogen.** Coherent with destiny. Acts and ideas that coincided with the Nazi ideology.

**schicksalserfüllt.** Conscious of the destiny of the racial type. Authentically German.

**schicksalsfremd.** Alien to destiny. Non-German.

**schicksalsgebunden.** Connected by fate. Conscious of racial (German) destiny.

**Schicksalskampf des deutschen Volkes.** The struggle of the German people as determined by fate. Used during World War II to encourage fighting to the end, especially against Russia.

**Schicksalskampf um Europa.** The struggle for the fate of Europe. *See also* Schicksalskampf des deutschen Volkes.

**schicksalsverbunden.** *See* schicksalsgebunden.

**Schießbuch.** Shooting book. Marksmanship record.

**Schießstand.** Shooting range. Murder site at Neuengamme where Soviet POWs were shot to death.

**Schiffchen.** Little ship. Military slang for overseas cap.

**"Schimpfen ist der Stuhlgang der Seele!"** "Complaining is the feces of the soul." Goebbel's slogan suggesting a purging of growing German dissatisfaction with the war.

**(von) Schirach, Baldur.** *See* Reichsstatthalter.

**Schlacht.** Battle. Strife, endeavor; government policy of effort campaign. *See also* Arbeitsschlacht; Ernährungsschlacht; Geburtenschlacht.

**Schlachtflieger.** Battle flyer. German fighter plane used toward the end of the war to attack enemy tanks.

**schlagartig.** All of a sudden. Striking by surprise was a Nazi technique to instill fear.

**"Schlagt den Weltfeind!"** "Beat the world enemy." SA slogan inciting violence against Jews.

**"Schlagt die Juden tot!"** "Beat the Jews to death." SA slogan inciting violence against Jews.

**Schlaraffia.** *See* Wilhelm-Busch-Gesellschaft.

**Schlauch.** Tube. The area at Belzec and Treblinka between the gas chamber and the barracks where Jews were stripped and beaten before being killed.

**Schleichessen.** Meal on the sly. Illegal restaurant meal during period of German rationing.

**Schleichfahrt.** Silent running. U-boat rigged to operate silently.

**Schleiferei.** Grinding. Drilling of Hitler Youth recruits.

**Schleuse.** Floodgate, air lock. Theresienstadt served as a holding area for Jews sent there en route to Auschwitz.

**(die) Schleuse.** Floodgate. SS financed organization that planned postwar escape from Germany of prominent Nazis.

**Schloß.** Castle. Reception area of Chelmno death camp.

**Schlucht.** Ravine. Burial location of the bodies of the murdered (mostly Jews) at various sites, the most notorious at Babi Yar, a ravine outside of Kiev. There, in September 1941, Ensatzgruppe C murdered between 30,000 and 40,000 prisoners (mostly Jews) on Yom Kippur.

**Schlüssel M.** Code M. German naval code.

**Schlußschein.** Final certificate. Sales permit for cattle and so on. *See also* Ablieferungspflicht.

**Schmachfriede.** Shameful peace. Versailles Peace Treaty.

**Schmeltjuden.** Schmelt Jews. In 1941, SS officer Albrecht Schmelt monopolized the forced labor of 50,000 Jews in Upper Silesia to work for the armaments industry.

**Schmelz.** Melted enamel. Jews and other people transferred from a labor camp to be murdered at a killing site.

**Schmelzghetto.** Smelting ghetto. Ghetto for so-called superfluous Jews to be held and then shipped to death camps.

**Schmetterling.** Butterfly. Code name for an air-defense guided missile under development that the Third Reich did not have time to put into use before the war ended.

**Schmitz-Werke.** Schmitz Works. Wehrmacht munitions factory using Jewish slave labor from Skarzysko-Zwangsarbeitslager, Poland.

**Schmuckstücke.** Pieces of jewelry. Female prisoners on the verge of death from starvation and/or disease at Ravensbrück. *See* Muselmann.

**Schmutzarbeit.** Dirty work. Many Germans did not want to deal with Jews in ghettos and concentration camps for fear of contamination.

**Schmutz und Schund.** Dirt and trash. *See also* jüdisch.

**Schmutz- und Schundbücher.** Dirt-and-trash books. *See also* Nacht der Feuer.

**Schnaps.** Liquor. Air force slang for gasoline.

**Schneekommando.** Snow unit. 1,000 priest-prisoners were assigned to shovel snow at Dachau, where they were not allowed to wear shoes and were ridiculed and beaten.

**schnell-.** Fast. Mobile (military prefix).

**Schnellarbeitsstahl.** High-speed steel (tool).

**Schnellbomber.** Fast bomber. Medium bomber.

**Schnellboot.** (S-Boot.) Fast boat. Motorboat equipped with torpedoes. Similar to the U.S. PT boat.

**Schneller Verband.** Fast unit. Motorized formation.

**Schobernhof.** Hans Frank's estate in south Germany where he sent food, goods, and artwork he stole from Poland while he was Governor-General of Poland. *See also* Generalgouvernement; Generalgouverneur.

**Scholle.** Ground, earth. Mystical for German soil and homeland. *See also* Blut und Boden.

**(Die) Scholle.** The Soil. Nazi film concerning the soil.

**schollengebunden.** Bound to the soil. An instinctive, mythical bond to the German soil.

**(der) schöne Adolf.** Handsome Adolf. Hitler, according to millions of German women.

**Schönheit der Arbeit.** The beauty of work. Estheticizing German workers' work areas. A department of the Nationalsozialistische Gemeinschaft Kraft durch Freude headed by Albert Speer.

**Schonungsblock/Sterbelager für kranke und entkräftete Häftlinge.** Recuperation block/death camp for sick and weak prisoners. At Neuengamme.

**Schonungslager.** Convalescence camp. Ironic for area of concentration camps where sick prisoners were kept until they died or were murdered.

**Schrage-Musik.** Hot, heavy (jazz) music. A German air force night fighter tactic in which several machine guns would shoot upward at an angle of 80 degrees to take advantage of the vulnerable underside of Allied bombers.

**Schreckladung.** Shock charge. Booby trap.

**Schreibgangwerk.** Writing-process work. Germanized for Schreibmaschine (typewriter).

**Schreibtischorder.** Desktop order. Directive written by Nazi officials who never saw the victim of the order face to face.

**Schriftenreihe biozentrischer Forschungen.** Publication series of bio-centric research. From 1935 to 1938, *Das deutsche Leben* (German Life) contained interpretations of German literature and philosophy from a bio-centric point of view. *See also* Arbeitskreis für biozentrische Forschungen.

**Schriftleiter.** Editor. Nazi-Germanized word for Redakteur.

**Schriftleitergesetz.** Editor Law. Law of April 10, 1933, that mandated that newspaper and magazine editors were to be German National Socialists and have "national characteristics." The law basically barred Jews and anti-Nazis from publishing.

**Schrifttum.** Literature. Nazi-Germanized word for Literatur.

**Schrifttumspflege.** Writing cultivation. Nazi censorship of all literature, including educational material.

**Schrifttumspreis.** Literature prize. Germanized for Literaturpreis.

**Schriftwalter.** Writing expert. Within a National Socialist office that published printed material, clerk or editor responsible for the political correctness of (ideological) content.

**Schrittmacher.** Pacesetter. From motorcycle racing, negative for promoting liberalism. Also, not sufficiently combating the spread of venereal disease.

**Schrumpfgermane.** Shrunken Teuton. Nickname for Goebbels and other Nazi Party members who were far from the ideal of the Nordic-Aryan man.

**Schufa.** *See* Schutzformation des Reichsbanners.

**Schuhtauschstelle.** Shoe exchange location. Place to exchange shoes during the war, because of the scarcity of shoes for German civilians.

**Schulgemeinde.** School community. Comprised of parents and teachers to guarantee the maintenance of education according to National Socialist principles.

**Schul-Jugendwalter.** School youth counselors. Ancillary teachers from the Hitler Youth organization in every German school.

**Schulung.** Training. Indoctrination, bring into alignment with National Socialism. Also, code name for Hitler's remilitarization of the Rhineland (*see* Rheinland).

**Schulungsabend.** Training evening. Ideological indoctrination of Nazi Party members.

**Schulungsamt.** Training office. *See also* Schulung.

**Schulungsburg.** Training castle. Indoctrination institution for Nazi Party functionaries.

**Schulungslager.** Training camp. Indoctrination institution to train groups of students, teachers, physicians, and other people.

**Schuma.** *See* Schutzmannschaften.

**Schundliteratur.** Trash literature. Category of children's literature as determined by the censorship authorities. *See Jugendschriften-Warte.*

**SCHUPO(S).** *See* Schutzmannschaft der Ordungspolizei.

**Schußzahlen erschießen.** To reach the goal (of the number of people to be) shot. To reach the quota of killing Jews and others through shooting them.

**Schuttpatron von Berlin.** Rubble patron of Berlin. Nickname for Goebbels instead of Schutzpatron (patron saint) after the 1942 and 1943 bombing raids on Berlin.

**Schutzabteilung.** (SA) Security Branch. Precursor of Sturmabteilung. *See also* Sturmabteilung.

**Schutzangehörige des Reiches.** Protected subjects of the Reich. Poles living in areas annexed by Germany, not part of the German people. Euphemism for slave laborers.

**Schutzangehöriger.** Protégé. Foreigner under German protection.

**Schützenloch.** Safety hole. Equivalent to the American and British foxhole. *See also* Fuchsloch.

**Schützenpanzerwagen.** Armored personnel carrier.

**Schütze.** A private in the army.

**Schutzformation des Reichsbanners.** (Schufa) Security Squad of the Reichsbanner. Social Democratic Party security units. *See also* Reichsbanner Schwarz-Rot-Gold.

**Schutzgerechtigkeit.** Right of protection. Justification for excluding Jews and other groups from legal protection.

**Schutzhaft.** Protective custody. Arbitrary internment of political opponents, Jews, and others in prisons and concentration camps as enemies of the people and of the state, allegedly to protect the nation. *See also* Reichstagsbrandverordnung.

**Schutzhaftbefehl.** Protective custody order. According to Nazi law, the legal basis for Schutzhaft.

**Schutzhaftjuden.** Protective custody Jews. Jews sent to concentration camps to be killed.

**Schutzhaftlager.** (SchHL) Protective custody camp. SS custody camp. Synonymous with concentration camp. *See also* Konzentrationslager.

**Schutzhaftlagerführer(in).** (Female) protective custody camp chief warden. At several German prisons and concentration camps.

**Schutzhäftling.** Protective custody prisoner. Prisoner kept in a concentration camp or Gestapo prison waiting for trial and death.

**Schutzhäftling Wehrmacht.** (SHW) Prisoner in protective custody of the army.

**Schutzhaftlagerführer.** Protective custody camp chief warden. At several camps. *See also* Lagerführer.

**Schutzjuden.** Protected Jews. Upper-class Jews in the Weimar Republic.

**Schutzkommando.** Security guard.

**Schutzmannschaft der Ordungspolizei.** (SCHUPOS) Detachments of Order Police. Pro-German auxiliary police forces in German-occupied countries. Pro-Nazi police used for security, police, and antipartisan activities, especially in Croatia, Estonia, Latvia, Lithuania, and Ukraine.

**Schutzmannschaften.** (Schuma) Security details. *See also* Schutzmannschaft der Ordungspolizei.

**Schutzpässe.** Protection passports. Spain, Sweden, and Switzerland gave papers to Hungarian Jews in 1944 to save them from death. *See also* Wallenberg-Paß.

**Schutzpolizei.** *See* Schutzmannschaft der Ordungspolizei.

**Schutzschein.** Protection certificate. Papers the Nazis allowed Judenräte to give to some ghetto Jews to save them temporarily from being rounded up and deported to concentration camps.

**Schutzstaffel.** (SS) Security Squad. These detachments were originally formed in 1925 as Hitler's personal guard. From 1929, under Himmler, the SS developed into the elite of the Nazi Party. SS members had to prove their racial purity back to 1700 and membership was also based on Aryan appearance. In mid-1934, they took over the political police and the concentration camps. Their goal was, in Nazi terms, to achieve a "Final Solution of the Jewish Problem." In reality units were used to round up and murder Jews and non-Jews. The elite Waffen-SS fought as German military units. For its emblem, the SS used two Teutonic runes—a parallel jagged double SS. The SS grew into a state within the state. Its divisions included the armed SS, or Waffen-SS, and the general SS, or Allgemeine-SS, which provided the guards and staff of the concentration camps. The SS contained Germanic units composed of Flemish, Danish, Dutch, and others from 1942 on. Later, as manpower demands grew greater, even units of Poles and Ukrainians, as well as a Turkic-Moslem unit who possessed the requisite racial qualities was formed.

*(Die) Schutzstaffel.* The Security Squad. Short-lived 1926 SS periodical.

**Schutzstaffel Fördernde Mitglieder.** (SS-FM) SS promoting members. In the 1920s and 1930s, these members did not need to pass the race standards, serve in the SS or in combat, nor swear an oath. They had only to support the SS financially. *See also* feiner Maxe.

**Schutzstaffelmann.** SS man. Man belonging to the SS. *See also* Schutzstaffel.

**Schutz- und Sportabteilungen.** Security and sport detachments. Organizations that became the Sturmabteilung.

**Schutzverband Deutscher Schriftsteller.** (SDS) (Nazi ideological) Organization to Protect German Writers. *See also* Reichsverband (Deutscher) Schriftsteller.

**Schutzverwaltung.** Protective administration. Country occupied by the Third Reich, formally independent, with native government, but under strict German supervision (e.g., Bohemia and Moravia). *See also* Neuordnung Europas; Protektorat Böhmen und Mähren.

**schwangere Frauen.** Pregnant women. A condition tantamount to a death sentence for Jewish women who arrived pregnant at Auschwitz. Non-Jews were sent to Ravensbrück for abortions.

**Schwarz.** Black. Code word for the occupation of Italy on September 9, 1943.

**Schwarze.** Blacks. An insulting allusion to the SS, referring to the color of their uniforms and associating them with black Africans, whom the Nazis and general German opinion looked at with contempt. Also, slang for prisoners called asocials and identified by a black triangle. *See also* asozial; Winkel.

**(der) Schwarze Bunker.** The black bunker. A wing of Block 3 at Buchenwald, entirely dark, locked, and without heat. Prisoners were locked up inside and brutally beaten, often killed.

**Schwarze Front.** Black Front. Organization of dissident Nazis. According to the April 1933 civil service law, a "Natural-Communist Movement." *See* Kampfgemeinschaft revolutionärer Nationalsozialisten.

**Schwarze Kapelle.** Black chapel, black band. Gestapo name for a group of Wehrmacht officers and civilians involved in several attempts to assassinate Hitler in 1943 and 1944. Major players were General Ludwig Beck, Chief of the Army's General Staff; General Friedrich Olbricht of the General Army Office; General Erich Hoepner; Major General Tresckow, a member of Army Group North; Colonel Henning von Tresckow; Major Fabian von Schlabrendorff, a lawyer; and civilians such as Ulrich von Hassell, the German Ambassador to Rome; Johannes Propitz, Prussian Minister of Finance; and Carl Goerdeler, the ex-mayor of Leipzig, who at one time was the conspirators' prime choice for Hitler's replacement. Other civilians involved in plotting against Hitler included Pastor Dietrich Bonhöffer and Father Alfred Delp. *See also* Flasche; Kreisauer Kreis; Walküre; 20. Juli.

**(das) Schwarze Korps.** (SK) The Black Corps. Synonym for the SS.

*(Das) Schwarze Korps.* The Black Corps. The SS weekly newspaper. Subtitled, Zeitung der Schutzstaffeln der NSDAP (Newspaper of the SS of the National Socialist German Workers' Party).

**schwarze Männer.** Black men. Army slang for tank crew.

**Schwarze Order.** Black Order. Himmler's SS. From the outbreak of World War II, black was worn only for ceremonial purposes, the Waffen-SS adopting the field-gray of the Germany army. In the concentration camps, from 1936 on, the Death's Head Units of the SS wore brown uniforms, although other SS men serving in the camps wore black. *See also* Totenkopfverbände; Waffen-SS.

**Schwarze Polizei.** Black Police. SS field police.

**Schwarze Reichswehr.** Black Reichswehr. Military units of volunteers sponsored by the German armed forces after the Versailles Treaty partially disarmed Germany. *See also* Fehmgerichte.

**Schwarze Schmach.** Black Shame. Black-African French troops occupying the Rhineland between wars.

**Schwarze Wand.** Black wall. Wall in front of which inmates were shot at Auschwitz I.

**Schwarzhören.** Illegally to listen to the radio. To listen to foreign broadcasts; punishable by death.

**Schwarz-Rot-Gold.** Black, red, gold. Colors of the Weimar Republic's flag. Hitler used these colors as indicative of the international conspiracies against Germany by the Catholic Church, Soviet Bolshevism, and, infecting the other two, international Judaism.

**Schwarz-Rot-Senf.** Black-red-mustard. Derogatory for the black-red-gold colors of the Weimar Republic's tricolor flag.

**Schweineecke.** Pig corner. Area of Flossenbürg concentration camp where those to be gassed were marked with a red cross on their foreheads, like pigs before slaughter.

**Schweinehund.** Pig-dog, bastard. Epithet often used against Jews inside and outside concentration camps. This oath and others were uttered by concentration camp guards who struck the Jew's head each time the oath was said. The Jew was expected to stand up straight with a fixed look forward.

**Schweineleistung.** Hog deliveries (by German farmers).

**Schweinemord.** Hog murder. Hog breeders killing their stock during World War I and during the first Nazi years to protest market regulations.

**schwer-.** Heavy (military prefix).

**Schwerarbeiter.** (German) worker performing heavy labor. Received increased rations during the war years. *See also* Bewirtschaftung.

**Schwerarbeiterkarte.** Card for worker performing heavy labor. Special ration card. *See* Schwerarbeiter.

**schweres Maschinengewehr.** (SMG) Heavy machine gun.

**Schwerpunkt.** Focal point. Center of attack.

**Schwerpunktbildung.** Building up the center point of a definitive action. Used both militarily and ideologically, indicating, for example, a decisive attack against the Allies or the Jews.

**Schwerstarbeiter.** (German) worker performing heaviest labor. Obtained additional food rations for working in the most extreme conditions (e.g., intense heat).

**Schwertleite.** Sword ritual. Ceremony during which Hitler Youth received their bayonets and became eligible for military service. *See also* Deutsches Jungvolk in der Hitlerjugend; Nationalpolitische Erziehungsanstalten.

**Schwertworte.** Sword words. Oath of German Youth boys. "Jungvolkjungen sind hart, schweigsam und treu. Jungvolkjungen sind Kameraden. Des Jungvolkjungen Höchstes ist die Ehre!" ("Boys of the German Youth are hard, silent, and faithful. Boys of the German Youth are good comrades. The highest [achievement] for boys of the German Youth is honor"). Also hard as steel, tough as leather, and fast as hound dogs. *See also* Deutsches Jungvolk in der Hitlerjugend; "Flink wie die Windhunde, zäh wie Leder, und hart wie Kruppstahl"; Hitlerjugend; Pimpf.

**Schwerverbrecher.** (S) Serious offender. Marked, in a concentration camp, by an S on a green triangle. *See also* Winkel.

**Schwimmwagen.** Floating car. Amphibious military vehicle with a propeller that swung down and connected directly to the crankshaft via a square-drive socket. The Schwimmwagen was made 4-wheel-drive in first gear so it could get out of the water more easily. *See also* Kübelwagen.

**Schwindelgas.** Swindle gas. A gas with an odor disguised as a different gas.

**Schwingblatt.** Swinging blade. Germanization of membrane.

**Schwingen.** Wings (of an aircraft).

**Schwulstzeit.** Era of pompousness. German language period from 1648 through the eighteenth century; Baroque period. *See also* Deutsche Sprache.

**SD.** *See* Sicherheitsdienst; Sicherheitsdienst des Reichsführers SS.

**SDG.** *See* Sanitätsdienstgrad.

**SD-Lager.** Security service camp. At Hertogenbosch.

**SDS.** *See* Schutzverband Deutscher Schriftsteller.

**VI F, 4A.** RSHA department at Sachsenhausen using Jewish forgers to counterfeit Allied and neutral-nation money. *See* Himmlerpfunde.

**Sechsstern.** Six-pointed star. *See also* Judenstern.

**Seehaus-Dienst.** Sea-house service. Code name for intelligence service of the Foreign Ministry that listened to foreign broadcasts.

**Seehund.** Seal. Midget U-boat.

**Seekriegsleitung.** (Skl) Naval War Command.

**Seekuh.** Sea cow. Navy slang for large, 700-ton, submarine.

**Seele.** Soul. A mystical life force based on (the German) race alone.

**Seelenbelastung.** Burdening of the soul. Effect on those who shot Jews and other people in prepared ditches. It became a motive for German technicians to develop a gas van designed to lessen the suffering of the murderers.

**Seelenbewirtschaftung.** Cultivation of souls. *See also* Menschenführung.

**Seelendurchmesser.** Soul diameter. Germanization of caliber.

**Seelenstil.** In the style of the soul. *See also* Seele.

**Seelentum.** Soulness. Character of the German people.

**Seelenwende.** Change of soul. Transition from a religious significance of soul to a racial National Socialist meaning.

**Seelenzelle.** Soul cell. Biological cell referring to how the German race was renewing itself, in the manner of cell multiplication.

**Seelöwe.** *See* Unternehmen Seelöwe.

**Sehrohr.** Seeing tube. Periscope.

**"Sei ehrlich!"** "Be honest." Directive carved into the cross beams of the barracks at Auschwitz.

**Sekretär des Führers.** Secretary of the Führer. Martin Bormann held this position. *See also* Stellvertreter des Führers.

**Sekretariat für das Sicherheitswesen.** Secretariat for Security Affairs. SS and SD coordinating unit for security in the Generalgouvernement. Second in authority only to Himmler in coordinating the murderous operation to destroy the Jews. *See also* Endlösung der Judenfrage.

**Sektor.** Sector, section. Different areas or fields within the National Socialist organization.

**Selbstauflösung.** Self-dissolution. Euphemism for the forced dissolution of German institutional organizations from 1933. *See also* Gleichschaltung.

**selbstfahr.** Self-propelled.

**Selbstgleichschalter.** Self-coordinator. A German who willingly accepted Nazi ideology.

**"Selbstmord durch Sprung aus dem Fenster."** "Suicide by jumping out of the window." Entry on death certificates and registries to conceal the murder of Jews and others in concentration camps. *See also* (gefälschte) Todesursachen; Todesfallsaufnahmen.

**Selbstmord-Kommando.** Suicide unit. *See also* Himmelfahrtskommando.

**Selbstreinigungsaktionen.** Self-cleaning operations. German-supported pogroms perpetrated by Ukrainian, Latvian, Lithuanian, and Estonian nationalists against Jews, justified as native revenge against Jewish oppression.

**Selbstschutz.** Self-defense. Paramilitary defense unit of Germans residing in Poland.

**Selbstschutzkräfte.** Self-Defense Forces. Germans on duty during air raids and emergency situations during the war years. *See also* Luftschutzgemeinschaft.

**Selbstversorger.** Self-supplier. During World War II, Germans, particularly self-sufficient farmers, who were independent of food ration cards. *See also* Teilselbstversorger.

**Selbstversorgung.** Self-sufficiency. *See also* Autarkie.

**Selbstverwaltung.** *See* Häftlingsselbstverwaltung.

**Selektion.** Selection. At concentration camps, sorting of male and female prisoners into groups such as slave laborers, the ill, and those for immediate murder.

**Semigranten.** Semitic emigrants. Derisive for prewar Jewish emigrants from Germany.

**Sendeleiter.** Radio-program director.

**Sendergruppe.** Network.

**Sennelager.** Extensive Wehrmacht training grounds near Paderborn, Germany.

**Septemberlinge.** Septemberlings. Goebbels' contemptuous term for those Germans who joined the Nazi Party after the September 1930 elections.

**September-Morde.** September murders. Polish mass murdering of ethnic Germans after Germany invaded Poland on September 1, 1939.

**seßhafte Kampfstoffe.** Permanent fighting material. War chemicals that settled on vegetation.

**Seuche.** Epidemic, scourge. Jews in Germany and in the world. *See also* Volksbazillus.

**Seuchengebiet.** Infested area. Nazi synonym for ghetto.

**Seuchensperrgebiet.** Epidemic zone. Nazi justification for closing off ghettos as an epidemic zone—a self-fulfilling prophecy since once the ghettos were closed and the inmates starving, they were more subject to typhus and other such epidemic diseases.

**SFK.** *See* Sanitätsführerkorps im SA-Sanitätsdienst.

**SG.** *See* Sondergerichte.

**SHD.** *See* Sicherheits- und Hilfsdienst.

**SHW.** *See* Schutzhäftling Wehrmacht.

**SichD.** *See* Sicherheits-Division.

**Sichelschnitt.** Sickle cut. Name for the Hitler-Mannstein 1940 Ardennes offensive intended to cut off Allied forces in Belgium. *See also* Fall Gelb.

**Sicherheitsdienst.** (SD) Security Service of the SS. Secret Service of the Nazi Party.

**Sicherheitsdienst des Reichsführers SS.** (SD, SS-SD) Security Service of the Reich Leader of the SS. The SS Security and Intelligence Service established in 1931 under Reinhard Heydrich to oversee political opponents and opposition political parties. In 1934 it became the Nazi Party's Intelligence Service. By 1936, it had become Germany's official intelligence service, in charge of national security, espionage, and counterespionage.

**Sicherheits-Division.** (SichD) Military Security Division.

**Sicherheitspolizei.** (Sipo) Security Police. Commanded by Heinrich Himmler as Reichsführer-SS und Chef der Deutschen Polizei. Included the SD, the Ordnungspolizei, the Kriminalpolizei, and the Gestapo. Their role was to pursue Jews, enemies, and opponents of the Third Reich. *See* Polizei.

**Sicherheits- und Hilfsdienst.** (SHD) Security and Aid Service. In response to World War II bombing raids in Germany, this official body provided assistance whenever civilian help was not sufficient.

**Sicherheitsverwahrungshäftlinge.** Protective-custody prisoners. Some Communists and trade-unionists arrested and placed in concentration camps.

**sicherstellen.** To guarantee, to secure. To require output from foreign war industry workers; to expropriate; to seize Jewish valuables.

**Sicherungslager.** (SiL) Security camp. One of the main categories of the SS concentration camp system.

**Sicherungsverwahrte.** (SV) Prisoners in protective custody. Prisoners classified as criminals who were transferred to the concentration camps often to be killed through labor. *See* Vernichtung durch Arbeit.

**sicherungsverwahrter Krimineller.** (SV) Criminal in protective custody. Ordinary criminal incarcerated in a concentration camp. Wore a triangle with the letter S. *See also* Winkel.

**Sicherungsverwahrung.** Preventive detention. Euphemism for concentration camp incarceration after a prison sentence.

**Sichtschutz.** Protection from sight. Camouflage.

**siedeln.** To settle. To return Germans to the German soil.

**Siedlerstellen.** Resettlement locations. New agricultural settlements of between thirty-five and forty acres established within Germany according to government settlement regulations. *See* Siedlungspolitik.

**Siedlungshelferin.** Female settlement helper. New position the Nazis created for women. They were responsible for the education, health, and household management of forty to 100 German settlement areas. *See* Siedlerstellen.

**Siedlungspolitik.** Settlement policy. Upon coming to power, the National Socialists introduced new regulations for the distribution and size of agricultural settlements. *See* Siedlerstellen.

**Siedlungsraum.** Settlement space. Creating space by moving Jews from areas of German-occupied Europe to the Lublin area.

**"Sieg des Glaubens."** "Victory of Belief." Motto of the Nazi Party rally in 1933 in response to Hitler's rise to power. Also, title of Leni Riefenstahl propaganda film.

**Siegerfriede.** Peace dictated by the victors. Allied victory over Germany in World War I.

**Sieges-Rune.** Victory rune. *See also* Sig-Rune.

**Siegfriede.** Peace through victory. German victory over the Allies with allusion to Nordic name Siegfried.

**"Sieg Heil!"** "Hail victory." From ancient Germanic times when the people hailed their gods. Nazi slogan and greeting, accompanied by salute. Equivalent to "Heil Hitler."

**"Sieg um jeden Preis!"** "Victory at any cost." Slogan on a 1942 German poster showing a soldier with his right arm raised and the Nazi flag large in the background.

**"(Der) Sieg wird unser sein!"** "Victory will be ours." Nazi slogan.

**Siemens.** The Siemens company used female slave labor at Ravensbrück.

*Signal.* Signal, call. German propaganda magazine edited by the High Command of the Wehrmacht with a distribution of 2.5 million; issued every two weeks from April 1940 to March 1945 in twenty different languages in 20,000 locations outside Germany.

**Sigrune.** *See* Sig-Rune.

**Sig-Rune.** Sowilo, or victory, rune. Runic letter and sign resembling an S. Single S was used by the Hitler Youth; double S by the SS. But the true sigrún (victory rune) was the rune of the god Thor. *See also* Runen; Schutzstaffel.

*Singkamerad: Schulliederbuch der deutschen Jugend.* Song Comrade: School Songbook for German Youth. Collection of German songs issued from 1934 on by the office of the National Socialist Teachers' Union. *See also* NS-Lehrerbund.

**Sinti.** *See* Zigeuner.

**Sipo.** *See* Sicherheitspolizei.

**Sippe.** Kinship, family, clan. Blood kin, belonging to the German-Aryan-Nordic race.

**Sippenältester.** (Male) head of clan.

**Sippenamt.** Clan offices. Government office to investigate the genealogical roots and racial health of SS members.

**Sippenbuch.** Kin or clan book. Special ID asserting the racial purity of each SS member. Book recording the family history of SS members.

**Sippenforschung.** Kinship research. Genealogy.

**Sippengedanke.** Clan/family way of thinking. Knowledge of the importance of the German family as biological basis of the German people. *See also* Volksgemeinschaft.

**Sippengemeinschaft.** Clan community. SS members and their families as the biological elite of the German people.

**Sippenhaft.** Punishment related to the clan, to the entire extended family. *See also* Sippenhaftung.

**Sippenhaftung.** Clan-liability arrest. A family's responsibility for the actions of one member. Used as a rationale for the punishment of resisters' extended families, usually by murder, for any act of opposition against the Third Reich. Especially for action taken against the families of the attempted assassins of Hitler in July 1944, the von Stauffenberg attempt, and at other times against members of the families of German military involved in plots against Hitler.

**Sippenpaß.** Clan (identification) papers. Based on this genealogical documentation, the Nazi government could investigate an individual's family connections for punitive actions in cases of wrongdoing. *See also* Sippenhaftung.

**Sippenpflege.** Kinship maintenance. Preservation of German kinship by promoting knowledge of blood community and healthy selection of mate.

**Sippenschande.** Shame of the clan. Marriage between a German and a Jew, Gypsy, or any (visible) minority.

**Sippschaftstafel.** Clan chart. A family genealogical chart that also contained the origins of family members by marriage.

**Sippung.** Pertaining to the clan. The family as the smallest unit of the German people.

*(Die) Sirene.* (The Air-Raid) Siren. Nazi periodical.

**Sittlichkeitsprozesse.** Immorality trials. Nazi legal attacks on the clergy in the 1930s, accusing them of sexual crimes.

**Sitzbereitschaft.** Sitting at the ready. Preparedness for instantaneous (military) action.

**Sitzkrieg.** Sitting war. Period between the end of the Polish campaign and the spring of 1940 with relatively little fighting between Germany, on the one hand, and Britain and France on the other. The period ended with the April 1940 German invasions of Denmark and Norway.

**SK.** *See* (das) Schwarze Korps; Strafkompanie.

**SK 1005.** *See* Kommando 1005.

**Skdo.** *See* Sonderkommando.

**Skl.** *See* Seekriegsleitung.

**SL.** *See* Straflager.

**SMG.** *See* schweres Maschinengewehr.

**Smolensk-Attentat.** Smolensk attempted assassination. *See also* Flasche.

**Sobibor.** Death camp located in the Lublin district of eastern Poland in Sobibor and close to Chelm. Sobibor opened in May 1942 and closed the day after a rebellion by its Jewish prisoners on October 14, 1943. The scene of incredible brutality perpetrated by the SS on the Jewish men, women, and children under their authority. At least 250,000 were killed there from all over German-occupied Europe, especially Poland and the Soviet Union. Some of the most infamous of the SS sadists associated with the camp were Christian Wirth, Fritz Stangl, Odilo Globocnik, and Gustav Wagner.

**Soldatensender.** Radio station for soldiers. German radio for German troops, broadcasting light music and news, mainly in German-occupied areas. *See also* Propaganda-Kompanien.

**Soldatensender Calais.** Soldier radio station (at) Calais. British station directing psychological propaganda at German armed forces.

**Soldatentum.** Soldiery. According to Nazi belief and training, bravery and military prowess were innate characteristics of the German soldier.

**soldatisch.** Soldier-like. Of soldierly bearing; important morale-building concept for home propaganda.

**Solf-Kreis.** Solf Circle. Anti-Hitler group of aristocratic Germans hosted by Hanna Solf. Infiltrated by the Gestapo in 1944, with most in the group murdered.

**Solidarität.** *See* Tag der nationalen Solidarität.

**Sonderabteilung der Kriegsmarine.** Special branch of the navy. Euphemism for German navy disciplinary unit. *See* Kriegsonderabteilung.

**Sonderaktion.** Special operation. SS or police roundup of Jews and/or other people to be murdered, or a selection of camp prisoners to be killed.

**Sonderaktion Nr. 1.** Special operation no. 1. Roundup and killing of Jews in hiding, Soviet POWs, and Poles who had aided Jews, by the antisemitic Polish National Defense Forces (Nardow Sily Zbronje, NSZ), paralleling the German raid on the Krakow-Ghetto in 1942.

**Sonderaufgabe.** *See* kriegswichtige Sonderaufgaben.

**Sonderauftrag.** Special task. *See also* Sonderbehandlung.

**Sonderausgleichsabgabe.** Special compensation payment. Additional German tax on Polish workers.

**Sonderbau.** Special room, building. Concentration camp brothel, camp infirmary, and death antechamber.

**Sonderbeauftragter.** Officer for a special task. Commissioner most frequently assigned to economic administration under 1936 law.

**sonderbehandelt.** (SB., S.B.) Specially treated. On prisoners' documents, code for to be murdered. Euphemism for "legal" execution of Nazi political adversaries; later, in concentration and death camps, mass killings of Jews, Poles, partisans, Russian POWs, the infirm, and other people without due process of law.

**Sonderbehandlung.** (SB.) Special treatment. *See also* sonderbehandelt.

**Sonderbehandlung 14 f. 13.** Special treatment 14 f. 13. Code placed on false insanity certificates and on files of "asocial prisoners" already in concentration camps to indicate prisoner to be murdered: Jews, Gypsies, Poles, and Russians. *See also* Euthanasie.

**Sonderdienst.** Special service. Volksdeutsche operating in Poland as guards in labor camps and as participants in murder operations against Jews.

**Sondereinheit.** Special unit. Attached to a division, corps, and so forth.

**Sondereinsatz.** Special task force. Concentration camp personnel committing mass murder of Jews. *See also* sonderbehandelt.

**Sondereinsatzkommando des SD.** Special task force of the Security Service (of the Reichsführers SS). Special police units that carried out mass murder of Jews in eastern Europe.

**Sondereinsatzkommando Eichmann.** Special Action Unit Eichmann. Unit commanded by Adolf Eichmann and responsible for the murder of hundreds of thousands of Jews who were rounded up and sent to Auschwitz and other camps.

**Sondererlaß.** Special decree. Exemption order for Poles and other non-Germans, except Jews, declared racially valuable (rassisch wertvoll) to be released from concentration camps to work in Germany, and thus spared murder. *See also* Eindeutschung.

**Sonderfahndungsbuch.** Special tracing book. Ledger of wanted persons lists compiled by the SD and the Gestapo and carried into Poland by each Eisatzgruppe; contained the names of prominent Polish political figures and individuals who had participated in Polish uprisings in East Upper Silesia in 1919–1921, as well as names of politically active Jews, members of both groups to be killed when apprehended. *See* Aktion Tannenberg; Einsatzgruppen; Einsatzgruppe z.b.V. für das oberschlesische Industrialgebiet.

**Sonderfahndungsliste-GB.** Special tracing list–Great Britain. Black list that Reinhard Heydrich gave SS Brigadeführer Walter Schellenberg of 2,300 prominent people to be arrested immediately on the success of the German assault on Great Britain, along with the establishment of six Einsatzgruppe, based in London, Bristol, Birmingham, Manchester, Liverpool, and Edinburgh to be led by Dr. Otto Six.

**Sonderfahrzeuge.** Special vehicles. *See also* Sonderwagen.

**Sonderführer.** Special leader. Geographers, anthropologists, meteorologists and others who became members of the military, received officers' rank, and were assigned special tasks.

**Sondergerichte.** (SG) Special courts. Nazi courts that tried political offenders against the Nazi state. From 1940, exclusively for war crimes without recourse to appeal. *See* Heimtückegesetz.

**Sonderhäftlinge.** Special prisoners. Diverse group of privileged, short-term, female prisoners at Ravensbrück consisting of Nazi women or wives of Nazis.

**Sonderkommando.** (Skdo) Special detachment. Jewish prisoners in the death camps who worked around the gas chambers and crematoria. Among other duties, they took the bodies from the gas chambers, retrieved any valuables the victims were able to hide on their bodies before being killed (including gold fillings), and then brought the bodies to be burned into the crematoria or to the pits to be buried. Also, Jewish forced-labor units used to burn bodies of Nazi murder victims at killing sites. Also, subdivision of Einsatzgruppen, generally smaller than Einsatzkommando. Also, special units assigned police and political functions in German-occupied eastern Europe.

**Sonderkommando Bothmann.** *See* Sonderkommando Kulmhof.

**Sonderkommando Dirlewanger.** Dirlewanger Special Unit. *See also* Dirlewanger Sonderbataillon.

**Sonderkommando Eichmann.** *See* Sondereinsatzkommando Eichmann.

**Sonderkommando Kulmhof.** Special Unit (at) Kulmhof. This unit oversaw mass murders at Chelmno. Also called Sonderkommando Lange and Sonderkommando Bothmann, after its commanders SS officers Hans Bothmann and Dr. Otto Lange.

**Sonderkommando Lange.** Special Unit Lange. SS squad employing mobile gas vans to murder the mentally ill in Poland. *See also* Aktion T-4; Euthanasie; Sonderkommando Kulmhof.

**Sonderkommando 1005.** *See* Kommando 1005.

**Sonderkommando Reinhard.** Special Unit Reinhard. SS administration in charge of Aktion Reinhard in the Generalgouvernement.

**Sonderkonto.** Special account. Bank account for Germans who received special pay for difficult tasks. *See also* Sonderzulage.

**Sonderkonto H.** Special Account H. Accounts established for all moveable assets of those Jews who, from 1942 on, were deported to Theresienstadt concentration camp. Assets were used allegedly to finance their new housing there. Only the Reich Main Security Office of the SS had access to this account.

**Sonderkonto W.** Special Account W. Established to pay for the deportation of Jews allegedly to cover all costs incurred. Only the Reich Main Security Office of the SS had access to this account.

**Sonderkost.** Special diet. Euphemism for Nazi starvation experiments on mentally and physically disabled Germans.

**Sonder-Kraftfahrzeug.** Special (military) motor vehicle.

**Sondermark.** Special (Reichs-)mark. Generic for different kinds of frozen and discounted German government money.

**Sondermaßnahmen.** Special measures. *See also* Sondermaßnahmen gegen Juden.

**Sondermaßnahmen gegen Juden.** Special measures against Jews. Mass murder of Jews by the Wehrmacht, Einsatzgruppen, and others in eastern Europe.

**Sondermeldung.** Special report. Term on German radio, signaling news of military victory.

**Sonderreferent.** Special Consultant. Adolf Eichmann's position as special adviser for deportation of Jews in office IV of the Central Reich Security Office.

**Sondersicherung.** Special security. Code word for special measures taken to ensure the security of Hitler and other high-ranking Nazis.

**Sonderstab Bildende Kunst.** Special Operations Staff for the Arts. Unit that seized Jewish art and cultural treasures in France. *See* Einsatzstab Reichsleiter Rosenberg für die Besetzten Gebiete.

**Sonderstufe SS.** (S, SS) Preferential priority of the Schutzstaffel for war projects.

**Sondertransport.** Special transport. Deportation of Jews to the east.

**Sonderungsraum.** Place of (natural) selection. Original home area of a race.

**Sonderunterbringung.** Special accommodation. Euphemism for mass killings at Auschwitz. *See also* Sonderbehandlung.

**Sonderwagen.** (S-Wagen) Special car. Code for poison-gas van used to transport and murder Jews at the same time. *See also* fahrbare Gaskammer.

**Sonderwechsel.** Special-bank bill. Advance-financing bill.

**Sonderzüge.** Special trains. Trains that carried the Jews to their death in eastern Europe even at the cost to the Nazis of endangering their war effort.

**Sonderzulage.** Special ration. Ration of cigarettes, alcohol, and/or money to those involved in the mass murder of Jews.

**Sonderzuteilung.** Special allotment. During World War II, Germans received extra rations for special food items, such as coffee, chocolate, and cigarettes; issued officially for war-related special occasions.

**Sonnenblume.** Sunflower. Code name for 1941 plan for Afrika Korps to attack British in Tripoli.

**Sonnenfeld.** Sun field. The central white area of the Nazi flag.

**Sonnenrad.** Sun wheel. Nordic sun wheel that Nazis used as a sun-wheel swastika. Also, symbol of the 15th SS-Panzer Division, Wiking.

**Sonnenwend.** Solstice. Code name for German offensive near Strasbourg. *See also* Nordwind.

*Sonntag—Alltag.* Sunday—Workday. Film demonstrating Nazi ideology of work.

**Sonnwendfeier.** Solstice festival. Nazi holiday of June 23 and winter festival around Christmas time.

**"so oder so."** "One way or another." Göring's reference to the settlement of the Jewish Problem by all means possible; that is, destruction of the Jews.

**Sopade.** Exiled German Social Democratic Party Organization.

**"Sous les débris de Berlin."** "Under the rubble of Berlin." In the last stages of World War II, Berliners sang this ironically titled song to the tune of "Sous les ponts de Paris" ("Under the Bridges of Paris").

**Sovog.** *See* Sozialistische Volksgemeinschft.

**Sowilo.** *See* Sig-Rune.

*So wird's gemacht.* That's How It's Done. 1944 film about German women during the war.

**Sowjetfeind.** Soviet enemy. Prominent on the German armed forces enemies list.

**Sozialausschuß.** Social Committee. 1938 German War Ministry committee analyzing the social consequences of war, such as wages, prices, taxes, social policy, and veterans' affairs.

**Sozialdemokratische Partei Deutschlands.** (SPD) Social Democratic Party of Germany. Allied with other political parties under the Weimar Republic.

**Sozialismus der Tat.** Socialism in action. Self-defined form of socialism practiced by the National Socialists in contrast to Bolshevism. Also, social actions of the Nazi regime to help Germans during the hard times of the war period.

*Sozialistische Aktion.* Socialist Action. Newspaper of the Social Democrats.

**Sozialistische Volksgemeinschft.** (Sovog) Socialist racial unity of the people. *See also* Volksgemeinschaft.

**Spanienkreuz.** Spanish Cross. Medal in gold, silver, or bronze awarded to the German volunteers who fought in the Spanish Civil War. *See also* Legion Condor.

**Spargel.** Asparagus (stalk). Navy slang for periscope.

**Sparingenieur.** Savings engineer. Materials control engineer, government-appointed expert in war industries.

**Sparmetall.** Rationed metal. Metal subject to allocation.

**Sparstoff.** Rationed material.

**sparstoffarm.** (Goods) made with few rationed materials.

**Spatensekte.** Spade sect. Ironic term for the German workforce whose symbol was a spade. *See also* Reichsarbeitsdienst.

**Spatz.** Sparrow. Code name for German jet fighter. *See also* Volksjäger.

**SPD.** *See* Sozialdemokratische Partei Deutschlands.

**Speichergas.** Stored gas. Bottled gas such as propane, butane.

**speichig.** Radial.

**Sperrbrechboot.** Barrier- or boom-breaking boat.

**Sperrgebiet.** Restricted area. *See also* Ghetto.

**Sperrgebiet-Raum.** Restricted-area space. Area not to be developed under any conditions.

**Sperrle-Befehl.** Sperrle order. In February 1944, Field Marshal Hugo Sperrle, German Commander in Chief of German Forces in German-occupied western Europe, issued several sets of orders concerning treatment of resisters, in particular the French Underground. It ordered commanders of German troops, if under attack, immediately to return fire even if civilians were put in danger, all civilians in the area were to be arrested, buildings from which the firing took place were to be burned down. No countermeasures would be considered too severe. Commanders were ordered to proceed with extreme severity and without any leniency. *See also* Oradour.

**Sperrlisten.** Restricted lists. Lists of names of Jews held in special camps, such as converted Jews, spouses of Germans, Mischlinge, Jewish citizens of neutral countries, Jews useful to Third Reich, and others. Most were killed in the end.

**Sperrmark.** Blocked Reichsmarks. After 1938, emigrating German Jews could keep only 25 percent of their assets; the remainder was held back in Germany.

**Sperrstempel.** Restriction stamp. Papers with special stamp allowing Dutch Jews temporary exemption from being deported to death camps.

**Spezialwagen.** Special car. *See* S-Wagen.

**Spiegelei.** Fried egg. Nickname for the German cross in gold; medal.

**Spielschar.** Play group. Selected members of the Hitler Youth who performed plays, songs, and dialogues during special gatherings and who wore distinctive uniforms.

**Spielscharen Hitlerjügend.** *See* Spielschar.

**Spieß.** Top kick. Sergeant in the Wehrmacht.

**Spießer.** Philistine, miserable little bourgeois. One of several negative terms Goebbels applied to the German middle class, along with Bürger and Bourgeois.

**(Die) Spinne.** The Spider. SS financed organization. *See also* (die) Schleuse.

**Spinnfaser.** Spin fiber. Synthetic fiber.

**Spinnstoffsammlung.** Cloth collection. During World War II, collection of used clothing and fabric.

**Spionageabwehr.** Counterespionage. Department in German Military Intelligence.

**Spital.** Hospital. At Neuengamme where tuberculosis experiments were carried out on Jewish children. *See* Krankenhospital.

**Splittergraben.** Splinter ditch. Trench that served to protect foreign workers from bombs. These workers were not allowed into German air-raid shelters.

**spontan.** Spontaneous. Adjective used by the National Socialists to conceal surreptitiously planned operations against their political opponents and Jews (e.g., the Reichskristallnacht pogrom of 1938).

**Sport.** Sport, athletics. Euphemism for several tortures devised by SS guards for inmates of concentration camps. *See also* Baumhängen; Bock.

**Sportabteilung.** (SA) Sport detachment. Precursor of Sturmabteilung.

**Sport-Palast.** Sports Palace. Berlin arena where Nazi leaders gave speeches to Party members.

**Sportwartin.** Sports leader. Female sports official for young girls.

**Sprachmittler.** Language communicator. Interpreter.

**Sprachregelung.** Language regulation. Special regulations determining the use of the German language by government officials and the press. Also, the Nazi code language for the carrying out and disguising the realities of German government actions and military operations. *See also* Reichspressekonferenz.

**Sprachzugehörige.** Those belonging to the language. Germans identified by language, but not by race.

**Sprechmaschine.** Speaking machine. Germanized for a record player or phonograph.

**Sprengboot.** Destruction boat. *See also* Schnellboot.

**Springkommandant.** Commander of a (German) military airport.

**Sprungverpflegung.** Parachutist's ration.

**"(Er) spurt wieder."** "(He) toes the line again." Applied to an individual who conformed and became submissive after punishment or torture.

**S-Rolle.** *See* Stacheldrahtrolle.

**S-Rune.** *See* Sig-Rune.

**SS.** *See* Schutzstaffel; Sonderstufe SS.

**SS-Anwärter.** SS candidate. Lowest rank of SS.

**SS-Aufseherin.** *See* Aufseherin.

**SS-Fallschirmjäger-Bataillon.** SS Paratrooper Battalion. SS battalion comprised of German volunteers who had been imprisoned for military infractions but who now could gain amnesty by order of Hitler.

**SSFHA.** *See* SS-Führungshauptamt.

**SS-FM.** *See* Schutzstaffel Fördernde Mitglieder.

**SS-Frauen.** SS Women. Female concentration camp overseers who were associated with the SS but not bona fide members of the SS, which was an all-male organization.

**SS-Freiwilligen-Division Wallonie.** *See* SS-Freiwillgen-Sturmbrigade Wallonie.

**SS-Freiwilligen-Sturmbrigade Langemarck.** *See* Langemarck.

**SS-Freiwilligen-Sturmbrigade Wallonie.** SS Volunteer Storm Brigade Waloon. Belgian volunteers under the SS-Sturmbannführer Léon Degrelle were employed on the Eastern Front to fight against the Russians.

**SS-Führer-Begleit Kommando.** *See* Führer-Begleit-Kommando.

**SS-Führungshauptamt.** (SSFHA.) SS Operations Administration. Administered all SS agencies except the Waffen-SS.

**SS-Galizien.** Galician SS. Ukrainian volunteer SS unit. Operated against partisans and Jews.

**SS-Grenadier.** SS rifleman, infantryman. Second lowest rank in SS.

**SS-Hauptamt.** SS Administration. Began operations in January 30, 1935. In charge of recruiting members for the SS, handling all SS offices in the vicinity, and all general procedures of the SS.

**SS-Heimwehr.** SS home army. An SS defense unit.

**SS-Lager.** *See* Lager-SS.

**SS-Mann.** A private in the SS.

**SS-Oberaufseherin.** Second highest rank for an SS woman in the concentration camps.

**SS-Panzergrenadier.** SS Mechanized Infantry. Elite SS divisions.

**SS-Panzergrenadier-Division Galizia.** *See* SS-Galizien.

**SS-Personal-Hauptamt.** SS Personnel Administration.

**SS-Regiment Westland.** SS military unit from Flanders.

**SS-SD.** *See* Sicherheitsdienst des Reichsführers SS.

**SS-Sicherheitsdienst.** *See* Sicherheitsdienst des Reichsführers SS.

**SS-SL.** *See* SS-Sonderlager.

**SS-Sonderlager.** (SS-SL) SS special camps. Special internment camps in Germany combining protective custody, concentration camps, and ghettos. Usually located on the outskirts of cities and guarded by the SS or uniformed city police. After 1935 these camps became depots for forced labor, genealogical registration, and compulsory sterilization. After 1939, they evolved into assembly centers for systematic deportation of Jews to concentration camps.

**SS-Standarte Nordwest.** SS Regiment Northwest. SS unit raised among the Belgian and Dutch.

**SS-Strafanstalten.** SS punishment facilities. SS military prisons at Danzig-Matzkau and Dachau.

**SS-Totenkopfring.** SS death's-head ring. Instituted by Himmler in 1934, the elite SS ring featured the runes and a death's head. It was a gift from the Reichsführer to reward senior SS officers. The accompanying citation read: "I award you the SS death's-head ring. The ring symbolizes our faithfulness to the Führer, our steadfast loyalty, our brotherhood, and comradeship. The death's head reminds us that we should be ready at any time to lay down our lives for the good of the Germanic people. The runes diametrically opposite the death's head are symbols from our past of the prosperity that we will restore through National Socialism. The two Sig-Runes stand for the SS. The swastika and the Hagal-Rune represent our unshakable faith in the ultimate victory of our philosophy. The death's head ring cannot be bought or sold, and must never fall into the hands of those not entitled to wear it. When you leave the SS, or when you die, the ring must be returned to the Reichsführer-SS. The unauthorized acquisition of duplicates of the ring is forbidden and punishable by law. Wear the ring with Honor! H. Himmler."

**SS-Totenkopfstandarten.** SS Death's-Head Regiments. Armed SS formations created at the beginning of the war to handle "special tasks of a police nature"; disbanded in 1941 with personnel absorbed into the Waffen-SS.

**SS-Totenkopfverbände.** (SS-TV) SS Death's-Head Units. Concentration camp guard units. Also, nucleus of SS-Panzerdivision-Totenkopf, a Waffen-SS unit.

**SS-TV.** *See* SS-Totenkopfverbände.

**SS- und Polizeiführer.** SS and Police Leader. Heinrich Himmler.

**SS- und Polizei-Gerichte.** SS and Police Court. For SS internal discipline.

**SS-Verfügungstruppen.** (SSVT) SS Special-Purpose Troops; troops at the disposal of (Hitler). SS ceremonial and security forces in the early 1930s. Militarized component of the SS in the prewar period. In the winter of 1939–1940 developed into the First SS Panzer Division, Leibstandarte-SS Adolf Hitler, the Waffen-SS unit that had sworn a loyalty oath directly to Hitler and were thus removed from Himmler's direct control. Also, used as Wehrmacht and SS concentration camp guards. *See also* Waffen-SS.

**SSVT.** *See* SS-Verfügungstruppen.

**SS-Werterfassung.** SS Valuables Control. Agency that gathered and shipped to Germany valuables left by deported Jews. Jews supervised by the SS had to perform this task.

**SS-Wirtschafts- und Verwaltungshauptamt.** (WVHA) SS Main Office for the Economy and Administration. Safeguarded autarky of the SS, oversaw SS troops; from 1942, controlled all concentration camps and was responsible for the allotment of slave labor. *See also* Deutsche Wirtschaftsbetriebe GmbH.

**Staatsakt.** State ceremony. Official ceremony with banners, parades, singing choirs, and speeches; during the war, often including interment ceremony, with caskets at the center.

**Staatsangehörige.** Belonging to the state. German subjects. Germans by nationality but of alien race. *See also* Reichsbürger; Reichsbürgergesetz.

**Staatsangehörige auf Widerruf.** Belonging to the state on probation. German citizens on probation.

**Staatsfeind.** Enemy of the state. German courts considered such individuals the worst offenders, and punishment was usually incarceration in concentration camps. During World War II, such individuals received the death penalty.

**staatsfeindlich.** Hostile to the state. Nazi category of those the Reich considered enemies of the German state and people. *See also* Staatsfeind.

**Staatsjugend.** (Stj) State youth. Code used in an individual's card file. Also, a law of 1936 declaring the Hitler Youth as the sole youth organization and charging it with the ideological and physical education of the young. *See also* Drei-Säulen-Theorie; Hitlerjugend; Volkskartei.

**Staatsjugendtag.** State Youth Day. Between 1934 and 1936, a Saturday off from school and reserved for Hitler Youth activities.

**Staatskassengutscheine.** Government coupons. Early Nazi economic notion substituting coupons for money. Hitler rejected it.

**Staatskrüppel.** State cripple. Colloquialism for unable to serve in the army. *See also* kriegsverwendungsfähig.

**Staatsnation.** State nation. Nation created by the state.

**Staatsnotstand.** State emergency. Used to justify Hitler's and the Nazi dictatorship and terror.

**Staatsoberhaupt des deutschen Reiches.** *See* Staatsoberhaupt des Großdeutschen Reiches.

**Staatsoberhaupt des Großdeutschen Reiches.** Head of State of the Greater German Reich. One of Hitler's titles. *See also* (Der) Führer.

**Staatsoberhauptgesetz.** Head-of-State Law. Law making Hitler the German Head of State, Leader, and Chancellor of Germany.

**staatspolitisch wertvoll.** Valuable according to state politics. Rating for German films that reflected Nazi ideology.

**Staatspolizei.** (Stapo) Prussian State Police before 1933. Afterward, merged into the Gestapo. *See also* Geheime Staatspolizei.

**Staatspolizei Außendienststelle.** (Stapo ADSt) State Police branch office.

**Staatsrasse.** State race. Dominant race of the Reich.

**Staatsvolk.** State people. *See also* Staatsrasse.

**Stab.** Headquarters, executive.

**Stabschef.** Chief of Staff.

**Stabschef der SA.** Chief of Staff of the SA. Ernst Röhm held this position (1930–1934).

**Stabshauptamt Reichskommissariat für die Festigung des deutschen Volkstums.** Headquarters of the Reich Commission for the Strengthening of the German People. Germanization department. *See also* Generalplan Ost.

**Stabshelferin.** Staff helper. Female office clerk in the German army usually in civilian clothing.

**Stabslager.** Staff camp. Living quarters for the administrative personnel of the concentration or POW camp.

**Stabsoffizier.** Staff officer.

**Stabsscharführer.** Sergeant-Major in the SS.

**Stabswache der SA.** Bodyguard, sentry post, of the Sturmabteilung. Paramilitary SA formation established early in 1934 by Ernst Röhm.

**Stabwache.** Bodyguard. Hitler's SA bodyguard, replaced by Leibstandarte-SS Adolf Hitler. *See also* Leibstandarte-SS Adolf Hitler; SS-Verfügungstruppen.

**Stacheldraht-Haus.** Barbed-wire house. A fenced-in, cage-like structure within the tent camp (Zeltlager) at Buchenwald concentration camp. Men and women inmates were left there at below freezing temperatures and without food and drink until they died.

**Stacheldrahtrolle.** (S-Rolle) Roll of barbed wire.

**Stadt der Auslandsdeutschen.** City of Germans from Outside Germany. Nickname for Stuttgart.

**Stadt der Bewegung.** City of the [Nazi] Movement. Hitler's name for Munich.

**Stadt der Jugend.** City of the [Nazi] Youth. Hitler's name for Landsberg.

**Stadt der Reichsparteitage.** City of the Reich Party Days. Hitler's name for Nuremberg.

**Stadthauptmann.** City chief. German civilian authority in Nazi-occupied Europe, in charge of local mayors and city officials and some ghettos and camps in his jurisdiction. In the ghettos, the Judenrat was responsible to him.

**Städtische Werkstätte.** City workshops. German-owned businesses in occupied Poland.

**Stadtwacht.** City guard. Former SA members drafted into this urban militia.

**Staf.** *See* Standartenführer.

**Staffel.** Staff. Administrative component of headquarters.

**Staffeln.** Units. Three units made up a Luftwaffe group. *See also* Gruppen.

**Staffelmann.** Staff man. *See also* Schutzstaffelmann.

**Stahlhelm.** Steel Helmet. Nationalist, conservative, veteran's organization (1918–1933). Incorporated into the SA in 1933.

**Stählerne Romantik.** Steel romanticism. Concept and slogan coined by Propaganda Minister Goebbels, who attempted to increase the German military and economic effort and production by emphasizing the synthesis of a retrospective utopia, cultural modernization, and science and technology.

**Stahlpakt.** Steel Pact. Mussolini's term for the May 1939 political and military friendship alliance between Germany and Italy.

**Stalag.** POW camp. *See also* Stammlager.

**Stalag 91.** Stammlager 91. Soviet POW camp at Bergen-Belsen.

**Stalingrad.** Russian city, scene of a climactic battle of World War II. The German losses in men and equipment changed the momentum on the Eastern Front. After this German defeat, most Europeans believed the Germans would not win the war.

**Stalingrad-Putsch.** Unsuccessful attempt to overthrow Hitler just before the German defeat at Stalingrad in January 1943.

**Stalin-Linie.** Stalin line. From 1939, the Soviet military's defensive line behind the USSR's western border; broken through by Germany in June 1941.

**Stalinorgel.** Stalin organ. Katushyn, a powerful Soviet multiple-rocket launcher.

**Stamm.** Stem/core. Unit of the Hitler Youth of about 600. *See also* Deutsches Jungvolk.

**Stammabschnitt.** Core section. Middle part of the ration card that contained name and number of the individual who was to obtain special rations. *See also* Bewirtschaftung.

**Stammgericht.** Special basic meal. During World War II, each German restaurant menu had to offer at least one special low-cost meal that could be obtained with one or no ration coupon.

**Stamm-HJ.** Core Hitler Youth. Group of Hitler Youth boys between the ages of fourteen and eighteen who had become members before the compulsory work duty. *See also* Reichsarbeitsdienst.

**Stammlager.** (Stalag) Main camp. Any main concentration camp, in contrast to subsidiary or satellite concentration or forced-labor camps; for example, Auschwitz 1, Stammlager (Stalag) VII A. Also, concentration camp for POWs.

**Standarte.** Standard, regiment. SA, SS, and other Nazi units. An SS Standarte unit contained about 3,000 men, equivalent to an army regiment.

**Standartenführer.** (Staf, STDF) Regiment leader. Colonel in the SS.

**Stander.** Sign post.

**Standesehre.** *See* Ehre.

**Standgericht.** Drumhead court-martial. Special court set up by Germans to try Poles and Jews in German-occupied Poland. Summary court-martials that

German military commanders had the emergency authority to create, permitting death sentences.

**Standortarzt.** Site doctor. Concentration camp doctor.

**Stapo.** Official abbreviation for the Gestapo. *See also* Geheime Staatspolizei; Staatspolizei.

**Stapo ADSt.** *See* Staatspolizei Außendienststelle.

**Stapoleit.** Staatspolizei(leit)stellen. *See* Geheime Staatspolizei.

**Stäte.** Archaic for Stätigkeit (steadfastness, reliability); a claimed characteristic of Nordic people.

**Station Z.** Mass-murder barracks used at Sachsenhausen concentration camp to murder thousands of prisoners. *See also* Sachsenhausen.

***Statistik des deutschen Reiches.*** Statistics of the German Reich. This book indicated the results of the German census, which in 1933 included statistics on those Germans who were Jews by religious affiliation, which was the only clear index of Jewishness.

**STBF.** *See* Sturmbannführer.

**STDF.** *See* Standartenführer.

**Steckbrief.** Arrest warrant. Reinhard Heydrich's order September 21, 1939, to Einsatzgruppen in Poland to arrest several categories of people, including Jews, Polish partisans, and other people, and send them to Buchenwald concentration camp.

**Stehgemeinschaft.** Standing community. Slang for queuing pool. Also, people reserving places for one another in the queues at various shops during the war years.

**Stehzelle.** Standing cell. Prisoners tortured, often to death, by being forced to stand in a cell too small to sit in.

**Steilgranate.** High-angle grenade. German armor-piercing artillery shell.

**Steinermark.** Himmler's private train.

**steingewordene Weltanschauung.** Worldview cast in stone. *See also* Bauten des Führers.

**Stellungnahme und Gedanken zum Generalplan Ost des Reichsführers SS.** Comments and thoughts on the Master Plan East of the Reichsführer SS. April 1942 RSHA minutes on the Germanization of the Soviet Baltic republics. *See also* Generalplan Ost.

**stellvertretender Gauleiter.** Deputy District Leader. *See also* Gauleiter.

**stellvertretendes Generalkommando.** Deputy General Command. Office of the Chief of the Reserve Army. *See* Ersatzheer.

**Stellvertreter des Führers.** Deputy Führer. Rudolf Hess was Hitler's Nazi Party Chief of Staff until he flew to Great Britain in May 1941. Later, Martin Bormann more or less replaced Hess as the Führer's secretary. *See* Minister der Reichsregierung mit Mitspracherecht in allen Bereichen; Sekretär des Führers.

**Sterbehilfe.** Death assistance. Mass murder of people with various hereditary diseases. *See also* Euthanasie.

**Sterbeurkunden.** Death certificates. Also official notices to relatives that inmates of concentration camps and other institutions had died.

**Sternjude.** Star Jew. *See also* Sternträger.

**Sternlager.** Star camp. *See also* Lager 2.

**sternlos.** Without star. Jews in Germany before having to wear the yellow-star badge from 1941.

**Sternträger.** Star carriers. Those German Jews who from 1941 had to wear the Yellow Star.

**Stiftungen.** Foundations, institutes. Organizations posing as research and scientific bodies were responsible for murdering thousands in the Euthanasia Program. *See also* Aktion T-4; Euthanasie.

**Stille Hilfe.** Silent help. *See also* (die) Schleuse.

**Stippangriff.** Slang for hit-and-run raid.

**Stj.** *See* Staatsjugend.

**Stockhiebe.** Beatings with a stick. Form of brutal punishment at Dachau and other camps that often resulted in death.

**stolzer Jude.** Proud Jew. Jacob Gens, chief of the Vilna-Ghetto Judenrat. *See* Judenältester.

**Stop-Preis.** Price ceiling. *See also* Preisstopverordnung.

**Storch.** Stork. Low-speed reconnaissance plane.

**Stoßtrupp.** Shock troop. World War I term adopted by Nazis, referring to those who guarded the stage when Hitler spoke publicly.

**Stoßtrupp Adolf Hitler.** Shock-Troop Adolf Hitler. Hitler's bodyguards, developed into the SS. *See also* Leibstandarte-SS Adolf Hitler.

**Strafappell.** Punishment roll call. Camp prisoners forced to stand at roll call, often after a prisoner escape, for almost a full day. Any failure to stand erect would be punished by death.

**Strafbataillon.** Punishment battalion. *See also* Bewährungsbataillon.

**Strafblöcke.** Punishment barracks. At concentration camps.

**Straferlaß.** Amnesty decree. 1939 Hitler decree exonerating individual SS men and SS units from prosecution for war crimes/atrocities against Jewish and non-Jewish civilians in Poland.

**Strafexerzieren.** Military exercises as punishment. *See also* Nebenstrafen.

**Strafexpedition.** Punishment expedition. Right-wing attacks on Communists after Hitler's victory in 1933, consisting of forcing victims to run a gauntlet on an oiled surface while being beaten with rubber clubs.

**Strafgefangenenlager.** (SGL) Punishment camps. Disciplinary camps for prisoners.

**Strafgesetznovelle.** Supplementary punishment law. June 28, 1935, law that established the principle: no crime without punishment. It replaced the older principle of German jurisprudence: no crime, no punishment without law.

**Strafkompanie.** (SK) Punishment company. At concentration and forced-labor camps, prisoners assigned to these companies were worked to death for the slightest infractions of the regulations.

**Straflager.** (SL) Punishment camp. *See also* Strafkompanie.

**Strafmaß.** Measure of punishment. Although there existed a rough guide for the punishment of concentration camp prisoners, there was no norm regarding the degree of punishment the SS could inflict on inmates. *See also* Disziplinar- und Strafordnung.

**Strafvollzugslager der Waffen-SS und Polizei.** Disciplinary camps of the armed SS and police. Camps for enlisted men and officers under disgrace. Many volunteered for hazardous duty in order to gain amnesty from these camps.

**Strahltyp.** Radiant type. Idealistic philosopher.

**Straßen des Führers.** Roads of the Führer. *See also* Reichsautobahnen.

**Straßenzellen.** Street cells. 1920s units of dedicated Nazis intended to defeat their Communist counterparts and win the battle of the streets.

**Streifendienst.** Patrol Service. Internal policing of Nazi paramilitary units. Also, Hitler Youth organization that served as a prerequisite to entrance into the SS, trained until eighteen years old by SS members.

**Streifendienst Hitlerjügen.** *See* Streifendienst.

**Streitbindung.** Argument resolution. Joining of two opposites.

**strengstens bestraft.** (SB., S.B.) Severely punished. Code for politically motivated killings. Victims were sent to concentration camps with SB stamped on their papers.

**Streudeutsche.** Scattered Germans. Ethnic Germans living among native non-German people.

**Streukegel.** Cone of dispersion.

**Streuung.** Dispersion. Distribution of subcontracts in the new Europe. *See also* (neue) Raumordnung.

**Struthof.** *See* Natzweiler-Struthof.

**Stubenälteste(r).** Senior prisoner in room. Senior barracks prisoner in a concentration camp.

**Stubendienst.** Room supervisors. Prisoners acting as room orderlies.

**Stücke.** Pieces. Dehumanizing for concentration camp inmates or corpses.

**Stück Gefangene.** Prisoners as objects. Bureaucratic for concentration camp inmates.

**Student.** Code name for 1943 operations in Italy. *See* Schwarz.

**Studentenkompanie.** Student company. Wehrmacht unit consisting of medical students and students of mechanical engineering.

**Stuf.** *See* Sturmführer.

**Stuka.** *See* Sturzkampfflugzeug.

**"Stunde der jungen Nation."** "Hour of the Young Nation." Title of weekly radio broadcast for German youth. *See also* Heimabend.

**Stundenklau.** Hour stealer. Figure on propaganda poster encouraging Germans to work instead of wasting time.

**Stunde X.** X hour. Zero hour.

**Sturm.** Storm. Assault unit of the SA, the SS, the NSFK, and the NSKK, of a few hundred men, equivalant to an army company.

**Sturmabteilung.** (SA) Storm Detachment. Also known as Storm Troopers and Brown Shirts, they were the uniformed and armed political combat troops of the Nazi Party, its main instrument for undermining democracy and facilitating Hitler's rise to power. The SA was the predominant Nazi terror and propaganda arm from 1923 until the "Night of the Long Knives" in 1934, when the leadership was killed off on Hitler's orders. They continued to exist throughout the Third Reich but were of little political significance after 1934, being used primarily for pre-military and post-military training. The SA numbered 15,000 in 1923, 400,000 by 1933, and 2.5 million by 1934. *See also* Nacht der langen Messer.

**Sturmbann.** Storm Unit. SA or SS unit equivalent to a battalion.

**Sturmbannführer.** (STBF) Major in the SS.

*(Der) Stürmer.* Wild Attacker/Stormer. An antisemitic German weekly published between 1923 and 1945 in Nuremberg by Julius Streicher. It was Hitler's favorite reading.

**Stürmerkasten.** *Der Stürmer* boxes. Public bulletin boards on which was fastened antisemitic material from Julius Streicher's newspapers. They served to encourage antisemitism and to put pressure on any German who still conducted business with Jews.

**Sturmführer.** (Stuf) Storm leader. Suffix for SS commissioned officers, from lieutenant to captain.

**Sturmgeschütz.** Storm gun. Self-propelled gun.

**Sturmlokal.** Storm local. Hangout for members of an SA-Sturm during the Weimar Republic.

**Sturmmann.** Storm man. Private first class in the SS.

**Sturmpionier.** Storm pioneer. Assault engineer.

**Sturmscharführer.** SS sergeant-major.

**Sturmtruppenleiter.** Storm troop leader. SA officer.

**Sturzkampfbomber.** *See* Sturzkampfflugzeug.

**Sturzkampfflugzeug.** (Stuka) German dive bomber JU 87, equipped with ear-deafening sirens for psychological impact on civilians and troops subject to its attack. It dove abruptly to drop bombs on troop concentrations and other front-line objectives. Without complete air mastery, it was vulnerable to interception.

**Stuttgart.** *See* Stadt der Auslandsdeutschen.

**Stutthof.** Concentration camp located near city of Danzig (Gdansk). Tens of thousands of prisoners were killed by means of torture, disease, and starvation, with many worked to death at the brick factory, the Focke-Wulff airplane plant, Deltahella submarine-machinery plant, and several other SS-sponsored industrial projects. At the end of the war, thousands more prisoners were murdered by means of death marches and mass drownings in the Baltic Sea.

**subjektive öffentliche Rechte des Einzelnen.** Subjective public rights of the individual. Nazi description of the Weimar Republic's Bill of Rights that was suspended by law on February 28, 1933. *See* Grundrechte.

**Suchaktion.** Search action. If a concentration camp prisoner was unaccounted for, all inmates had to stand at attention outside, often for hours no matter what the weather, while supervisory personnel conducted a search for the missing inmate.

**Sudetenland.** Area, bordering on Germany, formerly part of Austrian Reich. Predominantly populated by German-speaking people, it was given to Czechoslovakia after World War I because of its strategic location. Britain and France conceded this area to Germany at the Munich Conference in September 1938 following their appeasement policy. Germany annexed the rest of Czechoslovakia in March 1939.

**Sühneleistung.** Act of atonement, fine. *See also* Kontribution; Reichskristallnacht.

**Sühnemaßnahmen.** Atonement measures. Wehrmacht and SS rationale for the mass murder of hostages, mostly Jews and alleged Communists, by shooting or hanging in retribution for attacks on Wehrmacht soldiers.

**Sumpfkultur.** Swamp civilization, pre-classical Greek civilization. Negative for the democracies.

**Sumpfmenschen.** Swamp people. Derogatory for Russians.

**SV.** *See* Sicherungsverwahrte; Sicherungsverwahrter Krimineller.

**S-Wagen.** *See* Saurerwagen; Sonderwagen.

**Swastika.** *See* Hakenkreuz.

**Swing-Cliquen.** Swing cliques. Middle-class German youths, especially in Berlin, Hamburg, and other German cities, who did not belong to the Hitler Youth, marked by long hair and loose-fitting clothes, involved in prohibited American swing music, and opposed by the Hitler regime who saw them and their music as degenerate and un-German. Many were sent to concentration camps. *See also* Edelweißpiraten.

**Swing-Heinis.** Swing (music) Hanks. Groups of working-class youths interested in swing music and opposed by the Nazi regime. *See also* Swing-Cliquen.

**Swingjugend.** Swing youth. *See also* Swing-Cliquen.

**System.** Formal principle, constitution. Contemptuous for the Weimar Republic.

**System-.** System (as prefix). For example, Systempolitiker (system politicians, Weimar politicians).

**Systemrassen.** System races. According to German race–scientist Hans Günther, there were six major European races: Nordic, Aryan, Mediterranean (western), East Alpine, Slavic, and Balkan.

**Systemzeit.** Constitutional period. Negative for time of the Weimar Republic (1919–1933). *See also* System.

# T

**T.** Code for Treblinka concentration camp.

**T2.** *See* T.

**TII.** *See* T.

**T-4.** *See* Aktion T-4.

**Tafelmargarine.** Table margarine. A type of margarine introduced in 1939. *See also* Bewirtschaftung.

**Tag der Erfassung der Zigeuner.** Day of Gypsy Registration. August 2, 1942. Forced registration of Czech Gypsies, a prelude to the deportation and murder of those without permanent residence and occupation.

**Tag der Machtübernahme der NSDAP.** Day of the Nazi Party Takeover. January 30, 1933. When Hitler was appointed Reichs Chancellor. *See also* Machtübernahme.

**Tag der nationalen Arbeit.** *See* Feiertag der nationalen Arbeit.

**Tag der nationalen Erhebung.** Day of the National Uprising. Holiday celebrated on January 30 to celebrate Hitler's appointment as Reich Chancellor in 1933. *See also* nationale Erhebung.

**Tag der nationalen Solidarität.** National Solidarity Day. January 30 became a day of rallies and ceremonies celebrating Hitler's accession to power in January 1933.

**Tag des Bauern.** Farmer's Day. *See also* Erntedanktag.

**Tagesgabe.** Daily giving. Daily ration for Germans during the war.

**Tagesparole.** Daily word. From 1940, the Propaganda Ministry issued a twice-daily briefing at which the subject of the day of the Reich Publishing Chief was released with endless commentaries. The material amounted daily to ten or twelve closely typed pages, containing many prohibitions and few permissions. It prescribed the treatment of specified themes with regard to space, tone, headlines, and placement to the last detail. For example, when Roosevelt was described in the Nazi press as a gangster, criminal, or idiot, these expressions were officially prescribed.

**Tag von Potsdam.** Day of Potsdam. The first Nazi Youth Day, held in 1932; a crowd of 70,000 witnessed a seven-hour parade. *See* Reichsjugendtag.

**Taifun.** *See* Unternehmen Taifun.

**Tak.** *See* Tankabwehrkanone.

**Talmud-Hundertschaft.** The Talmud Hundred. Adolf Eichmann research unit begun at Theresienstadt concentration camp to investigate Jewish history and translate the Talmud into German. The Jews who were working on this project were murdered at Auschwitz before it could be completed.

**Talmud-Jude.** Talmud Jew. Derogatory for a religious Jew.

**Tankabwehrkanone.** (Tak) Antitank gun.

**Tankstärke.** Oil force. German oil reserves.

**Tannenberg.** Temporary Hitler headquarters in the Black Forest in the summer of 1940.

**Tannenbergbund.** Tannenberg League. Right-wing antisemitic movement organized by World War I General Erich Ludendorff (1925–1933). Some of its members would join the NSDAP. Tannenberg was a notable German victory in 1914.

**Taschenunterseeboot.** Pocket U-boat. Two-man U-boat carrying two torpedoes with a range of 300 miles.

**(Die) Tat.** The Action. Official publication of the Tatkreis. *See also* Tatkreis.

**Täterstrafrecht.** Law punishing the criminal. Nazi law punished the criminal, even the intent of the criminal, not the crime, as in Roman law. *See* Willensstrafrecht.

**Tätigkeitsabzeichen.** Action medal. Army decoration awarded for special tasks, for paratroopers, pilots, observers, and so forth.

**Tätigkeitsberichte.** Activity reports. Daily Einsatzgruppen reports of statistics and other information of mass murder of Jews and others.

**Tätigkeits- und Lagebericht.** (TLB) Activity and situation report.

**Tatkreis.** Action Circle. Rightist group under the Weimar Republic, hostile to democracy, advocating racism and German nationalism.

**Tauschgesuch.** Trade exchange. Advertisment for barter, offering of furniture, clothing, other essential goods in German newspapers during the war-ration period.

**tauchklar.** Clear to dive. Ready to submerge.

**Tauchzulage.** Diving ration. Bonus for submarine crew in action.

**tauglich.** Capable. Physically fit for classification and service in the German army. *See also* kriegsverwendungsfähig.

**tauglich 1.** Fit for front-line service.

**tauglich 2.** Fit for limited service.

**tauglich 3.** Conditionally fit for service.

**Tausendjähriges Reich.** Thousand-Year Reich. The envisioned duration of Nazi rule.

**Tausend-Mark-Grenze.** Thousand-mark border. Between 1933 and 1936, Hitler had closed the German-Austrian border because of the eviction of a German official from Austria. Travel to Austria was permitted only after paying 1,000 Reichmark to the Third Reich.

**TB.** *See* Totenbuch.

**Technische Lieferbedingungen.** (TL). Technical guidelines. *See also* Waffenamt.

**Technische Nothilfe.** (Teno, TN) Technical Emergency Service. Engineers acting as auxiliary police for civilian protection during air raids and disasters, and serving in field units in the Wehrmacht and the Waffen-SS.

**Technische Truppen.** Technical Troops. Special army detachments composed of miners, engineers, and so forth.

**Teigwaren.** Pasta. Collective term for all forms of noodles, spaghetti, and so on, used on ration cards during the war.

**Teilkommando.** (TK) Detachment.

**Teilselbstversorger.** Partial self-supplier. *See also* Selbstversorger.

**Telefunken.** The electronics manufacturer Telefunken used slave labor from Riga-Kaiserwald concentration camp.

**Teno.** *See* Technische Nothilfe.

**Teppichbeißer.** Carpet biter. Nickname for Hitler, who allegedly threw himself on the floor during fits of rage and bit the carpet.

**Teppichfresser.** Carpet eater. *See also* Teppichbeißer.

**Terezin.** *See* Theresienstadt.

**Terror.** Terror. All enemy actions against Nazi Germany, especially the Allied bombings from 1942 on. *See also* Terrorismus.

**Terrorismus.** Terrorism. All actions by the enemy against the NS-Reich were considered terrorist acts; for example, Allied bombing of Germany became Bombenterror. *See* Terror.

**Terroristen.** Terrorists. Official term for partisans. *See also* Partisanen.

**Tesch & Stabenow.** (Testa) Subsidiary of IG Farben, supplying Zyklon poison gas to concentration camps. *See also* Deutsche Gesellschaft für Schädlingsbekämpfung.

**Testa.** *See* Tesch & Stabenow.

**Testgebiet.** Test area. Proving ground. For example, during the second half of 1941, areas in eastern Poland, the Baltic countries, and the Soviet Union occupied by the German army where German death squads (Einsatzgruppen) killed Jews.

**Thanatologie.** The science of producing death. Description given during the postwar Nuremberg trials of the medical experiments performed during the Holocaust.

**Theresienstadt.** (Terezin) The City of Austrian Empress Maria Theresa. Nazi police prison, ghetto, and concentration camp located in Czechoslovakia, seventy miles from Prague. Terezin was not a sealed section of town, but rather an eighteenth-century Austrian garrison. It became a Jewish town, governed and guarded by the SS. When the deportations from central Europe to the death camps began in the spring of 1942, certain groups were initially sent to the ghetto in Terezin: invalids, partners in a mixed marriage and their children, and prominent Jews with special connections. They were joined by old and young Jews from the Czech Protectorate and later by small numbers of prominent Jews from Denmark, Holland, and Austria. Its large barracks served as dormitories for communal living; they also contained offices, workshops, infirmaries, and communal kitchens. The Nazis used Terezin to deceive public opinion in neutral countries and the Red Cross by tolerating a limited cultural life of theater, music, lectures, and art. Terezin, however, was only a temporary station on the road to the death camps; about 88,000 were deported from the camp to their deaths. In April 1945, only 17,000 Jews remained in Terezin, where they were joined by 14,000 Jewish concentration camp prisoners evacuated from camps threatened by the Allied armies. On May 8, 1945, Terezin was incidentally liberated by the Red Army. *See* Polizeigefängnis.

**Theresienstädter Kronen.** (Th-Kr) Theresienstadt crowns (Czech money). Money used at the ghetto of Theresienstadt that depicted Moses with long sideburns and a crooked nose. *See also* Ghettogeld.

**Theresienstädter Lager.** Theresienstadt camp. *See* Familienlager.

**Thing.** Festival. Old Germanic for open-air theater for the performance of organized festival plays.

**Thingspiel.** Festival play. Reich playwrights composed plays sanctioned by the government and performed before huge audiences in open-air theaters. *See* Thing.

**Thing(spiel)stätte.** Festival-play arena. For Nazi theater art form that emphasized military and pagan scenes presented out-of-doors to huge audiences.

**Th-Kr.** *See* Theresienstädter Kronen.

**Thule-Gesellschaft.** Thule Society. Nationalist, racisist, and antisemitic club in Munich just after World War I. Many of its members became prominent Nazis, including Rudolf Hess and Alfred Rosenberg.

**tibetanisches Gebet.** Tibetan prayer. Concentration camp torture of jamming pointed sticks under the fingernails.

**tiefgegliederte Abwehrstellung.** (Military) defense in depth.

**Tiergartenstrasse 4.** Address of a confiscated Berlin villa that became the Euthanasia Program's central administrative offices. *See also* Euthanasie.

**Tiger.** The largest German tank, introduced in 1943 (*see* Königstiger). Also, code name for German attack on French Maginot Line in June 1940.

*Tirpitz.* German battleship. Between 1942 and 1944 attacked several Allied convoys and survived several British sea and air attacks. Finally sunk in 1944.

**TK.** *See* Teilkommando.

**TL.** *See* Technische Lieferbedingungen.

**TLB.** *See* Tätigkeits- und Lagebericht.

**TN.** *See* Technische Nothilfe.

**Todesfallsaufnahmen.** Death certificates. Until 1940 certificates were sent to the German next of kin stating that prisoners in the concentration camp had died of heart failure or similar natural causes.

**Todeskampf.** Battle to the death, death agony. Word used in Nazi ideology.

**Todeskisten.** Death caskets. Goebbels' cynical term for the Polish ghettos.

**Todesmärsche.** Death marches. With the ending of the war in 1944 and 1945, the SS forced concentration camp inmates to march westward into Germany to use them for forced labor, to prevent their liberation, and to stop them from falling into Russian hands. A quarter of a million prisoners died or were killed on the way.

**Todesraum.** Death space. Limited eastern European space allotted to races deemed inferior once Germany won the war. Also, gas chamber.

**(gefälschte) Todesursachen.** Falsified cause of death. Cause of death registered on official documents that concealed the murder of prisoners in concentration camps. *See also* Todesfallsaufnahmen.

**Todeszug.** Death train. *See* Deportationszug.

**tödliche Gleichmacherei.** Deadly equality. The claim that all races were equal.

**Todt-Organisation.** *See also* Organisation Todt.

**Toebbens.** German firm that ran brush factories in the Warsaw-Ghetto.

**Topf und Söhne.** Company that used slave labor to build gas chambers and crematoria for the death camps.

**Torfverwertungs GmbH.** Peat Utilization Inc. SS company seeking to use peat as a fuel for Germany.

**Tornisterkind.** Knapsack child. Slang for child sired by a German soldier in a foreign country.

**totaler Krieg.** Total war. War that made no distinction between noncombatants and combatants, and with all the means and power of the whole nation mobilized for the war effort. An early nineteenth-century idea, it was popularized in the 1930s by General Erich Ludendorff, who wrote about war involving the whole people of a nation, and its soul and blood, as well as its army. The notion was fully adopted by the Nazis, especially by Goebbels in his Sport-Palast address of February 1943, where a very responsive audience agreed that war had to be total and radical. *See also* Generalbevollmächtiger für den totale Kriegseinsatz; Reichsbevollmächtigte für den totalen Kriegseinsatz.

**Totalevakuierung.** Total evacuation. Euphemism for mass murder of Jews in Poland.

**Totalität des Krieges.** *See* totaler Krieg.

**Totenbuch.** (TB) Death book. Register inaccurately recording murders and deaths at concentration camps.

**Totenburgen.** Death castles. Monumental memorials planned by the Nazis to honor their war dead.

**Totenjuden.** Jews of death. Jews in the Treblinka death camp assigned to dispose of bodies of Jews.

**Totenkopf.** Death's head. Symbol used by Waffen-SS units, the Waffen-SS tank corps, and the Totenkopfverbände, with slight variations among the symbols.

**Totenkopfring der SS.** *See* SS-Totenkopfring.

**Totenkopfstandarten.** *See* SS-Totenkopfstandarten.

**Totenkopfverbände.** (TV) Death's-Head Formations. Concentration camp guards under the direction of Theodor Eicke. As the military situation worsened, the more able-bodied members were transferred to the Waffen-SS. Their place was taken by older members of the SA and soldiers from the Wehrmacht and Waffen-SS who had been wounded and were no longer fit for active duty.

**Totenkopfwachsturmbanne.** Death's-Head Guard Battalions. Armed full-time component of the SS during the prewar period, tasked with guarding concentration camps and political prisons.

**Toten-Rune.** Death rune. Signified by an upside down Lebens-Rune. Printed on SS documents and SS gravestones next to date of death. *See also* Lebens-Rune.

**Totenvögel.** Death birds. Nazi Party officials whose function was to inform next of kin that their relative had been killed in action and to organize memorial ceremonies. Also, sarcastic reference to the German eagles represented on most military and Nazi Party uniforms.

**Traditionsgau.** Traditional district. Name for the area of Munich–Upper Bavaria from 1930 on.

**tragbarer Bevölkerungszuwachs.** Tolerable natural population increase. *See also* Eignungsprüfer.

**Träger.** Carrier. The relationship between the German individual and/or all Germans and National Socialist ideas and ideals.

**Träger des völkischen Willens.** Carrier of the people's will. The National-Socialist German Workers' Party and even the Führer were considered agents of a larger force.

**tragisch.** Tragic. Stereotypical adjective used in official death notices of civilians who were killed during Allied air raids on Germany.

**Tragschicht.** Basis.

**Tragschrauber.** Autogiro. Combination of a conventional aircraft and a helicopter.

**Trampelfäden.** Trample wires. Slang for trip wires.

**Tränenstoff.** Tear stuff. Tear gas.

**Transferstelle.** Transfer station. Agency in the Warsaw-Ghetto that controlled economic life, including restricting food supplies.

**Trans-Ocean.** Semi-official German news agency. Accused of spying in the United States and the first to announce the Allied landings in Normandy in June 1944. *See* Deutsches Nachrichtenbüro.

**Transport.** Deportation. Moving Jews and other people to concentration camps, labor camps, ghettos, death camps, or elsewhere to be murdered.

**Transportbeitrag.** Deportation fee. *See also* Mitgabegeld.

**Transportenblock.** Deportation barracks. Location for Muselmänner and other people marked for murder.

**Transportherde.** Deportation herd. Pejorative for German Jews deported to death camps.

**Transportjuden.** Deportation Jews. Jews destined for murder in the death camps.

**Transportkommando.** Transport unit. Concentration camp prisoners who cleaned freight cars after new prisoners had debarked.

**transportunfähig.** Unfit for deportation. Those too weak or old or sick to be moved easily to concentration camps and usually killed locally.

**"(in stolzer) Trauer."** "With proud mourning." Formulaic closing sentence in newspaper announcements of German soldiers killed in action.

***Trau keinem Jud' auf grüner Heid . . . Ein Bilderbuch für Groß und Klein.*** Don't Trust a Jew on the Green Heath . . . A Picture Book for Big Folks and Little Folks. One of the most prejudiced books of its kind, produced by Elvira Bauer in 1936 and published by the Stürmer Verlag. Contained antisemitic verses and crude, stereotypical illustrations.

**Trawniki SS.** 4,000 to 5,000 Ukrainians and Volksdeutsche trained in the SS-Ausbildungslager in Trawniki, south of Lublin, to run death camps. They also saw action destroying the Warsaw-Ghetto. *See also* Aktion Reinhard; Warschau-Ghetto.

**Treblinka.** Death camp located near a small village of the same name close to Warsaw on the Bug River in the General Government. Opened in July 1942, it was the largest of the Operation Reinhard killing centers. Almost a million Jews were murdered there, a large percentage from the Warsaw-Ghetto. The camp was able to kill about 10,000 Jews a day. In March 1943, Himmler visited the camp and ordered that the nearly 1 million bodies buried there be exhumed and burned. A revolt by the inmates on August 2, 1943, destroyed most of the camp, and the Nazis obliterated it in November 1943.

**Trennschleuder.** Separating spinner. Germanization of Zentrifuge (centrifuge).

**Treudienst-Ehrenzeichen.** Honor medal for loyal service. From 1938, award for German civilians having served their country by having worked several years for a firm.

**Treuegeld.** Loyalty money. Company bonus offered to German employees.

**Treuegelöbnis.** Loyalty oath. Public and communal oath to Hitler as a closing ritual after every Nazi rally.

**Treuhänder.** Trustees. Persons who operated expropriated Jewish and non-Jewish businesses and land, especially in Poland. *See also* Abwesenheitspfleger.

**Treuhänder der Arbeit.** Trustees of Labor. *See also* Reichstreuhänder der Arbeit.

**Treueid.** Loyalty oath. Every German civil servant had to swear this oath to Hitler. In August 1934, Hitler became Reichspräsident, as well as Chancellor and Head of the Nazi Party, when Hindenburg died, and at that time, all members of the Reich government and armed forces swore a personal loyalty oath to Hitler, no longer to the laws of the state. *See also* Fahneneid; Gesetz über das Staatsoberhaupt des Deutschen Reiches; Appendix: Treueid.

**Treuhansa.** *See* Hanseatische Vermögensverwaltungs- und Treuhand-Gesellschaft.

**"Treu und fest hinter dem Führer!"** "Loyal and steadfast behind the leader." Nazi propaganda slogan.

**Trichterfelde.** Shell-hole field. Sarcastic name given to the Berlin suburb Lichterfelde after bombing raids.

***Triumph des Willens.*** Triumph of the Will. Leni Riefenstahl's film of Hitler's Nazi Party Congress at Nuremberg in 1934.

**Trockengemüsebombe.** Dry-vegetables bomb. Concentrated, dehydrated vegetables dropped by parachute to besieged German troops.

**(der) Trommler.** The Drummer. Hitler nickname after the Hitler Putsch.

**Trommler und Sammler.** Drummer and Collector. Early Hitler self-description.

**Trostbriefe.** Letters of consolation. Formulaic letters to the families of victims of the Euthanasia Program. *See also* Euthanasie.

**Trupp.** Ten to twenty-man unit in the armed forces, approximately the size of a half platoon.

**Truppenbetreuung.** Troop care. During the war, government-organized performances and entertainment at the front and in Germany by famous German artists as a diversion for the troops.

**TV.** *See* Totenkopfverbände.

**T-4.** *See* Aktion T-4.

**Typ(us).** Type, norm, form. Racial variety and fate. *See also* Rasse; *Rasse und Seele.*

**Tyr-Rune.** Rune representing the Germanic god Tyr, god of war. Symbolic of leadership in battle. It appears as an arrow pointing upward. Often placed on the Hitler Youth proficiency badge and that of paramilitary officers, as well as on SS gravestones instead of crosses, for soldiers killed in action.

# U

---

**überbildet.** Overeducated. Over-intellectualized, too bookish, too rational. Nazi description of their opponents.

**Überfallskommando.** Search unit. Jewish police unit in Lodz-Ghetto.

**Überfremdung.** Foreign influence. Spiritual, foreign, un-German influence in the form of deceptive thinking and culture through Christianity and Judaism. Biological foreign influences from the introduction of foreign races and people. *See* artfremd.

**Übergangslager.** (ÜL) Temporary detention camp. A camp used as a stopping spot for reshipment of Jews to death camps.

**Übergangslösung.** Transition solution. Steps taken by high-ranking Nazi officials to achieve the so-called "Final Solution." Later, deportation of Jews preliminary to their transport to a death camp.

**Übergangsmaßnahme.** Transition measure. Placing or relocating the Jews in ghettos preliminary to their mass murder.

**Übermenschen.** Supermen. In Nazi ideology, the supreme examples of the human species, the German-Nordic-Aryans.

**Übernahmeschein.** Reception paper. Sales license, certificate that goods, especially food, were offered first to authorities. *See also* Ablieferungspflicht.

**übernationale Mächte.** Supranational powers. International agencies such as the Catholic church, the Freemasons, the Jewish "world conspiracy"; believed to be masterminds ruling the world.

**überrollen.** To roll over. To advance rapidly and overtake retreating troops.

**Überschiebung.** Overlapping. Of influence and authority.

**Übersetzungs- und Korrespondenzbüro.** Translation and correspondence office. Section of the Jewish Council's Office in the Warsaw-Ghetto and likely at other ghettos that corresponded with and translated for the German Reich government in Berlin.

**Übersiedlung.** Resettlement. Removal of Jews to death camps or mass-murder sites. *See* Umsiedlung.

**Übersiedlungsaktion.** Resettlement Operation. 1939 removal of Jewish men from Vienna to Poland for forced labor.

**überstellt.** Transferred. Note on prisoner's personal information card with the name of the concentration camp and date of arrival. *See* Häftlings-Personal-Karte.

**Übertragungsschein.** Transfer paper. Priority transferable to subcontractor or supplier.

**Über-Versailles.** Super Versailles. Goebbels' ironic propaganda reference to the Treaty of Versailles.

**U-Boot.** *See* Unterseeboot.

**Uckermark.** Youth concentration camp at Ravensbrück converted to women's concentration camp in 1939.

**Ufa.** *See* Universum-Film AG.

**Ufa-Film.** *See* Universum-Film AG.

**Uhu-Bücher.** Owl books. *See also* Uli-Taschenbücher.

**U-Jag.** *See* Unterseebootsjagdverband.

**u. k.** *See* unabkömmlich.

**UK-Stellung.** *See* Unabkömmlichstellung.

**ÜL.** *See* Übergangslager.

**Uli-Taschenbücher.** Uli Pocket Books. Of the Jewish Ullstein Publishing House, which the Nazis seized in 1934.

**Ullsteindeutscher.** Ullstein German. Pejorative for democratic and liberal journalist or politician, named after the Jewish Ullstein Publishing House, until seized in 1934.

**U-Mann.** *See* Unzuverlässiger Mann.

**Umbruch.** Deep-seated change. The new beginning in economics and politics stemming from Hitler's rise to power in 1933; National Socialist revolution.

**Umerziehung.** Reeducation, indoctrination. In 1933, more than 100,000 political enemies of the Reich were sent to concentration camps for ideological "reeducation."

**umgelegt.** Bumped-off. Mass-murdered.

**"umgesiedelt, Addresse unbekannt."** "Resettled, address unknown." *See also* umgezogen, Addresse unbekannt.

**"umgezogen, Addresse unbekannt."** "Moved, address unknown." Stamped on letters returned to senders by German postal authorities addressed to Jews already sent to concentration camps.

**UmL.** *See* Umsiedlungslager.

**umlegen.** Shift, bump off. In the jargon of the SA and the SS, to kill a Party enemy.

**umnageln.** To change nails. To adjust Russian railway tracks to German gauge.

**Umrassung.** Change of racial characteristics. Nazi race ideology described a positive change occurring when alien racial characteristics were superseded by Nordic ones.

**Umschichtung.** Regrouping (of society). Euphemism for deportation of Jews. *See* Umsiedlung.

**Umschlagplatz.** Transfer point. Assembly point in the ghetto, most notably the Warsaw-Ghetto, near the train station, where Jews were transferred to railroad cars heading to death camps. Or, in smaller towns, assembly point where Jews were murdered on the spot or selected to be moved to another location to be killed.

**Umschmelzmetall.** Metal for melting. Scrap metal.

**Umschulung.** Retraining. Reeducation to assure the Reich of a skilled labor supply.

**Umsiedler.** Resettler. Volksdeutsche resettling in Germany. Also, Jews and other people destined for deportation and murder.

**Umsiedlerzüge.** Resettlement trains. Trainloads of Jews deported from Germany or occupied Europe to death camps to be murdered.

**Umsiedlung.** Resettlement. Resettlement of Germans; forced deportation of Jews to ghettos and then to death camps in eastern Europe for mass murder.

**Umsiedlungsaktion.** Resettlement Operation. Deportation of Jews to eastern Europe for mass murder. Also, destruction of the Warsaw-Ghetto. *See also* Erste Aktion; Zweite Aktion.

**Umsiedlungskommando.** Resettlement Unit. Gestapo and SD units that murdered Jews in towns of eastern Europe.

**Umsiedlungslager.** (UmL) Resettlement camp. Euphemism for death camp.

**Umsiedlungsstab.** Resettlement Staff. Deportation board officers in charge of deporting entire Jewish communities to their death.

**Umvolkung.** Change of national loyalty, assimilation. Change the character of the people. Nazi policy opposed to Germans emigrating and foreigners entering Germany. Germanization of eastern European countries.

**Umvolkungspolitik.** Population transfer policy. Forced relocations.

**Umwandererzentrale.** *See* Umwandererzentralstelle.

**Umwandererzentralstelle.** (UWZ) Central Resettlement Office. Located in Lodz, this office facilitated the deportation of Jews and Poles to camps or ghettos to make room for ethnic Germans. Headed by Adolf Eichmann's assistant, Dieter Wisliceny.

**Umwanderungsstelle.** *See* Umwandererzentralstelle.

**unabkömmlich.** (u.k.) Indispensable. Germans exempted from military service because they were needed for other wartime duties (e.g., skilled workers, engineers, factory workers, miners, and some farmers).

**Unabkömmlichstellung.** (UK-Stellung) Exemption from military service. *See also* unabkömmlich.

**unbändig.** Unbounded. A superlative to describe the unbridled will, belief, courage, and so forth of National Socialism and its followers.

**Unbedenklichkeitsvermerk.** Entry (in documents) for safe passage. Official permit for such purposes as transferring foreign currency, receiving an exit visa, and so on.

**unbekannter Gefreiter und Meldegänger.** Unknown corporal and messenger. Positive cliché for Hitler's role in World War I.

**"unbekannt verzogen."** "Moved, address unknown." Euphemism for deportation of Jews to death camps.

**Unbesternter.** One without a star. Privileged Jew allowed not to wear a star in Germany after 1941 decree. *See also* Mischehen; privilegierte Juden.

**undeutsch.** Un-German. *See also* Aufklärungsfeldzug wider den undeutschen Geist.

**unerbittlich.** Pitiless. Goebbel's description of Hitler's persistent attitude toward the Jews.

**"unerwünschte Wiederkehr."** (u.W.) "Unwanted return." Noted on prisoners' documents indicating slave labor and then death.

**unerwünschter Bevölkerungszuwachs.** Undesirable natural increase. *See also* Eignungsprüfer.

**Ungeist.** *See* Aufklärungsfeldzug Wider den undeutschen Geist.

**Ungeziefer.** Vermin. Antisemitic name referring to the Jews.

**(der) unheilbare Kranke.** The terminally ill. Label for those too old, unable to work, or Nazi opponents who ended up murdered.

**Union.** Munitions factory run by the SS for Krupp in Auschwitz-Buna.

**Union Nationaler Schriftsteller.** National Writers' League. Name for the Reich German P.E.N. Club from 1934.

**Unionwerke.** *See* Union.

**Universum-Film AG.** (Ufa, Ufa-Film) Universe Film Company. Germany's largest film company. By 1937 controlled by the Ministry of Propaganda's Film Chamber and in turn controlled other German film production companies.

**unnütze Esser.** Useless eaters. *See also* unproduktive Esser.

**unproduktive Esser.** Unproductive eaters. Mentally and/or terminally ill Germans targeted for murder under the T-4 program. *See also* Euthanasie.

**unrassisch.** Not according to race. Un-German; whatever did not accord with Nazi ideology.

**UnschF.** *See* Unterscharführer.

**unser Doktor.** Our Doctor. Nickname for Goebbels, who held a Ph.D. in literature from Heidelberg University.

**"Unsere Ehre heißt Treue."** "Our honor is loyalty." SS motto engraved on SS belt buckles. *See also* "Meine Ehre heißt (meine) Treue!"

**"Unsere letzte Hoffnung: Hitler."** "Our Last Hope: Hitler." Nazi campaign slogan after the Depression hit Germany in 1929.

*Unser Wille und Weg.* Our Will and Way. Goebbels' monthly propaganda journal.

**Unstaat.** Unstate. Derogatory name for the Weimar Republic.

**untauglich für Wehrdienst.** Unfit for military service. *See also* tauglich.

**Unterabschnitt.** Branch of administrative subdistrict.

**Unterbann.** Hitler Youth Unit. *See also* Stamm.

**Unterführer.** Party functionary up to the rank of the local leader. Such a person usually had personal contact with the populace.

**Untergau.** Unit of League of German Girls. *See also* Bund Deutscher Mädel in der Hitlerjugend.

**Untergrund.** Underground. European opposition to the Third Reich.

**Unterkapo.** Assistant foreman (in concentration camps). *See also* Kapo.

**Unterkühlungsversuche.** Hypothermia experiments. Medical experiments on prisoners at Dachau to determine the chance of survival of German pilots whose planes had crashed into the sea. Prisoners were forced into tanks containing water of 2.5° C to 12° C (36.5° F to 53.6° F) or colder wearing a pilot's uniform. Life jackets prevented drowning.

**Unterkunftsleiter.** Accommodation leader. Hotel manager.

**(*Der*) *Untermensch*.** The Subhuman. Antisemitic publication with illustrations issued in 1941 by Himmler to Germans living in the German-occupied Polish territories (Volksdeutsche) to prevent fraternization with Jews. *See also* Untermenschen; Untermenschentum.

**Untermenschen.** Subhuman people. In the Nazi racial scheme, non-Aryans such as Jews, Poles, Russians, Serbs, Sinti-Romani, and Bolsheviks. Among the non-Aryans, the Jews were held to be the most dangerous group, the children of darkness, and the only true rivals of the Aryans, the children of light. The other non-Aryans were to serve as slaves to the Reich. A 1942 Race and Settlement head office pamphlet stated that subhumans only seemed biologically similar to Aryans because they had "hands, feet and a kind of brain, with eyes and a mouth." But they were "a completely different, dreadful creature, only a rough copy of a human being, with human-like facial traits but morally and mentally lower than any animal. Within this creature there is a fearful chaos of wild, uninhibited passions, nameless destructiveness, the most primitive desires, the nakedest vulgarity. For all that bear a human face are not equal. Woe to him who forgets it."

**Untermenschentum.** Subhumanness. According to Nazi race science, inferior races. Also, collective for Jews in eastern Europe. *See also* Untermenschen.

**Unternehmen Achse.** Operation Axis. Code name for German military plan based on the assumption Italy would withdraw from the war. Renamed from Operation Alarich.

**Unternehmen Alarich.** Operation Alarich. Code name for German occupation of Italy in 1943.

**Unternehmen Anton.** Operation Anton. Code name for the German occupation of Vichy, France, in November 1942. *See* Unternehmen Attila.

**Unternehmen Attila.** Operation Attila. Code name for German occupation of Vichy, France, in 1942. *See* Unternehmen Anton.

**Unternehmen Blau.** Operation Blue. Code name for spring and summer 1942 offensive in which the German army was to drive into the Caucasus to capture the Soviet oil fields.

**Unternehmen Braunschweig.** Operation Braunschweig. Renaming of Operation Blue. *See also* Unternehmen Blau.

**Unternehmen Donnerschlag.** Operation Thunderclap. Code name for Hitler's order to the German 6th Army to break out of Stalingrad.

**Unternehmen Felix.** Operation Felix. Code name for German plan to seize Gibraltar through Spain on November 20, 1940.

**Unternehmen Feuerzauber.** Operation Magic Fire. Code name for German assistance to Spanish General Francisco Franco during Spain's Civil War. Also, offensive against Leningrad.

**Unternehmen Herbstnebel.** Operation Autumn Mist. Hitler's last-minute change of code name for the German offensive in the Ardennes, December 1944. *See also* Unternehmen Wacht am Rhein.

**Unternehmen Himmler.** Operation Himmler. Reinhard Heydrich created a scheme to give Hitler a pretext for the German attack on Poland on September 1, 1939. On the night before the invasion, SD detachments disguised as Polish soldiers and guerrillas attacked a forestry station, destroyed a German customs building, and occupied the German radio station at Gleiwitz. After shouting anti-German slogans into the microphone, the SD (disguised as Poles) retreated, leaving behind a number of dead German concentration camp prisoners.

**Unternehmen Marita.** Operation Marita. Code name for German invasion of Greece in April 1941.

**Unternehmen Merkur.** Operation Mercury. Code name for the German air attacks on the island of Crete in April 1941.

**Unternehmen Nordlicht.** Operation Northern Lights. Code name for the German attack on Leningrad in 1942.

**Unternehmen Nordwind.** Operation North Wind. Code name for subsidiary German offensive in Alsace (winter 1944–1945).

**Unternehmen Panzerfaust.** Operation Bazooka. Code name for Hitler's plan to seize Admiral Miklós Horthy de Nagybánya's citadel residence in Budapest in case Hungary pulled out of its alliance with Germany.

**Unternehmen Regenbogen.** Operation Rainbow. The spring 1945 plan to scuttle most of the German navy. But on May 4 the Allies forced Admiral Karl Dönitz to withdraw this order, which he did, except that the U-boat commanders in the western Baltic scuttled their vessels anyway, amounting to 231 U-boats.

**Unternehmen Seelöwe.** Operation Sea Lion. Code name for the planned invasion of England (1940–1941).

**Unternehem Steinbock.** Operation Capricorn. German air attacks against London during the winter of 1943–1944.

**Unternehmen Taifun.** Operation Typhoon. Code name for the German offensive against Moscow in September 1941.

**Unternehmen Wacht am Rhein.** Operation Watch on the Rhine. Code name for December 1944 German Ardennes counteroffensive, which was called the Battle of the Bulge by the Allies.

**Unternehmen Walküre.** Operation Valkyrie. Failed plan by Hitler's officers to murder him on July 20, 1944, and take over the government. *See also* Schwarze Kapelle.

**Unternehmen Zitadelle.** Operation Citadel. Code name for the July 1943 Wehrmacht offensive in the Soviet Union.

**Unterrasse.** Sub-race. Used especially for Jews, deemed to belong to an inferior race. *See also* Untermenschen.

**unterrassisch.** Of inferior race. *See* Unterrasse.

**Unterscharführer.** (UnschF, USHF) Corporal in the SS.

**Unterseeboot.** (U-Boot) Undersea boat. Submarine. The Reich's most effective sea weapon during World War II.

**Unterseeboot machen.** To do the submarine. Slang for go into hiding.

**Unterseebootsjagdverband.** (U-Jag) German Naval Submarine-Hunter Unit.

**Unterseemutterschiff.** Underwater mother ship. Submarine tender launching a two-man midget submarine.

**Untersturmführer.** (U'Stuf, UstF) Second lieutenant in the SS.

**Untersuchungs- und Schlichtungsausschuß der Partei.** (USchlA) Investigation and arbitration committee of the Party. Supreme National Socialist Party Court with the power of life and death over Party members, headed by Major Walter Buch.

**Unterwanderung.** Infiltration of foreigners.

**untragbar.** Unbearable. Pejorative for Germans who were expelled from Nazi organizations.

**unzuverlässig.** Unreliable. Category used to classify German spies. *See also* A-Mann; H-Mann; U-Mann; V-Mann.

**Unzuverlässige.** Unreliables. SD agents open to bribes. *See* unzuverlässiger Mann.

**unzuverlässiger Mann.** (U-Mann) Unreliable man. German spy classified as unreliable and corrupt and who needed to be watched. *See also* A-Mann; H-Mann; V-Mann; Z-Mann.

**Urheber des 1. Weltkriegs.** Culprits of World War I: Jews, Socialists and Communists.

**Ursatz.** Germanization of axiom.

**USchlA.** *See* Untersuchungs- und Schlichtungsausschuß.

**USHF.** *See* Unterscharführer.

**Ustascha.** Croatian Nationalist Movement.

**UstF.** *See* Untersturmführer.

**U'Stuf.** *See* Untersturmführer.

**UTAG.** *See* Deutsche Umsiedlungs-Treuhand-GmbH.

**u. W.** *See* unerwünschte Wiederkehr.

**UWZ.** *See* Umwandererzentralstelle.

# V

**V.** Victory sign using upraised forefinger and middlefinger formed into a V. A German adaptation of the victory sign of the Allies. As a Wehrmacht newspaper put it: "V—the sign of our victory, the victory of good over evil, order over chaos, and the will to build over the destructive element of Jewry."

**VAA.** *See* Vertreter des Auswärtigen Amtes.

**Vaterland.** Fatherland. Usage discouraged in a press release of 1942. To be replaced by Heimat.

**Vaterländischer Schutzbund.** Fatherland Protection League. Organization that served as the basis of the Austrian Sturmabteilung.

**Vaterlandsverräter.** Fatherland traitor. *See also* Novemberverbrecher.

*VB.* *See Völkischer Beobachter.*

**VDA.** *See* Verein für das Deutschtum im Ausland. Volksbund für das Deutschtum im Ausland.

**VDB.** *See* Volksdeutsche Bewegung.

**V-3.** Long-range gun. Long-range smooth-bore gun designed to fire shells with up to a 10 kg (22 lb) high-explosive warhead and a range of 93 km. Most installations were bombed before the guns could be used. *See also* Vergeltungswaffen; Wunderwaffen.

**VE.** *See* Volksempfänger 301.

**V-1.** *See* Flugbombe V-1; Vergeltungswaffen; Wunderwaffen.

**veralmen.** To aluminize.

**Veränderungsnachweis.** Proof of change. *See also* Abgang.

**"Verantwortung von unten nach oben; Autorität von oben nach unten."** "Responsibility of subordinate to superior; authority from superior to subordinate." Göring's definition of the Führer principle. *See also* Führerprinzip.

**verarbeitet.** Processed, used up. Jews gassed to death in gas trucks in eastern Europe.

**Verband deutscher Vereine im Ausland.** Organization of German Associations Abroad. Headquartered in Berlin, this organization united people of German ethnic origin who lived outside of Germany.

**Verbastardierung.** Bastardization. The negative result of racial mixing within the German race.

**Verbindungsstab.** (Verb.St.) Liaison staff.

**Verbotszeit.** Forbidden time. Nazi Party internal name for the different laws against public speaking and gathering during the Weimar Republic after November 1923. Also, time period in 1932 during which the SA and the SS were forbidden.

**Verbrannte Erde.** Burned soil. Hitler's scorched earth order to all German troops retreating from the Soviet Union. Nothing was to be left standing.

**verbrecherische Befehle.** Criminal orders. Hitler and Wehrmacht orders justifying the murder of so-called criminals. They served as a basis for SS, Wehrmacht, Einsatzgruppen, and police mass murders of Jews and Communists in eastern Europe. *See* Kommissarbefehl.

**Verb.St.** *See* Verbindungsstab.

**Verbundwirtschaft.** Common economy. Pool for distribution of energy, combining privately and publicly owned utility.

**Verderb.** Spoilage. Waste.

**("Kampf dem) Verderb."** "Fight against spoilage. Don't waste." Slogan to promote reuse and recycling of goods and food.

**Verdichter.** Germanization of Kompressor (compressor).

**Verdienstorden vom Deutschen Adler.** (Adlerorden) German eagle merit medal. Military medal in five categories, introduced in 1937, bestowed on foreigners.

**verdrängt.** Evicted. *See* ausgesiedelt.

**Verdrängung fremden Volkstums.** Repression of foreign influences on the German people. Expulsion of inferior races, often leading to genocide.

**Verdunkelungsverbrecher.** Blackout criminals. Germans who committed criminal acts during an air-raid blackout, from looting to rape. Also, criminals whose offense was collusion. *See* Volksschädling.

**Verein für das Deutschtum im Ausland.** (VDA) Organization for Germans Abroad. *See also* Volksbund für das Deutschtum im Ausland.

**Vereinigte Stahlwerke.** United Steel Works. Largest steel company in Europe, headed by Albert Vögler, who strongly backed Hitler for the German chancellorship in the early 1930s.

**Vereinigte Vaterländische Verbände.** (VVV). United Fatherland Associations. Small party in the early 1920s associated with the Nazi Party.

**Verfallskunst.** Degenerate art. *See also* entartete Kunst.

**Verfallszeit.** Degenerate time. Slanderous for the period of the Weimar Republic.

**verfranzen.** To go astray. Air force slang. *See also* Franz.

**Verfügungstruppe(n).** (VT.) *See* SS-Verfügungstruppen.

**Vergasung.** Vaporization. Method of employing poison gas to murder Jews, Gypsies, political opponents, and other people.

**Vergasungskeller.** Gassing cellar. Gas chamber at death camps.

**Vergeltungsaktion.** Act of revenge. Pretext for mass murders of Jewish men, women, and children in eastern Europe by police battalions and Einsatzgruppen. Also, late in World War II, air attacks against England, especially referring to the reprisal weapons. *See also vergeltungsuaffen;* Wunderwaffen.

**Vergeltungsangriff.** Reprisal attack. *See also* Vergeltungsaktion.

**Vergeltungsbombe.** Revenge bomb, such as the V-1 and the V-2. Weapon used to bomb London and other English targets late in World War II. *See also* Vergeltungswaffen.

**Vergeltungsflug.** Reprisal flight. *See also* Vergeltungswaffen.

**Vergeltungsmaßnahme.** Reprisal measure. *See also* Vergeltungsaktion.

**Vergeltungsschlag.** Reprisal strike. *See also* Vergeltungsaktion.

**Vergeltungswaffe Eins.** Reprisal weapon one. *See also* Vergeltungswaffen.

**Vergeltungswaffe Zwei.** Reprisal weapon two. *See also* Vergeltungswaffen.

**Vergeltungswaffen.** (V-Waffe) Reprisal weapons. Rocket program in Peenemuende and Dora-Mittelbau concentration camps, whose slave labor made V-1 and V-2 rockets.

**Vergesellschaftung.** Nationalization. Nationalizing German trusts remained an unfulfilled point (No. 13 in the Nazi Party program). *See* Appendix: Parteiprogram: Fünfundzwanzig Punkte des nationalsozialistischen Programms.

**Vergiftung von Brunnen.** Poisoning of wells. Wehrmacht headquarters warned its troops to be on the watch for dangers from poisoned wells in eastern Europe.

**Verharrungstyp.** *See Rasse und Seele.*

**Verjudung.** Jewification. For centuries, the belief in the noxious Jewish influence on all aspects of German life. An often-used antisemitic propaganda term, for example, "Verjudung unseres Seelenlebens!" ("The Jewification of the Life of Our Souls"). From Hitler's *Mein Kampf.*

**Verkämpfung.** Obstinate fighting.

**Verkauf jüdischen Umzugsgutes Gestapo.** (Vugesta[p]) Sale of Jewish change-of-residence goods, Gestapo. Organization in Vienna that sold the property of deported Jews.

**Verköterung.** Muddiness. Racial degeneration.

**verkraften.** Germanization of mechanisieren (to mechanize).

**Verlagerung.** Transfer. Moving private and industrial property from cities to the countryside during the war.

**Verländlichung.** Raising the percentage of rural settlements.

**Verlegungsbescheid.** Transfer notice. *See also* Verlagerung.

**Verlobte mit Kind.** Fiancée with child. Had the same rights as a German soldier's wife. *See also* Brautkind.

**Verlobungsbefehl.** Engagement order. To get engaged to marry was considered a legal step for SS members so important that they had to report it to the Reichs-führer-SS three months prior to the marriage. *See also* Heiratsbefehl.

**Vermögensverwaltungs- und Rentenanstalt.** Property and Pension Administration. Agency created to seize all Jewish property in Holland.

**Vernegerung.** Blackened, niggered. The German racial soul contaminated with Black spirit. The mixture of German and Black blood. The influence on Germany of American language, literature, or jazz. *See also* Schwarze Schmach.

**Vernichtung.** Destruction, eradication, extermination. Intention of Nazi Germany to murder all Jews.

**Vernichtung durch Arbeit.** Destruction through work. Working Jews and other prisoners to death. Specifically, agreement of September 1942 between Himmler and Reich Minister of Justice Otto Thierack whereby some Jews and others serving in prisons were to be transferred to the SS so they could be worked to death.

**Vernichtung lebensunwerten Lebens.** Destruction of life unworthy of life. *See also* lebensunwertes Lebens.

**Vernichtungsanstalt.** Extermination facility. Unofficial term for death camps.

**Vernichtungskompanie.** Extermination company. Jews condemned to death at Dachau.

**Vernichtungslager.** (VL) Extermination camp. Unofficial term for death camp devoted primarily to the destruction of Jewish lives. The six major death camps were Auschwitz-Birkenau, Belzec, Chelmno, Lublin-Majdanek, Sobibor, and Treblinka. Jews arrived under the guise of resettlement or deportation. *See also* Konzentrationslager; Umsiedlung.

**Vernichtungsliste.** Extermination list. *See also* Richtlinien für das Verhalten der Truppe Rußland.

**Vernichtungsstelle.** Extermination center. Unofficial term for death camp devoted primarily to the destruction of Jewish lives. Only for internal Nazi conversations discussing the death camps. Often the word referred specifically to Auschwitz-Birkenau.

**Vernichtungsstelle 2.** Extermination center 2. Mass-murder site of Jews at the Ninth Fort in Kovno, Lithuania.

**Vernichtungsstrategie.** Extermination strategy. Nazi plan of complete destruction of all human and material resources in an enemy country. *See also* totaler Krieg.

**Vernichtungstransporte.** Extermination transports. Trains used to deport Jews to their deaths in eastern Europe.

**Verniederländerung.** Becoming like the Dutch. Germans losing their sense of history and instinct for conquest. *See also* Verschweizerung.

**Vernordnung.** Nordification. *See also* Aufnorden.

**Verordnung.** (VO) Order, decree.

**Verordnung des Reichspräsidenten zum Schutz von Volk und Staat.** Decree of the Reich President for the Protection of People and State. *See also* Reichstagsbrandverordnung.

**Verordnung gegen Volksschädlinge.** *See* Volksschädlingsverordnung.

**Verordnungsblatt des Reichsprotektorats Böhmen und Mähren.** (VOBl Prot) Regulations of the Reich Protectorate Bohemia and Moravia.

**Verordnung über das Kriegsausgleichsverfahren.** *See* Kriegsausgleichsverfahren.

**Verordnung über das Vermögen von Angehörigen des ehemals polnischen Staats.** Decree regarding the Property of Citizens of the Former Polish State. September 17, 1940.

**Verordnung über den Waffenbesitz von Juden.** Decree regarding Weapon Ownership by Jews. November 11, 1938, law preventing Jewish ownership of firearms.

**Verordnung über die Anmeldung des Vermögens von Juden.** Decree on the Registration of Jewish Property. April 24, 1938, law that required all Jewish property to be registered for future Aryanization.

**Verordnung über die Beschäftigung von Juden.** Decree regarding the Employment of Jews. October 3, 1941, forced-labor decree for Jews.

**Verordnung über die öffentliche Fürsorge der Juden.** Decree regarding Public Assistance for Jews. November 19, 1938, decree reducing public assistance for Jews.

**Verordnung über die Strafrechtspflege gegen Polen und Juden in den eingegliederten Ostgebieten.** Decree regarding the Application of the Penal Code to Jews and Poles in the Incorporated Eastern Territories. December 4, 1941, decree extending German penal code to Jews and Poles so that any criminal offense against Germans or Germany would result in a death sentence and/or being sent to a concentration camp. *See also* Volksschädlingsverordnung.

**Verordnung über die Zulassung von Ärzten zur Tätigkeit bei den Krankenkassen.** Decree regarding the Admission of Doctors to the National Health Insurance Service. September 8, 1937, decree excluding Jewish doctors from coverage.

**(Fünfte) Verordnung über die Zulassung von Zahnärzten und Dentisten zur Tätigkeit bei den Krankenkassen.** Fifth Decree regarding the Admission of Dental Surgeons and Dentists to Participate in the National Health Insurance Service. January 12, 1938, decree excluding Jewish dentists from coverage. One of many such decrees.

**Verordnung über eine Sühneleistung der Juden deutscher Staatsangehörigkeit.** Decree regarding an Atonement Fine for Jewish Subjects of the German state. November 12, 1938, law requiring the German Jewish community to pay a huge fine for damages they incurred while subject to the massive November 1938 Pogrom. *See also* Reichskristallnacht.

**(Dreizehnte) Verordnung zum Reichsbürgergesetz.** Thirteenth Regulation on the Reichs' Citizen Law. July 1, 1943, law that stated any infraction by Jews of German laws would be handled by the police, not by the courts. It essentially required that Jews be placed in police custody and required they be punished simply for being Jewish. Sent off to death camps, their property would revert to the Reich.

**Verordnung zur Abwehr heimtückischer Angriffe gegen die Regierung der nationalen Erhebung.** Regulation for the Defense of Insidious Attacks against the Government of the National Seizure of Power. March 1933 decree against criticizing the Nazi-controlled government. *See also* Gesetz gegen heimtückische Angriffe auf Staat und Partei und zum Schutz der Parteiuniformen.  ·

**Verordnung zur Ausschaltung der Juden aus dem deutschen Wirtschaftsleben.** Decree Eliminating the Jews from German Economic Life. November 12, 1938, order removing Jews from all business and labor activities in Germany.

**Verordnung zur Durchführung des Gesetzes über den Widerruf von Einbürgerungen.** Executive Decree of the Law concerning the Repeal of Naturalizations and the Adjudication of German Citizenship. This law of July 26, 1933, defined Jews from eastern Europe as "undesirable" and subject to denationalization.

**(Erste) Verordnung zur Durchführung des Luftschutzgesetzes.** (First) Decree to Implement the Air-Defense Law. September 1, 1939, order that Jews pay a special air-defense tax.

**verpolt.** Having become Polish. Germans in Poland who refused to return to Nazi Germany.

**Verrassung.** Race defilement. For Germans, negative biological impact of miscegenation with Jews and other non-Germans. *See also* Verjudung.

**(britischer) Verrat an Europa.** British betrayal of Europe. The belief that Germany would be surrounded, causing war in 1939 and making the world decide between British domination and a (German-dominated) new Europe. *See also* Neuordnung Europas.

**Verrechnungsabkommen.** Bank-clearing agreement (with a foreign country).

**Verrechnungsmark.** Compensation Mark. Mark held by foreign suppliers under clearing agreements. *See* Verrechnungsabkommen.

**Verrechnungsstelle.** Accounting office (for clearing and bartering transactions).

**Verreichlichung.** Creating one single Reich (government; and abolishing the provincial governments according to the 1934 restructuring law).

**verreist.** Gone on a trip. Euphemism for arrested and placed in a concentration camp in Germany.

**Versager.** Failures. Gypsies and others the Nazis considered racially inferior.

**Versager-1.** Failure (number) 1. Ironic for V-1 weapon. *See also* Flugbombe V-1; Vergeltungswaffen; Wunderwaffen.

**Versailler Diktat.** Versailles ultimatum. Versailles Treaty seen as unfairly forced on Germany. Pretext used by all those opposed to the Weimar Republic—especially, the National Socialists—to overthrow that government. Moreover, the Nazis employed this pretext as one of many to attack the German Jews as well as non-German Jews and other people, as organizing an anti-German conspiracy evidenced by the Versailles Treaty, its provisions for German loss of territory, change of government, arms limitations, and in particular the guilt clause and its attendant reparations requirement.

**Verschönerungsaktionen.** Beautification operations. Temporary beautification projects at Theresienstadt in June 1944. Done to impress the International Red Cross visiting the ghetto.

**Verschweizerung.** Becoming Swiss-like. Without a sense of history and passion for conquest.

**Verschwendung von Volksvermögen.** Wasting a people's wealth. *See also* Volksvermögen.

**verschworene Gemeinschaft.** Conspiracy community. Positive for the relationship between Hitler and the SS. Also, relationship among all Germans, suggesting unity during the war.

**verseucht.** Infested. During World War II, areas in eastern Europe with strong partisan activity.

**Verseuchung.** Contamination. Presence of Jews in Europe, particularly in eastern Europe.

**Versorgungsamt.** Social Benefits Office. Taken over by the Nazis and basing its services on racial principles.

**Versorgungsoffizier.** Social Benefits Officer. *See also* Versorgungsamt.

**Verstädterung.** Urbanization. The proportion of city dwellers in the whole of German society. The uprooting and resettling of cities according to the precepts of Blut und Boden, the principle that all racial Germans have the right to live on German soil.

**Verstärkter Grenzaufsichtsdienst.** Strengthened border control. Part of the Gestapo.

**Versteppung Europas.** Europe turning into prairie. Toward the end of World War II, Nazi fear of the Soviet Union's complete destruction of Europe if Germany lost the war.

**Verstrebung.** Strutting. Geopolitically to brace up an empire with military bases.

**Verstützung.** *See* Verstrebung.

**Versuchsabteilung der Reichsuniversität Straßburg.** Research Branch of Reich University of Strasbourg. Professor August Hirt selected Jews to be killed so that their skeletons could be used at the institute. *See also* Natzweiler-Struthof.

**Versuchspersonen.** Experiment persons, human guinea pigs. Prisoners chosen by SS doctors at concentration camps to be experimented on.

**VAA.** *See* Vertreter des Auswärtigen Amtes (VAA). Representative of the Foreign Office.

**Vertrauensfrau.** Confidante. Female shop steward in a German industry.

**Vertrauensleute.** Confidants. Trustworthy SD agents, loyal to the Nazi Party. *See* Vertrauensmann.

**Vertrauensmädel.** Young woman as intermediary. From 1935, young, Nazi-trained women served as ideological spokespersons between German companies and German youth.

**Vertrauensmann.** (V-Mann) Trusted man. Agent of the SD Intelligence Service. Spy or informer. Also, German Labor Front Trustees. *See also* A-Mann; Deutsche Arbeitsfront; H-Mann; U-Mann; Z-Mann.

**Vertrauensrat.** Confidence council. Representatives. Company committees required by law and consisting of the managers and workers, who decided on work-output improvement, accident prevention, working conditions, and so forth.

**vertrauliche Information der Parteikanzlei.** Confidential information from the Party Chancellery. Top-secret Hitler orders sent only to top Nazi officials.

**Verwaltungsführer.** Administrative officer. SS concentration camp officer.

**Verwendungszwang.** Utilization force. Obligation of companies to use German raw materials even if it meant poorer product quality.

**Verzichtfrieden.** Peace based on denial. Derogatory for the Versailles Treaty.

**Verzichtpolitiker.** Denial politician. Derogatory for the German politicians who signed the Versailles Treaty.

**VG, Vg.** *See* Volksgenossen.

**VGH.** *See* Volksgerichtshöfe.

**VH.** *See* Vorbeugungshäftling.

**Vichy.** City in France, location of authoritarian French government succeeding the Third Republic after the Germans conquered France in 1940. Controlling central and southern France and headed by Marshal Pétain and Pierre Laval. Vichy collaborated with the Nazis to round up and ship out Jews residing in Vichy to concentration camps in eastern Europe. In total, about 75,000 Jews residing in France, including those in the German-controlled northern and western sections of the country, were transported to death camps.

**Victoria-Zeichen.** Victory sign. *See* V.

**Viehjude.** Cattle Jew. Stereotype portraying Jews as greedy and ready to cheat farmers.

**Vierjahresplan.** Four-Year Plan. The first plan was established on February 1, 1933, just two days after Hitler's taking over power. The second plan, announced by Hitler at the Reichsparteitag at Nuremberg, began in 1936 and was suppposed to make Germany totally war-ready within four years by making the nation self-sufficient in raw materials and food supply, as well as improving the economy by initiating public works and financial aid to industry and agriculture.

*(Der) Vierjahresplan.* The Four-Year Plan. Publication of Göring's office for the Four-Year Plan.

**Vierling.** Four-barreled gun.

**Vierteljude.** Quarter Jew. A person with one Jewish grandparent. *See also* Mischlinge.

**14 f. 13.** Code word for the continuation of the Euthanasia Program. Concentration camp prisoners unable to work were also murdered under this program. *See also* Aktion T-4; Euthanasie; Sonderbehandlung 14 f. 13.

**Vierzehn Jahre der Schmach.** Fourteen shameful years. Negative for the period of the Weimar Republic (November 1918–January 1933).

**Villa Bechstein.** Building used as a guest house for visitors to Hitler's Berghof. *See also* Berghof.

**Virus-Haus.** Virus house. German nuclear research laboratory in Berlin.

**Vistra.** Name for synthetic fiber produced by the IG Farben Company. *See* Zellfaser.

**Vitamin B.** Slang for Beziehungen, connections, necessary to obtain scarce goods during the war.

**VK.** *See* Vorkommando.

**VKM.** *See* Vorkommando Moskau.

**VL.** *See* Vernichtungslager; Volksliste.

**VM.** *See* Volksdeutsche Mittelstelle.

**V-Mann.** *See* Vertrauensmann.

**VO.** *See* Verordnung.

**VOBl Prot.** *See* Verordnungsblatt des Reichsprotektorats Böhmen und Mähren.

**Vogel.** Bird. Derisive for Nazi eagle as the national emblem. *See also* Hoheitszeichen.

**Volk.** People, folk, nation, race. The German nation as a community defined and unified by blood, place, history, and language. *See also* Rasse; Schicksal; Volksgemeinschaft.

**"(Das) Volk der Führer ist, und der Führer das Volk ist."** "The people is the leader and the leader is the people." Rudolf Hess's mystical introduction of Hitler.

**"(Ein) Volk, ein Reich, ein Führer!"** "One people, one nation, one leader." Goebbels' slogan emphasizing the unity among the German people, Germany, and Hitler.

**Völkerbrei.** People mush. Derogatory for the mixture of many different peoples.

**Völkerchaos.** A chaos of people. Nazi vision of a mixing of different peoples that had to be struggled against and stopped. Also, war between Aryans and Jews.

**volkhaft.** Ethnic. Specific to the Volk.

*Volk im Werden.* A People in Progress. Nazi cultural periodical.

**völkisch.** Ethnic, racial, national. Antisemitic, racist, nationlist. A law of March 1934 ordered that all organizations training German youth had to stress four goals: physical, moral, intellectual, and racial.

**völkische Belange.** Interests pertaining to the Volk. German interests.

**völkische Erneuerung.** Racial renewal. Along with the Führerprinzip, basic goals of Nazi law.

**völkische Flurbereinigung.** Racial redistribution. The territorial consolidation and separation of racial groups. Hitler's and Himmler's attempts to rid areas of Poland of Poles and replace them with Aryan Germans.

*Völkische Kultur.* People's Culture. Nazi cultural periodical.

**Völkische Partei.** People's (Political) Party. A rightist party associated with Hitler's Nazi Party.

**völkische Politik.** Nazi policy toward Jews during the early years of the Third Reich, opposing the immigration and naturalization of eastern European Jews into Germany and advocating their expulsion from Germany. *See* Rassenpolitik.

*Völkischer Beobachter.* (*VB*) People's (National) Observer. Nazi Party newpaper, semiofficial organ of the Third Reich. First national German newspaper, published in Munich, Berlin, and Vienna.

**Völkischer Frauenorden.** People's Women's Order. *See also* Deutscher Frauenorden Rotes Hakenkreuz der NSDAP.

**völkisches Lebens.** Racial life. The security and victory of the German race was the overarching goal of the Nazi Party, state, armed forces, economy, and administration.

**volklich.** Pertaining to the Volk. Characteristically German.

**Volk ohne Raum.** People without space. The German people without the space they need to be self-sufficient. Taken from the title of an antisemitic and anti-English book by Hans Grimm of 1926, it became a code phrase for the Nazis. *See also* Autarkie; Lebensraum.

**Volksabstimmung.** Referendum. The national referendum the Nazis introduced by law in 1933 to replace federal elections.

**Volksartillerie-Korps.** People's Artillery Corps. German army artillery unit, organized after the last conscription call of 1944.

**Volksaufbau.** Race composition. Proportion of race groups in a population.

**Volksaufklärung.** Enlightenment of the people. *See also* Reichsminister(ium) für Volksaufklärung und Propaganda.

**Volksauto.** People's car. Prototype of the Volkswagen; project of Ferdinand Porsche. *See also* Volkswagen.

**Volksbazillus.** People's bacillus. Nazis saw Jews as microbes or bacteria attacking the health of the people. *See also* Volkskörper.

**Volksbefragung.** Plebiscite. It could award the government full power independent of the Parliament but not binding on the Führer.

**Volksbewegung.** People's Movement. The whole of the German people taking part in the National Socialist Movement.

**volksbiologisch.** Race-biological. Determined by race.

**Volksboden.** People's (German) soil. German ethnic region, territory settled, or formally settled, by Germans.

**Volksbüchereien.** People's libraries. Tens of thousands of Nazi Party lending libraries controlled by the Ministry of Education and Propaganda, meant to further Nazi ideology and strictly censor nonconforming literature.

**Volksbund für das Deutschtum im Ausland.** (VDA) Organization for Germans Abroad. Organization offering cultural and educational assistance abroad for German schools and institutions. Controlled by the Overseas Branch of the Nazi Party. *See* Auslandsorganisation der NSDAP.

**Volkscharakter.** People's character. *See also* volkisch.

**Volksdeutsche Bewegung.** (VDB) German Racial Movement. Nazi propaganda organization in Luxembourg.

**Volksdeutsche Mittelstelle.** (Vomi, VoMi, Vo-mi, VOM, VM) German Assistance Center. An SS organization instituted in 1936 by Rudolf Hess. This agency's goal was to enlist people of German ethnic origin to join the NS party. Later, it was responsible for Germanization of conquered countries, including aiding Germans abroad financially and materially. From 1941, it redistributed Jewish property and clothing from concentration camp victims.

**Volksdeutscher.** Ethnic German. A person of German ethnic origin without German citizenship or not living in Germany. Germans of foreign nationality.

**volksecht.** Racially authentic; German, Nordic.

**volkseigen.** Publicly owned, nationalized. Belonging to the German people.

**Volkseinheit.** People's unity. Utopian unity of all Germans of pure racial stock.

**Volksempfänger 301.** (V.E.) People's radios 30 January (allusion to the date of Hitler's appointment as Chancellor). Propaganda Ministry ordered these radios manufactured with just one frequency so that only government broadcasts could be received and foreign broadcasts excluded. Anyone broadening the reception capability of these radios was subject to the death penalty.

**(gesundes) Volksempfinden.** (Healthy) national feeling. Germans connected spiritually and emotionally, based on a shared common heritage.

**Volksertüchtigungsplan.** People's training plan. Pre-military and physical training for Germans.

**Volkserziehungsprogramm.** Folk education program. Educational program with short-term and long-range goals centralizing the vast network of the censorship apparatus with the general power structure of Party and State.

*Volksforschung.* People's Research. *See also Auslandsdeutsche Volksforschung;* Deutsches Ausland-Iinstitut.

**volksfremd.** Alien to the (German) people. Un-German in race, character, conduct, essence, and so forth.

**Volksfront.** People's front. Word used for propaganda purposes during the war.

**Volksführer.** Leader of the people. Hitler.

**(das) Volksganze.** Totality of the (German) people.

**Volksgebiet.** Territory settled by a people.

**volksgebunden.** Racially linked to the (German) people. Authentic.

**Volksgefolgschaft.** People's vassals. Nazi Party leaders who were supposed to act more responsibly and duty-bound than to enjoy their privileges of rank.

**Volksgeist.** Spirit of a people. The German way of thinking and feeling.

**Volksgemeinschaft.** People's community. The mystical unity of the blood-race of the national-German-Aryan community, which dominated all other beliefs, classes, parties, individual, and group interests. The central concept of National Socialist thought, it presented itself as the agent of national awakening, as a break with the shame of the World War I defeat, and as a chance to rebuild the German nation. Jews and others outside the racial community were excluded. Through persuasion and coercion, the Third Reich kept most—though not all—Germans loyal throughout World War II. They were expected to work for the community and for the honor and destiny of the German people contrasted with other peoples, and be prepared to die for the community and the spiritual mission of the German people.

**Volksgenossen.** (VG, Vg) Racial comrades. Members of the German community. *See also* Volksgemeinschaft.

**Volksgenossinnen.** Female racial comrades. Female members of the German community. *See* Volksgemeinschaft; Volksgenossen.

**"Volksgenossenschaft ist Rechtsgenossenschaft, Rechtsordnung ergreift jeden Untertan."** "Racial membership assures common rights, whereas law applies to everyone." Nazi jurists' rationale.

**Volksgericht.** People's Court. A court for those Germans accused of treason or race defilement (Rassenschande). The judges were professionals and members of the Nazi Party and the SS. Judgments were based on national and racial feeling. The chief judge was Roland Freisler, a passionate Nazi. *See* Blutrichter.

**Volksgerichte.** *See* Volksgerichtshöfe.

**Volksgerichtshöfe.** (VGH) People's courts. Nazi court system, established April 24, 1934, trying those charged with crimes against the German people, treason, or Rassenschande. *See* Volksgericht.

**volksgermanische Ergänzung.** Germanic race replenishment.

**Volksgermanische Erziehung.** Germanic race education.

**volksgermanische Führung.** Germanic race leadership, education. *See also* Germanische Freiwilligen Leitstelle.

**(Amt für) volksgermanische Führung.** Department for Germanic Race Leadership. Department VI of SS headquarters.

**Volksgeschwister.** The people's siblings. German brotherhood. *See also* Volksgenossen.

*Volksgesetzbuch.* The People's Book of Law. This book was supposed to redefine rights and responsibilities of each German and replace the so-called bourgeois law.

**Volksgliedschaft.** Race membership. Belonging to the German people.

**Volksgrenadier.** People's grenadier. From 1944, infantryman in the German army.

**Volksgrenzen.** Race borders. National borders not defined by politics but by race.

**Volksgröße.** Racial size, size of a people. Nazi concept that Germany would inevitably play a dominant role in Europe because of the size of its racial population.

**Volksgruppe.** Racial group. *See also* Volksdeutscher.

**Volksjäger.** People's fighter. Heinkel He-162, a lightweight jet fighter designed to be produced cheaply and in large quantity but too near the end of the war to be effective. Members of the Hitler Youth were intended to fly these planes.

**Volksjäger.** People's hunter. Toward the end of World War II, a German jet fighter designed by Ernst Heinkel but never used in regular service.

**Volkskameradschaft.** People's brotherhood, bond. National and racial sense of belonging together within the German community of people.

**Volkskampf.** People's battle. *See also* Volkskrieg.

**Volkskanzler.** People's Chancellor. Hitler as the guide of the German people.

**Volkskartei.** People's card file. Filing system, started in 1938, to keep track of all Germans between six and seventy years of age in order to draft them for labor and war duties. Divided into brown (for males) and blue (for females), file cards were ordered alphabetically and according to year of birth. File contained photo, fingerprints, handwriting sample, information on education and work, infirmities, civil status, languages spoken, expert knowledge, and skills. It followed the German individual automatically and invisibly with any change of address.

**Volkskirche.** People's church. Nazi idea of a church for Germans only, based on racial origin.

**Volkskörper.** People's body. The German people as a biological-racial unity, a single organism free of parisites and vermin, unlike Jews and other aliens, and hierarchically arranged.

**Volkskrieg.** People's war. Ideological race war fought by each German to secure more space for the Third Reich and German people in eastern Europe. Pretext for mass murder. *See also* Lebensraum.

**Volkskunde.** Folklore. The teaching of German folklore included preexisting anti-Jewish elements. *See also* Arbeitsgemeinschaft für deutsche Volkskunde.

**Volksliste.** (VL) *See* Deutsche Volksliste.

**Volksmeldedienst.** The People's Reporting Service. Every German was supposed to be trained to report and denounce defeatist and/or antigovernment utterances and actions.

**volksnah.** Near to the people. Adjective used to emphasize Hitler's accessibility to, and close contact with, the (German) people.

**Volksnation.** People nation. Racial nation.

**Volksnot.** Distress of a people. Public emergency; population pressure.

**Volksnotehen.** Racial emergency marriages. Plan to encourage male-female relationships whose goal was to produce children to replace the German population reduced by war deaths during World War II.

**Volksnummerung.** People's numbering. System, planned in 1944, for giving each individual German a number that would convey birth year and place, sex, and birth registration number. An identification number for life, it would appear on every official document.

**Volksoffizier.** People's officer, officer from the ranks. Flood of new officers in the expanded German Wehrmacht after 1935 were looked down on by the older professional officers from the Reichswehr. Also, German soldiers, twenty-five and younger, who were promoted to the rank of officer after two months of military service at the front; introduced late in 1944 due to high officer casualties. *See* Kriegsoffizier.

**Volksoffizier mit Arbeiter-Gesicht.** (Vomag) People's officer with worker's face. Army slang.

**Volksoffizier mit Obergefreiten-Niveau.** (Vomon) People's officer with the rank of a higher lance corporal. Army slang, soldier promoted from the ranks to the level of a lance corporal.

**Volksordnung.** The people's order. The only true (German) order.

**Volkspfleger.** The people's caretaker. Specially trained employee or civil servant of the welfare office.

**volkspolitische Aufgaben.** The people's political tasks. Pretext for mass murder in eastern Europe.

**volkspolitische Gefahren.** The people's political dangers. Threat to the German race nature by enemy POWs and Polish forced laborers.

**Volksreich.** People's Reich. Hitler's idealized Germany.

**Volksschädlinge.** Racial vermin, national pests, public enemies. During the Nazi rise to power, profiteers and usurers. In the 1930s, enemies of the German people, traitors to the nation; German citizens who opposed the Third Reich. With the outbreak of the war, individuals defined as looters and saboteurs. Also, a variety of un-German types, especially Jews and, in the Nazi perception, Jewish allies, homosexuals, and others. *See also* Volksschädlingsverordnung.

**Volksschädlingsverordnung.** Law against those deemed damaging to the people. Public-enemy law introduced in September 1939 against individuals in Nazi Germany who contravened war-economy regulations; such offenses were equated with high treason and could result in the death penalty. Later expanded to apply in German-occupied Poland, resulting in a death sentence and/or being sent to a concentration camp for anyone committing a criminal offense against Germans or Germany by taking advantage of "special circumstances." This amounted to awarding courts the arbitrary power of life or death over any of the occupied peoples. *See also* Verordnung über die Strafrechtspflege gegen Polen und Juden in den eingegliederten Ostgebieten.

**Volksschule.** *See* Oberstufe der Volksschule.

**Volksschwund.** Dwindling of a people. Depopulation.

**(kochende) Volksseele.** Boiling soul of the people. Propaganda term to justify the attacks on Jews during the November 1938 Pogrom. Later, during the war, used by the media to express outrage against Allied air raids on Germany. *See also* Reichskristallnacht.

**Volkssoldat.** Soldier of the people. From 1940, every German man who worked for the welfare of the German people. From 1944, applied exclusively to every member of the Wehrmacht as a representative of the people and of Nazi ideology.

**Volkssoziologie.** Volkish sociology. New interdisciplinary subject at the University of Berlin; closely linked to the expansionist policies in eastern Europe. *See also* Raumplanung.

**Volkssturm.** People's unit, national storm. German home guard of old men and boys, sixteen to sixty years old, instituted in October 1944 during the last months of the war.

**Volkstod.** Death of a people. Using scare tactics, the Reich government argued that if Germany lost the race war, then the declining birthrate and corruption of alien races would result in the death of the German people. *See* Euthanasie; Völkerchaos.

**Volkstum.** Nationality. Racial essence, ethnic, national, cultural identity. The German and closely related peoples as a divinely created entity, whose enemy was the Jew. Replaced Nationalität.

**Volkstum für das Deutschtum im Ausland.** National Association for Germans Living Abroad. SS organization for Germans outside of Germany.

**volkstum(s)politisch.** Racial and national political. Hitler expanded Himmler's duties to cover this area of Nazi policy just after the start of World War II.

**Volkstumsarbeit.** Work on race and nation. Nazi racial policy and activities in eastern Europe.

**Volkstumsgrenzen.** Racial boundaries. Refers to the divisions of German-occupied Poland based on racial principles.

**Volkstumskartei.** People's data file. Data bank, started in 1939 in Berlin, to register all non-Germans and German Jews. It contained name, birth date and place, profession, and degree of non-German blood.

**Volkstumsbewußtsein.** Consciousness of a people. Nazi belief that a people's sense of racial belonging will be retained even if they are not living within the racial group.

**Volkstumskampf.** A people's struggle for racial identity. National Socialist endeavor to maintain the Germanness of German groups outside of Germany.

**Volksüberdruck.** Excess population. High population density.

**Volksunterdruck.** Suppressed population. Low population density.

**Volksverdummer.** People's brainwasher. Nickname for German radios. *See also* Volksempfänger.

**Volksverdummung-1.** People's stultification (number) 1. Ironic for V-1 weapon. *See also* Flugbombe V-1; Vergeltungswaffen; Wunderwaffen.

**Volksvermögen.** A people's wealth. During World War II, German raw materials and energy were considered limited resources.

**Volksverräter.** Traitor to the people. Those who attacked the German nation or betrayed it by violating the Führer's commands and/or National Socialist laws and decrees. *See also* Volksgericht.

**Volksverratsgesetz.** Law against traitors to the people. *See also* Volksverräter.

**Volkswagen.** People's car. Originally, KdF-Wagen, Strength through Joy car. Designed by Ferdinand Porsche, this small, affordable family car was promised by Hitler to every German regardless of class, profession, or wealth. None were produced during World War II because of war production priorities, but it was an important Nazi propaganda idea. *See also* Kübelwagen.

**Volkswohlfahrt.** People's welfare. *See also* Nationalsozialistische Volkswohlfahrt.

**Volkswohnung.** People's apartment. New housing built during the Third Reich, with smaller apartments than those built earlier.

**Volkszugehörige.** Belonging to a people. Germans as defined by race.

*Volk und Rasse.* *People and Race.* Periodical concentrating on genetics and race.

**Vollalarm.** *See* Luftalarm.

**Vollfamilie.** Complete family. Hereditarily healthy German family with at least four children. *See* erbgesund.

**völlig untauglich.** Completely unfit. Unfit for military service and for labor service. *See* tauglich.

**Volljude.** Full-Jew. Based on the race law of 1933, a full-Jew was anyone who descended from even one fully-Jewish grandparent. The Nuremberg Laws of 1935 restricted the definition to a person with three or four religiously Jewish grandparents and who was raised in the Jewish community, despite the baptism of grandparents, parents, or the person in question. *See also* Mischlinge; (Dreizehnte) Verordnung zum Reichsbürgergesetz.

**volljüdisch.** Fully Jewish. *See also* Mischlinge; Volljude.

**Vollstreckungsschutz.** Stay of execution. Protection against seizure of land. *See* Erbhofgesetz.

**Vollzigeuner.** Full Gypsy. Based on the same principles as the definition of Volljude, a person with three or four Gypsy grandparents and who was raised in the Gypsy community. *See also* Beschäftigung von Zigeunern.

**VOM.** *See* Volksdeutsche Mittelstelle.

**Vomag.** *See* Volksoffizier mit Arbeiter-Gesicht.

**VOMI, VoMi, Vo-mi.** *See* Volksdeutsche Mittelstelle.

**Vomon.** *See* Volksoffizier mit Obergefreiten-Niveau.

**Voralarm.** *See* Luftalarm.

**Vorarbeiter.** Work foreman. Member of prisoner administration at a concentration camp.

**vorbeugende Verbrechensbekämpfung, Erlaßsammlung.** (VVB-E) Crime-prevention fight; collection of decrees.

**Vorbeugungshäftling.** (VH) Person imprisoned as a precautionary measure.

**Vorkommando.** (VK) Advance Unit.

**Vorkommando Moskau.** (VKM) Advance Unit Moscow.

**Vorläufiges Gesetz zur Gleichschaltung der Länder mit dem Reich.** Provisional Law for the Consolidation of the Provinces with the Reich. *See also* Ermächtigungsgesetz; Gesetz zur Gleichschaltung der Länder mit dem Reich.

**Vormerkschein.** Reservation paper. Statement of priority for machines.

**Vorsehung.** Providence. Hitler often expressed the idea that Providence looked out for him, a concept that served as a rationale for many of his beliefs and actions. He wrote in *Mein Kampf*: "Nations that make mongrels of their people, or allow their people to be turned into mongrels, sin against the Will of Eternal Providence."

**Vorsemestervermerk.** Pre-term endorsement. During the war, document attesting to German students' leaving university, having been conscripted to the army.

**Vorstoff.** Pre-material. Raw material or semifinished goods.

*Vorwärts.* Forward. Newspaper of the Social Democratic Party during the Weimar Republic.

**Vorzeigegeld.** Show money. Emigration fee that well-to-do Jews had to pay to authorities in order to leave Germany. These Jews were also forced to donate money to the Reich Jewish Organization to compensate allegedly for the emigration of poorer Jews who could not afford that sum.

**Vorzugslager.** Privileged camp. *See also* Theresienstadt.

**Vorzuweisungsliste.** Preassignment list. Racial classification list of ethnic Germans.

**VT.** *See* Verfügungstruppen.

**Vugesta(p).** *See* Verkauf jüdischen Umzugsgutes Gestapo.

**VVB-E.** *See* vorbeugende Verbrechensbekämpfung.

**VVV.** *See* Vereinigte Vaterländische Verbände.

**V-Waffe.** *See* Vergeltungswaffen.

**V-2.** Successor to the V-1, it was a long-range rocket powered by liquid oxygen and alcohol, having a 975 kg (2,150 lb) high-explosive warhead and a range of 320 km (200 mi). *See also* Fernrakete V-2; Vergeltungswaffen; Wunderwaffen.

# W

**WaA.** *See* Waffenamt.

**Wabo.** Wasserbombe. Water bomb. Depth charge used against submarines.

**Wachdienst.** Watch, sentry. Rural home guard. Also, elderly fire brigade.

**Wachenfels.** Hitler's house in Berchtesgaden in the 1920s.

**Wachmannschaft.** Guard Unit. Early SS concentration camp guards. *See also* Totenkopfverbände.

**Wachsturm.** Guard storm. Early SS concentration camp guards. *See also* Totenkopfverbände.

**Wacht am Rhein.** *See* Unternehmen Wacht am Rhein

**"Wacht am Rhein."** "Watch on the Rhine." German military song.

**Wachtmeister.** Captain of the guards. At concentration camps and other locations.

**Wachtruppe.** Guard Troops. Early SS concentration camp guards. *See also* Totenkopfverbände.

**Wachstumsspitze.** Strategic outpost. Economic expansion base.

**Wachtürme.** Watch towers. Guard towers along the periphery of concentration camps and other locations. *See also* Konzentrationslager.

**Wachverbände.** Guard formations. Early SS concentration camp guards. *See also* Totenkopfverbände.

**Waffenamt.** (WaA) Weapons Department. Army department that oversaw the German rearmament program—the testing and acceptance of weapons, equipment, and ammunition for the German armed forces. Also, German/Nazi stamp, equivalent to a MADE IN USA label. Representing an eagle perched on a wreath with a swastika in the middle, it denoted that the product was made for, and passed the standards of, the Weapons Department.

**Waffenfabrik Steyr-Daimler-Puch.** Steyr-Daimler-Puch Arms Manufacturing. The firm used slave labor at Lublin-Majdanek concentration camp.

**Waffenprüfämter.** (WaPrüf) Departments subsidiary to the Waffenamt, testing armaments for the Wehrmacht.

**Waffenrock.** Military tunic. Jacket of full-dress German army uniform with multicolored cords and silver embroidery.

**Waffen-SS.** Armed SS. Militarized units of the SS created in 1939. By 1945, of the nearly one million men in the Waffen-SS, almost half consisted of non-German SS volunteers from many countries in Europe. *See* germanische Freiwillige.

**(der) Waffen-SS.** (Of the) armed SS. Ranks of the Waffen-SS could be expressed as the Wehrmacht ranks, with this phrase added on; for example, leutnant der Waffen-SS.

**Waffen-SS-Arbeitskommando Berta.** *See* Kommando Berta.

**Wagen.** (Railroad) cars. Jews were deported to concentration camps, death camps, ghettos, and elsewhere by means of freight or cattle cars without water, food, or sanitation. Many Jews died en route and most others were murdered slowly or quickly on arrival at their destination.

**Wagen-Juden.** Wagon Jews. Jews using hand-drawn carts who were assigned to collect Jewish corpses from the streets in the large ghettos.

**Wahrheit.** Truth. In 1944 Goebbels equated Hitler with truth itself: "Hitler ist die Wahrheit selbst."

**Waldgänger.** Forest-goer. Partisans who fought the Germans in eastern European forests.

**Waldsee.** Forest lake. An imaginary idyllic location—in reality Auschwitz-Birkenau—from which the first deported Hungarian Jews in 1944 were deceived or forced into sending welcoming postcards to convince the remaining Hungarian Jews that death did not await them.

**Waldseekarten.** Forest-lake postcards. *See also* Waldsee.

**Walküre.** *See* Unternehmen Walküre.

**Wallenberg-Paß.** Wallenberg (protective) pass. A document resembling a Swedish visa, created by Raoul Wallenberg in his attempt to save Budapest Jews in 1944.

**Walli.** Code name for military intelligence and espionage in eastern Europe. Later taken over by Reich Main Security Administration, Espionage Department. *See also* Abwehr; Reichssicherheitshauptamt.

**Wallonie.** *See* SS-Freiwilligen-Strumbrigade Wallonie.

**Walter.** *See* Amtswalter.

**Wandervögel.** Birds of passage. German youth movement predating World War I. Back-to-nature, romantic, nationalistic, antisemitic.

**Wannsee-Konferenz.** Wannsee Conference. On January 20, 1942, at Lake Wannsee on the outskirts of Berlin, fourteen top Reich officials met to coordinate the total destruction of the European Jews, the so-called Endlösung der Judenfrage (Final Solution of the Jewish Problem). It was led by Reinhard Heydrich and secretaried by Adolf Eichmann.

**Wappen.** Emblem, coat of arms. Heraldic shield or decal worn on German military helmets.

**WaPrüf.** *See* Waffenprüfämter.

**Waren-Dollar.** Dollar equivalent of ASKI-Mark. *See also* ASKI-Mark.

**Warenverkehrsordnung.** Goods distribution regulation. Basic law of cartel control and planning.

**Warschauer Getto.** *See* Warschau-Ghetto.

**Warschau-Ghetto.** Warsaw-Ghetto. Established in November 1940, it held nearly 500,000 Jews at its height. About 45,000 Jews died there in 1941 alone, as a result of overcrowding, hard labor, lack of sanitation, starvation, and disease. During 1942, most of the ghetto residents were deported to Treblinka, leaving about 60,000 Jews alive. A revolt took place in April and May 1943, when the German armed forces, Waffen-SS, and police, as well as Polish police and Trawniki men, that is Ukrainian and ethnic German (Volksdeutsche) volunteers, attempted to raze the ghetto and deport the remaining inhabitants to Treblinka. Mordecai Anielewicz led the ZOB (Jewish Fighting Organization). The revolt was the first instance in occupied Europe of an uprising by an urban population, lasting longer than the following nations held out against the German armed forces: Poland, Norway, Denmark, Holland, Luxembourg, Belgium, and France.

**Warthegau/Wartheland.** The portion of western Poland annexed by the Third Reich after the outbreak of World War II in September 1939.

**"Wasche dich!"** "Wash yourself." Sign at Auschwitz.

**Wasserfall.** Waterfall. Code name for German ground-to-air missile program.

**wasserscheu.** Afraid of water. Adjective applied to Jews, implying their reluctance to clean themselves.

**Wasserschutzpolizei.** Water Safety Police. Police who patrolled German harbors, canals, and waterways.

**W-Bank.** *See* Wirtschaftsbank.

**W.Bef.** *See* Wehrmachtsbefehlshaber.

**WC.** Water closet, toilet. Nazi pun on the initials of Winston Churchill.

**WD.** *See* Wehrdienst.

**WE.** *See* Wehrertüchtigung.

**Wegegeld.** Travel money. Car fare and overtime pay for German workers living far from their place of work.

**Wehr.** Defense. Purpose of German armed forces according to the Allies in the Treaty of Versailles, replacing aggressive terms like Heer (army), Krieg (war), and Kampf (battle). Nazis expanded the concept of Wehr to mean "continuous readiness to fight and defend Germany." *See* Wehrmacht.

**Wehrabzeichen.** Military training badge.

**Wehrbau.** Military fortification.

**Wehrbauern.** Defense farmers. German farmers who lived in the eastern border areas had to assume border-defense duties.

**Wehrbetreuung.** *See* Truppenbetreuung.

**Wehrbezirkskommando.** Armed Forces District Command. Its goal was to draft as many men as possible into the German armed forces. *See also* Wehrmacht.

**Wehrdienst.** (WD) Duty in the armed forces. Abbreviation used in a person's card file. *See also* Volkskartei.

**Wehreinsatz.** Defense deployment. Mobilization for, employment in, temporary war work.

**Wehrersatzdienststelle.** Armed Forces Replacement Center. Wehrmacht recruiting office.

**Wehrertüchtigung.** (WE) Defense training. Used to describe paramilitary training of the elite of the Hitler Youth in guns, map reading, and sports.

**Wehrertüchtigungslager.** (WE-Lager) Defense training camp. 1940s camp for the training of the Hitler Youth for military and political service prior to basic-training camps.

**Wehrgedanke.** Defense thinking. The will to defend Germany as a basic principle of Nazi politics.

**wehrgeistig.** Pertaining to military theory. National Socialist youth were supposed to be trained in military theory as well as sports.

**Wehrgesetz.** Law concerning Armed Forces. Law of May 21, 1935, that barred Jews and Nazi opponents from military service.

**wehrhaft.** Soldier-like. Militant.

**Wehrhoheit.** Defense priority. The right of a state to build up its army; one of the key propaganda issues of the NSDAP after World War I in response to the restrictions of the Treaty of Versailles.

**Wehrkraft.** Defense force. All means, internal and external, that Germany could use to defend its vital interests.

**Wehrkraftzersetzung.** The destruction of military/defense strength. From 1938, any deviation from Nazi propaganda was seen as an attack on Germany and its Third Reich government. Attempts to paralyze or undermine the will of Germany or one of its allies to defend itself were severely punished. *See also* Kriegssonderstrafrechtverordnung.

**Wehrkreis.** (WK) Defense district. Recruitment and replacement district for the German army. Military district.

**Wehrkreisrangfolgeliste.** Defense-district ranking order. Priority list for war orders.

**Wehrkunde.** Defense information. Training to increase the will to fight. *See also* wehrgeistig.

**Wehrlandschaft.** Defense terrain. Strategic aspect of terrain.

**Wehrlehre.** Military science. Curriculum subject in schools and universities. *See also* wehrgeistig; Wehrkunde.

**WEHRM.** *See* Wehrmacht.

**Wehrmacht.** (WEHRM) Defense forces, armed forces. The Third Reich's army, navy, and air force. A military-ideological force designed to attack and destroy all of Germany's national, ethnic, and individual enemies first by military conquest of Europe, then by coercive occupation and ideological propaganda, collaborating with the SS, the SD, the Gestapo, and other police units especially in eastern Europe. From the start of World War II in Poland, some army units plundered, raped, mistreated, and shot Poles; burned synagogues; and tortured and massacred Jews. At this early stage of the war, Wehrmacht leadership saw this as a side effect of military conquest.

But the near-genocidal campaign in Poland served as a training ground for much more extensive collaboration between the German army and the Einsatzgruppen, the SD, and the Security Police in Russia from 1941 on in atrocities against the Jews. Letters from the front demonstrate that many German soldiers didn't need to be persuaded that the murder of Jews was justified because these soldiers had been preconditioned by their families, schools, churches, the Hitler Youth, and propaganda.

Some Wehrmacht generals unsuccessfully attempted to prevent their men from participating in the mass murders of Jews. But more typical were Field Marshal Walter von Reichenau, Commander in Chief of the 6th Army, orders: Not only were soldiers members of the Wehrmacht, they were also "the bearers of a pitiless völkisch ideology" who must exact a just atonement from the Jewish subhumans (jüdisches Untermenschentum). The Wehrmacht must liberate the German people from the Jewish threat, once and for all. General Hermann Hoth, Commander in Chief of the 17th Army, wrote in November 1941 that there existed an unbridgeable conflict between German soldierly tradition (Soldatentum) and Jewish thinking. The Wehrmacht must rescue Germany, indeed all of Europe, from the Jews, who support Bolshevism and aid partisans. In November 1941 General Erich von Manstein, Commander in Chief of the 11th Army, proclaimed that Jewish-Bolshevism must be exterminated once and for all. The German soldier must defeat Jewish-Bolshevism; he bears the racial idea and is the avenger of all atrocities on Germans, and must sympathize with a hard atonement demanded of Jewry. Several other Wehrmacht commanders equated Jews with Bolsheviks and partisans as well. *See also* Einsatzgruppen; Führerprinzip; Treueid.

**(Die) Wehrmacht.** The Defense/Armed Forces. German biweekly newspaper. Began publishing in 1937.

**Wehrmachtaufgaben.** Defense obligations. Military assignment of civilian organizations.

**Wehrmachtbericht.** Armed-forces report. Report issued daily by the Wehrmacht High Command. Consisted of official information about combat activities of all three military forces. *See also* Wehrmacht.

**Wehrmacht(s)helferinnen.** Armed forces helper. From 1940, young German women volunteers from the age of seventeen in Germany and in the German-occupied areas to aid the SS, the police, and army units in order to enable more men to fight on the war front. From 1943, obligatory service for females. By the end of the war, half a million German women were involved.

**Wehrmachtsführungsstab.** (WFSt) Armed Forces Operations Staff. Division of the Armed Forces High Command. Hitler's liaison to the army, under General Alfred Jodl. *See* Oberkommando der Wehrmacht.

**Wehrmachtsführungsstab Oberquartiermeister.** Armed Forces Chief of Staff for Quartermaster. In reality, Armed Forces Chief of Staff for Intelligence.

**Wehrmachtsamt.** Armed Forces Office. General Wilhelm Keitel's office replacing the Ministry of War. Keitel was made equivalent in rank and duties to a Reichsminister of War. Chief of the Armed Forces Department in the Reichs Ministry of War (Wehrmachtsamt im Reichskriegsministerium) from 1935 to 1938.

**Wehrmachtsbefehlshaber.** (W.Bef.) Armed Forces Commander. German commander of armed forces in occupied territory.

**Wehrmachtsfahrscheine.** Armed forces tickets. Receipts for truckloads of looted valuables from death-camp victims.

**Wehrmachtsgefolge.** Armed forces followers. Civil servants employed by the German Army in occupied areas.

**Wehrmachtsgut.** Armed forces goods, treasure. Ironic for deportation trains carrying Jews to death camps.

**Wehrmachtsnachrichtenverbindungen.** Armed forces communication links. Part of the Oberkommando der Wehrmacht.

**Wehrmachtsstab.** Armed Forces Staff. General Wilhelm Keitel's staff coordinating the three military services.

**wehrmachtverpflichtete Werkstätten.** Armed forces workshops. Civilian manufacturing firms under contract to the armed forces.

**Wehrmachtverpflichtungsschein.** Negotiable bill issued by the military. Advance payment on war contracts.

**Wehrmann.** Defense man. Civilian employed in home defense unit.

**Wehrmannschaften.** Defense Units. Reserve corps of ex-servicemen conducting defense training in the SA.

**Wehrmeldeamt.** (WMA) Defense Recruiting Office.

**Wehrpaß.** Military-service book. Military ID. Passport-like booklet each German man of military age was issued even if he did not serve.

**Wehrpflicht.** Compulsory military service. Instituted in Germany in 1935 for all German men between eighteen and forty-five.

**Wehrpolitische Vereinigung.** Defense Policy League. Ernst Röhm founded this paramilitary club in the 1920s to serve as the nucleus for the general staff of Hitler's future army.

**Wehrraum.** Defense space. *See also* Wehrlandschaft.

**Wehrsold.** Army pay. Soldiers' supplementary pay for front-line service.

**Wehrsport.** Defense sport. Paramilitary exercises for German boys, such as shooting, rigorous marches, and so on, conducted by the Nazi Party and aimed at training for war. *See also* wehrgeistig.

**Wehrstammbücher.** (WStB.) Wehrmacht personnel files. Military documents about German armed forces personnel, containing personal, family, and military data, such as education, profession, political background, health, decorations, legal and disciplinary punishment, wounds, and/or cause of death.

**wehrtauglich.** Fit for military service. *See* tauglich.

**wehrtüchtig.** *See* tauglich.

**Wehrüberwachung.** Conscription control. Supervision of conscription of eligible German men.

**wehrwichtige Firma.** (W-Firma) Essential defense firm. Any company important to the German war industry.

**wehrwichtiges Geschäft.** (W-Geschäft) Business important to the (German) war industry.

**Wehrwille.** Will to defend/fight. *See also* Wehrgedanke; Wehrkraft; Zersetzung.

**Wehrwirtschaft.** (WeWi) Defense (war) economy. The post–World War I ideological concept of the Germany economy as being a war economy even during peacetime. Also, the harnessing of the German economy for preparation for war.

**Wehrwirtschaftsamt.** Defense Economy Office. Armed forces staff devoted to economic matters.

**Wehrwirtschaftsführer.** Work leader in defense products factories. *See also* unabkömmlich; Wehrwirtschaft.

**Wehrwirtschafts- und Rüstungs(haupt)amt.** (Wi Rü Amt, WiRue) Defense Economy and Armaments head office.

**Wehrwissenschaft.** *See* Wehrlehre.

**wehrwissenschaftliche Zweckforschung.** *See* Institut für wehrwissenschaftliche Zweckforschung.

**Wehrwürdigkeit.** Eligible to do military service. Premise used for every racial German to serve in the army; Jews were excluded.

**weibliches SS-Gefolge.** SS Women's Auxiliary. *See also* SS-Frauen.

**weichende Erben.** Rescinding heirs. *See also* Erbhofgesetz.

**Weihe.** Honoring. Old German word Nazis used to suggest religious overtones for secular celebratory rituals.

**Weimar(er).** Used as a pejorative, applying to the ultraliberal culture and attitudes of the late Weimar Republic, especially in the capital city of Berlin.

**Weimarer Republik.** Weimar Republic. *See also* Zwischenreich.

**Weimarer System.** *See* Zwischenreich.

**Weinmond.** Wine month. October.

**Weiß.** White. Code name for the September 1, 1939, invasion of Poland that would begin World War II.

**Weiße Rose.** White Rose. This group of resisters to Nazism was led by University of Munich students Hans and Sophie Scholl and Christoph Probst and Professor of Philosophy Kurt Huber. They handed out anti-Hitler pamphlets and were arrested and murdered in 1943. The group may have taken this name because the white rose was the symbol of purity in Christianity.

**Weißruthenien.** (WR, wr) Old name for Belorussia. *See also* Ostland.

**weißruthenisch.** (wr.) *See* Weißruthenien.

**Weitere Nationalsozialistische Organsationen.** Other National Socialist organizations. A fourth category of Nazi organizations. Consisting of the Reich Labor Service (Reichsarbeitsdienst—RAD), subordinate to the Reich Labor leader (Reichsarbeitsführer), and the Flying Corps (NS-Fliegerkorps—FKNS), which was subordinate to the Reich Minister for Aviation. *See also* Gliederungen und Angeschlossene Verbände der NSDAP.

**Wel.** *See* Welteislehre.

**WE-Lager.** *See* Wehrertüchtigungslager.

**Welt.** World. In combination with other words, expressing a global or cosmopolitan attitude that Nazis deemed hostile. *See also* Weltpest.

**weltanschauliche Lage.** Ideological situation. Subject of reports of local SD officers in regard to German public opinion.

**weltanschauliche Prüfung.** Ideological scrutiny. Censorship.

**weltanschauliche Schulung.** (WS) Ideological education. Courses designed to teach Nazi ideology to students.

**Weltanschauung.** Worldview or ideology. The Nazi worldview that involved race, character, and destiny (Rasse, Charakter, und Schicksal) as a value system for the German people.

**Weltanschauungskampf.** *See* Weltanschauungskrieg.

**Weltanschauungskrieg.** Ideological war. A war fought by the German Wehrmacht against Germany's racial enemies during World War II.

**Weltanschauungsunterricht.** Teaching the ideological view. Schools taught Nazi ideology as a substitute for religion.

**Weltdienst.** World Service. Antisemitic Nazi news agency sponsored by the Nazi Propaganda Ministry.

*Weltdienst.* (WCI) World Service. Antisemitic journal sponsored by the Nazi Propaganda Ministry.

**Welteislehre.** (Wel) World ice science. The Nazis favored the glacial cosmogony of Hanns Hörbinger as an explanation for the beginning of the world.

**Weltfeinde.** World enemies. Racial opponents of Nordics-Aryans-Germans, in particular, Jews and Bolsheviks.

**Weltfurcht.** World fear. Fear of existence, fearful approach to life.

**weltgeschichtliche Mission.** Mission of world historical importance. Goebbels' propaganda campaign that the German nation's most important historical goal was to spread its racial ideas throughout the world.

**Welthauptstadt Germania.** World capital city Germania. Nazi plan to rebuild Berlin into the capital city of the world; Albert Speer's idea.

**Weltjude.** World Jew. Pejorative for world Jewry. *See also* Weltjudentum.

**Weltjudentum.** World Jewry. The Nazi fantasy of an international Jewish conspiracy that controlled the world.

*(Der) Weltkampf: Monatschrift für die Judenfrage aller Länder.* The World Struggle: Monthly Publication on the Jewish Problem in All Nations. Monthly magazine edited by Alfred Rosenberg, dealing in a pseudoscientific manner with what Rosenberg saw as the Jewish problem in all countries.

*Weltlitaratur.* World Literature. Official periodical of the Reichsführer-SS, supporting Nazi ideology.

**"Weltmacht oder Niedergang."** "World power or destruction." Hitler slogan.

**Weltparasit.** World parasite. Antisemitic term. *See also* Vernichtungsstrategie; Weltpest.

**Weltpest.** World plague. Jews perceived as a powerful, destructive, worldwide plague.

**weltpolitisches Dreieck.** World Political Triangle. The 1940 Tripartite Pact between Nazi Germany, Japan, and Italy in which each signatory promised to come to the aid of the other in the event of an attack by any state not yet at war. *See also* Antikominternpakt.

**"Weltvergifter aller Völker!"** "World poisoners of all peoples." Antisemitic Nazi Party campaign slogan before 1933.

**Wende.** Turning point. Goebbels' hope for a better turn of events in the war after a change in international politicians (e.g., the death of President Franklin Roosevelt in 1945).

**"(Und) wenn das Judenblut vom Messer spritzt, dann geht's nochmal so gut!"** "(And) when Jewish blood spurts from the knife, then things are going even better." Crude antisemitic slogan and SS song lyrics that made its way even into German schools, when on Saturdays, the teachers would lead the students in marching and singing it. *See* Appendix: Macht und Ehre—Sturmsoldates.

**"Wenn der Jude deutsch schreibt, lügt er!"** "When the Jew writes in German he lies." Antisemitic phrase often found on university bulletin boards in 1933.

**"Wenn die SS und die SA aufmarschiert."** "When the SS and the SA march up." Early Nazi marching song emphasizing the comradeship between the SS and the SA.

**"Wenn wir mit den Juden fertig sind, bist du deinesgleichen d'ran!"** "When we're through with the Jews, then it will be your turn." Hitler Youth slogan applied to enemies of the Third Reich.

**"Wer andern eine Grube gräbt, fällt selbst hinein."** "He who digs a hole for others will fall into it himself." Saying on barracks rafters at Auschwitz.

**"Wer beim Juden kauft, ist ein Volksverräter!"** "Whoever buys from Jews is a traitor to the (German) people." Motto of the German government's economic boycott of Jews in 1933.

**Werbeprogramm.** *See* Appendix: Parteiprogramm: Fünfundzwanzig Punkte des nationalsozialistischen Programms.

**Werberat der deutschen Wirtschaft.** Advertising Council of the German Economy. Public relations board coordinating business propaganda abroad and within the country.

**"Wer den Juden nicht kennt, kennt den Teufel nicht."** "He who does not know the Jew, does not know the devil." Antisemitic phrase placed in the newspaper showcases of *Der Stürmer*.

**werderichtig.** Genetically correct. Organic.

**"Wer flüstert, lügt!"** "He who whispers, lies." Slogan on propaganda posters to counteract the dissemination of rumors.

**"Wer Jude ist, bestimme ich."** "I decide who is and who is not a Jew." Statement attributed to Göring, and spoken fifty years earlier by Karl Lueger, mayor of Vienna and head of its Antisemitic Party. Personnel files of Wehrmacht members indicate that seventy-seven high-ranking armed forces officers came under the definition of Nazi laws as Jews or Mischlinge or were married to a Jew. Perhaps most prominent was Erhard Milch, General Field Marshal of the Air Force and Göring's deputy.

**Werkarbeit.** Work labor. *See also* Arbeit.

**Werk der Tat gewordenen Volksgemeinschaft.** The fruit of the labors of the community of the (German) people. *See also* Winterhilfswerk des deutschen Volkes.

**Werkehrenpflicht.** Honorable work duty. Voluntary service of German society women replacing female factory workers on leave.

**Werkeinsatzliste.** Work duty list. Priority list in engineering industries.

**Werkgenosse.** Fellow worker. Replacing Arbeitskollege (work colleague).

**Werkleiter.** Work Leader. Manager of industrial work in concentration camps. From 1942, person responsible for work efficiency and any failures.

**Werkluftschutz.** (WLS) Company air-raid shelter.

**Werkmann.** Workman. Worker.

**Werkschar.** Work unit. Oversight and propaganda group of the German Work Front. *See also* Deutsche Arbeitsfront.

**Werkschutz.** Work protection. Factory guards. *See also* Werkschutzkommando.

**Werkschutzkommando.** Factory-Protection Unit. Also, unarmed Jewish guards in ghetto factories in Poland.

**Werksparkasse.** Company savings bank.

**Werkstätte.** Workshop, studio. Artists workshop at Theresienstadt.

**Werkstoff.** Work material. Raw material.

**Werkverfeinerung.** Fine work. Processing of tool steel.

**"Wer sein Geld zum Juden schafft, zerstört die deutsche Wirtschaft."** "He who carries his money to the Jew, destroys the German economy." Poster slogan in 1933 to discourage Germans from buying in stores owned by Jews. *See also* Judenboykott.

**Werterfassung.** Property Collection. SS agency responsible for collecting Jewish property after Jews were moved out.

**Wertschein.** Value receipt. For gifts in kind. *See also* Winterhilfeswerk des deutschen Volkes.

**wertvollstes Gut des Volkes.** The most valuable good of the people. *See also* Arbeitskraft.

**Werwolf.** Werewolf. Along with the Stahlhelm, the most important defense formation in the 1920s (*see also* Stahlhelm). Also, unit of the Hitler Youth. Also, code name for Goebbels' plan for resistance to Allied occupation of Germany. Also, Hitler's headquarters in Ukraine in July 1942.

**Werwolf-Bund deutscher Männer und Frontkrieger.** Werewolf Alliance of German Men and Front Fighters. *See also* Werwolf.

**Weserübung.** Weser exercise. Code name for the German invasion of Denmark and Norway in April 1940.

*Westdeutscher Beobachter.* West German Observer. Nazi newspaper headquartered in Cologne.

**Westfeldzug.** Western campaign. Name for German military attack on Luxembourg, the Netherlands, Belgium, and France in 1940.

**westisch.** Western. One of the six races that allegedly comprised the Germans. Characteristics were large nose, small face, dark hair, and slender, as well as loving the homeland and being heroic. *See* dinarisch; fälisch; nordisch; ostbaltisch; ostische Rasse.

**westische Rasse.** Mediterranean, or western, race. According to Nazi pseudoscience, one of the European races. *See also* Systemrassen.

**Westmark.** Western Point. From 1941, name for the Saar region, the westernmost part of Germany, adjacent to France.

**Westwall.** Western wall. Ridiculed by Allies as the Siegfried Line, built between 1936 and 1939 in response to France's Maginot Line. Line of western German defense fortifications running from the lower Rhine to the Swiss border. North-south defensive military line roughly 400 miles long of concrete bunkers, gun emplacements, and tank traps in western Germany based on the World War I Hindenburg Line.

**Wewelsburg-Konferenz.** Wewelsburg Conference. Meeting of a dozen top SS generals, including Reinhard Heydrich, Erich Vondem Bach-Zelewski, and Kurt Daluege, called by Himmler in 1941 at Wewelsburg castle, where the invasion of Russia, resulting in millions of deaths, was discussed. *See also* Haus Wewelsburg.

**Wewelsburg Schloss.** *See* Haus Wewelsburg.

**WeWi.** *See* Wehrwirtschaft.

**W-Firma.** *See* wehrwichtige Firma.

**WFSt, WFst.** *See* Wehrmachtsführungstab.

**W-Geschäft.** *See* wehrwichtiges Geschäft.

**Wgr.** *See* Wirtschaftsgruppe.

**WH-.** Initials that, with the addition of numerals, identified German Army vehicles.

**WHW.** *See* Winterhilfswerk des deutschen Volkes.

**Wi.** *See* Wirtschaft.

**Wider den undeutschen Geist.** Against the un-German spirit. *See* Aufklärungs-feldzug wider den undeutschen Geist.

**Widerstand.** Opposition. Political, religious, and military resistance to Hitler and the Third Reich. *See also* (Der) Evangelische Kirchenkampf im Dritten Reich; Kreisauer Kreis; Sippenhaftung; Unternehmen Walküre; Wolfsschanze; 20. Juli.

**Widerstandsnest.** Resistance Nest. Wehrmacht tactical resistance center in World War II.

**Wiedereindeutschung.** Re-Germanization. The Germanization of Polish children. Secret racial abduction and indoctrination carried out by the SS in Poland. *See also* Deutsche Heimschulen; Heu-Aktion; Lebensborn; Ostkinder.

**Wiedererweckung des Artbewußtseins.** Reawakening of race consciousness. *See also* artbewußt.

**Wiedervereinigung.** Reunification. *See also* Anschluß.

**Wiedervernordung.** *See* Aufnordung.

**Wienergraben.** Vienna quarry. A quarry containing 186 steps at Mauthausen concentration camp. Prisoners were killed by being forced to carry huge stones rapidly up the stairs from the quarry or to jump from the top of the quarry cliff. *See also* Mauthausen.

**Wikingalter.** Of Viking age. German youth between twelve and fifteen years old.

**Wikinger.** Vikings. 5th SS-Panzer Division Viking comprised of Norwegian, Danish, Finnish, and Dutch volunteers. Associated with them was the runic symbol of the sun wheel, a version of the swastika.

**Wilddiebe-Kommando.** Poacher unit. *See also* Dirlewanger Sonderbataillon.

**wilde Einzelaktionen.** Unauthorized individual actions. Unsystematic attacks by individuals on Jews, rejected by Hitler as ineffectual and out of government control.

**wilde Euthanasie.** Unauthorized euthanasia. Euthanasia killings that occurred after the program was officially shut down. In reality, physicans were given wider range in choosing victims.

**wilde Jugendgruppen.** Unauthorized youth groups. *See also* Edelweißpiraten.

**wilde Konzentrationslager.** Unauthorized concentration camps. Created by individual SA members in basements and warehouses; dissolved in 1934 after the SS took control of the concentration camps. *See also* Nacht der langen Messer.

**wilde Lager.** *See* wilde Konzentrationslager.

**wilde Sau.** Wild sow. Military slang for confused battle situation. Also, code name for German air force night fighters flying without any radar, the pilot relying on eyesight alone.

**Wilhelm-Busch-Gesellschaft.** Wilhelm Busch Society. Camouflaged title for the former Schlaraffia, an organization promoting friendship, art, and brotherly love that was forbidden by the Nazis.

**Wilhelmstrasse.** Berlin street location of the Reich Chancellery, seat of the German government under the Third Reich.

**"(Der) Wille des Führers ist oberstes Gesetz."** "The leader's will is the supreme law." Principle on which Nazi law was based.

**Willensstrafrecht.** Punishment of the criminal will. Nazi law that punished the intent to commit a crime, not the crime itself. *See* Täterstrafrecht.

**Wille zum Kind.** The will to have a child. *See also* "Schenk dem Führer ein Kind."

**"(Vom) Wimpelträger zum Hakenkreuzritter!"** "From standard-bearer to knight of the swastika." Adolf-Hitler-Schule motto.

**windschnittig.** Wind sleek. Aerodynamic, streamlined.

**Winkel.** Triangle. Concentration camp triangular badges worn on the front and back of prisoner uniforms. *See also* Appendix: Winkel.

**Winkelried.** Name for a soldier who died in action in a one-man submarine. Named after Arnold Winkelried, a German-Swiss who in 1386 at the Battle of

Sempach opened the first gap in the Austrian lines by seizing a number of Austrian pikes, thus impaling himself and dying, so his comrades could get through.

**Wintergarten.** Winter garden, conservatory. Nickname for U-boat's antiaircraft platform.

**Wintergewitter.** Winter Storm. Code name for the unsuccessful German attempt to relieve the 6th Army at Stalingrad (December 1942).

*Winterhilfe.* Winter relief. *See also* Winterhilfswerk des deutschen Volkes.

**Winterhilfswerk (Büchlein).** Winter-Relief Program booklet. Given to those who contributed to the Nazi Party's Winter Relief charity. A different booklet was published each year. Typical titles were *Der Führer macht Geschichte* (The Führer Makes History), *Der Führer in den Bergen* (The Führer in the Mountains), *Des Führers Kampf im Osten* (The Führer's Fight in the East), as well as other titles on military campaigns and war heroes.

**Winterhilfswerk des deutschen Volkes.** (WHW) Winter-Relief Program of the German People. From 1933, under the auspices of Propaganda Minister Goebbels on behalf of the Nazi Party, money and material was collected to be distributed to the German needy. After 1942, distribution of confiscated property from Jews killed or deported to concentration camps.

**Winterkampfdenkzeichen.** Commemorative medal for winter combat. One of thirty-two army slang words for military decorations earned while fighting on the Eastern Front in freezing temperatures during 1941–1942. *See* Ostmedaille.

**Winterschlacht.** Winter battle. Battle at Stalingrad in the winter of 1942–1943. German advance into Russia stopped, and momentum of war changed against Germany.

**"Wir fahren gegen England."** "We are moving against England." A German march played by government radio after each German victory, real or imagined, over England.

**"Wir fahren nach Polen, um Juden zum [*sic!*] dreschen!"** "We're going to Poland to thrash the Jews." Slogan painted on German military trains headed to Poland indicating what the German soldiers planned to do when they got there.

**Wirkleistung.** Achievement of efficiency. Output.

**"Wir schaffen das neue Deutschland! Denkt an die Opfer."** "We're building the new Germany, think about the [Nazi] victims." Nazi campaign slogan indicating the Nazi fight against Social Democrats and Communists.

**"Wir sind Jüdische Schweine. Wir sind dreckige Juden. Wir sind Untermenschen."** "We are Jewish pigs. We are dirty Jews. We are subhumans." Austrian soldiers in Poland forced Jews to sing these lines.

**Wirtschaft.** (Wi) The economy, business. Hitler used the double meaning as propaganda when stating that capital serves business and economy serves the people.

(gebundende) Wirtschaft. Connected economy. Planned economy.

(ungebundende) Wirtschaft. Unconnected economy. Liberal, unplanned economy.

wirtschaftlich wertvoller Jude. (WWJ) Economically valuable Jew. Jews working for the German economy were to be the last to die.

Wirtschaftsbank. (W-Bank) Economy/business bank. German banks in occupied countries.

Wirtschaftsbeihilfe. Economic supplement. Financial aid for German families of owners of private enterprises and of freelance professionals to allow them to continue running their businesses during the war.

wirtschaftseigenes Futter. Feed from one's own economy. Farm-grown food.

Wirtschaftseinsatz Ost GmbH. Corporation to exploit eastern Europe.

Wirtschaftsgruppe. (Wgr) Group of companies.

Wirtschaftskammer. Business Chamber. Local, regional, state, and Reich organizations composed of members from all the trades.

Wirtschaftskartoffel. Economic potato. Standard, medium potato introduced in 1942.

Wirtschaftsoffizier. Economic officer. Officer accompanying the German occupation armies.

Wirtschaftsparasit. Parasite of the economy. After 1939, every German who committed a crime exploiting the wartime situation. *See* Volksschädlinge.

Wirtschaftsraum. Economic space. (German) living space, economic domain.

(SS-)Wirtschaftsring. (SS) Economic Circle. League of inactive SS members who paid contributions and were exempted from all service. *See also* feiner Maxe; Schutzstaffel Fördernde Mitglieder.

Wirtschaftssabotage. Economic sabotage. Criminal offense punishable by death for Germans who kept or invested their money outside the country.

Wirtschaftsschädling. Destroyer of the economy. Antisemitic slur.

Wirtschafts- und Verwaltungshauptamt. (WVHA) Economic and Administrative Main Office. Headed by SS General Oswald Pohl. It administered the concentration camps and controlled the economic enterprises of the SS in the camps and ghettos. *See also* Lagersystem.

Wirtsvolk. Host people. A nation harboring Jews.

Wi Rü Amt, WiRue. *See* Wehrwirtschafts- und Rüstungs(haupt)amt.

"Wir wurden dem Führer geschenkt!" "We were given to the Führer." Hitler Youth slogan.

**WK.** *See* Wehrkreis.

**WL.** *See* Wohnlager.

**WL-.** Initials that, with the addition of numerals, identified German air force vehicles.

**WLS.** *See* Werkluftschutz.

**WM-.** Initials that, with the addition of numerals, identified German navy vehicles.

**WMA.** *See* Wehrmeldeamt.

**Wochenabschnitte.** Weekly coupons. *See also* Lebensmittelkarten.

**Wochenbetreffnis.** Weekly ration.

**"Wo der Führer ist, ist der Sieg."** "Where the Führer is, there is victory." Nazi slogan.

*Wofür kämpfen wir?* What Are We Fighting For? 1944 publication by the Armed Forces Personnel Department, endorsed by Hitler; stressed the paramount importance of the race issue for the German armed forces.

**"Wohngebiet der Juden, betreten verboten."** "Jewish residential area, entrance forbidden." Sign Nazis placed at entrance of Lodz-Ghetto and other locations.

**Wohnlager.** (WL) Residence camp. Labor camp for French workers in Germany; (for example, Heinz Siebert Wohnlager.)

**Wohnraumblockade.** Residential-spaces blockade. The effect of Allied bombardment of German cities.

**Wohnsitzverlegung.** Change of address. Euphemism for the deportation of German Jews, mainly to Theresienstadt. Ghettoization.

**Wolfsangel.** Wolf hook. Germanic symbol that warded off werewolves. Used on various insignia of the Third Reich. Symbol of the 2d SS-Panzer Division (Das Reich), and Dutch SS volunteers in the 5th SS-Panzer Division (Wiking), SS-Freiwilligen-Standarte Nordwest, and the SS-Freiwilligen-Legion Niederlande.

**Wolfsschanze.** Wolf's Lair. Hitler headquarters in Rastenburg, East Prussia, where the unsuccessful attempt was made to assassinate him in July 1944.

**Wolfsschlucht.** Wolf's Gorge. Temporary Hitler headquarters in June 1940 in France.

**Wolgaorgel.** Volga organ. *See also* Stalinorgel.

**wollhaft.** Wool-like. Of synthetic wool.

**Wollstra.** Synthetic-wool product.

**Wonnemond.** Month of pleasure. May.

**Wortberichter.** Word reporter. Reporter's profession, in contrast to photojournalist.

**WR, wr.** *See* Weißruthenien.

**WS.** *See* weltanschauliche Schulung.

**WStB.** *See* Wehrstammbücher.

**Wühlarbeit.** Digging work. Derogatory for the agitation of opponents of the Nazi regime.

**Wunderwaffen.** (Wuwa) Miracle weapons. Toward the end of the war, Goebbels promised the German people new weapons (such as V-1 and V-2 rockets, V-3 long-range gun, and jet planes) to achieve victory, attempting to keep German public opinion behind the war effort. *See also* Vergeltungswaffen.

*Wunschkonzert.* (Musical) Request Program. 1940 Ufa film about a Luftwaffe lieutenant bonding with a woman who was to become his life partner. The happy ending, combining victory in war with happiness in the home front, was part of Nazi propaganda.

**Wunschkonzert für die Wehrmacht.** Request concert for the armed forces. From 1939 until 1944, every Sunday between 4 and 8 P.M., radio concerts transmitted to civilians in Germany and soldiers at the front, creating a bond between them.

**Wunschprogramm.** *See* Wunschkonzert für die Wehrmacht.

**wurzellos.** Without roots. Negative for city people.

**Wüstenfuchs.** Desert Fox. Popular nickname for General Erwin Rommel.

**Wuwa.** *See* Wunderwaffen.

**WVHA.** *See* SS-Wirtschafts- und Verwaltungshauptamt; Wirtschafts- und Verwaltungshauptamt.

**WWJ.** *See* wirtschaftlich wertvoller Jude.

# X

**X-Gerät.** X equipment. German-bomber radio-navigational equipment.

**X-Zeit.** X time. Zero hour.

# Z

**Z.** *See* Zigeuner; Zivil.

**Zählappell.** Counting roll call. A roll call in addition to the morning and evening roll call of camp prisoners as a further harassment. *See also* Appell.

**"zäh wie Leder."** "Tough as leather." *See also* Schwertworte.

**ZAL.** *See* Zwangsarbeitslager.

**Zapfer.** Barman. Gas-pump attendant.

**Zapfwart.** *See* Zapfer.

**Zaunkönig.** Fence king, wren. Nickname for acoustic torpedo.

**Zast.** *See* Zentralauftragsstelle.

**zbV.** *See* zur besonderen Verwendung.

**Zegrost.** *See* Zentralstelle Grenzschutz-Ost.

**Zeilappell.** *See* Zählappell.

**Zeitenwende.** Change of era. Nazis used "Zw vor" in place of B.C. and "Zw nach" in place of A.D.

**Zeitfreiwillige.** Temporary volunteers. *See also* Freikorps; Schwarze Reichswehr.

**Zeitfunk.** Broadcast (of current events). Political radio program.

**Zeitgeschehen.** *See* Geschehen.

**zeitlich tauglich.** *See* tauglich 3.

**Zeitschreiber.** Chronograph.

*Zeitschrift für Geopolitik.* Journal for Geopolitics. Karl Haushofer's periodical devoted to geopolitics. *See also* Geopolitik.

*Zeitschrift für Rassenkunde.* Journal for Race Science. Specializing in Nazi material on race, especially Jews and Slavs, published in Stuttgart (1935–1939).

*Zeitschrift für Sozialismus.* Journal for Socialism. Social Democratic periodical.

**Zelle.** Cell. Nazi unit, about 200 families. *See also* Betriebszelle.

**Zellenleiter.** Cell leader. Lowest level of important Nazi Party officials. Responsible for 200 families and immediately superior to the Blockwart. *See also* Blockwart; Zelle.

**Zellfaser.** Synthetic cellulose fiber. *See also* Vistra.

**Zellhaut.** Cellular skin. Cellophane.

**Zellpack.** Cellulose derivative. Used in the production of fabric.

**Zellwolle.** Synthetic wool made of cellulose to replace wool and cotton.

**Zeltlager.** (Tent) camp. Part of larger concentration camps, surrounded by barbed wire, used either to house extra prisoners or to perform special tortures and murders.

**zementierte Verteilung.** Cemented distribution. Complete economic control of the economy, with the government determining both suppliers and customers.

**Zentralamt.** Central office. *See also* Planungsamt.

**Zentralamt für jüdische Auswanderung.** Central Office for Jewish Emigration. Modeled on Adolf Eichmann's similar office in Vienna, it was created in 1939; Reinhard Heydrich was appointed to head it. A department of the Central Resettlement Office, its main function changed from forced migration before the war to deportation of Jews to be murdered in death camps. *See also* mwandererzentralstelle.

**Zentralamt zur Lösung der Judenfrage in Böhmen und Mähren.** Central Office to Plan and Prepare for Resolution of the Jewish Problem in Bohemia and Moravia. Founded in 1939 in Prague by Adolf Eichmann.

**Zentralauftragsstelle.** Central Office for Allocations. Main agency in charge of allocating ordnance to German armed forces in France, Belgium, and Holland.

**Zentrale für Handwerkslieferungen.** Main Office for Work Supply. A German business that bought factories in the ghetto areas of Poland. Part of the deal was the inclusion of Jewish forced labor.

**zentrales Museum der ausgelöschten jüdischen Rasse.** Central Museum of the Extinguished Jewish Race. An uncompleted museum devoted to the Jews, Jewishness, and Judaism in Prague.

**Zentralforschungsinstitut.** Central Research Institute. Goebbels' agency that included all of the Third Reich's anti-Jewish agencies.

**Zentralhandelsgesellschaft Ost.** (ZO) Central Trading Company East.

**Zentralkomitee der Boykottbewegung.** Central Committee of the Boycott Movement. Nazi organization that planned economic boycotts against Jews in the 1930s.

**Zentralkomitee der Kommunistischen Partei.** (ZK) Central Committee of the Communist Party. Controlling body of the German Communist Party and chief political German enemy of the Nazis.

**Zentralstelle.** Central office, central station. Coordinating bureau; also place where (Amsterdam) Jews met to be deported.

**Zentralstelle für jüdische Auswanderung.** *See* Reichszentralstelle für jüdische Auswanderung.

**Zentralstelle Grenzschutz-Ost.** (Zegrost) Headquarters for Border Security in the East.

**Zentralverlag der NSDAP.** Central Publishing House of the NSDAP. Publisher Franz Eher issued all official party literature, including the *Völkische Beobachter*. *See (Die) Kunst im Dritten Reich*.

**(Das) Zentrum.** The Center. *See* Deutsche Zentrumspartei.

**Zeppelin.** Code name for the headquarters of the German Army High Command (*see* Oberkommando des Heeres). Also, code name for German deception operations in the Balkans in 1943.

**Zeppelinfeld Stadion.** *See* Reichsparteitagsgelände.

**Zeppelinfeldtribune.** *See* Reichsparteitagsgelände.

**zerkreuzen.** To cross and destroy. To ruin a people (Germans) by interbreeding.

**Zerrungsbogen.** Overdrawn bow. Strategic area under pressure.

**zerschmeißen.** To break apart. Air force slang for to crash.

**zersetzende Literatur.** Decomposing literature. *See also* Nacht der Feuer.

**Zersetzung.** Decay, decomposition, demoralization, disruption. The Nazi belief in the assault on Germany by the international Jewish conspiracy—defined as Germany's major ideological-racial-political enemy—and by its allies on the German attempt at world domination. Also, a legal term for the undermining of the will to resist. *See* Wehrwillen.

**Zerstörer.** Destroyer. Naval vessel and air interceptor; heavily armed fighter plane used to attack ground targets.

**Zerstörergeschwader.** Luftwaffe heavy-fighter squadrons.

**Zeughaus.** Armory. Berlin arsenal, site of March 1943 aborted attempt on Hitler's life by German Army Intelligence Officer Colonel Rudolph von Gersdorff at the Hero Remembrance Day ceremonies.

**Zeugungshelfer.** Procreation assistant. (German) husband.

**"Ziehen und drücken."** "To pull and press." To avoid enemy aircraft by pulling up and then diving.

**Zielraum.** Target area. Air force objective.

**Zigeuner.** (Z) Gypsies. A collective term for Romani and Sinti people. Most Gypsy men, women, and children were considered asocial and a people of an alien and criminal race, and the Nazis deported hundreds of thousands of them to concentration camps, where they were mistreated and murdered. The Reich did not pursue those Gypsies who were regarded as having permanent residence and work—those in Poland, the Crimea, and Latvia excepted—and some Gypsy men were allowed to serve in the Wehrmacht until early in World War II. In concentration camps, Gypsies were treated similarly to the Jews. *See also* Endlösung der Judenfrage; Regelung der Zigeunerfrage aus dem Wesen der Rasse heraus in Angriff zu nehmen.

**Zigeunerfrage.** Gypsy problem. *See also* Erlaß zur Bekämpfung der Zigeunerplage; Regelung der Zigeunerfrage aus dem Wesen der Rasse heraus in Angriff zu nehmen.

**Zigeunerkinder.** Gypsy children. Considered uneducable. This would lead to concentration camps and death.

**Zigeunerlager.** Gypsy concentration camp. Separate camps set up in Germany as early as 1936. Also, area at various concentration camps devoted to Roma and Sinti. *See also* SS-Sonderlager.

**Zigeuner, Neger oder ihre Bastarde.** Gypsies, niggers, or their bastards. The Reich Ministry of the Interior determined it needed to apply race laws to Gypsies and Blacks in Germany to prevent their marriage to Germans and to prevent the birth of mixed offspring.

**Zigeunersippenarchiv.** Gypsy kinship file.

**Zigeuner und nach Zigeunerart lebende Personen.** Gypsy and people living Gypsy-style. Romani and Sinti and any others interpreted by the Nazis as Gypsies. Considered asocials, foreign to the racial community. *See also* Gemeinschaftsfremde.

**(Brechung der) Zinsknechtschaft.** Breaking of the subjugation to interest, breaking interest bondage. Nazi campaign to change or destroy the aspect of the capitalist system that, allegedly under Jewish influence, ruined department stores, banks, and small businesses by charging interest on loans.

**Zitadelle.** Citadel. *See* Unternehmen Zitadelle.

**Zittermokka.** Trembling mocha. Very strong coffee issued to the German population after an Allied air raid.

**ZivAL.** *See* Zivilarbeitslager.

**zivil.** (Z) Civilian. Stamp on goods meant for civilian economy. Developed a Nazi meaning of unheroic.

**Zivilarbeitslager.** (ZivAL) Civilian work camps. Camps owned by German companies mostly of non-Jewish prisoners, with minimal rent for the workers paid to the SS. *See also* Lagersystem.

**Zivilisation.** Civilization. The humanitarian, escapist, unpolitical concept of culture, synonymous with a weak way of living rejected by Germany's warlike state.

**(jüdisches) Zivilisationsliteratentum.** (Jewish) civilization literature. The work of any writer the Nazis disliked.

**Zivilpole.** Polish civilian. Polish citizen working in Nazi Germany voluntarily or as forced labor.

**Zivilversorgungsschein.** Civil supply papers. Civil-service preference certificate granted to ex-servicemen of Wehrmacht and SS.

**Zivilverwaltung.** (Z.V.) Civil administration. Of a German-occupied nation.

**ZL.** *See* Zweiglager.

**ZM+, ZM(+).** (Zigeunermischling mit vorwiegend zigeunerischem Blutanteil [Mixed Gypsy person with predominantly Gypsy blood]) Abbreviation used in a person's card file. *See also* Volkskartei.

**ZM-, ZM(-).** (Zigeunermischling mit vorwiegend deutschem Blutanteil [Mixed Gypsy person with predominantly German blood]) Abbreviation used in a person's card file. *See also* Volkskartei.

**Z-Mann.** *See* Zubringer, Zuträger.

**ZO.** *See* Zentralhandelsgesellschaft Ost.

**Zöglinge.** Pupils. SS auxiliary antiaircraft brigades composed of fourteen to seventeen year olds. In 1944, even so-called non-Aryan boys and girls were forcibly recruited.

**Zossen.** Army Command Headquarters south of Berlin.

**Zossen-Putsch.** German generals contemplated an attempt to overthrow Hitler shortly after the defeat of Poland in 1939. They hesitated and the plot dissolved.

**Z-Plan.** German naval plan to build a surface fleet to challenge the British navy. 1938 plan by Hitler and the Naval High Command envisaged the creation of a fleet of 10 battleships, 15 pocket battleships, 5 heavy and 24 light cruisers, 4 aircraft carriers, 68 destroyers, 90 torpedo boats, and 249 submarines.

**Zubringer.** (Z-Mann) Informant. Special agent who brought information to the SD.

**Züchtung.** Breeding. The creation of a German racist elite through eugenics and race health.

**Zuchtwart.** Breeding master. Nazi eugenics official who controlled the breeding of healthy German children of pure race.

**"Zuerst ausnutzen und dann ausrotten."** "First exploit and then exterminate." Inscription on several of the forced-labor camps in Poland remaining after 1943. *See also* Vernichtung durch Arbeit.

**Zug.** Platoon. A thirty- to forty-man subunit of an army company. Also, train.

**Zugänge.** Incoming individuals. Forms at concentration camps with date of arrived transport on top, and below a list of newly arrived individuals, their names, date and place of birth, and profession. *See* Zugang.

**Zugangsbaracke.** Entry barracks. Quarantine area for new prisoners at concentration camps.

**Zugführer.** Train leader. Teacher in an elite Nazi school.

**Zugwache.** Train guard. Military troop-train and supply-train guard.

**Zulassungsmarke.** Permission stamp. Permit needed to send parcels exceeding 100 grams to German soldiers.

**zur besondern Verwendung.** (zbV) For special purpose, for special use. Wehrmacht, SS, and air force term.

**zurückschlagen.** To hit back. Hitler's propaganda term for the German attack on Poland in 1939 that started World War II. *See also* Unternehmen Himmler.

**zur Verfügung.** At the disposition of. Armed Forces Reserves.

**Zusammenballung.** Crowding together. Grouping as many Jews as possible into a few ghettos, resulting in the death of many, before the survivors were sent to killing sites or death camps.

**Zusatzarbeit.** Overtime work. Brutally enforced extra hours Jews had to work every day in the concentration camps and ghettos.

**Zusatzname.** Additional name. From January 1939, Jews not having a typical Jewish name had to add to their given names either Abraham or Israel for men and Sara or Sarah for women.

**Zuteilung.** Portion. The amount of hard-to-get goods that one could obtain with a ration card. *See also* Sonderzuteilung.

**Zuträger.** (Z-Mann) Informant of the Security Service. *See also* A-Mann; H-Mann; U-Mann; V-Mann.

**Z.V.** *See* Zivilverwaltung.

**Zwangsarbeit.** Forced labor. Divided into slave labor from concentration camps and ghettos (mostly Jewish and earmarked for death) and forced labor of non-Jewish civilians (living in labor camps) and forcibly conscripted labor from German-occupied countries as well as POWs to work in Germany and German-occupied Europe. From 1942, Germany used millions of slave and forced laborers in agriculture and industry, enabling the German war economy to succeed in meeting its goals. *See* Bunawerke; Lagersystem; Vernichtung durch Arbeit.

**Zwangsarbeitslager.** (ZAL) (Jewish) forced-labor, or slave-labor, camp. Sometimes synonymous with ghetto; often transformed into a concentration camp (e.g., Krakow-Plaszow).

**Zwangsarisierung.** Forced aryanization. Confiscation of Jewish property in Germany and Austria ordered by Reichsmarschall Hermann Göring after the November 1938 Pogrom. *See also* Arisierung; Reichskristallnacht.

**Zwangsentjudungsverfahren.** Forced removal of Jews. Process of complete elimination of Jews from the German economy (1933–1939).

**Zwangsgemeinde.** Forced community. In occupied Europe, Jews were forced into Jewish communities, no matter how assimilated they were before this time.

**Zwangsglaubenssatz.** Forced dogma. Alfred Rosenberg's word for Christian beliefs.

**Zwangslauflehre.** Forced path patterns. Mechanical motion, determinism.

**Zwangssterilisation.** Forced sterilization. *See also* Gesetz zur Verhütung erb-kranken Nachwuchses.

**Zwangstod.** Forced suicide. Suicide as one of the Nazi techniques for dealing with political embarrassment; for example, Rommel was forced to commit suicide after the discovery of his involvement in the von Stauffenberg attempt to assassinate Hitler. *See also* 20. Juli.

**Zwangsverkauf.** Compulsory sale. Following the numerous collective deportations of Jews, Jewish property had to be sold. When the Reich Society of Jews in Germany, for example, was finally disbanded, the Nazis immediately confiscated the entire property as hostile to the state. *See* staatsfeindlich.

**20. Juli.** July 20. The most dramatic of several attempts to kill Hitler. On this date in 1944, Colonel Claus von Stauffenberg, a highly decorated German war hero, attempted to blow up Hitler along with most of his top military and political cohorts—Heinrich Himmler, Hermann Göring, Joachim von Ribbentrop, Adolf Heusinger, Alfred Jodl, and Wilhelm Keitel—at his headquarters at Wolf's Lair. Even though von Stauffenberg's bomb exploded, Hitler suffered only minor injuries and his top-level advisers were either left unhurt or were not present. Numerous military officers and civilians were involved in the plot. Among those executed were General Ludwig Beck, former Armed Forces Chief of Staff; Admiral Wilhelm Canaris, Head of the Abwehr; General Helmuth Stieff, Head of the Organization Branch of the Oberkommando des Heeres; General Eduard Wagner, First Quartermaster General of the Army; General Paul von Hase, Commandant of Berlin; Count Wolfron Helldorf, Commander of the Berlin Police Force; General Erich Fellgiebell in communications; General Erich Hopner; General Hans Oster; General Karl von Stulpnagel; General Henning von Tresckow; Field Marshals Erwin von Witzleben and Erwin Rommel. Prominent among civilians executed were the Jesuit priest Alfred Delp, Hans von Dohnanyi, Dr. Karl Gördeler, Ulrich von Hassell, Dr. Julius Leber, Graf Helmut von Moltke, Adam von Trott zu Solz, and Peter Yorck von Wartenburg. The Nazis murdered more than 5,000 people accused, most falsely, of involvement in the plot. *See also* Abwehr; Schwarze Kapelle; Sippenhaftung; Unternehman Walküre; Wolfsschanze.

**Zweckentfremdung.** Usage for a different purpose. Illegal diversion of raw materials intended for defense purposes; wastage.

**Zwecksparkasse.** Savings bank for a specific purpose. For example, savings bank for financing the building of family houses.

**zweibeiniges Viehzeug.** Two-legged cattle. Reinhard Heydrich's term for Slavic people in Germany's New European Order. *See also* Europäische Neuordnung.

**Zweiglager.** (ZL) Branch camp. Many large concentration camps had branch camps associated with the main camp, where prisoners were used as forced labor. Auschwitz had at least two dozen branch camps, possibly ten times this number.

**2004.** Underground factory where Flossenbürg concentration camp inmates built Messerschmidt figher planes under barbarous conditions.

**Zweite Aktion.** Second operation. Deportation of Jews from the Warsaw-Ghetto to the Treblinka death camp in January 1943. Called off after four days due to Jewish armed resistance. *See also* Erste Aktion; Umsiedlungsaktion.

**Zweites Gesetz zur Gleichschaltung der Länder mit dem Reich.** Second Law concerning the Coordination of the Provinces with the Reich. April 1933 law allowing Hitler to control Germany's provincial governors. *See also* Gleichschaltung.

**Zweite Verordnung zur Durchführung des Gesetz über die Änderung von Familiennamen und Vornamen.** The Second Decree for the Implementation of the Law concerning the Change of Family and First Names. August 17, 1938, law explaining more fully the law changing German-Jewish names. *See also* jüdische Vornamen.

**Zwischeneuropa.** In-between Europe. Slavic countries between Germany and Russia.

**Zwischenreich.** In-between Reich. The Weimar Republic, considered an illegitimate government falling between the Second Reich and the Third Reich.

**Zwischensystem.** In-between system, interregnum. *See also* Zwischenreich.

**Zw nach.** After change of era. *See also* Zeitenwende.

**Zwölf Sätze der Deutschen Studentenschaft.** Twelve principles of the German student body. Antisemitic proclamation of 1933.

**Zw vor.** Before change of era. *See also* Zeitenwende.

**Zyklon.** Cyclone. Brand name for an insecticide (hydrogen cyanide or Prussic acid) manufactured by Deutsche Gesellschaft für Schädlingsbekämpfung (DEGESCH), and Tesch & Stabenow (Testa), both subsidiaries of IG Farben. It interferes with the body's ability to use oxygen and is one of the most poisonous substances known. *See also* Deutsche Gesellschaft für Schädlingsbekämpfung; Tesch & Stabenow; Zyklon-A; Zyklon-B.

**Zyklon-A.** Cyclone A. A water-based delivery system for the chemical Zyklon, or cyanide-chloride, which, when dissolved in water, creates the deadly gas hydrogen cyanide. This murder delivery system was rarely used, except at Natzweiler-Struthof and Sachsenhausen concentration camps. *See also* Zyklon; Zyklon-B.

**Zyklon-B.** Cyclone B. An air-based delivery system for the chemical Zyklon (hydrogen cyanide). Pellets of Zyklon were shipped in airtight containers that sublimated into the poison gas hydrogen cyanide when released into the air at room temperature (at least 75° F, 25° C), the deadly gas having a faint odor of bitter almonds. Zyklon as a gas (Zyklon-B) was utilized to murder people in the Euthanasia Program, and in October 1941 it was employed on Soviet prisoners of war. Most notoriously, the gas was used to kill millions of men, women, and children (most Jews and also people of most European nationalities and religions) in gas chambers, especially the six death factories in Poland. *See also* Zyklon; Zyklon-A.

# APPENDIX

# MAJOR CONCENTRATION CAMPS AND GHETTOS

*(Overall, some estimate more than 10,000 concentration camps and 500 ghettos across Europe.)*

**Germany**
Arbeitsdorf
Bergen-Belsen (2 satellite camps)
Börgermoor
Breslau
Buchenwald (nearly 200 satellite camps and external slave-labor units)
Dachau (nearly 200 satellite camps and external slave-labor units)
Dieburg
Dora-Mittelbau (32 satellite camps)
Esterwegen (1 satellite camp)
Flossenbürg (nearly 100 satellite camps and external slave-labor units)
Groß-Rosen (more than 100 satellite camps)
Gundelsheim
Herzogenbusch (13 satellite camps)
Moringen
Neuengamme (96 satellite camps and external slave-labor units)
Papenburg
Peenemuende
Ravensbrück (45 satellite camps and external slave-labor units)
Sachsenburg
Sachsenhausen (74 satellite camps and external slave-labor units)
Stutthof (176 satellite camps)
Wewelsburg

**Austria**
Mauthausen (50 satellite camps and external slave-labor units)

**Belgium**
Breendonck

**Bohemia and Moravia**
Theresienstadt (9 satellite camps)

**Estonia**
Vivara (27 satellite camps)

**Finland**
Kangasjarvi
Koveri

**France**
Argeles
Aurigny
Brens
Drancy
Gurs
Les Milles
Le Vernet
Natzweiler-Struthof (70 satellite camps and external slave-labor units)
Noé
Récébédou
Rieucros

Rivesaltes
Suresnes
Thill

**Holland**
Amersfoort
Ommen
Vught (12 satellite camps and external
    slave-labor units)
Westerbork (transit camp)

**Hungary**
Budapest

**Italy**
Bolzano
Fossoli
Risiera di San Sabba

**Lattvia**
Dundaga
Eleje-Meitenes
Jungfernhof
Lenta
Riga-Ghetto
Riga-Kaiserwald (29 satellite camps)
Shavli
Spilwe

**Lithuania**
Aleksotaskowno
Kaunas (14 satellite camps)
Kovno-Ghetto
Palemonas
Pravieniskès
Vilna-Ghetto
Vilnius
Volary

**Morocco and Algeria Vichy Camps**
Abadla
Ain el Ourak
Bechar
Berguent
Bogari
Bouarfa

Djelfa
Kenadsa
Meridja
Missour
Tendrara

**Norway**
Baerum
Berg
Bredtvet
Falstadt
Tromsdalen
Ulven

**Poland**
Auschwitz (51 satellite camps)
Auschwitz-Birkenau (Oswiecim-
    Brzezinka) (extermination camp)
Auschwitz-Monowitz/Auschwitz-Buna
Belzec (extermination camp; 1
    satellite camp)
Bialystok
Bierznow
Biesiadka
Chelmno (Kulmhof) (extermination
    camp)
Czestochowa
Czwartaki
Dzierzazna
Groß-Rosen-Rogoznica (77 satellite
    camps)
Huta-Komarowska
Janowska
Kielce
Krakau-Ghetto
Krakow-Placzow (10 satellite camps)
Lodz-Ghetto
Lodz (Litzmannstadt)
Lublin-Majdanek (extermination
    camp; 14 satellite camps)
Lwów (German: Lemberg)
Mielec
Pawiak (prison)
Piotrkow
Plaszow (work camp but later became
    satellite camp of Lublin-Majdanek)

Poniatowa
Pustkow (work camp)
Radogosz (prison)
Radom
Rzeszow-Ghetto
Schmolz
Schokken
Sobibor (extermination camp)
Stutthof-Sztutowo (40 satellite camps
    and external slave-labor units)
Treblinka (extermination camp)
Warschau-Ghetto
Wieliczka
Zabiwoko (work camp; no satellite
    camp known)
Zakopane

**Russia**
Akmétchetka
Balanowka
Bar
Bisjumujsje
Bogdanovka
Brody
"Citadelle" (near Lvóv)
Czwartaki
Daugavpils
Domanievka
Edineti
Kielbasin (or Kelbassino)
Khorol
Klooga
Kolomyia
(Lvóv) Lemberg
Mezjapark

Minsk-Ghetto
Novogrudok
Pinsk
Ponary
Rawa-Russkaja
Salapils
Smolensk
Strazdumujsje
Yanowski
Vertugen
Vitebsk

**Yugoslavia**
Banjica
Brocice
Chabatz
Danica
Dakovo
Gornja reka
Gradiska
Jadovno
Jasenovac
Jastrebarsko
Kragujevac
Krapje
Kruscica
Lepoglava
Loborgrad
Sajmite
Sisak
Slano
Slavonska-Pozega
Stara-Gradiska
Tasmajdan
Zemun

# RANKS

**Heer** *(In order of rank)*
Grenadier
Obergrenadier
Gefreiter
Obergefreiter

Stabsgefreiter
Unteroffizier
Unterfeldwebel
Fähnrich
Feldwebel

Oberfeldwebel
Hauptfeldwebel
Oberfähnrich
Stabsfeldwebel
Leutnant
Oberleutnant
Hauptmann
Major
Oberstleutnant
Oberst
Generalmajor
Generalleutnant
General der . . .
Generaloberst
Generalfeldmarschall

**Waffen-SS** *(In order of rank)*
SS-Schütze
SS-Oberschütze
SS-Sturmmann
SS-Rottenführer
SS-Unterscharführer
SS-Scharführer
SS-Oberscharführer
SS-Hauptscharführer
SS-Stabsscharführer
SS-Sturmscharführer
SS-Untersturmführer
SS-Obersturmführer
SS-Hauptsturmführer
SS-Sturmbannführer
SS-Obersturmbannführer
SS-Standartenführer
SS-Oberführer
SS-Brigadeführer
SS-Gruppenführer
SS-Obergruppenführer
SS-Oberstgruppenführer
Reichsführer-SS

**Luftwaffe** *(In order of rank)*
Flieger
Gefreiter
Obergefreiter
Hauptgefreiter

Stabsgefreiter
Unteroffizier
Unterfeldwebel
Feldwebel
Oberfeldwebel
Stabsfeldwebel
Leutnant
Oberleutnant
Hauptmann
Major
Oberstleutnant
Oberst
Generalmajor
Generalleutnant
General der . . .
Generaloberst
Generalfeldmarschall
Reichsmarschall

**Kriegsmarine** *(In order of rank)*
Matrose
Matrosengefreiter
Matrosenobergefreiter
Matrosenhauptgefreiter
Matrosenstabsgefreiter
Maat
Obermaat
Fähnrich zur See
Feldwebel
Stabsfeldwebel
Oberfeldwebel
Oberfähnrich zur See
Stabsoberfeldwebel
Leutnant zur See
Oberleutnant zur See
Kapitänleutnant
Korvettenkapitän
Fregattenkapitän
Kapitän zur See
Kommodore
Vizeadmiral
Konteradmiral
Admiral
Generaladmiral
Grossadmiral

# SS DIVISIONS

1st SS-Panzer Division (Leibstandarte Adolf Hitler)
2nd SS-Panzer Division (Das Reich)
3rd SS-Panzer Division (Totenkopf)
4th SS-Panzergrenadier Division (Polizei)
5th SS-Panzer Division (Wiking)
6th SS-Gebirgs Division (Nord)
7th SS-Freiwilligen-Gebirgs Division (Prinz Eugen)
8th SS-Kavallerie Division (Florian Geyer)
9th SS-Panzer Division (Hohenstaufen)
10th SS-Panzer Division (Frundsberg)
11th SS-Freiwilligen-Panzergrenadier-Division (Nordland)
12th SS-Panzer Division (Hitlerjugend)
13th Waffen-Gebirgs Division der SS (Handschar) (kroatische Nr. 1)
14th Waffen-Grenadier Division der SS (ukranische Nr. 1)
15th Waffen-Grenadier Division der  SS (lettische Nr. 1)
16th SS-Panzergrenadier Division (Reichsführer SS)
17th SS-Panzergrenadier Division (Götz von Berlichingen)
18th SS-Freiwilligen-Panzergrenadier-Division (Horst Wessel)
19th Waffen-Grenadier Division der SS (lettische Nr. 2)
20th Waffen-Grenadier Division der SS (estnische Nr. 1)
21st Waffen-Gebirgs Division der SS (Skanderbeg)
22nd Freiwilligen-Kavallerie Division der SS (Maria Theresa)
23rd Waffen-Gebirgs Division der SS (Kama) (kroatische Nr. 2)
23rd SS Freiwilligen Panzergrenadier Division ("Nederland")
24th SS-Gebirgs Division (Karstjäger)
25th Waffen-Grenadier-Division der SS (ungarische Nr. 1) (Hunyadi)
26th Waffen-Grenadier-Division der SS (ungarische Nr. 2) (Hungaria)
27th SS-Freiwilligen-Panzergrenadier Division (Langemarck)
28th SS-Freiwilligen-Panzergrenadier Division (Wallonien)
29th Waffen-Grenadier-Division der SS (russische Nr. 1)
29th Waffen-Grenadier-Division der SS (italianische Nr. 1)
30th Waffen-Grenadier-Division der SS (weissruthenische Nr. 1)
31st SS-Freiwilligen-Grenadier Division
32nd SS-Freiwilligen-Grenadier Division (30 Januar)
33rd Freiwilligen-Grenadier-Division der SS (ungarische Nr. 3)
33rd Waffen-Grenadier-Division der SS (Charlemagne)
34th Waffen-Grenadier-Division der SS (Landstorm Nederland)
35th SS-Polizei-Grenadier-Division
36th Waffen-Grenadier-Division der SS (Dirlewanger)
37th SS-Freiwilligen-Kavallerie-Division (Lützow)
38th SS-Panzergrenadier-Division (Nibelungen)

# WINKEL (TRIANGLE)

*(Concentration camp triangular badges
worn on the front and back of prisoner uniforms.)*

two triangles, including one yellow, composing a Star of David (Jew)
pink (homosexual)
red (political prisoner)
black (asocial)
brown (Romani [Gypsy])
green (criminal)
purple (Jehovah's Witness)
blue (emigrant who had illegally left Germany and then returned)

# NAZI SONGS

**"Horst-Wessel-Lied"**
*[Also called "Die Fahne hoch!"]*
Die Fahne hoch!
Die Reihen dicht geschlossen!
SA marschiert mit ruhig festem Schritt.
Kameraden, die Rotfront und Reaktion erschossen,
Marschiern im Geist in unsern Reihen mit.
Die Straße frei den braunen Bataillonen!
Die Straße frei dem Sturmabteilungsmann!
Es schaun aufs Hakenkreuz voll Hoffnung schon Millionen,
Der Tag für Freiheit und für Brot bricht an.
Zum letztenmal wird nun Appell geblasen.
Zum Kampfe stehn wir alle schon bereit.
Bald flattern Hitlerfahnen über alle Straßen.
Die Knechtschaft dauert nur noch kurze Zeit.
Die Fahne hoch!
Die Reihen fest geschlossen!
SA marschiert mit ruhig festem Schritt
Kameraden, die Rotfront und Reaktion erschossen,
Marschiern im Geist in unsern Reihen mit.

**"Horst-Wessel-Song"**
Raise the flag high!
Close the ranks tight!
Storm Troopers march,
With firm and steady step.
Souls of the comrades

Shot by Reds and the Reaction
Are in our ranks
And march along in step.
Open the roads
For the brown battalions,
Open the roads
For the storm trooper.
In hope, the eyes of millions
Are raised to the swastika
Dawn breaks for freedom and bread.
This is the final
Bugle call to arms.
Already we are set,
Prepared to fight.
Soon Hitler's flags will wave
Over every street.
Enslavement ends.
We'll soon set things right.
Raise the flag high!
Close the ranks tight!
Storm Troopers march,
With firm and steady step.


## Macht und Ehre—Sturmsoldaten

Ihr Sturmsoldaten, jung und alt, nehmt die Waffen in die Hand,
Der Jude haust ganz fürchterlich in das deutsche [sic] Vaterland,
War einst ein junger Sturmsoldat, der dazu ward bestimmt,
Daß er sein Weib und Kind verlassen muß, verlassen muß geschwind.

Alte Weiber weinen fürchterlich, junge Mädchen noch viel mehr.
So leb denn wohl mein geliebtes Kind, wir sehen uns nimmermehr
Wenn der Sturmsoldat ins Feuer zieht, ja da hat er frohen Mut,
Und wenn das Judenblut vom Messer spritzt, dann geht's nochmal so gut.


## Might and Honor—Storm Soldiers

You storm soldiers, young and old, take your weapons in your hand,
The distusting and terrifying Jew lives everywhere in the German fatherland.
Once there was a young storm soldier who had
To leave his wife and child; he had to leave fast.

Old women cry terribly, young girls even more.
So farewell my dear child, we'll never see each other again.
When the storm soldier marches into battle, he is cheerful,
And when Jewish blood drips from his knife, things are even better.

**In München sind viele gefallen**
In München sind viele gefallen,
in München waren viele dabei
Es traf vor der Feldherrnhalle
Deutsche Helden das tödliche Blei

Sie kämpften für Deutschlands Erwachen,
Im Glauben an Hitlers Mission
Marschierten mit Todesverachten
In das Feuer der Reaktion,

In München sind viele Gefallen,
Für Ehre, für Freiheit und Brot,
Es traf vor der Feldherrnhalle
Sechzehn Männer der Märtyrertod,

Ihr Toten vom neunten November,
Ihr Toten wir schwören Euch,
Es leben noch viele tausend Kämpfer
Für das Vierte, das Großdeutsche Reich.

Ihr Sturmsoldaten jung und alt,
Nehmt die Waffen in die Hand,
Der Jude dringt ganz fürchterlich
In das deutsche Vaterland.

**Many Fell in Munich**
Many fell in Munich.
Many were there in Munich
In front of the Feldherrnhalle.
German heroes were shot to death.

They fought for Germany's awakening,
Believing in Hitler's mission.
They marched defying death
Into the fire of the Reaction.

Many fell in Munich
For honor, for freedom, and bread.
In front of the Feldherrnhalle,
Sixteen men died as martyrs.

You dead from the ninth of November,
You dead, we promise you this:
Many thousands of fighters are left
For the Fourth and Greater German Reich.

You storm soldiers, young and old,
Take weapons into your hands.
The disgusting and terrifying Jew is invading
The German fatherland.

**Das Jungvolk-Lied**
Wir sind die Hitlerjungen;
Wir stehn nie hinten an;
Vom deutschen Geist durchdrungen,
So steh'n wir unsern Mann.
Sieg Heil! Sieg Heil! Sieg Heil!
Voll Hoffnung stürmt die Jugend
Ins dritte Reich hinein,
Das Vorbild unsrer Tugend
Soll Adolf Hitler sein.
Sieg Heil! Sieg Heil! Sieg Heil!
Sind wir erst Deutschlands Wehre,
Dann soll die Losung sein:
Für Deutschlands Ruhm und Ehre,
Da setzen wir uns ein.
Sieg Heil! Sieg Heil! Sieg Heil!
Zur Einigkeit und Treue,
Da ging der Weg sehr steil.
Jetzt rufen wir aufs Neue:
"Großdeutschland lebt! Sieg Heil!"
Sieg Heil! Sieg Heil! Sieg Heil!

**The Young People's Song**
We are Hitler boys,
We never come last;
Filled with the German spirit
We stand behind our man.
Sieg Heil! Sieg Heil! Sieg Heil!
Full of hope the youth storm
Into the Third Reich,
The model of our virtue.
Adolf Hitler must be.
Sieg Heil! Sieg Heil! Sieg Heil!
We are Germany's last line of defense.
Then our motto will be:
For Germany's glory and honor,
We will fight.
Sieg Heil! Sieg Heil! Sieg Heil!
For unity and loyalty.
The road was very steep;
But now we're shouting again:

"Great Germany is alive, Sieg Heil!"
Sieg Heil! Sieg Heil! Sieg Heil!


**Deutschland erwache!**
Deutschland erwache aus deinem bösen Traum!
Gib fremden Juden in deinem Reich nicht Raum!
Wir wollen kämpfen für dein Aufersteh'n.
Arisches Blut soll nicht untergehn!
All diese Heuchler, wir werfen sie hinaus.
Juda, entweiche aus unserm deutschen Haus!
Ist erst die Scholle gesäubert und rein,
Werden wir einig und glücklich sein.
Wir sind die Kämpfer der N.S.D.A.P.
Treudeutsch im Herzen, im Kampfe fest und zäh.
Dem Hakenkreuze ergeben sind wir.
Heil unserm Führer, Heil Hitler dir!


**Germany awaken!**
Germany, awaken from your nightmare!
Give alien Jews no space in your Reich!
We will fight for your resurrection.
Aryan blood must not perish!
All these hypocrites, we'll throw them out.
Jew, get out of our German house!
Once our soil is clean and pure,
We'll be unified and happy.
We are the warriors of the NSDAP.
True Germans in our hearts, solid and tough in our battles.
We are devoted to the Swastika.
Hail our Führer, Heil Hitler.


**Deutschlandlied. Das Lied der Deutschen**
Deutschland, Deutschland über alles,
Über alles in der Welt,
Wenn es stets zum Schutz und Trutze
Brüderlich zusammenhält.
Von der Maas bis an die Memel,
Von der Etsch bis an den Belt—
Deutschland, Deutschland über alles,
Über alles in der Welt!


Deutsche Frauen, deutsche Treue,
Deutscher Wein und deutscher Sang
Sollen in der Welt behalten
Ihren alten schönen Klang.

Uns zu edler Tat begeistern
Unser ganzes Leben lang—
Deutsche Frauen, deutsche Treue,
Deutscher Wein und deutscher Sang!

Eingkeit und Recht und Freiheit
Für das deutsche Vaterland!
Danach laßt uns alle streben
Brüderlich mit Herz und Hand!
Einigkeit und Recht und Freiheit
Sind des Glückes Unterpfand—
Blüh im Glanze dieses Glückes,
Blühe, deutsches Vaterland!

**Germany Song. The Song of the Germans**
Germany, Germany above everything,
Above everything in the world,
When it always stands together
In protection and defiance as brothers.
From the Maas to the Memel,
From the Etsch to the Belt—
Germany, Germany above everything,
Above everything in the world.

German women, German loyalty,
German wine and German song
Shall in the world keep
Their old beautiful sound.
And to noble action inspire
Our whole life long—
German women, German loyalty,
German wine and German song!

Unity and Rights and Freedom
For the German Fatherland!
Let us all strive for that
Brotherly with heart and hand!
Unity and Rights and Freedom
Are the foundations of happiness—
Bloom in the glow of this happiness,
Bloom, German Fatherland.

(Only the first stanza was used by Nazi Germany. Postwar Germany has retained
the *Deutschlandlied* as the national anthem, but uses only the third stanza, which
emphasizes unity, justice, freedom, and brotherhood.)

## PARTEIPROGRAMM:  FÜNFUNDZWANZIG PUNKTE DES NATIONALSOZIALISTISCHEN PROGRAMMS

### February 24, 1920

1. We demand the union of all Germans in a Great Germany on the basis of the principle of self-determination of all peoples.
2. We demand that the German people have rights equal to those of other nations; and that the Peace Treaties of Versailles and St. Germain shall be abrogated.
3. We demand land and territory (colonies) for the maintenance of our people and the settlement of our surplus population.
4. Only those who are our fellow countrymen can become citizens. Only those who have German blood, regardless of creed, can be our countrymen. Hence no Jew can be a countryman.
5. Those who are not citizens must live in Germany as foreigners and must be subject to the law of aliens.
6. The right to choose the government and determine the laws of the State shall belong only to citizens. We therefore demand that no public office, of whatever nature, whether in the central government, the province, or the municipality, shall be held by anyone who is not a citizen.

    We wage war against the corrupt parliamentary administration whereby men are appointed to posts by favor of the party without regard to character and fitness.
7. We demand that the State shall above all undertake to ensure that every citizen shall have the possibility of living decently and earning a livelihood. If it should not be possible to feed the whole population, then aliens (noncitizens) must be expelled from the Reich.
8. Any further immigration of non-Germans must be prevented. We demand that all non-Germans who have entered Germany since August 2, 1914, shall be compelled to leave the Reich immediately.
9. All citizens must possess equal rights and duties.
10. The first duty of every citizen must be to work mentally or physically. No individual shall do any work that offends against the interest of the community to the benefit of all.

Therefore we demand:

11. That all unearned income, and all income that does not arise from work, be abolished.
12. Since every war imposes on the people fearful sacrifices in blood and treasure, all personal profit arising from the war must be regarded as treason to the people. We therefore demand the total confiscation of all war profits.
13. We demand the nationalization of all trusts.
14. We demand profit sharing in large industries.

15. We demand a generous increase in old-age pensions.
16. We demand the creation and maintenance of a sound middle class and the immediate communalization of large stores which will be rented cheaply to small tradespeople, and the strongest consideration must be given to ensure that small traders shall deliver the supplies needed by the State, the provinces, and municipalities.
17. We demand an agrarian reform in accordance with our national requirements and the enactment of a law to expropriate the owners without compensation of any land needed for the common purpose, the abolition of ground rents, and the prohibition of all speculation in land.
18. We demand that ruthless war be waged against those who work to the injury of the common welfare. Traitors, usurers, profiteers, and so forth are to be punished with death, regardless of creed or race.
19. We demand that Roman law, which serves a materialist ordering of the world, be replaced by German common law.
20. In order to make it possible for every capable and industrious German to obtain higher education, and thus the opportunity to reach into positions of leadership, the State must assume the responsibility of organizing thoroughly the entire cultural system of the people. The curricula of all educational establishments shall be adapted to practical life. The conception of the State Idea (science of citizenship) must be taught in the schools from the very beginning. We demand that specially talented children of poor parents, whatever their station or occupation, be educated at the expense of the State.
21. The State has the duty to help raise the standard of national health by providing maternity welfare centers, by prohibiting juvenile labor, by increasing physical fitness through the introduction of compulsory games and gymnastics, and by the greatest possible encouragement of associations concerned with the physical education of the young.
22. We demand the abolition of the regular army and the creation of a national (folk) army.
23. We demand that there be a legal campaign against those who propagate deliberate political lies and disseminate them through the press. In order to make possible the creation of a German press, we demand:
    (a) All editors and their assistants on newspapers published in the German language shall be German citizens.
    (b) Non-German newspapers shall only be published with the express permission of the State. They must not be published in the German language.
    (c) All financial interests in or in any way affecting German newspapers shall be forbidden to non-Germans by law, and we demand that the punishment for transgressing this law be the immediate suppression of the newspaper and the expulsion of the non-Germans from the Reich.
        Newspapers transgressing against the common welfare shall be suppressed. We demand legal action against those tendencies in art and literature that have a disruptive influence upon the life of our folk, and that any organizations that offend against the foregoing demands shall be dissolved.

24. We demand freedom for all religious faiths in the state, insofar as they do not endanger its existence or offend the moral and ethical sense of the Germanic race.

   The party as such represents the point of view of a positive Christianity without binding itself to any one particular confession. It fights against the Jewish materialist spirit within and without and is convinced that a lasting recovery of our folk can only come about from within on the principle:

COMMON GOOD BEFORE INDIVIDUAL GOOD

25. In order to carry out this program we demand: the creation of a strong central authority in the State, the unconditional authority by the political central parliament of the whole State and all its organizations.

   The formation of professional committees and of committees representing the several estates of the realm, to ensure that the laws promulgated by the central authority shall be carried out by the federal states.

The leaders of the Party undertake to promote the execution of the foregoing points at all costs, if necessary at the sacrifice of their own lives.

Munich, 24th February 1920                 For the Party Committee:  Anton Drexler

Contributions should be sent to the Head Office:  Corneliusstraße 12 (Tel. 23620) Business Hours 9–12 (am), 2–6 (pm)

## TREUEID (LOYALTY OATH)

Ich schwöre bei Gott diesen heiligen Eid, daß ich dem Führer des Deutschen Reiches und Volkes Adolf Hitler, dem Oberbefehlshaber der Wehrmacht, unbedingten Gehorsam leisten und als tapferer Soldat bereit sein will, jederzeit für diesen Eid mein Leben einzusetzen.

I swear this holy oath before God, that for the Führer of the German Reich and People Adolf Hitler, Commander in Chief of the Armed Forces, I will be prepared at all times to carry out my duties with absolute obedience as a courageous soldier, to risk my life in absolute obedience to this oath.

## MONATSNAMEN (MONTH NAMES)

*The Nazis tried to replace conventional month names using some old Germanic names for each month of the year (old month name/new month(s) name).*

Januar/Eismond, Hartung (ice moon)
Februar/Hornung

März/Lenzing, Lenzmond (spring moon)
April/Ostermond (Easter moon)
Mai/Wonnemond (delight moon)
Juni/Brachet, Brachmond (plow moon); Sommermond (summer moon)
Juli/Heuet, Heumond (hay moon)
August/Ährenmonat, Erntemond (grain moon); Ernting (harvest moon)
September/Herbstmond, Scheiding (autumn moon)
Oktober/Gilbhard, Weinmond (wine moon)
November/Nebelmond, Nebelung (fog moon)
Dezember/Juhl, Christmond (Christ moon); Julmond (yule moon)


# CHILDREN'S PRAYER

*Poem in form of a children's prayer by H. Sommer*
*with illustration in a 1936 school primer.*

**Gebet**
Schütze Gott, mit deiner Hand
unser liebes Vaterland!
Gib zu seinem schweren Werke
unserm Führer Kraft und Stärke!
Wende unsres Volkes Not:
Arbeit gib und jedem Brot.

**Prayer**
Protect, God, with your hand
Our dear fatherland.
Give strength and power to our Führer,
And help him in his difficult task.
Turn away our nation's sorrow,
Give all of us work and bread this morrow.


*Hitler's maxims in a 1936 school primer.*

Der Führer spricht:
Lerne Opfer bringen für dein Vaterland!
Wir sind vergänglich, aber Deutschland muß leben!
In deinem Volke liegt deine Kraft.
Ihr müßt treu sein, ihr müßt mutig sein, ihr müßt tapfer sein,
und ihr müßt untereinander eine einzige große,
herrliche Kameradschaft bilden!
Adolf Hitler

The Führer speaks:
Learn to make sacrifices for your fatherland.
All of us will have to die but Germany will live.
In your folk community lies your strength.
You must be faithful, you must be courageous, you must be heroic,
And you must create with each other one big
Glorious comradeship.
Adolf Hitler

*Example of how German children learned the alphabet from the school primer*
**Von Drinnen und Draußen** *(From Inside and Outside).*

E Ei—E EI
Eintopf—Sonntag
Ein topf  Sonn tag
Eine  Schüssel. Eine dicke Suppe.
Ei ne Schüs sel. Ei ne di cke Sup pe.
Geben spenden—arm reich
Ge ben spen den—arm reich
Ei ne Sup pe nur. Ja, a ber ei ne di cke  Sup pe.
Ei ne Schüs sel. Ein topf.
Mut ter soll auch Sonn tag ha ben.
Es ist we nig zu spü len. Em ma und El la spü len.
Wir op fern—Op fer sonn tag.

E Ei—E EI
A one-course dish—on Sundays.
A bowl. A thick soup.
Give donate—poor rich.
Just a soup. Yes, but a thick soup.
A bowl. One pot.
Mother, too, shall have Sunday.
There are few dishes to wash. Em ma and El la wash.
We sacrifice—Sacrifice Sunday.

# Select Bibliography

**English**

Betz, Werner. "The National-Socialist Vocabulary." In *The Third Reich*, edited by Maurice Baumont, John Fried, and Edmond Vermeil, 784–796. New York: Frederick Praeger, 1955.

Blumenthal, Nachman. "On the Nazi Vocabulary." *Yad Vashem Studies* 1 (1957): 49–66.

———. "Action." *Yad Vashem Studies* 4 (1960): 57–96.

———. "From the Nazi Vocabulary." *Yad Vashem Studies* 6 (1967): 69–82.

Burke, Kenneth. *The Philosophy of Literary Form: Studies in Symbolic Action*. Berkeley: University of California Press, 1973.

Edelheit, Abraham, and Hershel Edelheit. *History of the Holocaust: A Handbook and Dictionary*. Boulder, CO: Westview Press, 1994.

Epstein, Eric, and Philip Rosen. *Dictionary of the Holocaust: Biography, Geography, and Terminology*. Westport, CT: Greenwood Press, 1997.

Esh, Saul. "Words and Their Meanings: 25 Examples of the Nazi-Idiom." *Yad Vashem Studies* 5 (1963): 133–168.

Friedlander, Henry. "The Manipulation of Language." In *The Holocaust: Ideology, Bureaucracy, and Genocide*, edited by Friedlander and Sybil Milton, 103–114. Millwood, NY: Kraus International Publications, 1980.

Hamilton, L. *The BBC German Vocabulary German-English/English-German*. London, New York, Toronto, 1947.

*Handbook on German Military Forces*. 1945. Reprint with an introduction by Stephen E. Ambrose. Baton Rouge: Louisiana State University Press, 1990.

Hutton, Christopher M. *Linguistics and the Third Reich: Mother-tongue Fascism, Race, and the Science of Language*. New York: Routledge, 1998.

Klemperer, Victor. *I Will Bear Witness: A Diary of the Nazi Years 1933–1941*. Translated by Martin Chalmers. New York: Random House, 1998.

Lang, Berel. "Language and Genocide." In *Act and Idea in the Nazi Genocide*. Chicago: University of Chicago Press, 1990, 81–102.

Mieder, Wolfgang. " 'As if I were the master of the situation': Proverbial Manipulation in Adolf Hitler's *Mein Kampf*." In *The Politics of Proverbs: From Traditional Wisdom to*

*Proverbial Stereotypes*. Madison: University of Wisconsin Press, 1977; and in *De Proverbio* 1(1) (1995).

———. "Language and Folklore of the Holocaust." In *The Holocaust: Introductory Essays*, edited by David Scrase and Wolfgang Mieder, 93–106. Burlington: The Center for Holocaust Studies at the University of Vermont, 1996.

Neuburger, Otto. *German-English Dictionary of German Administrative Terms: Civil Affairs Guide, War Department Pamphlet No. 31–169*. Washington, DC: Government Printing Office, 1944.

Paechter, Heinz. *Nazi-Deutsch: A Glossary of Contemporary German Usage*. New York: Frederick Ungar, 1944.

Snyder, Louis. *Encyclopedia of the Third Reich*. New York: Paragon House, 1989.

Steiner, George. *Language and Silence: Essays on Language, Literature, and the Inhuman*. New York: Athenaeum, 1982.

Taylor, James, and Warren Shaw. *Dictionary of the Third Reich*. New York: Penguin, 1997.

Wodak, Ruth, ed. *Language, Power, and Ideology: Studies in Political Discourse*. Amsterdam/Philadelphia: John Benjamins, 1989.

Young, John Wesley. *Totalitarian Language: Orwell's Newspeak and Its Nazi and Communist Predecessors*. Ann Arbor, MI: University of Michigan, Bell and Howell, 1994.

Zentner, Christian, and Friedemann Bedürftig. *The Encyclopedia of the Third Reich*. Translated and edited by Amy Hackett. New York: Macmillan, 1991.

## German

Bauer, Gerhard. *Sprache und Sprachlosigkeit im "Dritten Reich."* Köln: Bund-Verlag, 1988.

Bendavid, Abba. *Übersetzung und Transkription deutscher und nazistischer Wörter*. Jerusalem, 1961.

Berning, Cornelia. "Die Sprache der Nationalsozialisten." *Zeitschrift für deutsche Wortforschung* 18 (1962).

———. *Vom "Abstammunsnachweis" zum "Zuchtwart": Vokabular des Nationalsozialismus*. Berlin: de Gruyter, 1964.

Berning, Cornelia Schmitz-. *Vokabular des Nationalsozialismus*. New York: de Gruyter, 1998.

Bork, Siegfried. *Mißrauch der Sprache: Tendenzen nationalsozialistischer Sprachregelung*. Bern: Francke, 1970.

Brackmann, Karl-Heinz, and Renate Birkenauer. *NS-DEUTSCH: "Selbstverständliche" Begriffe und Schlagwörter aus der Zeit des Nationalsozialismus*. Straelen/Niederrhein: Straelener Manuskripte Verlag, 1988.

Brückner, Wolfgang. *"Arbeit macht frei" Herkunft und Hintergrund der KZ-Devise*. Opladen: Leske and Budrich, 1998.

Diekmann, Walther. *Sprache in der Politik: Einführungen in die Pragmatik und Semantik der politischen Sprache*. Heidelberg: Carl Winter Universitätsverlag, 1975.

Doerr, Karin. " 'To Each His Own' (Jedem das Seine): The (Mis-)Use of German Proverbs in Concentration Camps and Beyond." *Proverbium* 17 (2000): 71–90.

Ehlich, Konrad, ed. *Sprache im Faschismus*. Frankfurt am Main: Suhrkamp, 1987.

Heinßen, Jürgen. "Das Lesebuch als politisches Führungsmittel. Ein Beitrag zur Publizistik im Dritten Reich." Ph.D. dissertation, University of Münster, 1963.

Henningsen, Jürgen. *Bildsamkeit, Sprache und Nationalsozialismus*. Essen: Neue Deutsche Schule Verlagsgesellschaft, 1963.

Hoffend, Andrea. "Bevor die Nazis die Sprache beim Wort nahmen: Wurzeln und Entsprechungen nationalsozialistischen Sprachgebrauchs." *Muttersprache* 97 (1987): 257–299.

Jäger, Siegfried. *Faschismus, Rechtsextremismus, Sprache: Eine kommentierte Bibliographie.* Duisburg: Duisburger Institut für Sprach- und Sozialforschung, 1989.

Jäger, Siegfried. *Text- und Diskursanalyse.* Duisburg: Duisburger Intitut für Sprach- und Sozialforschung, 1989.

Kammer, Hilde, and Elisabet Bartsch. *Lexikon Nationalsozialismus: Begriffe, Organisationen, und Institutionen.* Reinbeck bei Hamburg: Rowohlt Taschenbuch, 1999.

Kämper, Heidrun, and Hartmut Schmidt, eds. *Das 20. Jahrhundert: Sprachgeschichte—Zeitgeschichte.* Berlin: Walter de Gruyter, 1998.

Kinne, Michael, and Johannes Schwitalla. *Sprache im Nationalsozialismus: Studienbibliographien Sprachwissenschaft 9.* Heidelberg: Julius Groos, 1994.

Klemperer, Victor. *Ich will Zeugnis ablegen bis zum letzten: Tagebücher 1933–1945.* Vol. 1 and 2, edited by Walter Nowojski. Berlin: Aufbau-Verlag, 1995.

———. *LTI: Notizbuch eines Philologen.* 1957; Reprint, Leipzig: Reclam, 1996.

Maas, Utz. *Als der Geist der Gemeinschaft eine Sprache fand: Sprache im Nationalsozialismus. Versuch einer historischen Argumentationsanalyse.* Opladen: Westdeutscher Verlag, 1984.

Marek, Michael. "Wer deutsch spricht, wird nicht verstanden!" Der wissenschaftliche Diskurs über das Verhältnis von Sprache und Politik im Nationalsozialismus. *Archiv für Sozialgeschichte* 30 (1990).

Maurer, Friedrich, and Heinz Rupp, eds. *Deutsche Wortgeschichte.* 3 vols. New York: Walter de Gruyter, 1974–1978.

Maurer, Friedrich, and Friedrich Stroh. *Deutsche Wortgeschichte.* Berlin: Walter de Gruyter, 1959.

Mieder, Wolfgang. "Sprichwörter unter dem Hakenkreuz." In *Deutsche Sprichwörter in Literatur, Politik, Presse, und Werbung.* Hamburg: Buske, 1983, 181–201.

———. " '. . . als ob ich Herr der Lage würde': Zur Sprichwortmanipulation in Adolf Hitlers *Mein Kampf*." *Deutsche Redensarten, Sprichwörter und Zitate: Studien zu ihrer Herkunft, Überlieferung und Verwendung.* Vienna: Edition Praesens, 1995, 183–208.

———. "In lingua veritas": *Sprichwörtliche Rhetorik in Victor Klemperers Tagebüchern 1933–1945.* Vienna: Edition Praesens, 2000.

Müller, Claus. *Politik und Kommunikation: Zur politschen Soziologie von Sprache, Sozialisation, und Legitimation.* München: List Verlag, 1975.

Römer, Ruth. *Sprachwissenschaft und Rassenideologie in Deutschland.* München: Wilhelm Fink, 1989.

Sauer, Christoph. "Sprachpolitik und NS-Herrschaft: Zur Sprachanalyse des Nationalsozialismus als Besatzungsmacht in den Niederlanden 1940–1945." *Sprache und Literatur in Wisschenschaft und Unterricht* 14 (1983): 80–99.

Sauer, Wolfgang. *Der Sprachgebrauch von Nationalsozialisten vor 1933.* Hamburg: Helmut Buske, 1978.

Seidel, Eugen, and Ingeborg Seidel-Slotty. *Sprachwandel im Dritten Reich: Eine kristische Untersuchung faschistischer Einflüsse.* Halle [East Germany]: VEB Verlag Sprache und Literatur, 1961.

Simon, Gerd. " 'Ihr Mann ist tot und läßt Sie grüßen': Hans Ernst Schneider alias Schwerte im Dritten Reich." *Sprache und Literatur* 27 (1996): 82–119.

Steinke, Klaus, ed. *Die Sprache der Diktaturen und Diktatoren.* Heidelberg: C. Winter, 1995.

Sternberger, Dolf, Gerhard Storz, and W.E. Süskind. *Aus dem Wörterbuch des Unmenschen.* Hamburg: Claassen, 1957.

Straßner, Erich. *Ideologie-Sprache-Politik: Grundfragen ihres Zusmmenhangs.* Tübingen: Niemeyer, 1987.

Voigt, Gerhard. "Bibliographie: Die deutsche Sprache in der Zeit des Nationalsozialismus." *Praxis Deutsch* 10 (1983): 4–6.

Wagner, Hans. *Taschenwörterbuch des Nationalsozialismus.* Leipzig: Verlag Quelle und Meyer, 1934.

Weiss, Peter. "Laokoon oder Über die Grenzen der Sprache." In *Rapporte.* Frankfurt am Main: Suhrkamp, 1968.

Wiese, Benno von, and Rudolf Henß, eds. *Nationalismus in Germanistik und Dichtung: Dokumentation des Germanistentages in München vom 17. Bis 22. Oktober 1966.* Berlin: Erich Schmidt, 1967.

Wigger, Arndt. "Bibliographie: Sprachwissenschaft und Faschismus." *Osnabrücker Beiträge zur Sprachtheorie* 21 (1982): 105–119.

Wulf, Joseph. *Aus dem Lexikon der Möder: "Sonderbehandlung" und verwandte Worte in nationalsozialistischen Dokumenten.* Gütersloh: Sigbert Mohn, 1963.

Zabel, Hermann. " 'Es spricht der Ortsgruppenführer': Zum Sprachgebrauch eines NS-Funktionärs." *Wirkendes Wort* 37 (1987): 407–418.

Zentner, Christian, and Friedemann Bedürftig. *Das Große Lexikon des Dritten Reiches.* Südwest Verlag, 1985.

## About the Authors

ROBERT MICHAEL is Professor of European History at the University of Massachusetts Dartmouth, where he has taught the Holocaust for 25 years. He has published over 50 articles on the Holocaust and anti-Semitism and several books, including *The Holocaust Chronicle* (1999) and *The Holocaust: A Chronology and Documentary* (1998). He is a recipient of the American Historical Association's James Harvey Robinson Prize for the "most outstanding contribution to the teaching and learning of history in any field" (1997).

KARIN DOERR teaches German at Concordia University in Montreal, is a research associate at the Montreal Institute for Genocide Studies, and a teacher at the Simone de Beauvoir Institute for Women's Studies. Her lastest research involves Holocaust survivors and their recollections of the German language from the Hitler period.